Zimbabwe
Botswana & Namibia

Zimbabwe, Botswana & Namibia – a travel survival kit

1st edition

Published by
Lonely Planet Publications
Head Office: PO Box 617, Hawthorn, Vic 3122, Australia
Branches: PO Box 2001A, Berkeley, CA 94702, USA and London, UK

Printed by
Singapore National Printers Ltd, Singapore

Photographs by
Deanna Swaney (DS)
Myra Shackley (MS)
Greg Herriman (GH)
Tony Wheeler (TW)
Richard Perry (RP)
Geoff Crowther (GC)
Jules de Cinque (JdC)

Front cover: Mitch Reardon, The Photo Library, Sydney

First Published
February 1992

Safari Guide Illustrations by
Matt King

Although the authors and publisher have tried to make the information as
accurate as possible, they accept no responsibility for any loss, injury or
inconvenience sustained by any person using this book.

National Library of Australia Cataloguing in Publication Data

Deanna Swaney.

Zimbabwe, Botswana & Namibia – a travel survival kit.

1st ed.
Includes index.
ISBN 0 86442 119 2.

1. Zimbabwe – Description and travel – 1981 – – Guide-books. 2.
Botswana – Description and travel – 1981 – – Guide-books. 3.
Namibia – Description and travel – 1981 – – Guide-books. I.
Shackley, Myra, 1949- II. Title.

916.804

Deanna Swaney

After completing her university studies, Deanna Swaney made the standard European tour and has been addicted to travel ever since. Despite an erstwhile career in computer programming, she managed intermittent forays away from encroaching yuppiedom and, at first opportunity, made a break for South America where she wrote Lonely Planet's *Bolivia – a travel survival kit*. Subsequent travels led through an erratic circuit of island paradises – Arctic and tropical – and resulted in three more travel survival kits: *Tonga, Samoa* and *Iceland, Greenland & the Faroe Islands*.

Deanna, who enjoys the company of moose and bears back home in Alaska, found furry diversity – from marauding monkeys to bamboozling baboons, latex-hungry hyaenas to elegant elephants – while researching the Zimbabwe and Botswana sections of this book. Her current projects have sent her back to Bolivia and Brazil for further wildlife encounters.

Myra Shackley

Myra Shackley was once a professional archaeologist and spent her early working life crawling round caves in deserts all over the world. In this capacity she spent a total of three wonderful years in Namibia, conceiving a lifelong passion for that beautiful country. She now runs a travel company and teaches tourism planning and management at Nottingham Business School, England. Her major research interests are in the environmental impacts of tourism, particularly with wildlife management issues.

From Deanna Swaney

I'd especially like to thank Ernst, Annemarie and Isa Gruenfeld of Bulawayo for their apparently boundless hospitality and for providing me with a place to call home in Africa. Similarly, thanks are due to Lollie and Theo Nel of Bulawayo for their assistance and kindness at both Bulawayo and Hot Springs. Also in Bulawayo, Val Bell helped with loads of useful information. Beat Accorsi of Shamwari Safaris and Russell & Colleen of

Black Rhino Safaris seem to infectiously enjoy what they're doing in Hwange and Matobo national parks and their experience and expertise are greatly appreciated.

Thanks also to Marisa Mowszowski of Melbourne for her expert contribution to the section on Zimbabwean music and to Lucy Mow for her interest in the workings of the book. Also thanks to Tony Hunter of Melbourne and Danny Forton of Petts Wood, UK, for their input.

Mike Brown and Aaron Ndlovu of Bulawayo are appreciated for their help with transport to some outlying areas. Thanks to Barry of UTC at Vic Falls who helped with some transportation logistics and to Helge

Haniger of Kasane, Botswana, for his gracious assistance during my visit there. Richard Naisbitt of Centenary supplied some useful information on northern Zimbabwe.

In Gaborone, Robert and Pam Colegrave went out of their way to help with the book and endured a good measure of my frustration with this project, as well; their patience and kindness won't be forgotten. Thanks also to Jan and Eileen Drotsky of Shakawe for their generosity and casual outlook, to Nigel Cantle of Merlin Services for going loads of extra miles when the Hilux refused to, and to master mechanic Cecil Wright for coming to the rescue.

Quite a few travellers considerably enlivened and enlightened my time in Africa: Sue & Debra Tan of Melbourne, Alex Sloan of Bulawayo via Memphis, Rudie, Simon & Martin (who helped choke down the Drotsky's Delight), Matthias Haffner of Ulm, Germany, Adam Hunter & Sam Forsyth of Pommieland North, and Tom Montague, the only penguin man in Toongabbie. Readers' letters from Ms/Mr Ballin of Exeter and Sindre Johan Ottesen of Gaborone both provided welcome additions to the text as well.

Finally, special thanks to my father, Earl Swaney, and also to Robert, who provided the incentive to complete this project right on schedule.

From Myra Shackley

I would like to thank all my friends and colleagues in Namibia who fostered my love of the country and contributed so much useful background information for this book. Particular thanks go to Mary Seely, Director of the Namib Desert Research Station at Gobabeb, and Antje Otto from the State Museum, Windhoek.

Nottingham Business School provided an elastic teaching schedule within which a last fieldwork visit was accomplished and the kindness of my colleagues Chris Ryan and Katie Evans is much appreciated.

Representatives of the Ministry of Wildlife, Conservation & Tourism provided

useful background information, as did the many Namibians in all walks of life with whom I have come in contact over the years. I'm also grateful to my editors at Lonely Planet for their patience as I wrestled my thoughts into house style, and to my collaborator Deanna Swaney who shares my view of Namibia as the jewel of Africa.

From the Publisher

This first edition of Zimbabwe, Botswana & Namibia was edited by Rick Bouwman and David Meagher. It was carried through to production by Greg Alford. Proofing was done by Greg Alford and Michelle de Kretser. Mapping, design, cover design and illustration was done by Greg Herriman. Additional mapping was carried out by Tamsin Wilson, Chris Lee Ack, Graham Imeson and Glenn Beanland. Additional illustrating was done by Margeret Jung and Kelly Enthoven, and title page illustrations by Margaret Jung. Safari Guide layout (*roar!*) was done by Valerie Trellini.

The Safari Guide was originally written by Hugh Finlay and Geoff Crowther; additional material was supplied by the authors of this book. Special thanks to Matt King for the Safari Guide illustrations, and to David Meagher for *scientific* checking of the Safari Guide. Thanks also to Sharon Wertheim for compiling the index.

Warning & Request

Things change, prices go up, schedules change, good places go bad and bad ones go bankrupt – nothing stays the same. So, if you find things better or worse, recently opened or long since closed, please write and tell us about it.

Between editions, when it is possible, we'll publish the most interesting letters and important information in a Stop Press section at the back of the book.

All information is greatly appreciated, and the best letters will receive a free copy of the next edition or any Lonely Planet book of your choice.

Contents

Map Legend

BOUNDARIES

— ·· — ·· — ....International Boundary
— · — · — ....Internal Boundary
+ + + + + + + + ...National Park or Reserve
- - - - - - - - - ....The Equator
· · · · · · · · · · · · · · · ....The Tropics

SYMBOLS

◉ NEW DELHI ....National Capital
● BOMBAY ....Provincial or State Capital
● Pune ....Major Town
• Borsi ....Minor Town
■ ....Places to Stay
▼ ....Places to Eat
⌷ ....Post Office
✈ ....Airport
i ....Tourist Information
⊖ ....Bus Station or Terminal
66 ....Highway Route Number
☪ ✝ ✝ ......Mosque, Church, Cathedral
∴ ....Temple or Ruin
✚ ....Hospital
☀ ....Lookout
⛺ ....Camping Area
⚊ ....Picnic Area
⌂ ....Hut or Chalet
▲ ....Mountain or Hill
..............................Railway Station
..............................Road Bridge
..............................Railway Bridge
..............................Road Tunnel
..............................Railway Tunnel
..............................Escarpment or Cliff
..............................Pass
..............................Ancient or Historic Wall

ROUTES

........Major Road or Highway
- - - - - - - - - - .... Unsealed Major Road
..............................Sealed Road
- - - - - - - - ..... Unsealed Road or Track
..............................City Street
+ + + + + + + + + + ...Railway
━●━ ....Subway
· · · · · · · · · · · · · · ....Walking Track
- - - - - - - - - - ....Ferry Route
+ + + + + + + + + + ...Cable Car or Chair Lift

HYDROGRAPHIC FEATURES

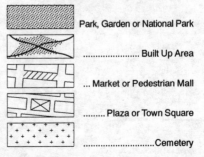

..............................River or Creek
..............Intermittent Stream
........Lake, Intermittent Lake
..............................Coast Line
..............................Spring
..............................Waterfall
..............................Swamp

..............Salt Lake or Reef

..............................Glacier

OTHER FEATURES

Park, Garden or National Park

..............................Built Up Area

... Market or Pedestrian Mall

.........Plaza or Town Square

..............................Cemetery

Note: not all symbols displayed above appear in this book

Introduction

Forming an east-west band across southern Africa, Zimbabwe, Botswana and Namibia are three distinctly different countries, each with its own unique topography, government and people. On the map they're scarcely noticed, overshadowed by the familiarity of Kenya further north and the political unpopularity of their southerly neighbour, South Africa. Many of today's visitors will have first known them as Rhodesia, Bechuanaland and Southwest Africa, but all have recently emerged as independent nations and in shedding their colonial governments, have also assumed new identities.

Zimbabwe is the most populated and perhaps best known of the three. The name is still associated with the violent war and subsequent uprisings that resulted in its break from the racially unethical Rhodesian regime and the establishment of majority government. Nevertheless, it has now been independent for over a decade and has enjoyed a stable peace for nearly as long,

While it's not without problems, Zimbabwe is a beautiful and relatively safe country that pleasantly caters to all budgets from shoestring to Sheraton. What's more, the Zimbabweans are a friendly and easy-going lot who have accomplished wonders with their world-famous music, sculpture and traditional crafts. Their bright cities of Harare and Bulawayo, which boast a variety of museums, parks, markets, restaurants and nightclubs, provide well-organised urban breaks from the uncertainties of African travel.

In the hinterlands, one encounters a wealth of natural and cultural attractions. The greatest crowd puller is of course Victoria Falls, but Zimbabwe enjoys other equally appealing – but distinctly pristine and untouristed – destinations which include some of Africa's finest game parks, packed with the diverse creatures that represent the essence of the continent to much of the world. Then there are the lovely eastern highlands – more

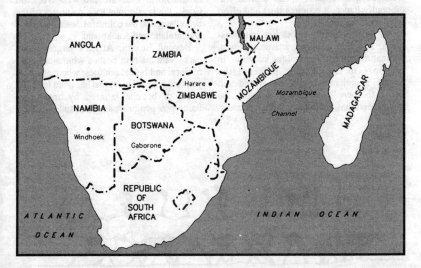

like Canada or England than the rest of Africa – and the ruins of Great Zimbabwe, sub-Saharan Africa's greatest ancient capital. In the south are the extraordinary hoodoo rocks and painted caves of Matobo National Park and beneath them, an encouragingly healthy population of black and white rhino.

To the west of Zimbabwe is Botswana, truly an African success story. A long-neglected British protectorate, Botswana achieved its timely independence under democratic rule in 1966 and immediately thereafter, discovered in the Kalahari three of the world's richest diamond-bearing formations. While politically and ideologically it affiliates itself with its fellow Black majority-governed states, it maintains trade relations with South Africa and enjoys enlightened nonracial policies and health, educational and economic standards unequalled in Black Africa.

Beyond the narrow eastern corridor where the capital Gaborone, and the majority of the population, transport and development are concentrated, Botswana is a country for the intrepid traveller. A largely roadless wilderness of vast spaces – savannas, desert, wetlands and saltpans – and myriad traditional villages, it requires time and effort to enjoy to its fullest.

All its economic success has put Botswana, also rich in game, artistic tradition, and natural appeal, in a unique situation. In response to the need to preserve the country's national natural assets and still derive the benefits offered by tourism, the government has instituted a policy of court-ing only high-cost, low-impact tourism. As a result, the best of Botswana is inaccessible to shoestring travellers. Mid-range budgets are accommodated in places by inexpensive camping sites and there is still reasonably priced access to the country's primary tourist draw, the anomalous wetlands of the Okavango Delta.

Newly independent Namibia, wedged between the Kalahari and the chilly South Atlantic, is a country of practically unlimited potential and promise. Rich in natural resources and unquestionably spectacular beauty, it has also inherited a solid modern infrastructure and a mixed diversity of cultures and national origins: Herero, San, Khoi-Khoi, Kavango, Wambo, Afrikaner, German, Asian and others.

Namibia's attractions are unparalleled. Well known only in southern Africa, its fine bushwalking opportunities, rugged seascapes, quaint European and African cities and villages, and nearly unlimited elbow room have largely been ignored by outsiders. Along the coast stretches the Namib Desert with its brilliant red dunes and the surprising oasis of Sossusvlei. In the south is the immense Fish River Canyon, and in the north-west are the wild Skeleton Coast, the mysterious rock paintings of the Brandberg and the colourful desert ranges of Damaraland and Kaokoland.

Beyond Etosha, Africa's largest game park, Namibia also hosts a whimsical array of floral and faunal oddities; where else will you find a 'dead' plant that has lived for 1200 years or beaches shared by antelopes, flamingos, penguins, sea lions and ostriches!

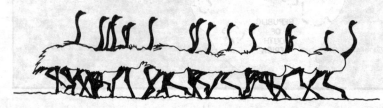

Facts about the Region

HISTORY
Prehistory

Southern Africa's human history reaches back through the millennia to the first rumblings of humanity on the planet; the countries covered in this book contain an archaeological record of the world's earliest inhabitants. In geologic time, the last two million years or so comprise the Pleistocene era – the last ice age – and although no ice reached southern Africa, its effects were manifested in a series of climatic shifts of varying length which formed the background for human evolution.

Continuing controversy amongst scholars makes it difficult to determine the latest opinion on who evolved into whom, but most accept that the earliest human-like creatures were a group of upright-walking 'hominids' who became established nearly four million years ago in the savannas of southern and eastern Africa. At least one advanced variety of these small creatures eventually developed rudimentary tool-making abilities around 1.3 million years ago, allowing people to hunt rather than just scavenge for food. This, combined with a series of climatic changes in the region, alternating wet or dry trends lasting thousands of years each, led to an increase in brain size, changes in body form and a growing population.

The next clearly identifiable stage is an early form of man called *homo erectus* or 'man who stands upright', whose camps and stone tools are found scattered throughout the region. One archaeological site in the Namib Desert provides evidence suggesting that these early people were hunting the ancestors of present-day elephants and butchering their remains with stone hand-axes as early as 750,000 years ago. The tools of the era were large and clumsy affairs but by 150,000 years ago, the people were using lighter stone points, projectile heads, knives, saws and other finer tools useful for various hunting and gathering activities.

In Namibia, middle Stone Age sites are widespread and suggest that certain groups hunted only particular species and that many were nomadic as well. The plains of the Namib Desert are carpeted with artefacts from this period and there have been many archaeological excavations of middle Stone Age cave sites there.

By the middle Stone Age, which lasted until 20,000 years ago, the Boskopoid people, the primary human group in southern Africa and presumed ancestry of the present-day San (traditionally known as Bushmen, although there is some controversy over the use of this name nowadays), had progressed into an organised hunting and gathering society. Use of fire was universal, tools – now made from wood and animal products as well as stone – had become more sophisticated, and natural pigments were being used for personal adornment.

Between 20,000 and 30,000 years ago, southern Africans made sudden and significant progress in their standard of tool manufacture; tools became smaller and better designed and finer workmanship greatly increased hunting efficiency and allowed time for further innovation and artistic pursuits. This stage is known as the microlithic revolution because it was characterised by small flake working of microliths, or small stones. These are accompanied by clear evidence of food gathering, consumption of shellfish and working of wood, bone and ostrich eggshell beads.

There are caves and rock shelters, particularly in Namibia's Brandberg mountains, where several metres of archaeological deposits from this period have been discovered. Not all these late Stone Age people used microliths, however, and although some believe that they were

13

ancestors of the modern Khoisan groups – San (Bushmen) and Khoi-Khoi (Hottentot or Nama) – it hasn't been conclusively confirmed. What is well substantiated, however, is that from around 800 BC, the hunting and gathering people of the late Stone Age began producing pottery and occupied rock shelters and caves all over southern Africa.

The artistic traditions and material crafts of these people are evidenced by their use of pigments. Although they'd been used for bodily ornamentation for thousands of years, they now found their way into the earliest rock paintings; whether the San or some other group were directly responsible for the paintings, however, remains a matter of dispute. Although the artistic tradition in southern Africa chronologically and stylistically coincides with that of Europe, the spreading Sahara probably precluded any contact between the cultures and there's no substantial evidence supporting a theory of mutual influence.

As would be expected, most rock painting reflected the people's interaction with the natural element. Some were stylised representations but the majority portray faithfully and skilfully the people and animals of the region: hunters, giraffes, elephants, rhinos, lions, antelopes and so on in red, yellow, brown and ochre.

Although the earliest works have long faded, flaked, and eroded into oblivion, the dry climate and their normal location in sheltered granite overhangs have preserved

many of the more recent ones. No reliable method of dating these paintings has yet been devised but anthropological studies have used the content, skill level, and superposition of the paintings to identify three distinct stages.

The earliest paintings seem to portray a period of gentle nomadism during which people were occupied primarily with the hunt. Later works suggest peaceful incursions by outside groups, perhaps Bantu or Khoisan (from whom the San and Khoi-Khoi/Nama are descended). During this stage, many significant paintings were produced, revealing great artistic improvement.

The final stage indicates a decline in the standard of the paintings; either a loss of interest in and facility with the genre or imitation of earlier works by subsequently arriving peoples. For the archaeologist, there are considerable difficulties in relating the paintings to the cultural sequences preserved in soil layers of caves and rock shelters but recent advances in radiocarbon dating are beginning to shed some light.

Early Bantu Groups

The archaeological connection between the late Stone Age people and the first Khoisan arrivals isn't clear but it is generally accepted that the earliest inhabitants of Botswana and Namibia were San, nomadic people organised into extended family groups who were able to adapt to the severe terrain. The San seem to have come under pressure from the Khoi-Khoi with whom they share a language group. The Khoi-Khoi were tribally organised people who raised stock rather than hunted and who were probably responsible for the region's first pottery production. They seem to have migrated from the south and gradually displaced and absorbed the San in Namibia and dominated the country until around 1500 AD. Their descendants still live in Namibia but few maintain a traditional lifestyle. The Topnaar of the Kuiseb River area are today probably the closest to the early traditions.

During the early Iron Age, between 2300 and 2400 years ago, rudimentary farming

Three gatherers, Gwangwadza

techniques appeared on the plateaux of south-central Africa. Whether the earliest farmers were Khoisan who'd settled into a stationary existence or migrants fleeing the advancing deserts of northern Africa remains in question but the latter is the favoured hypothesis. The arrival of these farmers in southern Africa marked the beginning of the tribal structure and the beginning of the group known as the Bantu, meaning 'man'. These people would more accurately be called 'Bantu-speaking' since the word actually refers to their language group. It has become a term of convenience for the Black African peoples and the grouping is as ill-defined as 'American' or 'Oriental'.

The first agriculturalists and iron workers of definite Bantu origin are known as the Gokomere culture. They settled the temperate savannas and cooler uplands of Zimbabwe and were the first occupants of the Zimbabwe site, the appeal of which as a natural fortification could not have been overlooked.

Between 500 and 1000 AD, the Gokomere and subsequent groups developed gold-mining techniques in the region and produced progressively finer quality ceramics, jewellery, soapstone carvings and textiles. Cattle ranching became the mainstay of the community and earlier San groups gradually disappeared from the scene, either retreating to the west or being enslaved and absorbed into Bantu society, a process which continues to the present day.

As early as the 11th century, some foundations and stonework were already in place at Great Zimbabwe and the settlement, generally regarded as the nascent Shona society, came into contact with Swahili traders who'd been plying the coast of what is now Mozambique for over four centuries. They traded African gold and ivory for glass, porcelain and cloth from Asia; Great Zimbabwe thereby became the capital of the wealthiest and most powerful society in south-eastern Africa. The hilltop acropolis at Great Zimbabwe came to serve not only as a fortress but as a shrine for the worship of Mwari, the pre-eminent Shona deity.

In about 1600, the Herero people, Bantu-speaking pastoralists, arrived in Namibia from the Zambezi Valley and occupied the north and west of the country, coming into conflict with the Khoi-Khoi with whom they competed for the best grazing lands and water sources. Eventually all the indigenous groups submitted to the aggressive Herero, who displaced not only the San and Khoi-Khoi, but also the Damara people, whose origins are unclear.

It is thought that the Nama people of present-day Namibia are descended from the early Khoi-Khoi groups who had held out against the Herero; in the 1870s and 80s, there were violent clashes. A new Bantu group, the Wambo, probably descended from people who had migrated from eastern Africa over 500 years earlier, had now settled in the north along the Okavango and Kunene rivers.

For the history of the colonial and postcolonial periods, see Facts About the Country – History for each country in this book.

FAUNA

This section deals with reptiles, birds, fish and insects native to Zimbabwe, Botswana and Namibia. Larger animals are identified in the colour Safari Guide at the back of the book.

Reptiles

Africa's reptile extraordinaire is the Nile crocodile. Female crocodiles lay up to 80 eggs at a time, depositing them in sandy areas above the high-water line. After three months' incubation in the hot sand, the babies emerge. Newly hatched crocs are avocado green in colour and, like avocados, darken as they age to nearly black.

Other reptiles to watch for – but which shouldn't inspire bush paranoia – are snakes. Southern Africa has a complement of both venomous and harmless snakes, 76 varieties in all, but most fear humans (they fear anything larger than they are) and travellers will be lucky to even see one.

The largest snake – and one that is harmless to humans – is the python, which grows to over five metres in length. It is found mainly in eastern Zimbabwe from the lowveld north to Nyanga and subsists mainly on small mammals.

There are a host of other harmless snakes – the bush snake, the green water snake, the mole snake, and so on – and quite a few venomous sorts. The most sinister-looking – and for good reason – is the flat, fat and bloated gaboon viper. It has a massive triangular head and grows to over a metre in length. Although it's not common, watch for it on walking tracks in the eastern highlands of Zimbabwe; its bite means bye-bye unless antivenin is administered immediately, and that's an unlikely prospect around those parts.

The related puff adder also enjoys sunning itself on mountain tracks. It reaches about one metre in length and although it isn't as hideous-looking as the gaboon viper, it's responsible for most snakebite poisoning in Zimbabwe. The puff adder isn't aggressive but because it's so lethargic, hikers should take care not to inadvertently kick one out of its sweet dreams.

Zimbabwe also boasts four species of cobra: the forest cobra, the rinkal, and the Egyptian cobra, all of which reach over two metres in length, and the metre-long Mozambique spitting cobra which can spit a stream of venom up to three metres. It aims for the eyes.

Other venomous snakes include the common vine snake, both the green and black mamba, and the *boomslang* (Afrikaans for tree snake), a slender two-metre aquamarine affair with black-tipped scales.

Lizards are ubiquitous in southern Africa from Zimbabwe's eastern highlands to Namibia's Kaokoland and from the bathroom ceiling to the kitchen sink. The largest of these is the *leguaan* or water monitor, a docile creature that reaches over two metres in length, swims and spends a lot of time lying around waterholes, perhaps dreaming of being a crocodile. A smaller version, the savanna leguaan, inhabits kopjes (small hills) and drier areas. Also present in large

numbers are geckos, chameleons, legless snake lizards, rock-plated lizards and a host of others.

Birds

Although southern Africa offers an adequate sampling of LBJ's ('little brown jobs'), it is also home to an array of colourful and exotic bird life. The following are only a few of the most interesting and frequently encountered species.

Dove Southern Africa has several species of dove including the African mourning dove and the emerald spotted wood dove. Some visitors are enchanted, some haunted, and some perturbed by the endless and repetitious cooing of doves in the bushveld but nearly everyone agrees that if there's one sound evocative of Africa, this is it.

Guinea Fowl The roadrunners of Africa, guinea fowl are most often seen either rooting around in the dirt or retreating from following vehicles. Many African drivers take the challenge and try and run them down for a meal but the 'bush chickens' normally recognise imminent defeat and take to the air at the crucial moment.

Grey Lourie The grey lourie, the original sticky-beak, is an ordinary-looking grey bird with a notable crest. It is most most often seen perched in an acacia tree surveying the scene. The lourie's distinctive 'Go-away' call, delivered in the whining tones of a spoilt child, is welcomed by the hunted but predators consider it rather inauspicious, hence its nickname, the 'warning bird'.

Crowned Crane This dandified black and white crane, sporting a distinctive yellow crown of stiff feathers, primarily inhabits the higher plateau regions. Like the Japanese crane, its mating ritual includes a series of dances.

Secretary Bird The dour office hand of the feathered set is named for its strong resemblance to a 19th-century British desk jockey with a clutch of quill pens tucked behind the ear. A relative of the eagle, this spindly character reaches 150 centimetres in length and subsists mainly on small reptiles, rodents, and insects. You'll most often see it strutting detachedly around grassland areas of western Zimbabwe and northern Botswana.

Bustard Also known as the great or kori bustard, the bustard is Africa's largest flying bird. It rarely flies, however, preferring to stride slowly and proudly across the savanna, making itself particularly vulnerable to predators (including humans).

Secretary Bird

Weaverbird Several species of these lively little birds are present in southern Africa. With their sharply pointed bills they construct and attach sac-like grass nests to branches and reeds. Placed on the western sides of trees due to prevailing weather patterns, these nests can serve as orientation devices for befuddled human wanderers.

Eagle Southern Africa boasts 17 species of eagle, including the bateleur, tawny, martial and several snake eagles. The best known, the African fish eagle, has a particularly haunting and memorable cry. It feeds almost exclusively on fish and can frequently be seen kamikaze diving for dinner along the Zambezi, Chobe and Okavango rivers and in larger dams.

Marabou Stork Ominously resembling an undertaker in a long-tail coat, the lovably hideous marabou stork is a carrion eater that spends most of its time perched in dead straggly trees doing gangly vulture imitations. It's most easily observed in game parks where the best leftovers are found.

Cattle Egret These are those graceful white birds that like to go hitchhiking on the backs of cattle and game.

Hornbill These noisy and awkwardly top-heavy birds are instantly recognisable by the shape of their bill which is nearly as large as their bodies. They come in many colours and sizes and nearly every southern African habitat supports at least one variety.

Ostrich, Vulture, and Flamingo These are included in the Safari Guide at the end of the book.

Fish

Zimbabwe has 117 species of fish. Not all are native to the country – many were introduced by anglers during the colonial period – but every liquid habitat in Zimbabwe has its own piscine community and angling remains a popular pastime and food source.

The swift streams of the eastern highlands abound with rainbow, brown and brook trout and the area's dams are stocked by the trout hatchery at Nyanga National Park. In Lake Kariba and the Zambezi Valley, several species of bream, *vundu* or catfish, chessa, and the 'fighting' tiger fish are the most sought after; while the main fishing dams hold bream, yellowfish, barbel, black bass, bottlenose, Hunyani salmon and carp.

Those interested in fishing seasons and licence fees should contact the Zimbabwe National Anglers' Union in Harare or one of the 70 or so angling societies throughout the country. Local tourist offices are the best sources of information.

Insects & Spiders

Although southern Africa doesn't enjoy the profusion of bug life found in countries further north, a few interesting specimens buzz, creep, and crawl around the place. Over 500 species of colourful butterflies – including the African monarch, the commodore, and the citrus swallowtail – are resident as well as many fly-by-night moths.

Some of the more interesting buggy types include the large and rarely noticed stick insects, the also large (and frighteningly hairy) baboon spider, and the leggy chongalolo, a millipede that grows as long as your foot.

More garden variety insects like ants, stink bugs, grasshoppers and locusts sometimes find their way into deep fat and are served as a snack and protein supplement.

Nuisance insects include malarial mosquitoes, especially profuse in the Zambezi Valley, and the tsetse fly, which carries sleeping sickness, which is found in the lowveld and around Zimbabwe's Lake Kariba. There are also various stinging insects like the striped hornet, a stringy evil-looking thing which is actually a variety of house wasp.

CULTURE
Etiquette

Short of public nudity or openly vocal criticism of the government, there aren't really any unforgivable (to foreigners, anyway) faux pas that must be avoided. A few courtesies, however, all straightforward, may greatly improve a foreigner's chances of acceptance by the local community, especially in rural areas.

The African handshake consists of three parts: the handshake you're probably used to, followed by the linking of bent fingers while touching the ends of upward-pointing thumbs, finishing off with a repeat of the conventional handshake. Verbal greetings in rural areas are often accompanied by a clap of the hands, the characteristics of which will be determined by the circumstances. For those out of earshot, it is customary to offer just a smile and a pleasant wave, even if you're just passing them in a vehicle.

As in most traditional societies, a success-ful journey into old age is an accomplishment worthy of respect and elders are treated with deference; their word should not be questioned and they should be accorded maximum courtesy. Teachers, doctors, and other professionals often receive similar treatment.

Likewise, persons occupying positions of authority – immigration officers, government officials, police, village chiefs, and so on – should be dealt with pragmatically. Zimbabwe, Botswana, and Namibia aren't as bad as most neighbouring countries – indeed, officials are normally refreshingly open and friendly – but if you cross them or strike a nerve, all that may change. It's one thing to stand up for your rights but blowing a fuse or undermining an official's judgement or authority or insulting their ego will probably only serve to waste time, tie you up in red tape, and inspire closer scrutiny of future travellers.

At the other end of the spectrum, children rate very low on the social scale. They're expected to do as they're told without complaint and defer to adults in all situations. It is considered rude for a child to occupy a seat in a bus, for example, if adults are standing. Foreigners, however, are normally exempted. Similarly, southern Africa is largely still a man's country and a Black man won't normally give up his seat to a woman, never mind that she's carrying a baby and luggage and minding two toddlers. It makes one wonder what they must think of the Whites and foreigners who habitually do.

When visiting rural settlements, it's a good idea to request an audience with the chief to announce your presence and request permission before setting up camp or wandering aimlessly through a village. You'll rarely be refused. Women should dress and behave modestly. Visitors should also ask permission before drawing water from community bore holes.

Lone travellers may be looked upon with suspicion, women because they should be home rearing families and men because in many areas, White foreigners are potentially all South African spies. It may help to carry convincing photographs of your home and family or evidence of some non-espionage-related profession.

Most travellers will have the opportunity to share an African meal sometime during their stay and will normally be given royal treatment and a seat of honour. Although concessions are sometimes made to foreigners, table manners are probably different from what you're accustomed to, so it may be a good idea to prepare yourself. The African staple, maize or sorghum meal, is the centre of nearly every meal. It is normally taken with the right hand from a communal pot, rolled into balls, dipped in some sort of relish – meat gravy or vegetables – and eaten. As in most societies, it is considered impolite to scoff food or to be stingy with it.

Finally, if you do visit a remote community, please tread lightly and leave as little lasting evidence of your visit as possible. Reciprocation of kindness is one thing but superficial altruism is another. Indiscriminate distribution of gifts from outside, however well intentioned, tends to create a taste for items not locally available, erodes well-established values, robs people of their pride and in extreme cases, creates villages of dependent beggars. If you don't have time to observe and emulate local custom, consider the way one would express goodwill toward strangers and fellow human beings at home and do likewise here.

Africans & Foreigners

Despite the racial turmoil of the past, especially in Zimbabwe, White European travellers need not fear vindictive attitudes or vengeful violence against Whites. Most Zimbabweans have adopted an attitude of 'forgive, forget, and get on with it' in response to past misdeeds on the part of the Rhodesian government.

A most disconcerting aspect of African/White foreigner relations for many travellers, again especially in Zimbabwe, is the deference they will receive from most local people. Thanks to years of colonialism, many people have been conditioned to respond to Whites in a subservient manner; they will frequently address men as 'Boss' and women as 'Madame'. Since these terms were once required signs of respect (and unfortunately still are under some circumstances) most people don't consider the implications of such words and their use comes more or less naturally. You may choose to ignore them but it's probably better, in the interest of easing conversational tensions, to simply explain that you prefer to be addressed by your Christian name.

Conversely, many Westerners, perhaps due to fear of crossing cultural boundaries or to assumptions of guilt by national origin, tend to respond to Black Africans of similar age or social standing more formally than they would a friend (or even a European stranger) in their home country. While the elderly and people in positions of authority should be accorded such courtesy, an affected 'arm's length' attitude is easily detected and can result in communication breakdowns.

Foreigners of African origin will be faced with a different set of concerns. Among Black Africans, people of African origin often aren't accorded as much cultural or linguistic tolerance as White travellers. To some, it will seem inconceivable that a Black person would speak English, French, or whatever as a first language and have no knowledge of, for instance, Setswana, Shona or Sindebele. Inability to communicate in the local language may be interpreted as conceit – a 'selling out' if you will – to the 'Rich White' culture. Once this novelty is carefully explained, however, you will be enthusiastically accepted.

Facts for the Visitor

WHAT TO BRING & WHEN TO GO

What items will need to be brought from home will depend on your intended budget, itinerary, mode of travel, time of visit and length of stay. While travelling as light as possible is always a good idea if you want to enjoy yourself, some items will be required if you can't splash out on hotel accommodation.

There are four items no budget traveller in southern Africa should be without: a tent, a sleeping bag, a torch (and plenty of batteries) or candle lantern, and a universal drain plug. The tent and sleeping bag will keep accommodation costs to a minimum, the light source will allow you to remain awake past 6 pm in the winter/dry season, and the drain plug will give you access to bathtubs in a region of few showers and even fewer drain plugs.

Backpacks are usually recommended as the most practical and useful carry-all; internal-frame packs don't get battered around or broken quite as easily, but some walkers think that framed packs are more comfortable over long distances – cooler and better balanced. Buy the most sturdy and well-made pack that you can afford, paying special attention to the strength of zippers, straps and tabs. A small padlock to secure the bag's contents from opportunistic thieves is a good idea, though some people say that it may encourage people to take the whole bag! Take some plastic bags to protect against moisture and dust. Generally, a khaki or military-green bag is not recommended. It's best not to resemble, however fleetingly, a soldier or mercenary, especially in border areas near Mozambique or Zambia.

All three countries covered by this book lie in the tropics. However, there is a broad range of climatic conditions, varying from the cool, almost English, climate of Zimbabwe's eastern highlands to the heat and dust of the Namib Desert and the tropical

humidity along the Zambezi. The year is generally divided into dry and wet seasons.

If you're travelling in the dry period between May and August and plan to camp or spend any time in the Kalahari or Namib deserts, along the Namibian coast or in Zimbabwe's eastern highlands, bring a range of clothing. You can expect T-shirt weather during the day across most of the region but overnight temperatures can dip below freezing and even at Hwange or Victoria Falls, mornings and evenings can be quite chilly. You won't need thermal underwear but a light jacket, a woolly jumper, a hat, a pair of gloves and some warm socks would be welcome. For walking in the bush, a pair of gaiters is also useful – first, to fend off thorns and annoying little seeds that cling to every passing thing, and second, to offer some basic protection from snakes.

In summer the Namib Desert can get extremely cold at night (below freezing), so a down jacket is a good idea if you're camping out. The southern coast around Lüderitz and the northern part of the Skeleton Coast are also very windy all year round, and a jacket and warm socks are a good idea. Take a tracksuit or something similar for mornings and evenings in game parks, with shorts for the daytime. If you're planning to do any walking in the Namib, take track shoes or desert boots, as sandals are unsuitable unless your feet are *really* tough!

During the rainy season or if you plan to do any bushwalking in the eastern highlands, bring waterproofs and sturdy footwear. A bathing costume will also come in handy for swims in lakes and pools of the eastern highlands and in hot springs and public pools (elsewhere, intentions to swim are likely to be foiled by bilharzia – see Health). If you're travelling in the deserts, the Zambezi, Chobe or Okavango valleys, or during the summer/wet season, bring some cool lightweight cottons (women should read the Women Travellers discussion later in this chapter).

People in Windhoek (Namibia) tend to dress more formally than in the rest of the country and the region, so it's worth taking some respectable clothes for town living. In outlying areas of Namibia the farmers tend to be conservative; and too-short shorts or swimwear will definitely not be well received.

For camping and bushwalking, it may be a good idea to carry a lightweight stove, preferably one which will run on petrol, since white gas (Shellite) isn't always readily available, especially in Zimbabwe. As for butane (Camping Gaz, Bleuet etc) stoves, there are, to my knowledge, two shops in Harare which sell butane cartridges for them: Fereday & Son on Robert Mugabe Rd and the pet shop near the railway station (you cannot carry the cartridges on aeroplanes).

There's no problem with obtaining batteries, camping gas or similar supplies in Namibia, and you can buy everything you need in Windhoek. Smaller towns may have a more limited range. Although tap water may be drunk in Namibia, ground water contains bilharzia; bushwalkers and visitors to rural areas should carry steritabs.

Additional items which will come in handy are a small travel alarm, a Swiss Army-style knife, a clothes line, a basic first-aid kit, a water bottle and water purification tablets, a towel, a sewing kit, photographic equipment and all the film you'll be needing; and enough batteries to power all the gadgetry for the duration of your stay if you're spending any time in Zimbabwe. Zimbabwe-made batteries will power a small torch for a minute or two but in a Walkman, they've been known to expire in under 10 seconds!

TIME
Zimbabwe, Botswana and Namibia are two hours ahead of Greenwich Mean Time. Therefore, when it's noon Saturday in southern Africa, it's 10 am Saturday in London, 5 am Saturday in New York, 2 am Saturday in Los Angeles and 8 pm Saturday in Sydney.

ELECTRICITY
Electricity in southern Africa is generated at 220 volts AC so for use of US appliances you'll need an adaptor. Both round and rectangular three-prong plug sockets are in use.

FILM & PHOTOGRAPHY
The first rule for photographers visiting southern Africa, especially Zimbabwe, is bring everything you'll be needing from home. Where available, camera equipment and film are prohibitively expensive.

In Zimbabwe, film is virtually unobtainable although one shop in Harare does sell Ektachrome slide film but you'll find travellers willing to sell their souls for a roll of Kodachrome 64. Fujichrome and Agfachrome are similarly unheard of. At Victoria Falls and selected tourist shops, you can buy Kodacolor 110 print film. Low-quality Eastern European print film is available in a few places. In Botswana and Namibia, film is normally available in the cities, but it is very expensive.

If you want to score some excellent wildlife shots effortlessly, a good lightweight 35 mm SLR camera, an ultraviolet filter, and a 70 to 200 mm zoom or telephoto lens should do the trick. If your subject is nothing but a speck in the distance, try to resist wasting film on it (unless you have a super lens) but keep the camera ready. Anything can happen at any time.

When photographing out of doors, be sure to take light readings on the subject and not the brilliant African background or your shots will all turn out underexposed. Likewise for people shots: dark African faces will appear featureless if you set the exposure for background light.

As in most places, the quest for the perfect 'people shot' will prove a photographer's greatest challenge. While many Africans enjoy being photographed, others will be put off. They may be superstitious about your camera, suspicious of your motives, or simply interested in whatever economic advantage they can gain from your desire to photograph them. The main point is that you must respect the wishes of the locals, however photogenic or colourful, who may be camera-shy for whatever reason. Ask permission to photograph if a candid shot can't be made and don't insist or snap a picture anyway if permission is denied.

Often, people will allow you to photograph them provided you give them a photo for themselves, a real treasure in rural Africa. Understandably, people are sometimes disappointed not to see the photograph immediately materialise. If you don't carry a Polaroid camera, be sure to make it clear that you'll have to take their address and send the photo by post once it's processed.

Although officials in Zimbabwe, Botswana and Namibia aren't nearly so paranoid about photography as their counterparts in most other African countries, photographing bridges, airports, military equipment, government buildings and anything that could be considered strategic or susceptible to sabotage is taboo.

HEALTH
Travel health depends on predeparture preparations, day to day attention to health-related matters, and the manner of handling medical emergencies if they do arise. Although the following health section may seem like a who's who of dreadfully unpleasant diseases, your chances of coming down with something serious in Zimbabwe, Botswana, or Namibia are slight. If you take the recommended jabs, faithfully pop your antimalarials (especially if you're headed further north in Africa!), and use common sense, there shouldn't be any problems.

Predeparture Preparations
Health Insurance A travel insurance policy to cover theft, loss and medical problems is a wise idea. There is a wide variety of policies and your travel agent will have recommendations. The international student travel policies handled by STA or other student travel organisations are usually good value. It's always important, however, to check the small print:

● Some policies specifically exclude 'dangerous activities' which can include scuba diving, motorcycling or even trekking. If these activities are on your agenda, such a policy would be of limited value.

● You may prefer a policy which pays doctors or hospitals directly rather than requiring you to pay first and claim later. If you must claim after the fact, however, be sure you keep all documentation. Some policies ask you to phone (reverse charges) to a centre in your home country where an immediate assessment of the problem will be made.

● Check on the policy's coverage of emergency transport or evacuation back to your home country. If you have to stretch out across several airline seats, someone has to pay for it!

Medical Kit It's a good idea to carry a small, straightforward medical kit. Most medicines are available in Zimbabwe, Botswana and Namibia but most pharmacies will refuse to dispense drugs without a doctor's prescription. Malaria treatments are the exception and pharmacists will hand out chloroquine or Fansidar based on a description of the symptoms.

A possible medical kit could include:

1. Aspirin or paracetamol – for pain or fever
2. Antihistamine (such as Benadryl) – useful as a decongestant for colds and allergies, to ease itching from insect bites, or to prevent motion sickness
3. Antibiotics – useful if you're travelling off the beaten track. Most antibiotics are prescription medicines
4. Kaolin and pectin preparation such as Pepto-Bismol for stomach upsets and Imodium or Lomotil to bung things up in case of emergencies during long-distance travel
5. Rehydration mixture – for treatment of severe diarrhoea. This is particularly important when travelling with children.
6. Antiseptic liquid or cream and antibiotic powder for minor injuries
7. Calamine lotion – to ease irritation from bites and stings
8. Bandages and band-aids
9. Scissors, tweezers, and a thermometer – but remember that you cannot transport mercury thermometers on airlines
10. Insect repellent, sunblock (15+), suntan lotion, chap stick and water purification tablets (or iodine)
11. Sterile syringes are recommended for travel in Africa due to the AIDS risk. Be sure you have at least

one large enough for a blood test – those normally used for injections are too small.

Ideally, antibiotics should be administered only under medical supervision and should never be taken indiscriminately. Overuse of antibiotics can weaken your immune system and can reduce the drug's efficacy in the future. Take only the recommended dosage at the prescribed intervals and continue using the antibiotic for the prescribed period, even if you're feeling better sooner. Antibiotics are quite specific to the infections they will react with so if you're in doubt about a drug's effects or suffer any unexpected reactions, discontinue use immediately.

When buying drugs anywhere in Africa, be sure to check expiry dates and storage conditions. Some drugs available there may be no longer recommended or even be banned in other countries.

Health Preparations Make sure you're healthy before embarking on a long journey, have your teeth checked and if you wear glasses or contacts, bring a spare pair and a copy of your optical prescription. Losing your glasses can be a real problem but in southern Africa, you can have a new pair made with little fuss.

At least one pair of good-quality sunglasses are essential, as the glare is terrific and dust and blown sand can get into the corners of your eyes. A hat, sunscreen lotion and lip protection are also essential.

If you require a particular medication, take an adequate supply as it may not be available locally. Take the prescription with the generic rather than brand name so it will be universally recognisable. It's also wise to carry a copy of the prescription to prove you're using the medication legally. Customs and Immigration officers may get excited at the sight of syringes or mysterious powdery preparations.

Immunisations Vaccinations provide protection against diseases you may encounter along the way. For entry into Zimbabwe or Botswana, a yellow fever vaccination

certificate is required if you're coming from a more northerly African country. Most commonly recommended for travel to southern Africa are typhoid, tetanus DPT, polio, and meningitis vaccines as well as gamma globulin as protection against hepatitis. Some physicians will also recommend a cholera vaccine (and many African countries still require it) but its effectiveness is minimal.

Namibia theoretically requires a Yellow Fever certificate for entry but this is not always enforced. You would, however, be crazy to go there without the vaccination and are also seriously recommended to have a hepatitis A jab.

Cholera Although many countries require this vaccine, it lasts only six months and is not recommended for pregnant women.

Tetanus DPT Boosters are necessary at least every 10 years and are highly recommended as a matter of course

Typhoid Protection lasts for three years and is useful if you are travelling for longer periods in rural tropical areas. The most common side effects from this vaccine are pain at the injection site, fever, headache, and a general unwell feeling.

Gamma Globulin Gamma globulin is not a vaccination but a ready-made antibody which has proven successful in reducing the chances of contracting infectious hepatitis (hepatitis A). Because it may interfere with the development of immunity, it should not be given until at least 10 days after administration of the last vaccine needed and as near as possible to departure due to its relatively short-lived effectiveness – normally about six months.

Yellow Fever Protection lasts for 10 years and is recommended for all travel to Africa. You usually need to visit a special yellow fever vaccination centre. Vaccination isn't recommended during pregnancy, but if you must travel to a high risk area, it is still probably better to take the vaccine.

Basic Rules
Food & Water Care in what you eat and drink is the most important health rule; stomach upsets are the most common travel health problem but the majority of these upsets will be minor. Don't be paranoid about sampling local foods – it's all part of the travel experience and shouldn't be missed.

Although many African countries have problems with contaminated water, tapwater is safe to drink in Zimbabwe, Botswana and Namibia. Care should be taken when drinking from rural bores, however, since many have been tested and the water is considered fit only for cattle. Except in the Okavango Delta and in a few areas of Zimbabwe's eastern highlands, surface water (ie from rivers, lakes and ponds) should not be drunk untreated due to the risk of contamination by bilharzia.

Namibia, however, is a very healthy country. The water supply is good and clean even in outlying areas although you may find it very salty in the desert where it is essential to drink from two to five litres of water daily. Never travel anywhere without water and ensure that you top up your water container at every opportunity as the next tap may be a long way away.

You may, however, on occasion need to rely on surface water or rural bores which may be contaminated. The simplest way to purify suspect water is to boil it for eight to 10 minutes. Simple filtering won't remove all dangerous organisms so if you can't boil suspect water, it should be treated chemically. Chlorine tablets (Puritabs, Steritabs and other brand names) will kill many but not all pathogens. Iodine is very effective and is available in tablet form (such as Potable Aqua) but follow the directions carefully and remember that too much iodine will be harmful.

If you can't find tablets, tincture of iodine (2%) or iodine crystals may be used. Add two drops of tincture of iodine per litre or quart of water and let stand for 30 minutes. Iodine crystals can also be used to purify water but this is a more complicated and dangerous process since you first must prepare a saturated iodine solution. Iodine loses its effectiveness if exposed to air or damp so keep it in a tightly sealed container. Flavoured powder will disguise the normally foul taste of iodine-treated water and is an especially good idea for those travelling with children.

When it's hot, be sure to drink lots of liquids. Excessive sweating can lead to loss of salt and cause muscle cramping. Failure to urinate or dark yellow urine is a sign of dehydration. Always carry a bottle of water on long trips.

Reputable brands of bottled water or soft drinks are normally fine although sometimes water bottles are refilled and resold – check the seals before buying. In rural areas, take care with fruit juices since water may have been added. Milk should be treated with suspicion as it is often unpasteurised. Boiled milk is fine if it is kept hygienically and yoghurt is always good. Tea or coffee should also be okay since the water used was probably boiled.

Salads and fruit should be washed with purified water or peeled where possible. Ice cream is usually OK but beware of ice cream that has melted and been refrozen. Thoroughly cooked food is safest but not if it has been left to cool or if it has been reheated. Take great care with shellfish or fish and avoid undercooked meat. If a place looks clean and well-run and the vendor also looks clean and healthy, then the food is probably all right. In general, look for places that are packed with locals.

In Namibia, food hygiene is not usually a problem and you are unlikely to get gut bugs from dirty food. The only thing to watch for is frozen foods bought from stores in rural areas where they may not have been kept at the right temperature. Do not try to keep fresh meat or fish for more than a day without an icebox, or more than three days even in cool conditions. No fresh food will last more than a few hours in the desert unless you have an icebox.

Vegetarians find it particularly difficult to travel in Africa since most of the inexpensive fare is based upon meat; vegetable dishes politely concocted for vegetarian foreigners are normally bland or stodgy. Eggs and groundnuts, both good sources of protein, are readily available in southern Africa and fresh breads and vegetables can be found nearly everywhere but to form an interesting meal from them, you'll probably have to resort to self-catering.

Sun, Heat & Exertion

Sunburn In the tropics or the desert you can be quickly sunburnt, even when it's cloudy. Use a sunblock and take extra care to cover skin which rarely sees the sun. A hat will protect your face and scalp and zinc oxide will prevent a burnt and peeling nose. In Namibia, sun protection products are widely available in stores and garages as well as chemists. Do not be deceived on a foggy or windy day on the coast – you can get just as burnt through a layer of fog.

Prickly Heat Prickly heat is an itchy rash caused by excessive perspiration trapped under the skin. It usually strikes those newly arrived in a hot climate whose pores have not opened enough to accommodate profuse sweating. Frequent baths and application of talcum powder will help relieve the itch.

Heat Exhaustion Dehydration or salt deficiency can lead to heat exhaustion. Take time to acclimatise to high temperature and be sure to drink sufficient liquids. Salt deficiency, which can be brought on by diarrhoea or nausea, is characterised by fatigue, lethargy, headaches, giddiness and muscle cramps. Salt tablets will probably solve the problem. Anhidrotic heat exhaustion, caused by inability to sweat, is quite rare but can strike even those who have spent some time in hot climates.

Heatstroke This serious, sometimes fatal, condition can occur if the body's thermostat breaks down and body temperature rises to dangerous levels. Continuous exposure to high temperatures can leave you vulnerable to heatstroke. Alcohol intake and strenuous activity can increase chances of heatstroke, especially in those who've recently arrived in a hot climate.

Symptoms include minimal sweating, a high body temperature (39 to 40° C), and a general feeling of unwellness. The skin may become flushed and red. Severe throbbing headaches, decreased coordination, and aggressive or confused behaviour may be signs of heatstroke. Eventually, the victim will become delirious and go into convulsions. Get the victim out of the sun, if possible, remove clothing, cover with a wet towel and fan continually. Seek medical help as soon as possible.

Motion Sickness Eating very lightly before and during a trip will reduce the chances of motion sickness. If you know you're susceptible, try to find a place that minimises disturbance, near the wing on aircraft or near the centre on buses. Fresh air almost always helps but reading or cigarette smoking (or even being around someone else's smoke) normally makes matters worse.

Commercial motion sickness preparations, which can cause drowsiness, have to be taken before the trip; after you've begun feeling ill, it's too late. Dramamine tablets should be taken three hours before departure and scopolamine patches (which are available only by prescription in most places) should be applied 10 to 12 hours before departure. Ginger can be used as a natural preventative and is available in capsule form.

Diseases of Insanitation

Diarrhoea Sooner or later – unless you're exceptional – you'll get diarrhoea so you may as well accept the inevitable. Depending on how much travelling you've done and what your guts are used to, it can be merely the result of a change of food. If you've spent all your life living out of sterilised, cellophane-wrapped packets and tins from the local supermarket, you'll have a hard time until you adjust.

There are lots of flies in Africa – flies which live on various wastes produced by humans and other animals. In most places, local people shit fairly indiscriminately whenever the urge takes them. Rural facilities are rare or unspeakable and sewage treatment isn't always top rate. Most gut infections stem from the connection of food and shit via flies. In Namibia, there are very few public lavatories but facilities provided in petrol stations and cafes are usually clean. If you need to make use of the bush ensure that no paper or sanitary products are left behind. These will immediately be dug up by jackals and in semidesert soils they will take decades to biodegrade.

If and when you get a gut infection, avoid rushing off to the chemist and loading up on antibiotics. It's too harsh a treatment and you can build up a tolerance to them through overuse. Try to starve the bugs out first. If possible, eat nothing, rest and avoid travelling (or pop an Imodium or Lomotil to plug the drain). Drink lots of liquids – diarrhoea will cause dehydration and may result in stomach cramps due to a salt imbalance in the blood. Chewing a small pellet of paregoric, a stronger version of Milk of Magnesia, will relieve the pain of the cramps.

If you can't hack starvation, keep to a light diet of dry toast, biscuits and black tea. To keep up your liquids, drink bottled water or lemonade. Once you're headed towards recovery, try some yoghurt but stay away from sweets, fruit, and dairy products.

If you don't recover after a couple of days, it may be necessary to visit a doctor to be tested for other problems which could include giardia, dysentery, cholera and so on.

Giardia This is prevalent in tropical climates and is first characterised by a swelling of the stomach, pale-coloured faeces, diarrhoea, frequent gas, headache and later by nausea and depression. Many doctors recommend Flagyl (metronidazole) tablets (250 mg) twice daily for three days. Flagyl, however, can cause side effects and some doctors prefer to treat giardiasis with two grams of Tinaba (tinadozole), taken in one fell swoop to knock the bug out hard and fast. If it doesn't work the first time, the treatment can be repeated for up to three days.

Dysentery This serious illness is caused by contaminated food or water and is characterised by severe diarrhoea, often with blood or mucus in the stool, and painful gut cramps. There are two types: bacillary dysentery, which is uncomfortable but not enduring, and amoebic dysentery which, as its name suggests, is caused by amoebas. This variety is much more difficult to treat and is more persistent.

Bacillary dysentery hits quickly and responds well to antibiotics but amoebic dysentery builds up more slowly and is more dangerous. You cannot starve it out and, left untreated, it will worsen and permanently damage your intestines. If you see blood in your faeces over two or three days, seek medical attention. A stool test will be necessary to verify dysentery but if no medical care is available, the normally prescribed treatment for bacillary dysentery is tetracycline. For amoebic, it's good old Flagyl (see the preceding discussion of diarrhoea).

Cholera The cholera vaccine is between 20% to 50% effective according to most authorities, and can have some side effects. Vaccination is not usually recommended for, nor is it legally required by, the countries covered in this book, but some other countries (eg Tanzania, Rwanda, Nigeria) sometimes strongly recommend vaccination at borders. If you are travelling further afield, and want to avoid unplanned-for jabs, it may be worth getting a shot before you leave.

During 1991, a large epidemic of the disease was reported in South America, and there was also an outbreak in Zambia. Keep up to date with information about this and other diseases by contacting travellers' clinics or vaccination centres, and avoid areas where there are outbreaks.

Cholera is characterised by a sudden onset of acute diarrhoea with 'rice water' stools, vomiting, muscular cramps and extreme weakness. You need medical attention but your first concern should be rehydration. Drink as much water as you can – if it refuses to stay down, keep drinking anyway. If there is likely to be an appreciable delay in reaching medical treatment, begin a course of tetracycline which, incidentally, should not be administered to children or pregnant women. Be sure to check the expiry date since old tetracycline can become toxic.

Viral Gastroenteritis This is not caused by bacteria but, as the name implies, a virus. It is characterised by stomach cramps, diarrhoea, vomiting and slight fever. All you can do is rest and keep drinking as much water as possible.

Hepatitis This incapacitating disease is caused by a virus which attacks the liver. Hepatitis A is contracted through contact with contaminated food, water, toilets, or individuals. The victim's eyes and skin turn a sickly yellow and urine orange or brown. An infected person will also experience tenderness in the right side of the abdomen and a loss of appetite.

If you contract infectious hepatitis (hepatitis A) during a short trip to Africa, you probably should make arrangements to go home. If you can afford the time, however, and have a reliable travelling companion who can bring food and water, the best cure is to stay where you are, find a few good books and only leave bed to go to the toilet. After a month of so, you should feel like living again. Drink lots of fluids and keep to a diet high in proteins and vitamins. Avoid alcohol and cigarettes absolutely.

Type A can be caught by eating food, drinking water or using cutlery or crockery contaminated by an infected person.

The best preventative measure available is a gamma globulin jab before departure from home and booster shots every three or four months thereafter while you're away (beware of unsanitary needles!) A jab is also in order if you come in contact with any infected person; and if *you* come down with hepatitis, anyone who has been in recent contact with you should take the shot too.

Hepatitis B, formerly known as serum hepatitis, can only be caught by having sex with an infected person or by skin penetration such as tattooing or using the same syringe. If type B is diagnosed, fatal liver failure is a real possibility and the victim

should be sent home and/or hospitalised immediately. Gamma globulin is not effective against hepatitis B.

A vaccine does exist for hepatitis B, but it is not readily available and is extremely expensive. It consists of a course of three shots over a period of six months.

A variant of the B strain, called hepatitis C, now also exists. Transmission and symptoms are similar to hepatitis B; however, there is presently no vaccine against hepatitis C. It is not very common, though, and should not be of too much concern to travellers.

Typhoid Contaminated food and water are responsible for typhoid fever, another gut infection that travels the faecal-oral route. Vaccination against typhoid isn't 100% effective. Since it can be very serious, medical attention is necessary.

Early symptoms are like those of many other travellers' illnesses – you may feel as though you have a bad cold or the flu combined with a headache, sore throat and a fever. The fever rises slowly until it exceeds 40°C while the pulse slowly drops. These symptoms may be accompanied by nausea, diarrhoea or constipation.

In the second week, the fever and slow pulse continue and a few pink spots may appear on the body. Trembling, delirium, weakness, weight loss and dehydration set in. If there are no further complications, the fever and symptoms will slowly fade during the third week. Medical attention is essential, however, since typhoid is extremely infectious and possible complications include pneumonia or peritonitis (burst appendix).

When feverish, the victim should be kept cool. Watch for dehydration. The recommended antibiotic is chloramphenicol but ampicillin causes fewer side effects.

Worms Worms are common in most rural tropical areas and a stool test when you return home isn't a bad idea if you think you may have contracted them. They can live on unwashed vegetables or in undercooked meat or you can pick them up through your skin by walking barefoot. Infestations may not be obvious for some time and although they are generally not serious, they can cause further health problems if left untreated. Once the problem is confirmed, over-the-counter medication is available to rid yourself of it.

Diseases Spread by People & Animals

Tetanus This potentially fatal disease is found in undeveloped tropical areas and is difficult to treat but is easily prevented by vaccination. Tetanus occurs when a wound becomes infected by a bacterium which lives in human or animal faeces. Clean all cuts, punctures, and bites. Tetanus is also known as lockjaw and the first symptom may be difficulty in swallowing, a stiffening of the jaw and neck followed by painful convulsions of the jaw and whole body.

Rabies Rabies is found all over Africa. It is caused by the bite or scratch of an infected animal. Dogs are particularly notable carriers. Any bite, scratch or even lick from a mammal should be cleaned immediately and thoroughly. Scrub with soap and running water and then clean with an alcohol solution. If there is any possibility that the animal is infected, help should be sought. Even if the animal isn't rabid, all bites should be treated seriously as they can become infected or result in tetanus. A rabies vaccination is now available and should be considered if you spend a lot of time around animals.

Meningococcal Meningitis Sub-Saharan Africa is considered the 'meningitis belt'. The disease is spread by close contact with people who carry it in their throats and noses. They probably aren't aware they are carriers and pass it around through coughs and sneezes. This very serious disease attacks the brain and can be fatal. A scattered blotchy rash, fever, severe headache, sensitivity to light and stiffness in the neck preventing nodding of the head are the first symptoms. Death can occur within a few hours so immediate treatment with large doses of

penicillin is vital. If intravenous administration is impossible, it should be given intermuscularly. Vaccination offers reasonable protection for over a year but you should check for reports of recent outbreaks and try to avoid affected areas.

Bilharzia This is caused by blood flukes, minute worms which live in the veins of the bladder or large intestine. The eggs produced by adult worms are discharged in urine or faeces. If they reach water, they hatch and enter the bodies of a certain species of freshwater snail where they multiply for four or more weeks and are then released into the snail's watery home. To survive, they must find and invade the body of a human being where they may develop, mate and reoccupy the veins of choice. They lay eggs and the cycle starts over. The snail favours shallow water near the shores of lakes and streams and are most abundant in water polluted by human excrement. Generally speaking, moving water poses less risk than stagnant water but can still be a problem.

Bilharzia is quite common in Africa. To avoid contracting it, stay out of rivers and lakes – the streams of Zimbabwe's eastern highlands and Botswana's Okavango Delta are significant exceptions. Since the intermediate hosts – snails – live only in fresh water, there's no risk of catching bilharzia in the sea. If you are likely to drink water from a suspicious source, refer to the discussion of water purification earlier in this section. The disease is painful and causes persistent and cumulative damage by repeated deposits of eggs. If you suspect you have it, seek medical advice as soon as possible – look for blood in the urine or faeces that isn't associated with diarrhoea.

Diptheria Diptheria can appear as a skin infection or a more serious throat infection. It is spread by contaminated dust coming in contact with the skin or being inhaled. About the only way to prevent the skin infection is to keep clean and dry – not always easy in Africa. The throat infection is prevented by vaccination.

Gonorrhoea & Syphilis Sexual contact with an infected partner spreads a number of unpleasant diseases. While abstinence is 100% effective, use of a condom will lessen your risk considerably. The most common of these diseases are gonorrhoea and syphilis which in men first appear as sores, blisters or rashes around the genitals and pain or discharge when urinating. Symptoms may be less marked or not evident at all in women. The symptoms of syphilis eventually disappear completely but the disease continues and may cause severe problems in later years. Antibiotics are used to treat both syphilis and gonorrhoea.

AIDS AIDS is another issue. It is prevalent in Africa to a degree unfamiliar to most Western travellers and should be a major concern to all visitors. The statistics, especially for Zimbabwe, are both frightening and difficult to accept. The latest press release by the Medical Advisory Services for Travellers Abroad in London states of Zimbabwe:

3,134 AIDS cases officially (4,000 unofficially) reported to date. 60% of Zimbabwean soldiers and 30% to 50% of hospital patients are HIV positive. Up to 20% of the population are thought to be carriers of the virus. 5.18% of blood donations are said to be HIV positive. Casual sexual intercourse is very risky. Risk is reduced but not eliminated by the use of a condom.

AIDS is a death sentence and will continue to be until a cure is found – and that may not be for a while. Although in the West it is most commonly spread through intravenous drug abuse and male homosexual activity, in Africa it is transmitted primarily through heterosexual activity.

Known colloquially as 'Slim', AIDS is prevalent in East Africa – some areas of Uganda are already being depopulated by it – and has spread southward. Of the countries covered in this book, Zimbabwe has the worst statistics but it is also spreading rapidly through neighbouring countries.

Most people affected by the AIDS virus are not aware they have it and hospitals are likely to diagnose their symptoms as something more mundane. The obvious way to

best avoid the disease is to remain celibate. Not everyone can – or is inclined to be. If you do have sex in Africa, cut the risk by using a condom. Even then, as the press release warned, you are still far from 100% safe.

You can also pick up AIDS through blood transfusions. Zimbabwe, Botswana and Namibia currently claim that all blood donations are screened for AIDS but if you can help it, don't take any chances. It is also possible to pick up the virus through injection with an unsterilised needle. If you must have an injection, either provide your own sterilised syringe or make absolutely sure it is either new or properly sterilised.

Insect Borne Diseases

Malaria Malaria is caused by the blood parasite *plasmodium* which is transmitted by the nocturnal *anopheles* mosquito. Only the females spread the disease but you can contract it through a single bite from an insect carrying the parasite. The best – but hardly 100% effective – preventative is a course of antimalarials which are normally taken two weeks before, during and several weeks after travelling in malarial areas. Also, since the mosquitoes bite at dusk, you can best avoid bites by covering bare skin and using an insect repellent. Insect screens on windows and mosquito nets on beds offer some protection, as do mosquito coils. The areas of greatest risk include the Zambezi and Chobe valleys, the Caprivi Strip, and most of western Zimbabwe. Malaria is also a serious problem everywhere in Namibia except on the coast and the local variety is resistant to the drug chloroquine if it is used alone.

The malaria parasite mutates rapidly and although pharmacology manages to keep one step ahead of it, advice on which antimalarials you'll need to take goes out of date very quickly. Your doctor or travellers' health clinic will have access to the latest information. Currently, the recommended prophylaxis for Zimbabwe, Botswana and Namibia is chloroquine although it will be of no use in nearby Malawi where the local strain is highly resistant to chloroquine.

Every traveller I met who'd visited Malawi had suffered a bout of malaria.

Some strains, particularly *plasmodium falciparum*, can be fatal if not immediately and properly treated. Malarial symptoms include (in this order) gradual loss of appetite, malaise, weakness, alternating shivering and hot flashes, diarrhoea, periodic high fever, severe headache, vomiting and hallucinations. If you develop malarial symptoms, seek medical advice immediately. If you have plasmodium falciparum and reach the headache stage, you may be in serious danger. If you are not within reach of medical attention, the treatment for all strains (until you can reach a doctor) is one single dose of four tablets (600 mg) of chloroquine followed by two tablets (300 mg) six hours later and two tablets on each subsequent day. As an alternative (requisite for chloroquine-resistant strains) take a single dose of three tablets of Fansidar. *Never* use Fansidar as a prophylaxis.

Myiasis This very unpleasant affliction is caused by the larvae of the Tumbu fly which lays its eggs on damp or sweaty clothing. The eggs hatch and the larvae burrow into the skin, producing an ugly boil as it develops. To kill the invader, place drops of hydrogen peroxide, alcohol or oil over the boil to cut off its air supply, then squeeze the boil to remove the bug. However revolting the process, at this stage the problem is solved.

Trypanosomiasis (Sleeping Sickness) This is another disease transmitted by biting insects, in this case the tsetse fly. Like malaria, it's caused by minute parasites which live in the blood. The risk of infection is very small and confined to only a fraction of the tsetse fly's total range, which includes western Zimbabwe and the Zambezi and Chobe valleys. The flies are found only south of the Sahara but the disease is responsible for the absence of cattle and horses from large tracts of central Africa. The fly is about twice the size of a common house fly and recognisable from the scissor-like folding of its wings at rest.

The disease is characterised by irregular fevers, abscesses, local oedema (swelling caused by excess water retention in body tissue), inflammation of the glands and physical and mental lethargy. It responds well to treatment.

Yellow Fever Yellow fever is endemic in much of Africa but only the northern extremes of the area covered by this book – the Zambezi and Chobe valleys and north-eastern Namibia. This viral disease, which is transmitted to humans by mosquitoes, first manifests itself in fever, headache, abdominal pain and vomiting. There may appear to be a brief recovery before it progresses into its more severe stages when liver failure becomes a possibility. There is no treatment apart from keeping the fever as low as possible and avoiding dehydration. The yellow fever vaccination, which is highly recommended for every traveller in Africa, offers good protection for 10 years.

Typhus Typhus is spread by ticks, mites or lice and begins as a severe cold followed by a fever, chills, headache, muscle pains, and rash. There is often a large and painful sore at the site of the bite and nearby lymph nodes become swollen and painful.

Trekkers in southern Africa may be at risk from cattle or wild game ticks. Seek local advice on areas where ticks are present and check yourself carefully after walking in those areas. A strong insect repellent can help and regular bushwalkers should consider treating boots and trousers with repellent.

Ticks are particularly common in the bush in Namibia but not all varieties carry disease. They are generally found where animals have grazed and the worst places are inviting shady thorn trees in the grasslands, or (unfortunately) some picnic spots. Tick bite fever is definitely something to be avoided so camping or picnicking in such areas is a bad move. If you are suspicious, watch for little round grey ticks about the size of a thumbnail which drop on your head from the branches.

Cuts, Bites, & Stings

Cuts & Scratches Skin punctures can easily become infected in hot and humid climates and may resist your body's efforts to heal them. Treat any cut with an antiseptic solution or cream and mercurochrome. Where possible, avoid using bandages, which keep wounds moist and encourage the growth of bacteria.

Snakebite To minimise chances of being bitten, always wear boots, socks and long trousers when walking through undergrowth. A good pair of canvas gaiters will further protect your legs. Don't put your hands into holes and crevices and be careful when collecting firewood.

Puff adders are the most common cause of snake bite in southern Africa. They especially like the loose sand in dry river beds and it is a good idea always to wear stout footwear rather than sandals in such locations. The Namib also has a sidewinder adder which is reputedly always fatal and anyway a good idea to avoid. I've known someone who was bitten and survived but he happened to be near medical attention at the time.

Snakebites do not cause instantaneous death and antivenenes are usually available, but it is vital that you make a positive identification of the snake in question or at very least, have a detailed description of it. Keep the victim calm and still, wrap the bitten limb as you would for a sprain and then attach a splint to immobilise it. Tourniquets and suction on the wound are now comprehensively discredited. Seek medical help immediately and if possible, bring the dead snake along for identification (but don't attempt to catch it if there is a chance of being bitten again). Bushwalkers who are (wisely) concerned about snakebite should carry a field guide with photos and detailed descriptions of the possible perpetrators.

Insect & Spider Bites & Stings Bee and wasp stings are usually more painful than dangerous. Calamine lotion offers some relief and ice packs will reduce pain and swelling. In southern Africa, any large and hairy spider will deliver a painful bite as will several smaller black ones; fortunately, none are fatal.

There are no dangerous spiders in Namibia with the exception of some, small harmless-looking grey spiders that live under rocks in the central Namib. The species has only recently been discovered but is a good reason for taking care when fossicking.

Women's Health

Gynaecological Problems Poor diet, lowered resistance due to use of antibiotics, and even contraceptive pills can lead to vaginal infections when travelling in hot climates. To prevent the worst of it, keep the genital area clean, wear cotton underwear and skirts or loose-fitting trousers.

Yeast infections, characterised by a rash, itch and discharge, can be treated with a vinegar or lemon juice douche or with yoghurt. Nystatin suppositories are the usual medical prescription. Trichomonas is a more serious infection which causes a discharge and a burning sensation when urinating. Male sexual partners must also be treated and if a vinegar and water douche is not effective, medical attention should be sought. Flagyl is the most frequently prescribed drug.

Pregnancy Most miscarriages occur during the first trimester of pregnancy so this is the most risky time to be travelling. The last three months should also be spent within reasonable distance of good medical care since serious problems can develop at this stage as well. Pregnant women should avoid all unnecessary medication but vaccinations and malarial prophylactics should still be taken where possible. Additional care should be taken to prevent illness and particular attention to diet and proper nutrition will significantly lessen the chances of complications.

WOMEN TRAVELLERS

Southern Africa is one place in the developing world where it's possible for women to meet and communicate with local men –

Black or White – without necessarily being misconstrued. That's not to say the 'loose foreigner' stigma that prevails in so many countries hasn't arrived to some degree but White Zimbabweans have done a lot to refute the image that women of European descent are willing to hop into bed with the first taker. Neither does it mean you won't get a lot of attention if you sally into a bar or a disco unaccompanied. Generally, however, sober men are polite and respectful and if it's obvious you're not interested, you won't have to fend off roving tentacles while conversing or dancing.

Keep in mind that some degree of modesty is expected of women; short sleeves are fine but hemlines shouldn't be much above knee-level. To avoid unwanted attention, prevent sunstroke and keep cool, it's probably best to cover as much as possible. Namibia, however, is probably more conservative than Zimbabwe and Botswana, especially in Windhoek and the north. Wearing beach clothes is not acceptable, except in Swakopmund.

The threat of sexual assault isn't greater in southern Africa than it would be in Europe but women should do their best to avoid wandering alone through parks and backstreets, especially at night.

Although these countries aren't as dangerous as Kenya, hitching alone in Zimbabwe and Botswana cannot really be recommended. Hitching alone in Namibia is definitely not recommended. In all three countries, you should be prepared to refuse a lift if the driver is visibly intoxicated (a sadly common condition) or the car is chock-a-block with men and there's not a female in sight. Similarly, if you're alone, don't accept lifts from military transport vehicles – they'll almost always stop for you – unless you don't mind an uncomfortable amount of male attention. It's best not to hitch at night, of course, and to find a companion for trips through wild and sparsely populated areas. Use common sense and things should go well.

DANGERS & ANNOYANCES
Large Animals
The threat of attack by wild animals in Africa is largely exaggerated and problems are extremely rare but compliance with a couple of rules will further diminish the chances of a close encounter.

The five animals most potentially dangerous to humans have been grouped into a sort of game hunter's checklist known as the 'Big Five' – lion, leopard, buffalo, elephant and rhino. Since they're normally abroad only at night, you'd have to be extremely fortunate to see a leopard, let alone have problems with one. Because rhinos are so rare these days, the threat of a rhino charge is negligible. If for some reason you are caught out, the advice normally given is to face the charge and step to one side at the last moment. The rhino can't really see you and will have too much forward momentum to turn quickly, anyway. If you're with other people, be sure the entire group steps to the same side or there could be complications.

Although buffalo are docile while in a herd, individuals who've somehow become estranged from buffalo society can be more

irritable. Avoid such animals. If you do encounter one in the bush, however, back quietly away without making any sudden moves until you're out of sight. If there is a charge, head for the nearest tree or dive into the bushes posthaste.

Lions, though rarely interested in humans, have been known to attack on occasion. If you're camping out in the bush, be sure to zip your tent up completely and if you hear a large animal outside, lie still even if it brushes against the tent. This is easier said than done, of course, but lions don't really know what to make of tents and normally leave them alone. If you encounter a lion (or especially a lioness) while walking in the bush, try to avoid an adrenalin rush (also easier said than done); whatever you do, don't turn and run. If you respond like a prey species, the lion could react accordingly.

Unless you're in a vehicle, elephants are best avoided. Although they certainly aren't bloodthirsty creatures – they're vegetarian – it's been said that an elephant never forgets. An individual that's had trouble from humans previously may feel the need to take revenge. Their size alone will probably put you off approaching them anyway. When camping, don't keep fresh fruit – especially oranges – in your tent, since it will attract elephants.

Other large animals which can be dangerous to humans are the crocodile and the hippo. It's often repeated that hippos kill more humans in Africa than any other animal. Like elephants, they aren't vicious but they are large. When boating or canoeing, watch for signs of hippos and steer well away from them. Never pitch a tent in an open area along an otherwise vegetated riverbank or shoreline; this will probably serve as a hippo run. Hippos spend most of their time underwater munching tender bottom-growing plants but when it's time to surface or to enter or leave the water, they don't much mind what's in their way.

The Nile crocodile has provided hours of hair-raising campfire tales and can be worthy adversaries. Although not as large as their Australian counterparts, the crocs, which spend most of their time lying motionless around waterholes or on riverbanks minding their own business, grow up to four metres in length and have been known to cause problems for the careless.

Visitors should take care not to swim in rivers or waterholes where crocs (or hippos!) are present – if local advice is not available, assume there are crocs and don't swim (you'll be also be avoiding bilharzia) and use extreme caution when tramping along any river or shoreline. Crocodiles aren't readily recognisable as such; when they're snoozing in the sun, they look more like logs or branches.

Crocodiles are an especial problem in Kavango and Caprivi in northern Namibia where there is said to be one for every two metres of bank. Watch someone setting off in a canoe and a pair of eyes will rise from the water and follow them across the river.

Hyaenas are also potentially dangerous, although when they're menacing, they're normally just after your food. Hyaenas aren't particularly fussy eaters, either. They will eat boots, food and other equipment left outside a tent and they have been known to gnaw off headlamps and door handles from vehicles. One cheeky character at Zimbabwe's Mana Pools National Park spent several hours one night subduing one of Deanna's car tyres.

You will certainly hear hyaenas in the Namib Desert Park and may suffer from their unwanted attentions. Myra once had a hyaena urinate on her tent pole but he didn't seem anxious to investigate the contents of the tent. There are 'scare' tales that hyaenas will eat your face if it is sticking out of a sleeping bag without a tent, but this has never been authenticated (as far as we know).

Hunting dogs can also be quite vicious but they are very rarely seen.

Poachers

Although few travellers wander far enough from the beaten routes to encounter poachers, a warning is still probably in order. Each of the three countries covered in this book likes to blame the other two, as well as

Zambia, Mozambique and South Africa, for their wildlife poaching problems.

Wherever their origin, elephant and rhino poachers are ruthless businesspeople in pursuit of the high prices commanded for rapidly dwindling supplies of animal products such as ivory and especially rhino horn. The latter is a necessary component in the sheaths of Yemeni dagger handles and is mistakenly believed by some Oriental cultures to have aphrodisiac properties. Both markets shell out big money for the commodity and as long as someone will pay (and the product isn't yet extinct), someone else is going to risk their neck to provide it.

Nearly all African countries have a 'shoot to kill' policy with respect to poachers so the culprits are understandably jumpy about anyone seen travelling in the remote bush where they practice their heinous trade. Anything that stands between a poacher and their profits will be as endangered as the prey itself.

ACTIVITIES
Safaris & Game Viewing
If you're an average visitor to southern Africa, you're planning at least one foray into the bush to meet the endearing faces you've come to know over the years through National Geographic specials and nature programs. Although the term 'safari' may conjure up the image of a single-file procession of adventurers stalking through the bush behind a very large elephant-gun, modern usage allows a broader spectrum of connotations. The word, which means 'we go' in Swahili, may refer to river rafting, bushwalking, horseback riding, even warming your bum in a train or aeroplane!

Most safaris are the game-viewing sort, however. Because the majority of game parks are off limits to those without vehicles, independent travellers can still appreciate game-viewing activities without having to shell out for car hire. Don't be put off by a glance at prices for overseas-booked safaris. Most of these are tailored for those who want all the comforts of home and are willing to pay dearly for them. There are numerous

more affordable mid-range adventures including guided camping and bushwalking safaris which will be outlined in in pertinent chapters.

Shoestring travellers, however, may be frustrated by the rules and regulations that appear to be designed specifically to keep them out. There is no public transport into the parks, hitching on park roads is forbidden, and individual walking tours and bush camping are prohibited in Zimbabwe, except at Mana Pools where the permit system makes access without a vehicle extremely awkward. Persistence, however, will normally pay off and I never met anyone who really wanted to see the parks and failed. Hitching may be prohibited in the parks, but hours spent waving your thumb outside the gates may result in a lift that takes you precisely where you want to go. I've even had lifts from park rangers who were more interested in chatting about my holiday than about the evils of hitching!

In Namibia, though, park officials tend to be not nearly so liberal in interpreting the law – see Facts for the Visitor in the Namibia chapter for more details.

Canoeing & Rafting
The upper Zambezi River below Victoria Falls offers some world-class white water and below Lake Kariba, a more lethargic Zambezi accommodates those who prefer to take their thrills more slowly. Raft trips may be done either on the Zimbabwe or Zambia side. For further details, refer to the Victoria Falls section.

Other companies run lower Zambezi camping and canoe safaris which run from three to nine days along the river between Kariba and Kanyemba on the Mozambique border, highlighted by overnight stops in Mana Pools National Park.

None of these trips are particularly inexpensive and nonresidents must pay in foreign currency or show bank receipts totalling at least the amount of the trip.

Bushwalking & Hiking
Some of the best and most popular

bushwalking areas – Nyanga, Vumba, and Chimanimani national parks – are in the Zimbabwe's eastern highlands. There you can spend an afternoon or a week walking, camping and enjoying the forests, streams and the country's highest peaks. For the more motivated, Outward Bound operates a climbing and abseiling school at the foot of the Chimanimani mountains. Other excellent hiking areas include Matobo National Park near Bulawayo, Matusadona National Park near Kariba and the newly opened Mavuradonha Wilderness in northern Zimbabwe.

Hiking safaris in the game parks are available through several companies but they are typically booked up far in advance by South African university students so if you want to participate, make reservations early. Backpackers Africa, which tends toward the expensive, offers guided bushwalking trips through Chizarira, Matusadona, Kazuma Pan and through some pretty wild areas along the Zambezi River. For further information, contact Backpackers Africa (☎ 735712), 5th Floor, Karigamombe Centre, PO Box 3961, Harare. Kalambeza Safaris, which operates from Victoria Falls, offer much tamer walking safaris lasting from a couple of hours to all day. Their address is Kalambeza Safaris (☎ 4480, fax 4644), PO Box 121, Victoria Falls.

Guided walks are also available from rangers in a couple of the Zimbabwe national parks, especially Hwange and Chizarira.

In Namibia, some of the Parks without 'dangerous' animals such as Hardap Dam and the Naukluft allow bushwalking. Others, including Fish River Canyon and Waterberg Plateau Park, feature organised and accompanied hikes with rangers, which are good value but must be booked well in advance at the Nature Conservation office in Windhoek.

The main Namib Desert Park is not fenced off and you can walk anywhere you like as long as you take sensible precautions because of the extreme heat and dryness. Remember that you need a Nature Conservation permit to venture off the main road on foot.

Rail Safaris

For serious rail buffs with a lot of ready cash, Rail Safaris in Zimbabwe offers four-day and nine-day steam rail tours using 1st-class and Luxury carriages. Prices range from Z$1000 for one person all the way up to Z$10,000 for a compartment accommodating up to four people. For further information, contact Rail Safaris (☎ 736056, fax 708554), PO Box 4070, Harare, Zimbabwe.

Train journeys in Namibia are rather more utilitarian. The trip from Windhoek to Swakopmund should be a scenic wonder but it's run overnight so you don't get to see a lot. Moreover, the rail track between Walvis Bay and Swakopmund is laid on a bed of sand which sometimes shifts and the whole system has been known to close down when there's a specially bad east wind.

Horseback Riding

If you're acquainted with equine sports (or would like to be), you may want to try your hand in Zimbabwe's national parks and game reserves. Animals aren't frightened by horses and don't normally notice the rider so you'll be able to approach them without causing alarm. Most national parks and many other game reserves operate daily guided Pony Trails through game lands and other areas of interest. They normally charge about Z$6 for a 1½ hour trip.

Riding is possible in Namibia at the various game farms but as yet the only way round the National Parks is by vehicle.

Getting There & Away

AIR

Southern Africa isn't exactly a hub of international travel nor is it an obvious transit point along the major international routes; air fares to or from Europe, North America and Australia certainly reflect that. About the only relief you'll get are fares for the low season which fortunately coincides with the nicest weather there anyway.

Low-season fares to southern Africa from Europe and North America are typically applicable in April and May while high season is between July and September. The rest of the year, with the exception of the several weeks around Christmas, which is considered high season, falls into the shoulder season category.

Airline Tickets

Economy-Class Tickets Buying a normal economy-class ticket is usually not the most economical way to go, though they do give you maximum flexibility and the tickets are valid for 12 months. Also, if you don't use them, they are fully refundable, as are unused sectors of a multiple ticket.

APEX Tickets APEX stands for Advance Purchase Excursion fare. These tickets are usually between 30% and 40% cheaper than the full economy fare but there are restrictions. You must purchase the ticket at least 21 days in advance (sometimes more) and must stay away for a minimum period (normally 14 days) and return within a maximum period (90 or 180 days). Stopovers are not allowed and if you have to change your dates of travel or destination, there will be extra charges to pay. If you have to cancel altogether they are not fully refundable and the refund is often considerably less than what you paid for the ticket. To avoid loss, take out travel insurance to cover you.

Round-the-World Fares Round-the-world (RTW) tickets have become all the rage in

the past few years; basically there are two types – airline tickets and agent tickets. An airline RTW ticket is issued by two or more airlines that have joined together to market a ticket which takes you around the world on their combined routes. Within certain time and stopover limitations, you can fly pretty well anywhere you choose using their combined routes as long as you keep moving in approximately the same direction east or west. Compared to the full-fare tickets, which permit you to go anywhere you choose on any IATA airline as long as you don't exceed the maximum permitted mileage, these tickets are much less flexible. They are, however, much cheaper.

The other type of RTW ticket, the agent ticket, is a combination of cheap fares strung together by an enterprising travel agent. These can be cheaper than an airline RTW ticket but the choice of routes may be quite limited. However, most RTW tickets you'll find which include southern Africa will be of this type. If you want to include southern or eastern Africa on a RTW routing, you'll probably wind up flying into Nairobi from India or London or to Harare from Australia or London.

Student Discounts Some airlines offer student card holders 20% to 25% discounts on their tickets. The same often applies to anyone under the age of 26. These discounts are generally only available on ordinary economy-class fares. You wouldn't get one, for instance, on an APEX or a RTW ticket since these are already discounted.

Bucket Shop Tickets At certain times of the year and/or on certain sectors, many airlines fly with empty seats. This isn't profitable and it's more cost-effective for them to fly full even if that means having to sell a certain number of drastically discounted tickets. They do this by off-loading them onto 'bucket shops', travel agents who specialise in discounted fares. The agents, in turn, sell them to the public at reduced prices. These tickets are often the cheapest you'll find but you can't purchase them directly from the airlines. Availability varies widely, of course, so you'll not only have to be flexible in your travel plans, you'll also have to be quick on the mark as soon as an advertisement hits the press.

Most of the bucket shops are reputable organisations but there will always be the odd fly-by-night operator who sets up shop, takes your money and then either disappears or issues an invalid or unusable ticket. Be sure to check what you're buying before handing over the dough.

Bucket shop agents advertise in newspapers and magazines and there's a lot of competition – especially in places like Bangkok and London which are crawling with them – so it's a good idea to telephone and ascertain availability before rushing from shop to shop. Naturally, they'll advertise the cheapest available tickets but by the time you get there, those may be sold out and you may be looking at something slightly more expensive.

Children's Fares Airlines will usually carry babies up to two years of age at 10% of the relevant adult fare, and some carry them free of charge. Reputable international airlines usually provide nappies (diapers), tissues, talcum and all the other paraphernalia needed to keep babies clean, dry and half-happy. For children between two and 12 years of age, the fare on international flights is usually 50% of the regular fare or 67% of a discounted fare. These days, most fares will probably be considered discounted.

To/From Europe
Bucket Shop Tickets There are bucket shops by the dozen in London, Paris, Amsterdam, Brussels, Frankfurt and a few other places. In London, several magazines with lots of bucket shop ads can put you on to the current deals. The best ones are:

Trailfinder A magazine put out quarterly by Trailfinders (☎ (071) 603-1515 from 9 am to 6 pm Monday to Friday UK time or fax (071) 938-3305 anytime), 42-48 Earls Court Rd, London W8 6EJ, UK. It's free if you pick it up in London but if you want it mailed, it costs UK£6 for four issues in the UK or Ireland and UK£10 or the equivalent for four issues in Europe or elsewhere (airmail). Trailfinders can fix you up with all your ticketing requirements as well. They've been in business for years, their staff are very friendly and we highly recommend them.

Time Out (☎ (071) 836-4411), Tower House, Southampton St, London WC2E 7HD, is London's weekly entertainment guide and contains travel information and advertising. It's available at bookshops, newsagents and newsstands. Subscription enquiries should be addressed to Time Out Subs, Unit 8, Grove Ash, Bletchley, Milton Keynes MK1 1BZ, UK.

TNT Magazine (☎ (071) 937-3985), 52 Earls Court Rd, London W8, UK. This is a free magazine which can be picked up at most London Underground stations and on street corners around Earls Court and Kensington. It caters to Aussies and Kiwis working in the UK and is therefore full of travel advertising.

In these magazines, you'll find discounted fares to Harare and Johannesburg as well as other parts of Africa. Many of them use Aeroflot or Eastern European and Middle Eastern Airlines but most of the best deals will land you up in Nairobi.

A word of warning, however: don't take the advertised fares as gospel truth. To comply with advertising laws in the UK, companies must be able to offer *some* tickets at their cheapest quoted price, but they may only have one or two of them per week. If you're not one of the lucky ones, you may be looking at higher priced tickets. The best thing to do is begin looking for deals well in advance of your intended departure so you can get a fair idea of what's available.

Non-Discounted Tickets About the cheapest consistently available fare directly to southern Africa from Europe is the long and laborious London to Harare flight on Balkan Bulgarian Airlines, stopping in both Sofia (Bulgaria) and Lagos (Nigeria). If there are no delays, the flight takes about 24 hours. Given the bare-bones service, combined with typically severe overbooking and an obstinate reluctance to change reservations or tickets, it may be worthwhile to pay for something more reliable. The low-season return fares start at about £500 return. High-season one-way fares are as low as £320.

Another inexpensive deal is on Zambia Airways from London to Harare which advertises a low-season APEX fare of £595 return or £843 high season. To Gaborone or Windhoek, you'll pay approximately £200 more.

British Airways, which flies on Monday and Friday between London and Harare, advertises low-season APEX fares starting at £550 but you must stay at least three months.

Kenya Airways flies twice weekly from London or Frankfurt to Harare via Nairobi. This leg can be included in some round-the-world packages. Ethiopian does one weekly run from London via Addis Ababa, Ethiopia and Mt Kilamanjaro, Tanzania. South African Airways has daily flights between London and Johannesburg with connections to Harare five days a week and twice weekly to Gaborone.

On Tuesdays, UTA runs a once-weekly direct flight from Paris to Gaborone, Botswana.

Namib Air operates a twice-weekly flight (Thursday and Saturday) direct to Windhoek international airport from Frankfurt which takes about 10 hours. No charter flights are currently allowed into Namibia although rumours suggest that limited operations by a German-based charter company Harpag Lloyd will be allowed in 1991. The Frankfurt route tends to be expensive unless you are based in Germany; it will certainly be cheaper to get a scheduled flight to Johannesburg, Cape Town, Harare, Lusaka or Gaborone and then either pick up a Namib Air connection or travel overland.

To/From North America

In the USA, the best way to find cheap flights is by checking the Sunday travel sections in the major newspapers such as the *Los Angeles Times* or *San Francisco Examiner-Chronicle* on the west coast and the *New York Times* on the east coast. The student travel bureaux – STA or Council Travel – are also worth a go but in the USA you'll have to produce proof of student status and in some cases be under 26 years of age to qualify for their discounted fares.

North America is a relative newcomer to the bucket shop traditions of Europe and Asia so ticket availability and the restrictions attached to them need to be weighed against what is offered on the standard APEX or full economy (coach) tickets.

It may well be cheaper in the long run to fly first to London on Virgin Airways (for around US$225 one way) or another inexpensive airline then buy a bucket shop ticket from there to Africa. Do some homework before setting off, however. All the magazines specialising in bucket shop advertisements in London (details are in the previous discussion under To/From Europe) will post copies so you can study current pricing before you decide on a course of action.

Otherwise, the only direct routing between North America and southern Africa – that is, one that doesn't require you to go via Europe – is Zambia Airways' flight from New York to Lusaka, Zambia, with one stop in West Africa. From Lusaka, you can make easy air connections to either Harare or Gaborone. Lusaka is quite near the Zimbabwe border and overland travel is also possible. If you're not a seasoned traveller, however, be warned that Lusaka may not be the best place to introduce yourself to Africa so think seriously about purchasing a connecting flight from there to Harare or elsewhere in southern Africa.

To Namibia, it will certainly be cheaper to get a scheduled flight to either Johannesburg, Cape Town, Harare, Lusaka or Gaborone and then either pick up a Namib Air connection or travel overland.

To/From Australia & New Zealand

Australians and New Zealanders are at a distinct disadvantage because there are very few route options directly to Africa. On Monday and Thursday, Qantas and Air

Zimbabwe fly a combined service to Harare direct from Sydney and Perth, Australia. They return to Sydney via Perth departing several hours after landing in Harare. These flights connect directly to a South African Airways flight to and from Johannesburg. There are no direct flights from New Zealand to southern Africa so Kiwis will first have to get to Sydney.

Although the return flight between Australia and Harare is quite expensive – around A$2700, one-way flights are available as part of a RTW package fare for which substantial discounts are available. If you just want a one-way ticket, for about A$1300 you can fly from Sydney to Singapore on British Airways (with a stopover in Singapore), then Singapore to Mauritius with Air Mauritius (for another stopover), and finally Mauritius to Harare.

It does make sense for Australasians to think in terms of a RTW ticket or a return ticket to Europe with a stopover in Nairobi. RTW tickets with various stopovers can still be found for as little as A$2100. The best publications for finding good deals are the Saturday editions of the daily newspapers such as the *Sydney Morning Herald* and the Melbourne *Age*. Also, try the student travel agencies (STA Travel) which have branches at universities and in all the state capitals.

It may well work out cheaper to buy a routing through Singapore since from there, there are several possibilities for reaching Africa including via Mauritius in the Indian Ocean. Discuss your options with several travel agents before buying because many have had very little experience with inexpensive routings to Africa; but you'll probably land up in Nairobi and still have to find your way overland or on another airline to southern Africa.

To/From Asia

The only reasonable way to travel between India or Pakistan and Africa is to fly. There are marginal bucket shops in New Delhi, Bombay and Calcutta. In New Delhi, Tripsout Travel, 72/7 Tolstoy Lane, behind the Government of India Tourist Office, Janpath, is recommended. It's very popular with travellers and has been in business for many years. If you're coming on this route, you'll have to resign yourself to flying into Nairobi on Air India and continuing from there on another carrier or overland to southern Africa.

To/From Elsewhere in Africa

Since Harare is the major hub between Nairobi and Johannesburg, many intra-Africa flights to Zimbabwe, Botswana and Namibia will be routed through there but there aren't really any bargain fares – you do get a few breaks for advance purchase but that's about it – so it won't be worth spending much time shopping around.

Kenya Airways and Air Zimbabwe fly between Harare and Nairobi two and three times weekly for around Z$680 each way. Air Mauritius has one direct weekly flight from Mauritius to Harare and three more with connections through Johannesburg. To fly between Harare and Antananarivo, Madagascar, you must make connections in Mauritius.

Both Air Zimbabwe and Air Tanzania do the run between Harare and Dar es Salaam, Tanzania. Air Zimbabwe and Air Malawi fly to/from Lilongwe, Malawi, six times weekly for Z$200 each way. Linhas Aéreas de Moçambique flies to/from Maputo and Beira in Mozambique. Zambia Airways and Air Zimbabwe each do three weekly trips between Harare and Lusaka, Zambia. South African Airways and Air Zimbabwe connect Harare with Johannesburg, Cape Town and Durban.

To continue on to Botswana, Air Botswana and Air Zimbabwe both have flights between Harare and Gaborone. Air Zimbabwe also flies on Friday between Harare and Windhoek, Namibia. Namib Air has flights on Wednesday and Friday between Harare and Windhoek and also has many flights to South Africa. See the Getting There & Away sections for each country later in this book for more details.

LAND

With the exception of the Israel-Egypt connection, all overland travel to Africa will have to be done through Europe and even that will involve a ferry crossing at some point.

Whether you're hitching, taking a bus or travelling by train across Europe, you should decide which of the two routes south through Africa you want to take – through the Sahara from Morocco or Algeria to West Africa or up the Nile from Egypt to Uganda and Kenya. It's impossible to overland between the two routes in North Africa due to the roadblock imposed by Libya so those wishing to travel between Morocco, Algeria or Tunisia, and Egypt will have to fly. Also bear in mind that even the fortunate travellers who can somehow wangle a Sudanese visa won't be able to overland south of Khartoum due to the civil war, there so the Nile route will probably entail a flight between Cairo – or at best from Khartoum – and Kampala or Nairobi.

From Nairobi, there are several options for reaching Zimbabwe, Botswana and Namibia. The most popular route seems to be the TanZam Railway between Dar es Salaam, Tanzania, (accessible by bus or plane from Nairobi) and Kapiri Mposhi, Zambia, from where it's possible to pick up another train on to Lusaka and Livingstone. It's extremely inexpensive for the distance travelled – around US$40 at the time of writing – but be prepared for a slow pace and uncomfortable conditions.

Another option takes you across Tanzania to Kigoma on Lake Tanganyika, then by steamer to Mpulungu, Zambia, and overland to Chitipa, Malawi, or Lusaka, Zambia. It's also possible to enter Zambia at Nakonde or Malawi between Mbeya and Karonda. There's no public transport along the latter route so it will require hitching.

Other possibilities from Nairobi include travelling through Uganda, Zaïre, Rwanda and Burundi, catching the Lake Tanganyika steamer from Bujumbura, Burundi, and connecting up with the previously outlined route at Mpulungu, Zambia.

The final option – which could require months – is a very long and tedious route through Uganda or Burundi and Zaïre to Zambia. Once you've completed it, you may not feel like travelling any further!

Once you're in Zambia, however, it's fairly straightforward getting to Lusaka or Livingstone and entering Zimbabwe at Chirundu, Kariba or Victoria Falls, or Botswana at Kazungula. For further information on these routes, see the Getting There & Away chapter in the Zimbabwe section where you'll also find details of the Tete Corridor route from Malawi to Zimbabwe via Mozambique.

TOURS
Overland Companies

Although the days of doing Cairo-to-the-Cape are over for the time being due to unrest in Sudan, quite a few overland operators have taken up the trans-Sahara route through Algeria and West Africa, across the Central African Republic, Zaïre and Uganda to Kenya and on to Zimbabwe, Botswana and South Africa. These trips are very popular, but aren't for everyone. They are designed primarily for first-time travellers who feel uncomfortable striking out on their own or to those who prefer guaranteed social interaction to the uncertainties of the road. If you have the slightest inclination toward independence or would feel confined travelling with the same group of 25 or so for most of the trip (quite a few normally drop out along the way), think twice before booking something like this.

If you'd like more information or a list of agents selling overland packages in your home country, contact one of the following Africa overland operators, all of which are based in the UK (Exodus and Encounter also have offices in Australia, New Zealand, USA and Canada):

Dragoman, Camp Green, Kenton Rd, Debenham, Suffolk IP14 6LA (☎ (0728) 861-133, fax (0728) 861-127)

Encounter Overland, 267 Old Brompton Rd, London SW5 9JA (☎ (071) 370-6845)

Exodus Expeditions, 9 Weir Rd, London SW12 0LT (☎ (081) 673-0859, fax (081) 673-0779)

Guerba Expeditions, 101 Eden Vale Rd, Westbury, Wiltshire BA13 3QX (☎ (0373) 826-611, fax (0373) 838-351)

Hann Overland, 201/203 Vauxhall Bridge Rd, London SW1V 1ER (☎ (071) 834-7337, fax (071) 828-7745)

Top Deck, Top Deck House, 131/135 Earls Court Rd, London SW5 9RH (☎ (071) 244-8641, fax (071) 373-6201)

Namibia Tours

A number of overseas tour companies feature Namibia on their itineraries. Trips vary in length and route, but usually include the Namib area, the coast near Swakopmund, Etosha National Park and Lüderitz, although some are now beginning to offer Kavango-Caprivi as well. Most operate small coaches or minibuses, and some companies have self-guided itineraries with prebooked accommodation. Many overseas operators have flight/tour packages.

Tour Operators UK tour operators running tours to Namibia include:

Skyway World Travel Ltd, 34 Notting Hill Gate, London W11 (☎ (071) 602-6751, fax (071) 229-9031)

SAR Travel, 266 Regent St, London W1R 5DA (☎ (071) 287-1133, fax (071) 287-1134)

African Encounter, Bonaventure Tour Operators, 306 Upper Richmond Rd West, London SW14 7JG (☎ (081) 392-1589)

Explore Worldwide Ltd, 1 Frederick St, Aldershot, Hants GU11 1LQ (☎ (0242) 344161, fax (0252) 343170); offices also in Belgium, Denmark, Switzerland, Australia, New Zealand, Hong Kong, USA and Canada

World Tracks Ltd (Africa), 12 Abingdon Rd, London W8 6AF (☎ (071) 937 3028)

GETTING AROUND

For information about travelling between the various countries covered in this book, consult the Getting There & Away section for each country.

Zimbabwe

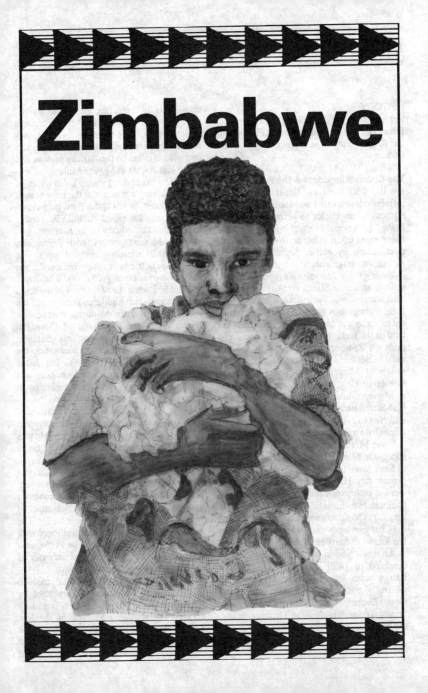

Facts about the Country

HISTORY

For history prior to the Great Zimbabwe era, refer to the History section in the Facts about the Region chapter at the beginning of this book.

The Shona Kingdoms & the Portuguese

By the 15th century, Great Zimbabwe's influence had crested and started to decline. Although reasons for its ultimate desertion in the 1500s remain something of a mystery, those most often cited are overpopulation, overgrazing by cattle, popular insubordination, and fragmentation of the realm.

During Great Zimbabwe's twilight period, several scattered Shona dynasties began to drift away from the ruling dynasties and form autonomous states. The most prominent of these was Mutapa which occupied the land of the Karanga people. After a series of raids on Zambezi Valley tribes, it took in most of northern and eastern Zimbabwe and much of Mozambique. Their powerful *mambo* or king, Mutota, came to be known as Mwene Mutapa or 'the great raider' and his Mutapa Empire grew wealthy by policing and taxing the trade routes between Zimbabwe and the coast.

Upon Mutota's death in 1450, his son and successor, Motope, moved the seat of empire to Fura Mountain just 50 km or so north of present-day Harare. Mutota's successor, a weaker character called Nyahuma, lost the southern two-thirds of Mutapa territory (and his life) to Motope's son, Changa, founder of the Changamire dynasty which would spawn the Rozwi dynasty in the late 1600s.

Another Shona kingdom, the Torwa, emerged in 1480 in south-western Zimbabwe with its capital at Khami. It is generally considered the successor to the Great Zimbabwe state and its ruling class amassed considerable wealth from cattle and the ongoing gold trade.

In 1502, the Portuguese voyager Vasco da Gama landed at Sofala on the Mozambique coast. Shortly thereafter, Europeans arrived on the scene in the form of Portuguese traders who learned from the Swahili typically exaggerated tales of unlimited wealth and golden cities on the African plateau and of the vast empire of Mwene Mutapa (Monomatapa to European tongues), custodian of King Solomon's mines and the long-sought land of Ophir. In 1512, the Portuguese government sent the exiled Antonio Fernandez to ascertain the validity of the rumours.

Over the next century, both Portuguese and Swahili traders exploited squabbles among the Africans to their own ends: the collection of as much gold as could be carted off. In 1565 when the Mambo of Manyika (a state in the eastern highlands) challenged the incumbent Mwene Mutapa, Portuguese forces under the command of Francisco Barreto, governor of loosely defined Portuguese East Africa, attempted to help the Mwene Mutapa seize Manyika but failed miserably and had to resort to bribery and manipulation of African ruling classes in order to gain influence over the interior.

In 1629, Mwene Mutapa Kapararidze tried and failed to muster sufficient support to drive the Portuguese out for good. He was summarily replaced by Mwene Mutapa Mavura, a Catholicised Portuguese vassal, and Iberian interests were not only preserved but given free reign. Their grip was broken, however, by the southern state of Guruhuswa and the Changamire dynasty which attacked Mutapa and deposed the puppet leader. The new Mwene Mutapa formed an alliance with the Changamire and forced the Portuguese to retreat to Mozambique and stay out of African politics for the time being.

Meanwhile, in 1684 the Torwa dynasty in the south-west was forcefully absorbed by the Changamire (the clan which began by conquering southern Mutapa in the late 1400s). This resulted in the creation of the Rozwi state which took in over half of present-day Zimbabwe and had its capital at

Danangombe (Dhlo-Dhlo). Its power and influence continued until 1834 when Nguni forces under Soshangane and Zwangendaba invaded from the south, stormed the Shona fortifications, and assassinated the Rozwi leader.

The Ndebele

After Portuguese influence had withered, various Shona groups remained in control of most of present-day Zimbabwe. South of the Limpopo River, however, a number of loosely associated Sotho-speaking Bantu tribes, the Nguni, competed for territory and power.

In 1780, in a bid to command a larger and more respectable force, the chief of the Mtetwe clan, Dingiswayo, set about forcibly confederating them. In 1818, however, an ambitious youngster called Shaka from a minor clan engineered the commander's death and took control of the (by now) ruling Mtetwe. He renamed it 'Zulu' after his own humble clan and launched into a campaign of military despotism and expansionism that would reverberate through all of southern Africa.

As the Zulu plundered and conquered their way across Natal, some Nguni tribes fled northward on the *mfecane*, an African version of the Exodus. They ploughed their way through existing political entities and by the 1820s, one contingent, the Soshangane, had reached southern Mozambique and eastern Manyika. It established the Gaza state, installed a ruthless and oppressive military government, and more or less enslaved the local population. Gaza was finally reined in by Portuguese forces in the late 1800s after official international recognition of Portuguese control in Mozambique.

In the 1830s, further west, Rozwi was mown down and its government, dismantled by the forces of Zwangendaba, headed for greener pastures in present-day Zambia, Malawi, and points north. Rozwi's final chapter, however, was written by the Ndebele ('those who carry long shields') under command of Mzilikazi, chief of the

Xumalo (the 'x' is pronounced as a click against the front teeth; this word is sometimes spelt 'Kumalo'). Mzilikazi and a band of his followers had fled northward after his father was executed for failing to hand over to Shaka the spoils of a cattle raid.

Along his way, Mzilikazi peacefully encountered the missionary Robert Moffat, who'd posted himself to what is now South Africa, and took a beating in several scrapes with northbound Boer trekking parties. Upon reaching the Matobo (Matopos) hills near present-day Bulawayo, Mzilikazi established a settlement and adopted a policy of total confederation of all Nguni tribes within his sphere of influence before continuing northward, perhaps to assess the potential of the country beyond the Zambezi River. Upon his return, he found the *induna*, or captains, had elected a new chief – Mzilikazi's son. Legend has it that those involved were promptly executed for treason on the hill called Thabas Indunas north-east of Bulawayo, effectively cementing consolidation of the Ndebele state.

Mzilikazi ultimately set up his capital at Inyati 60 km north of Bulawayo, and in 1859 allowed Robert Moffat and his son John Smith Moffat to establish a London Missionary Society mission nearby. Although Mzilikazi never was much taken with Christianity and refused to convert, he initially afforded the foreigners the full measure of Ndebele hospitality. He took exception, however, to the Moffats' preaching that even the lowliest of the Ndebele had access to God's personal attention and relations began to break down. Moffat left Inyati in 1864 and Ndebele interest in Christianity remained lukewarm.

During the 1850s, missionary and geographer David Livingstone passed through Ndebele territory and briefly made his home there with his wife, Mary Moffat, the daughter of Robert Moffat. But Livingstone couldn't help gazing dreamily northward toward the Congo Basin and the source of the Nile; whether it was a case of religious fervour or simply wanderlust remains a matter of dispute. Leaving his family in the care of the London Missionary Society, he set off toward his 'presumptuous' meeting with Stanley in Ujiji, Tanzania.

After Mzilikazi's death in 1870, his son Lobengula ascended to the throne and relocated the Ndebele capital to Bulawayo. In the meanwhile, European opportunists – gold seekers and ivory hunters – from the Cape were already making forays into Shona and Ndebele territory. Frederick Courteney Selous' reports of gold workings (albeit abandoned ones!), artist Thomas Baines' gold find in Mashonaland and Adam Renders' 1868 'discovery' of Great Zimbabwe launched a wholesale European grab for the region's presumed wealth.

Enter the British

Perhaps the best known opportunist of them all was Cecil John Rhodes, who had made his fortune in South Africa's Kimberley diamond fields and was keen to take the Queen's interests – and his own enterprise – into the potentially rich and exploitable country north of the Limpopo. From there, he envisioned a broad corridor of British territory stretching north to south across Africa and a railway from Cairo to the Cape, providing elbow-room, access and appeal for wholesale colonisation and the eventual British-style 'civilisation' of the African continent.

In 1888, Rhodes managed to wangle the Rudd Concession with the Ndebele leader Lobengula (Lobengula heard a deliberately mistranslated version – he would never have agreed otherwise) permitting British mining and colonisation of lands between the Limpopo and the Zambezi while at the same time prohibiting any Boer activity in Matabeleland. In exchange, the king would receive £100 monthly, 1000 rifles, 10,000 rounds of ammunition, and a riverboat. Lobengula had apparently hoped the concession to Rhodes would also eliminate European competition for minerals and thereby limit the number of prospectors and roustabouts entering his territory. In fact, it had just the opposite effect.

In 1889, Rhodes formed the British South

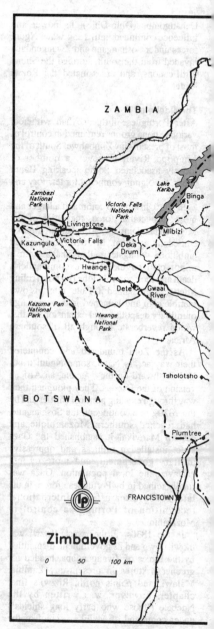

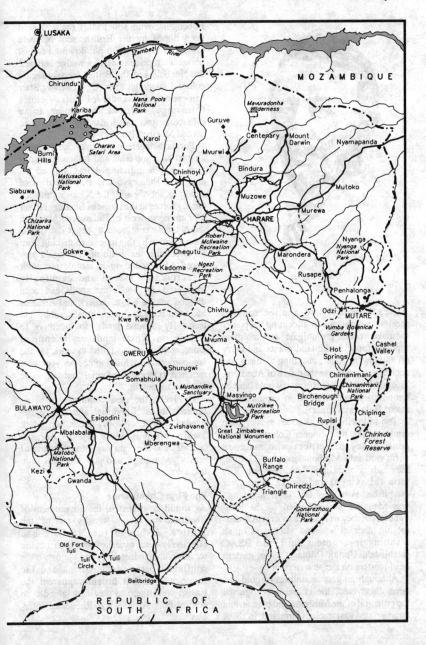

Cecil Rhodes

Africa Company and applied for and received a royal charter allocating the power to 'make treaties, promulgate laws, maintain a police force...make land grants and carry on any lawful trade', installing on his board such heavyweights as the dukes of Abercorn, Fife and Earl Grey (a trio who would later be temporarily memorialised in the names of major Bulawayo streets).

The following year, Rhodes mustered an army of 500, the 'Pioneer Column', and a contingency of settlers who marched northward into Mashonaland. On 27 June, they hoisted the Union Jack over Fort Victoria (Masvingo) and on 12 September established Fort Salisbury. Their next target was Manyika, still occupied by the Portuguese, but they were able to coerce Africans to join their efforts and after a skirmish resulting in a border shift, the BSAC established Umtali (Mutare) as an eastern headquarters on the new frontier.

Although no great quantities of gold had been discovered, the colonists recognised the potential of the Mashonaland plateau and appropriated vast tracts of farmland. In 1893,

Lobengula, who still hadn't realised he'd been duped by the British, sent Ndebele raiders to Masvingo to put down a band of Shona attempting to drive a wedge between the Ndebele and the British by sabotaging colonial telegraph lines. One Leander Starr Jameson, commander of Fort Victoria (Masvingo), mistook this action as an offence against the British and prepared to invade Matabeleland.

For the Ndebele, it was an unequal contest against superior arms and Lobengula, anticipating a humiliating defeat, burned his capital at Bulawayo and fled. He died of smallpox shortly after the Ndebele thrashed enemy forces at the Battle of Shangani River 150 km north-west of Bulawayo. Although the Ndebele continued to resist the BSAC forces, which by this time were striking from all directions, the death of Lobengula produced a marked drop in morale and their effectiveness waned and eventually foundered. By 1895, the spoils had been divided among White settlers, and Africans had been relegated to marginal scrubby and tsetse fly-infested lands, an incentive to remain on White lands as indentured workers. Those who failed to work for the landowner at least four months per year were required to pay a substantial 'hut tax' to be allowed to remain.

By 1895, the new country was being referred to as 'Rhodesia' after its heavy-handed founder. Shortly thereafter, Mark Twain wrote in *More Tramps Abroad*: 'Rhodesia is the right name for that land of piracy and pillage, and puts the right stain upon it'.

The First Chimurenga

As would be expected, the government of Rhodesia was set up 'for, by, and of' the Whites. Although the Ndebele had effectively been squashed and their bovine wealth commandeered by the victors, trade continued between the Shona and the Europeans until it became apparent the British were there to stay and intended to control both African and Rhodesian interests.

Recognising the weakness of the BSAC army after an abortive raid against Kruger's Boers in the Transvaal in March 1896, the Ndebele came back with a vengeance, gathering forces and single-mindedly aiming to drive the enemy from their land forever. This warlike spirit proved contagious; by June, the Shona, traditional enemies of the Ndebele, had joined in, calling it Chimurenga, the War for Liberation.

This jihad-like crusade was led by two African *mhondoro* or spiritualists, Nehanda Charwe Nyakasikana (a woman) and Sekuru Kaguvi, who preached solidarity and cooperation among both the Shona and Ndebele. Although the revolt gained some momentum, it was effectively stalled when the leaders were captured and hanged in 1897. The Nehanda's parting words, 'my bones will rise again', prophesied the Second Chimurenga which culminated in Zimbabwean independence.

The Ndebele indunas conferred with the BSAC and came to an agreement of sorts but the fragmented Shona groups were only quelled after violent BSAC persuasion. An all-White Legislative Council was installed to govern the colony in 1899.

At this point, lasting European control of the region seemed ensured and immigration then began in earnest. By 1904 there were some 12,000 European settlers in the country and double that number by 1911. In 1922, a referendum was held in which Whites voted to become a self-governing colony under 'Responsible Government', rather than a province in the Union of South Africa (the Cape and Natal combined with the conquered Boer Republics of Transvaal and Orange Free State). The following year the BSAC, realising that Rhodesian profits were not meeting expectations, happily handed Southern Rhodesia over to the British crown.

Although the colony's constitution was in theory nonracial, suffrage was based on British citizenship and annual income and only a few Blacks qualified. Taxation was introduced and the wholesale exploitation of African labour kept the mines and farms humming the White government's tune. In the 1930s, White supremacy was legislated by the Land Apportionment Act which excluded Africans from ownership of the best farming land and by a labour law in 1934 which called for separate development of the races (Zimbabweans also refer to this by the Afrikaans term *apartheid*). It prohibited Blacks entering into skilled trades and professions or settling in White areas (including all towns and cities), thereby leaving them dependent on the whims of White landowners and commercial bosses for their livelihood.

Rumbles of Nationalism

The first Black resistance to their unequal status surfaced in the 1920s and 30s with the formation of the Rhodesia Bantu Voters' Association, the Southern Rhodesia Native Association and the Southern Rhodesia African National Congress. These represented only middle-class Africans (as the name of the first implies – only the middle class could vote), and sought to reform the system rather than dismantle it. They were effectual only in that they raised Black consciousness of the realities of inequality.

Abysmally poor wages and conditions led to the gradual radicalisation of the African labour force. During the 1940s, active resistance surfaced in the form of the African Voice Association, headed by Benjamin Burombo. Nationalistic fervour was fanned with the passage of the Native Land Husbandry Act of 1951 in which common pasture land on native reserves was divided into smallholdings and allocated to individual families, some of whom were recent evictees from White lands. Herd sizes were necessarily reduced to the number that could be grazed on the tiny individual plots.

By the time Southern Rhodesia, Northern Rhodesia and Nyasaland were politically joined in 1953 into the Federation of Rhodesia and Nyasaland, mining and industrial concerns favoured a more racially mixed middle class as a counterweight to the increasingly dissatisfied labour force. Pressure from the British government eliminated several of the economic segregation policies and allowed Blacks to enter skilled professions and work in city centres but no concessions were made to the sort of one-man-one-vote system the nationalist movements envisioned.

Meanwhile, White farmers, skilled workers and businesspeople perceived that growing nationalistic sentiments posed a threat to their privileged status. When Garfield Todd, the Federation's prime minister, attempted to satisfy some of the more moderate African demands, he was thrown out. The same thing happened to his successor in 1962, following the approval of a new constitution which envisaged a vague African-European parity sometime in the distant future, an unacceptable position as far as most Whites were concerned.

In Salisbury in 1955, the City Youth League was formed by the most adamant nationalist leaders and two years later merged with the Southern Rhodesian African National Congress to form a new ANC under the leadership of labour activist Joshua Nkomo. Although the organisation was banned in 1959, it continued for a short time under the guise of the National Democratic Party, during which period the resistance turned to violent uprising in the form of *zhii* or 'vengeful annihilation of the enemy' in response to the State of Emergency declared on 26 February 1959. Protests, labour strikes and sabotage punctuated this violent period of organised unrest. The government responded by banning the party and, tragically, taking violent and deadly action at one Bulawayo rally. Unfazed, the NDP re-emerged on 17 December 1961 as the Zimbabwe African People's Union (ZAPU) with Joshua Nkomo again at the helm.

Predictably, ZAPU was banned after a few months, accused of sponsoring rural vandalism and sabotage. In 1962 the newly elected ultra-right-wing government (Winston Field's Rhodesian Front Party) countered by banning Black assemblies and political debates and instituting a mandatory death sentence for arson.

Nkomo bantered about the possibility of setting up a government in exile but internal disputes caused a rift in ZAPU and the dissident members, including Robert Mugabe, Ndabaningi Sithole and Leopold Takawira, were ousted and shortly thereafter formed the Zimbabwe African National Union (ZANU). After squabbles between the two in the aftermath of the Federation's 1963 breakup – which later resulted in the independence of Northern Rhodesia (Zambia) and Nyasaland (Malawi) – both ZAPU and ZANU were banned and most of the leadership imprisoned.

Ian Smith & UDI

In April 1964, Ian Smith took over both the Rhodesian Front and the presidency and began actively pressing for Rhodesian independence. British prime minister Harold Wilson countered by outlining a series of requisite conditions which had to be met before Britain would even consider cutting the tether, including guarantees of internal racial equality, evidence of a charted course toward majority rule and majority sanction of the prospect of independence. In 1965, realising he had as much chance as a snowball in hell of securing such concessions from the White constituency, Smith pressed for a Unilateral Declaration of Independence from Britain. In the election of May 1965, Smith's party picked up all 50 seats in government and UDI was declared in December.

Britain reacted by declaring Smith's action illegal and imposing economic sanctions in an attempt to bring him to heel. The UN eventually (1968) voted to make these sanctions mandatory, but with South Africa openly assisting Smith and Mozambique still under colonial rule, the loopholes were enormous. The sanctions were ignored by most Western countries and even by some British companies (including British Petroleum) and action that was intended to force Smith to the negotiating table failed miserably. The Rhodesian economy actually prospered; sanctions provided the incentive to increase and diversify domestic production. In fact, laws were passed to restrict

ZANU poster

nationalists were able to establish bases there and escalate the conflict. Following suit, ZAPU (combined with South Africa's ANC) set up its own ZIPRA (Zimbabwe Peoples' Revolutionary Army) bases in Zambia and training camps were organised in Tanzania.

The increasingly organised nationalist movements didn't faze Smith nearly so much as Britain's refusal to budge on the issue of independence. His response was to submit a new constitution guaranteeing Blacks eight out of 66 seats in parliament but Britain, intent upon hearing the will of the people, organised the Pearce Commission to solicit Black African opinion before it considered taking any action. Despite the Rhodesian Front's massive and costly campaign to secure Black acceptance of the new constitution, the Smith government – which had apparently been on holiday from reality for some time – was surprised to find its scheme summarily and forcefully thrown back in its face.

As the liberation movement gained momentum, Josiah Tongogara, commander of ZANLA (Zimbabwe African National Liberation Army), ZANU's military forces, went to China for Maoist tactical training. As a result, the civilian public was drafted into cooperation; young men operated as *mujiba* scouts, serving as messengers, and women *zwimbwido* assisted and cooked for guerrilla troops. When the government got wind of all this, it set up 'protected villages' and, to shield them from 'intimidation', forcibly relocated those suspected of helping or harbouring guerrillas and terrorists.

Nationalist forces struck with ever-increasing ferocity throughout the country: ZANLA from Samora Machel's Mozambique and ZIPRA from Kaunda's Zambia, and Whites, most of whom had been born in Africa and knew no country but Rhodesia, gradually began to realise the gravity of their situation. Many abandoned their homes and farms, particularly in the eastern highlands, and emigrated to South Africa or the Commonwealth countries. It finally dawned on Ian Smith that all might not be well in Rhodesia.

export of profits and to impose import controls. Smith staunchly refused to even countenance any concessions and considered the revocation of UDI and especially acceptance of majority rule entirely out of the question. 'Never in a thousand years,' he declared, would Black Africans rule Rhodesia.

Given such intransigence, both ZANU and ZAPU decided that only by armed conflict could power be wrested from Smith and his Rhodesian Front. On 28 April 1966 (now known as Chimurenga Day), the Second Chimurenga began when ZANU guerrillas launched an attack on Rhodesian forces at Chinhoyi, north-west of the capital. Although this and subsequent guerrilla actions failed due to lack of cohesion and vulnerability of training facilities within the country, after Frelimo liberated substantial areas of neighbouring Mozambique, ZANU

The Lisbon Coup and subsequent overthrow of the fascist regime in Portugal in April 1974, which brought independence, pseudo-Marxism and eventual chaos to both Angola and Mozambique, altered completely the balance of power in the area. It forced such powers as the USA and South Africa to reappraise their positions in southern Africa and surprisingly, both advised Smith to accommodate the nationalists.

On 8 December 1974, at Lusaka, Zambia, the various nationalist groups were united under Abel Muzorewa's African National Congress. On 11 December on the Zambezi Bridge at Victoria Falls, the unlikely duo of South Africa's John Vorster and Zambia's Kenneth Kaunda persuaded Smith to call a ceasefire and release from detention the highest ranking members of the nationalist movement – Nkomo, Sithole, and Mugabe among them – to allow peace negotiations to begin.

The talks, however, were hardly peaceful and broke down in an atmosphere of recrimination between Smith and the nationalists on one hand and between nationalist leaders on the other; ZANU split, Joshua Nkomo had differences with ANC leader Muzorewa and was expelled from the organisation, and Robert Mugabe, a highly respected former teacher and 10-year detainee under Smith, made his way to Mozambique where he replaced Sithole as the leader of ZANU. The following year, ZANU chairman Herbert Chitepo was assassinated in Lusaka by Rhodesian intelligence.

Nationalist groups continued to fragment and re-form in an alphabet soup of 'Z' acronyms. In January, 1976, at Geneva, ZANU and ZAPU were induced to form an alliance known as the Patriotic Front, with Sithole and Muzorewa leading separate delegations. Although the hoped-for spirit of cooperation between the two was never realised, the Patriotic Front survived in name. Similarly, ZIPRA and ZANLA combined to form ZIPU (Zimbabwe People's Army) under Rex Nhongo.

At this stage, Ian Smith, faced with wholesale White emigration and a collapsing economy, was forced to change his strategy to one of internal settlement. Both Sithole and Muzorewa were persuaded to join a so-called transitional government in which the Whites were to be guaranteed 28 out of 100 parliamentary seats as well as a veto over all legislation for the next 10 years. In addition, White property would be guaranteed and White control of the armed forces, police, judiciary and civil service would continue. In exchange, Patriotic Front guerrillas would be granted amnesty. The effort was a dismal failure, as could have been expected, and indeed only resulted in escalation of the violence. To salvage the settlement, Smith entered into clandestine negotiations with Nkomo, offering to ditch both Sithole and Muzorewa, but Nkomo wouldn't be swayed.

Finally, with support for Smith waning among the White population and the country's largest fuel depot sabotaged by Patriotic Front guerrillas, Smith opted to call a general election by both Blacks and Whites. On 1 May 1979, he handed the office of Prime Minister over to Muzorewa, who was effectively a puppet, and opened up 50% of European-designated lands to people of any race; government structure was, however, much the same as that proposed under the 'internal settlement'. The changes weren't taken very seriously; no one was cheering and international diplomatic recognition of Zimbabwe-Rhodesia, as it was now called, wasn't forthcoming. At best, a few countries regarded Zimbabwe-Rhodesia as simply a passable transitional government.

Independence

In Britain, the Conservatives won the 1979 election and Margaret Thatcher immediately began pressing for a solution to the Rhodesian problem. It was finally decided that any new constitution would have to be satisfactory to Britain and be ratified in free and well-monitored elections. On 10 September 1979, the delegations met at Lancaster House in London to draw up a constitution

Robert Mugabe

factions got down to the business of jostling for position in the queue for power.

In the carefully monitored election of 4 March 1980, Mugabe and ZANU won 57 of the 80 seats available to Blacks, Nkomo's ZAPU party 20, and Muzorewa's UANC only three. Zimbabwe joined the ranks of Africa's independent nations from this date, under an internationally recognised majority government headed by Robert Mugabe. In Salisbury (Harare) on 16 April 1980, the Reverend Canaan Banana was officially sworn in as first president of independent Zimbabwe and Robert Mugabe took the helm as prime minister.

Despite the long and bitter struggle, Mugabe displayed restraint and kept vengeful tendencies at bay in the new society. The remaining Whites were a nuisance but he wasn't keen to throw out the baby with the bathwater and lose their wealth, technical expertise and access to foreign investment, all necessary to the fulfilment of the dream he, as a committed Marxist, had of the creation of a one-party socialist state. He appointed White ministers of agriculture and commerce & industry, made assurances that 'there is a place for everyone in this country...the winners and the losers', and that he aimed not to bring about a new Mozambique or a new Kenya, but a new Zimbabwe. The economy soared, wages increased and basic social programs – notably education and health care – were reformed or established.

It was a promising start, but the euphoria and the optimistic sense of national unity brought on by independence quickly faded. There was a resurgence of the rivalry between ZANU and ZAPU which escalated into armed conflicts between supporters of the two parties. Mugabe ordered five prominent Nkomo supporters arrested in 1980 and ousted Nkomo from his cabinet position in 1981. Tensions were further inflamed by the arrest of the Minister of Manpower Planning, Edgar Tekere, for the alleged murder of a White farmer. Although he was found not guilty, his political career was derailed.

satisfactory to both the Patriotic Front represented by Nkomo and Mugabe and the Zimbabwe-Rhodesia government, represented by Muzorewa and Smith. Also attending were Kenneth Kaunda and Julius Nyerere, to encourage the Patriotic Front towards a settlement, and Margaret Thatcher, who would pressure Smith to compromise. For several months, the talks accomplished nothing; Mugabe, who wanted ultimate power in the new government, refused to make any concessions whatsoever.

After 14 weeks of talks and some heavy-handed coercion by the British, the racially imbalanced Lancaster House Agreement, which guaranteed Whites (3% of the population) 20 of the 100 seats in the new parliament, was reached. The agreement also stipulated that private landholdings could not be nationalised or appropriated without adequate compensation, a more logical 'concession' to Whites than the race-dictated imbalance in parliamentary representation. Despite the agreement's failings, the way for independence was paved and the various

More recently, Nkomo was accused of plotting to overthrow the government and there was a resurgence of guerrilla activity in Matabeleland, the area from which ZAPU draw the bulk of its support. In early 1983, Mugabe sent in the North Korean-trained Fifth Brigade to quell the disturbances but instead of quelling, they launched into an orgy of killing to which several thousand civilians fell victim; villagers were gunned down and prominent members of ZAPU were systematically eliminated in order to rout out dissidents. Essentially, the conflict was a tribal one between the majority Shona (largely ZANU supporters) and the minority Ndebele (largely ZAPU supporters).

Nkomo meanwhile fled to England and was to remain there until Mugabe, realising Zimbabwe's enemies were watching with interest as internal strife threatened to escalate into civil war, publicly relented and guaranteed his safe return, then began the talks which would result in the combining of ZANU and ZAPU. An amnesty was offered to the dissidents and the entire affair, but not the underlying discontent, was thereby masterfully swept under the rug.

Recent Developments

Despite the tragic examples of Kaunda's Zambia, Nyerere's Tanzania, and the violently oppressive revolutionary government in Mozambique, Mugabe still dreams of transforming Zimbabwe into a one-party state. The long overdue abolition in mid-1988 of the law guaranteeing 20 parliamentary seats to Whites, the imposition of strict and strangling controls on currency, foreign exchange and trade and, in April 1990, a review of White land ownership guarantees (after the British-brokered constitution expired on the 10th anniversary of independence) all seemed to indicate steps in this direction.

The late 1980s were characterised by scandal and government corruption. Some MPs and cabinet ministers were loudly professing socialism, a few sincerely, but many of the same group were privately greasing their own palms. In 1988, the government was linked with shady practices at the Willowvale automobile assembly plant near Harare. The corruption was exposed by the press and students at the University of Zimbabwe launched a protest against Mugabe having allowed dirty government to exist in Zimbabwe when he'd expressly pledged it would never happen. Mugabe felt threatened by the uprising, cut off some areas of university funding and refused to restore them until the students admitted their mistake. Late 1990 saw further student unrest when riot police resorted to tear gas to break up a demonstration protesting a proposed increase in government control over University of Zimbabwe policy.

Some particularly dirty business surrounding the March 1990 elections revealed similar facets of the president. The newly formed ZUM (Zimbabwe Unity Movement) party under the leadership of Edgar Tekere, which promoted a free-enterprise economy and a multiparty democratic state, played mouse to the elephant and challenged ZANU in several electorates. Like the elephant, Mugabe overreacted and engineered some last minute gerrymandering to waylay any possible ZUM victories. Shortly following the election (a ZANU landslide all around) the ZUM candidate who'd shown promise in the Gweru North electoral district, Patrick Kombayi, was wounded in an apparent assassination attempt and anyone having ties with ZUM quickly sought a low profile.

The White land issue, the bugbear of the Mugabe government, also resurfaced when the Zimbabwe government announced a plan to resettle half of the country's White-owned farmlands by the year 2000. Since independence, only 10 million acres had been purchased and 51,000 families resettled, far short of the original goal. The government sought another 15 million acres for the resettlement of 110,000 more families, leaving 15 million acres for more efficient commercial farming ventures.

The proposed methods of land takeover, however, have been loudly protested by the Commercial Farmers Union (made up of primarily White farmers): the lands would be subject to price controls set by the government (also, incidentally, the buyer), each farmer would be allowed to sell only one farm, absentee landlords would be prohibited, land could not be sold to foreigners unless they had skills needed in Zimbabwe, and farmers would be compensated in Zimbabwe dollars rather than foreign currency, preventing their leaving the country after selling out.

Although Mugabe publicly continues to pay lip service to his resettlement scheme, one official, recognising the commercial farmers' gripes, admitted the government does not want to 'kill the goose that lays the golden eggs' or frighten away foreign investors. It looks as if the land reformists are on their way back to the drawing board. The National Farmers Association and the Zimbabwe National Farmers Union (both primarily non-White organisations) have suggested that resettlement be handled on a mutually willing buyer and seller basis and that the government offer easy terms loans to allow small or peasant farmers to purchase their own land.

The most recent development in the one-party state issue came in August 1990, when, at a Central Committee meeting 22 of 26 members voted against continuation of the idea. They argued that introducing a one-party state at a time when the worldwide trend is in the opposite direction could be interpreted as a step backward and severely affect Zimbabwe's credibility in the eyes of potential investors.

Their efforts were negated in late 1990 and early 1991, however, when the government decided that 50% of the lands held by White commercial farmers would be redistributed to Black subsistence farmers. Unfortunately, this will remove the source of the majority of Zimbabwe's foreign exchange earnings and furthermore, such racially based policies threaten to invite criticism from overseas and thwart investment schemes.

GEOGRAPHY

Zimbabwe is a landlocked country in south central Africa. It's situated entirely within the tropics – between 15°S and 22°S latitude – but most of Zimbabwe consists of highveld and middleveld plateau lying between 900 and 1700 m above sea level. The country enjoys a remarkably temperate climate. It is bound on the north-west by Zambia, on the east and north-east by Mozambique, on the south-west by Botswana, and on the south by South Africa. Four countries – Zambia, Zimbabwe, Botswana and Namibia – come within 100 metres of each other at the country's westernmost extreme.

Zimbabwe's maximum width is 725 km while north to south it stretches 835 km. The total land area is 390,310 square km, roughly half the size of Australia's New South Wales or the same size as the British Isles with an extra Scotland thrown in.

A low ridge passing along the Mvurwi Range in the north-east to the Matobo Hills in the south-west marks the divide between two of Africa's greatest watercourses, the Zambezi in the north and the Limpopo and Save in the south. The former, consisting mostly of plateau, gently slopes away from the ridge then drops dramatically to the broad plain of the Zambezi Valley in the north-east and into the tangled hills and valleys around Lake Kariba in the north-west. The plateau landscape is characterised by bushveld dotted with small rocky outcrops or *kopjes* and bald knob-like domes of slickrock known as *dwalas*.

The hot, dry lowveld of southern Zimbabwe consists of the relatively flat savanna lands of the Save Basin, sloping almost imperceptibly toward the Limpopo River.

The only significant mountainous region is the eastern highlands which straddles the Zimbabwe-Mozambique border from the Nyanga region in the north to the Chimanimani Mountains in the south. Zimbabwe's highest peak, Nyangani, rises 2592 metres near the northern end of the range.

FLORA & FAUNA

The following section contains information on flora and smaller animals. Larger animals and birds are discussed in detail in the Safari Guide at the back of the book.

Flora

Author TV Bulpin wrote of Zimbabwe 'there is not a more picturesque part than the wild garden of trees and aloes and flowering plants that lies between the Limpopo and Zambezi rivers...'

Despite Bulpin's assessment, Zimbabwe's background vegetation cover is undeniably rather uniform throughout. Most of the central and western plateau country is covered in bushveld – thorny acacia savanna and *miombo* – or dry open woodland. The drier lowlands of the south and south-east are characterised by lower thorny scrub and baobab.

Generalisations, however, fail to convey the richly colourful array of species that enliven this plain canvas: towering cactus trees resembling pipe-organs, 30 diverse species of aloe (which flower in the cool, sunny days of midwinter), spreading poinsettia shrubs as big as cottages, flowering jacaranda, hibiscus, citrus trees, jasmine, banana trees, flame trees, bougainvillaea and a host of other succulents, tropical flowers, palms and perennials.

The eastern highlands and their unique climatic conditions provide another botanical environment altogether. The higher slopes around Nyanga are draped with very un-African pine forests – some admittedly planted by the paper industry – and down the eastern slopes of the Vumba where Zimbabwe spills into Mozambique, one can find stands of tropical hardwood forest complete with ferns and lianas.

Those after Africa's archetypal Tarzan jungles, however, will have to go to Zaïre or keep within 100 metres of Victoria Falls, where the constant misty spray has created a lush stand of tropical rainforest.

Game Parks

For travellers whose ideal African adventure would include rambling through forest and savanna bushlands pursuing and photographing the menagerie that symbolises wild Africa to armchair dreamers worldwide, Zimbabwe is where it can be realised. Without the commercial conveyor belt feeling of Kenya, the expense of Botswana or Tanzania, the elite crowds of South Africa, or the political uncertainties of most other countries, Zimbabwe's wilderness game parks offer pristine wildlife habitat, large animal populations and as much variety of species as any place on the continent. In fact, 13% of Zimbabwe's surface area is protected or semiprotected wildlife habitat, either fully-fledged national parks or unfenced national safari areas.

Hunting & Conservation Practices

Although it may seem sacrilegious to mention both hunting and conservation in the same breath, Zimbabwe's official – and internationally unpopular – policy is one of 'sustained yield use'; that is, limiting hunting to the level of natural growth in the game population. The government needs foreign exchange and sees in its wildlife resources an abundant and relatively painless method of acquiring it. Safari areas allow game hunting and the government cites their

Elephants

ability to annually net millions of dollars in foreign exchange as justification for their existence and therefore, for the conservation of wildlife.

Revenues from hunting on communal lands, where wildlife can become a nuisance to subsistence farmers, are channelled back into the affected communities in the form of schools, hospitals and other infrastructure.

In addition to the national parks and reserves, many private ranches double as game reserves. Some are open to big game hunting in order to both finance the operation and make a profit.

Despite the rhetoric about all the benefits of sustained yield and the resulting windfall in government coffers, it's difficult to fathom anyone deriving more pleasure from stalking Zimbabwe's wildlife to destroy and stuff it than to simply watch and photograph it. Those who can't restrain themselves, however, should direct enquiries to the Provincial Warden – Hunting Division (☎ 707624), Dept of National Parks and Wildlife Management, PO Box 8365, Causeway, Harare or to The Registration Office (☎ 706511), PO Box 8052, Causeway, Harare.

On a more positive note, Zimbabwe does seem to realise the value of wild lands and preservation of habitat for their aesthetic as well as their economic values. Since the turn of the century, the human population has grown from 500,000 to over eight million and as pressure to develop and farm wild lands to sustain the growing population increases, so too does the need for retreat from all the chaos.

In an effort to instil in schoolchildren, particularly urban dwellers, the value of wilderness and wildlife appreciation, several amateur conservation groups have taken the initiative to purchase small protected reserves in urban areas, primarily for the purpose of education – Mukuvisi Woodlands near Harare, Cecil Kop near Mutare, and Tshabalala near Bulawayo.

Culling

Another practice which remains highly controversial is the Zimbabwe National Parks Department's culling of elephants. Although it's done humanely – entire herds are destroyed rather than individuals to prevent emotional stress on the survivors – many argue that nature should simply be allowed to take its course.

The flaw in this argument, according to officials, is that humans have interfered so drastically with lands outside game reserves – setting up farms and veterinary control fences, grazing domestic stock, and clearing the tasty bushland trees that elephants bulldoze, uproot, and devour in staggering quantities – the herds haven't the ability to spread out as they'd be inclined to in a no-human-interference scenario. For evidence of the destruction that results from elephant overpopulation, you need only look at Botswana's Chobe National Park which has four times the ideal elephant population. In places, the bush appears to have experienced nuclear holocaust.

GOVERNMENT

The legislative body of the Republic of Zimbabwe consists of the executive president, and a parliament made up of the Senate and the House of Assembly. The president, is elected by the members of parliament and serves a six-year term. He is the official head of state and commander-in-chief of the armed forces. Currently, executive president Robert Mugabe's ZANU party is in undisputed control of the national government.

The Senate consists of 40 senators; 36 of these are chosen by the electoral college and four are appointed by the president. A Senate Legal Committee has power to investigate legislative goings-on. The House of Assembly consists of 100 representatives or members of parliament who are elected by the constituency of the district being represented every five years.

The judicial branch of government is made up of a Tribunal consisting of both General and Appellate Divisions, with power in both civil and criminal matters. The chief justice is appointed by the president in

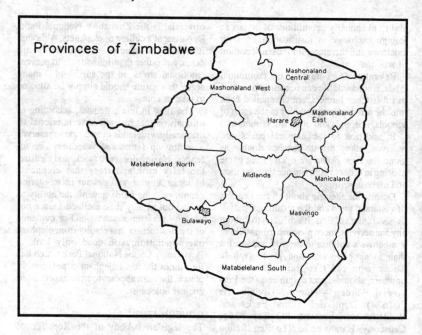

Provinces of Zimbabwe

Mashonaland West • Mashonaland Central • Harare • Mashonaland East • Matabeleland North • Midlands • Manicaland • Bulawayo • Masvingo • Matabeleland South

council with the prime minister. Appellate justices are appointed by the president in concordance with the Judicial Commission.

Zimbabwe is divided into eight provinces, each of which has its own local government headed by a state-appointed governor.

ECONOMY

Although about 80% of Zimbabwe's population is dependent upon agriculture, it accounts for only 20% of the GNP because the majority of farmers operate on the subsistence level while many larger, commercially viable farms are being purchased by the government for resettlement purposes. Interestingly, less than 15% of arable land is currently under cultivation.

The staple food crop is maize, while cotton, both burley and virginia tobacco (tobacco is the largest export earner in the economy), citrus fruits, wine grapes (Zimbabwe's white wines are palatable but

the reds still have a long way to go!) and sugar cane are the primary cash crops. The sugar cane, which is grown in the lowveld, is turned into table sugar, molasses and 40 million litres of ethanol annually. Ethanol is blended with petrol and used as fuel to supplement the imported petrol entering the country through the carefully guarded but vulnerable pipeline through the Beira corridor.

Livestock, the major indication of wealth in precolonial Zimbabwe, remains a major commodity. The country is nearly self-sufficient in terms of milk, beef, poultry, pork and mutton. In addition, more than a million goats roam the communal lands (grazing them into wastelands) and provide subsistence-level protein. Game ranching, particularly of antelope, is also currently on the increase.

Mining interests account for around 40% of Zimbabwe's exports; gold is the major earner. Coal, chromite, nickel, asbestos, copper, iron ore and tin are also exported in significant quantities.

Forestry is also an up-and-coming venture, especially in the eastern highlands, where vast tracts of softwood forests have been planted and are being harvested for pulp, and in the south-west where mahogany and teak provide raw materials for railway construction and a growing furniture industry.

Tourism, while on the increase, has not yet recovered from the setback it experienced during the war. Although hordes of package tours descend on Victoria Falls, reports of sporadic violence since then have put off many of those who would prefer to wander further. Although these concerns are entirely out of proportion to the real dangers – Zimbabwe is far more secure than Kenya, for example – it will be a while before the tourist industry becomes a major player in the foreign exchange arena. The plus side of this is, of course, that visitors won't have to endure close encounters with their own kind. This will certainly change in the near future – so hurry!

POPULATION & PEOPLE

In 1985, Zimbabwe's population was officially estimated at 8.4 million, a substantial increase over the 4.8 million recorded by the 1969 census. Most of the people are of Bantu origin, 76% belong to various Shona groups (Ndau, Rozwi, Korekore, Karanga, Manyika and Zezuru) occupying the eastern two-thirds of the country, 18% are of Ndebele stock (including the Kalanga) living primarily in south-western Zimbabwe, and the remainder are divided between Batonka (2%) of the upper Kariba area, Shangaan or Hlengwe (1%) of the lowveld, Venda (1%) of the far south, and European (2%).

The European population has declined steadily, with an average of 17,000

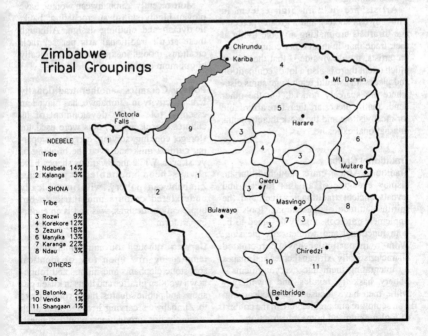

Zimbabwe Tribal Groupings

NDEBELE

Tribe

1 Ndebele 14%
2 Kalanga 5%

SHONA

Tribe

3 Rozwi 9%
4 Korekore 12%
5 Zezuru 18%
6 Manyika 13%
7 Karanga 22%
8 Ndau 3%

OTHERS

Tribe

9 Batonka 2%
10 Venda 1%
11 Shangaan 1%

emigrants annually immediately following independence. Their numbers have now stabilised at about 100,000. In addition, there are about 25,000 people of mixed European and African descent and 10,000 Asians, primarily of Indian origin.

The average annual population growth rate is currently 3.5% and the average life expectancy is 57 years.

ARTS

Visitors are normally surprised by the scope and degree of artistic talent Zimbabweans seem to take for granted and eventually become immune to the sort of quality that at home would be considered a work of genius; from even the humblest practical ceramic pot or basket created in a remote village emerges evidence of artistic sensitivity and attention to detail. Arts centres in Harare and Bulawayo are taking this potential seriously and seeking out the greatest talents for special training.

Artists are held in high esteem in Zimbabwean society and a greater percentage of artists are making a viable living at their trade than in most other countries. For the artists, the down side is that there is so much talent there is also a lot of competition and pieces that would fetch huge sums elsewhere are scarcely noticed. On the other hand, quality pieces are therefore affordable for most visitors and the work thereby gains international exposure.

Traditional Crafts

Traditional African crafts, though utilitarian, display a degree of art that reflects and reveals ancient traditional values and the spiritual attitude of the culture. Tools and implements are consciously designed to be both functional and aesthetically pleasing. Women in particular have perpetuated characteristically African themes and shapes by integrating them into everyday items – pottery, basketry, textiles, and jewellery – while men have focused on woodcarving, iron sculpture and architecture in the context of tool-making and home construction.

Textiles & Basketry Even before Arab traders brought cloth from India, Zimbabweans were spinning and weaving garments from wild cotton that grew on the plateau and making blankets, mats and clothing from strands of the soft and pliable tree bark known as *gudza*. This art is still practised today.

The quality of woven baskets in Zimbabwe is phenomenal and the patterns well thought out and beautifully symmetrical. As in many cultures, baskets are used for a variety of purposes, from trapping fish underwater to storing and carrying food and belongings. They are even used as table service.

A number of materials – *imizi* grass, reeds, *ilala* palm, and sisal – are utilised and the characteristic earth-tone dyes are derived from a variety of tree barks. The largest baskets, which typically contain well over a cubic metre, are a favourite with tourists who take them home to use as laundry hampers.

More recently, Zimbabwean women have proven highly skilful at crocheting, batik, tie-dyeing and clothing design. Although these aren't traditional arts per se, their creations, though inexpensive, are typically of optimum quality.

Pottery Ceramics, another traditionally female activity in Zimbabwe, has played an essential role in the development of its cultures. As elsewhere, pots were used for storage, cooking, serving, carrying, preparing curdled milk and even the brewing of yeast beer. While their various shapes have always been undoubtedly practical, Zimbabwean pottery, with its typically understated colours and intricate but unpretentious designs, was and is an enduring art form.

Carving Although souvenir hunters will be tempted by row upon row of identical soapstone elephants and hippos and rough-hewn wooden giraffes and lions in kitsch gift shops and public squares, there's much more to Zimbabwe's carving heritage than such assembly-line productions would suggest.

Such tools as hoes, axe handles, ladles, bowls, and penis sheaths (umncwado) were all carved from wood in simplistic and practical designs. Spear, knobkerrie and dagger handles were decoratively rendered and shields were mounted on a carved wooden frame. Even small canoes were typically hewn out of a single bit of wood.

Carved mutsago or umqamelo (Shona and Ndebele words for 'headrest') were considered emblematic of family responsibility and headrests of distant ancestors are passed down male lines and called upon to evoke ceremonially the spirits of earlier owners. Various theories have arisen about the extent of their early use – whether for afternoon rests, protection of elaborate coiffures, or as concessions to the comfort of the elderly. Now, their worth lies primarily in their antique or heirloom value.

Wooden stools, whose expertly intricate decorations reach their highest level in the Batonka culture of western Lake Kariba, are carved from a single piece of wood. Historically, only men were allowed to sit on them and male heads of household used them as a 'throne' from which to oversee family affairs.

Divining devices or hakata are carved from bone, wood or ivory and are used to forecast future events, determine guilt and communicate with ancestors in traditional rural areas. There are four tablets in a set: chirume which has a male value, kwami with a female value, nhokwara with 35 triangular cuts representing good luck, and chitokwadzima which represents bad luck and bears the image of a crocodile. Interpretations are made by a reader based on the tablets' configuration after being thrown.

Shona Sculpture

Although it's a relatively recent addition to Zimbabwe's cultural arts – it has no functional or ceremonial value and therefore wasn't significant in traditional society – Shona sculpture has garnered most of the laurels as far as international recognition is concerned. It isn't simply considered great African art but great art in the broadest sense.

Although the movement is known as Shona sculpture, the Shona tribe has no exclusive rights to the genre and smaller tribal groups are participating as well. Today's sculpture has been evolving over the past 30 years or so, a product of welding African themes and ideas with European artistic training.

African folklore provides themes for a majority of the work and pieces are populated by stylised animals, gods, spirits, ancestors and totems as well as deeply emotional humans heavily involved in life. One recurring theme is the metamorphosis of man into beast, the prescribed punishment for violation of certain social interdictions – such as making a meal of one's totem animal. Most of the work is superb.

Four of the major practitioners these days are considered to be among the world's greatest living sculptors. John Takawira, highly acclaimed in Europe, is known for his facility with a number of forms, sizes and themes. Minimalist Nicholas Mukomberanwa, on the other hand, has tended to utilise consistently bulky masses while striving to simplify the designs into only their essential components. The third, Henry Munyaradzi, learned his art at the Tengenenge colony in northern Zimbabwe. Although his pleasant and instantly recognisable works seem reminiscent of the cubist tradition and he's been highly successful, he risks becoming repetitious and therefore ineffectual. Bernard Matemera, Tengenenge's best known artist, experiments with deliberately surreal dimensions and forms, testing responses. In 1986, he won a major international award in India.

In addition to these, Zimbabwe has hundreds of exceptionally talented sculptors chiselling away, many at schools, art centres, and sculpture communities around the country.

Music

Traditional Music Music has always been a given in traditional Zimbabwean culture. The melody and rhythm of repetitive chant-

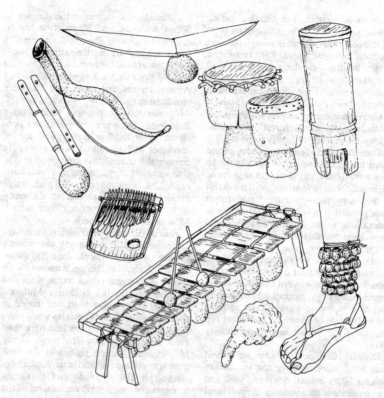

Top right: (clockwise) drums, majaka, hosho, marimba, mbira, wooden flutes, hwamanda & dimbwa

ing becomes a mesmerising declaration of unity between the singers, while individuality is sustained by the various parts being harmonised. Shared song has served as an evocation and confirmation of solidarity in common struggles, whether battle with a neighbouring tribe, cooperation on a successful harvest, or confrontation with natural disaster. Moreover, African stories and legends are punctuated by musical choruses in which the audience participates and social events – weddings, funerals, and religious ceremonies, harvests, and births – are each accompanied by unique songs.

Only recently has the rest of the world begun to take notice of African music – especially since the release of Paul Simon's *Graceland* album – and most modern Zimbabwean artists use traditional music as a base for new musical direction.

Zimbabwe's traditional musical instruments, though fashioned from natural materials on hand, produce an array of effects. The best known is the marimba or xylophone which creates tones similar to those in Western music and is often used for pieces with strong European influences. The keys of the best marimbas are made from the hard wood of the *mwenje* tree of northern Mozambique which produces optimum resonance. Sound boxes are normally made of dried gourds.

Another instrument which is enjoys popularity among souvenir hunters as well as musicians is the *mbira* or thumb piano. It was originally used to accompany historical epics set to music. Although there are several variations, most mbira consist of 22 to 24 narrow iron keys mounted in rows on a wooden sound board. The player plucks the ends of the keys with the thumbs or specially grown thumbnails. An accomplished mbira player is known as a *gwenyambira*.

Percussion instruments include an array of rattles and drums. Rattles can be made of seeds, gourds and even bottle caps. *Hosho* (maracas) rattles are held in the hands while *magagada, majaka, madare* (bells), and Ndebele *mahlwayi* rattles are attached to the legs and ankles of dancers. The *ngoma*, a tapered cylindrical drum made from the *mutiti* or 'lucky bean' tree, is found in all sizes. Although the standard skin covering these days is cowhide, the optimum skins are considered to be zebra and *leguaan*. To achieve maximum resonance, drums are treated with beeswax and dried over a flame before a performance.

Probably the oddest percussion instrument ever used in Zimbabwe was the *mujejeje*, the 'stone bells'. Many stones in granite kopjes around the country have exfoliated in such a way that when struck, they'll resound with a lovely bell-like tone. Historically, special occasions were held around these stones in order to take advantage of this novel musical opportunity. The most famous of these can be seen today at the Khami ruins near Bulawayo.

The wind grouping is represented by several types of flutes, including pan pipes and the *nyanga* or 'horn' which is, logically, fashioned from the horn of an animal. Although traditional string instruments have been used historically in Zimbabwe, mostly bow-shaped like the Shangaan *makweyana*, they are rarely played these days.

Pungwes The exact origin of the commonly used word *pungwe* is unknown but is believed to be derived from the word *ngwe* which means 'from darkness to light'. It was first used in the 1960s and referred to all-night urban discos. During the Second Chimurenga (1972-80), however, all-night celebrations of nationalistic unity between villagers and guerrillas, accompanied by morale-inspiring song and dance, came to be known as pungwes. Nowadays, any sort of event, ordinarily a disco or musical performance, may be advertised as a pungwe, meaning it begins in the evening and carries on through the night.

Popular Music Marisa Mowszowski writes: In Shona culture, as in so many African cultures, music is incorporated into almost every aspect of life. Through traditional songs, stories are told, games are played and important lessons passed from generation to generation. These songs use the traditional rhythmic structures of Zimbabwean music and are often accompanied by various percussion instruments (such as dried gourd rattles and skin drums), the mbira, marimbas and the nyanga.

In the period between WW II and the start of Zimbabwe's war of independence in the early 1970s, little attention or interest was afforded by the music industry to these traditional musical forms. Musically, Zimbabwe was inundated with foreign material – from Swing in the 1940s through South African pennywhistle in the 1950s to Otis Redding and other American soul music in the 1960s. Many local groups, including some of today's famous names such as Thomas Mapfumo and Oliver Mtukudzi, began their careers doing Beatles and Elvis covers!

To the great benefit of Zimbabwean music lovers, the war of independence inspired musicians to write, perform and record original protest songs, which were based on traditional Shona sounds, transposed onto Western instruments. These songs, known as Chimurenga, form the musical basis for much of Zimbabwean popular music today. Particularly in Harare, there is no shortage of excellent groups performing their own variations on this essentially Zimbabwean style, mostly with lyrics sung in Shona. Some of the best musicians have been snapped up by overseas audiences – the Bhundu Boys with their fast *jit* dance music went international in 1987 and Thomas Mapfumo's records are sold all over the world – but the majority of them are still there in Harare; very fortunate indeed for the traveller!

Zimbabwe has also over the past decade become a kind of asylum for South African exiles – there are quite a number of musicians hanging around there until the time is right to return to their homeland. This and the fact that so many American and European bands tour Zimbabwe in lieu of South Africa combine to make Harare one of Africa's great musical centres. One way to tap into what's current and popular is to take your own transistor radio and tune in to one of the Shona stations which play great local and not-so-local music.

As well as popular Shona and Shangaan styles, there is a strong market for Zaïrean music, which tends to be based on the rhumba beat. In fact, so admired is the rhumba that Zimbabwean record shops have four categories for African music: local, South African, reggae and rhumba. The general rule is: if it's not local or South African, you'll find it under rhumba! There's some great West African music around, too. Try the Pop Shop on the corner of First St and Baker Ave in Harare – the men in the shop are as helpful and enthusiastic as they come and if you ask them to play something local, they may even dance to it as you listen!

Music Venues The easiest way to find out who's playing where is to look in the entertainment section of the newspaper. The lesser-known but often equally exciting bands usually advertise through posters around the outskirts of town and by the railways. Most hotels have a band playing there on a regular basis and charge Z$10 or Z$15. Popular venues in Harare are the Mushandira Pamwe Hotel in Nyandoro Rd, Highfields, the Queens Hotel on the corner of Robert Mugabe Rd and Kaguvi St and the Playboy Night Club in Union Ave (a little more expensive than the others). In Bulawayo, try the Bulawayo Sun Hotel or 'Z' International in the Show Grounds.

Groups & Musicians Some of Zimbabwe's better-known music names include Thomas Mapfumo and the Blacks Unlimited, Oliver Mtukudzi (currently bandless, but bound to be playing somewhere!), The Four Brothers, New Black Montana (in the Mapfumo genre), Robson Banda and the Black Eagles, Joseph Mutero and Steve Dyer. Bands, however, are constantly breaking up, changing members and changing names, so don't be discouraged if you can't find a group you know of – those men in the record shop can be a useful source of information! Or just keep your eye out for the posters to get an idea of who's around.

Literature

Prior to the 1960s, most of Zimbabwe's literature was produced by the White sector of the population. Popular novelists like Cynthia Stockley and Gertrude Page wrote simplistic but well-received novels during the early part of the century. The first work to express scepticism of Rhodesia's social structure was *The Bay Tree Country*, penned by Arthur Cripps, a British-born poet and missionary, in 1913. In the same vein, in 1950, Doris Lessing produced *The Grass is Singing*.

Although both Shona and Ndebele oral tradition had perpetuated a large body of stories, legends, songs and poetry, the first written works by Black authors didn't appear in print until the publication (in Shona) of *Feso* by S Mutswairo in 1956. The first published Ndebele novel was *Umthawakazi* by P S Mahlangu, which appeared in 1957. Subsequent works by both groups are polarised into those dealing with precolonial traditions, myths and folk tales and those focusing on the social and political experiences of Black Africans under a White regime. Although numerous protest pieces were written during the following 10 years, the first serious treatise of the topic was Stanlake

Top: Hippo (GC); Rhinos (GH)
Middle: Elephant (front view) (GH); Elephant (rear view) (GH); Lion (GH)
Bottom: Zebra (JdC), Cheetah (GH)

Top: Kokerboom (quivertree) (DS); Cactus tree (DS)
Middle: Poinsettia (DS); Welwitschia plant (DS); Baobab (DS)
Bottom: Red Hot Poker (DS); Grass (DS)

Samkange's *On Trial for my Country* in 1966.

Zimbabwean independence in 1980 brought an end to oppression-inspired literature, however, and although some anticlimactic axe-grinding still goes on, most independence era literature has focused on the liberation effort and the struggles to build a new society. Thanks to increasing literacy rates, better education and higher wages over the past decade, Zimbabwean literature is enjoying a boom. New novels, nonfiction and poetry titles in English, Shona and Ndebele are appearing frequently and are being studied as serious literature, as evidenced by the University of Zimbabwe's offering a university degree in Shona literature.

For information on some other titles and players, refer to the Books & Bookshops discussion in the Facts for the Visitor chapter.

RELIGION
Christianity
Between 40% and 50% of Zimbabweans belong to Christian churches but their belief system is characterised more by a hybrid of Christian and traditional beliefs than by dogmatic Christianity.

In 1859, Reverend Robert Moffat of the London Missionary Society established Zimbabwe's first Christian mission at Inyati near Bulawayo. He was followed by Black African representatives of the Dutch Reformed Church from South Africa and the Jesuits who set up their headquarters at Lobengula's Kraal in Matabeleland in 1880. Anglicans and Methodists came later. All the Protestant groups set up schools, medical facilities, and agricultural assistance.

Many Zimbabwean Christians identify with some Protestant sect – the result of numerous early missions zealously competing for converts – but the Roman Catholic church, with 800,000 members in Zimbabwe, claims more adherents than any of the various Protestant denominations which include Methodist, Salvation Army, Seventh-Day Adventist, Dutch Reformed,

Presbyterian, Congregational, Episcopalian, North American fundamentalist groups and a number of exclusively African splinter organisations.

Although the Portuguese first brought Catholicism to Zimbabwe in 1561, it wasn't a recognised presence until 1890 and only became a significant force in the 1950s. In 1972, the Church established the Catholic Commission for Justice and Peace to monitor human rights violations within the country and promote peace and justice. Although it was most active during the Second Chimurenga, it has continued its work to the present day. Another organisation, the Catholic Development Commission, is working to upgrade socioeconomic conditions in rural areas. The church also operates a number of private schools around the country.

Mwari Cult
The majority of Zimbabweans profess traditional religious beliefs as well as those introduced by Europeans. The Mwari Cult, a monotheistic animist belief system which entails ancestor worship and spiritual proxy and intercession, has predominated at least since the height of Great Zimbabwe. Because of its rather clandestine nature, however, little is actually known about the scope of its current influence. Of the numerous Mwari cave shrines in Zimbabwe, only the Matonjeni grouping near Bulawayo – Njelele and Wirarani in the Matobo and Dula near Esigodini – are thought to be still active. These shrines remain officially off limits to outsiders.

The original concept of Mwari, the supreme deity, was probably brought by southward migrating Bantu groups who arrived in Zimbabwe during the 1300s. The new religion spread quickly across southern Africa and took a firm hold. In fact, it was one of the few elements of the Rozwi Empire that survived the Nguni invasions of the early 1800s and the conquering Ndebele were themselves absorbed into the Rozwi religion. Even Christianity could not displace it and converts to European sects took it that Mwari and the Christian God were one and the same. In Shona, the Christian God is still known as Mwari.

Mwari theology is quite simple. Occasionally referred to as Musiki (Creator), Musikavanhu (Origin of Man), or Nyadenga (Father of the Skies), Mwari is the unknowable supreme being. He speaks to his human subjects (or victims) through The Voice of Mwari, a cave-dwelling oracle who is most often female. The oracle is not only responsible to serve as a vehicle for divine will but also to serve as intercessionary between the spirits, the god and the people, especially in cases of natural disaster or outside aggression – both considered deserved punishments for religious infractions. It was the oracle, in fact, that received the go-ahead to begin the First Chimurenga in 1896.

Midzimu, Mhondoro & Mambo

Although Mwari is the head honcho, followers also believe that spirits of their ancestors or *midzimu*, all the way back to the *tateguru* (the common ancestors who lived at some hazy point in the distant past and ultimitely deliver messages to Mwari), continue to inhabit the human world. These spirits, for whom afterlife status is determined by tenure, retain a great deal of influence over the physical world. A person with happy midzimu will be kept out of harm's way while those whose forbears are dissatisfied may meet with all sorts of misfortune.

When that happens, a medium is contacted and the disgruntled ancestor is identified. Normally, a *bira* or family gathering is held in which the unhappy mudzimu (singular form of midzimu) is invited to enter the victim's body, state the complaint and make suggestions for remedying the problem. If all goes well, the victim becomes the family *svikiro* or medium for the now appeased mudzimu.

The mhondoro ('lion' in Shona) operate under much the same principle as the midzimu but rather than confining attentions to their descendants, the mhondoro are often territorial spirits and can affect entire communities of people. When a problem such as a plague or drought strikes, these are the spirits who must be consulted.

Svikiros of individual mhondoro spirits may appear erratically through many generations. Due to their ferocity and fearlessness, they are normally associated with a lion character, hence their name, and the svikiro of a mhondoro effects the aspect of a lion. Prior to the fall of Rozwi, it was most often the Rozwi mambo or king who served as the svikiro. Although his ravings were normally indecipherable to the lay populus, they were easily interpreted by the Mwari priesthood.

In the early 1800s, one mambo managed to fun afoul of Mwari himself, a particularly serious infraction for someone in his position. It wasn't long before the Offended made known to the priests that Rozwi was doomed and would soon fall at the hands of outsiders. Shortly thereafter, the Nguni invasions began.

LANGUAGE

The official language of Zimbabwe – that used in government, legal and business proceedings – is English but it is a first language for only about 2% of the population. The rest of the people are native speakers of some Bantu language, the two most prominent of which are Shona, spoken by 76% of the population, and Ndebele, spoken by 18%.

Shona, which is actually a collection of numerous Bantu dialects, is spoken in the central and eastern parts of the country. The 'high' dialect and the one used in broadcasts and other media is Zezuru which is indigenous to the Harare area.

Ndebele is spoken primarily in Matabeleland in the western and south-western parts of Zimbabwe. It is derived from the Zulu group of languages and is not mutually intelligible with Shona.

Another dialect, Chilapalapa, is actually a pidgin of Ndebele, English, Shona, and Afrikaans, among other things, and is used primarily as a lingua franca for communication between employers and employees. It isn't overly laden with niceties and it's a safe bet that Zimbabweans would prefer to hear straight English than this aberration.

Pronunciation

Since both Shona and Ndebele were first written down by phonetic English transliteration, most letters are pronounced as they would be in English. The major exception are the Ndebele 'clicks', drawing of the tongue away from the front teeth (dental), slapping it on the roof of the mouth (palatal), or drawing it quickly sideways from the right upper gum (lateral). Each of these come in four different varieties: voiced, aspirated, nasal, and aspirated nasal. For interest only – non-native speakers rarely get the hang of this – the following table outlines standard transliterations of each of these sounds:

	voiced	aspirated	nasal	aspirated/nasal
dental	gc	ch	nc	ngc
palatal	gq	qh	nq	ngq
lateral	gx	xh	nx	ngx

Other Ndebele differences of note include:

b pronounced implosively
th is aspirated like the t in 'tarmac'
o is like aw in 'law'
m when placed before a consonant at the beginning of a word is pronounced as a little hum
n when placed before a consonant at the beginning of a word, it's a hum with an n sound

Shona differences of note:

dya pronounced 'jga', as near to one syllable as possible
tya this one is 'chka', also say quickly
sv this is similar to the Chinese (Pinyin) x. If that's not familiar, say 's' with your tongue touching the roof of your mouth
zv similar to sv but say 'z' instead of 's'
m, n same as in Ndebele when placed before a consonant at the beginning of a word

Although most urban Zimbabweans have at least a little knowledge of English, many rural dwellers' English vocabulary is very limited, so it may help to know a few pleasantries in the local lingo. Even those Zimbabweans who speak English well will normally be pleasantly surprised to hear a foreigner make an attempt to speak a few words of Shona or Ndebele.

The following is a very basic list of words and phrases to get you started. The first translation given is Shona. The second is Ndebele. If two translations are given for the same word or expression, the first is used when speaking to one person, the second with more than one.

Greetings & Civilities

Hello (initial)
Mhoro/Mhoroi
Sawubona/Salibonani
Hello (reply)
Ahoi
Yebo
How are you?
Makadii?/Makadi-ni?
Linjani?/Kunjani?
I am well
Ndiripo.
Sikona.
Thank you
Ndatenda/Masvita
Siyabonga kakulu
Welcome
Titambire
Siyalemukela
Good morning
Mangwanani
Livuke njani
Good afternoon
Masikati
Litshonile
Good evening
Manheru
Litshone njani
Please
Ndapota
Uxolo
Goodbye (person staying)
Chisarai zvakanaka
Lisale kuhle

Goodbye (person leaving)
Fambai zvakanaka
Uhambe kuhle

Useful Words & Phrases

What is your name?
Unonzi ani zita rako?
Ibizo lakho ngubani?

My name is...
Ndini...
Elami igama ngingu...

I would like...
Ndinoda...
Ngicela...

How much?
I marii?
Yimalini?

I am from...
Ndinobva ku...
Ngivela e...

Where is the station?
Chiteshi chiri kupi?
Singapi isiteshi?

When does the bus/train/car leave?
Bhazi/chitima/motokari richaynda rihni?
Izawuhamba nini bhasi/isitimela/imoto?

yesterday
nezuru
izolo

tomorrow
mangwana
kusasa

today
nhasi
lamhla

What time is it?
Dzava nguvai?
Yisikhati bani?

men/women
varume/vakadzi
amadoda/abafazi

yes/no
ehe/aiwa
yebo/hayi

friend
shamwari
mngane

small/large
diki/guru
okuncane/ncinyane

Sir/Madam
changamire/mudzimai
umnimzana/inkosikazi

boy/girl
mukomana/musikana
umfana/inkazana

market/shop
musika/chitoro
imakethe/isitolo

Food & Drink

bread
chingwa
isinkwa

meat
nyama
inyama

fish
hove
ininhlanzi

beef
mombe
nkomo

chicken
huku
nkukhu

potatoes
mbatatisi
amagwili

vegetables
muriwo
imbhida

ground nuts
nzungu
amazambane

butter
bhata
ibatha

salt
munyu
isaudo

sugar
shuga
ushukela

eggs
mazai
amaqanda

maize
chibage
umbila

maize porridge (grits)
sadza
sadza

fruit
michero
izithelo

beer
doro/whawha
utshwala

coffee
kofi
ikofi

tea
ti
itiye

milk
mukaka
ucago

water
mvura
amanzi

Animals

giraffe
twiza
ntundla

dog
imbwa
nja

buffalo
nyati
nyathi

impala
mhara
mpala

hippopotamus
mvuu
mvubu

horse
bhiza
ibhiza

goat
mbudzi
mbuzi

rabbit
tsuro
mvundla

baboon
gudo
ndwangu

zebra
mbizi
ndube

leopard
mbada
ngwe

rhinoceros
chipembere
ubhejane

monkey
bveni
nkawu

elephant
nzou
ndhlovu

lion
shumbai
silwane

hyaena
bere
mpisi

warthog
njiri
ungulube yeganga

Days of the Week

Sunday
svondo
ngesonto

Monday
muvhuro
umbulo

Tuesday
chipiring
olwesibili

Wednesday
chitatu
ngolwesithathu

Thursday
china
ngolwesine

Friday
chishanu
ngolwesihlanu

Saturday
mugovera
ngesabatha

Numbers

one
potsi
okukodwa
two
piri
okubili
three
tatu
okutathu
four
ina
okune
five
shanu
okuyisihlanu
six
tanhatu
okuyisithupha
seven
nomwe
okuyisikhombisa
eight
tsere
okuyisitshiyangalo mbila
nine
pfumbamwe
okuyisitshiyangalo lunye
ten
gumi
okuli tshumi

Zimbabwean English

In addition to the indigenous languages, Zimbabweans have some unique ways of expressing themselves in English. Some words have been adopted from Afrikaans, Shona or Ndebele, some are common words adapted to local usage, and others are entirely new. The following is a rundown of several you can expect to encounter:

ablutions block – a building which contains a loo, bath, washing up area, and sometimes a shower. It's also known as an 'amenities block'.

babalass – a hangover; those who indulge in *chibuku* are particularly vulnerable.

bashas – thatched A-frame chalets

bhundu – in Australia this would be called 'the bush'. Elsewhere, it's known as 'the tules', 'the sticks', the 'boonies', etc.

biltong – dried and salted jerked meat that can be made from just about anything from eland or ostrich to mutton or beef.

blair toilet – high-tech dunny developed in Zimbabwe and used in rural areas. It has an odd spiral long-drop with a black-painted interior to drive flies up air vents toward daylight where they are trapped in a mesh just short of freedom.

boerevoes – a spicy Afrikaner sausage which ranges from the consistency of mince meat to solid and bricklike. No braai could be without it.

braai – a barbecue which normally includes several varieties of meat grilled on a braai stand or pit. The braai is a southern African institution, particularly among Whites.

buppies – Black yuppies

chibuku – the 'beer of good cheer'. Both inexpensive and revolting, this grain and yeast concoction is stored in large vats at beer halls and is served up in buckets. It's good for a quick euphoria and a debilitating babalass.

Comrade (or Cde) – a Marxist title used primarily by the media when referring to Black Zimbabwean citizens, especially government officials.

dam – in Zimbabwe, a dam is what other English speakers would call a reservoir.

dam wall – what other English speakers would call a dam.

daga hut – a traditional African round house consisting of a wooden frame covered with mud and manure walls reinforced with straw, also known as 'pole and daga hut'.

donkey boiler – it may sound cruel but it has nothing to do with donkeys. It's an elevated water tank positioned over a wood fire and used to heat water for baths and showers.

Dutchman – a White Zimbabwean or South African of Afrikaaner descent. It's always used in a derogatory manner and offence is always taken, so be forewarned.

gap it – to 'split' in the sense of making a quick exit.

guti – dank and drizzly weather that can afflict the eastern highlands in the winter.

Izzit? – this most closely translates as 'Really?' and is used without regard to gender, person, or number of the subject. Therefore, it could mean 'Is it?', 'Are you?', 'Is he?', 'Are they?', 'Is she?', 'Are we?', etc.

just now – reference to some time in the future but intended to imply some degree of imminence. It could be half an hour from now or two days from now.

kopje – pronounced 'coppie', this translates from Afrikaans as 'little hill'. In Zimbabwe, any old heap of rocks qualifies.

kraal – Afrikaans version of the Portuguese *curral*. It can refer to either an enclosure for livestock or a fortified village of daga huts.

kroeksesters – small doughnuts dripping in honey – very gooey and figure-enhancing.

Malawi shandy – a nonalcoholic drink made from lemonade, ginger ale, and Mazoe orange.

Mazoe orange – sickly sweet orange cordial made from citrus grown in the Mazoe area. It's a Zimbabwe staple.

mopani worms – also known as *gonimbrasia belina*, these lovely larval delicacies are available in mopani trees and some Zimbabwe markets.

não faz mal – Portuguese expression meaning 'it doesn't make bad', used in Zimbabwe as 'no problem'.

nownow – definitely not now but sometime sooner than 'just now'.

peri peri – ultra-hot pepper-based sauce that will usurp the flavour of your *sadza ne nyama*.

PK – the WC, the toilet

pronking – gleeful leaping by several species of antelope, apparently for the sheer fun of it.

Rhodey – a normally derogatory term for a White Zimbabwean. It's roughly the equivalent of 'ocker' or 'redneck' in Aussie and the US.

robot – no, not R2-D2. It's just a traffic light.

rock shandy – a wonderful nonalcoholic concoction made of lemonade, soda water and bitters.

rusks – although Pommies already know about these from their teething days, for the benefit of others, rusks are solid bits of bread that North Americans would save for the Thanksgiving turkey or throw out long before they reached such a state. They're often flavoured with cinnamon or raisins and made masticable by immersion in coffee or tea.

shebeen – an illegal drinking establishment cum brothel. Nonregulars are unwelcome without an invitation.

Snice! – equivalent of 'Wow!'

Sus! – the opposite of 'snice'. Roughly the equivalent of 'yuck'.

TAB – 'That's Africa, baby.' Standard utterance when things are AFU, that is, not going according to plan.

TIZ – 'This is Zimbabwe'. Same connotation as TAB.

Tonkies – Rhodey word for members of the Batonka tribe.

TWOGs – acronym for 'third world groupies', used by White Zimbabweans in reference to foreigners who travel to underdeveloped countries and consciously sink to the lowest level of local society.

veld – open grassland, normally in plateau regions. One variation, 'bushveld', has the grassland replaced with thorn scrub.

vlei – any low open landscape, sometimes marshy.

Ziko ndaba – Zimbabwean version of the Swahili *Hakuna matata*. Has the same meaning as 'Não faz mal'.

Facts for the Visitor

VISAS & EMBASSIES

Visas are not required by nationals of Commonwealth countries, members of the European Community, Japan, Norway, Sweden, Switzerland or the USA. A valid passport is required by everyone. South African citizens do require visas. Visa requirements occasionally change, so if you're not sure whether you need one, direct enquiries to the Zimbabwe embassy in your home country or the Chief Immigration Officer, Private Bag 7717, Causeway, Harare, Zimbabwe.

Immigration officials are normally immovable about onward tickets – although a ticket out of a neighboring country or even Kenya will usually suffice – and they rarely ask to see your money or credit card unless you cannot produce a ticket. If you're entering by bus or rail, a return ticket via the same route will sometimes work but it's best not to count on it; they'll normally want a ticket back to your home country. Miscellaneous Charge Orders are not acceptable.

Those who front up at the border without an onward ticket may be refused entry entirely or carefully scrutinised for 'sufficient funds'. Some may even be required to pay a refundable deposit in cash or travellers' cheques which can run to as much as US$1000. The biggest concern will be getting it back when you leave. There's no worry about the officials absconding with the money – things thankfully don't work that way in Zimbabwe – but they may possibly return it in Zimbabwe dollars (at the official rate) just before you're due to leave and you're only permitted to carry Z$40 out of the country.

On the immigration form, you'll be asked for the name of your hotel or address in Zimbabwe. In the interest of minimising hassles, it's probably best not to write 'camping' or 'don't know'. It would be better to select the name of a mid-range hotel in Harare or the next city you'll be visiting whether you've booked it or not. If you state an intention to visit friends in Zimbabwe, you'll be expected to provide names, addresses, telephone numbers and any other details the officer may want to know.

The average maximum length of stay granted will be about three months although that can be extended to a maximum of six months at any immigration office. But, anyone initially requesting a length of stay longer than about two weeks will normally be given a slip of paper called a Notice to Visitor (NTV). If you get one, you'll have to fill in details of your intended itinerary and list addresses where you'll be staying. You'll be required to produce this document upon exit from the country.

If you want to avoid red tape – especially if you're just on holiday – don't write 'journalist' on your immigration form. Otherwise, you'll be issued with a 24-hour visa and required to apply for a temporary employment permit from the Ministry of Home Affairs. On the other hand, this could be useful (especially if you are on assignment!). The 14-day work permit requires only about two hours' effort to secure and you're issued with a press card. The office is on the 7th floor, Liquende House, Baker Ave, in Harare. Unlike most immigration offices elsewhere, this is normally an efficient and pleasant operation.

Zimbabwe Diplomatic Missions

Zimbabwe is diplomatically represented abroad at the following missions:

Canada
    High Commission of Zimbabwe, 112 Kent St, Place de Ville Tower B, Plastaville, Ottawa, Ontario KIP 5PT
France
    Ambassador of Zimbabwe, 5 Rue de Tilsitt, Paris 75008
Germany
    Ambassador of Zimbabwe, Victoriastrasse 28, 5300 Bonn

Kenya
     High Commission of Zimbabwe, 6th Floor ICDC Building, PO Box 30806, Nairobi
Japan
     Ambassador of Zimbabwe, 11-23 Minami Azabu, 3-Chome, Mulatoku, Tokyo 106
Sweden
     Ambassador of Zimbabwe, Oxtoget 5, 10290 Stockholm
UK
     High Commission of Zimbabwe, Zimbabwe House, 429 The Strand, London WC2 O5A
USA
     Ambassador of Zimbabwe, 2852 McGill Terrace NW, Washington, DC 20008
Zambia
     High Commission of Zimbabwe, 4th Floor, Ulendo House, Cairo Rd, Lusaka

Foreign Embassies in Zimbabwe

Countries with diplomatic representation in Zimbabwe include:

Australia
     Karigamombe Centre, 4th Floor, 53 Samora Machel Ave, PO Box 4541, Harare
Austria
     Room 216, New Shell House, 30 Samora Machel Ave, Harare
Botswana
     Southern Life Building, Jason Moyo Ave, Harare
Canada
     45 Baines Ave (cnr Moffat St), PO Box 1430, Harare (☎ 73 3881/2/3/4/5)
Denmark
     2nd Floor, 30 Robson Manyika Ave, Harare
Egypt
     7 Aberdeen Rd, PO Box A433, Avondale, Harare
France
     Ranelagh Rd nr Orange Grove Dr, PO Box 1378, Highlands, Harare (☎ 46 001) – note: the French Embassy issues visas for Côte d'Ivoire, Senegal, Burkina Faso, Central African Republic and Gabon. Check with them for information on visas for other formerly French West African countries.
Germany
     14 Samora Machel Ave, PO Box 2168, Harare (☎ 73 1955/6/7/8)
Ghana
     11 Downie Ave, Belgravia, Harare
Italy
     7 Bartholomew Close, PO Box 1062, Greendale, Harare (☎ 48 190, 47 200/79)
Japan
     Commercial Union House, Baker Ave, Harare
Kenya
     95 Park Lane, Harare

Malawi
     Malawi House, 42-44 Harare St, PO Box 321, Harare
Mozambique
     152 Herbert Chitepo Ave, Harare
Namibia
     See Zambia
Netherlands
     47 Enterprise Rd, Highlands, Harare (☎ 73 4528)
New Zealand
     6th Floor, Batanai Gardens, 57 Jason Moyo Ave, PO Box 5448, Harare (☎ 72 8681/2/3/4/5/6)
South Africa Trade Mission
     Temple Bar House, Baker Ave, PO Box 121, Harare
Spain
     16 Phillips Ave, PO Box 3300, Belgravia, Harare (☎ 73 8681/2/3)
Sweden
     42 Orange Grove Dr, Highlands, Harare
Switzerland
     Southampton House, Union Ave, Harare
Tanzania
     23 Baines Ave, PO Box 4841, Harare
UK
     Stanley House, Jason Moyo Ave & First St, Harare
USA
     172 Herbert Chitepo Ave, PO Box 3340, Harare
Zaïre
     24 Van Praagh Ave, Harare
Zambia
     Zambia House, Union Ave, PO Box 4698, Harare (note: the Zambian High Commission is responsible for issuing Namibian visas until Namibia has established diplomatic representation in Harare)

Visas for other Countries

If you're after visas for other African countries, Harare is the best place in southern Africa to get them. Requirements are constantly changing but nearly all require a fee – some must be paid in US$ – and multiple passport-sized photos. If you plan to do a lot of border hopping, carry a stack of them.

South Africa If you're after a South African visa, turn up at the Trade Commission early or you won't make it into the office before the noon closing time. The queue begins forming at dawn and is soon winding around the block. The free visa takes between five and seven days to issue and will be stamped in a loose-leaf folder if you so desire (who wouldn't?).

Those planning to visit Tanzania or Zambia later, however, should be warned that a visit to South Africa will just about cancel your chances of entering those countries unless you have two passports. Even without a South African visa in your passport, entry or exit to or from Zimbabwe, Botswana, Namibia, Lesotho, or Swaziland through South African borders are easily recognisable and with those stamps, you'll be denied access. Even travellers who've had 'lost' passports reissued in Harare have had problems. Officials simply assume – often correctly – that the bearer has visited South Africa and had a new passport issued to hide the evidence. Similarly, don't be caught carrying any rand, even if it's just from Namibia.

Kenya Single entry Kenya visas require two passport photos, are issued in two days and cost Z$25 but multiple entry visas take one month to issue. If you plan on multiple entries, it's much less hassle to buy a single entry visa and change it in Nairobi upon arrival. Transit visas cost Z$14.

Kenya is only concerned about South African stamps if they're less than 90 days old. I guess they figure after 90 days you'll be adequately purged of whatever dreadful stuff may have rubbed off on you there.

Mozambique A Mozambique transit visa costs Z$20 at last notification and is good for one trip through the Tete corridor to Malawi. The consulate is open between 8 am and noon on weekdays. You'll need a passport-sized photo and the visa will be issued in 48 hours to one week. The number of travellers waiting around Harare for this visa, checking the consulate daily, are phenomenal. It's a kind of personal triumph when one comes through and is cause for celebration. Tourist visas are now available for trips between Mutare and Beira. They cost Z$25 and are issued in two weeks. Take a photocopy of your passport to leave with them.

Zambia Citizens of Commonwealth countries won't need a visa for Zambia unless they've been resident in East Africa and are of Indian, Chinese, Pakistani or Bangladeshi descent. South Africans and citizens of the former Eastern Bloc need a preissued visa as well. At the time of writing, citizens of other countries can be issued visas at the border for 100 kwacha (Z$10 at the official rate). Those day tripping to Zambia at Victoria Falls are subject to the same visa requirements but their visa will be issued only for the day of travel unless otherwise requested, in which case it is valid for 21 days.

Zaïre Applications are accepted any time between 8 am and 5 pm Monday to Friday but visas are issued only on Tuesday and Thursday. A visa valid for one month from day of issue costs US$20 and a three-month visa is US$24. You'll need two passport-sized photos. If you don't have exact change, demand a receipt stating the amount paid and the amount due back. It will normally take them a couple of days to scrape it together.

DOCUMENTS

Yellow fever vaccination certificates are required of those entering Zimbabwe from more northerly African countries where the disease is endemic. Cholera and smallpox vaccines are required of those entering Zimbabwe from an infected area.

Visitors won't need an international driving licence in Zimbabwe. Driving licenses from Zambia, Malawi, Namibia, South Africa, Botswana, and Swaziland are valid until their expiration dates and other foreign licences are valid for 90 days.

CUSTOMS

Visitors may import a maximum of Z$200 in non-trade items, excluding personal effects. Those over 18 years of age can also bring in up to five litres of alcohol, two of which may be spirits. Firearms may be imported but must be declared at the border.

Motor vehicles may be imported temporarily as long as they bear current number plates and are licensed, registered and titled in the home country.

If you're visiting with a pet, you should apply to the Director of Veterinary Services, PO Box 8012, Causeway, Harare, Zimbabwe, several months in advance of your visit.

MONEY

All brands of travellers' cheques in US$ or UK£ may be easily exchanged for Zimbabwe dollars at any bank. Banks are open Monday, Tuesday, Thursday, and Friday between 8.30 am and 2 pm. On Wednesday, they close at noon and on Saturday they're open from 8.30 to 11 am. The exchange desk at Harare airport is open whenever there's an incoming flight. Hotel reception desks will sometimes exchange currency but the service is normally reserved for hotel guests and a significant commission is taken.

Credit cards – American Express, Diner's Club, MasterCard and Visa, as well as Eurocheques – are accepted by establishments catering to tourists and business people. Petrol credit cards – even those issued by oil companies represented in Zimbabwe – aren't accepted at all.

When purchasing currency with a credit card, you may only take Z$20 worth of foreign currency per transaction although you can buy as many official rate Zimbabwe dollars as you like. Be prepared to wait awhile until authorisation comes through, especially in smaller towns. Barclays Bank handles Visa transactions.

It's also possible to purchase foreign currency travellers' cheques but it never works out to a good rate since the transaction is converted through Zimbabwe dollars and each conversion yields a commission for the bank. Funds transferred to Zimbabwe from outside the country can only be received in official rate Zimbabwe dollars or foreign currency travellers' cheques – at the same loss ratio as when buying travellers' cheques outright.

Currency

The unit of currency is the Zimbabwe dollar (Z$1=100 cents). Notes come in denomin-

ations of two, five, 10 and 20 dollars. Coins are valued at one, five, 10, 20 and 50 cents, and Z$1.

The value of the currency is artificially controlled by the government and therefore, import or export of banknotes is limited to Z$40 per person per visit. In theory, all currency, including travellers' cheques, must be declared upon arrival and, also in theory, without this form in good order you won't be permitted to export more than US$20 in foreign currency. Customs occasionally also asks to see bank receipts as you leave, as proof you've exchanged your foreign currency at the official rate, so don't throw them away. You'll also need bank receipts to convert leftover Zimbabwe dollars back into hard currency when you leave the country.

In reality, the only place currency declarations are consistently distributed is Harare airport. Elsewhere, border posts only sporadically have a stock of them and you'll rarely get one. Similarly, they're only occasionally scrutinised on departure because very few travellers have one to begin with.

If you plan to stay in hotels or participate in organised activities such as rafting, canoeing, or what have you, you'll need to pay in foreign currency or produce bank receipts totalling at least the amount you're spending.

Exchange Rates

A$1	=	Z$4.05
UK£1	=	Z$9.10
US$1	=	Z$5.55
¥100	=	Z$4.08
DM1	=	Z$3.22
SFr1	=	Z$3.57
FFr1	=	Z$0.92
NZ$1	=	Z$2.94
C$1	=	Z$4.76
SAfR1	=	Z$1.89
BotP1	=	Z$2.44

Costs

Even using the official rate of exchange, Zimbabwe is not an expensive country unless you're taking advantage of the big hotels, fine dining and package safaris that support the bulk of the country's tourist industry. Unfortunately, rock-bottom cheap accommodation doesn't exist outside major centres where there are youth hostels and a couple of crash pads, or the national parks where small cabins rent for a pittance. Travellers who want to see the country on a minimal budget, therefore, will have to take advantage of the camping grounds and caravan parks found in nearly every town and national park.

Food is very reasonably priced and those eating at small local establishments or self-catering will be able to eat heartily on a very tight budget. A meal of the Zimbabwean staple, *sadza ne nyama* (mealies with meat relish), in a local eatery will set you back between Z$1.50 and Z$2. Big hotels offer all-you-can-eat buffet meals and if you're really hungry, you can get good value out of the Z$10 to Z$12 they'll cost.

Any item which must be imported and therefore purchased with foreign exchange will be extremely expensive. Zimbabweans will save for years to purchase a bang box or a television, for example, which will normally set them back thousands of dollars. Even cheap digital watches are incredibly expensive and would make well-appreciated gifts for helpful locals. Consumer goods produced in Zimbabwe on the other hand, although rarely of optimum quality, are very affordable.

Consumer taxes are also fairly substantial: 16% on retail items, excluding food and 19% on 'luxury' items such as electronic equipment, airline tickets, furniture and automobiles. There is also a 15% tax on hotel rooms, safaris and other tourist services. Those going the upmarket route can avoid this expense by booking and paying for all such items before leaving home.

Tipping

Tips of approximately 10% are more or less expected by taxi drivers and in tourist-class hotels and restaurants. Some establishments automatically add a 10% service charge to the bill, however, which replaces the gratuity.

Black Market

Although it's not as straightforward as in some other African countries, the black market in foreign currency is thriving and will yield double or more the official rate. The best rates are available in Harare. Since Zimbabwean citizens and residents aren't permitted to export more than Z$450 per year, effectively precluding holidays outside the country, many have established foreign bank accounts where they stash any hard currency they can get. All the standard international currencies are accepted including Aussie, Kiwi and Canadian dollars, Botswanan pula, South African rand, Italian lira, and so on. Many individuals will exchange travellers' cheques as well as cash.

I'm not officially recommending taking advantage of the black market but anyone planning to go this route should realise it's essential that things remain extremely discreet. It's especially best to avoid contacts travellers all seem to know about; it's almost certain the police know as well, and that the contact will be required to turn in a certain percentage of clients in order to remain in business. The penalties for illegal currency dealings are severe, so take heed!

Departure Tax

For nonresidents over 12 years of age, the airport departure tax is US$10 per person. If you're paying at the airport, it must be paid in US currency in US$20 notes or less. You can prepay the departure tax in Zimbabwe dollars at any commercial bank at the official rate but you'll have to produce bank receipts proving you've exchanged the money legitimately.

Zimbabwe residents pay Z$10 airport departure tax.

CLIMATE & WHEN TO GO

The thing that surprises most about Zimbabwe's climate is that it's not as hot as its latitude would suggest. Although it lies entirely within the tropics, the country is draped over a high plateau averaging 900 metres above sea level and, during the dry season, enjoys a pleasantly temperate climate. Winters (May to September) are like luscious Mediterranean summers with warm, sunny days and cool, clear nights. There is never any snow, not even in the eastern highlands, but overnight frosts and freezing temperatures are not uncommon anywhere on the plateau. It is also the best time for game viewing since animals tend to gather around the pans and never stray far from water sources.

The lowveld and the Zambezi Valley experience hotter and more humid temperatures but during the winter months there is still a minimum of rainfall.

Although spring and autumn aren't really obvious as seasons, throughout the winter the highveld mopane trees change colours and provide touches of orange, yellow and red reminiscent of a European or North American autumn.

Most of Zimbabwe's rain falls in brief afternoon deluges during electrical storms in the summer months (October to April) and bring only fleeting relief from the typically miserable humidity. Although temperatures rarely break the 30°C mark, the air feels heavy and oppressive.

Zimbabweans and residents of neighbouring countries travel mainly during winter school holidays from mid-April to mid-May and from early August to mid-September. The latter is the more popular, so if you like crowds, that's the time to go. On the other hand, June is the coolest and quietest month of the year and many businesses close down for lack of activity. July is chilly but things begin to pick up again. Although quite a few winter-weary Europeans and North Americans venture southward between November and February, it's not the best time of year in Zimbabwe and activities will be limited by climatic unpleasantness.

TOURIST OFFICES
Local Tourist Offices

Several publicity associations around the country distribute brochures, maps and pamphlets about their respective areas. Although some are considerably more helpful and better organised than others, they can at least provide up-to-date information on any new developments in their area.

Bulawayo
> Bulawayo Publicity Association, City Hall, Fife St, Bulawayo (☎ 60867)

Gweru
> Gweru Publicity Association, City Hall, Livingstone Ave, Gweru (☎ 2226)

Harare
> Harare Publicity Association, African Unity Square, PO Box 1483, Harare (☎ 705085)

Kadoma
> Kadoma Publicity Association, PO Box 86, Kadoma (☎ 2747)

Kariba
> Kariba Publicity Association, PO Box 86, Kariba (☎ 328)

Kwe Kwe
> Kwe Kwe Publicity Association, PO Box 115, Kwe Kwe

Masvingo
> Masvingo Publicity Association, PO Box 340, Masvingo (☎ 3380)

Mutare
> Manicaland Publicity Association, Market Square, Milner Ave, PO Box 69, Mutare (☎ 64711)

Victoria Falls
> Victoria Falls Publicity Association, Stand 412, Parkway/Livingstone Rd, PO Box 97, Victoria Falls (☎ 4202)

Overseas Representatives

Germany
> Zimbabwe Fremdenverkehrsamt, Steinweg 9, 6000 Frankfurt am Main 1

South Africa
> Zimbabwe Tourist Board, Upper Shopping Level, Carlton Centre, Johannesburg 2000

Switzerland
> Zimbabwe Fremdenverkehrsamt, Ifangstrasse 111, CH-8153, Rumlang, Zurich

UK
> Zimbabwe Tourist Board, Zimbabwe House, 429 The Strand, London WC2R OSA

USA
> Zimbabwe Tourist Board, Suite 1778, 35 East Wacker Drive, Chicago, Illinois

Central Booking Offices

To minimise red tape and expend an economy of effort while planning an independent tour around Zimbabwe, it's best (and in some cases necessary) to book accommodation, tours, national park camping sites, hire cars and what have you at central booking offices in Harare and Bulawayo. Some of the more useful addresses include:

National Parks Central Booking Office, Travel Centre, 93 B Stanley Ave, PO Box 8151, Causeway, Harare (☎ 706077)

National Parks Bulawayo Booking Agency, 140 A Fife St, PO Box 2283, Bulawayo (☎ 63646)

Zimbabwe Sun Hotels Central Booking Office, PO Box 8221, Causeway, Harare (☎ 736644, fax 734739)

Zimbabwe Tourist Development Corporation Hotels Central Reservations Office, PO Box 8052, Causeway, Harare (☎ 706511)

Cresta Hotels Central Reservations Office, fax 794655), PO Box 2833, Harare (☎ 794641)

Harare Sheraton Reservations Office, PO Box 3033, Harare (☎ 729771, fax 796678)

United Touring Company, United House, 4 Park St, PO Box 3914, Harare (☎ 793701)

Avis Car Hire, 5 Samora Machel Ave, Harare (☎ 720351)

Europcar/Echo Car Hire, 19 Samora Machel Ave, PO Box 3430, Harare (☎ 706484)

Hertz Rent-a-Car, United House, Park St, PO Box 2914, Harare (☎ 792791)

BUSINESS HOURS & HOLIDAYS

Shops are generally open between 8 am and 5 pm Monday to Friday, with early closing on Wednesday in some places and lunch closing from 1 to 2 pm. Saturday hours are 8 am to 12 noon. Petrol stations open up at 6 am and the majority close down at 6 pm although several in Harare and Bulawayo keep later hours. Banks are open between 8.30 am and 2 pm Monday to Friday, except Wednesday when they close at noon, and from 8.30 to 11 am on Saturday. Postal services are available from 8.30 am to 4 pm Monday to Friday and 8.30 to 11.30 am Saturday.

Public Holidays

1 January
> *New Year's Day*

March or April
> *Good Friday, Easter Sunday, Easter Monday*

18 April
> *Independence Day*

1 May
> *Workers' Day*

25 & 26 May
Africa Days
11 & 12 August
Heroes' Days & Defence Forces Day
25 December
Christmas Day
26 December
Boxing Day

POST & TELECOMMUNICATIONS
Post

Harare is probably the best place in this part of the world to send and receive mail. There are direct flights to and from Australia and Europe and although delays do occur, the system is relatively efficient and it's not like Lusaka (Zambia) where you risk arrest for even approaching the post office. It's still a good idea to register anything of value, however. Registration costs only Z$1 for anything under Z$50 in value.

Poste restante services are available in all major cities and towns but Harare is probably the best and most efficient of the lot. Have mail sent to you c/o Poste Restante, GPO, Inez Terrace, Harare, Zimbabwe.

Telephone

The Zimbabwean telephone system may be a butt of jokes but it is improving all the time. Local calls are the most notorious. Although there is no shortage of public telephone boxes, the frequent foul-ups in local services combined with staggeringly crowded party lines will generally mean long queues waiting to use the phone, especially in Bulawayo and Harare. Local calls cost 15 cents, and to party lines they're 15 cents for each three minutes. Zimbabwe's country code is (263).

To make an overseas call, you'll either have to phone from a private telephone (hotels charge double or triple the official rates!) or carry a large stack of Z$1 coins to the telephone box with you. There are no telephone offices where charges can be paid after the call. Collect calling is available to a few countries but only from private lines. Calls to Australia, most of Western Europe and North America cost Z$14.70 for the first three minutes and Z$4.90 for each minute thereafter. To other places, including New

Zealand, you'll pay Z$19.50 for the first three minutes and Z$6.50 for each extra minute.

TIME

Zimbabwe is two hours ahead of Greenwich Mean Time. Therefore, when it's noon Saturday, it's 10 am Saturday in London, 5 am Saturday in New York, 2 am Saturday in Los Angeles and 8 pm Saturday in Sydney.

ELECTRICITY

Electricity is generated at 220 volts AC, so for use of US appliances you'll need an adaptor. Both round and rectangular three-prong plug sockets are in use.

LAUNDRY

All mid-range hotels in Zimbabwe offer laundry services to their guests for very reasonable prices while upmarket hotels tend to charge significantly more. If you're camping or staying in hostels, there are commercial laundries/dry cleaners in Harare and Bulawayo. Those on the strictest of budgets will be pleased to find that nearly all camping grounds are equipped with laundry sinks (but you'll need your own universal drain plug to use them).

BOOKS & MAPS
History

An Introduction to the History of Central Africa – Zambia, Malawi, and Zimbabwe by A J Wills, Oxford University Press, 4th Edition, 1985. The word 'introduction' in the title is a bit misleading. Although it's a little disorganised, this 500-page book, generally considered the best work on the history of the region, will probably tell you more than you ever wanted to know on the subject.

History of Southern Africa by Kevin Shillington, Longman Group, Harlow, Essex, 1987. Although the focus of this history is South Africa, Botswana and Namibia, it does discuss the prehistoric aspects of the entire region and details events that have effected Zimbabwe and its neighbours.

Great Zimbabwe Described & Explained

by Peter Garlake, Zimbabwe Publishing House, Harare 1982. An attempt at sorting out the history, purpose and architecture of the ancient ruins at Great Zimbabwe.

Mapondera 1840-1904 by D N Beach, Mambo Press, Gweru, 1989. This biography of Kadungure Mapondera, a descendent of the Changamire and Mutapa dynasties, who resisted settler encroachment into north-eastern Zimbabwe.

Mugabe by Colin Simpson & David Smith, Pioneer Head, Salisbury, UK, 1981. Biography of Robert Mugabe tracing his rise to the office of executive president of Zimbabwe.

The Struggle for Zimbabwe: the Chimurenga War by David Martin & Phyllis Johnson, Faber, London, 1981. This popular history of the Second Chimurenga describes in detail the Zimbabwean perspective of the tragic war that led to the country's independence. It is also available in Zimbabwe in an edition published by Zimbabwe Publishing House.

If you're particularly interested in the colonial history of Zimbabwe in particular or Africa in general, there are several biographies and diaries of such figures as Robert Moffat, David Livingstone, Cecil John Rhodes, Frederick Courteney Selous, Leander Starr Jameson, and so on which should be available at your local library.

Literature & Fiction

There are currently several established and emerging names in Zimbabwean literature whose works are available in the Heinemann African Writers Series, Longman African Classics, and a couple of locally published series. My favourite – and one which shouldn't be missed by any visitor to Zimbabwe – is Tsitsi Dangarembga's *Nervous Conditions*, first published by the Women's Press, London, 1988, and subsequently by the Zimbabwe Publishing House, Harare. Set in eastern Zimbabwe, it's the tale of a young Black woman attending a mission school in 1960s Rhodesia. It's available in the bookshop at the Harare Sheraton.

Also worthwhile are the works of Charles Mungoshi, one of Zimbabwe's first internationally recognised Black writers, who masterfully captures the despair and hopelessness of Black Africans in pre-independence Rhodesia. His most highly acclaimed work is *Coming of the Dry Season*, originally published by Oxford University Press in 1972 and again by the Zimbabwe Publishing House, Harare, after independence. If you like this one, look for his other works which are published in the Heinemann African Writers' Series. They are available at most Zimbabwe bookshops.

Other Black writers to watch for include Dambudzo Marechera, John Munoye, Ngugi and John Nagenda. The late Stanlake Samkange, whose 1967 book *On Trial for my Country* raised the ghosts of both Lobengula and Cecil John Rhodes, is a favourite. Also, *Bones* by Chenjerai Hove is a highly acclaimed account of a soldier in the Liberation war; it's worthwhile but at times gets a bit clichéd.

Doris Lessing, the most widely known serious writer to examine the Rhodesian experience and expose its inequalities, sensitively portrays the country and its people in *The Grass is Singing*, published in the Heinemann African Writers Series in 1973. She's also done two anthologies of African stories, *Sun Between Their Feet* and *This was the Old Chief's Country*, both published in 1979 by Panther Books. Once you're used to her style, you'll want to read more – and she has many works to choose from!

Most visitors to Zimbabwe will probably have read at least one novel by Wilbur Smith, who was born in what was Northern Rhodesia and has written nearly a score of adventure novels set in southern Africa, past and present. Although they aren't exactly great literature, they are page-turners and are good for diversion. Those which take place in Zimbabwe include *A Falcon Flies*, *Men of Men*, *The Angels Weep*, *The Leopard Hunts in Darkness* and *A Time to Die*. The last two are currently banned in Zimbabwe primarily because they side with the Ndebele factions, expose some of the gruesome realities of the war in Mozambique, and speculate in some detail about corruption in the Zimbabwe government.

Travel Guides

Africa Calls Handbook of Zimbabwe by Mark & Hazel Igoe, Roblaw Publishers, Harare. This is more like an expanded tourist office brochure than a guidebook. There's a fair amount of information and lots of advertising for tourism-related services. Several spinoffs from this book are available as well, including titles on Victoria Falls, Kariba and the Zambezi River. The same publisher also does *The Mobil Guide to the National Parks of Zimbabwe*, which has good background information on the parks but for practical info, the photocopied national parks handouts are better.

Zimbabwe & Botswana – the Rough Guide by Barbara McRae and Tony Pinchuck, Harrap Columbus, London, 1990. If you're the sort that carries two guidebooks, this is a good choice. The research is solid and it's got a lot of good background information but the writers' politics are more up front than most readers will appreciate.

Discovery Guide to Zimbabwe by Melissa Shales, Michael Haag Ltd, London, 1989. Although it's necessarily sparse on information – nearly half of each page is left blank – this is a good general guide to Zimbabwe and covers most of the major attractions adequately.

Backpacker's Africa – East and Southern by Hilary Bradt, Bradt Publications, London, 1989. This contains a pretty good rundown of hiking possibilities in Zimbabwe.

Language

There are several English/Shona and English/Ndebele dictionaries available in Zimbabwe bookshops. If you're interested in picking up a bit of Shona, the pamphlet-sized book *Fambai Zvakanaka muZimbabwe – Have a Nice Trip in Zimbabwe* offers some basic grammar and vocabulary. It's available only in Zimbabwe.

Art & Music

Shona Sculpture by F Mor, Jongwe, Harare, 1987. Although the photographs in this full-colour production are superb, it seems the Italian author was more keen to practice artsy-fartsy hyperbole than convey any real information about the works in question. The text seemed utterly inaccessible; maybe I'm just out of touch.

The Material Culture of Zimbabwe by H Ellert, Longman Zimbabwe, Harare, 1984. The most complete coverage of all aspects of Zimbabwe's material crafts cultures, both ancient and modern, including weapons, musical instruments, tools, pottery, jewellery, basketry and so on.

The Painted Caves – An Introduction to the Prehistoric Art of Zimbabwe by Peter Garlake, Modus Publications, Harare, 1987. Explanations and locations of major prehistoric rock art sites in Zimbabwe. This is an essential companion for anyone searching out Zimbabwe's prehistoric art works.

Images of Power – Understanding Bushman Rock Art by David Lewis-Williams, Thomas Dawson, 1987. Comprehensive treatment of rock art sites in southern Africa and educated speculation about its history and meaning.

Serima by Albert B Plangger, Mambo Press, Gweru, 1974. A history and outline of the beautiful Serima Mission near Masvingo and its modern sculptural and woodcarving traditions.

Roots Rocking in Zimbabwe by Fred Zindi, Mambo Press, Gweru, 1985. Good coverage of Zimbabwe's pop music scene including background information on the music itself and data on all the major players.

Other

A Concise Encyclopaedia of Zimbabwe edited by Denis Berens, Mambo Press, Harare, 1988. This isn't a history book per se, but any historical event that may be of interest is covered in this excellent collection of information snippets. It also includes entries on government, politics, religion, climate, wildlife, etc.

Robert's Birds of Southern Africa by Gordon Lindsay, New Holland Press, London, 1988. Although this is a requisite book for birdwatchers travelling through southern Africa, be warned it's not a featherweight volume. Although not so comprehensive, the much more luggable *Bundu Guide* published by Longmans in Zimbabwe is available at some Kingston's outlets.

Field Guide to the Mammals of Southern Africa by Chris & Tilde Stuart, New Holland Press, London, 1989. A well-illustrated field guide to just about any furry thing you're likely to encounter in this part of the world.

Bookshops

Although Zimbabwe offers a wide range of reading materials and well-stocked bookshops compared to most African countries, there's nothing like what you'd find at home or even in neighbouring Botswana. Most of the books available are published locally and foreign imports are prohibitively expensive so if you need pulpy paperback novels to while away long nights in a tent, bring a few from home and resign yourself to trading with other travellers or with the book swaps in Harare and Bulawayo to keep yourself in a steady supply of reading material.

Otherwise, you can get acquainted with the local literature, much of which is very good. Quite a few foreign writers and researchers have heard the call of Africa and set about committing it to ink, but recently the Africans themselves are beginning to realise their unique perspective also needs to be heard.

The country's largest popular bookshop chain is government-owned Kingston's, which has outlets of varying quality in most cities and towns. For the largest selection of Zimbabwe-related topics, try the Grass Roots Bookshop in Harare. It's a bit odd – there's an entire wall devoted to Marxism and Leninism (maybe you can pick up something cheap at this stage) – but you'll also find a variety of African literature and lots of African-perspective works on history, economy, politics, music, languages and the natural history of both Zimbabwe and the entire continent.

Maps

City plans of Harare, Bulawayo and Masvingo are available at tourist information offices, but plans of other towns are much more difficult to come by. Most publicity bureaux offer photocopied national parks maps for about 50 cents each. If you'll be spending a lot of time exploring Harare, you may want to pick up a copy of the detailed *Greater Harare Street Guide* which has large-scale maps of all neighbourhoods. It's available from the Harare Publicity Bureau on African Unity Square for Z$9.95.

The best readily available national map is the colourful tourist office production distributed at publicity bureaux. It doesn't show all that much detail, especially on minor routes, but is probably enough for most visitors' purposes. The best available road map is the information-packed *Michelin #955 Central and Southern Africa*.

The office of the Surveyor General (☎ 794545) in Electra House on Samora Machel Ave, Harare, sells 1:50,000 ordnance survey topographic sheets covering the entire country for Z$4 per sheet. They also offer a range of other thematic maps including a colourful 1:15,000 Harare street plan for Z$1.50. The salesperson may ask to check your ID when purchasing maps but usually, they only want your name and home address on the chit. The postal address is PO Box 8099, Causeway, Harare, Zimbabwe.

MEDIA

Newspapers & Magazines

The two daily papers published in Zimbabwe – the Bulawayo *Chronicle* and the Harare *Herald* – are both long on local, national and especially sports news; international events get short shrift. The Friday *Financial Gazette* offers a modicum of outside news but the best source of information about world events will probably be *Time* and *Newsweek*, both of which are available from street vendors (check the dates before buying!) and bookshops in Harare and Bulawayo. Hotel gift shops often stock international newspapers as well.

The Catholic monthly magazine *Moto* published by Mambo Press is probably the most interesting of Zimbabwe's periodicals and covers national, cultural and political issues. It was first published in 1959 and became a weekly newspaper in 1971. *Moto* was banned by the Smith government in 1974 but resurfaced to become one of the most influential pre-independence influences on the Black population.

Africa Calls Worldwide, a travel and general interest magazine published in Harare, offers some light reading about sights, arts, wildlife, dining and other tourism-related issues. It's published bimonthly and available internationally by subscription. For further information, contact *Africa Calls Worldwide*, Modus House, 27-29 Charter Rd, PO Box 66070, Kopje, Harare, Zimbabwe.

Radio & TV

Radio and television are overseen by ZBC, the Zimbabwe Broadcasting Corporation. There are currently two television stations and four radio stations in Zimbabwe. TV 2 and Radio 4 are funded by the government; both are commercial-free and education-oriented. Radio 1 broadcasts interviews in English and emphasises classical music. Radio 2 focuses on African music and broadcasts primarily in Shona but also in Ndebele. Radio 3 broadcasts mainly in English and plays popular top 40-style music.

BBC World Service broadcasts four times daily. For specific times and frequencies, contact the BBC African Service bureau (☎ 793961) on the 4th floor of Frankel House, Second St, Harare. The Voice of America is also available twice daily. If you have good conditions, or a good receiver, you will also be able to pick up Radio Australia's South East & North Asian service.

DANGERS & ANNOYANCES

Racism

Although Zimbabwe has been independent for some time now, it will soon be apparent to visitors that racism based on skin colour and tribal origin still exists and the fact that the country is governed by the Shona majority has had little effect on old habits. It is tempting to sweep the issue under the rug and present Zimbabwe in the image its tourist industry would most appreciate – that it's a free country where all races and tribes are treated equally – but that's simply not the case.

The situation is not, as many foreigners are conditioned to believe by the Western media, merely an issue of Black and White. Although the economic disparity between those of European and African origin is more obvious and exploitation is still pathetically rampant, the long-standing animosity between the majority Shona and the minority Ndebele is just as serious and has caused untold grief.

Therefore, throughout this section on Zimbabwe, efforts will be made to present things as they are, or at least as they appear to be, with as little editorialising as possible. I hope that no offence is taken – none is intended toward anyone – at the mention of issues many would prefer to avoid.

Police & Military

Compared to most African countries, Zimbabwe's police and military presence is neither obvious nor intimidating. If you're driving, the most hassle you're likely to get is being asked for food or money at routine roadblocks. If you offer something, you will get a smile and thanks. Otherwise, the officers normally tell you to have a nice day and wave you on.

The Zimbabwe military wear green soldierly uniforms and are easily recognisable – they'll often be carrying an automatic weapon. The police normally wear khaki – long trousers in the winter and shorts in the summer – with peaked caps. Traffic police wear all-grey uniforms. Other units wear grey shirts and blue trousers or all-blue uniforms with white caps.

Most police are both friendly and courteous and problems are very rare; should you encounter an officer behaving in an unprofessional manner, note their name and ID number. If the offence is serious, it should be reported to the Public Relations Officer at the Central Police Station in Harare.

Land Mines

Those intending to travel in the eastern highlands of Zimbabwe, particularly around Mutare and Chimanimani National Park, should note that there is danger of encountering land mines and unexploded ordnance in the area.

The mines were planted along the border both by Renamo rebels from Mozambique and by the Zimbabwe military in hopes of discouraging cross-border forays during the height of guerrilla activity in Mozambique. Some ordnance may even date back to the Second Chimurenga. Despite efforts by the Zimbabwe authorities to remove the devices, it is generally believed that mines still exist in considerable numbers, since they are regularly detonated by wild animals. The well-publicised 1989 fatality near Skeleton Pass in Chimanimani National Park should provide sufficient warning to hikers tempted to wander off marked tracks.

If you do find yourself away from well-trodden areas, be wary of earth that appears to have been disturbed, don't touch anything vaguely resembling weaponry, and tread as lightly as possible.

Con Artists & Scams

Operating primarily in Harare and to a lesser extent in Bulawayo and Victoria Falls, con artists bilk tourists out of staggering amounts of money and often the victims don't even realise they've been taken. There are a million fabricated sob stories, all tailored to separate you from some of your cash. There's no reason to be paranoid – they're not all that common – but those who remain alert should manage to avoid the worst of them.

Theft

Apart from the previously mentioned scams, which give the alert victim a fighting chance, theft isn't much of a problem in Zimbabwe. Places which warrant caution, particularly at night, are bus terminals, crowded discos and the big parks in Harare and Bulawayo. Camping grounds and caravan parks have guards posted to watch over campers' belongings but occasionally things do go missing so it's not a good idea to leave valuables in your tent. If you have a car, don't leave tempting items anywhere in sight while you're away from it.

WORK

Although it isn't impossible to secure permission to work in Zimbabwe, neither is it easy and the officials definitely prefer that intending workers organise the permit in their home country. If you've simply run out of money, however, and have a skill that is in demand, you may be able to convince them that your case warrants hardship considerations (keep in mind that clueing them in to such a situation will also qualify you for deportation). At this stage, it's best to seek out an employer, secure a solid job offer, and then set about arranging a permit with the prospective employer's help.

Upper or A level teachers, especially science teachers, engineers, computer experts and medical personnel, will have the most luck. Professions for which there are sufficient qualified Zimbabwean citizens such as nurses or primary teachers will have less chance of being granted a permit.

At the present time, teachers in Zimbabwe are permitted to teach up to the level they have completed. A university degree and/or education certificate are not necessary to teach A level courses but those so qualified will command a higher starting salary than those who've completed only A levels. If you're really committed to teaching in Zimbabwe and are prepared for a challenge, you can improve your chances of success by offering to accept a posting in a rural area.

Wages in Zimbabwe are very low by European, North American or Australasian standards and salaries are paid only in Zimbabwe dollars. In some cases, you may be permitted to export up to one-third of your salary but special permission will have to be granted. Otherwise you're subject to the same currency controls as Zimbabwean citizens (see Money). Especially if you're working for the government, be prepared to wait months for a pay cheque; the system doesn't work as smoothly as it could. The normal teaching contract is for an extendible two years.

Private colleges pay better than government schools (usually about twice the salary), but require teachers to hold at least a four-year degree. The two best colleges in Harare are Speciss College on Herbert Chitepo and ILSA Independent College on Fife Ave. Paid leave at both government and private schools amounts to about four months annually.

Recent sources indicate that all applications for permanent residence and work permits must be accompanied by a doctor's letter or certificate stating the applicant has had a recent chest x-ray and shows no evidence of tuberculosis.

HIGHLIGHTS

Zimbabwe has a lot to offer and to enjoy it thoroughly will require more time than most travellers allow. If you're in a real hurry, visits to a few outstanding places and experiences can provide a sampling of the best Zimbabwe has to offer. Those who must keep to a rigid itinerary may want to include some of the following:

Victoria Falls Zimbabwe's number one attraction, Victoria Falls is included on most whirlwind Africa tours so the tourist district can get crowded but the falls themselves remain lovely and unspoilt.

Hwange National Park Hwange is the most easily accessible of Zimbabwe's game parks and offers the greatest variety and concentration of game. It nevertheless remains relatively uncrowded and offers accommodation for all budgets.

Great Zimbabwe Ruins The former capital of Great Zimbabwe is sub-Saharan Africa's greatest archaeological site. It's also a surprisingly serene place to relax for a few days of camping and exploring.

Chimanimani National Park Chimanimani contains Zimbabwe's wildest and most rugged mountain wilderness. There are no roads in the park but lots of hiking tracks offer the best bushwalking country in Zimbabwe.

Matobo National Park The kopje-studded terrain and weird balancing rocks of the Matobo Hills near Bulawayo shelter hundreds of caves and rock paintings. The park is also the best place in the world to see white rhino.

Mana Pools National Park More remote than Hwange, Mana Pools is one park where visitors are permitted to strike out alone on foot. Since access is awkward, most travellers arrive by canoe safari along the Zambezi River.

Nyanga National Park The 'civilised' mountain country of Nyanga and the wilderness of adjoining Mtarazi Falls National Park make this area *the* highland escape for upper-crust Harare dwellers.

Lake Kariba Few visitors are overwhelmed by Kariba but Zimbabweans seem to believe it's paradise on earth so who can argue? Around the lake there's good fishing, boating, game viewing and camping.

Vumba National Park The forests and botanical gardens of Vumba offer good walking opportunities and far-ranging vistas across nearby Mozambique.

Domboshawa & Ngomakurira Both these sites, just 30 km from Harare, offer good hiking over beautiful lichen-covered domes as well as the opportunity to see lots of rock paintings.

Bulawayo Museum of Natural History If you have an interest in geology, palaeontology, anthropology, zoology or history, don't miss this, by far the best of Zimbabwe's museums. It's worth an all-day ramble through and the surrounding gardens are good for lounging and allowing the information to filter in.

Mzilikazi Arts & Crafts Centre This practical art centre just outside Bulawayo reveals the scope and amount of artistic talent to be found in Zimbabwe. Although a lot of their stuff is repetitious, some of it is positively inspired.

ACCOMMODATION

Unfortunately for budget travellers, Zimbabwe doesn't have much to offer between camping and lower mid-range hotels. There are youth hostels in Harare and Bulawayo and several doss houses popping up in Harare, Bulawayo and Mutare but beyond that, budget accommodation is limited to national park cabins and chalets.

Camping

All larger cities and towns have well-maintained caravan parks with space for both caravans and tent camping. Most are exceptionally clean and all offer toilet and bath facilities. Some even have showers, and at the most popular ones there's an attendant on duty 24 hours a day so your belongings are reasonably secure when left inside your tent.

Camping grounds are also available in the national parks and recreation areas where you'll find braai pits, hot showers and sometimes specially planted grassy areas for tent camping. At Hwange Main Camp, however, they seem to have got it backwards – caravans are allotted the big grassy lawn areas while tents may only be erected in cement-solid dirt. Make sure you bring tent pegs that are up to the challenge. Even when it's disguised by grass, the typically cast iron Zimbabwe earth tends to resist the wimpy aluminium sort. National Parks camping sites with toilets and baths normally cost Z$10 per site, accommodating up to six people. Those without amenities cost only Z$6 per site.

Camping in rural areas or communal lands is usually prohibited or discouraged. If you wish to camp in these places, be sure to secure permission from property owners or villagers before setting up camp.

Hostels & Crash Pads

Harare and Bulawayo each have a youth hostel but they're somewhat dilapidated and are characterised by distinctly Rhodesian attitudes. Alternative budget accommodation includes private homes which have been converted into dormitory-style accommodation. If they're full, you'll often be given the option to sleep on the floor or wherever until space becomes available. Although such establishments are completely above board, the police sometimes like to keep an eye on them so it may be a good idea to keep a low profile if you're doing anything that may interest them.

National Parks Accommodation

Besides the camping grounds, national parks offer several types of accommodation. Chalets, the most basic, provide furniture, fridges, cooking implements (but no crockery or cutlery), bedding, towels and lighting.

Cooking is done outside the main unit and amenities are communal. One bedroom chalets cost Z$10, two rooms cost Z$15. Cottages add both kitchens and private baths and cost Z$15 for one-bedroom units or Z$20 for two rooms. The lodges are fully self-contained and serviced by national park staff and cost only about Z$20 per bedroom. All three types offer one or two bedroom units with two beds per room.

Hwange, Matusadona and Mana Pools also offer exclusive camps which will accommodate varying numbers of people and cost on an average of Z$50 per night.

During high season, national parks accommodation is very popular and should be booked in advance through the central booking offices in Harare or Bulawayo if you want to be certain of a place. Half the fee is payable upon booking and the balance is due 30 days before you arrive. If you've paid for accommodation and can't arrive before 5.30 pm, phone and inform the attendant or you'll forfeit the booking and the money.

Hotels

If you want a quiet place to crash, the cheapest hotels are probably best avoided. Their regular patrons are normally more interested in sex and swill than in sleep so the noise level remains fairly constant. Not only could snoozing prove difficult, you may encounter misunderstandings with the personal services squads, so be warned.

Middle-range accommodation is comfortable, adequate and, in most cases, reasonably priced. But unless you're prepared to pay for five stars, a holiday will be more enjoyable for those with a *laissez-faire* attitude. Life moves more casually in Zimbabwe than in Europe or North America and perhaps that's one of the reasons it's such an appealing place.

Middle to upper-range hotels in Zimbabwe are rated on a zero to five-star scale based on an elaborate points system for service, cleanliness and amenities. Most mid-range hotels have either one or two stars and will average Z$70 to Z$90 for a double room. Three-star hotels will range from

Z$80 to Z$130 for a double. In four and five-star hotels, foreigners must pay in US$ and at a higher rate – as much as 30% more – than Zimbabwe residents. At cheaper places, Zimbabwe dollars will be accepted provided bank exchange slips for the amount of the bill can be produced.

FOOD

Zimbabwean cuisine, the legacy of bland British fare combined with normally stodgy African dishes, makes for some pretty ordinary eating. The dietary staple sadza or white maize meal porridge forms the basis upon which nearly all meals are built. The second component is meat (or nyama – sadza with meat gravy is known as sadza ne nyama) which is both plentiful and inexpensive.

Fruits and vegetables are limited but what's available is quite good. Gem squash, a type of marrow, is delicious and popular. Tomatoes, cucumbers, maize, pumpkins, courgettes (zucchini), and tropical fruits such as papayas, mangoes and bananas are also inexpensive and plentiful.

Zimbabwe is one of the world's great producers of beef, which is available nearly everywhere. Chicken is also a staple and on occasion, game meat, including kudu, crocodile and impala, is available. In the rural communal lands, people eat lots of goat and mutton. The most popular fish include bream from Lake Kariba and the anchovy-like dried *kapenta*, also from Kariba. Trout is a speciality in the eastern highlands and is superb.

Normally anonymous dried meat or *biltong*, which can be anything from beef to kudu or ostrich, is usually delicious and makes a great snack. It can be deceptively salty so don't eat too much unless you have lots of water handy.

Buffets

For those with hearty appetites who aren't on the strictest of budgets, nothing can beat the hotel buffets for value. For breakfast, you can get unlimited fresh and tinned fruit, cereals, breads, porridge, bacon, sausage, eggs, cheese, yoghurt, coffee, and so on for an average of Z$12. Lunch buffets normally include salads, several meat dishes, casseroles and desserts for a similar price although in some places, vegetarians can opt out of the meat for a significant reduction. At the Holiday Inn in Harare, for example, a vegetarian lunch costs only Z$6.50 compared to nearly twice that for the full board.

Although all-you-can-eat dinners are rare, the buffet braai at the Victoria Falls Hotel shouldn't be missed if you can at all swing it. This is the original pig-out with table after table of wonderful European and African dishes, meats, salads, casseroles, breads and myriad sweets. The three or four hours you'll spend gorging and socialising are worth every bit of the Z$25 price.

Self-Catering

If you insist on shopping at supermarkets, self-catering will be easier in Botswana than in Zimbabwe. That's not to say that Zimbabwe doesn't offer some variety and quality but there are production problems and shortages are not uncommon. Normally, no amount of running around town will turn up an ingredient in short supply. If one shop doesn't have it, chances are none of them do.

Township markets/bus terminals, although limited in their variety of fruits and vegetables, are good for picking up fresh inexpensive produce.

Fast Food

Bus terminals also brim with cheap and greasy snack stalls where you can pick up groundnuts, corn on the cob, eggs, sweets, and even deep-fried beetles. Basic cooked meals are available in a central eating area of the markets but aren't really recommended for those who have a weak stomach or functional olfactory receptors.

One step up are the Mom & Pop style takeaways which serve chips, sausages, meat pies, sandwiches, burgers and so on. Some offer a wider variety of fare and are excellent value. Next up the scale (although not necessarily better) are the fast food chains, the most prominent of which are Wimpy and Chicken Inn, found all around the country.

Restaurants

In the major cities, especially around transportation terminals, you'll find lots of small eating halls which serve up plain but filling fare – normally some form of sadza ne nyama – for just a dollar or two. These places are normally happy to try their hand at vegetarian fare as well, but it doesn't always work out well. The best they'll probably manage is sadza overlain with tinned baked beans, boiled cabbage and onions, or a boiled green known as *rabe* (which is the best of the lot).

Near the central business districts are a variety of pleasant little coffee houses. International cuisine – Italian, Chinese, Greek, Indian and so on – are available primarily in Harare and Bulawayo. All the big tourist hotels harbour expensive restaurants serving European dishes – mostly the meat, potatoes and two vegies variety – and a couple of elegant places around the two major cities admirably attempt gourmet cuisine with the limited available ingredients.

There are normally dress restrictions in bars and restaurants after about 4 pm but the definition of the standard 'smart casual dress' will vary from place to place. At very least, it excludes anyone wearing jeans or thongs and men are expected to turn up in sports jackets and ties.

DRINKS
Nonalcoholic Drinks

The first thing to remember about soft drink consumption in Zimbabwe is that the bottle is worth more than the drink inside. Bottles represent hard foreign currency and aren't taken lightly. A coke drunk on the spot costs a mere 30 cents, but if you want to take it away in the bottle, you'll pay at least a 50 cent deposit – that is if the establishment will let the bottle out of sight at all; normally, to take a bottle one must exchange an empty. Cheaper places must obey the laws of bottle conservation themselves; they are only sold as many bottles of soft drink as they can supply empties to the distributor.

Southern Africa's refreshing contribution to liquid enjoyment is the shandy, which comes in two varieties. The Malawi shandy is comprised of ginger beer, Angostura and soda water with ice and lemon. The rock shandy is a smoother alternative, replacing the ginger beer with lemonade.

Also popular is Mazoe Orange, a ubiquitous orange cordial that fills the noncarbonated drink niche. Many travellers love it; others find it too sticky sweet.

If you just want a glass of water, which is safe to drink straight from the tap in Zimbabwe, order a Zambezi cocktail. If you want to add something to this tired little joke which nevertheless still gets a lot of mileage in Zimbabwe, tell them to hold the bilharzia (or the crocs, or whatever...groan!).

Hot Drinks

Although both tea and coffee are grown on plantations in the eastern highlands, the best of it is for export and not readily available in the country. A few restaurants, which will be identified in the regional chapters, serve real local or imported coffee but what you'll normally get, including in most of the big hotels, is a revolting instant coffee and chicory blend known as Daybreak. Coffee lovers should give it a wide berth.

Although it isn't the optimum quality stuff, Nyanga tea, which is available throughout the country, is quite good.

Alcohol

The alcoholic concoction of the Zimbabwean masses is *chibuku*, which, as its advertising asserts, is 'the beer of good cheer'. Chibuku is not at all tasty. Served up in buckets which are passed between partakers, it has the appearance of hot cocoa, the consistency of thin gruel, and a deceptively mellow build-up to the knockout punch. The usual pretence for drinking it is to mess one's self up as cheaply as possible and at that, it succeeds on a grand scale. Since it's brewed from indigenous ingredients – yeast, millet, sorghum and mealie meal – it can also be used for ceremonial purposes.

You probably wouldn't go into a pub and order chibuku – it just isn't done. Chibuku is drunk mainly in high-density township beer halls – a significant male social scene in Zimbabwe – or in shebeens, those not quite legal drinking establishments to which admission is reserved for invited guests. Unescorted women will feel uncomfortable in either sort of place.

One step below chibuku is *skokiaan*, a dangerous and illegal grain-based swill spiked with whatever's lying around. It was common 50 years ago but is fortunately no longer popular.

The beer you're probably more used to is also available in the form of lager, which is always served cold – or at least as cold as they can get it. The most popular brand is Castle, which is excellent, followed by Lion and the misnamed Black Label – most beer in Zimbabwe is unlabelled and you have to look at the bottle cap to find the brand name. There seems to be some debate about whether this anonymity is due to cost-cutting measures at the breweries or just the inferior glue used to affix labels to the bottles.

Although Zimbabwe's climate isn't ideal for grapes, it does sustain a limited wine industry centred on the area east and southeast of Harare. The largest winery, Mukuyu, is in Marondera. Although there are some palatable white wines available, the reds range from bad to disastrous and the primary reason for drinking them at all is the price; you'd have to be relatively wealthy to pay the steep duties levied on imported wines.

Spirits are also available in varying qualities and imports are relatively expensive. The local produce is cheaper and in most cases bearable, but Zimbabwean ouzo, whisky and brandy are all a little odd.

THINGS TO BUY

Curio shops in Zimbabwe dispense a remarkable amount of tourist kitsch. Notwithstanding the many soapstone, mahogany or ebony giraffes and lions that line the footpaths on city squares, sculpture is a new and well-received form of expression in Zimbabwe. The big-name sculptors will naturally command high prices but there are sculpture gardens, arts centres and gallery shops in Harare and Bulawayo where you can pick up some competent work by budding artists for very competitive prices.

Precious and semiprecious stones such as malachite, verdite, serpentine and low-grade emeralds are carved or set into jewellery and make pleasant mementos. If you're intrigued by unusually beautiful natural patterns and 'meditation' pieces, some of the most interesting stone specimens are polished into egg-shaped chunks and sold for about Z$10.

Another recent artistic manifestation is crochet, and magnificently intricate lace table coverings and bedspreads are hawked for peanuts – as low as Z$20. Competition and therefore the lowest prices seem to be concentrated in the Kariba area but it would be hard to avoid guilt pangs paying so little for the considerable time and expertise involved in their creation.

Baskets also display a rare level of skill and facility with design and are excellent value, sold along roadsides and in shops nationwide. The speciality around Binga and the upper Zambezi are Batonka stool seats with their roughly carved wooden bases. These are a real speciality item and not easy to come by but if you're looking for something unusual to take home, they're an excellent choice. They're more readily available in Victoria Falls than in the area of origin.

On the issue of ivory, although carvings sold in tourist shops around Zimbabwe will come with a certificate stating it's 100% culled ivory – certainly don't buy anything without such a statement or it won't be allowed back in your home country – it may still be best to avoid sustaining the market which keeps poached ivory profitable.

Getting There & Away

This chapter covers access into Zimbabwe only from neighbouring countries. Information about reaching southern Africa from elsewhere on the African continent and from other continents is outlined in the regional Getting There & Away chapter at the beginning of the book.

BORDER CROSSINGS

All land border crossings are open between 6 am and 6 pm daily except Beitbridge (South Africa) which stays open until 8 pm and the Plumtree rail border with Botswana which opens any time a train passes.

There are three land crossings into Zambia at Chirundu, Kariba and Victoria Falls. The Kazungula ferry crossing between Zambia and Botswana is just two km or so from the Zimbabwe/Botswana border post at Kazungula, and 55 km west of there (also in Botswana) is the Namibian border post at Ngoma Bridge. To or from Mozambique there are crossings at Mutare and Nyamapanda. The only crossing into South Africa is at Beitbridge. To Botswana, you can cross at Plumtree (by road or rail) or at Kazungula, west of Victoria Falls.

TO/FROM BOTSWANA

There are two major border crossings between Botswana and Zimbabwe, one at Kazungula-Kasane and the other at Plumtree, which has both road and rail crossings.

The rail crossing between Plumtree and Francistown is probably the most relaxed for entering and leaving Zimbabwe. There are so many people to process on the train that searches/questions/hassles are normally kept to a minimum. When entering Zimbabwe on the train, the immigration officer will process you at Plumtree but you must then clear customs at the station in Bulawayo. Travellers will normally be able to get away with saying 'nothing to declare' and marching on past the sinuous and stagnant queue

of hapless Zimbabwe residents awaiting scrutiny for contraband.

Those travelling from Zimbabwe by rail to either Botswana or on to South Africa will have to show their passport when booking the ticket. Keep in mind that your Zimbabwe dollars are worthless on the international train so be sure to have some Botswanan pula (or other hard currency) before setting out.

Express Motorways operates a couple of buses daily between Francistown and Bulawayo. In western Zimbabwe, there's a daily tourist bus between Kasane and Victoria Falls which costs a very off-putting Z$65 each way. Hitching is possible but occasionally there'll be long waits.

TO/FROM MALAWI
Via Mozambique

The most direct route between Malawi and Zimbabwe is across the infamous Tete Corridor between Zobue, Malawi, and Nyamapanda, Zimbabwe. Quite a few travellers these days are opting to avoid Zambia's high crime rate and confrontations with its corrupt and paranoid officials and take their chances with the MNR (Mozambique National Resistance).

Convoys of up to 60 trucks make the journey in either direction daily except Sunday, taking anywhere from 14 to 24 hours. Since there's a lot of MNR guerrilla activity in this area, every convoy is accompanied by an army escort.

You can pick up a Mozambique transit visa in Lilongwe, Malawi for 22.50 kwacha and two passport-sized photographs. From Blantyre, you can hitch to the border at Zobue and arrange a lift in a convoy truck or van. At the time of writing, the price hung at around 80 kwacha per passenger but as demand for transport increases, so does the price. Going the other direction, plan on paying at least Z$80.

If you're headed *to* Malawi, you may be able to arrange transport in advance through the Trans-Africa truck depot on Dagenham Rd in Willow Park, Harare, but the route is becoming popular enough that there should be no problem finding something in Nyamapanda. The trucks collect there the night before and depart as early as 6 the following morning. Mozambique transit visas are available at the Mozambique consulate in Harare which is open 8 am to noon weekdays. They cost Z$20 and require one passport photograph. They may be issued in as little as 48 hours but allow more time; some people have waited for as long as five to seven days.

Also keep in mind that those entering Malawi must comply with a rather strict national appearance code. Women must wear skirts or dresses at all times and men may not wear beards or hair below collar length. Those who do will be obliged to face the hair-hacker posted at the border to reform deviates. If you'd rather hang onto your locks, look around Harare for a cheap wig.

Despite the military assistance, this trip is not for the nervous traveller. It's rough and potentially hazardous. Although the route is well guarded, the MNR still manages to plant the odd land mine and evidence of detonations is visible along the road. Also, there seems to be some competition between drivers to reach the head of the convoy (seems odd – is there some sort of prestige attached to discovering new land mines?) so expect some hair-raising moments jockeying for position. At Tete, the strategic Zambezi bridge has been damaged so often by MNR saboteurs that only one vehicle is permitted to cross at a time. If that's not enough, the drivers – poor over-stressed buggers – will probably stop several times along the way for a friendly arm-bending session.

Furthermore, spares are unavailable along the way so if the vehicle you're travelling in breaks down or exhausts its spare tyre supply and is left behind, there's a very real danger of MNR guerrilla attack by night.

Via Zambia

United Transport Malawi/Express Motorways offers a direct weekly bus service between Lilongwe and Harare. It leaves Lilongwe at 1.30 pm Tuesday, stops briefly in Lusaka, Zambia, and at the Zambia/Zimbabwe border at Chirundu, and arrives in Harare at 1.30 pm Wednesday. Going the other way, it departs from Harare at 8.30 am Thursday and returns to Lilongwe via Chirundu and Lusaka, arriving at 8.30 am Friday. The one-way fare is Z$105.27.

This bus is certainly the most hassle-free way to speed across Zambia. For those who aren't put off by hassles, however, it's possible to take a bus from Lilongwe to the Zambian border, catch a mini-bus to Chipata, Zambia, and then another bus into Lusaka. From Lusaka, United Bus Company of Zambia (UBZ) does crowded daily trips into Harare via Chirundu. Alternatively, you can catch a UBZ bus to Livingstone and cross into Zimbabwe at Victoria Falls.

TO/FROM SOUTH AFRICA

The only border crossing between Zimbabwe and South Africa is at the Limpopo River in Beitbridge. Although there are direct bus connections to Harare or Bulawayo from Johannesburg, due to lengthy delays and hassles at Beitbridge, most travellers prefer to take the rail line across Botswana from Johannesburg to Bulawayo. It's also a relatively easy matter to find lifts over the border but South African immigration and customs officials don't seem to like hitchhikers and can be painful, so be warned.

The best time to cross the border from Zimbabwe into South Africa is around 12.30 pm when the shift is changing and the officials often can't be bothered to take too much trouble scrutinising you. Likewise after 7.45 pm just before the border closes; they're ready to go home without delay.

Customs are very tight going either way. Zimbabwean officials realise that Zimbabweans go to South Africa to buy up items which are unavailable or prohibitively expensive in Zimbabwe and try to smuggle them back in without having to pay the high duty, risking confiscation of the goods. Searches are thorough and if you're on a bus

– or behind a bus – expect to be delayed here for hours. If you're a foreigner entering Zimbabwe from South Africa and expect to return, declare all photographic equipment, radios, Walkmans etc on the form provided and be sure to include serial numbers just in case.

There's a Translimpopo/Express Motorways coach service from Johannesburg to Harare via Bulawayo on Monday, Wednesday and Friday at 10 pm, for a rather steep R145.50 considering that elsewhere their 'five-star service' wouldn't rate any stars at all. It supposedly arrives at Meikles Hotel in Harare at 7 pm the following day but don't count on it. Delays at the border and frequent equipment failure will both extract their toll on the schedule. Going in the other direction, the buses leave Meikles Hotel in Harare at 6 pm on Monday, Wednesday, Friday and Saturday. They stop at Bulawayo early in the morning on Tuesday, Thursday, Saturday and Sunday, picking up passengers at the city hall car park on Leopold Takawira Ave beside City Hall Square.

TO/FROM NAMIBIA

There's no direct overland route between Namibia and Zimbabwe but the most straightforward way to travel between the two is between Namibia's Caprivi Strip and Victoria Falls via Botswana. The trip will entail driving or hitching first to Katima Mulilo in the Caprivi Strip and thence to the relaxed Botswana border crossing at Ngoma Bridge. It's normally not a difficult hitch along the free transit route across Chobe National Park (you won't be subject to the preposterous park fees unless you turn off onto the tourist route) to Kasane. From there, it's six km to the border post at Kazungula and then about 60 km on a good road to Victoria Falls. For information on this border crossing, refer to the To/From Botswana description.

TO/FROM ZAMBIA

Between Zambia and Zimbabwe, there are three border crossings: Chirundu, Kariba and Victoria Falls, all of which are open from 6 am to 6 pm daily. For obvious reasons, most travellers cross at Victoria Falls. For those entering Zambia, this is the most relaxed of the three crossings.

If you're only going over for the day to see the Zambia side of Victoria Falls, Zambian officials normally aren't fussed about onward tickets, sufficient funds or South African stamps in your passport. If you need a Zambian visa, it can be purchased at the border for Z$10 and can normally be validated for up to 21 days, if you request it. But some travellers have reported being refused more than a single-day visa at the border post, so those who need a longer one should play it safe and secure their visa in Harare. The Zimbabwe side will baby-sit your excess Zimbabwe dollars (over Z$40) while you're in Zambia and return them when you pass back through.

If you're in Zambia wanting to cross for the day to visit the Zimbabwe shore of Victoria Falls, you'll have to go through standard Zimbabwe customs and immigration procedures. You'll probably be asked for an onward ticket as well, but this may be waived if it's obvious all your gear is sitting in Zambia. Don't count on it, however.

The Chirundu crossing lies along the main route between Harare and Lusaka. There are usually two buses per day in either direction, leaving Lusaka at 6 am and 4.30 pm and taking about 10 hours. The United Transport Malawi express bus departs from Lusaka for Harare on Wednesday at 2.25 am. It leaves Chirundu at 8 am and arrives in Harare at 1.30 pm. From Harare to Lusaka, it departs at 8.30 am Thursday and arrives in Lusaka at 5.05 pm, passing Chirundu at 3.05 pm.

Getting Around

At independence, Zimbabwe inherited good rail links between all major centres and a superb network of tarred roads which, although they've deteriorated considerably over the past few years, are still among the best on the African continent.

What Zimbabwe lacks, however, is sufficient foreign exchange to purchase and maintain public transport commensurate with the quality of its infrastructure. Spares are either unavailable or difficult to find and although Zimbabweans are adept at jury-rigging repairs, there remains a serious shortage of equipment. Consequently, transport delays are probably best taken with a relaxed attitude and those depending upon public transport may want to avoid working schedules too tightly.

One corollary of the transport shortage is that buses will run only where there is sufficient demand to justify running them. Travellers wishing to strike out into the wilder areas of the country – national parks, for instance – will have to find alternative means. The masses aren't going that way; most locals visiting the national parks have their own vehicles and the bulk of the tourists are booked onto prearranged tours which include transport.

NAME CHANGES

Since independence in 1980, the Zimbabwe government has attempted to rid the country of the nomenclature bestowed upon it by the colonial power. City names were the first to change and in 1990, they really got down to brass tacks and began changing names of streets, dams, parks, rivers, military installations and anything else with a colonial-sounding name. Ironically, Rhodes-like, Robert Mugabe's name is cropping up on street signposts with some frequency these days. The following is a list of city name changes. Street name changes will be included in sections dealing with individual cities.

Old Name	New Name
Balla Balla	Mbalabala
Belingwe	Mberengwa
Bulalima-Mangwe	Bulilima-Mangwe
Chipinga	Chipinge
Dett	Dete
Enkeldoorn	Chivhu
Essexvale	Esigodini
Fort Victoria	Masvingo
Gatooma	Kadoma
Gwelo	Gweru
Hartley	Chegutu
Ingezi	Ngezi
Inyanga	Nyanga
Inyazura	Nyazura
Mangula	Mhangura
Marandellas	Marondera
Mashaba	Mashava
Matepatepa	Mutepatepa
Mazoe	Mazowe
Melsetter	Chimanimani
Miami	Wami
Mrewa	Murewa
Mtoka	Mutoko
Nkai	Nkayi
Nuanetsi	Mwenezi
Que Que	Kwe Kwe
Salisbury	Harare
Selukwe	Shurugwi
Shabani	Zvishavane
Sinoia	Chinhoyi
Sipolilo	Guruve
Somabula	Somabhula
Tjolotjo	Tsholotsho
Umniati	Munyati
Umtali	Mutare
Umvukwes	Mvurwi
Umvuma	Mvuma
Urungue	Hurungwe
Vila Salazar	Sango
Wankie	Hwange

AIR

Air Zimbabwe, the national carrier, flies domestic routes between Harare, Bulawayo, Kariba, Victoria Falls, Masvingo, Hwange National Park, Gweru and Buffalo Range (Triangle/Chiredzi).

Foreigners may purchase Air Zimbabwe domestic (but not international) flight tickets with Zimbabwe dollars.

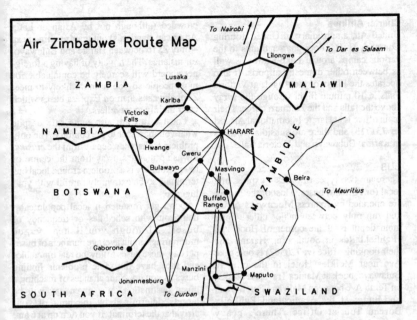

Air Zimbabwe Route Map

Fares

The following fare table is in Zimbabwe dollars based on one-way economy-class fares.

Harare							
76	Bulawayo						
81	157	Buffalo Range					
61	137	142	Kariba				
120	79	201	80	Victoria Falls			
46	117	127	107	166	Gweru		
53	129	29	114	17	99	Masvingo	
106	106	187	68	30	152	159	Hwange

Air Zimbabwe Offices

Air Zimbabwe has a number of offices and agents all over the country.

Bulawayo
Treger House, Jason Moyo St, PO Box 1000, Bulawayo (☎ 72051)

Buffalo Range (Triangle)
Lowveld Travel, 77 Knobthorne Rd, Chiredzi (☎ 295)

Gweru
Musgrove & Watson Castlemarine, PO Box 1347, Gweru (☎ 3316)

Harare
City Air Terminal Reservations, cnr Third St & Speke Ave, PO Box 1319, Harare (☎ 794481)

Hwange National Park
United Touring Company, Hwange Safari Lodge, PO Box DT-5792, Dete (☎ 24)

Kariba
Kariba Airport, PO Box 13, Kariba (☎ 213)

Masvingo
United Touring Company, Great Zimbabwe Hotel, Masvingo (☎ 2131)

Victoria Falls
Air Zimbabwe Terminal, Victoria Falls (☎ 316)

Charter Airlines

United Air, a subsidiary of United Touring Company (UTC) does charter flights to the various camps around Lake Kariba as well as between other domestic airports. It also operates the Flight of the Angels at Victoria Falls, a 10 minute flight through the spray above the falls and the Zambezi gorge. Their main office is at Harare International Airport (☎ 731713) and there are subsidiary offices in Kariba, Bulawayo and Victoria Falls.

BUS

There are two types of buses – express and local (or African) buses. Most of the former are operated by Express Motorways Africa and run only between major cities. Their main depot is at the corner of Hood and Highfield Rds in Southerton, Harare, and their booking office (☎ 720392) is on Speke Ave near Meikles Hotel in the city. In Bulawayo, book at Manica Travel (☎ 69293) on Tenth Ave between Main and Fort Sts and in Mutare at the Manicaland Publicity Bureau Tourist Office. There's heavy demand for seats so it's wise to book in advance.

Express buses are relatively efficient, operating according to published timetables and making scheduled snack and toilet stops along the way. An Express Motorways bus leaves Harare for Bulawayo at 7.45 am on Monday, Wednesday, Friday and Saturday and at 1 pm on Thursday and Sunday, calling at Chegutu, Kadoma, Kwe Kwe, Gweru and Insiza en route. They leave Bulawayo at 7.45 am on Tuesday, Thursday and Saturday and at 1 pm on Monday and Sunday. The one-way fare is Z$34. Ajay Motorways also runs between Harare and Bulawayo.

Between Bulawayo and Victoria Falls, there's an express bus which departs on Monday, Wednesday and Friday. Other express services include Harare to Mutare (3¾ hours), Bulawayo to Masvingo (4 hours) and Harare to Kariba (6 hours).

Local buses, on the other hand, go just about everywhere. They can be slow – although I've known them to beat the 'express' service on occasion – and fairly crowded (although not by Asian or Latin American standards) but they're ultra cheap – only Z$16 between Harare and Bulawayo, for instance. The novelty of having a foreigner aboard will scarcely be containable for most people so you're more likely to meet Zimbabweans than on Express buses which cater mainly to travellers.

Local buses are also quite safe despite what you may hear to the contrary. The only problem is that they depart from the *musika*, township markets away from the centre of town. Robbery is a problem around local bus terminals so be extremely careful with your luggage.

Don't get flustered if local people can't help you with schedules or frequency of buses. Although you'll hear vague murmurings about average numbers of buses per day, these buses follow no real timetables and they have the same problems finding buses as you do. Your chances of reaching a given destination on a given day will be largely determined by the hour of your arrival at the terminal. If you turn up at 6 am, you'll have a good chance of catching the first – and often the only – bus of the day headed in that direction. This is less of an issue between major population centres, however, since buses depart when full throughout the day, usually until mid-afternoon.

TRAIN

Zimbabwe has a good network of railways connecting most major centres. They're very cheap, especially in third or economy class, which is available on all but express runs. For internal journeys, bookings open 30 days prior to departure but those travelling to Botswana or South Africa can book up to 90 days in advance.

The majority of trains in Zimbabwe run at night and, because of the relatively short distances, move very slowly in order to arrive at a convenient hour of the morning. Sleeping compartments and bedding are quite inexpensive and good for a comfortable night, especially if you've been camping and sleeping on the hard earth for a

Top: Herero women, Gcangwa, Botswana (DS)
Bottom: Chapungu Kraal, Harare, Zimbabwe (TW)

Top: Beach dance, Swakopmund, Namibia (DS)
Bottom: Tswana chief and children, Tsodilo Hills, Botswana (DS)

while. Sexes are separated at night unless you reserve a family compartment or a coupé (two-person compartment) in advance for an additional charge. Women who want to sleep may do well to pay the extra charge for a coupé, anyway. Although 2nd-class compartments are intended to hold six adults, children aren't counted and most Zimbabwean women will have at least one baby. Chances of sound sleep will be fairly slim under such circumstances.

Zimbabwe, along with China and India, is one of the last countries in the world to use steam locomotives on regularly scheduled services and the romantic jaunt between Bulawayo and Victoria Falls is considered one of the world's great rail journeys. The rolling stock includes 1920s passenger cars, complete with brass and wood-trimmed interiors even in 2nd class. What's more, it's cheap – just Z$26.40 in 2nd-class and Z$37.80 in 1st.

Questions about fares or schedules may be directed to the enquiries desks at the stations in Harare (☎ 700011, after hours 700033), Bulawayo (☎ 363111, after hours 322284), and Victoria Falls (☎ 391).

Timetables
Harare to Mutare Fares between Harare and Mutare are Z$24.15 1st-class, Z$16.80 2nd-class and Z$7 economy. Trains go daily at the following times:

Station	Departs
Bulawayo	7.00 pm
Dete (Hwange Park)	2.00 am
Hwange	3.34 am
Victoria Falls	7.30 am

Station	Departs
Victoria Falls	5.30 pm
Hwange	9.12 pm
Dete (Hwange Park)	11.13 pm
Bulawayo	7.05 am

Bulawayo to Harare There is a choice of day and night trains on this route. Night trains have all classes Monday to Thursday and on Saturday. On Friday and Sunday, there are 1st and 2nd-class cars only.

Exclusively economy-class trains depart from Harare and Bulawayo at 8 pm on Friday and Saturday and arrive in Harare at 6 am and Bulawayo at 5.35 am the following morning. Daytime trains pull only 2nd and economy-class carriages.

Between Bulawayo and Harare, the 1st-class fare is Z$41.40, 2nd is Z$28.80 and economy-class costs Z$12.

Station	Departs	
Bulawayo	9.00 pm	8.00 am
Gweru	1.10 am	11.30 am
Kwe Kwe	2.27 am	12.34 pm
Kadoma	4.00 am	1.46 pm
Harare	7.00am	4.00 pm

Station	Departs	
Harare	9.00 pm	8.00 am
Kadoma	12.01am	10.24 am
Kwe Kwe	1.21 am	11.39am
Gweru	3.00 am	1.07 pm
Bulawayo	6.40 am	4.10 pm

Bulawayo to Victoria Falls Service between Bulawayo and Victoria Falls is by steam locomotive. The 1st-class one-way fare is Z$41.40, 2nd is Z$28.80, and economy costs Z$12.

Station	Departs	Station	Departs
Harare	9.30 pm	Mutare	9.00 pm
Marondera	11.50 pm	Nyazura	11.15 pm
Macheke	12.50 pm	Rusape	12.20 am
Rusape	3.23 am	Macheke	2.49 am
Nyazura	4.01 am	Marondera	4.00 am
Mutare	6.00 am	Harare	6.00 am

Bulawayo to Gaborone, Mafikeng & Johannesburg Daily trains run between Bulawayo and Lobatse, Botswana. On Tuesday, it continues on to Mafikeng and Johannesburg in South Africa, returning on Thursday. Although people will assure you the daily train to and from Lobatse has a buffet car attached, it normally doesn't so bring along whatever you'll be needing to eat or drink.

The 1st-class fare between Bulawayo and Gaborone is Z$86.60. To/from Johannesburg, it's Z$155.60, and all the way to Cape Town is Z$315.40. The 2nd-class fares between Bulawayo and Gaborone,

Johannesburg and Cape Town are Z$63.54, Z$105.50 and Z$231.70. If you're going through to Cape Town from Zimbabwe and want to pay the whole thing in Zimbabwe dollars, you'll have to purchase the entire ticket at once. Also, although stopovers are permitted en route, if you want to skip any part of the rail journey outside of Zimbabwe, you'll have to produce bank exchange receipts for the proper amount at the time of purchase.

Station	Departs	
	Daily	Tuesday
Bulawayo	11.25 am	11.10 am
Plumtree	3.53 pm	2.05 pm
Francistown	6.26 pm	3.51 pm
Palapye	10.09 pm	7.11 pm
Mahalapye	12.50 am	10.45 pm
Gaborone	6.10 am	1.30 am
Lobatse	8.20 am	3.25 am
Ramatlhabama	–	5.00 am
Mafikeng	–	6.30 am
Johannesburg	–	12.45 pm

Station	Departs	
	Daily	Thursday
Johannesburg	–	1.30 pm
Mafikeng	–	9.00 pm
Ramatlhabama	–	9.30 pm
Lobatse	4.14 pm	10.40 pm
Gaborone	6.30 pm	1.04 am
Mahalapye	12.15 am	5.15 am
Palapye	1.57 am	6.32 am
Francistown	6.00 am	9.56 am
Plumtree	8.55 am	12.14 pm
Bulawayo	12.20 am	2.25 pm

Bulawayo to Chiredzi The slow train between Bulawayo, Triangle and Chiredzi, which pulls freight cars and economy-class carriages, leaves Bulawayo at 9.25 pm daily and arrives in Chiredzi at 3.55 pm the following day. The service leaves Chiredzi at 5.40 pm daily and arrives in Bulawayo at 1.35 pm the following day.

CAR & MOTORBIKE

The ideal way to travel around Zimbabwe is in a private vehicle. You can stop where you like, visit game parks at leisure, and reach places not served by public transport. Motorbikes also perform well on Zimbab-

we's open highways but they aren't permitted in game parks. In Zimbabwe, like the rest of southern Africa, traffic keeps to the left.

Foreign-registered vehicles can be imported temporarily free of charge and third party insurance is available at the border if you're not already covered.

A driving licence from your home country is sufficient for a visits of up to 90 days. If your licence isn't in English, you must produce an authenticated translation and a photograph when entering the country.

Naturally, you'll have to be on the lookout for African wildlife on the roads – elephants will saunter onto the pavement without warning and a collision would be fatal for the car. Likewise, antelope and other game can appear out of nowhere. On communal lands the highways become footpaths for people and their domestic animals; if you run down a suicidal goat or sheep with a vehicle, you will be expected to financially compensate the owner.

Rental

Hiring a vehicle in Zimbabwe can be expensive so those on a tight budget will have to be part of a group to make it worthwhile. On the other hand, it's really the most feasible way of touring the national parks unless you have loads of time to wait around for lifts. Rental vehicles are in short supply, however, so if you're planning to go this route, make bookings well in advance.

You must have a valid driving licence and be at least 23 years old to hire a vehicle in Zimbabwe. Due to the shortage of spares, vehicle rental agencies won't allow you to take their equipment into Mana Pools National Park or anywhere away from paved roads in the eastern highlands.

Transit Car & Truck Hire (Bulawayo), Europcar and Avis offer unlimited km with a minimum rental period of six days (seven days for Europcar) starting at Z$140 per day plus insurance. For less time, they charge Z$61 per day plus 75 cents per km. If you're hiring for fewer than six days but plan to do a lot of driving in that time, it may still work out better to take the six day rate than pay the per km charges. Avis allows vehicles to be picked up or dropped at Harare, Bulawayo, Kariba, or Victoria Falls. Hertz requires a minimum rental period of 10 days to qualify for unlimited kms and charges a standard Z$100 for drop-off at other than the hire location.

For all rental agencies, the collision damage waiver is an additional Z$10 per day and if you don't take it, you'll have to increase your additional deposit. At the time of writing, petrol, which in Zimbabwe is fossil fuel blended with sugar cane ethanol, costs Z$2.54 per litre. The three major car hire companies – Avis, Hertz, and Europcar – accept their own credit cards as well as American Express, MasterCard, Diners Club and Visa.

Rental Agencies Below are the names and addresses of all the car hire firms in Zimbabwe.

Avis
  Samora Machel Ave, Harare (☎ 720351)
  99 Robert Mugabe Way, Bulawayo (☎ 68571)
  Oasis Service Station, Kariba (☎ 2555)
  Livingstone Way/Mallet Dr, Victoria Falls (☎ 2532)
Europcar/Echo
  19 Samora Machel Ave, PO Box 3430, Harare (☎ 706484)
  Sheraton Hotel, Harare (☎ 700080)
  9a Africa House, Fife St, PO Box 2320, Bulawayo (☎ 67925)
  1 Crawford Rd, PO Box 897, Mutare (☎ 62367)
Hertz
  4 Park St, Harare (☎ 704915)
  Meikles Hotel, Harare (☎ 793701)
  George Silundika St & Fourteenth Ave, Bulawayo (☎ 74701)
  Bulawayo Sun Hotel, Bulawayo (☎ 61402)
  Zimbank Bldg, Victoria Falls (☎ 2203)
  Manicaland Publicity Bureau, Mutare (☎ 64711)
  Caribbea Bay Hotel, Kariba (2453)
  Founders House, Robert Mugabe St, Masvingo (☎ 2131)
  Hwange Safari Lodge, Hwange National Park, Dete (☎ 393)
  Lowveld Travel, Chiredzi (☎ 2295)
Transit Car & Truck Hire
  Corner of Twelfth St & Fife Ave, PO Box FM 260, Bulawayo (☎ 76495)

Purchase
Unless you're loaded and staying for an extended period, buying a vehicle in Zimbabwe will be an unreasonable option. Not only are vehicles expensive, they're also in short supply. Those intent upon purchasing a vehicle to drive around Zimbabwe will find it much cheaper and easier to buy a car in South Africa, especially Johannesburg, secure the necessary paperwork, and then return to South Africa to sell it when you're finished. You won't be able to sell a vehicle in Zimbabwe without officially importing it and paying a substantial duty.

BICYCLE
All major routes in Zimbabwe are surfaced and in excellent repair. The shoulders are often sealed and separated from the mainstream of vehicular traffic by painted yellow lines – instant bicycle lanes. Although there are certainly rough hilly bits, the relatively level landscape over much of the country (at least where the roads are) will further facilitate long-distance cycling. Bicycles are not permitted in game parks, though.

The predictable climate helps cyclists considerably. Winter weather especially is ideal, with cool, clear days and what wind there is normally comes in the form of a gentle easterly, rarely strong enough to hinder cycling activity. Although distances between towns and points of interest are long by European standards, there are plenty of small stores between towns where you can stop for a drink and a friendly chat.

If you're riding a lightweight bicycle, bear in mind that next to nothing is available in terms of spares, not even in Harare. Local cycles use 26 or 28 inch tyres so you can sometimes find these but 27-inchers or 700C are impossible to obtain. Bring with you all the tools and spares you think may be necessary. The two best cycle shops in Harare are Zacks on Kenneth Kaunda Ave opposite the railway station and nearby Manica Cycles on Second Ave. Bicycles may be rented in Harare, Bulawayo and Victoria Falls.

HITCHING

Hitching is easy in Zimbabwe and is many locals' standard means of transport. It is a good opportunity to meet Zimbabweans and many travellers consider it easier and more reliable than the local buses. Don't hesitate to accept lifts from either White or Black drivers but do ascertain whether or not payment is expected before getting in. Hitching at night isn't advisable.

Although it's better to hitch in pairs, it is possible for women to hitch alone, especially if there are women and/or children in the car. Think twice, however, before accepting a lift from a car full of men. It's also best to ascertain the driver's degree of sobriety before setting off. Drunken driving is a serious problem in Zimbabwe.

It's important to note that away from the main road system vehicles are few so if you're headed for the hinterlands, plan on walking and waiting. Even on some major highways – the approaches to Beitbridge from Masvingo or Bulawayo or the long haul from Bulawayo to Victoria Falls – there isn't an abundance of traffic. What vehicles do happen along, however, are more than likely to offer a lift.

In cities or towns, the best place to solicit lifts is at petrol pumps, especially at the last station before the open road where everyone heading your direction will be stopping to top up the tank. Don't feel bad about asking; locals do it as well, and it's a good straightforward way to select just the right lift and determine prices.

BOAT

Since Zimbabwe is a landlocked country, the only boats of any consequence are the three ferries that operate on Lake Kariba between Kariba town and Binga or Mlibizi near the western end of the lake. They're handy especially if you want to do a circular tour of Zimbabwe without having to retrace your steps between Victoria Falls and Bulawayo. For further information on both ferries, see the discussion under Kariba in the Northern Zimbabwe chapter.

LOCAL TRANSPORT

To/From the Airport

Harare's international airport is 15 km from the centre of town. Taxis will cost approximately Z$17 to Z$18. Air Zimbabwe buses which run every half an hour between the airport and the Air Zimbabwe office near Meikles Hotel cost Z$5. Both Meikles and Sheraton offer free shuttle buses for guests.

There are no hotel booking facilities at the airport but currency exchange is available whenever international flights arrive.

Bus

Both Harare and Bulawayo have city bus services connecting the centre with suburban areas. In either city, try to board the bus at the terminus if at all possible. Otherwise, it will be packed to overflowing. Once people are hanging out the windows and doors, the driver won't bother to stop to pick up more. Local bus fares are currently about 15 cents.

Emergency Taxi

Emergency taxis are easily recognised – just look for clunky stripped-down Peugeot station wagons with 'emergency taxi' haphazardly painted on one door. The name has nothing to imply about the urgency of their condition; most just keep plugging along against all odds. They're licensed to operate only within city limits along set routes and charge a standard nationwide rate of 60 cents to anywhere they're going. Their routes aren't advertised, however, so you'll have to ask for help from the driver or one of the numerous locals certain to be milling around them at terminals.

Taxi

By Western standards, city and suburban taxis are inexpensive in Zimbabwe, generally less than Z$5 to or from anywhere in the city centres and Z$8 to Z$15 into the Harare or Bulawayo suburban areas. Most are metered but if you're boarding at a railway station or bus terminal, especially if you're headed for a hotel, drivers will often forego the meter and offer competitive fixed prices.

TOURS

Tours of all sorts – bushwalking, rail tours, canoe and raft trips, sightseeing, game viewing and even all-inclusive lounging around – are available throughout Zimbabwe in all price ranges from local and foreign tour operators and travel agencies. Details on what's available in each region of the country will be outlined in the respective chapters.

Harare

Whatever Harare lacks, it can be safely assumed Zimbabwe doesn't have. The capital and heart of the nation in nearly every respect, Harare, with a population of nearly one million in its metropolitan area, was bequeathed a distinctly European flavour by its White colonisers.

History

The first Shona inhabitants of the marshy flats near the kopje where Harare stands today called themselves Ne-Harawa after the regional chief, whose name meant The One Who Does Not Sleep. The Mbare, under rule of the lower Chief Mbare, controlled the kopje itself. Later, another small clan led by Chief Gutsa settled in what is now Hillside, south-east of the city centre. When the inevitable clash between the two groups came, latecomer Gutsa emerged victorious, killing his rival Mbare and sending the Mbare people packing off into the rugged north-west above the Zambezi Valley.

On 13 September 1890, the Union Jack was raised at the present site of African Unity Square and the anticipated settlement was named Fort Salisbury after British Prime Minister, Robert Cecil, the Marquis of Salisbury. A fort was built and things got off to a rocky start; the subsequent rainy season brought lean times and an unusually high incidence of malaria. The subsequent winter brought the first influx of White settlers from the south, arriving to collect on promises of fertile farm lands and lucrative gold claims along the Zambezi.

More White settlers and merchants arrived and began developing the low-lying lands immediately east of the kopje. Shortly thereafter, the government decided the higher ground to the north-east was eminently more suitable and attempted to relocate the entire settlement. Those entrenched at the kopje refused to budge, however, and the two areas developed separately, hence the distinct clash in street grids

between Causeway and Kopje. Even so, they inevitably merged into one city. Black African workers were forced to remain outside the settlement proper in the area of present-day Mbare which remains the heart of the high-density working-class suburbs.

Salisbury was officially proclaimed a municipality in 1897 and was recognised as the colony's capital in 1923. In 1935, it was granted city status. Through WW II and the Federation of Rhodesia and Nyasaland, business and industry boomed. The city continued to grow until 1965 when Ian Smith and his UDI cast a tarpaulin of uncertainty over the country's biggest construction site.

Salisbury languished through the war but at independence in 1980, things began to pick up. The city summarily became the capital of the new Republic of Zimbabwe and was renamed Harare, a mistransliteration of Ne-Harawa, the early regional chief's name, which had been in use among local Blacks for some years.

Orientation

Central Harare is quite compact, making it a breeze to travel around on foot. Most of the trendy shopping activity is found in and around the First St Mall; the area of Causeway bounded by Samora Machel Ave, Robert Mugabe Rd, Fourth St and Julius Nyerere Way. The higher density peripheral business district south and west of the core area contains more crowded streets and smaller, cheaper shops and businesses.

Since central Harare is formed by the collision of two grids, the street pattern isn't entirely straightforward. On the Causeway grid, streets run roughly north and south whilst avenues run east and west. On the Kopje grid, streets run in both directions except where they are extensions of avenues from the Causeway grid.

Jason Moyo Ave is the heart of the central booking office scene and anyone organising a trip out into the provinces will find themselves tripping around here first. Here also are the Air Zimbabwe office and the Harare Publicity Bureau tourist office, conveniently placed on African Unity Square.

Chancellor Ave Warning Chancellor Ave, a short stretch of the street known in the city as Seventh St and further out as Borrowdale Rd, is the site of both the Executive President's residence and the State House. It is off limits and blocked with barriers between the hours of 6 pm and 6 am. The trigger-happy guards are under official orders to fire without question upon any person or vehicle entering this area during those hours.

Street Name Changes The most important thing to remember when orienting yourself in Harare is that many of the major street names changed in early 1990.

Old Name	New Name
Beatrice Rd/Watt/ Stuart Chandler Way	Simon Mazorodze Rd
Forbes Ave	Robson Manyika Ave
Golden Stairs Rd	Second St Extension
Gordon Ave	George Silundika Ave
Harare/Beatrice Rd	Masvingo Rd
Harari Rd North	Harare Rd
Harari Rd South	Mbare Rd
Hatfield Rd/ Prince Edward Dam Rd	Seke Rd
Kings Crescent	Julius Nyerere Crescent
Mackenzie Rd/Mainway/ Mcneilage Rd	Masotsha Ndlovu Way
Manica Rd/Umtali Rd	Robert Mugabe Rd
Moffat St	Leopold Takawira St
Montagu Ave	Josiah Chinamano Ave
Mazoe St	Mazowe St
Mtoko Rd	Mutoko Rd
North Ave	Josiah Tongogara Ave
Pioneer St	Kaguvi St
Queensway North/ Queensway Rd	Airport Rd
Queensway Rd beyond Mazorodze Rd	Chitungwiza Rd
Rhodes Ave	Herbert Chitepo Ave
Salisbury Dr	Harare Dr
Salisbury Way	Harare Way
Sinoia St	Chinhoyi St
Sir James McDonald Ave	Rekayi Tangwena Ave
Stanley Ave	Jason Moyo Ave
Victoria St	Mbuya Nehanda St
Widdecombe Rd	Chiremba Rd

Information

The best source of information about daily events in Harare is the booklet *What's on in Harare*, published monthly and distributed by the Harare Publicity Association. *The Visitor*, a monthly tourist newspaper published in Harare and distributed by the Publicity Bureau, contains tourism-related advertising and snippets of information in Harare and Zimbabwe but doesn't go into any depth.

Sporting, cinema, and cultural events are also outlined in the local daily, the *Harare Herald*.

For the time of day, phone 93.

Tourist Offices The Harare Publicity Association (☎ 705085) has its office on Second St at the south-west corner of African Unity Square but you'll have to persevere to get much out of them. In addition to their monthly publication, *What's on in Harare*, they distribute pamphlets and advertising about attractions in the immediate area and even a few from around the country. The mailing address is PO Box 1483, Causeway, Harare.

Nationwide information is best obtained from the Zimbabwe Tourist Board (☎ 793666) at the corner of Jason Moyo Ave and Fourth St. They're open from 8 am to 1 pm and 2 to 4.30 pm and are generally more helpful than the Publicity Association. National Parks information and bookings are available next door at the National Parks Office (☎ 706077), 93b Jason Moyo Ave, PO Box 8151, Causeway, Harare.

For climbing, trekking, birdwatching and bushwalking information, contact the Mountain Club of Zimbabwe. The phone numbers of members conducting monthly climbing and bushwalking outings are listed in *What's on in Harare*. Visitors are always welcome to participate.

Money All banks change US$ and £sterling cash and travellers' cheques and are open, as in the rest of the country, on Monday, Tuesday, Thursday and Friday from 8.30 am to 2 pm; on Wednesdays they close at noon

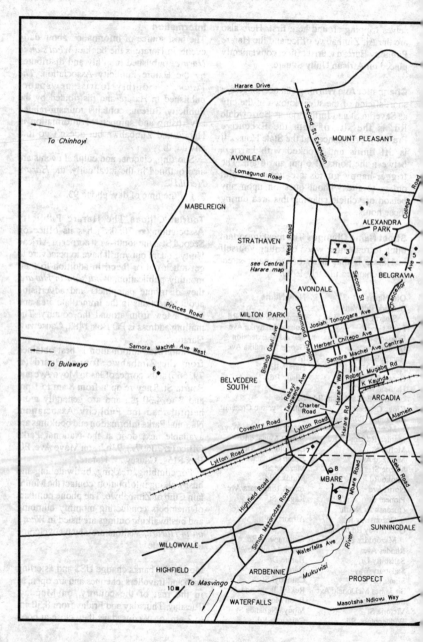

To Chinhoyi

Harare Drive

MOUNT PLEASANT

AVONLEA

Lomagundi Road

Second St Extension

MABELREIGN

STRATHAVEN

West Road

College Road

ALEXANDRA PARK

BELGRAVIA

see Central Harare map

AVONDALE

Second St

Chancellor Ave

Princes Road

MILTON PARK

Drummond Chaplin

Josiah Tongogara Ave

Herbert Chitepo Ave

Bishop Gaul Ave

To Bulawayo

Samora Machel Ave West

Samora Machel Ave Central

BELVEDERE SOUTH

Rekayi Tangwena Ave

Charter Road

Robert Mugabe Rd

Harare Way

K Kaunda

ARCADIA

Alamein

Harare Rd

Coventry Road

Lytton Road

Lytton Road

MBARE

Highfield Road

Simon Mazorodze Road

Mbare Rd

Seke Road

SUNNINGDALE

WILLOWVALE

Waterfalls Ave

Mukuvisi

River

PROSPECT

HIGHFIELD

To Masvingo

ARDBENNIE

WATERFALLS

Masotsha Ndlovu Way

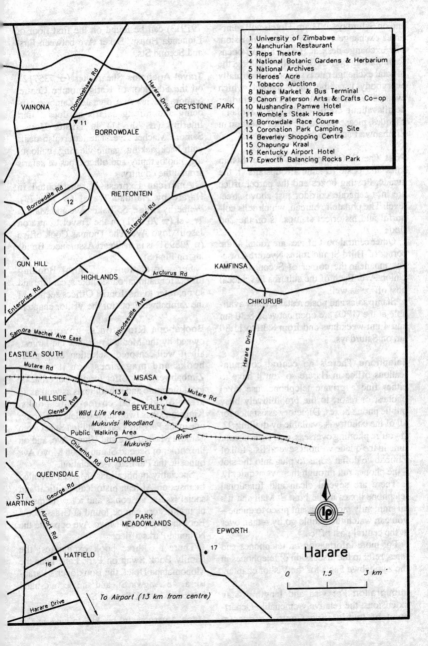

1 University of Zimbabwe
2 Manchurian Restaurant
3 Reps Theatre
4 National Botanic Gardens & Herbarium
5 National Archives
6 Heroes' Acre
7 Tobacco Auctions
8 Mbare Market & Bus Terminal
9 Canon Paterson Arts & Crafts Co-op
10 Mushandira Pamwe Hotel
11 Womble's Steak House
12 Borrowdale Race Course
13 Coronation Park Camping Site
14 Beverley Shopping Centre
15 Chapungu Kraal
16 Kentucky Airport Hotel
17 Epworth Balancing Rocks Park

VAINONA

GREYSTONE PARK

Donnybestawe Rd

Harare Drive

BORROWDALE

▼11

RIETFONTEIN

Borrowdale Rd

12

Enterprise Rd

GUN HILL

HIGHLANDS

Arcturus Rd

KAMFINSA

Enterprise Rd

Rhodesville Ave

CHIKURUBI

Samora Machel Ave East

Harare Drive

EASTLEA SOUTH

Mutare Rd

MSASA

13 ▲

Mutare Rd

HILLSIDE

Glenara Ave

14 ◆
BEVERLEY

Wild Life Area
Mukuvisi Woodland
Public Walking Area
Mukuvisi

◆15

River

CHADCOMBE

Chiremba Rd

QUEENSDALE

ST
MARTINS

George Rd

PARK
MEADOWLANDS

Airport Rd

EPWORTH

HATFIELD

16 ■

● 17

Harare

0   1.5   3 km

To Airport (13 km from centre)

and on Saturdays at 11 am. Hotels will sometimes exchange currency for a commission. The exchange desk at Harare airport opens for incoming flights. Generally speaking, the official exchange rate is so poor that virtually everybody uses the black market, which eventually finds most visitors. For further details about credit cards and travellers' cheques, please turn to the Money section in Zimbabwe Facts for the Visitor.

Post The GPO is on Inez Terrace. Stamp sales and poste restante are upstairs in the arcade. Posting boxes and the parcel office are in a separate corridor just above street level. The philatelic bureau, which sells colourful and historical stamps, is on the 2nd floor.

Other central post offices are found at the corner of Third St and Julius Nyerere Crescent and near the corner of Second St and Union Ave. Each of the suburbs has a local post office as well.

Stamp sales and poste restante (only available at the GPO) are open between 8.30 am and 4 pm weekdays and from 8.30 to 11.30 am on Saturdays.

Telephone There's no central communications office in Harare so you'll have to either find a private telephone, use hotel phones, or resort to the prohibitively busy public phone boxes. Directory assistance for all of the country is available by dialling 92. If you're phoning overseas, don't waste your time in the queue without several fists full of Zimbabwe dollar coins to plug into the slot – the phones run through them very quickly.

There are several clean and functional telephone boxes in the First St Mall and it's an eminently more pleasant place to queue – you can watch the people go by – than over at the central post office.

For more information on telephones and rates, refer to the discussion of telephones in the Zimbabwe Facts for the Visitor chapter.

Immigration For visa and length-of-stay extensions, the relatively amenable Department of Immigration Control office (☎

791913) can be found on the first floor of Liquenda House, Baker Ave between First and Second Sts.

Travel Agencies Shearwater (☎ 735712), on the 5th floor of Karigamombe Centre, Samora Machel Ave, operates Zambezi canoeing and rafting safaris as does Safari Interlink (☎ 700911), in Trustee House, Samora Machel Ave. The latter also deals with backpacking, game viewing, ballooning, photography and other types of safaris around the country.

American Express is represented in Harare by Halmac Travel (☎ 725673), Wetherby House, 55 Baker Ave and Manica Travel (☎ 703421) in the Travel Centre on Jason Moyo Ave. The Thomas Cook office (☎ 728961) is in the Pearl Assurances Building on First St.

For information on Central Booking offices for national parks, hotels, car hire and so on, refer to the Tourist Offices section of the Zimbabwe Facts for the Visitor chapter.

Bookshops Kingston's, government-owned by the Media Trust, has the largest, albeit well-censored, selection of popular books and magazines you'll find in Zimbabwe. They offer foreign paperbacks, local literature and school texts as well as an array of gift and coffee-table books. Kingston's has two major outlets in Harare: one in the Parkade Centre at First St between Samora Machel Ave and Union Ave, and on the corner of Second St and Jason Moyo Ave opposite the Publicity Association.

Speciality publications, Marxist-oriented treatises on African historical, political and social issues, art books and a few items on natural history can be found at Grass Roots Bookshop on Jason Moyo Ave opposite the National Parks office.

There are three book exchanges: the Family Book Swap on Park Lane near the Monomatapa Hotel, the Booklover's Paradise at 48 Angwa St, and the second-hand bookshop at 26C Second St.

Maps A very useful booklet to have is *The*

Greater Harare Street Guide, a gazetteer of large-scale maps including the city centre and all the suburbs. It's available for Z$9.95 from the Harare Publicity Association.

You may want to pick up a copy of the *Central Harare* map from the Surveyor General (☎ 794545) for Z$1.50. The office is on the ground floor of Electra House, Samora Machel Ave.

If you're hiring a car from Avis, ask for their useful central city plan.

Left Luggage You can deposit luggage at the Air Zimbabwe office on Jason Moyo Ave for Z$1 per piece per day or at the railway station for 60 cents per day. The railway station left-luggage deposit is open Monday to Friday from 6 am to 1 pm and 2 to 9.30 pm. On Saturday, it's open from 6 am to 10 pm and on Sunday from 5.30 to 9.30 pm.

Although both the crash pads, Sable Lodge and Paw Paw Lodge, offer safe luggage storage, the youth hostel in Harare is currently not a secure place to leave your things, locked up or otherwise. The situation could change, however, so ask other travellers.

Laundry There is no public laundrette in Harare but there are several dry cleaning services around the city centre. Try American Tailors beside the Surveyor General's office on Samora Machel Ave. If you're staying in a mid-range hotel, you can utilise their laundry services, which will cost about Z$2 for a T-shirt and Z$3 to Z$5 for trousers. The big hotels will charge considerably more.

The caravan park has a laundry sink where you can scrub away at will but you'll need a universal drain plug to use it.

Camping Equipment Limited camping equipment, including butane canisters for Bleuet stoves, is available at Fereday & Sons on Robert Mugabe Rd between First St and Angwa St. If you'd rather just hire camping equipment, Rooney's Hire Service (☎ 792724) at 144 Seke Rd (Julius Nyerere Way extension), about 1½ km south of the railway station, offers just about anything you could possibly need.

Emergency Services Police, fire and ambulance services are available by dialling the emergency number 99. For nonemergency police calls, phone 733033.

Parking Multistorey parking garages, known as parkades, may be found on Julius Nyerere Crescent near the GPO and between Union and Samora Machel Aves on First St. They're open from 6 am to 11 pm. Metered parking is available all over the city and you'll normally be able to find a spot after only a brief search.

National Archives

Founded in 1935 by the Rhodesian government, the National Archives are the repository for the history of both Rhodesia and modern Zimbabwe. It's on Ruth Taylor Rd, just off Borrowdale Rd about three km north of the centre.

In the upstairs foyer is some striking artwork done by Zimbabwean children, and the Beit Trust Gallery displays colonial period historical artefacts and photos as well as original early opportunists' and explorers' accounts. The downstairs foyer contains revolving exhibits and a biographical display of Zimbabwean war heroes. In separate rondavels are old photos and newspaper clippings from the Second Chimurenga, one containing general war information and the other saluting the exploits of ZANU.

They're open from 7.45 am to 4.30 pm Monday to Friday and from 8 am to noon on Saturday and admission is free. The aloe gardens out the front alone are worth the trip out there. To get there, take the Borrowdale or Domboshawa bus from the market square terminal. The Archives are well signposted on Borrowdale Rd as you head north out of town.

Queen Victoria Museum

The best part about this small and easily digestible rundown on the history of life and rocks in Zimbabwe are the concrete creatures standing guard out front. Although this museum isn't as good as its superb Bulawayo counterpart, it's pleasant enough for an hour or so and certainly worth the 20 cent admission charge.

The museum is in the Civic Centre complex between Pennefather Ave and Rotten Row. It's open from 9 am to 5 pm daily, including weekends.

National Gallery of Zimbabwe

This museum is the final word on African art and material culture from around the continent. It was founded in 1957 around a core of works by European artists and was augmented several years later by the fruits of an African sculptors' workshop established by Frank McEwen, the museum's first director. On the ground floor are drawings and paintings, some from the original collection and others added during the late colonial and postcolonial eras. Although there's nothing gripping about most of it, there are a few gems.

In contrast, the display of vibrant and earthy African art and material culture on the first floor is captivating. It's a storehouse of insight into a private Africa normally hidden from European eyes.

Visiting thematic exhibitions are often good and the annual Baringa/Nedlaw competition is open to artists from around the country. If it's on while you're in town, it offers a glimpse at the possible futures of Zimbabwean art.

The museum shop sells art-related publications, crafts, and consigned sculptural works (those placed in the gallery by the artist, who pays the vendor a commission on sale) by both the masters and newcomers for corresponding prices. The museum is open Tuesday to Sunday from 9 am to 12.30 pm and from 2 to 5 pm. Admission is 50 cents.

African Unity Square

This square in the city centre was originally known as Cecil Square in honour of the British Prime Minister, when Fort Salisbury was founded in 1890.

The footpaths in the square were intentionally laid down in the pattern of the Union Jack. The new name of the square now serves as a tribute to the 1988 unity between ZANU and ZAPU.

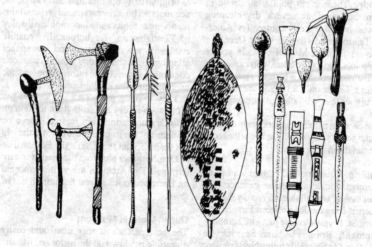

Weapons & Tools: handaxes, spears, shield, knobkerrie, daggers, hoes, adze

Harare Gardens

Harare Gardens, the city's largest park, is a green expanse of lawns and gardens, and even a mini rainforest. It's a popular picnic spot and a quiet haven from the city bustle just a block to the south. Clustered around the Monomatapa Hotel at its southern edge are the National Gallery, an open-air theatre, and the Les Brown Swimming Pool. Near the northern entrance on Herbert Chitepo Ave are a children's playground, an open-air restaurant and teahouse and a bowling club. On weekends, there's music at the bandstand and wedding parties stroll through, posing for photographs.

In the middle is an island-like stand of rainforest which contains a miniature model of Victoria Falls and the Zambezi Gorges. Below the falls is a small pond, evidently representing Lake Kariba.

On weekends, an arts and crafts market is held – mainly just a conveniently transplanted version of what's normally available at Mbare. It's sometimes improved by impromptu musical performances.

Despite its outwardly peaceful atmosphere, Harare Gardens is notorious for both rip-offs and rape, the latter primarily after dark; women should especially avoid short-cutting across it at night. During the daytime, watch your things carefully and however appealing it may be, don't fall asleep on the lawn if you have anything to lose.

Greenwood Park

This neighbourhood park at Herbert Chitepo Ave and Seventh St contains a children's fun park with a miniature railway and cable car. It operates on Saturday from 2 to 5 pm and Sunday from 10 am to 1 pm and 2 to 5 pm. It's also open on Monday, Wednesday and Friday during school holidays between 9 am and noon. South of Herbert Chitepo Ave is a football pitch where there'll nearly always be something going on. Visitors are welcome to watch or even join the game if they'd like.

Kopje

The granite hill rising above the south-west corner of central Harare (the area called Kopje as opposed to Causeway) was once the capital of Chief Mbare, and at its foot the White pioneers first set up their shops and businesses. Access to the summit, where the Eternal Flame of Independence was lit on 18 April 1980, is from Bank Street and Rotten Row. Points of interest below are indicated by small scopes fixed at the lookout.

National Botanic Gardens

The 58 hectare Botanic Gardens between Belgravia and Alexandra Park contain examples of the diverse flowers and greenery that thrive in Harare's pleasant climate. Most of the botanical species found in Zimbabwe are represented as are specimens from around Africa and elsewhere. The National Herbarium (☎ 303211) at Downie Rd and Sandringham Drive is a botanical research centre and dispenses advice and information to gardeners and plant enthusiasts by appointment. There's a map of the gardens' layout at the parking area off Sandringham Drive south of the herbarium.

The gardens are about a 25 minute walk north of Herbert Chitepo Ave along Fifth St or Second St Extension. Alternatively, you can take a northbound bus along Second St Extension, get off at Downie Ave, where there's a signpost pointing the way to the gardens, and walk two blocks east to the herbarium. Admission is free and the gardens are open daily between sunrise and sunset.

Historic Buildings

If you're interested in Harare's colonial architecture, look for a copy of the book *Historical Buildings of Harare* by Peter Jackson, published by Quest Publishing, Harare, 1986. It can be hard to find, so if it's not in the shops, contact the publisher (☎ 704076) at Makomva House, 107 Leopold Takawira St.

Market Hall The old market hall, built in 1893, is at the corner of Bank and Mbuya Nehanda St at Market Square bus terminus near the Kopje. It still serves as a market and is currently in the process of renovation.

Parliament Buildings At the corner of Baker Ave and Third St are the Parliament Buildings which were conceived as a hotel in 1895 and did short stints as a Rhodesian Army barracks and a post office before being taken over by the Legislative Assembly in 1899. The building has undergone several renovations but is still used by the Senate and Assembly for official proceedings and will be until the new Parliament buildings are completed on the Kopje, which is still a few years off by all present indicators.

Those interested in the weekly guided tours and an explanation of government operations or in gallery seats during sessions should apply to the Chief Information Officer (☎ 700181), Parliament of Zimbabwe, PO Box 8055, Causeway, Harare.

Anglican Cathedral The first church in Harare was constructed African-style of mud and pales by Canon Balfour in 1890 on the corner of Second St and Baker Ave. On the same site today is the Anglican Cathedral of St Mary & All Saints, a not particularly inspiring granite-block structure designed by South African architect Sir Herbert Baker. It was begun in 1913 and not completed until 1964; part of the delay has been attributed to a dispute over the shape of the bell tower (which wasn't completed until 1961). The architect originally proposed a Great Zimbabwe-like conical tower but the idea was turned down in favour of the square dungeon-like thing.

Town House Elsewhere, the Town House (☎ 706536), which dates back to 1933, is Harare's town hall. This primarily Italian Renaissance structure on Julius Nyerere Way near the GPO houses the mayoral, City Council and town clerk's offices. The centrepiece of the gardens is a colourful floral clock. If you'd like a look around the interior, phone for an appointment.

Mukuvisi Woodlands

The nearest thing to a zoo in Harare is Mukuvisi Woodlands, a 265 hectare wood-land reserve seven km east of the city. Of the total area, 156 hectares are natural *msasa* parkland for picnics, walking and birdwatching. The remaining area has been set aside as a game park where zebra, sable, wildebeest, giraffe, elephant, warthog and impala roam free. There used to be a rhino but it's now been removed for its own safety. Guided two hour foot safaris through the game area are conducted on Saturday afternoons at 2 pm, on Sunday at 8 am, and on Wednesday at 2 pm for Z$5 per person. If you're there at any other time, there's a game-viewing platform overlooking the waterhole where you can while away an hour or two watching the animals. Admission to the platform is Z$1. Proceeds go to Mukuvisi Woodlands trust for the upkeep of the park.

Mukuvisi is a 20 minute walk from the caravan park along Glenara Ave South; caravan park attendants will explain the quickest route over the railway line. From the centre, take the Msasa bus from Market Square terminus or the Greendale bus from Rezende St terminus and ask the driver to drop you as near to Mukuvisi as possible.

Chapungu Kraal

If not for its sculpture garden and weekend African dance performances (Saturday at 3 pm and Sunday at 11 am and 3 pm), Chapungu Kraal wouldn't rate the Z$5 admission charge or even the effort of getting out there.

The name Chapungu is the Shona word for the bateleur eagle, the spirit messenger for the Shona people. The sculptural displays are accessible in a half-hour guided tour which leads you through the motivation behind the granite, jasper, verdite etc works of Zimbabwe's most renowned artists.

Chapungu (☎ 47472) is open daily from 6.30 am to 4.30 pm at Doon Estate, 1 Harrow Rd, Beverley East, Msasa. It's within easy walking distance of the caravan park but about 8 km from the centre of Harare. Take the Greendale bus to the caravan park from the Rezende St terminus and walk from there or hitch east on Mutare Rd past the Beverley shopping centre and Chicken Inn. Turn right into the industrial area and after a sharp right turn, pass through the security gate at the Sorbaire sign.

Epworth Balancing Rocks

Although there are better examples of balancing rocks all over Zimbabwe, the ones at Epworth, 13 km south-east of Harare are probably the most famous. The big attraction is the group known as the Bank Notes, catapulted to rock stardom when they were featured on Zimbabwe paper currency. If you're not interested in paying the Z$2 admission to the park, however, there are plenty of free balanced rocks across the road which are just as interesting to explore.

To get there, take the Epworth bus from the Fourth St and Jason Moyo Ave terminus and get off at either Munyuki Shopping Centre or the turnoff to Epworth Primary School. From the latter, it's 500 metres further along the road to the park entrance. You'll be surrounded by the balancing boulders – and Epworth kids – for the entire walk. By car, follow Robert Mugabe Rd east from the centre and turn right on Chiremba Rd, which will take you directly to Epworth.

Heroes' Acre

On a hill overlooking Harare, the obelisk of Heroes' Acre serves as a monument to the ZIPRA and ZANLA dead during the struggle for liberation from the Rhodesian oppressor. It contains the tombs of the war heroes of the fighting and is the future site of a war museum. This North Korean-designed canonisation of the dead heroes as well as the Leninisation of Robert Mugabe is quite an impressive production.

If you can avoid being swept away by the propaganda, Heroes' Acre is worth a visit. You must first apply for a permit from the Ministry of Information, Room 514 of Liquenda House on Baker Ave which, if you check out politically, will be issued immediately. To reach Heroes' Acre, which is five km from the centre out on the Bulawayo Rd, catch the Warren Park bus from the terminus just west of Chinhoyi St along Samora Machel Ave. Admission and guided tours of the site are free.

Tobacco Auctions

Zimbabwe is one of the world's largest producers of tobacco, currently the country's largest single foreign exchange earner. Harare serves as the tobacco trading centre of southern Africa. The world's largest tobacco auction floor on Gleneagles Rd in Willowvale, eight km from Harare, was constructed in 1986. Auctions are held daily between April and October (exact dates will vary from year to year depending on the harvest) from 8 am to noon. During a single day an average of 16,000 bales will change hands, one every six seconds. Visitors are welcome to watch proceedings and guided tours of the floor as well as the lowdown on the complex tobacco industry are available at the site. Take the Highfields bus from the corner of Fourth St and Robert Mugabe Rd.

For further information and confirmation of trading activity, contact the Tobacco Sales Floor (☎ 68921) or the Tobacco Marketing Board (☎ 66311).

Harare Agricultural Show

The Harare Agricultural Society Show, held at the Harare show grounds near the Sheraton near the end of August, is the national showcase for agricultural, commercial and manufacturing industries, a bit like a state fair in the midwestern USA. It was first held in 1897 as a cattle and produce show and has grown into an annual event attracting over 150,000 spectators and 150 commercial exhibitions along with traditional dance performances, live music and military demonstrations. Check with the Publicity Bureau for dates and scheduled events.

Sports

The Olympic-sized Les Brown Swimming Pool between Harare Gardens and the Monomatapa Hotel is open daily 10 am to 6.30 pm from late August to early May. The rest of the year, hours are 11 am to 4 pm. It costs 50 cents for as long as you'd like to swim.

Another variation on swimming is available at Waterwhirld, with water slides and an artificial beach less than two km east of the centre along Samora Machel Ave.

Golf is also popular in Zimbabwe and green fees are some of the world's least expensive – 18 holes for around Z$10 on weekdays and Z$20 on weekends. Clubs may be hired at clubhouses for around Z$10 per day and caddies will cost about Z$5 per game. There are seven courses in the Harare area alone, including the internationally acclaimed Royal Harare Golf Club on Josiah Tongogara Ave, just a 20-minute walk north of the city centre. Those who prefer miniature golf will find a course at Waterwhirld.

For information on tennis and squash, contact the Harare Sports Club (☎ 791151). Squash court bookings can be made by phoning 722234; for tennis court bookings, call 724424.

Organised Tours

The United Touring Company (UTC) offers several day tours in and around Harare. The tours depart from Meikles Hotel and should be booked through UTC (☎ 793701), corner of Park St and Jason Moyo Ave, PO Box 2914, Harare.

There's a Scenic City Tour for Z$40 per person, which takes in the central area including African Unity Square, the Kopje, and Mbare Market. In season (April to October), it includes the Tobacco Auction Floors, while the rest of the year, it includes Epworth Balancing Rocks instead. A Cultural City Tour for the same price includes the National Archives, the Queen Victoria Museum, the National Gallery and Matombo Gallery. Both of these operate daily, the former at 8.45 am and the latter at 1.45 pm, allowing you to participate in both on the same day.

Another, which departs at 1.45 pm daily visits Chapungu Kraal and Mukuvisi Woodlands. It also costs Z$40.

Other tours include Ewanrigg National Park, Larvon Bird Gardens, the Lion and Cheetah Park and Lake McIlwaine Game Park. These tours will be described in the discussion of those sights.

Places to Stay – bottom end

Camping At the lowest priced end of the accommodation scale is the camping ground in Coronation Park (☎ 46282) seven km east of the centre along Mutare Rd (which merges with Samora Machel Ave out of town so you can take either route to get there). Most people try to hitch, which isn't too difficult but the Manara and Greendale buses from the Rezende St terminus pass it and the Msasa bus from the Market Square terminus will get you within a couple of minutes' walk of the site. Showers, baths and public telephones are available. Camping sites cost about Z$4.50 for up to four campers and Z$1 for each additional person.

Hostels The *Harare Youth Hostel* (☎ 796436) at 6 Josiah Chinamano Ave probably isn't the ideal place to stay. Security isn't very good, but it does offer cooking facilities and YHA members pay only Z$5 for dormitory rooms. The hostel is closed from 10 am to 5 pm daily and the kitchen closes at the 10 pm curfew. At least there are no chores to do.

At 95 Selous Ave is the normally overcrowded crash pad *Sable Lodge* (☎ 726017). If no rooms are available, they'll make room. Until the police put an end to it, they even allowed tent camping on the lawn. If a rare room comes available, it'll cost Z$12 per person. Otherwise, you'll pay Z$10 wherever you wind up sleeping.

Friendly and laid-back, they sell beer, soft drinks and snacks out the back. If you like lazing around the pool and meeting other travellers, this is the place to go but there are frequent police raids. Be discreet about anything you'd rather keep to yourself, even with fellow travellers.

The third inexpensive option is *Paw Paw Lodge* (☎ 724014, Mrs Washaya) at 262 Herbert Chitepo Ave. It's a very friendly operation with clean dormitory-style accommodation. If you opt to hire linen, a bed costs Z$15 per person; it's Z$12 if you have your own sleeping gear. Mattresses on the floor cost Z$10. They have a lounge and cooking facilities for guests and there's no curfew but drugs and alcohol are prohibited inside.

A few educational and volunteer hostels in Harare allow travellers to stay when space is available and/or an invitation has been made from someone within the relevant organisation, but don't make plans around them. A particularly quiet hostel open to women only, with rooms available between school terms, is *Bromley House* (☎ 724072) at 182 Herbert Chitepo Ave opposite Harare Gardens. It costs Z$10 per person for a room or Z$12 for bed and breakfast.

Although the *YMCA* (Toc-H) men's hostel was once popular and offered good cheap accommodation, the situation there has changed and the place would be wisely avoided.

Hotels For the sake of a breakdown, bottom-end hotels are those charging less than Z$50 for a single room. Most of the bottom-end hotels in Harare are noisy and double as brothels so lone women who'd prefer not to risk being misconstrued may want to look for accommodation elsewhere.

The most popular and central of these is the *Elizabeth Hotel* (☎ 708591) at the corner of Julius Nyerere Way and Robert Mugabe Rd. Single rooms cost Z$45.10, doubles are Z$70.20, both with shared facilities. Rooms with showers but no toilets cost Z$72. The Elizabeth offers disco music nightly until at least 11.30 pm and often hosts local bands, but cover charges are imposed.

Next in popularity is the *Queens Hotel* (☎ 738977), Kaguvi St, in the town centre near the corner of Robert Mugabe Rd, which has a bar and disco music Monday to Friday until 11.30 pm and pungwe performances in the garden by live local bands (subject to a cover charge) on Friday and Saturday nights. Singles/doubles cost Z$45/60. A double with bath is Z$70.

The *Earlside* (☎ 730003) at the corner of Fifth St and Selous Ave is quiet but also quite centrally located. The outside looks seedier than it really is so don't be put off by appearances. Singles/doubles will set you back Z$35/50. Double rooms with private

bath cost Z$65. There's a swimming pool and a dining room where you get set lunches and dinners for Z$6.50 each.

The *Russell Hotel* (☎ 791894) at 116 Baines Ave and its annexe, the *City Limits* at the corner of Second St and Baines Ave, are very good value for money. For singles/doubles with bed and breakfast, private baths, radio, telephone, and a pool (at the Russell, which may be used by guests of either building), they charge Z$52/73 at the main building and Z$42/58 at City Limits.

Another option is the *Hotel International* (☎ 700332) at the corner of Baker Ave and Fourth St. It's well located but doesn't have a pool or television. Bed and breakfast in singles/doubles with shared bath costs Z$50/60. With private bath, doubles only are available for Z$70.

At 9 Harare St near the southern end of the Kopje between the centre and Mbare is the *Federal Hotel* (☎ 706118). It's the most distinctly African of all the inexpensive places. Prices are similar to those of the Queens Hotel.

The *Elmfield Lodge* (☎ 724014) at 111 Fife Ave is run by the same management as the Paw Paw Lodge mentioned in the discussion of hostels. Both single and double rooms are available for Z$30 and Z$50 respectively.

Places to Stay – middle
Mid-range hotels in Harare are for the most part very nice and, while not luxurious, they're more than adequately comfortable. Although they don't require payment in hard currency as the top-range hotels do, guests paying in Zimbabwe dollars must still produce bank exchange receipts for at least the amount of the bill. The prices given here are for foreigners. Zimbabwe residents can expect to pay at least 25% less.

Few visitors will disagree that the *Bronte Hotel* (☎ 796631), at 132 Baines Ave, as far as atmosphere is concerned is Harare's finest. It's clean, surrounded by gardens and set back from a quiet street. There are a pool and bar on hand for relaxation and they even have monthly rates for those who can't tear

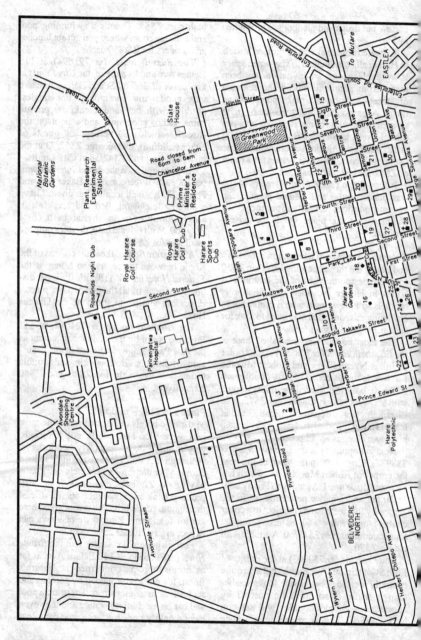

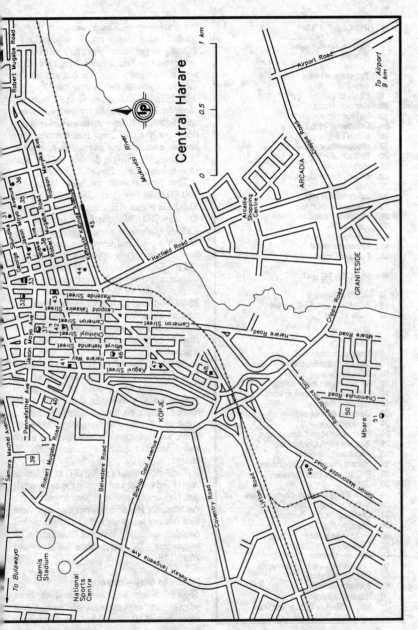

Central Harare

themselves away. The downside is that it's booked out at least a month in advance so, unless you get lucky, you can't just turn up and expect to find a room. Singles/doubles with private bath, including bed and breakfast, cost Z$68/88. Suites cost Z$105.

A friendly alternative is the *Courteney Hotel* (☎ 706411) at the corner of Selous Ave and Eighth St. It has a secluded and relaxing pool area, the Old Crow Bar, a coffee shop and an excellent but expensive restaurant, (L'Escargot). Single/double rooms with private baths cost Z$66/80.

The one-star *Terreskane Hotel* (☎ 7007031) on Fife Ave between Second and Third Sts offers singles/doubles with baths for Z$65/80. Without baths, rooms cost Z$55/70. Family rooms go for Z$150. There's a pool and television lounge and a bar out the front where you can sit in the sun.

The *Selous Hotel* (☎ 727940) at the Coimbra Portuguese Restaurant, at the corner of Selous Ave and Sixth St, costs Z$60 single and Z$70 double. Breakfast will cost an extra Z$7. The place has little to recommend it, however, apart from the chicken available at the restaurant, which is legendary.

At the corner of Fourth St and Samora Machel Ave, the *Executive Hotel* (☎ 792803), formerly a block of flats, offers private baths, telephones and TV in every room. There's no pool but they do have a sundeck. Singles/doubles cost Z$65/85. There's a restaurant which is open for lunch and dinner but there's a minimum Z$6.50 charge.

The *Ambassador* (☎ 708121) at 88 Union Ave is pretty nice and right at the brink of all the Causeway activity; the foyer of the Ambassador House next door displays some nice African sculpture and painting. Singles/doubles, including bed and breakfast, with telephones, TV and private baths go for Z$95/148.

Places to Stay – top end

Top-end hotels here are defined as those whose least expensive single rooms cost more than Z$100 per night. The only luxury international-class hotels, however, are the Sheraton, Meikles and the Monomatapa. They all employ a two-tier pricing scheme by which foreigners pay higher rates than Zimbabwe residents. Although most rooms will have been booked and paid for overseas, those settling accounts at the time of departure will be expected to pay in hard foreign currency; prices here are therefore given in US$. Again, foreigners will pay substantially higher rates than Zimbabwe residents.

Straddling the mid-range and top-end categories quality-wise, the three-star *Cresta Oasis* (☎ 704217, fax 794655) at 124 Baker Ave (the entrance is on Union Ave between Fifth and Sixth Sts) offers marginal luxury and a quiet location. Non-Zimbabwe residents will pay US$55 per person for a standard room including bed and breakfast.

The Oasis' relative, the four-star *Cresta Jameson* (☎ 794641, fax 794655), on Samora Machel Ave at Park St, is very nice and is right in the centre of things in high-rise Harare. Foreigners pay US$76 a single and US$90 a double; all rooms have private facilities, and the rates include breakfast.

On Samora Machel Ave between Fifth and Sixth Sts is the *Holiday Inn* (☎ 795611, fax 735695), which is pretty much like Holiday Inns everywhere. Single rooms cost US$80 and doubles US$100.

Meikles Hotel (☎ 795655, fax 707754) on Jason Moyo Ave, claims five stars but is stuffy and slack with service. They charge US$105 for a single room and US$121 for a double. Suites cost Z$168 a single and $192 a double.

Of Harare's three five-star hotels, the *Harare Sheraton* (☎ 729771, fax 796678) and conference centre, between Samora Machel Ave and the end of Pennefather Ave, is the largest, newest and most pretentious but isn't the most expensive in town. A standard double room costs US$120 (no singles are available) while the Presidential Suite is US$510. There are all the standard amenities; exclusive shops, hairdressers, gourmet restaurants, upmarket pubs and the like.

Harare's most expensive hotel is the *Monomatapa* (☎ 704501) on Park Lane backed up by Harare Gardens. Standard single rooms cost US$109, and doubles cost US$145 without breakfast, which will set you back an extra Z$13 per person.

Places to Stay – suburban & out of town
The *Mushandira Pamwe Hotel* (☎ 64355) at Nyandoro Rd, Stand 4806 in Highfields sits between a couple of local music venues but it's an expensive taxi ride from the centre of town. Likewise, the one-star *Nyagonzera Skyline Motel* (☎ 67588 Beatrice), on the Masvingo Rd about 19 km from Harare, offers excellent live music performances but transport can be problematic or expensive for those without their own vehicles.

The *Kentucky Airport Hotel* (☎ 506550) on St Patrick's Rd, Hatfield, has been recommended. It costs Z$45/70 for a single/double including breakfast.

On an entirely different plane is *Carolina Wilderness* (☎ 29565 Norton), a resort 25 km from Harare off the Bulawayo Rd, offering luxury lodges and game viewing on a private game reserve. Advance booking is essential. For reservations and information, phone or write to Carolina Wilderness Lodge, PO Box W83, Waterfalls, Zimbabwe.

Nameless informal accommodation (☎ 791881 ext 242 day, 882794 evening) is available in the pleasant suburb of Borrowdale close to the bus lines. There's a dormitory with kitchen facilities for Z$12 per person and a private double room and bath for Z$35. The only catch is that it's open only between 5 pm and 7.30 am.

Places to Eat
Breakfast, Snacks & Light Meals All over the city centre you'll find takeaways selling chips, burgers, 'samoosas' (as samosas are known in Zimbabwe), soft drinks and other standard takeaway fare. Try *Dagwood's* in the First St Parkade for sandwiches and sadza ne nyama. If you're looking for cheap African fare, the takeaways in the Kopje area of town are good – try the *Tafara Cafe*, a nice local hangout at the corner of Albion and

Robert Mugabe Rds where African music blares at all hours.

A full breakfast of cereal, juice, eggs, bacon, sausage, toast, and (not recommended) coffee or tea at *The Cottage Pie* in the Courteney Hotel, especially convenient if you're staying at Sable Lodge, will cost only Z$3.50 per person.

Fast food chains represented in Harare include *Wimpy* and *Chicken Inn*, both on the First St mall, but neither is anything special. Next door to the Chicken Inn is the affiliated *Bakers Inn* where you can buy sticky pastries and doughnuts. Another Chicken Inn can be found at Beverley Shopping Centre not far from the Coronation Park Caravan Park.

Real brewed coffee is available at *Brazita's* in the First St Parkade but its demeanour is a bit aloof so don't plan a lingering conversation over a slow cuppa. The nearby *Le Paris* at the Samora Machel Ave side of the Parkade also has good coffee and is better for a chat. On sunny afternoons, try the reasonably priced teahouse in Harare Gardens.

Another quality coffee shop is *Europa* in Throgmorton House on Samora Machel Ave. Both Le Paris and Europa offer light meals and sandwiches as well as coffee and snacks. For gooey pastries, there's the *Boulangerie-Patisserie* in the Sheraton lobby. The baguettes and brown breads aren't bad.

Natie's Grill in the First St Mall has a pretty nice set breakfast with chips, two eggs, sausage, bacon, grilled tomato and coffee or tea for Z$7. For lunch they offer a varied light menu – ham, steak, chicken, burgers, chips, waffles and so on – most of it good. It's only open until 4.30 pm weekdays and 1 pm on Saturday.

The *Lido* at 51 Union Ave has been recommended for burgers and their Z$6 set breakfast special. Another pleasant alternative is the *Terrace Restaurant* on the third level of Barbour's Department Store where you'll find decent lunches and a fresh-air view. It's one place where they don't mind if you sit in the sun, drink coffee and write postcards to your heart's content. The small and dank coffee shop in the basement is also okay for snacks and coffee but you miss out on the sun and fresh air.

Buffet Meals Most of the big hotels put on extravagant (for Zimbabwe) buffet meals which could easily become a budget traveller's mainstay. In the morning you can try the large English or continental breakfast fare or wait until midday for the lunch version. Most agree that one or the other will satisfy appetites for most of the day.

The best buffets in Harare are found at the Sheraton, Meikles, the Monomatapa and the Holiday Inn. An all-you-can-eat English breakfast at the Holiday Inn, the cheapest of these, will cost Z$10; Z$7 if you prefer just a continental breakfast. Their lunch buffet, which includes a variety of salads, meat dishes, casseroles and desserts, costs Z$12.50. Vegetarians who prefer only salad dishes will get by paying Z$6.50 per person. If you'd rather just pig out at the dessert table, you'll pay only Z$3. The other big hotels offer similar options for only slightly more, with the Sheraton having the top price of Z$14 for the buffet English breakfast and slightly more for the lunch.

Restaurants Although there isn't much for the gourmet in Harare – imported foods are hard to come by and restaurant owners squabble over smuggled shipments of Mozambique prawns, for example – there is a surprising number of very good and relatively inexpensive restaurants.

One of the most popular restaurants with travellers, not only because it's around the corner from the Youth Hostel, is *Guido's Trattoria* in the Montagu Shopping Centre at the corner of Harare St and Josiah Chinamano Ave. Each evening they offer a pasta speciality for around Z$8 and a meat dish for about Z$14 as well as pizza and other Italian standbys. The salads are superb as well, and you'd be hard-pressed to find a better inexpensive restaurant in Harare. Don't miss their espresso and cappuccino. Guido's serves lunches between noon and 2 pm and opens for dinner at 6.30 pm.

Almost as good as Guido's is *Demi's* (☎ 7723308), near the corner of Speke Ave and Leopold Takawira St, which specialises in Greek cuisine, including a wonderful Greek salad. It's open for lunches and takeaways between 10 am and 2.30 pm weekdays and for dinners Monday to Saturday from 6.30 to 10.30 pm. Harare's other Greek restaurants are the *Aphrodite Taverna* (☎ 35500) at Strathaven Plaza, Strathaven and the *Acropolis* in Avondale, which also serves reportedly superior Greek meals for under Z$15 per person.

Another excellent option is the friendly and reasonably priced *Bombay Duck* (☎ 721487), an Indian curry house at 7 Central Ave near Third St. It's open for dinner nightly except Sunday and covers most of the standard Indian specialities. They also have a takeaway next door where you can buy curries and rice for around Z$4. If you have a vehicle or don't mind a taxi ride into the suburbs, another Indian option is the *Sitar* (☎ 729132) in Newlands Shopping Centre on Enterprise Rd.

The new *Spago's* (☎ 791894) in the Russell Hotel on Baines Ave comes highly recommended for its Italian cuisine and reasonable prices. Their salads and garlic bread are made all the tastier by real filtered coffee and they serve some of the nicer Zimbabwean wines, as well.

If you're looking for Chinese, there are two options in the city centre, both on Robert Mugabe Rd within a few metres of each other: the *Bamboo Inn* (☎ 705457), which is probably the better or the two, and the *Mandarin* (☎ 726227). For a different Oriental twist, try the *Manchurian* (☎ 36166), next to the Reps Theatre on Second St Extension in Avondale, which serves Mongolian cuisine.

The Carvery (☎ 702484) upstairs in the Fife Ave Shopping Centre at the corner of Sixth St and Fife Ave, which serves both lunches and dinners, specialises in steak and beef dishes. The works including a starter, main course, dessert and coffee will set you back Z$22. Another steak house, *Womble's* (☎ 882747) at Ballantyne Park Shopping Centre, is a favourite hangout for local White youth.

If you're not interested in meat, highly recommended vegetarian fare is available at *The Homegrown* (☎ 703545) at the corner of Speke Ave and Leopold Takawira St. This is a real rarity in Africa so enjoy it while you're in Harare. Meals cost Z$9.50 but an all-you-can-eat salad bar is only Z$2.50. Lunches are served noon to 2 pm Monday to Friday and dinners from 6.30 to 10 Monday to Saturday. Live music is sometimes featured during dinner.

The *Coimbra* (☎ 700234) at 61 Selous Ave serves Portuguese fare but, according to locals, the only reason to go is for their barbecued chicken which is reputedly excellent. For upmarket French cuisine, try *Le Français* (☎ 302706) at the Arts Complex in Avondale. For dinner, it's open daily except Sunday. Mexican food, or as close to it as you'll find in Zimbabwe, is served at the new *Taco's Restaurant* on Union Ave near the Playboy Night Club. There you'll find a filling three-course meal for less than Z$20.

All the big hotels and some smaller ones offer both fine dining and mid-range restaurants. *La Chandelle* for gourmet fare and *Harvest Garden* for more down-to-earth meals, both in the Sheraton, are highly recommended for financial blowouts. *L'Escargot* (☎ 706411) at the Courteney Hotel is also touted as one of the country's finest and highly acclaimed. *Alexander's* (☎ 700340) at 7 Livingstone Ave serves the highest priced, but arguably the best, food in town.

Entertainment

The best place to find information on upcoming events is the monthly tourist office booklet *What's on in Harare* which lists cultural, sports and musical events which they deem of interest to tourists. More obscure venues and cinema schedules are normally listed in the *Herald*.

A couple of warnings: unfortunately, unaccompanied women may encounter some uncomfortable situations at live music venues, discos and most drinking establishments, so unless you're the type who's prepared to face them head on, find a partner or stay away. Drink tends to lighten fingers as well as hearts so anyone dancing at a crowded performance or disco would be wise to leave their wallet and other valuables with a member of your group back at the table.

Secondly, upmarket pubs and hotel bars require 'smart casual' dress. That's normally interpreted as jackets for men, skirts or suits for women, and no trainers (joggers, sandshoes), thongs (flip-flops), denims or T-shirts.

Cinema There is no shortage of cinema in Harare – there are 11 movie houses and two drive-ins. Most cinemas run three or four screenings of American films, primarily in the afternoon and evening. Check the *Herald* for daily listings.

Theatre Harare doesn't have much in the way of theatre but Gallery Delta, an all-round venue in the courtyard of the Strachan Building at 76 Robert Mugabe Rd, occasionally comes up with some quality theatrical, artistic and musical exhibits and productions. If you're interested in what's on, phone 792135 or check the most recent *What's on in Harare* for the current month's activities.

Harare Reps, which stage some entertaining albeit middle of the road productions, have their auditorium 40 minutes' walk from the centre in the Belgravia Shopping Centre at Thurston Lane and Second St Extension, Avondale. Advance bookings for Reps productions is through Spotlight (☎ 724754) in Chancellor House, Samora Machel Ave. Occasionally Harare also stages performances by visiting theatre groups which normally use the Seven Arts Theatre, a large cinema also in Avondale.

Live Music Most travellers interested in the local music scene come to Harare looking for a pungwe, an all-night drinking and dancing musical performance, by one of Zimbabwe's

top musicians. Since the Publicity Bureau doesn't normally stock such information, the best bet is to watch for posters wrapped around signs and poles – primarily in the Kopje area of town – which announce upcoming events. All venues impose a cover charge for live musical events and some even charge for disco music.

For the best opportunity to hear local bands – although there's not much quality control so you do get the occasional dud – try one of the Central African Hotels Group hotels on a Friday or Saturday night. The Queen's and Elizabeth seem to lead the pack with the Federal Hotel following just behind. If you're very lucky, an internationally known name like Thomas Mapfumo or Oliver Mutukindzi may drop by for a session.

The garden of the Nyagonzera Skyline Motel (☎ 67588) at km 19 of the Beatrice-Masvingo Rd is also a popular nightspot and frequently attracts some superb talent. Unfortunately, it's a long way from town and there's no public transport running at the hours you'd be needing it so a hefty taxi fare will be the only option for those without their own transport. Anyway, phone in advance to ascertain whether the trip out is worth the effort.

For a reasonable chance of hearing such greats as the Bhundu Boys, Thomas Mapfumo & the Blacks Unlimited or Ilanga, try the weekend gigs at Job's Night Spot, owned by Job Kadengu; it's in the Wonder Shopping Centre on Julius Nyerere Way between Kenneth Kaunda and Robson Manyika Sts.

For the more intrepid, the three nightclubs in and around the Mushandira Pamwe Hotel out in Highfields have live bands on weekends and at least one will probably be offering something of interest; you'll have to catch a taxi out there.

Marimba bands, including the renowned Jairos Jiri Marimba Band, give free performances in the bandstand at Harare Gardens. Local bands also play at the drinking halls at Mbare market on Saturday afternoons. Men will find them interesting cultural scenes but lone women should steer clear.

Bigger musical events such as national celebrations or concerts by foreign stars normally take place in the National Stadium. For the latter, half of Zimbabwe seems to descend upon Harare so it will be vital to book tickets well in advance, an option not available to most travellers.

Discos & Drinking Spots The best daytime drinking spot is probably the front patio at the Terreskane Hotel.

The Elizabeth Hotel and Queens Hotel offer African and Western disco music nightly until 11.30 and both are great places to meet and party with locals but sound systems are less than optimum. Most of the drinking spots are in hotel bars – the Bird & Bottle in the Ambassador Hotel on Union Ave has been recommended. For a more sedate drinking experience, try the Old Crow Bar at the Courteney Hotel on Eighth St and Selous Ave or the pubs at one of the four or five-star hotels.

The Playboy Night Club at 40 Union Ave has been recommended for music and drinking. Sarah's, on the first floor of the CABS building at Jason Moyo Ave and Park St, offers alcohol and pop/New Wave music. It also serves as a pick-up joint and theft isn't uncommon.

If you're more conservative, try Your Place at 99 Robert Mugabe Rd which has been described as a Rhodies' boozing joint, pretty tacky and usually crammed full; a live band usually features. They serve meals as well as drinks and locally it's considered a rather upmarket haunt.

For the young and mode-conscious White set, there's Rosalind's in Avondale Shopping Centre. Trendy dress and hairstyle are obligatory.

Spectator Sports One of the most popular sports in Harare is horse racing and chances are interested visitors will be able to catch one of Mashonaland Turf Club's 41 annual meets at the Borrowdale Park track. The Harare area boasts 600 active thoroughbred

horses. Alternatively, trotting races are held every Sunday at the National Trotting Club's Waterfalls Stadium on Hatfield Rd.

Sporting events, which are announced in the *Herald*, are held regularly at the Chinese-constructed National Stadium a few km west of the centre out along the Bulawayo Rd (take Samora Machel Ave).

Things to Buy

All the big hotel gift shops and a plethora of souvenir and curio shops around the centre dispense locally made crafts and souvenirs of varying quality. While they're convenient, they're not normally the cheapest way to go and often, similar or superior items can be found at lower-overhead outlets around town.

For real works of art, particularly the Shona sculpture for which Zimbabwe is famous, the National Gallery and several commercial galleries offer a variety of names and prices.

Commercial Sculpture Galleries In addition to the shop at the National Gallery, several galleries and crafts shops sell original African art and skilled craft work. Those inspired by Shona sculpture can find original creations at several commercial galleries around town. The four major ones deal primarily in works by known sculptors.

Stone Dynamics at 56 Samora Machel Ave specialises in serpentine and verdite works by older well-known and established artists. Vukutu Gallery, north of town on the corner of Harvey Brown Ave and Blakiston St, is in a pleasant old suburban home. Besides sculptural works by well-knowns and newcomers, they also deal in handicrafts. At 114 Leopold Takawira St is Matombo Gallery which also emphasises big names but also devotes space to emerging talents.

Out in the eastern suburbs at Doon Estate, 1 Harrow Rd, Msasa, is The Gallery of Shona Sculpture at Chapungu Village. The sculptures are spread around a large, grassy lawn, there's a nice lake, and easy-going sales people. The only drawback is the Z$5 admission charge but it does buy you a guided tour of the gardens and a spoon-fed appreciation for the thinking behind some of the works. It's open daily from 9 am to 4.30 pm. For more info, see the discussion of Chapungu earlier in this chapter.

Crafts & Practical Items Plenty of reasonably priced crafts outlets exist around Harare. The best and cheapest are found at Mbare market where stall upon stall of carvings and practical items as well as kitsch souvenirs can be purchased at negotiable prices. Alternatively, try the National Handicraft Centre, open Monday to Saturday from 9.30 am to 5 pm, at the corner of Grant and Chinhoyi Sts in Kopje. You'll also find crafts pedlars set up in Harare Gardens and along Jason Moyo Ave in the centre of town.

The cheapest T-shirts in the centre are at Zimcraft Co-operative Shop in the First St Parkade where you'll pay at least 30% less than at Rado Arts, a trendy but expensive gift shop on the First St mall.

The Jairos Jiri Crafts Shop, which benefits disabled Zimbabweans, is in the Park Lane Building on Julius Nyerere Cres opposite the National Gallery. At the Danhiko Project School on Mutare Rd opposite the Nite-Star Drive-in Cinema, you'll find a variety of locally made clothing and carpentry items for sale at well below shop prices. Otherwise, check out the shops selling inexpensive African print clothing around the area of South Ave and Kenneth Kaunda Ave near the railway station.

See also the discussions of the Cold Comfort Farm Society and Mbare in the Around Harare section.

Getting There & Away

Air There are direct domestic Air Zimbabwe flights between Harare and Bulawayo, Buffalo Range, Kariba, Victoria Falls, Gweru, Masvingo and Hwange National Park. For more details, refer to the Zimbabwe Getting Around chapter. Information about getting to Harare from other countries is found in both the Zimbabwe and regional Getting There & Away chapters.

Airline offices in Harare include:

Air Botswana, Suite 501, Jameson Hotel, Union Ave (☎ 703132)
Air India, Batanai Gardens, First St & Jason Moyo (☎ 700318)
Air Malawi, Throgmorton House, Samora Machel Ave & Julius Nyerere Way (☎ 706497)
Air Mauritius, 13th Floor, Old Mutual Centre, Third St & Jason Moyo Ave (☎ 735738)
Air Tanzania, Lintas House, Union Ave (☎ 706444)
Air Zimbabwe, City Air Terminal, cnr Third St & Speke Ave (☎ 737011)
Balkan Airlines, Trustee House, 55 Samora Machel Ave (☎ 729213)
British Airways, Batanai Gardens, cnr First St & Jason Moyo Ave (☎ 794616)
Ethiopian Airlines, Central African Building Society Centre, Jason Moyo Ave (☎ 790705)
Ghana Airways, 2nd Floor, Royal Mutual House, 45 Baker Ave (☎ 703335)
Kenya Airways, Batanai Gardens, cnr First St & Jason Moyo Ave (☎ 792181)
KLM, 1st Floor Harvest House, Baker Ave (☎ 705430)
Linhas Aereas de Moçambique, Chancellor House, 69 Samora Machel Ave (☎ 703338)
Lufthansa, Mercury House, 24 George Silundika Ave (☎ 707606)
Qantas, 5th Floor, Karigamombe Centre, 54 Union Ave (☎ 794676)
Royal Swazi Airline, 6 Chancellor House, 69 Samora Machel Ave (☎ 730170)
Swissair, Hungwe House, 69 Jason Moyo Ave (☎ 707712)
TAP Air Portugal, 5th Floor Prudential House, cnr Angwa St & Speke Ave (☎ 706231)
UTA, 95 Jason Moyo Ave (☎ 703868)
Zambia Airways, Pearl Assurance Building, First St (☎ 793235)

Bus The Ajay's Express (☎ 703421) terminal is at the Monomatapa Hotel while Express Motorways (☎ 720392) operates from the Air Zimbabwe Building on the corner of Third St and Jason Moyo Ave.

Ajay's departs for Bulawayo on Tuesday, Thursday and Sunday at 8 am and 2 pm and on Monday, Wednesday and Saturday at 11 am and 5 pm. From Bulawayo to Harare, they leave from the Bulawayo Sun Hotel, running on Monday, Wednesday, Friday, Saturday and Sunday at 8 am and 2 pm and on Tuesday at noon and 6 pm. On Monday, Wednesday and Friday, Express Motorways leaves at 7.45 am and on Tuesday, Thursday and Sunday at 1 pm. On Saturday they operate at both 7.45 am and 1 pm. In the other direction, they leave Bulawayo City Hall at 7.45 am on Tuesday, Thursday and Saturday, at 1 pm on Monday, Wednesday, Friday and Sunday, with an additional Sunday departure at 4 pm. The one-way fare with either company is Z$41.

To Mutare, Express Motorways departs Monday, Wednesday, and Friday to Sunday at 7.45 am and returns on the same days at 1.30 pm, for Z$22 each way. To Victoria Falls, you'll have to change buses in Bulawayo, entailing at least an overnight stop. For other destinations, check with the individual companies for their latest schedules.

Long-distance 'African' or 'Black' buses depart from the extensive Mbare musika in Mbare township, five km from the centre. To smaller villages, there may only be one bus daily and chances are, it will depart at or shortly after 6 am. Although buses to Bulawayo depart into the afternoon, if you're headed to Masvingo, Kariba, Mutare or elsewhere, the closer to 6 am you arrive, the better your chances are of getting a seat. The buses aren't normally as crowded as you may expect, but at weekends and holidays, they're packed to overflowing. There are large signs at the terminal indicating the buses' destinations, grouped according to which road they'll be taking out of the city – Mutare, Beatrice or Bulawayo Rds.

As enjoyable and interesting as the locals' buses can be, finding the right bus can strain otherwise mellow natures. Travellers and locals alike are often assailed by touts who will cluster around and create confusion, some physically grabbing and dragging people in several directions at once to get them on one bus or another, others hoping to separate travellers from their luggage. To avoid the worst of it, try not to get rattled, don't reveal your destination when asked and hold tightly to your luggage all the while. If things do become uncomfortable, sit down

long enough to regain your composure before continuing. If you need help finding a particular bus, it may be best to ask a woman or an older man.

Fares between Harare and Mutare or Masvingo are only Z$10 and between Harare and Bulawayo, Z$15. Between the main centres, there are normally buses running at least hourly. Some of the best companies are Tenda, Phumulani, Tauya, Shu-Shine, Zimbabwe Omnibus and the ominously named Tombs Motorways.

Information on buses to Harare from Zambia, Malawi and South Africa is included in the Zimbabwe Getting There & Away chapter.

Train The railway station is at the corner of Kenneth Kaunda Ave and Second St. Trains run daily between Harare and Bulawayo and between Harare and Mutare. Timetables and fares are detailed in the Zimbabwe Getting Around chapter.

The reservations office is open from 8 am to 1 pm and 2 to 4 pm Monday to Friday and from 8 to 11.30 am Saturday. The ticket office opens Monday to Friday between 8 am and 1 pm, 2 to 4 pm, and 7 to 9.30 pm. On Saturdays, you can buy tickets from 8 to 11.30 am and 7 to 9.30 pm. On Sundays, it's only open between 7 and 9.30 pm.

Getting Around

To/From the Airport Transport between the city and the airport is straightforward. The Air Zimbabwe bus departs hourly from the city airline terminal at the Air Zimbabwe office on the corner of Third St and Jason Moyo Ave. There are also hourly trips from the international airport into town. For a taxi to or from the airport, expect to pay about Z$20 each way for up to four people.

Meikles Hotel and the Sheraton each provide complimentary airport shuttles for their guests.

Bus Harare city buses, which exist primarily to connect the city centre with the suburban areas during the daytime, are very crowded so if you want to use them heading away from the centre, catch them at a bus terminus, one of the five central city stations. Your chances of squeezing on – or even inspiring a driver to stop for you – are inversely proportional to the number of stops you are from the terminus. If your destination isn't anywhere near the end of the line, the return trip could be problematic. The bus fare is about 15 cents.

The five central termini are Market Square between Harare and Mbuya Nehanda Sts, Robert Mugabe Rd between Fourth and Fifth Sts, at the corner of Angwa St and Robson Manyika Ave, on Rezende St between Jason Moyo and Baker Aves, and Speke Ave between Cameron and Chinhoyi Sts. Buses to Mbare intercity bus terminal depart from the Angwa and Robson Manyika terminus.

Taxi Taxi stands are found in front of all hotels, on the corner of First St and Baker Ave, on Samora Machel Ave near First St, and on Union Ave between Angwa St and Julius Nyerere Way. Although there are hundreds of maverick taxis, official services include Rixi Taxi (☎ 707707 or 724222), A1 Taxi (☎ 706996) and Cream Line Taxis (☎ 703333).

To or from anywhere in the city centre will cost between Z\$5 to Z\$7. Trips into the suburbs will run between Z\$15 and Z\$18, to the airport about Z\$20. Taxi meters all run at different speeds and controls are nonexistent but Rixi, based at the corner of Samora Machel Ave and Harare St, seems to be the best company.

If you want to have a go at working out the emergency taxis, the most reliable places to find one are around the corner of George Silundika Ave and Fourth St or on Rezende St between Jason Moyo and Baker Aves. Emergency taxis cost 60 cents from anywhere to anywhere along their fixed routes.

Bicycle Harare, compact and mostly flat, lends itself well to exploration by bike but watch the equipment pretty closely while you're stopped anywhere.

Bikes may be hired at Pedal Pushers (☎ 702069), 46 Samora Machel Ave beside

Livingstone House. Sable Lodge (☎ 726017) at 95 Selous Ave also hires bikes. Expect to pay around Z\$3.50 per hour or Z\$12 per day.

Around Harare

MBARE

Although Mbare, less than five km from the centre, is technically little more than a Harare suburb, it's probably the only one that's worth visiting in its own right. A particularly good time to go is Sunday afternoon; while the rest of the city shuts down, Mbare keeps on buzzing.

When Harare was called Salisbury, Mbare was known as Harare Township, named after the Shona chief Mbare who was headquartered on the Kopje.

All Mbare's activity is centred on the musika, Zimbabwe's largest market and busiest bus terminal. Between 6 am and 6 pm, it constantly bustles, crowded with shoppers, travellers, and sales and business people. Shoppers can find everything from second-hand clothing and appliances to herbal remedies, African crafts and jewellery. Fresh fruit and vegetables can be bought in the local produce stalls at a fraction of supermarket prices.

Also of interest in Mbare is the Canon Paterson Art Centre on Chaminuka Rd, founded by the Bulawayo reverend in the 1940s. Here you can watch artists carving soapstone, verdite, wood and serpentine into the souvenirs you'll find for sale throughout the country. Naturally, you can also purchase the items at the centre for substantial savings over what you'd pay elsewhere.

To reach Mbare from the centre, take the municipal bus from the Angwa St and Robson Manyika Ave terminus. Taxis for up to five passengers will cost between Z\$4 and Z\$6 each way, depending on your bargaining skills.

For information on the intercity bus terminal at Mbare musika, read the discussion under Getting There & Away for Harare.

EWANRIGG BOTANICAL GARDEN

This small and loosely defined national park 40 km north-east of Harare consists of an elaborate 40 hectare botanical garden and 200 hectares of woodland. The main attraction is the garden which is best known for its aloes, cacti and palm-like cycads. In addition to the flowering plants, there's a stand of bamboo, an herb garden, a water garden and an arboretum. On weekends it can be pretty crowded, so for solitude visit during the week. Available facilities include picnic tables, braai pits, water taps, toilet blocks and firewood. No camping sites are available in the vicinity. Admission is Z$1 per person.

Getting There & Away

To get there on public transport, take the Shamva bus from Mbare as early in the morning as possible and ask to be dropped at the Ewanrigg turnoff, from where it's a three km walk to the gardens. You can also hitch from the city about 20 km north-east along the Mutoko Highway (Enterprise Rd) to the Shamva turnoff (route A15), and then another 20 km to the Ewanrigg turnoff.

Mermaid's Pool

This small resort is six km from the Ewanrigg turnoff in a nice vegetated spot. There are picnic sites, a petrol pump, a stone water slide and occasional live musical performances. Admission is Z$3 per person. To get there, follow the directions to the Ewanrigg turnoff. If you're on the Shamva bus, stay aboard for four more km to the signposted gravel turning to the left and walk the remaining two km to the resort.

HARARE TO LAKE McILWAINE

Lion & Cheetah Park

The Lion and Cheetah Park (☎ 6437 Norton) 24 km from Harare just off the Bulawayo Rd is the only place in the area to see big cats. It's on a large private estate which also boasts a population of baboons and crocodiles. Admission is Z$10 per vehicle containing up to 8 people and Z$2.50 for each additional adult. It's open from 8.30 am and 5 pm.

Since walking and hitching aren't permitted, you'll have to arrive in a private vehicle or take a United Touring Company (☎ 793701) tour from Meikles Hotel in Harare. A three hour tour of the Lion and Cheetah Park combined with Larvon Bird Gardens departs every day except Thursday at 9.30 am and costs Z$50 per person. A four hour tour combining the Lion and Cheetah Park with Lake McIlwaine Game Park, leaving Harare at 9 am and 2 pm daily, costs Z$55 per person. The UTC office is at 4 Park St and Jason Moyo Ave in Harare.

Snake Park

The Snake Park, owned by the same folks as the Lion and Cheetah Park, lies 11 km from Harare on the Bulawayo Rd. Admission is Z$5 per person but unless you're passing by anyway or have a particular fascination, it's not worth a special trip out there. Any Bulawayo-bound bus passes the Snake Park. It's open daily from 8.30 am to 5 pm.

Larvon Bird Gardens

Larvon Bird Gardens, 17 km south-west of town on the Bulawayo Rd, is worthwhile especially if you're a birdwatcher heading off into the bush and want to familiarise yourself with southern African species. Over 400 species are on display. They operate a bird orphanage and a conservation reserve as well. It's a sensitive set-up with larger birds allowed some room to roam while waterfowl enjoy a pleasant natural lake. It's open weekdays except Thursday from 10 am to 5 pm and on weekends from 9 am to 5 pm. Admission is Z$5 for adults and Z$3 for children under 12. On weekends, a tea garden beside the lake serves light snacks and drinks.

To get there, drive out along the Bulawayo Rd or take any Bulawayo-bound bus from Harare and ask to be dropped at the Oatlands Rd turnoff. From the intersection, it's just one km to the entrance. Larvon Bird Gardens is also included in a UTC tour, described in the discussion of the Lion and Cheetah Park.

Cold Comfort Farm Society

The Cold Comfort Farm Society (☎ 703372)

is an artists' cooperative 13 km from the centre on the Bulawayo Rd. They produce African tapestries from local wool and natural dyes which are sold for very reasonable prices. It's open to visitors from 7 am to 5 pm Monday to Saturday.

ROBERT McILWAINE RECREATIONAL PARK

Lake McIlwaine is a popular weekend spot with Harare people. The 5500 hectare national park 32 km south-west of Harare is centred around 57 sq km Lake McIlwaine, a reservoir created by the 1952 damming of the Manyame – then known as Hunyani – River. It was named for Sir Robert McIlwaine, first chairman of the board of National Resources. The water level has been quite low for several years now and the shore is becoming choked with rapidly spreading water hyacinth.

North Shore

The commercialised northern shore of Lake McIlwaine is lined with private boat harbours and special interest group camps, all with big iron gates and fences. Fishing, boating, water-skiing and boozing are the appeal here.

Admiral's Cabin, which has picnic sites and a snack bar, charges Z$2 admission to the shoreline. Those without their own water craft can hire motorboats for Z$25 per hour, pontoon boats for Z$40 and paddle canoes for Z$3 to Z$5.

For a look at the 'strategic' and zealously guarded dam wall, stroll from Hunyani Hills Hotel along the lake shore and through the Mazowe Sailing Club, less than half an hour each way.

Game Park & South Shore

Most of the southern shore of the lake belongs to the 1600 hectare game park where many species of antelope, zebra, giraffe, and white rhino may be observed; overall, though, the game viewing is pretty marginal. Admission is Z$1 for day use and Z$3 for a multiday pass. Ranger-guided 1½ hour pony

1	Store
2	Tea Garden
3	Yacht Club
4	Hunyani Hills Hotel
5	National Parks Caravan Park
6	Lakeside Caravan Park
7	The Admiral's Cabin
8	Spillway Restaurant
9	Game Park Entrance Gate
10	MOTH Park
11	Rock Paintings
12	Pax Park Guide Camp
13	Public Mooring Site
14	Ranger's Office
15	Chalets
16	Lodges

safaris cost Z$6 per person and operate twice daily from the reception office at the chalets.

Rock Paintings Bushman's Point at the end of the southern shore drive has been designated a picnic site and walking area within the game park. The rock paintings above the lake shore just beyond the traffic turnaround are worth a look if you're out that way. Most of the figures in the scene are human including hunters, dancing women and a row of 13 kneeling figures of undetermined sex. Also interesting is the representation of a tree being felled but perhaps the most relevant painting is of several large fish, completed long before the lake just beneath them was even a gleam in some ancient angler's eye.

Other rock paintings in the game park, such as those at Crocodile Rock, Pax Park and Ovoid Rock, are accessible only with a park service guide.

Places to Stay & Eat

North Shore The *Hunyani Hills Hotel* (☎ 2236 Norton), PO Box 2852, Harare, is the park's only hotel. Single/double rooms cost Z$45/60 and family rooms are Z$80. It's a nice enough setting and the restaurant and tea house are pleasant.

The national park camping ground beside the hotel offers camping sites, accommodating up to six people, for Z$10 including use

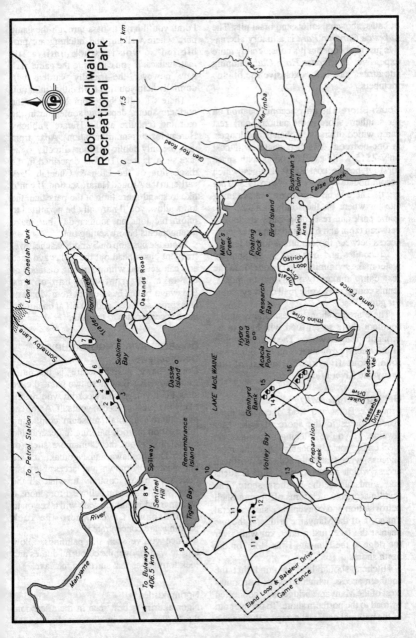

Robert McIlwaine
Recreational Park

of baths, showers, toilets and braai pits. The *Lakeside Caravan Park* is a luxury alternative just next door but it's considerably more expensive. The *Trader Horn Club* camping site further east is for exclusive use of club members.

South Shore The only accommodation on the southern shore is the national park rest camp which offers both chalets and lodges. A one-bedroom, two-bed chalet will cost only Z$15 while two bedrooms with space for four people cost Z$20. Lodges which accommodate up to six people cost Z$70 per night. There is no camping or caravanning site anywhere on the southern shore. The game park and rest camp gates are locked between 6 pm and 6 am and non-emergency access between those hours is forbidden.

Crocodiles and bilharzia in the shallow water make swimming a very poor idea. The rest camp makes two swimming pools, tennis courts and a volleyball court available for guests' use.

There are no shops or restaurants on the southern shore so all food will have to be brought from elsewhere. The nearest shop is at the Shell petrol station on the Bulawayo road about five km north-east of the Manyame River bridge.

Getting There & Away

From the Bulawayo road, there are three access routes to the shore of Lake McIlwaine. If you're hitching, especially on weekends, you'll probably have the most success with Oatlands Rd, the northern access which passes Larvon Bird Gardens and winds up at the northern shore. The middle access, which turns off from a Shell petrol station and convenience store several km north of the Manyame bridge, is the one nearest the lake, just a three km walk over the ridge to the Hunyani Hills Hotel on the north shore.

Hitchers should bear in mind that the southern access, which turns off just southwest of the Manyame bridge, isn't connected by road to the northern shore. To get in or out of the national park rest camp or Bushman's Point, you'll have to pass through the game park where walking and hitching are prohibited so you're stuck until a lift materialises. If you can get to the game park gate, however, the friendly wardens will normally help you find a lift either in or out.

There's a daily bus from Mbare to the northern shore, departing sometime in the morning (enquire at the Harare Publicity Bureau for current information). Apart from that, the only public transport directly to the lake shore is the UTC tour described in the discussion of the Lion & Cheetah Park earlier in the Around Harare section. If you'd like to spend more time at the park than the tours allow, you'll normally be permitted to rejoin the tour on another day but make arrangements before setting out.

From the bus stop on Samora Machel Ave, frequent buses head out the Bulawayo road and can get you within striking distance of the lake. Alternatively, hop on any Bulawayo-bound bus – either from Mbare or an express service – and get off at one of the three access routes to the lake.

DOMBOSHAWA & NGOMAKURIRA

Domboshawa

Domboshawa, nearer Harare, is the more frequently visited of these two painted cave sites, but if you go on a weekday, you're still likely to have the place to yourself. At the car park there's a small museum containing information on rock painting in general and speculation about the Chinamora sites (of which Domboshawa and Ngomakurira are the most well known and accessible) but there's no motel, contrary to what all the signs would have you believe. From there, a well-marked 15 minute walk will take you to Domboshawa Caves where the rock paintings are concentrated.

Once you've seen the paintings, allow time to wander over the colourful domes and rock formations that surround the cave.

Ngomakurira

Ngomakurira is best seen in the afternoon, due to glare caused by direct sunlight on the paintings. Its romantic name means 'the mountain of drums' after the acoustic effect created by the natural form of the stone; it's believed that the reverberations one hears there are the beating drums of festive spirits. It's generally agreed that Ngomakurira offers the finest easily accessible rock paintings in Zimbabwe.

Once you've reached the rock, the route to the best paintings on the eastern side isn't exactly straightforward. From the base of the hill, walk around the northern end to a small valley containing a stream bed. Follow it up to the foot of the orange lichen-stained cliff that rises to the dome's eastern summit. The paintings are found at its base. While you're there, don't forget to try and coax a performance out of the spirit drummers – they'll always comply if you start pounding first.

In addition to these two popular sites, there are numerous other examples of rock paintings in the Chinamora area. For further information and directions to the more

obscure sites, refer to *The Painted Caves* by Peter Garlake, which is available at Kingston's in Harare.

Getting There & Away

To reach Domboshawa, you can take the Bindura via Chinamora bus from Mbare musika, get off at the turnoff four km north of Domboshawa village (30 km north of Harare), and walk the remaining one km to the base of the rock. The same bus continues on to the Sasa Rd turnoff. Ngomakurira lies just two km east of there. Alternatively, you can reach the former by taking the Domboshawa bus from Mbare to Domboshawa village and walking the from there to the site. Either bus can also be caught on Seventh St – known further out as Chancellor Ave and Borrowdale Rd – in Harare if they aren't full at that stage. Hitching will be difficult beyond Domboshawa village.

Northern Zimbabwe

If the high incidence of prehistoric rock paintings around the present town of Mutoko is any indication, north-eastern Zimbabwe has been inhabited for millennia. In the mid-1500s, the name of the small mountain Fura, now known as Mt Darwin, was taken by early Portuguese arrivals to be a corruption of 'Ophir' and for several centuries, Europeans rampantly speculated that the 'Empire of Monomatapa' guarded the biblical land of Ophir and the elusive mines of King Solomon. The British who arrived in the late 19th century settled the Harare area because they believed the country immediately south of the Zambezi to be as rich in minerals and precious metals as the Kimberley and Witwatersrand regions of South Africa.

Later, this wild country attracted the exiled and dispossessed of other regions, including the people of the defeated chief Mbare who had ruled from the Kopje at present-day Harare, and the charismatic 19th-century Shona outlaw, Mapondera, who died in prison on a hunger strike after admitting defeat in his attempts to resist encroaching colonial rule.

The North-East

NYAMAPANDA

The only reason anyone goes to Nyamapanda is to connect with the 'gun run' across Mozambique's Tete Corridor to Malawi. Trucks intending to join the convoy gather in the evening and depart across the border between 6 and 7 the following morning. There is no public transport to Nyamapanda from Harare so you'll have to rely on hitching but, as would be expected, there is a fair amount of commercial traffic along the route. For details on this trip, refer to the discussion of Malawi in the Zimbabwe Getting There & Away chapter.

TENGENENGE

Although it's well off the trampled route, travellers with an appreciation of Shona sculpture and a bit of spare time will enjoy a visit to Tengenenge farm, the remote sculptors' community near the Zambezi Escarpment, about 20 km north of Guruve.

The community today is the realised vision of tobacco farmer Tom Blomefield who discovered Great Dyke chrome on his land during UDI and from it earned enough money to abandon farming and concentrate on his consuming interest in art. In 1966, local soapstone sculptor Crispen Chakenyoka revealed deposits of magnificent black serpentine in the hills surrounding the property; fate had seemingly dictated that Blomefield's focus would be on sculpture.

Although Tengenenge lay in an area of severe conflict during the Second Chimurenga, Blomefield respected the guerrillas' cause as well as their spiritual motivation and was left to peacefully carry on his work.

More and more artists were welcomed and provided with food, tools, stone and exhibition space and by the time the formal school closed in 1979, over 500 sculptors had lived and worked there, among them such names as Sylvester Mubayi, Bernard Matemera and Henry Munyaradzi.

Tengenenge is still supported by the sale of artists' works as well as outside sponsorships and it is continuously on the lookout for new talent. Some of the original artists remain and maintain farms at the community while others have established studios nearer their market. Visitors are welcomed and are invited to stroll through the extensive sculpture gardens. On the farm, there should be no problem finding a camping site. Availability of food at the site is uncertain so bring along what you'll be needing.

Getting There & Away

There's no public transport directly to Tengenenge. Coming from Mbare, take the bus

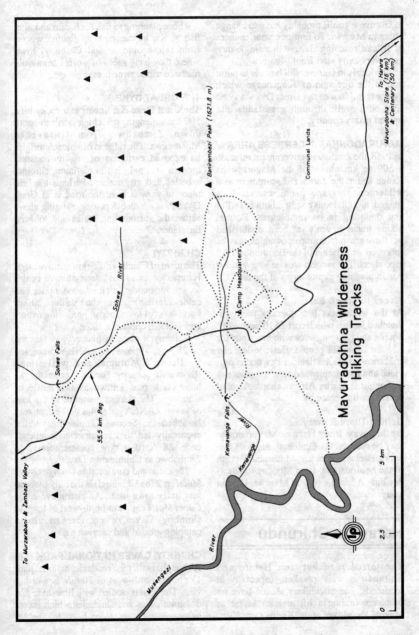

to Guruve – you'll probably have to change buses in Mvurwi. To improve your chances of at least reaching Guruve in a single day, get a very early start from Mbare.

The locals in Guruve will be able to point you in the direction of Tengenenge which lies near the foot of the Great Dyke, a good five hour walk through grasslands and upland msasa country.

MAVURADONHA WILDERNESS AREA
In 1988, the Zimbabwe government set aside a 500 sq km chunk of the Mavuradonha Range above the Zambezi Escarpment as a wilderness area and game reserve. It is rugged, mountainous country, both beautiful and daunting in its remoteness. Formal hiking tracks haven't yet been established but there are numerous routes which may be followed with the aid of the Banirembezi A3 topo sheet. The rangers will be happy to aid you in planning explorations of the area.

Places to Stay & Eat
At the wilderness headquarters there are thatched *bashas* which cost Z$10 per night a double and camping sites with braai pits for Z$5 for up to six people. Basic toilets and cold showers are available. Firewood is provided and food staples and basic supplies can be bought at nearby African shops. Alcohol is very hard to come by.

Getting There & Away
By highway from Harare, Mavuradonha may be reached via Centenary in about two hours. Fuel is available at Muzarabani, north of the headquarters, from Monday to Saturday but on Sunday only at Mvurwi, 115 km away.

Harare to Chirundu

The tarred road between Harare and Chirundu is well travelled, especially at weekends, and hitchhikers should have no problems finding a lift at least as far as Makuti, the village at the Kariba turnoff.

Those planning to fish for bream and tiger fish at Kariba can pick up fishing worms from salespeople around Chinhoyi town where they hang sacks of worms from little roadside tripod structures.

THE GREAT DYKE
The Great Dyke is a line of low rocky hills 500 km in length, stretching north to south down Zimbabwe from Guruve to Mberengwa. The ridge is of volcanic origin, an exposed extrusion of erosion-resistant igneous material, rich in platinum, chrome, asbestos and magnesium. Perhaps the best place to view it from the road is at Great Dyke Pass which offers long-ranging views across the surrounding maize and tobacco farmlands.

CHINHOYI
The town of Chinhoyi, 120 km north-west of Harare, serves as the administrative centre for the surrounding rich tobacco, maize and cattle-farming region. Alaska mine, 20 km north-west of town, began producing export quantities of copper in 1959.

Chinhoyi's place in history was secured on 28 April 1966, when ZANLA forces, led by Bernard Mutuma, and well-armed Rhodesian Security Forces met in the 12 hour clash now known as the Battle of Chinhoyi. The skirmish resulted in the loss of seven ZANLA guerrillas and effectively launched the Second Chimurenga which eventually led to Zimbabwean independence. 28 April is now commemorated in Zimbabwe as Chimurenga Day.

The clean and comfortable *Orange Grove Motel* (☎ 2785 Chinhoyi) is the only place to stay in the town itself. An alternative is the *Caves Motel* eight km north-west of town at Chinhoyi Caves, where there is also a camping ground and caravan park.

CHINHOYI CAVES NATIONAL PARK
Although small, this 'roadside' national park 1½ hours north-west of Harare is worth a visit. The area is riddled with limestone and dolomite caves and sinkholes which recent evidence indicates have been in use for

storage and refuge by local people for nearly 1500 years.

The main pool is popularly called Sleeping Pool or Chirorodzira (Pool of the Fallen). The 'fallen' were local people intentionally chucked into the formidable hole by the invading Nguni tribes in the early 19th century. In 1887, colonial hunter Frederick Courteney Selous arrived to find the area occupied by the subjects of Chief Chinhoyi. He took the Swiss-cheese-like landscape, similar in appearance to the modern copper mines at Alaska (just a couple of km away), to be result of ancient mine workings.

Divers have discovered a submarine passage leading from the Bat Cave, a subchamber of Dark Cave, to another room known as Blind Cave.

The park is open during daylight hours year round and admission is Z$1 per person. Petrol is available at the hotel.

Places to Stay & Eat

The *Caves Motel* (☎ 2340 Chinhoyi) at the park entrance charges Z$60/90 for singles/doubles including a set breakfast. The camping and caravan site adjacent to the park costs Z$6 per night for up to six people. Firewood is available for Z$3 per bundle.

Getting There & Away

The park entrance is right on the Harare-Chirundu road, eight km north-west of Chinhoyi town. From Harare, take any Kariba or Chirundu bus and get off at the Caves Motel.

KAROI

Karoi, the centre of the commercial tobacco growing Makonde district, may serve as a break for those hitching between Harare and Kariba or Chirundu. Accommodation includes the *Karoi Hotel* (☎ 317 Karoi) which has an attached restaurant and bar and a new caravan park beside a pleasant dam just out of town.

The town lies near the eastern terminus of the long and rattling unsurfaced track to Matusadona, Siabuwa and the western end of Lake Kariba. There are generally unreliable daily buses between Karoi and Binga via Siabuwa. Enquire locally for further information, especially since the westbound bus leaves Karoi at varying small hours of the morning.

MAKUTI

Makuti sits on the edge of the Zambezi Escarpment, 66 km from Kariba. The tiny settlement is little more than a motel, a road junction and the last petrol station before Kariba. This is also the last petrol available if you're driving into Mana Pools National Park.

Apart from the rather dilapidated pub beside the petrol station, the *Cloud's End Hotel* (☎ 526 Makuti) sees most of Makuti's activity. It's a favourite of Harare-dwellers who've taken off for Kariba after work on Friday. There's a swimming pool and a reasonable dining room which serves up a mean buffet breakfast. Single/double rooms cost Z$70/95.

MARONGORA

In the hills near the lip of the Zambezi Escarpment, Marongora is the administrative centre for Mana Pools National Park. Visitors lacking private vehicles – who are necessarily denied prebooking for Mana Pools accommodation in Harare – will probably find Marongora their best prospect for both transport and accommodation. All visitors to Mana Pools must stop at the Marongora office *before 3.30 pm* on the day of their entry into the park to secure a park entry permit but they must have both accommodation in the park and a means of transport before permits will be issued. If you haven't prebooked park accommodation in Harare and lodges or camping sites are still available – and you have secured a guaranteed lift – the rangers here can sort it out for you.

There's no camping site in Marongora so if you have to wait a day or two to get into the park, you can either stay at the *Cloud's End Motel* (☎ 526 Makuti) at Makuti about 10 km south, or ask the rangers for advice and permission to camp somewhere in the area. Campers should carry water since surface water is scarce and likely to be contaminated with giardia and bilharzia.

CHIRUNDU

This uninspiring little border town on the Zambezi is one of several put-in points for Zambezi canoe safaris. It also serves as a final respite for travellers contemplating a headlong plunge into the uncertainties of travel in Zambia.

Chirundu is known for its abundance of game close at hand. One correspondent has written of the place: 'Do *not* go walking, even down to the river, or you are liable to get eaten. Just sitting by the side of the road you see plenty of big game and every day elephants come to drink out of the swimming pool'. One crosses the river into Zambia on the Otto Beit Bridge. The border is open from 6 am to 6 pm.

Places to Stay & Eat

The *Chirundu Valley Motel* (☎ 618 Chirundu) is good value. Single/double units with bath rent for Z$50/65 and rondavels are Z$35/50; both include a full buffet breakfast. The floodlit camping site near the river offers basic amenities for only about Z$4 per site. Wildlife is profuse here, so campers should exercise due caution – keep your tent zipped at night, stay away from hippo runs and, if at all possible, don't venture outside after dark.

Powerboat excursions on the Zambezi are available; enquire at the hotel desk for latest details.

Getting There & Away

As you'd expect, there's a fair amount of commercial traffic along this main route between Harare and Lusaka (Zambia) so hitching won't be as difficult as the area's remoteness would otherwise suggest.

The weekly United Transport express bus between Harare, Lusaka and Lilongwe, Malawi, stops for several hours at Chirundu. Southbound, it arrives at 4.25 am Wednesday and departs at 8 am. Northbound, the bus reaches Chirundu at 2.05 pm and leaves an hour later.

There are also daily buses between Harare and Chirundu from Mbare musika. Alternatively, you can use the more frequent Kariba buses which pick up and drop passengers at Makuti. Between there and Chirundu, you'll have to hitch.

The Middle Zambezi

Apart from Chirundu and Mana Pools National Park, this stretch of river is inaccessible from the Zimbabwe highway system by ordinary vehicle. In fact, the river *is* the highway system for many people. Several canoe safari companies have taken advantage of its appeal to visitors as a route into the wilderness and set up three to nine day trips taking in various stretches of the river between Kariba and Kanyemba on the Mozambique border.

MANA POOLS NATIONAL PARK

Mana Pools is magnificent but if allowed only a quick glance the park may disappoint; the landscapes aren't overwhelming and as far as wildlife density is concerned, Mana Pools pales in comparison to Hwange. Even so, UNESCO has designated Mana Pools and neighbouring Chewore Safari Area a World Heritage Site.

Information

Opening & Permits Despite rumours to the contrary, Mana Pools was not opened to year-round visitation in 1990. It is open only during the dry season, 1 May to 31 October.

Everyone entering Mana Pools National Park will have to first secure a permit to enter. The first step is to book accommodation through the National Parks Central Booking Office in Harare (or through the alternative method outlined in the discussion of Marongora earlier in this chapter). In order to book accommodation, you'll have

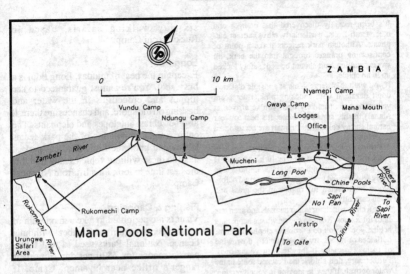

to sufficiently demonstrate to the office attendant that you have transport into the park. They'll ask something like 'How do you intend to get there?'. If you reply that you're hitching, you'll be refused accommodation because hitchhikers aren't permitted in the park. If you say 'We've rented a car', you'll still be refused because rental agencies don't allow their vehicles into Mana Pools on the grounds that the road is too rough.

Hitchhikers' only options will be to convince them that a local friend has loaned you a vehicle – then somehow get to the park on the day you've paid for – or hitch to Marongora and hope there's a camping site available when you arrive. If you're catching a lift with a friend, you can be added to their permit at Marongora.

To get the permit, you must turn up at the Marongora office before 3.30 pm on the day you plan to enter the park. Once the permit is issued, you'd also better get to the ranger's office near Nyamepi camp later that day or a search may be mounted! En route, the permit will be scrutinised no less than four times before you reach the Zambezi – at Marongora, at the park turnoff, at the park

boundary, and at the ranger headquarters – so don't even consider trying to sneak past without one. And once you've arrived, don't lose it; you'll have to produce it three more times to get out of the park.

Game Viewing on Foot Perhaps Mana Pools' greatest appeal lies in its concession to those who want to walk in the African bush. Some people won't be able to get enough bushwalking while others, especially after a tense night of unsettling noises, may be put off by the prospect. If you can't muster the nerve to strike out on foot, no points will be tallied against you; walking at Mana Pools is meant to be an enjoyable experience.

While the risks are very real and the (often sensationalised) stories reiterated in travellers' haunts Africa-wide can get pretty gory, the reality is that humans have safely coexisted with African wildlife for aeons and generations of bush wisdom are at the disposal of modern visitors. Although caution is warranted, paranoia is not and following time-honoured (and some relatively new) guidelines will practically ensure only pleasant encounters:

- It's been recently discovered that oranges and other fresh fruits, particularly citrus, attract elephants. Although park rangers make a point of confiscating oranges brought into the park, all sweet-smelling fruit should be kept safely locked up in a vehicle.
- If you want to observe game at a visible distance, don't dazzle it with shocking pink, fluorescent yellow or even (unlikely once you've arrived at Mana!) freshly scrubbed white. It's best to wear natural earthy colours the animals are accustomed to seeing.
- Try to stay out of heavy bush or high grass where you can't observe what may be lurking ahead. If you must pass through such areas, climb a tree every so often and have a good look around before proceeding. Watch for ripples in the grass and listen carefully.
- Keep a close watch for larger animals and scan tree lines for felines. Keep an eye on what's happening behind you. If you do encounter elephants, lions, buffaloes or rhinos, try to pass quietly downwind of them, especially if they're with young ones. Furthermore, don't block their escape route to the water or bush. If they're moving in your direction, move quietly away but never run, especially in the case of large cats. Your retreat may trigger their reflex to give chase.
- While avoiding the big guys, don't forget to watch where you're putting your feet. Snakes also thrive along the middle Zambezi.
- When walking along river banks, beware of logs that could turn out to be crocodiles and steer away from hippo runs. Before drawing water from any source, make a slow and careful assessment of what's occupying the water in question.
- Don't even think about swimming in the Zambezi.
- Keep a good distance from all animals and don't be seduced into carelessness by what may appear to be the ultimate photo opportunity. On foot, you're lucky to approach within even telephoto range.
- Although the milky way of the Zambezi nights will tempt you to try sleeping in the open, it's not a good idea. Lions, elephants and hyaenas are all known to prowl around camping sites at night so it's a good idea to zip your tent and stay quietly inside. The obvious corollaries to this are to drink liquids in moderation before bedtime and use the loo before crawling into the sack.
- For further animal-related advice, refer to the discussion of Dangers & Annoyances in the Facts for the Visitor chapter at the beginning of the book.

If you prefer more structured exploration Backpackers Africa (☎ 735712, fax 735716 Harare), PO Box 3961, Harare, offers four to six day walking safaris, based in Ruckomechi Camp.

Long Pool

Except in the heat of midday, Long Pool is a busy spot. You're almost guaranteed to see hippos and crocodiles in the water and basking on the shore, and chances are there'll also be zebras, antelopes and elephants. The entire human population of the park seems to descend upon the Long Pool car park at dusk so those without vehicles may find this the best time to look for a lift from Nyamepi Camp.

Fishing & Canoeing

Visitors are permitted to take a maximum of six fish per day from the Zambezi without a licence. National Parks used to rent three-person canoes for Z$30 per day from their ranger's office near Nyamepi Camp. If you're interested, check whether they're still available.

Places to Stay

Most visitors will wind up staying at *Nyamepi Camp* near the park headquarters. Although advance booking is advised – and essential during Zimbabwean and South African school holidays – cancellations and low periods will sometimes allow last-minute bookings from Marongora.

Nyamepi camping sites cost Z$10 for up to six people each and there are showers, baths, toilets and sinks. Firewood is available for Z$3 per bundle, but due to ecological concerns, national parks request that, if possible, campers bring their own stoves or fuel from elsewhere. Individual collection of firewood is prohibited.

In addition to Nyamepi, there are several other smaller camping areas. *Muncheni*, eight km west of the ranger office, has four camping sites each of which cost Z$10. *Gwaya Camp* or 'Old Tree Lodge' near the national park lodges is available for Z$20 for groups of up to 12. *Ndungu Camp*, 11 km west of Nyamepi Camp, has two camping sites, and costs the same as Gwaya.

Vundu Camp, an exclusive camp 13 km

Hippo

upstream from the ranger's office, offers sleeping quarters, a kitchen, a living area and ablutions block. It's rented out in six-day blocks for Z$120, accommodating up to 12 people. This is the only exclusive camp with hot water and showers.

There are two national park lodges with eight beds each just a short distance west of the ranger office. They rent for Z$90 per night but they are very popular and must be booked well in advance – up to six months prior – if you're arriving during school holiday periods.

There are no shops or restaurants anywhere in the park so hikers and campers will have to be self-sufficient.

Luxury Camps *Ruckomechi Camp*, an upmarket luxury facility operated by Shearwater near the western boundary of Mana Pools, offers cottages with private baths and catered meals. It's accessible by vehicle, plane, boat and canoe. Some of the Zambezi canoe safaris use it as a scheduled stop. Children under 12 are not permitted. Bookings should be made through Shearwater (☎ 735712, fax 735716 Harare), PO Box 3961, Harare.

Yet more upmarket is *Chikwenya Camp* just outside park boundaries at the confluence of the Sapi and Zambezi Rivers. All-inclusive double rooms cost Z$542 per night. Air transfers are Z$140 per person each way. Book through Island Reservations (☎ 2253 Kariba), PO Box 2081, Kariba.

Getting There & Away
To reach the vicinity of Mana Pools by bus, follow the instructions outlined in the Chirundu section; get off at Marongora to find a lift into the park and pick up your permit. From Marongora, the Chirundu road continues northward to the lip of the Zambezi Escarpment then steeply descends 900 metres into the broad Zambezi Valley. The Mana Pools turnoff lies just below the escarpment.

Once past the turnoff gate, it's a long, corrugated, low-visibility route, primarily through dense and thorny *jesse* scrub, to the Nyakasikana park entrance at the Ruckomechi River. Once across the bridge, sign in at the boom gate and then turn left. Everyone has to check in at the ranger office before proceeding to their lodge or camping site.

If you have a vehicle and would like to share petrol and expenses to Mana Pools from Harare, post notices at the youth hostel, Sable Lodge and Paw Paw Lodge or check those places regularly for travellers interested in doing the trip. You'll be enthusiastically received by those who might have given up hope of ever getting there!

The alternative access to Mana Pools is by canoe from Chirundu.

ZAMBEZI CANOE SAFARIS

A growing number of operators are taking advantage of the Zambezi's wilderness appeal and organising multiday canoe safaris for tourists who want to enjoy a little soft adventure. The entire possible route extends from Kariba to Kanyemba on the Mozambique border and is normally done in stages: Kariba to Chirundu, Chirundu to Mana Pools and Mana Pools to Kanyemba. Any west to east combination of these is possible if your pockets are deep enough.

If only one stage is possible, however, the Chirundu to Mana Pools segment offers a diversity of game as well as good scenery. If you have more time and money, Mana to Kanyemba could be added. The motivated can go for the entire nine day Kariba to Kanyemba trip.

Hippos and crocs will be seen almost constantly but the guides seem to know where the big guys most often lurk and steer clear accordingly. Canoe safaris all camp on the river banks but participants aren't permitted to wander more than 50 metres from the river unless you're lucky enough to get one of the rare guides trained and licensed to lead foot safaris as well, a real plus if you can manage it. August and September are peak months for wildlife viewing along the banks.

While operators are happy to arrange transfers between the put-in and take-out points and either Harare or Kariba, transport is normally not included in the already painful cost of these trips. Prices quoted do include meals, however. Foreigners will have to pay in US$ unless they can produce bank receipts proving legal purchase of the equivalent in Zimbabwe dollars. Use the following table as a general guide to prices:

Stage	Days	Nights	Price US$
Kariba-Chirundu	3	2	300
Chirundu-Mana Pools	4	3	420
Mana Pools-Kanyemba	5	4	650
Kariba-Mana Pools	5	5	600
Chirundu-Kanyemba	6	6	700

Kariba to Chirundu

Since Kariba is so easily accessible, this stage is the most convenient for those who will be satisfied with just an introduction to the Zambezi. Unfortunately, the highlight of the trip, Kariba Gorge, is quickly left behind and there's comparatively little game along the shore until you're nearly upon Chirundu.

Chirundu to Mana Pools

The most popular and, game-wise, most interesting stage is the three or four day paddle from Chirundu to and through Mana Pools National Park. The river is broad and flat and allows canoeists to safely paddle within close range of the abundant wildlife. Overnight stops in the national park will normally include Vundu, Nyamepi and Nyamatusi camps.

Mana Pools to Kanyemba

This stage is the wildest and most thrilling of the three options. Leaving Mana Pools, the river slides along between Zimbabwe's Chewore Safari Area and Zambia's North Luangwa National Park then passes through a region of low and nondescript hill country before picking up a bit and slotting between the high walls of 30 km long Mupata Gorge, a dramatic slice in the Chewore Mountains.

Beyond the gorge, nearer Kanyemba, lies the territory of the Va Dema, also known as the Three-Toed Tribe, Zimbabwe's only nonagricultural society. (The moniker is derived from a genetic mutation affecting a small percentage of families.) Although many have been resettled in the area's communal lands, some retiring and independent Va Dema, who have been somewhat successful at eluding persistent Western anthropologists, still manage a living hunting local wildlife and gathering wild foods.

Canoe Safari Companies

Shop around when arranging your Zambezi trip. Different operators use different camps and employ different approaches. All their canoe guides are licensed and most are knowledgeable and experienced in the bush.

Most canoe safaris operate between April or May and October or November, but since demand for these trips is so great and participation is limited, a couple of them operate year-round. Single travellers may be able to squeeze in a booking a month in advance but if you're travelling with several people, three to six months advance booking is recommended, especially if you're wanting to travel during peak months or school holidays. Safari Interlink booking agents (☎ 700911 Harare), Trustee House, 55 Samora Machel Ave, PO Box 5920, Harare, can offer the best guidance. They also have an office in London at 27-31 Jerdan Place, SW6 1BE, UK (☎ 071-381 5229).

Buffalo and Goliath Safaris, especially, have been highly recommended by independent travellers. Upmarket patrons tend more toward the Shearwater approach which offers the soft option of Ruckomechi Luxury Camp in Mana Pools instead of the rougher national parks camping sites. All operators use 5.7 metre Canadian-designed fibreglass canoes:

Backpackers Africa (☎ 735712, fax 735716 Harare), PO Box 3961, Harare, offers canoe safaris through Mana Pools combined with walking trips through the park.
Buffalo Safaris (☎ 2645 Kariba), PO Box 113, Kariba, offer three to 10 day trips on various stages between Kariba and Kanyemba. They also operate canoe trips around Sanyati Gorge and the Sampakaruma Islands at Lake Kariba.
Goliath Safaris (☎ 30623 Arcturus), PO Box 294 Chisipite, Harare, are highly recommended. They tend to be the least 'routine' of the operators and are gaining popularity among travellers.
Shearwater (Same telephone and address as Backpackers Africa). Shearwater offers the widest range of itineraries and accommodation options, covering the entire route from Kariba to Kanyemba.

Eastern Lake Kariba

KARIBA

It's only natural that ocean-starved upper-class Zimbabweans take to Kariba like – well – fish take to water. The strict currency controls are irrelevant here, so while foreigners flock to Victoria Falls, Zimbabweans who can afford the luxury of a holiday – mostly Whites and professional Blacks – spend their leisure time and Zimbabwe dollars fishing, relaxing and puttering around the lake.

Budget travellers, on the other hand, may not find Kariba terribly interesting. The most interesting sights are dispersed about the lake; transport is expensive and accommodation mostly exclusive. Kariba town itself, an unconsolidated two-level jumble with no definable character, is of little interest and the sticky-hot, filthy Mahombekombe township beside the lake could well be the country's least appealing. If you can't afford to join the 'beautiful people' you may not want to burden yourself with too much time here.

Orientation & Information

Kariba's lack of an overall plan leaves it with a distinctly disjointed geography. The area normally known as 'Kariba' stretches for over 10 km along the lakeshore between the airport and the Zambian border. There's no central area devoted to tourism and all the upmarket hotels seem to intentionally keep their distance from their competitors. The central camping site and boat harbour are separated from the main highway by Mahombekombe, the African township where the post office, shops and bus terminal are found. The bank, shopping centre, cinema, country club, bakery and supermarket are all in Kariba Heights, a cooler and more prestigious neighbourhood disappearing into the clouds 600 metres above the rest of town.

Tourist Office The Kariba Publicity Bureau at the dam wall observation point is next to

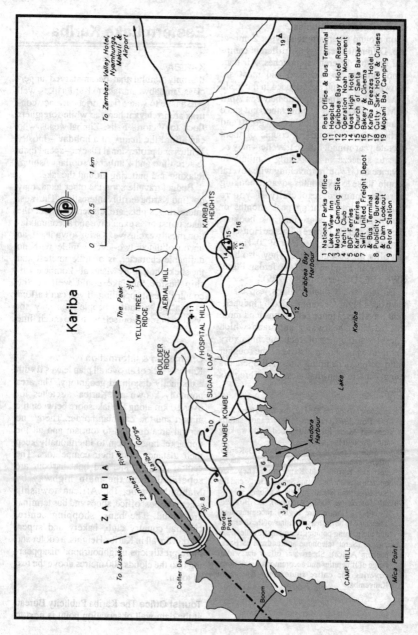

Kariba

To Lusaka
To Zambezi Valley Hotel,
Nyamhunga, Makuti &
Airport

ZAMBIA

Zambezi River
Kariba Gorge
Coffer Dam
Border Post
Boom

The Peak
YELLOW TREE RIDGE
AERIAL HILL
BOULDER RIDGE
SUGAR LOAF
HOSPITAL HILL
KARIBA HEIGHTS
MAHOMBE KOMBE
CAMP HILL
Mica Point

Lake Kariba
Caribbea Bay Harbour
Andora Harbour

0   0.5   1 km

1	National Parks Office
2	Lake View Inn
3	Moths Camping Site
4	Yacht Club
5	Kariba Ferries
6	Kariba Fries
7	Swift United Freight Depot & Bus Terminal
8	Publicity Bureau
9	Petrol Station
10	Post Office & Bus Terminal
11	Hospital
12	Caribbea Bay Hotel Resort
13	Operation Noah Monument
14	Most High Hotel
15	Church of Santa Barbara
16	Bakery & Cinema
17	Kariby Breezes Hotel
18	Cutty Sark Hotel & Cruises
19	Mopani Bay Camping

useless for information but they do sell some unusual walking sticks carved in the shape of Nyaminyami, the Zambezi River god, as well as various kitsch souvenirs. Most worthwhile are the beautiful crocheted tablecloths and bedcovers sold by local women at the observation point (for ridiculously low prices). One feels guilty purchasing so much time and creativity for the pittance they're asking.

Climate Kariba is hot. During the summer months, you can anticipate average temperatures of 38°C accompanied by stifling humidity and frequent rain. During the winter months – June to August – expect daytime temperatures of around 25°C.

Dam Wall

On 17 May 1960, with the Queen Mother officiating, the switch was flipped on the first Kariba generator. Until Egypt's Aswan High Dam was completed in 1971, the Kariba project was Africa's largest.

You can visit the dam wall between Zimbabwe and Zambia by leaving your passport at Zimbabwe immigration and walking right onto the wall, as it vibrates to the rhythm of the 700 megawatt generators that power most of Zimbabwe and Zambia. The arching 579 metre wide dam wall rises 128 metres above the Zambezi River and Kariba Gorge. The structure contains over one million cubic metres of concrete which, at the base, is 24 metres thick.

The best overall view can be had from the observation point less than one km uphill from the Shell petrol station near the border post. From the lake, boaters aren't permitted past the nets and floating markers at the gorge entrance. The vulnerability of the dam wall is of grave concern to both Zimbabwe and Zambia and the military guards of both countries take these boundaries very seriously.

Church of Santa Barbara

The circular Church of Santa Barbara in Kariba Heights is dedicated to the patron saint of engineers as well as the Virgin Mary and St Joseph, the patron saint of carpenters. It was built by workers from Impresit (the Italian company which built Kariba Dam) in memory of their 86 colleagues who perished during construction. A stone plaque lists their names.

The open circular shape of the building represents a coffer dam; the open walls are a concession to the climate. Inside are two sculptures of Carrara marble, one of St Catherine and the other of St George, the latter a copy of the renowned original by Donatello.

Operation Noah Monument

The rising lake waters caused problems not only for the Batonka people but also for animals trapped on intermediate islands threatened with inundation by the rising Kariba waters.

Word of the situation got around and the resulting public outcry encouraged the Rhodesian government to assign Rupert Fothergill and a team of 57 wildlife personnel to effect a rescue project. They worked throughout the dry season – March to December, 1959 – tracking, trapping and relocating over 5000 creatures of at least 35 species including reptiles (even black mambas!) and small mammals as well as lions and rhinos. The project, dubbed Operation Noah after a similar operation quite a few years earlier, resulted in artificially dense concentrations of game on the southern shore and in the stocking of Matusadona National Park with game.

A monument commemorating the efforts behind Operation Noah has been erected at the lake viewpoint point in Kariba Heights.

Crocodile Park

Kariba's crocodile park is beyond the airport about 20 km out of town and so not convenient for anyone without a vehicle. Admission is Z$5 and it's open 8 am to noon and 2 to 5 pm daily except Monday.

Activities

Water Sports The presence of crocodiles and bilharzia in Lake Kariba may put a damper on any water activities you may have had planned, although the beach at Caribbea Bay seems to be pretty well protected and they do allow swimming.

Caribbea Bay hires out sailboards for Z$4/15/25 per hour/half-day/full day, canoes (Z$2/8/12), paddleboats (Z$2/20/35) dinghies (Z$2/20/35) and rowboats (Z$5/15/ 20). In addition, you'll have to pay Z$5 per person to get into the complex.

Launching from Caribbea Bay's private yacht harbour costs Z$20. Moorings and vehicle parking each cost Z$2 per 24 hours.

Power boats may be hired through UTC. They charge Z$70 for half a day, that is from 6 am to noon or noon to 5 pm, not including petrol. All-day hire is Z$90 and if you need fish bait, they charge an extra Z$8.

Yacht Rental Yachts which sleep up to four adults may be rented for individual cruising on the lake from Kariba Yachts at the Cutty Sark Hotel Marina. They charge US$60/ Z$105 per day not including food although catering for two/four people is available for an additional Z$45/90 per day. This is a fairly popular option so it would pay to book in advance through their central booking office in Harare. From April to September phone (☎ 736789 Harare) or write to Cutty Sark Marina, PO Box 80, Kariba, Zimbabwe. Between October and March, call (☎ 50305 Harare) or write to Kariba Yachts, 6 Fairfield Rd, Hatfield, Harare, Zimbabwe.

For a *lot* more money, you can hire a yacht and crew from several operators in Kariba; contact Blue Water Charters (☎ 369), PO Box 78, Kariba, or Lake Safaris (☎ 475), PO Box 34, Kariba.

Organised Tours Lots of safari companies operate day tours from Kariba. One of the more popular is the misnamed Matusadona Picnic Cruise (it doesn't go to Matusadona at all) which leaves Cutty Sark jetty at 9.30 am and returns in the afternoon in time for the airport transfer to the Harare flight. It costs Z$45 per person for the cruise and a picnic lunch aboard. Slightly cheaper is the

Lake Safaris Islands Cruise (☎ 2474), PO Box 34, Kariba, which costs only Z$35 for the full day; it doesn't include lunch though.

UTC (☎ 2453), PO Box 93, Kariba, offers a Kariba town tour for Z$20, departing at 10.30 am from Cutty Sark, 10.45 am from Caribbea Bay, and 11 am from Lake View Inn. Morning or evening game drives through the Charara Safari Area cost Z$35 per person and depart at 5.30 from Lake View Inn and 15 and 30 minutes later from Caribbea Bay and Cutty Sark respectively.

In addition, UTC and Cruise Kariba (☎ 2697), PO Box 1, Kariba, do two daily booze cruises, the Siesta Cruise which costs Z$10 and departs from Cutty Sark jetty at 2 pm (returning in time for the airport transfer) and the Sunset Cruise, costing Z$15 and leaving the same place at 4.30 pm.

Speciality Trips If you want five days cruising the length of Kariba in the floating hotel MV *Manica* or several days hopping around the Zambezi Valley in a Catalina flying boat or a week of fishing from a houseboat on the lake, there's a safari for you. For the first option, contact Manica Touring Services (☎ 736091 Harare), PO Box 429, Harare. The Catalina is operated by Nostalgia Safaris (☎ 738999 Harare), 1 Raleigh St, PO Box 89, Harare. If the houseboat is more your speed, talk to Lake Wilderness Safaris (☎ 2645), PO Box 113, Kariba.

Places to Stay – bottom end
The bottom end at Kariba is primarily camping. The most popular with travellers is the relatively convenient *MOTHS Holiday Resort* (☎ 2809), near the yacht club just 20 minutes walk from Mahombekombe township. Several travellers have written to report theft from tents here, but management has recently installed floodlighting in an attempt to thwart the worst of it. You can also camp at the *Lion's Club* site just up the hill for the same price, but it's not always attended and security could be a problem. Although most visitors just camp for Z$4.50 per night, there are also chalets available which cost Z$14.40 per person; double rooms are Z$24. For

The other camping site is the National Parks operated *Nyanyana Camp* (☎ 2337) at the mouth of the Nyanyana River in the Charara Safari Area. It's five km down a dirt road from the main Makuti-Kariba road, about 30 km out of town. This is the best option for those who prefer to immerse themselves in the literally wild side of Kariba. Baths, showers and toilets are available. Camping and caravan sites with braai pits cost Z$10 for up to six people. Prebookings through the National Parks Central Booking Office in Harare are advisable if you're visiting on a weekend or holiday. Buffalo Safaris (☎ 2645), PO Box 113, Kariba, offers all-inclusive organised tours, game drives and lake cruises using Nyanayana as a base.

Caribbea Bay used to have a permanently crowded caravan park charging Z$25 per site and an additional Z$10 per person. In fact, so much drunken partying went on, they had to close it down due to the impact of the noise levels on other guests. There are plans to relocate it at a safe distance from the main resort across their private yacht harbour.

Places to Stay – middle

Cutty Sark (☎ 2321) at Mopani Bay affords a good view of distant hills. It's a way out of town but quieter for it. Singles/double cost Z$68/120, all rooms including breakfast. *Kariba Breezes Hotel* (☎ 2433) is similar to the Cutty Sark, perhaps even a bit nicer, and charges the same prices.

Then there's the *Most High Hotel* (☎ 2964). Well, it is at the highest altitude of the lot but the name of this Christian mission hotel on the peak at Kariba Heights actually represents more religious connotations. It's clean, quiet and friendly and the view is excellent. Alcohol is forbidden, however, and smoking is only permitted in the gardens outside. They charge Z$65 per person, including bed and an amazing breakfast.

The *Zambezi Valley Hotel* (☎ 2926), in the Nyamhunga suburb near the airport, is just the opposite of quiet. If you're looking for African-style boozing and all-night disco music, this should be your haunt. They

Giraffe

rooms and chalets, bookings are always advisable but during weekends and school holidays, they're essential. The postal address is PO Box 67, Kariba, but you can also book in at the MOTHS office.

Little tin huts at the yacht club rent for Z$20 a double but they're unbearably hot in Kariba's climate and should only be considered an option by those stranded without a tent.

Those who prefer more peace, quiet and the occasional exciting encounter with wildlife should try *Mopani Bay Caravan Park* (☎ 2485) on the lakeshore about two km from the Cutty Sark Hotel. Developed sites (ie with braai pits) cost Z$5.50 per person plus Z$4 per site. Undeveloped sites for tenting and caravanning cost Z$4 per person. They're pretty cagey about the undeveloped sites so you have to specifically request one.

charge Z$81/90 for singles doubles. Lone women may want to give it a miss.

Places to Stay – top end

The upmarket hotel is *Caribbea Bay* (☎ 2453), which can get nearly as noisy as the Zambezi Valley Hotel but the boozing here is Rhodey-style. This sparkling monument to pseudo-Mexican stucco architecture could have been the inspiration for the Eagles' *Hotel California*. With its beach, palm trees, tennis courts and casino, it aims to fulfil holiday fantasies by transporting patrons away from Africa to an imaginary tropical paradise Somewhere Else.

For many, the casino is Caribbea Bay's real attraction. Monte Carlo or Las Vegas it's not but die-hards and amateurs alike can either become absorbed with roulette and blackjack or just relax while feeding hungry one-armed bandits.

Nonresidents pay US$80/120 for singles/doubles. Zimbabwe residents pay Z$98/176. Breakfast costs an additional Z$10.50. To get past the boom, nonguests will have to pay Z$5 per person to visit the restaurant lie on the fairly nice beach or even just look at the place.

The well-located *Lake View Inn* (☎ 2411) offers average accommodation and a glorious view. Nonresident rates for singles/doubles including breakfast are US$52/104. Residents pay Z$70/130.

Places to Stay – Zambian shore

Although the Zimbabwean side is more popular, it's also possible to stay on the Zambian side of Kariba but if you're planning a lot of activities on the Zimbabwean side, the border post and currency and visa requirements could make the international commuting inordinately awkward. Still, if you pay in Zambian kwacha, accommodation works out cheaper than comparable pickings in Zimbabwe.

The self-catering *Eagle's Rest Chalets* (☎ 52 Siavonga) in Siavonga East comes highly recommended. The chalets, which rent for US$15 per night, are equipped with bedding, electricity, a fridge and a shower and toilet block with hot water but cooking implements are not provided. Although Eagle's Rest was once a popular camping site, camping is no longer permitted. To get there, take the Siavonga turnoff and follow the signs. It's about four km off the main road.

Also at Siavonga is the *Government Rest House* which costs US$12 per person (at the official rate) and serves meals and alcohol but the place lacks the views and tranquillity of the chalets. The bus to Lusaka departs from here at 5 am daily so guests will have a chance of getting a seat.

Another option is the more upmarket *Lakeside Lodge* in Siavonga West.

Places to Eat

One of the best places for cheap eats is the *Country Club* in the Heights where a large hearty spread will cost about Z$7. Ignore the 'members only' sign; people have been ignoring it for years.

The most convenient (if you're not staying at Kariba Heights) and cheapest snacks, groceries and sadza ne nyama are available in Mahombekombe township and the beer hall there sometimes offers live music. In the Heights is the more upmarket *Emerald Butchery and Supermarket* as well as an excellent bakery.

All the hotels have dining rooms with prices pretty much proportional to their room rates. The *Cutty Sark* does a good buffet breakfast for Z$8.50. *Lake View Inn* offers a magnificent view from their patio and it's just a quick jaunt up the hill from the MOTHS camping site.

Pedro's at Caribbea Bay bravely makes an attempt at Mexican cuisine but fails miserably. If you're craving a taco, go see the folks at the *Most High Hotel* in Kariba Heights who occasionally put on a genuine taco feed for North American visitors in need of a Mexican fix. They also offer big buffet breakfasts for Z$10 and set menu dinners – typically enormous home-cooked-USA-country-style – for Z$18 per person.

Getting There & Away

Air Air Zimbabwe has a daily flight from Harare to Kariba, departing at 9 am and arriving at 9.45 am. From Victoria Falls via Hwange, another daily flight departs at 2.50 pm and arrives at 4.30 pm. From Kariba to Hwange and Victoria Falls, the flight departs at 10.05 am, arriving at Hwange at 10.55 am and the Falls at 11.45 am. To Harare, there's a daily flight at 4.50 pm, arriving at 5.35 pm.

Warning: Zimbabwe, especially for flights to Kariba, seem to have rules of its own when it comes to airline scheduling. Although the plane to Harare officially departs at 4.50 pm, don't check in any later than 3.45 if you can help it. If the pilot gets antsy to go, waiting passengers are boarded, the plane is filled with standbys and they're off, sometimes as early as 4 or 4.15 pm. Confirmed passengers arriving later are out of luck.

Bus Several daily buses connect Kariba with Mbare musika in Harare but there is no express service. The Kariba bus terminal is in Mahombekombe township.

Hitching The road between Harare and Kariba is relatively well travelled all the time but your lifts may tend to be short ones unless you go at the weekend. Hitching will be especially easy late Friday night and Saturday morning where the bulk of weekend traffic will be passing through. Naturally, Sunday afternoon or evening will be the optimum time for heading in the other direction.

Ferry There are two ferries linking the eastern and western ends of Lake Kariba. The more popular is the 22 hour journey on one of the two Mlibizi car ferries – the large *Sea Lion* and the smaller *Sea Horse* – which charge Z$127 per person for cabin space. Vehicle space costs around Z$100 and is normally booked up more than two months in advance. Despite that, walk-ons won't have any problem getting on the ferry at the last minute if they aren't travelling with a vehicle; I've never heard of anyone being turned away. There is an average of one weekly sailing per ferry, although during peak periods more runs are added. From Kariba, the ferry departs on Monday from Andora Harbour and departs from Mlibizi on Tuesday morning. For bookings and current scheduling information, contact Kariba Ferries Ltd (☎ 65476 Harare, 2475 Kariba), PO Box 578, Harare, Zimbabwe.

Without a vehicle, reaching Mlibizi at the western end of the ferry route can be tricky. It will entail catching the more or less daily Binga bus (some days there are two buses!) from Dete Crossroads near Hwange on the Bulawayo to Victoria Falls road. Ask to be dropped at the turnoff to Binga and then begin the 15 km walk down the washboard track to Mlibizi. It's hot, dry and dusty so carry plenty of water. You may get lucky and catch a lift if your visit is synchronous with the ferry departure but don't count on it. Going the other way, hitching will undoubtedly be easier since nearly everyone on the ferry will have their own vehicle.

The Safari Office Services (☎ 4571 Vic Falls) in Victoria Falls will provide transport between Victoria Falls and the ferry terminal at Mlibizi but there have to be at least four passengers who can spare Z$150 each.

The other ferry, a local operation, is run by the District Development Fund or DDF (☎ 2694 Kariba), and is based at Andora Harbour. It links Kariba, Bumi Hills and Binga on an average twice monthly. Due to frequent breakdowns, however, it doesn't run according to any real schedule so you'll just have to be lucky to catch up with it. It cost Z$26 for spartan but adequate accommodation. The trip takes 2½ days and there are no cabins aboard. Passengers either sleep on the boat and cope with the swarms of mosquitoes or stay on shore. There's no food available on the boat – although they do have a cooker to boil water for sadza – so bring all you'll be needing from elsewhere.

There are one or two buses daily between Dete Crossroads and Binga. The road is currently being asphalted, so although the trip was extremely rough at the time of reearch, major improvements are forthcoming.

Getting Around

To/From the Airport UTC does transfers between the airport and the town for Z$10 per person each way. They meet all incoming flights. For the Hwange/Victoria Falls flight, they leave the Lake View Hotel at 8.30 am, Caribbea Bay at 8.45 and the Cutty Sark at 9. If you're flying to Harare, meet them at the Lake View at 3 pm, Caribbea Bay at 3.15 and the Cutty Sark at 3.45.

Bus & Taxi A viable but less convenient alternative is the bus which connects the Swift United Freight Depot with Nyamhunga suburb near the airport, stopping en route at Mahombekombe and Kariba Heights. It seems to appear about every 30 to 60 minutes.

Taxi services (☎ 2454) at Kariba are operated from Caribbea Bay Resort.

Hitching Those without vehicles are at a significant disadvantage here and walking around sprawling, up-and-down Kariba makes for a hot, tiring and time-consuming experience. Fortunately – or unfortunately, depending upon your perspective – most of the locals are in the same boat so hitching has become the standard city transport system. Normally, you shouldn't have to wait more than a few minutes for a lift from one area of town to another. The downside is that even these areas sprawl a bit and that, combined with the convoluted road and street patterns, will still guarantee you a fair amount of exercise.

AROUND LAKE KARIBA
Lake Resorts

The 'biggie' lake resorts outside of Matusadona National Park are Fothergill Island, Spurwing Island, Bumi Hills and Tiger Bay. These four, which cater to just about every budget range except the lowest, try to maintain a sense of isolated luxury; guests will be able to enjoy the bush and its wilder residents close at hand while still enjoying the comforts of home.

Bumi Hills Safari Lodge (☎ 353), PO Box 41, Kariba, which belongs to the Zimbabwe Sun hotels group, is a beautiful but pricey three-star wilderness resort west of Matusadona National Park. It caters primarily to an upmarket crowd looking for low-key adventure; organised fishing, game viewing, water sports, bushwalking and other activities are available. Those who'd like to escape even further into high finance can opt to visit their Water Wilderness Camp, which offers accommodation on houseboats in a nearby estuary.

Accommodation and meals cost around US$100 per person per day and game viewing is an additional Z$50 per day. Air transfers are about Z$100 return from Kariba to Bumi Hills. The resort is also accessible by 4WD vehicle over a long and poor track from the Siabuwa road. Bookings should be made through the Zimbabwe Sun central reservation office in Harare. A weekly DDF ferry connects Bumi Hills with Andora Harbour in Kariba but if you're in need of the luxury level afforded by Bumi Hills, it's a safe bet you won't like this ferry!

Fothergill Island Resort (☎ 2253), PO Box 2081, Kariba, is in a very bushy area on Fothergill Island, just offshore from Matusadona National Park. (Actually, since the lake's level has been so low in recent years, at the time of writing both Fothergill and Spurwing islands are actually peninsulas.) The camp has a bar, pool, fishing, canoe rentals, game viewing on foot and by vehicle, and an airstrip. With food, accommodation and all activities included, they charge Z$188 per person per day. Transfers to or from Kariba cost Z$40 per person each way. Fothergill Island is also accessible on a more or less weekly DDF ferry from Andora Harbour.

Nearby *Spurwing Island* (☎ 2466), PO Box 101, Kariba, is a bit smaller and less expensive than Fothergill but offers similar amenities. The biggest advantage Spurwing has over Fothergill is its sparser vegetation, which results in better game viewing. Tent accommodation including meals runs to Z$80 per person; add another Z$35 for game viewing. Boat transfers cost Z$40 each way.

The name of *Tiger Bay* (☎ 569), PO Box

102, Kariba, refers to Kariba's fighting tiger fish and not stray Asian big cats. Its thatched chalets sit beside the Ume River just outside the Matusadona National Park boundary. As the tiger fish connection would suggest, the emphasis here is on tiger fishing and equipment is available for hire. Boat/air transfers to Tiger Bay cost Z$40/60 per person each way. Singles/doubles including meals cost Z$95 per person.

MATUSADONA NATIONAL PARK

Matusadona covers nearly 1500 square km on the southern shore of Lake Kariba, sandwiched between the Sanyati, which lies in a pronounced gash between rumpled peaks, and the Ume, a broad islet-studded watercourse. Much of the wildlife displaced by the waters of Lake Kariba eventually settled down in the Matusadona area and game populations are therefore predictably dense.

Fishing is the most popular activity at Matusadona. Each October, the Kariba International Tiger Fishing Tournament is held at the mouth of Sunyati Gorge. You'll also find lots of walking opportunities along rivers

and gorges and near the shore along 4WD tracks but it would be wise to note the profusion of large and intimidating animals thereabouts.

Organised Tours

Backpacker's Africa leads strenuous six day walking tours along the Gubu Trail through Matusadona National Park. The route follows the Gubu River from the road up into the Matusadona Mountains and down into Sanyati Gorge at the park's eastern boundary. This trip, which must be paid for in foreign currency, is quite expensive and books up well in advance. If you're interested in a go at it, contact Backpacker's Africa (☎ 735712 Harare), Shearwater Adventures, 5th Floor, Karigamombe Centre, PO Box 3961, Harare.

Places to Stay

The National Parks Department operates two camping sites, both with showers, baths, toilets and laundry sinks, near the lakeshore – one along the Sanyati River and the other at park headquarters at Tashinga. A site at either of these will cost Z$6 per night for up to six people. Camping equipment may be hired inexpensively at both sites but Tashinga offers a wider variety of gear. On all counts, advance booking is advised.

In addition to the two main sites, three exclusive camps accommodating up to 12 people for six days cost only Z$300. Advance booking from Harare is essential. *Ume* and *Mbalabala* are both near Tashinga beside the Ume River, and *Muuyu* is near Elephant Point about seven km further east. Each of these camps consists of two two-bedroom units with three beds in each room, a bathroom and toilet, kitchen, dining room, and storeroom. A refrigerator, a stove, all cooking implements, linen and lighting are provided.

Another option is *Sanyati Lodge* (☎ 703000 Harare), PO Box 2008, Kariba, a resort at the mouth of Sanyati Gorge near the park's eastern boundary. It's a quiet spot that runs exclusively on solar power and accommodates a maximum of only eight people.

Getting There & Away

Access to the park is tricky no matter how you look at it. The Karoi, Siabuwa, Binga bus only skirts the southern boundary of the park and won't get you any closer than 82 km from the Tashinga park headquarters. Even with your own vehicle, most of the year you'll need 4WD for the final bit into Tashinga. Those entering by road have to pay Z$5 per person for a weekly entry permit.

One option is to try hitching a lift on a boat from Andora harbour or the Caribbea Bay marina to Tashinga. Of course, once you've reached the park, you're still faced with the logistics of arranging a trip back, a much easier prospect if you're staying at Tashinga rather than Sanyati. Take lots of extra food, however, in case the wait proves longer than anticipated.

The final option is to connect with either of two weekly DDF freight ferries, one of which stops at Tashinga en route to Bumi Hills. The other winds up at Sanyati. Enquire at the DDF office near Andora Harbour for anticipated schedules and prices.

Eastern Highlands

Few first-time travellers to Zimbabwe expect to find anything like the eastern highlands, but once they have discovered them, fewer still can get enough of them. The narrow strip of mountain country that forms Zimbabwe's easternmost extreme isn't the Africa that normally crops up in an armchair traveller's fantasy but surprises can be the most pleasant fringe benefits of really being there.

Transport isn't particularly reliable in the eastern highlands, so without a vehicle a rapid tour of the region would require a great deal of luck hitching or connecting with infrequent buses. What's more, the transport system in places exists primarily to connect the region to Harare and to provide access to communal lands in western Manicaland. The areas of greatest interest to most travellers aren't linked up.

MARONDERA

Although it isn't actually in Manicaland, if you arrive during the dry winter season, you'll be able to catch your first whiffs of high country pine amidst the eucalyptus at Marondera (population 22,000), just 72 km east of Harare. Marondera has the highest altitude of any Zimbabwean town and its temperate climate is ideal for maize, sheep, European garden vegetables and deciduous orchards.

The latest agricultural development in Marondera is viticulture. Marondera wines are produced by the Mukuyu division of Monis wineries. Okay, the climate isn't ideal but it's the nearest Zimbabwe has and it allows Zimbabweans to enjoy wine without having to pay prohibitive excise duties on imported products. The white wines haven't been too bad of late. The reds, however, can be given a summary miss unless you're fond of red punch.

The wineries, just half an hour's drive from Marondera along the Ruzawe road, offer both tours and tastings but the place is rather difficult to reach without a private vehicle.

On the main road through town, you can buy inexpensive handmade textiles and carpets at the Gatehouse Training Centre, a cooperative organisation which provides training for unskilled unwed mothers.

Malwatte Farm House

The Malwatte Farm House & Tea Room (☎ 3239 Marondera), 10 km east of Marondera, has been highly recommended for its hospitality. It's a great place to stop for tea, coffee, snacks or meals while en route to or from the eastern highlands. There's also a gift shop. It's open daily from 8 am to 5 pm Monday to Friday and evenings on weekends. Some travellers I met were permitted to camp there in what they reported was a lovely setting. If you're interested, phone in advance for information on the current situation.

Markwe Cave Paintings

The difficult-to-reach Markwe paintings portray a host of human figures involved in various unidentified tasks interspersed with a menagerie of animal forms. Reaching Markwe is almost impossible without your own vehicle and the site probably isn't worth the considerable time you'd have to wait for lifts when there are other more easily accessible cave paintings around. Coming from Harare, turn right on Watershed Rd about two km west of Marondera. After three km, turn left on Bridge Rd and follow it for about 35 km, then turn left at the unpaved but sign-posted Markwe turnoff. After four more km, turn right at the farmhouse and continue nearly one km to the base of a small hill, above which you'll find the cave containing the painted panel.

If Markwe is too far afield for your taste, another less impressive panel can be found on a large rock behind the Macheke railway station about 35 km east of Marondera.

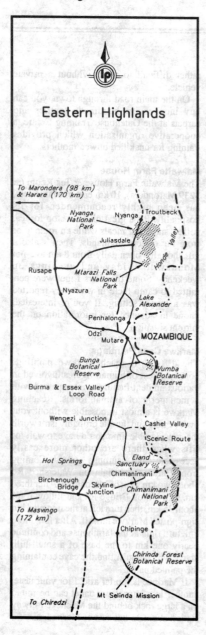

Eastern Highlands

To Marondera (98 km)
& Harare (170 km)

Nyanga
National Park — Nyanga — Troutbeck

Juliasdale

Honde Valley

Rusape — Mtarazi Falls
National Park

Nyazura

Lake Alexander

Penhalonga

Odzi

Mutare — MOZAMBIQUE

Bunga Botanical Reserve

Vumba Botanical Reserve

Burma & Essex Valley Loop Road

Wengezi Junction

Cashel Valley

Scenic Route

Hot Springs

Eland Sanctuary

Chimanimani

Birchenough Bridge

Skyline Junction

Chimanimani National Park

To Masvingo (172 km)

Chipinge

Chirinda Forest Botanical Reserve

To Chiredzi

Mt Selinda Mission

Places to Stay

The *Hotel Marondera* (☎ 4005 Marondera) is okay but unless you're really stuck, it's probably better to continue on to Harare or Rusape for the night.

RUSAPE

This small town of 9000 people between Marondera and Mutare lies in a prime tobacco-growing region amid scenic dwala domes and kopjes. It is the junction of the routes between Harare and Mutare or Nyanga. Apart from the unusual Diana's Vow rock painting nearby, however, there's really nothing specific to see.

Diana's Vow Rock Paintings

There are quite a few imaginative explanations behind the intriguing rock painting at Diana's Vow, Zimbabwe's answer to Namibia's White Lady of the Brandberg. Most of them are unlikely and entirely incompatible with the artists' likely perspective.

Some flights of fancy have shown a reclining white king. Others construe a dead king wrapped mummy-like, his funeral procession dancing him into the world beyond. The most accepted interpretation states that the scene is indeed connected with the sable antelope and the dancers have entered their trance-like state in order to generate potency in the central figure, represented by the large object on his back.

Places To Stay

The hotel *Balfour* (☎ 2945 Rusape) is relatively inexpensive and more pleasant than the hotel in Marondera. The one-star *Crocodile Motel* (☎ 2404 Rusape) on the main road is another option. Camping is available at the *Rusape Dam Caravan Park* 10 km south of town.

Getting There & Away

If you'd like to see the paintings, you'll either need a private vehicle or a lot of time (and luck) waiting for lifts. The paintings are found beneath a rock overhang a couple of hundred metres from the gate of Diana's Vow

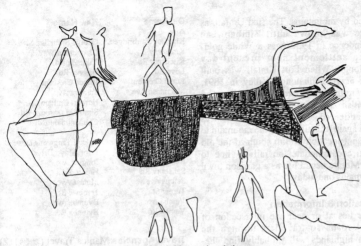

Diana's Vow rock paintings

Farm. To get there from Rusape, turn off the Harare-Mutare Rd toward Juliasdale on route A14. After 29 km, turn left on Constance Rd and follow it for 12 km to the intersection of Silver Bow Rd, where you turn left again. The farm entrance is just a couple of hundred metres ahead on your left.

ODZI

The primary interest of Odzi, a tobacco-growing and tungsten-mining village 30 km west of Mutare, is the remarkable *Mapor Estates* (☎ 13 Odzi), c/o B Holman, PO Box 98, Odzi, 16 km south of the village.

Mapor hasn't yet been 'discovered' by the hordes but all who've visited provide rave reviews of the hospitality, camping facilities, swimming pool and even the tasteful reading material in the loos! There are good opportunities for bouldering and rock climbing as well as exploration on foot or horseback (the horses have been described as 'rather marginal') in the surrounding hills, which contain numerous caves and rock paintings. Mapor is a working tobacco farm and during the right season you'll be able to observe the harvesting, drying or curing processes.

There's a small store selling basics and petrol. Braai pits and cooking facilities (but no meals) are available. Day visits cost Z$1.50 per person, overnight camping is Z$5 per person. Guesthouse accommodation must be arranged in advance.

Getting There & Away Turn south at the bridge just west of the Odzi River, 32 km west of Mutare. Continue six km along this road to Odzi post office and turn left at the sign marked 'Maranke-Mapembe'. After 10.5 km, you'll reach a left turning signposted 'Mapor Estate'. Travel a further 2.5 km along this road to another signposted left turn and follow the signs into the farmhouse.

If you don't have private transport, you can reach the Odzi River bridge on any Harare-Mutare bus. Without a vehicle, you can phone Mapor Estates in advance and arrange a time to be picked up (for a minimal charge) from the bridge or walk the six km to Odzi post office and phone from there.

MUTARE

Mutare, Zimbabwe's fourth-largest city, is beautifully situated in a bowl-like valley surrounded by mountains. The first Umtali, as Mutare was known until Zimbabwean independence in 1980, was a White gold-mining settlement near present-day Penhalonga. When Fort Umtali was built further down Penhalonga Valley in 1891, following the 1890 border dispute between the British and Portuguese, the name was commandeered. In 1896, the town was shifted again, this time over the mountain to its present location 16 km south of the old fort, to accommodate the railway line to Beira. Mutare began life as a garrison town and remains one today.

Orientation & Information

Mutare lies at or near the intersection of several roads so travellers through the eastern highlands will probably find themselves passing through at least once.

The helpful Manicaland Publicity Bureau office (☎ 64711) on Market Square near the corner of Herbert Chitepo St and Robert Mugabe Ave will be able to help you with most queries, but they don't have much info about the routes and frequency of buses departing for other eastern highlands destinations from Sakubva musika.

Street Name Changes Even more than the two larger cities, Harare and Bulawayo, Mutare made an effort early in 1990 to purge itself of any and all British or 'colonial' sounding street names. Even 'Love Rd' was changed!

Old Name	New Name
Aerodrome Rd/ Victory Ave	Aerodrome Rd
Allan Wilson Rd	Leopold Takawira Rd
Cecil Ave	Independence Ave
Churchill Rd/Milner Ave	Robert Mugabe Ave
Coghlan Ave	Robson Manyika Ave
Cowley Place	Simon Mazorodze Place
Crawford Rd	Josiah Tongogara Rd
Devonshire Rd	Makoni Rd
Earl Grey Ave	Gukurahundi Ave
Eickoff Ave	Chimoio Ave
Evans Rd	Nyadzonya Rd
Guide Ave	Eighth Ave
Jan Smuts Drive	Magamba Drive

Old Name cont.	New Name
Kingsley Fairbridge St	George Silundika St
Kingsway	Chamunika Way
Kitchener Rd	Takunda Rd
Love Rd	Batanai Rd
Lundi Crescent	Runde Crescent
Macintosh Ave	Tatonga Ave
Main St	Herbert Chitepo St
Meikle Rd	Simon Mazorodze Rd
Melsetter Rd	Chimanimani Rd
Moffat Ave/Circular Drive	Rekayi Tangwena Drive
Rhodes Drive	Jason Moyo Drive
Rudland Ave	Jongwe Ave
Salisbury Rd	Harare Rd
Selous Ave	Mutasa Ave
Turner St	Tembwe St
Vumba Ave	Bvumba Ave
Vumba Rd	Bvumba Rd

Travel Agencies Manica Travel (☎ 64112) at 92 Herbert Chitepo St near Second Ave serves as the American Express representative and transport booking agent for Mutare.

Bookshops If you're headed into the mountains and want to pick up some reading material, try the Book Centre in the Norwich Union Centre on Herbert Chitepo St. They stock a reasonable selection of light-reading foreign novels and Zimbabwean publications. There's also a small book exchange beside Manica Travel on Herbert Chitepo St.

Mutare Museum

If you have some time in Mutare don't miss the museum, which is a very well-mounted conglomeration of exhibits – geology, history, anthropology, technology, zoology and the arts. There's even a snake collection and a series of dioramas of Manicaland landscapes and wildlife.

Also, check out the collection of 16th to 19th century armaments, the stone, iron and agricultural age archaeological exhibits, and the transportation museum. Out the back, there's an active beehive, cut away for easy viewing, and a walk-in aviary with over 500 birds.

The museum, which is within easy walking distance of the city centre, is open from 9 am to 5 pm daily; admission costs 20 cents.

Main Park & Aloe Garden

Mutare's Main Park and Aloe Garden are great for a sunny afternoon read or a picnic on the lawns. In the aloe garden, which blooms in midwinter, approximately 250 species native to Zimbabwe and Madagascar are represented, including prehistoric cycad palms.

Utopia House Museum

Utopia House was the home of Kingsley Fairbridge (1885-1924), a colonial poet and founder of Fairbridge Farm Schools for homeless and neglected children. The home was built in 1897, but to make it more typical of a colonial homestead the museum has been restored and refurnished in a 1920s style. The statue of Kingsley Fairbridge that once overlooked Christmas Pass has been moved to the Utopia garden. The museum, which is on Jason Moyo Drive, is open 2.30 to 4.30 pm on Saturday and Sunday.

Cross Kopje

A short track leads from Circular Drive east of town to the top of this small hill overlooking the Mozambique border. The cross on the summit is a memorial to black Zimbabweans and Mozambicans who died in the WW I East Africa campaigns. To get there, follow Milner Ave east past the park to Park Rd. Turn left and carry on one block to Vintcent Ave where you turn right. It soon becomes Circular Drive, which passes near the foot of Cross Kopje.

Mutare Heights Lookout

Mutare Heights offers a view of the entire bowl. There's a steep footpath up from Murambi suburb but it's easier to hitch up to Christmas Pass and walk the six km or so from there to the top along the road.

Murahwa's Hill

The national trust nature reserve on Murahwa's Hill, which consists of a single rock kopje, is a nice place to spend a day wandering and getting lost on the maze of routes around it. There are some rock paintings and the ruin of an iron-age village but the real attractions are the views and access to nature so near Mutare. Although leopards are believed to inhabit the reserve, they're rarely seen but you'll probably see a monkey or two.

Access is from Magamba Drive near the Agricultural Show Grounds or on Old Pass Rd above the Wise Owl Motel.

Cecil Kop & Thompson's Vlei

This 1700 hectare game reserve which abuts the Mozambique border is a reasonable 3.5 km walk from town. Visitors without vehicles can visit Tiger's Kloof Dam – follow Herbert Chitepo St north from the centre. About one km after it turns into Arcadia Rd, you'll come to the dam parking area. Climb the small hill, pay your Z$1 admission, and proceed to the wildlife viewing area. If you're interested in the zoo-like nature of this game reserve, the best time to visit is between 4 and 4.30 pm when the animals – giraffes, elephants, zebras, buffalo and a range of antelope – congregate for feeding time.

Those with vehicles can drive into the Thompson's Vlei section of the reserve to see zebras, monkeys, nyala, wildebeest, buffalo, warthogs and the usual antelope range – impala, kudu, waterbuck, duiker and so on. Not far from the entrance gate is a pan with a game-viewing platform. Without a vehicle, you may be able to hitch a lift from the entry gate off Circular Drive.

One admission ticket will get you into both sections of the park, but an extra Z$2 is charged for your vehicle at Thompson's Vlei. Don't wander anywhere near the fence along the eastern boundary – this is the Mozambique border and this 'no-man's land' is riddled with land mines.

La Rochelle Botanical Gardens

La Rochelle in Imbeza Valley is the former estate Sir Stephan and Lady Virginia Courtauld bequeathed to the nation upon Lady Courtauld's death in 1972. There is a

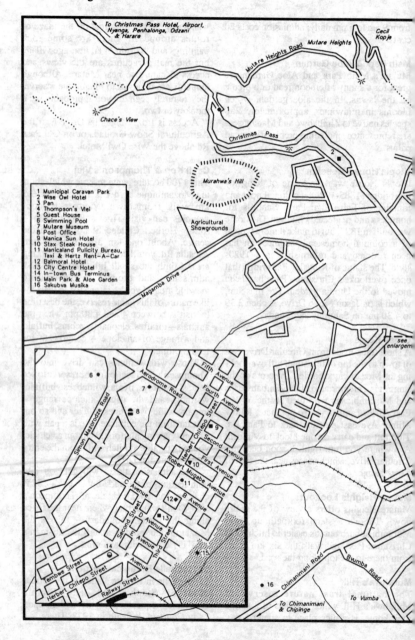

1 Municipal Caravan Park
2 Wise Owl Hotel
3 Pan
4 Thompson's Vlei
5 Guest House
6 Swimming Pool
7 Mutare Museum
8 Post Office
9 Manica Sun Hotel
10 Stax Steak House
11 Manicaland Publicity Bureau, Taxi & Hertz Rent-A-Car
12 Balmoral Hotel
13 City Centre Hotel
14 In-town Bus Terminus
15 Main Park & Aloe Garden
16 Sakubva Musika

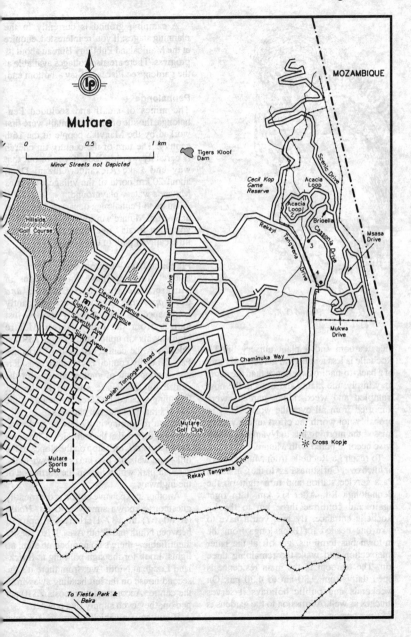

Barred Owl

nice tearoom and a plant nursery but La Rochelle is less a botanical garden and more of a back-to-nature experience than the name may imply; the plants and trees in the now trampled and weed-ridden gardens were imported from all over the world. They're probably not worth the effort unless you've missed the morning bus to Nyanga or otherwise become bored with Mutare.

To reach La Rochelle from Mutare, drive or hitch over Christmas Pass to the Christmas Pass service station and turn right on the Penhalonga Rd. After six km, turn right again and continue three km to the La Rochelle entrance. By bus, you'll have to take one headed for Penhalonga from the in-town bus terminus, get off at the latter intersection and walk the remaining three km. The tearoom in the main residence is open daily from 9.30 am to 4.30 pm. On weekends and public holidays it serves lunches as well. Admission to the gardens is Z$1 per person.

A camping ground is currently in the planning stages; if you're interested, enquire at the Manicaland Publicity Bureau about its progress. There are also cottages available at the garden; see Places to Stay – bottom end.

Penhalonga

The mines of small and secluded Penhalonga, the site of the first Umtali, were first worked by the Manyika people in the 16th century. The turn-of-the-century tin church is certainly worth a look if you're out that way and Lake Alexander/Odzani Dam, about 20 km north of the village, serves as Mutare's watery playground.

Buses to Penhalonga depart several times daily from Mutare's in-town bus terminus. If you want to stay overnight, there's a nice little caravan park in the village.

Places to Stay – bottom end

Budget travellers have three options in Mutare. The *Municipal Camping and Caravan Park*, although very pleasantly landscaped, is unfortunately located just metres from the noisy Harare-Mutare highway, six km uphill (and a Z$7 to Z$9 taxi ride) from the centre just below Christmas Pass. The city council is currently considering development of another site nearer the centre but plans are still up in the air. Camping sites cost Z$6 each, including the use of braai pits and hot showers.

If you're coming in by bus from Harare, ask to be dropped at the summit of Christmas Pass – drivers won't stop on the slopes of the hill – and walk the two km or so down to the caravan park which lies on the north side of the highway.

Another inexpensive option is the friendly guesthouse known simply as *Guest House* (☎ 60467) at 137 Herbert Chitepo St, between Ninth and Tenth Aves. It isn't easily identifiable – there's no number, no sign, no lights. Look for the sign pointing to Strickland Lodge at Ninth Ave; from there it's the second house on the left heading away from the centre. Accommodation costs Z$10 per person; they even supply flea powder.

If you have a vehicle, there are six quiet

cottages available for Z$20 per night at *La Rochelle* (☎ 250 Penhalonga), PO Box 34, Penhalonga, in the Imbeza Valley about 20 km from Mutare. For more information see the discussion of La Rochelle Botanical Garden.

The cheapest hotel option is the seedy but adequate *Balmoral Hotel* (☎ 61435) on C Ave. Rooms cost Z$25 single or double without private bath or toilet.

Next up the price scale but definitely down the quality scale is the *City Centre Hotel* (☎ 62441) at the corner of Herbert Chitepo St and D Ave. Singles/doubles cost Z$30/50. Formerly known as the Little Swallow Hotel and still occasionally referred to as such, this place is a real dump and the city is currently threatening to pull its licence unless they clean it up a bit.

Places to Stay – middle

Over on the other side of Christmas Pass 10 km from town is the colonial-style *Christmas Pass Hotel* (☎ 63818). There's a garden and a swimming pool in a quiet setting for those into out-of-town relaxation. Singles/doubles cost Z$65/110 with breakfast included.

The *Wise Owl Motel* (☎ 64643) is a way out from the centre on Robert Mugabe Rd (Christmas Pass Rd). It's clean and offers good mid-range value if you have a private vehicle. Single/double rooms including breakfast will cost Z$65/100.

Places to Stay – top end

The only top-end accommodation in Mutare is the *Manica Sun*, one of those cast-in-a-mould expense account hotels, at the corner of Herbert Chitepo St and Aerodrome Rd. Singles/doubles for nonresidents cost US$60/90. Zimbabwe residents pay Z$70/130.

Places to Stay – out of town

Other bottom-end, mid-range and top-end accommodation is available in the Vumba area east of Mutare. For specifics, refer to the section on Vumba later in this chapter.

Places to Eat

If you're after a cheap plate of sadza ne nyama, try the *Little Swallow Inn* on Herbert Chitepo St where it'll cost you less than Z$3. Alternatively, try the *Zvinoira* on E Ave near Herbert Chitepo St for similar fare.

The nicest mid-range restaurant is the friendly *Stax Steak House* in the Norwich Union Centre Arcade which, despite its name, serves everything from chicken curry to burgers and lots in-between. Their set breakfast is inexpensive and excellent or you can get a Belgian waffle piled with cream and berries. It's one of the few places in town open for dinner and if you're into slabs of beef, don't miss it.

The *Wise Owl Motel* restaurant has also been recommended for great Z$10 dinners.

A good option for lunch or snacks is *Meikles Department Store*, also on Herbert Chitepo St, a favourite of the 'old school' and a real Mutare institution. It's unfortunately not open for dinner.

For light lunches or tea in a slightly pretentious crafts shop, try *Jenny's Cottage* at 130 Herbert Chitepo St. *Dairy Den* in the arcade on Herbert Chitepo St is Mutare's fast food representative. It's not bad for takeaway lunches, ice cream and greasy fare but it's only open until early evening.

The breakfast buffet at the *Manica Sun* hotel is one of the best in the country. For Z$7.70, the continental version offers a selection of fresh fruit, breads, pastries, cereals and cheeses. The Z$11.50 full English breakfast adds sausage, bacon, kidneys, eggs and fried potatoes. They also serve lunches and dinners.

Entertainment

There are two very popular pubs in town, the Portuguese Club and the Motoring Club. The City Centre Hotel offers riotous drinking nightly with live performances in the beer garden on Saturday and Sunday afternoons.

Mutare also has a cinema showing primarily rubbishy North American films. The Courtauld Theatre provides a venue for conservative local theatrical productions. Both are near the Civic Centre Complex on Robert Mugabe Ave.

There's also an Olympic-sized swimming pool near the Civic Centre complex on Robert Mugabe Rd. It opens daily except Mondays from 6 to 7 am and 10 am to 5 pm, from late August to mid-May. Admission is 30 cents for as long as you'd like to swim.

Getting There & Away

Air There is no scheduled air service to or from Mutare.

Bus The in-town bus terminus is between Herbert Chitepo and Tembwe Sts near F Ave. If you're coming from Harare or other points over Christmas Pass, be sure to get off here unless you want to get to the Sakubva musika bus station several km from the centre in Sakubva township. Chances are that buses entering Mutare from the south will be swamped upon arrival at Sakubva and won't continue on to the in-town bus terminus, although some do. Never mind; there are plenty of local buses from Sakubva into the centre and taxis only charge Z$4 or so – bargain or try to find one with a functional meter.

For the seven hour trip to Harare, buses leave hourly from the in-town terminus. From Sakubva musika, there are daily (except Saturday) buses to Nyanga for only Z$4 at around 6 am but arrive earlier if possible. There is also at least one daily bus to Harare, Birchenough Bridge, Honde Valley, Cashel Valley, Chipinge and Masvingo and periodic service to Chiredzi, Triangle and Beitbridge. To reach Bulawayo from Mutare, you first need to get to Masvingo.

The elusive Chimanimani bus goes quite literally whenever the driver feels like it – normally two or three times per week. More reliable but time-consuming ways to reach Chimanimani from Mutare include taking a Chipinge bus, getting off at the intersection seven km north of Chipinge, and hitching to Skyline Junction and thence Chimanimani Village. Alternatively, take any bus passing through Birchenough Bridge, get off at

Wengezi, 67 km south of Mutare, hitch to Skyline Junction and then down to Chimanimani. Allow a very long day for either of these options.

Most daily buses leave Sakubva between 6 and 7 am and it's a long nine km slog from the caravan park to the musika. If you're departing early and staying at the caravan park, it may be a good idea to prearrange a morning taxi pickup (☎ 63344, 63166) the previous night.

An Express Motorways bus runs five times a week between Harare and the Manica Sun hotel in Mutare, a trip of four to five hours.

Train The easiest way to travel between Harare and Mutare is by overnight train. The service departs from Harare nightly at 9.30, arriving in Mutare at 6 am. From Mutare, it leaves at 9 pm and arrives at 6 am in Harare. The 1st-class fare is Z$24.15, 2nd class is Z$16.80, and economy is Z$7.

The reservations and ticket office are open from 8 am to 12.30 pm and 2 to 4 pm weekdays.

Getting Around

There are taxi stands at Sakubva Market, the in-town bus terminus, the Manica Sun Hotel and near the publicity association. You can phone for a taxi on 63344 or 63166. Urban buses run between Sakubva musika and the centre.

Car rentals are available at the Hertz Rent-a-Car (☎ 64784) office in the Manicaland Publicity Bureau building.

Nyanga Area

The tame highlands around Nyanga have long been the summer holiday spot for heat-weary Harare dwellers. Well, at least for those who could afford the luxury of a few days fishing and vegetating in the mountain country.

Nyanga National Park, around which the region revolves, is more a popular and developed resort area than a real wilderness although some remote bushwalking is available around the perimeter, especially in the park's southern extremes. Adjoining Mtarazi Falls National Park, which is little more than an afterthought appended to Nyanga, is completely undeveloped – there's not even a camping area – and the only vehicle access is a steep, rutted track leading to the park's namesake attraction. Just east lie the tropical agricultural lowlands and tea estates of the Honde Valley.

JULIASDALE

Piney Juliasdale, it seems, is little more than a holiday cottage settlement and a repository for scattered hotels and private cottages in need of a town somewhere in their address. From the centre, inasmuch as Juliasdale has one, there are good westward views across the farm lands, intermittent forests and granite domes. The village boasts a petrol station, a post office, and a couple of small shops. On the highway between Juliasdale and the Nyanga Park entrance is Claremont Orchard Shop where you can purchase trout and locally grown apples.

Places to Stay

Camping is available for Z$5 per tent at *Rupurara Farm*, an unspoilt tract of real estate with good mountain views and bushwalking opportunities. The friendly farmer, Frank, also opens extra rooms in his home for Z$10 per person.

The *Brondesbury Park Hotel* (☎ 342 Juliasdale), PO Box 8070, Rusape, is actually 30 km from Juliasdale on the road to Rusape. This three-star hotel charges approximately Z$100/120 for singles/doubles including breakfast and dinner and use of the swimming pool, tennis courts and bowling green. A golf course adjoins the grounds.

Nearer town, the recommended *Pine Tree Inn* (☎ 25916 Juliasdale), PO Box 1, Juliasdale, has a reputation for its excellent meals. Singles/doubles, including all meals, cost around Z$60/110.

The *Montclair* (☎ 231 Juliasdale), which

boasts one of Zimbabwe's three casinos (the others are at Kariba and Vic Falls), attracts upmarket tourists and Zimbabwe's elegant crowd with all its trappings of luxury: tennis courts, a swimming pool, croquet, horseback riding, golf and so on. (Even so, if I had the money to spend on such a hotel, I'd opt instead for Troutbeck north of the national park.) Rooms cost around Z$90 a single and Z$150 a double for residents. Foreigners are required to pay higher rates in US$.

There are also a couple of private cottages providing accommodation: *Silver Rocks Holiday Farm* (☎ 21719 Juliasdale), PO Box 27, Juliasdale, which is 10 km along the road to Rusape; and *Punch Rock Chalets* (☎ 24424 Juliasdale), PO Box 30, Juliasdale, near the Pine Tree Inn.

NYANGA NATIONAL PARK

Although it can hardly be described as pristine – nearly all the naturally occurring vegetation in easily accessible areas was cleared for farming long ago – the 33,000 hectare Nyanga National Park is a scenically distinct enclave in the eastern highlands. Cecil Rhodes fell in love with it and, as only he could have done, bought it for his own residence. Not surprisingly, the park, like the entire country, acquired his name; it's still sometimes referred to by locals as Rhodes Inyanga.

Nyanga streams and lakes are stocked with rainbow, brook and brown trout. Trout fishing licences cost Z$2 per day or Z$7 per week, although higher rates apply to Gulliver and Saunyami (Purdon) dams. Guided 1½ hour horseback tours are available around the archaeological sites above the Nyanga (Rhodes) Dam area for Z$6. Bookings (☎ 274 Nyanga) should be made at the parks office near Nyanga Dam.

Around Nyanga Dam

The Nyanga National Park service centre focuses on the Nyanga Dam area, which also served as the location of the estate homestead. Indeed, Rhodes' stone cottage residence stands surrounded by English gardens and imported European hardwoods

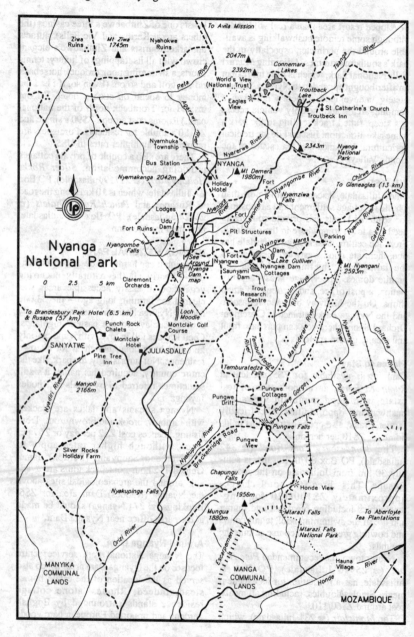

Nyanga National Park

0   2.5   5 km

Top: McIlwaine Recreational Park, Zimbabwe (TW)
Bottom: Chimanimani Mountains, Zimbabwe (DS)

Top: Nalatale Ruins, Zimbabwe (DS)
Left: Matobo National Park (DS)
Right: Mtarazi Falls, Mtarazi National Park (DS)

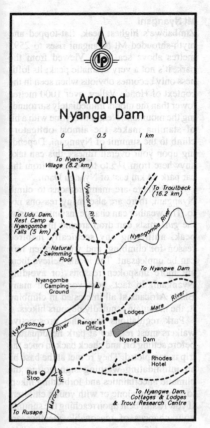

Around Nyanga Dam

0   0.5   1 km

To Nyanga Village (8.2 km)

To Troutbeck (16.2 km)

To Udu Dam, Rest Camp & Nyangombe Falls (5 km)

Nyanora River

Nyangombe River

Natural Swimming Pool

To Nyangwe Dam

Nyangombe Camping Ground

To Nyangwe Dam

Nyangombe River

Mare River

Lodges

Ranger's Office

Nyanga Dam

Rhodes Hotel

Bus Stop

Marora River

To Nyanga Dam, Cottages & Lodges & Trout Research Centre

To Rusape

beside the small artificial lake that bears his name. Near the lodges is the National Parks office (☎ 274 Nyanga), open 7 am to 6 pm daily.

Rhodes Museum The Rhodes Museum, which occupies Cecil Rhodes' old stables, is worth a good peruse. Although one would expect devotion to the coloniser himself, it does dedicate space to positive facets of Black African history; the struggles of the Second Chimurenga and its spirit-inspired elements and the good works of Zimbabwean war hero and philanthropist

Rekayi Tangwena. Then of course there are the obligatory Rhodes relics! The museum is open every day except Monday from 9 am to 1 pm and 2.30 to 5.30 pm; it's closed during the month of June.

Natural Swimming Pool Between the Nyanga Dam complex and the Nyangombe camping area is a natural wide spot below a cascade in the Nyangombe River. There's a sandy beach, unofficially known as Brighton Beach, a green lawn, changing rooms and bilharzia-free swimming for anyone prepared to brave the chill mountain water.

Pit Structures Although there are pit structures strewn haphazardly around the Nyanga landscape, the reconstructed pit structure near Nyanga Dam may help put the architecture into perspective. For comparison, also take a look at the similar but unrestored pit structure in a grove of trees behind the main pit. These particular sites have been dated back to the 1500s.

The most plausible explanation is that the dry stone-walled pits were used as corrals for small livestock: goats, sheep, pigs or small cattle. The entrances were through tunnels; the animals were kept in (and protected) by pales extending through the floor of the family hut, which was built on a level stone platform above the tunnel. Smaller stone platforms surrounding the pit were probably used as foundations for grain storage huts.

Chawomera Fort A nice morning hike from the Nyanga Dam area is to Chawomera Fort, about six km up the Nyangombe River; there's a well-defined path along the north bank. Alternatively, if you have a vehicle, the fort is more easily accessible from the Troutbeck road. Like Nyanga Fort, the Chawomera Fort is another of the series of lookouts that stretch across the Nyanga region. Although they resemble defence structures, it's more likely they served as simple lookouts.

Udu Dam Udu Dam, just over two km west of Nyanga Dam, lies at the bottom of a grassy valley. The lodges at Udu Dam are A-frame basha huts; visitors can swim in a convenient pool of the Udu River but if you're not a camp guest, you may attract suspicion if you wander through there. Rowboats may be hired for Z$2 per hour.

Both the Udu Valley and surrounding hills make for easy walking country and you'll be rewarded with a high incidence of unexcavated ancient ruins. There aren't any tracks so ask the parks personnel at the camp to direct you to the most interesting sites.

Nyangombe Falls Just outside the Nyanga Park boundary, the Nyangombe River tumbles white over terraced stacks and plunges into a steep, shallow gorge.

The falls are just a five km walk from the Nyangombe camping ground, two km from Udu Dam, with good mountain scenery all around. Wear strong, treaded shoes because the climb down from the car park, although short, is steep and slippery. The best views are had by following one of the several well-worn tracks to the right as you approach the river. Stay off the rocks near the falls, however, since the flowing water fosters the growth of moss which can be deadly slick.

Nyangwe (Mare) Dam Trout Research Centre At the Trout Research Centre near Nyangwe Dam one can learn from the experts about breeding and hatching rainbow and brown trout to stock Zimbabwe Rivers. They conduct free 15 minute tours of the site whenever there's interest.

Nyangwe Fort Although Nyangwe Fort and other hilltop enclosures have traditionally been ascribed to defence, closer scrutiny has revealed that implicit features in their structures would have precluded their use for that purpose.

The main enclosure, full of storage hut platforms and overgrown in places with aloes and msasa trees, is surrounded by five smaller fort-like enclosures. Nyangwe is just a two km walk from Nyangwe Dam along a very marginal yet motorable road.

Mt Nyangani

Zimbabwe's highest peak, flat-topped and myth-shrouded Mt Nyangani rises to 2593 metres above sea level. Viewed from the park, it's not a very dramatic peak; its loftiness only becomes obvious when seen in the context of Honde Valley, over 1000 metres lower than the moors immediately surrounding the mountain. Nearly everyone with a bit of stamina makes the almost obligatory climb to the summit of Nyangani. Depending upon your overall fitness, this can take anywhere from 1½ to three hours from the car park 14 km east of Nyanga Dam.

While there are many reasons to climb Nyangani, there are also many reasons not to. The weather can change instantaneously; the *guti* mists can drop around the marshy peak, nullifying any scenically inspired reason for climbing, and wind-driven rain can be unpleasant. The locals believe there are more unspoken reasons for avoiding Nyangani. In fact, you won't find many Black Africans at all interested in climbing it; the mountain reputedly devours hikers.

Park regulations state that prospective walkers must register at park headquarters before setting off and check back in once the trip is completed. They're met at the base by an intimidating warning sign noting the climatic uncertainties and forbidding hikers to venture up alone or with young children. If you're still bent upon reaching the summit, your chances of reasonable weather are increased if you set out as early as possible. Those without a vehicle should easily find a lift from the camping ground or park headquarters but should still be prepared to walk the 15 km if necessary.

Mt Nyangani to Honde Valley Walk

For a fairly easy – but not entirely straightforward – three or four day walk, you may want to consider the increasingly popular route from Mt Nyangani down into the Honde Valley, from where you can connect with a Mutare-bound bus.

From the car park at the base of Mt Nyangani, there's a southbound track skirting the base of the mountain. Once you've reached the summit of Mt Nyangani, either descend to the car park the way you came, then follow the track southward, or descend from the summit on the south-western slope of the mountain to strike the track approximately four km south of the car park.

About 12 km south of the car park, the track widens into a motorable road which, after 10 km of excellent views along the lip of the escarpment, descends into the upper reaches of Pungwe Gorge at Pungwe Drift. It would be unusual to run into anyone else along this lonely stretch.

Here are some recently rebuilt National Parks lodges which were destroyed during the Second Chimurenga and a one hour return side-trip to the top of 240 metre Pungwe Falls. The bilharzia-free eddies above the falls are good for swimming. Between Pungwe Drift and the falls are several possible camping sites with plenty of fresh water available from the hell-bound Pungwe River. The most favoured site is the sand bar near Pungwe Drift.

From Pungwe Drift, walk the road back up onto the escarpment and follow it all the way to the car park at Mtarazi Falls. There's not a lot of traffic but there are a couple of breaks along the way. The first is Pungwe View where a magnificent vista of the gorge, the falls and the now-distant Mt Nyangani opens up along a short detour from the main road. About four km beyond the Mtarazi Falls turnoff is Honde View, which offers a panorama of Honde Valley nearly 1000 metres below and the Mozambique frontier.

After three more downhill km, you'll arrive at the Mtarazi Falls car park from where it's less than a km along a footpath to a view of Mtarazi Falls, the second highest in Africa at 762 metres, as it plunges over the escarpment. Again, the best place to camp is along the river above the falls but campers should try to keep a low profile since it isn't officially sanctioned.

The steep nine km farmworkers' track – there are actually several tracks – over the escarpment and down into Honde Valley begins several hundred metres from the Mtarazi Falls car park. It's a little tricky to

find but the isolated car park attendant would probably welcome the opportunity to chat with visitors and offer direction. To meet with the Honde Valley road about one km above Hauna, take the right fork where the track branches on the way down.

Nyamziwa Falls

Nyamziwa Falls lies just over one km north of the northern loop road between Nyanga Dam and Mt Nyangani, an easily walkable five km from the latter. The upper part of these falls resembles an immense slippery slide. It's a great spot for a couple of hours relaxation on a sunny day, especially after a morning climb of Mt Nyangani.

Troutbeck

If you're not concerned about cash outlay, try the *Troutbeck Inn* (☎ 305 Nyanga), founded by Irishman Major Herbert McIlwaine at an altitude of 2000 metres. The food is 100% typically English – cream teas, Yorkshire puddings and game pies – with an atmosphere and the weather to match. Tradition has it that the log fire roaring in the main hall has been going since the hotel was founded in 1950! There's tennis, swimming, shooting, squash courts, a golf course, a private lake for trout fishing, lawn bowls and stables. Dinner, bed and breakfast are included in the prices which are around Z$100 per person.

If you're staying in Troutbeck, also have a look at the pretty Church of St Catherine-in-the-Downs in Troutbeck village.

World's View

World's View, atop the Troutbeck Massif, is 11 winding km up the mountain road from posh and prestigious Troutbeck Hotel. As its name implies, this national trust site affords a far-ranging view across northern Zimbabwe. Visitors must pay 25 cents upkeep fee to use the landscaped site's lawns and picnic facilities.

Since World's View is on nearly everyone's Nyanga itinerary, hitching shouldn't be a problem unless you go in June when the whole park seems to close down.

Buses from Nyamhuka township are so occasional that you'd have little hope of connecting with one. If you have time, it's possible to walk back to the main park road; a steep four km footpath winds down the massif scarp from World's View and meets the road north of Nyanga village.

Nyanga

Separated from the Nyamhuka township by a km of highway, Nyanga conspires to unsettle visitors with its manicured gardens and hedges, its village common, small library and stone church, all beneath the towering Troutbeck Massif. Brits may even feel pangs of nostalgia.

Besides the hotel, Nyanga has a petrol station, an excellent weaving cooperative, a small grocery store and a bottle store. Fresh vegetables are available from the gardener living behind the hotel.

Nyamhuka township, of an entirely separate character, is the terminal for the bus to and from Mutare, Rusape and Harare. When you've had enough nostalgia and are again longing for Africa, a visit to Nyamhuka should do the trick! There are a couple of shops and stalls selling inexpensive food and a more relaxed atmosphere than you're likely to find anywhere else in the Nyanga highlands.

Pungwe View & Pungwe Gorge

If you're driving or walking the back roads between Nyanga and Mtarazi Falls, stop at the Pungwe View turnoff and have a look down dramatic Pungwe Gorge, just inside the southern boundary of Nyanga National Park.

Coming from the Pungwe viewpoint, approximately four km along Scenic Rd north of Pungwe View is the turning down to Pungwe Drift and its recently restored lodges. Plan on at least an hour if you're walking from the viewpoint. From the Drift, it's an easy and pleasant half-hour walk downstream to some pools immediately above the falls.

Continuing north-east from Pungwe Drift, the track climbs back onto the moors. After

10 km or so, it deteriorates a bit and 12 km later connects with the Mt Nyangani car park. Those hiking the route from Mt Nyangani to Honde Valley will cross the Pungwe River at Pungwe Drift as a matter of course.

Places to Stay

Camping The National Parks' *Nyangombe Camping and Caravan Site* lies between the Nyangombe River and the highway. It's full of big piney woods, reminiscent of a US national park, and is very nice with hot showers, baths, braai pits and toilets. Tenting or caravanning costs Z$10 per site.

Camping in other areas of the park is officially prohibited and unofficially tolerated but be discreet about it. The park administration may find it difficult to imagine anyone wanting to engage in such activities as overnight hiking trips but they don't organise sting operations to reel in violators. Mt Nyangani is a special case; climbers are technically required to register at headquarters before making the trip but they're also expected back to sign out the same day. If you're climbing Nyangani en route to Pungwe Gorge, you'll have to forego the registration process and just lie as low as possible.

Lodges & Cottages Cosy National Parks lodges are available at Udu Dam, Nyanga Dam and Nyangwe Dam, all within a few km of the main park service area. At Nyangwe and Nyanga Dams, two-bedroom lodges rent for Z$40 per night; a one-bedroom one costs Z$20. At Udu Dam, they cost Z$50 or Z$40 for one room. At Pungwe Drift near the southern extreme of the park are two remote lodges which cost the same as those at Mare Dam and can also be booked through the park offices.

Near the head of Pungwe Gorge are the rudimentary *Brackenridge Cottages* (☎ 26321 Juliasdale). There are no shops or services nearby. When booking, enquire about what you'll need to bring from elsewhere.

Hotels The *Nyanga Holiday Hotel* (☎ 336 Nyanga), at the end of the road through Nyanga village, is a small and basic but friendly alternative to camping or to the stuffy Rhodes Nyanga Hotel in the park. The equally basic restaurant isn't bad and when it's cold outside, they'll let you curl up with your meal beside the log fire in the lounge. There's even a piano for anyone feeling musically inspired. Single/double rooms go for Z$60/90.

Outwardly, the one-star *Rhodes Nyanga Hotel* (☎ 377 Nyanga) near Nyanga Dam, with its tropical verandah and well-kept gardens, seems an appealing option. Its pretentious nature, however, provides perhaps a suitable tribute to its namesake, who once lived on the site. Budget travellers aren't particularly welcome in this staunchly colonial environment. If you can't be dissuaded, rooms with shared baths, including dinner, bed and breakfast, cost Z$50/90 for singles/doubles. With your own bath, you'll pay Z$60/100. Rondavels are also available for Z$90 a double. Breakfast buffets cost Z$8 per person. Like the associated museum, the hotel is closed during June.

For information on the *Troutbeck Inn*, which deserves separate treatment, refer to the discussion earlier in this section.

Places to Eat

Apart from the hotel dining rooms, there isn't much available in way of prepared food. The shop in Nyanga village and the market food stalls in Nyamhuka township provide options. For snacks, try *Nyamano Farm* at Troutbeck which sells fresh dairy and farm produce. To get there, take the road north of Troutbeck and turn left at the top of the hill past the 'jersey cow' sign, then turn left again at the signposted gate.

NORTH OF NYANGA

The highland areas north of Nyanga, which hold the greatest concentration of precolonial ruins in Zimbabwe, are for the most part accessible only by private vehicle. Since some of the best ruins lie only about 22 km from Nyanga village, walking would be

straightforward were the area traversed not used as a Frelimo guerrilla training zone. Permission to pass through must be arranged with BMATT (☎ 350), the British Military Advisory Training Team, at 3 Duiker Drive in Nyanga village.

Ziwa & Nyahokwe Ruins

The most extensive area of ruins is the Ziwa complex, sprawling sparsely over 80 sq km. Formerly known as Van Niekerk's Ruins, after the Boer who showed them to archaeologist Randall McIver in 1905, they are now called after 1745 metre Ziwa Mountain (in turn named after Sa Ziwa, a Karanga chief from the last century) which rises in their midst.

The parallel walls, housing platforms, agricultural terraces, circular enclosures, pit corrals and the disjointed rubble that litters the intermediate ground are thought to be evidence of a Karanga agricultural community, everyday farmers closely associated for defence purposes. With the exception of some excavation of artefacts, these post-Great Zimbabwe ruins have remained pretty much as their inhabitants left them. Stone seats and built-in grinding niches are in evidence.

Getting There & Away

As mentioned previously, BMATT permission will be necessary to reach Ziwa Ruins by the shortest route, the road turning west from the main road between the Troutbeck turnoff and Nyanga village (see the Nyanga map). The other option is to continue 14 km north of Nyanga village along the main road and turn west. After five km, you'll come to the turnoff for Nyahokwe ruins (which lie one km north). From there, it's 13 more km to Ziwa. If you have a few days, it's possible to walk but hitching will be nigh unto hopeless.

MTARAZI FALLS NATIONAL PARK

Tiny Mtarazi Falls National Park lies just south of Nyanga National Park and is, for practical purposes, a part of the same entity.

The central attraction, 762 metre Mtarazi

Falls, is little more than a trickle of water that reaches the lip of the escarpment and non-chalantly plummets over the edge, passing out of sight in long cascades through the forest below.

From the main Mutare-Nyanga route, take the Honde Valley turnoff, bearing left onto Scenic Road after two km or so. The right turning to the falls will be 16 occasionally rough km from there. Follow that road for seven km to the car park, from which it's a one km or so walk down through intermittent forest and grass to the most spectacular vantage points.

Although hitching won't be impossible, be prepared for long waits and keep in mind that most drivers visit Mtarazi Falls as an obligatory stop on their Nyanga tour. For more information, check out the description of the Mt Nyangani to Honde Valley walk in the Nyanga National Park section.

Honde View

Drivers along the road toward Mtarazi Falls aren't normally aware of the sharp escarpment that drops off to their left. Then they pull off at Honde View, scramble over the rocks to the edge and receive a dramatic awakening when they behold a patchwork of agricultural patterns in the broad Honde Valley below.

HONDE VALLEY

A favourite of MNR raiders, the picturesque Honde Valley sits vulnerably estranged from the rest of Zimbabwe by the Nyanga Mountains. This low-lying and well-watered basin, a world apart from the cool highlands immediately west, is ideal for growing coffee, tea and tropical fruit.

With a private vehicle, it's possible to visit the Aberfoyle Tea Estates where the majority of Zimbabwe's export tea is grown. There's a good road which turns off 27 km south of Juliasdale, winding and twisting through pine forests for 30 km until it drops off the escarpment into the valley. From near Hauna village there are views and difficult foot access to the bottom of Mtarazi Falls. The tea estates, where you can find accommodation

at *Aberfoyle Country Club*, lie another 30 km north-east of Hauna.

From Sakubva musika in Mutare, buses depart daily for Hauna in Honde Valley in the morning but won't take you as far as the tea estates.

VUMBA MOUNTAINS

The Vumba Mountains 28 km south-east of Mutare are characterised by cool, forested highlands alternating with deep, almost jungled valleys. In Manyika, the name Vumba (or Bvumba as it will be preferably spelt in the near future) means simply 'mist' and chances are you'll have the opportunity to determine the name's validity.

Altar Site Ruins

A few km south-east of Mutare just north off the Vumba road is a small archaeological site amid msasa trees. Although there's not much left of Altar Site ruin, excavators speculate that it may have once served as a provincial capital of the Great Zimbabwe state sometime around 1450.

Vumba & Bunga National Botanical Reserves

The Vumba and Bunga Botanical reserves are two small protected enclaves just over 30 km from Mutare in the Vumba Mountains. The loosely defined Bunga Botanical Reserve, which offers no facilities, contains 39 hectares straddling the Vumba road.

Until the 1950s, the Vumba section was the very English private estate of former Mutare mayor Fred Taylor, and was known as Manchester Gardens. It consists of 200 hectares of sloping ground, 30 hectares of which are beautifully manicured and well-maintained as Botanical Gardens. The remaining 170 hectares is unspoilt indigenous bushland, embodied in the Vumba Botanical Reserve.

From the gardens, where one finds an international sampling of botanical wonders as well as the obligatory teahouse and wide lawns, there are far-ranging views over the hills to the tropical lowlands of Mozambique

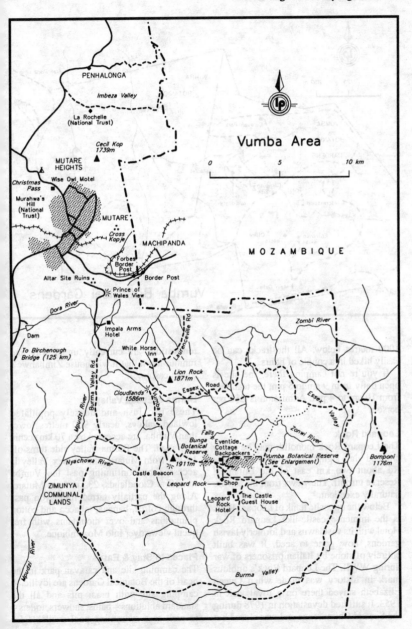

Vumba Area

0   5   10 km

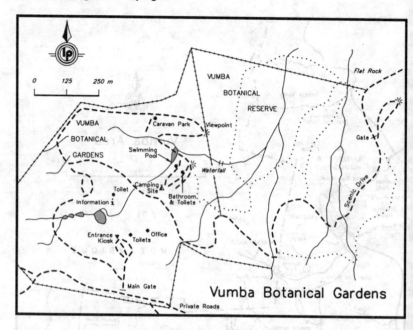

Vumba Botanical Gardens

1000 metres below. All the tracks can be easily hiked in a couple of hours.

If you're not camping there, the site is open daily from 9 am to 5 pm; the teahouse from 10 am to 4 pm. Admission is Z$1 per person.

Leopard Rock

The Leopard Rock monolith may be easily climbed via a signposted track from Vumba Rd about two km east of the Botanical Reserve turnoff. The views from the top are naturally excellent.

Below the opposite flank of Leopard Rock is the immense castle-like Leopard Rock Hotel with its vast lawns and formerly lavish gardens, now gone to seed. It was built entirely of stone by Italian prisoners of war during WWII. The Leopard Rock's dubious mark in history was made when Queen Elizabeth stayed there on a royal visit in 1953. It suffered devastation in 1978 during the Second Chimurenga and was closed but renovations are currently under way and rumour has it that it will house Zimbabwe's fourth casino.

Burma & Essex Valleys

These two lush and densely populated lowland valleys, nearly 900 metres lower than Vumba, are accessed by a 70 km scenic loop road. The Burma Valley side turns off 12 km from Mutare while Essex Valley is accessed by continuing past the Vumba turnoff at Cloudlands, 23 km from Mutare. Along the partially tarred route you pass through coffee, banana, tobacco and cotton plantations and over mountains with frequent views over into Mozambique.

Places to Stay & Eat

The camping site and caravan park in the heart of the Botanical Gardens are idyllic. A camping site with braai pits and all the standard ablutions – baths, showers, toilets – as well as a swimming pool available for guests' use will cost only Z$10 per night for up to six occupants. It's one of those places most people would be happy to disappear for a few days so if you have a tent, this is your opportunity.

Vumba's only budget accommodation, *Eventide Cottages* alias *The Backpackers* – because the sign out front reads 'Accommodation for Backpackers' – would be worthwhile even if it weren't in the heart of the misty mountains just 20 minutes walk from the Vumba Botanical Reserve. Cooking facilities are provided and there's a lovely and quiet garden area out the front. Dormitory-style beds cost Z$15 per person, including linen. The newest addition is a bungalow with four dormitory-style rooms and shared facilities for Z$10 per night. It's all topped off with a cosy fireplace and sunny patio area. The owner, Mr Peter Hancock, is a well-travelled conversationalist who is currently hoping to establish an organic ecosystem on the property and market the produce.

For self-caterers, there's a small shop which sells staples and basics about 2½ km from Eventide Cottages. Head east from the Vumba Botanical Garden turnoff and turn right at the next opportunity.

If you want something a bit more plush, there are several options. At any given time, you'll find about a dozen private cottages and guesthouses scattered across the region. The constantly changing list is available from the Manicaland Publicity Bureau in Mutare; they change so frequently it would be futile to list them here.

The exception is *The Castle* (☎ 210320) which is so impressive that it's become an eastern highlands institution. It's housed in a secluded hilltop castle at Leopard Rock just eight km from the Vumba Botanical Gardens. To secure a reservation, you must book well in advance. They accept only six guests per night, all of whom must be more or less in the same party since bathroom facilities are shared. The management spares nothing to provide a cosy and luxurious stay and all meals, home-cooked, are included. It's an ideal splurge if you can manage to squeeze in. Singles cost Z$105, doubles Z$180, but it's well worth it.

Another recommended doss is *Colombarg Guest Cottage* (☎ 64635) just 18 km from Mutare at the Essex Road turnoff. They have space for four people in one double and two bunks but you have to take your own food. The entire place rents for Z$40 per day with a minimum stay of two days.

Apart from the guesthouses, there are two hotels between Mutare and Vumba. Nearest town is the *Impala Arms* (☎ 60722), which is quite average and costs Z$60/95 for singles/doubles but its pub is a local favourite. The other, a posher place, is the *White Horse Inn* (☎ 60325) on Laurenceville Rd, known for its elegant dining room and excellent French cuisine. Nice dress is required. Single/double rooms cost Z$85/115.

BIRCHENOUGH BRIDGE

This 378-metre-long bridge over the braided Save River was designed by Ralph Freeman, who was also responsible for Sydney's 'Coat Hanger' (the Sydney Harbour Bridge). It was named after Sir Henry Birchenough, chairman of the Beit Trust which financed its construction in 1935, and whose ashes now lie in one of the bridge's towers. The strategic structure, which appears on Zimbabwe's 20 cent coin, is guarded day and night against Mozambican insurgency. Photography is prohibited from the span itself.

The bus terminal here is the connection point for services between Harare, Mutare, Chipinge, Chimanimani, Masvingo, and even Chiredzi and Beitbridge.

Places to Stay

Birchenough Bridge has a single hotel, the *Birchenough Bridge Hotel* (☎ 225819 Chipinge), where single/double rooms cost Z$40/78. It's pretty seedy but the staff is friendly and there's a nice little dining room but don't expect *haute cuisine*; try the sadza. There's no camping ground in town but the hotel will allow campers to set up on the lawn where they'll have a front row view of the bridge itself.

HOT SPRINGS

Hot Springs at Nyanyadzi, 32 km north of Birchenough Bridge, shouldn't be missed. Its beautiful and peaceful setting in the communal lands between the dry highlands and the Odzi River combines with a natural hot spring and swimming pool to make an ideal spot for a few days of relaxing. Fishing is available in the dam. Reduced to a heap of rubble during the war, the chalets, camping area and facilities are now being rebuilt and a more upmarket resort and small white-water rafting operation are planned for the river bank.

Camping or caravanning costs Z$10 per person including use of the hot springs. Chalets rent for Z$60 per night; day use costs Z$3 per person. There's a small shop and snack bar on the site and a restaurant is planned for the near future.

Bookings can be made by phoning 75270 Bulawayo. To reach Hot Springs without a vehicle, take any bus between Mutare and Birchenough Bridge. The resort is just 100 metres from the highway.

CHIMANIMANI

The name Chimanimani is derived from the Manyika name for a place that must be passed single file, presumably referring to the narrow gap where the Msapa River flows through the range between Zimbabwe and Mozambique, followed closely by a narrow footpath. The name has been enlarged to include the entire mountain range and since shortly after independence, the village as well.

Information

Although there's no tourist information office, the reception people at the Chimanimani Hotel distribute maps, brochures and local advertising and can help with your questions. At the cooperative shop opposite the post office you can pick up a Z$5 copy of the *Milkmaps Guide*, a pamphlet listing some hill-walking options around the village. Proceeds benefit the local health services.

Eland Sanctuary & Nyamzure

Although most visitors drive through the 18 square km eland sanctuary around the slopes of Nyamzure (more commonly known as Pork Pie Hill), the energetic will find it's a great place to spend a few hours exploring on foot.

The sanctuary was established to contain eland and other antelope who found it hard to resist young shoots of maize, coffee and pine saplings in the surrounding agricultural and timber lands. Tan-coloured eland are Africa's largest antelope, reaching heights of nearly two metres and weighing in at 600 kg. They share the sanctuary with duiker and klipspringer as well as waterbuck, baboons and zebra.

If you're walking from town, turn left at the T-junction just north of the post office then right at the first turning. Keep walking north from there five km to the car park at the base of Nyamzure (it isn't too difficult to work out how this hill came to be called Pork Pie; it looks almost edible). From the car park, you can follow the well-defined route to the summit, an altitude gain of only 120 metres, or wander at will over the hills and ridges back to the village.

Bridal Veil Falls

Bridal Veil Falls, a slender 50 metre drop on the Nyahodi River, is in a lush setting six km from Chimanimani. There's a rough and winding road leading in from Chimanimani village but it's also an easy and pleasant walk. Camping isn't officially permitted on the green lawns.

Follow the road from the village out of town past the two general stores, then six more km as it twists, climbs and descends around wooded slopes down to the parking area. To make a longer walk out of the trip, continue along the road two km past the falls until you reach a cattle grid. From there, turn left up the fence line to the ridge; there, turn left again along the southern boundary of the eland sanctuary and follow it for four km. Descend the ridge to the road, and turn left. This road will meet the Bridal Veil Falls road less than a km from Chimanimani Village.

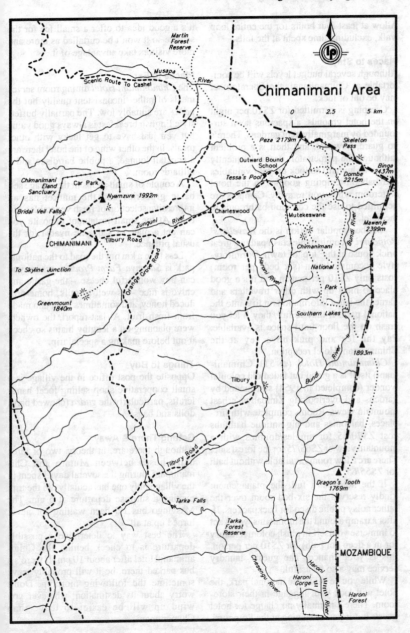

Chimanimani Area

Martin Forest Reserve

Scenic Route To Cashel

Musapa

River

Peza 2179m

Skeleton Pass

Outward Bound School

Tessa's Pool

Binga 2437m

Dombe 2215m

Chimanimani Eland Sanctuary

Car Park

Nyamzure 1992m

Charleswood

Mutekeswane

Mawenje 2399m

Bridal Veil Falls

Zunguni River

CHIMANIMANI

Tilbury Road

Chimanimani

To Skyline Junction

Orange Grove Road

Haroni River

National

Park

Greenmount 1840m

Bundi River

Southern Lakes

1893m

Tilbury

Bundi River

Tilbury Road

Dragon's Tooth 1769m

Tarka Falls

Tarka Forest Reserve

MOZAMBIQUE

Chesengu River

Haroni Gorge

Haroni River

Haroni Forest

0   2.5   5 km

Allow at least four hours for the entire loop walk, excluding time spent at the falls.

Places to Stay

Although several budget levels will be comfortable at Chimanimani, the Sheraton set may be out of luck.

Camping is permitted for Z$10 per night on the hotel grounds, a spacious lawn surrounded by marginally kept gardens. There's no guard, however, and theft is a problem (although the perpetrators are as frequently simian as human) so lock up your valuables and baboon-tempting goodies in the hotel storeroom while you're away. Campers are permitted to use the common bathrooms in the hotel.

Another popular option is the *Travellers' Potpourri*, a comfortable crash pad in a great brick house at the 'top' of town. Dormitory-style accommodation (six beds per room) costs only Z$10 per person and it's a good place to meet up with other travellers and garner the latest information on lifts into the national park. If they're full, they'll let you crash on the floor until space is available. Pay the fee and pick up a key at the Chimanimani Hotel reception.

Chimanimani Hotel (☎ 511 Chimanimani) itself is a grand but faded old colonial wonder (completed in 1954) surrounded by gardens and overlooking Zimbabwe's best mountain views. Rooms complete with fireplaces, balconies and big antique bathtubs cost Z$70/85 for singles/doubles with a mountain view or Z$65/75 for the forest side. There are a few rooms available without bath for Z$55/65.

If the hotel isn't full, the management kindly reserves the six-bed room over the rather noisy public disco for backpackers. If, after a tramp around the mountains, you want to immerse yourself in plush colonial luxury (or in a deep hot bath) for Z$10 per person, this is your chance. The guests' laundry service may also be useful.

While you're off in the national park, the hotel will lock your luggage in their storeroom. There's normally no charge for hotel guests but if you're staying at the Potpourri,

it's a good idea to offer a small fee for the service so it won't be curtailed as more and more visitors take advantage of it.

Places to Eat

The *Chimanimani Hotel* dining room serves meals of rather inconsistent quality but the prices are suitably low. The partially buffet-style English breakfast is always good value but you just have to get lucky with other meals. In the other wing of the hotel there are a cocktail lounge, a public bar/disco and a billiards room.

A couple of small shops in the village sell basic groceries and the market has an impressive selection of fresh vegetables and fruit. At the small restaurant opposite you can get a plate of sadza ne nyama for the usual pittance.

Less than a km out the road to the national park is *Saranya Farm Produce* where you can buy wonderful cheese – the garlic and chive is nice – as well as milk, home-produced honey, and sometimes even jam made from fresh fruit. At last report, the owners were planning on a lengthy hiatus so check it out before making a special trip.

Things to Buy

Opposite the post office in the village is a small cooperative shop selling local handicrafts, particularly the *gudza* (chewed bark) dolls and bags.

Getting There & Away

Although there are, in theory, two or three daily buses between Mutare and Chimanimani, during the several days I spent in the village only one bus actually did the trip, making a surprise departure at 5 am. The Masvingo bus I'd been waiting for never turned up at all.

The best way to determine a possible departure is to check behind the Chimanimani Hotel after about 10 pm. If there's a bus parked there, be it will probably leave sometime the following morning. Don't worry about its destination; wherever you wind up will be easier to leave than Chimanimani.

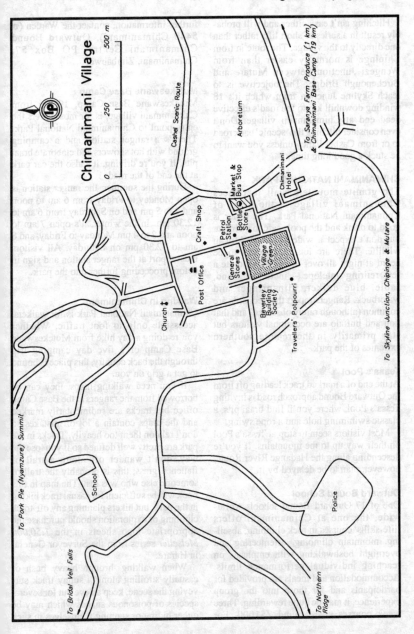

Chimanimani Village

0   250   500 m

To Saranga Farm Produce (1 km)
& Chimanimani Base Camp (19 km)

Cashel Scenic Route

Arboretum

Market &
Bus Stop

Chimanimani
Hotel

Craft Shop

Petrol
Station
Bottle
Store

General
Stores

Village
Green

Post Office

Beverley Building
Society

Church

Travellers' Potpourri

To Skyline Junction, Chipinge & Mutare

To Pork Pie (Nyamzure) Summit

School

Police

To Bridal Veil Falls

To Northern
Ridge

Hitching isn't easy either and will probably result in a series of short lifts rather than one directly to the village. The route in from Chipinge is normally easier than from Wengezi Junction between Mutare and Birchenough Bridge. The objective is to reach Skyline Junction from which it's 18 winding downhill km to the road's effective dead end at Chimanimani village. Don't even consider hitching the 'scenic' back road to or from Cashel Valley unless you want to be stuck a good long time.

CHIMANIMANI NATIONAL PARK
The granite mountain wall that faces Chimanimani village is the heart of Chimanimani National Park. The water is good to drink and the pools safe to swim in, but don't expect a wide range of African wildlife. There are lots of baboons to be heard at night all over the park and quite a few retiring antelope – including eland, sable, blue duiker, klipspringer and waterbuck. Rangers report that leopards are common (although rarely observed) and that lion and buffalo are occasional visitors but stay primarily in the remote southern extremes of the park.

Tessa's Pool
At the end of a marked track leading off from the Outward Bound approach road is inviting Tessa's Pool, where you'll find braai pits, a classic swimming hole and a rope swing.

Most visitors seem to stop at Tessa's Pool on their way up to the mountains. If you're descending along the Hadange River Route, however, plan to be delayed by it.

Outward Bound School
One of 17 Outward Bound schools worldwide, the one at Chimanimani offers 'life-skills' courses in rock climbing, abseiling, mountain climbing, orienteering and overnight bushwalking with emphasis on reaching individual performance limits. Accommodation and meals are provided for participants and for those into the group experience, it may be quite rewarding. Three week courses cost around Z$1000. For

further information, contact the Warden (☎ 5440 Chimanimani), Outward Bound Chimanimani Centre, PO Box 57, Chimanimani, Zimbabwe.

Mutekeswane Base Camp
Mutekeswane Base Camp, 19 km from Chimanimani village, is for most hikers the entry point to Chimanimani National Park. There's a ranger station and a camping ground with hot showers and elaborate braai pits. If you're driving, it's also the car park at the end of the road.

During the summer, the ranger station is open Monday to Friday from 6 am to noon and 2 to 5 pm and on Saturday from 6 am to 12.30 pm. In the winter, it's open 7 am to noon and 2 to 4 pm Monday to Friday, and 8 am to 12.30 pm on Saturday. All visitors must report at the ranger station and sign in before proceeding further into the park.

Walking in Chimanimani
Chimanimani National Park is for walkers, accessible only to foot traffic. Whether you're doing a day hike from Mutekeswane Base Camp or a five day camping trip through the back country, this place is bound to get a grip on you.

If you need walking maps, they can be borrowed from the rangers at the Base Camp office but tracks are rudimentarily marked and the maps contain a lot of mistakes so don't rely on them too heavily. Tracks in the park are pretty well defined so if you lose the way, don't wander off along a trail of flattened grass; this is probably the trail of someone else who was lost. The map in this book will be sufficient for casual track hiking in the park, but hikers planning any off-track climbing or exploration should purchase the appropriate topo sheets in the *1:50,000 Melsetter* series from the Surveyor General in Harare.

When walking through heavy bush or casually strolling along a sunny track surveying the scene, keep an eye out for several species of poisonous snakes which may be either hiding or sunning themselves in such

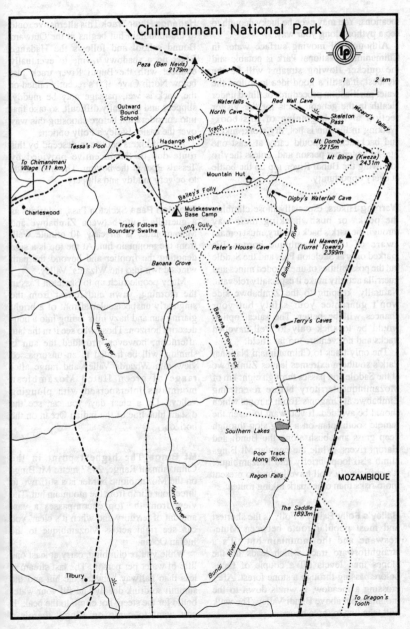

Chimanimani National Park

0   1   2 km

Peza (Ben Nevis)
2179m

Outward
Bound
School

Waterfalls

North Cave

Red Wall Cave

Skeleton
Pass

Wizard's Valley

Tessa's Pool

Hadange River
Track

To Chimanimani
Village (11 km)

Mountain Hut

Mt Dombe
2215m

Mt Binga (Kweza)
2431m

Charleswood

Bailey's Folly

Digby's Waterfall Cave

Mutekeswane
Base Camp

Track Follows
Boundary Swathe

Long Gully

Peter's House Cave

Mt Mawenje
(Turret Towers)
2399m

Banana Grove

Bundi River

Terry's Caves

Haroni River

Banana Grove Track

Southern Lakes

Poor Track
Along River

Ragon Falls

MOZAMBIQUE

Haroni River

The Saddle
1893m

Bundi River

Tilbury

To Dragon's
Tooth

locations. You may even be lucky enough to see a python along your way.

Although all moving surface water in Chimanimani National Park is potable and the quicker flowing streams will be the cleanest, it's still a good idea to follow the water purification procedures outlined under Health in the general Facts for the Visitor section at the beginning of this book. Walking in the sun is hot, dry work; hikers and backpackers should carry at least one litre of water per person and, unless they're following the Bundi River, top up the bottle at every opportunity.

Warning Hikers, especially those climbing the peaks or bushwhacking their way through the park's back country, must remain aware of the Mozambique border. It's marked only at Skeleton Pass and the Saddle but the possibilities of unexploded mines and guerrilla activity make it especially relevant. Naturally, keeping to the Zimbabwe side won't guarantee your safety but your chances will be better. The safest option would be to stick only to well-travelled tracks and not venture too far afield.

The only track to Chimanimani National Park's southern extremes leaves Zimbabwe at the Saddle and passes through eight km of Mozambique territory before re-entering Zimbabwe at Dragon's Tooth, a route which should be avoided. If you want to reach the remote south, plan on a long slog through deep grass and bush along the Bundi and Haroni rivers. While the popular Mt Binga climb also loops briefly into Mozambique, it's sufficiently well travelled not to present more risks than other park hiking routes.

Bailey's Folly Bailey's Folly is the shortest and most popular route between Mute-keswane and the mountain hut. It's a straightforward track which leads up the slopes then levels off a couple of times before passing through a stone forest. After crossing a meadow, it winds down to the mountain hut above Bundi Valley. The walk will take two to three hours.

Hadange River Track This alternative route to the mountain hut begins at the Outward Bound school and follows the Hadange River up a shadowy ravine to eventually connect with the Bundi River track just below North Cave. If it's recently rained or the track is wet, passage may be muddy, slippery and generally difficult, so take that into consideration before choosing this way over the easier Bailey's Folly option.

A lot of hikers choose to descend by this route due to the incentive provided by Tessa's Pool at the bottom. The track tends to be very muddy and slippery.

Skeleton Pass Skeleton Pass, notorious as a guerrilla route between Zimbabwe and Mozambique, is an easy 40 minute walk from the mountain hut. At the top is a sign denoting the frontier and beyond the path winds down into the Wizards' Valley.

Many people ruch up to Skeleton Pass in the morning, yawn and retreat from the singularly unspectacular affront of a bright glaring sun and hazy hills fading into a non-descript horizon. Those who see it in the late afternoon, however, provided the sun is shining, will be treated to an unsurpassed view into Wizards Valley and range after range of green fluted Mozambican mountains interspersed with plunging valleys. On a clear day, you can see the distant blue line of the Indian Ocean on the horizon.

Mt Binga The highest point in the Chimanimani Range, 2437 metre Mt Binga on the Mozambique border is a stiff two to three hour climb from the mountain hut. The view from the top encompasses a vast amount of territory and when it's clear, you can see right across Mozambique to the Indian Ocean.

While you're climbing, carry at least one litre of water per person. The last stream is less than halfway between the hut and the summit so drink deeply and fill your water bottle for the steep, hot climb to the peak. If you want to camp on Binga, there's a reasonably level site 150 to 200 metres below the peak but no water is available.

Southern Lakes Little more than wide spots in a U-turn bend of the Bundi River, the murky pools known as Southern Lakes provide a nice lunch spot or, if you have a tent, a passable camping site. The obvious mountain rising to the east is Mt Mawenje, formerly known as Turret Towers.

From Southern Lakes, another track heads south-east toward the Saddle. Following the river another four km south along a not-so-clear track, you'll come to Ragon Falls. It's not a bad day trip from Southern Lakes but nothing terribly exciting.

The Saddle The Saddle, at 1893 metres, is another pass into Mozambique. To get there, cross the Bundi River between the first and second Southern Lakes and walk north along the river until you reach a steep track leading up the slope. From there, it's about an hour to the top.

Banana Grove The Banana Grove Track is named for the banana-like strelitzia trees that grow along it as well as the hillside banana plantation half an hour's walk from trail's end at base camp. It's a gentler ascent than the more popular Bailey's Folly, but is also a longer route to the mountain hut so this track is most often used by hikers returning to base camp from the hut via Southern Lakes.

To connect with it from Mutekeswane, descend steeply from the south side of the road about 250 metres west of the ranger station. At the bottom, you'll cross a small and disagreeable swamp then follow the up-and-down fire swathe to a place known as Dead Cow, where the track turns sharply to the left and winds upward through a rocky ravine to the first level of peaks. From there, it's just a matter of following the downward-trending track into the Bundi Valley at the northernmost Southern Lake. Allow about five hours for this hike.

Heading for Mutekeswane Base Camp from the mountain hut, watch carefully on your right as you approach the first Southern Lake or you'll miss the red-earth track that climbs steeply about 30 metres above the main river route before levelling off. Allow seven to nine hours for the walk from the mountain hut back to Mutekeswane via Southern Lakes and Banana Grove.

Places to Stay
Unless they have a vehicle or are very lucky with a lift to Mutekeswane Base Camp, most people entering Chimanimani National Park will spend their first night camping at Base Camp, where the rise is so steep the camping sites are on stone-walled terraces in the hillside. From there you'll have great vistas of nearby forested hills and the red-earth coffee plantations beyond. Amazingly, hot baths and showers are available (although there's no electricity in the ablutions block so take your own light!). Overnight charges of Z$10 per night are payable at the Mutekeswane Ranger Station.

Unless you're keen to really get away from people, there's no need to carry a tent through the park. Over the first range of peaks a two to three-hour hike from base camp is the Bundi Valley which is overlooked by a classic stone mountain hut complete with wooden bed bases, propane cooking rings (but not cutlery or cooking implements) and cold showers. The hut will comfortably sleep 20 to 30 people but only at weekends and holidays will there ever be that many around. An attendant lives just over the rise from the hut and comes around nightly to chat and collect the Z$3 fee from each visitor.

Alternatively, the Bundi Valley is riddled with small caves and rock overhangs ideal for camping. The nicest and most accessible ones are near the northern end of the valley. North Cave, a 30 minute walk from the mountain hut, overlooks the waterfall and affords a great view out the entrance to the highest peaks. At the top of the waterfall is a pool good for a swim and Red Wall Cave is a 10 minute walk further along. If you plan to camp in either of these, get an early start from base camp since they are the first to be occupied.

A similar distance down the valley from the hut is Digby's Waterfall Cave, where the river provides a swimming hole, and beyond that, there is Peter's House Cave. Still further along, perhaps one km north of Southern Lakes and at least a two hour walk from the hut, is Terry's Cave which is divided into two rooms by an artificial stone wall. It's on the eastern side of the river and not easy to find but there is a faint track leading to it from the river.

Getting There & Away

It seems only a matter of time before some enterprising individual with a ute (utility truck) realises the transport gap between Chimanimani village and the Mutekeswane Base Camp and sets up a shuttle service. Currently, however, those without a private vehicle should resign themselves to the 19 km road walk to Mutekeswane. It's not an unpleasant prospect but will take a day in either direction.

Set out from Chimanimani village along the Tilbury road for nine km to Charleswood. There, turn left at the coffee plantation and immediately take the right fork. After five km, you'll come to the Outward Bound/Tessa's Pool turnoff. From there, it's a further five km to Mutekeswane.

Some get lucky with hitching – your best chances will be on an army, National Parks or agricultural school vehicle or on a tractor with local farmers. If you're in a hurry, enquire at the Chimanimani Hotel. They're sometimes aware of government workers or guests who may be headed that way.

Don't believe rumours of a regular bus going as far as Charleswood. It's far more the exception than the rule.

CHIPINGE

Named after a local chief, Chipinge lies in the heart of a rich agricultural district. Dairying is important but the real wealth of the town comes from export coffee and tea plantations. There's a coffee research institute just off the Mt Selinda road as well

as wattle extraction and logging activities on the surrounding hillsides. Many of the local commercial farmers are of Afrikaner heritage, descendants of the Boers who arrived with the Moodie Trek.

Places to Stay & Eat

The *Chipinge Hotel* (☎ 2226 Chipinge) has certainly seen better times but unless you're set up for camping, it's your only option. Singles/doubles with attached bath will cost Z\$40/80, without bath Z\$35/70. The hotel restaurant is pretty average but again, there isn't much choice unless you'd like to take advantage of the market snacks, the supermarkets or the *Busi-Grill* snack bar.

The camping ground beside the river about 500 metres west of town is in a secluded spot away from the confusion of the centre.

Getting There & Away

Chipinge is really nothing to go out of your way for but it is the gateway to the Mt Selinda area and hitchhikers to or from Chimanimani are often stuck there. The bus terminal at market square three blocks east of the main street serves Birchenough Bridge, the lowveld, adjoining communal lands and, occasionally, Chimanimani. There are also three or four buses daily to both Mutare and Masvingo and frequent service to nearby Mt Selinda.

MT SELINDA

The village of Mt Selinda sits in a hollow on a hilltop above the Chipinge district coffee plantations. It's centred around a health mission founded by the American Board of Commissioners in 1893 and developed over the years into a vocational and agricultural training centre. If you like monuments, Swynnerton's Memorial is just north of the road into the village. It commemorates the work of the 19th century British naturalist and entomologist who settled in Melsetter (Chimanimani) to catalogue local bugs and flora.

Chirinda Forest Botanical Reserve

Similar to the Vumba but further off the trodden track is the Chirinda Forest Botanical Reserve, a 949 hectare slice of tropical hardwood forest. There are lots of tracks into the forest but the Big Tree route, an obvious track off the Mt Selinda road just up the 'tree tunnel' from the mission hospital, is the most popular. The Big Tree is claimed to be Zimbabwe's biggest tree, a 1000 year old, 66 metre high and 15 metre round behemoth of the species *khaya nyasica* or red mahogany. Stands of both red and forest mahogany, ironwood and other large trees are found throughout the forest reserve, particularly along the walking route known as Valley of the Giants.

There are no amenities or camping facilities at the forest reserve but in a pinch, campers could easily melt into the trees without detection; remember to take water.

Getting There & Away

From Chipinge, frequent but unscheduled buses do the 30 km run to and from Mt Selinda but hitching is a better option. The road may be sparsely travelled but since Mt Selinda sits at the end of the line (the road continues into Mozambique but the border is closed), everyone will know where you're going. If they're charging, agree on a fee before climbing aboard.

The Midlands & South-Eastern Zimbabwe

With the exception of Great Zimbabwe, the Midlands and south-eastern Zimbabwe aren't endowed with any overwhelmingly scenic or interesting sites. If you're on a rushed tour through the country, you probably won't want to linger in the area. For those with more time, however, there are some interesting places to be discovered and the sort of person that seeks out areas regarded by the tourist industry as dull and uninteresting will have the opportunity to live it up.

MANYAME DAM RECREATIONAL PARK

Just 40 km west of Harare, the nine sq km Manyame Dam (formerly known as Darwendale-Lake Robertson) National Recreational Park provides some of the most productive and diverse fishing in Zimbabwe, offering five species of bream, tiger fish, Hunyani salmon and more. Fishing permits are available from the National Parks Central Booking Office in Harare. The dam was constructed in 1976 to supply water to the capital.

There are picnic areas and camping sites with braai pits, hot water and all facilities. Camping sites cost Z$10 per party of up to six people. While there is no public transport to the dam you can get to Darwendale or Norton on buses from Harare and try to hitch but prospects aren't good except at weekends and holidays.

KADOMA

The name of this small town means 'silent' in Ndebele. It was founded in 1906 as a magnesite, nickel, copper and gold-mining town but the emphasis today is on Zimbabwe's cotton textile industry. With a population of 50,000, Kadoma boasts weaving, spinning and dyeing mills as well as a cotton research institute and a textiles training facility.

There isn't much to keep tourists busy

although the colonial architecture in the centre is nice enough and worth a look if you're in town anyway.

Places to Stay

Kadoma is proud of its three-star *Kadoma Ranch Motel* (☎ 2321, fax 2325 Kadoma), situated 'in the heart of Zimbabwe' on the Harare-Bulawayo road. Single/double rooms including breakfast cost approximately Z$70/90.

On Union St in the centre is the cheaper but still pleasant one-star *Speck's Hotel* (☎ 3302 Kadoma). The *Grand Hotel* (☎ 4035 Kadoma) on Herbert Chitepo St at the square doubles as a brothel.

SEBAKWE & NGEZI NATIONAL RECREATION AREAS

These twin dams in central Zimbabwe between the Harare-Masvingo and Harare-Bulawayo roads are primarily of interest to the fishing crowd. Unlike the more popular dams nearer Harare, however, they see very few visitors. Visitors should be warned that both dams are bilharzia breeding grounds so swimming is clearly not recommended.

The dam wall is being increased in height by seven metres. Once the new lake level is reached, Sebakwe Dam will be the fourth largest lake in the country. Until work is complete, Sebakwe will be open for day use only. Entry costs Z$1 per person per day. Sebakwe lies 10 km from the Kwe Kwe-Mvuma road; the turnoff is 18 km east of Kwe Kwe.

Ngezi, about 70 indirect highway km north of Sebakwe, is the larger of the two parks and quite a long way from anywhere – 90 km by road west of Chivhu and 93 km east of Kwe Kwe. Developed camping and caravan sites are available for Z$12 per site, accommodating up to six people. Lodges with space for four may be rented for Z$40

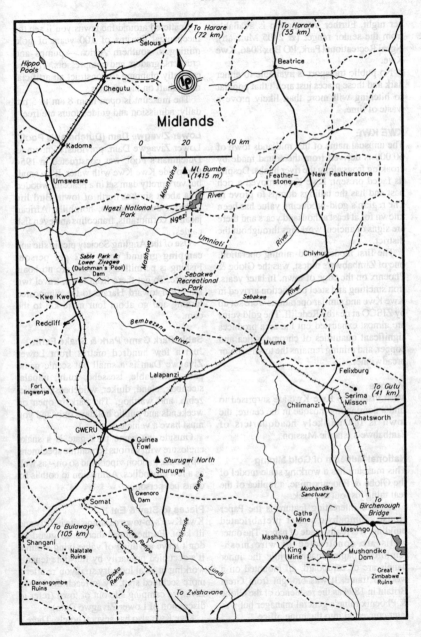

Midlands

0   20   40 km

To Harare
(72 km)

To Harare
(55 km)

Selous

Beatrice

Hippo
Pools

Chegutu

Kadoma

Umsweswe

Mt Bumbe
(1415 m)

Featherstone

New Featherstone

Mashavo Mountains

Ngezi River

Ngezi National
Park

Ngezi

Umniati River

Chivhu

Sable Park &
Lower Zivagwe
(Dutchman's Pool)
Dam

Sebakwe
Recreational
Park

Sebakwe River

Kwe Kwe

Redcliff

Bembezana River

Mvuma

Fort
Ingwenya

Lalapanzi

Felixburg

To Gutu
(41 km)

Serima
Misson

Chilimanzi

Chatsworth

GWERU

Guinea
Fowl

Shurugwi North

Shurugwi

Chironde Range

Longwe Range

Mushandike
Sanctuary

To
Birchenough
Bridge

Somat

Gwenoro
Dam

Gaths
Mine

Ghoko Range

Mashava

Masvingo

To Bulawayo
(105 km)

Shangani

Nalatale
Ruins

King
Mine

Mushandike
Dam

Danangombe
Ruins

Lundi

To Zvishavane

Great
Zimbabwe
Ruins

per night. Further information is available from the senior ranger (☎ 2405 Munyati), Ngezi Recreational Park, PO Box 8046, Kwe Kwe.

No public transport is available to either park and these places just aren't that popular so hitching will more than likely prove a waste of time.

KWE KWE

The unusual name of this midlands town of 60,000 is derived from the sound made by croaking frogs along the river banks. Despite its faded present, Kwe Kwe enjoyed a rich past and has the tailings dumps to prove it. The region's gold-producing value has been known for at least a thousand years and there are signs of ancient workings throughout the district.

The first modern gold-mining operation, one of Zimbabwe's oldest, was the Globe & Phoenix on the edge of town. In later years, iron smelting and steel production arrived in Kwe Kwe and similar operations were set up by ZISCO at nearby Redcliff. The gold veins are almost exhausted but the area produces significant quantities of chrome, silica and copper, and mining remains the town's major breadwinner.

Mosque

Most visitors to Kwe Kwe are surprised to find a dominating mosque in the centre; the town is the unlikely headquarters of Zimbabwe's Islamic Mission.

National Museum of Gold Mining

This museum has a working scale model of the Globe & Phoenix mine, a replica of the real thing just out the back.

Another interesting feature is the Paper House, Zimbabwe's first prefabricated building. It is really made of paper. The outer walls are constructed of wire mesh-reinforced papier mâché while the inner panels are of cardboard, all mounted on a wooden frame. It was brought from Great Britain in 1894 as the residence of the Globe & Phoenix mine's general manager but was later converted into the mine office.

Scattered around the lawns you'll see the mechanical detritus of 100 years of gold mining in southern Africa – pumps and crushers, graders and compressors. They're currently planning to construct an artificial mine shaft on the grounds.

The museum is open from 8 am to 5 pm daily; admission and guided tours are free.

Lower Zivagwe Dam (Dutchman's Pool)

Lower Zivagwe Dam, previously known as Dutchman's Pool, was constructed in 1954 to provide Kwe Kwe with water. It's a small but very pretty dam set in a peaceful wooded area about six km north of town. Bird life includes ducks, herons, hornbills, African jacanas, cormorants, francolins and even fish eagles.

Use of the Angling Society picnic site and camping ground costs Z$2 per person. Fishing is permitted but there are no boats for hire. To get there from town, travel two km north toward Harare to the signposted turning and go about four more km to the dam.

Sable Park Game Park & Snake Farm

Just a few hundred metres from Lower Zivagwe Dam is a small but scenic game park with sable, tsessebe, kudu, impala, steenbok, eland, duiker, wildebeest, dassie, zebra, and warthog. The park is open on weekends and public holidays only and you must have a vehicle.

Outside the game park gate is a snake enclosure with various serpentine specimens – pythons, gaboon vipers and so on – as well as a few crocodiles. Admission to both is 65 cents per person.

Places to Stay & Eat

Kwe Kwe's in-town camping site is dirty and ill kept. Furthermore, there's no guard so don't leave anything of value lying around. It's occupied primarily by full-time tenants working in local industry so if you're after a more secluded spot, try to reach the Lower Zivagwe camping site out of town (refer to discussion of Lower Zivagwe Dam).

Kwe Kwe also has several hotels. There's

nothing really outstanding value-wise but they'll do in a pinch. The three-star *Golden Mile Motel* (☎ 3711 Kwe Kwe) is the most popular of the lot. Singles/doubles cost about Z$60/80, without breakfast. Alternatively, the *Shamwari Hotel* (☎ 2387 Kwe Kwe), on First St in the centre, is a bit cheaper but it is only one-star. Next down the scale is the similarly one-star *Sebakwe Machipisa Hotel* (☎ 2981 Kwe Kwe), also in the centre. The *Phoenix Hotel* (☎ 3748 Kwe Kwe) on Second St is the local bottom end in just about every way.

Getting There & Away

The Ajay and Express coach terminal is at the Golden Mile Motel, two km south of town on the Bulawayo road. Other bus services operate from the market.

Trains between Harare and Bulawayo pass through Kwe Kwe daily at 2.27 am and 12.34 pm northbound and at 1.21 and 11.39 am southbound. The nearest air services are at Gweru, 62 km south.

GWERU

Gweru, Zimbabwe's third-largest city with 105,000 residents, isn't a travellers' destination but almost everyone on the overland circuit of Zimbabwe will pass through it at some stage and comment on its friendly small-town feel. The original name, Gwelo, was believed to mean 'steep' in the vernacular, possibly in reference to the sloping banks of the Gweru River. Growth began in earnest in 1902 with the arrival of the Harare-Bulawayo railway line. On 18 June 1914, the settlement gained municipal status but Gweru didn't become an official city until October 1971.

Information

Tourist Office You'll find the Gweru Publicity Bureau (☎ 2226 Gweru) in the town hall at the corner of Eighth St and Robert Mugabe Way. It's open from 8 am to 4.30 pm Monday to Friday. Although limited printed matter is available, the staff are friendly and happy to answer specific questions.

Travel Agency American Express is represented in Gweru by Manica Travel (☎ 3316) at Meikles on the corner of Robert Mugabe Way and Fifth St.

Midlands Museum

The Midlands Museum near the corner of Eleventh St and Lobengula Ave is primarily dedicated to the evolution of military and police history and technology in the country from the earliest tribal warfare through the Rhodesian years and to modern Zimbabwe. Given only that description, it's safe to say most travellers would be inclined to give it a miss but it's not as bad as it sounds. In fact, as museums go, it's quite informative. Of particular interest are the descriptions of pre-colonial weapons and warfare, and the displays of military and police uniforms from way back. The aviation exhibits are being expanded into a national aviation museum.

The museum is open from 8 am to 5 pm daily. Admission is 20 cents.

Stock Exchange

On Main St between Robert Mugabe Way and Leopold Takawira Ave is the colonial-style Stock Exchange. Constructed in 1898, it is Gweru's oldest building. While you're in the neighbourhood, have a look at the Boggie Memorial Clock Tower, which can't be missed since it blocks Gweru's two main streets.

Antelope Game Park

The zoo-like antelope game park nine km from Gweru is a small enclave containing most of the antelope species present in Zimbabwe as well as giraffe, zebra and other game. Large cats are kept in a separate enclosure.

The only way to get there is by private vehicle. Head out the road toward Bulawayo (Robert Mugabe Way). Turn right on Tratford Rd at the Fairmile Motel, then left on Bristol Rd and follow it out of town through Mkoba township. The park is open from 10 am to 5 pm daily, with feeding at 3 pm. Admission costs Z$2.50 per person.

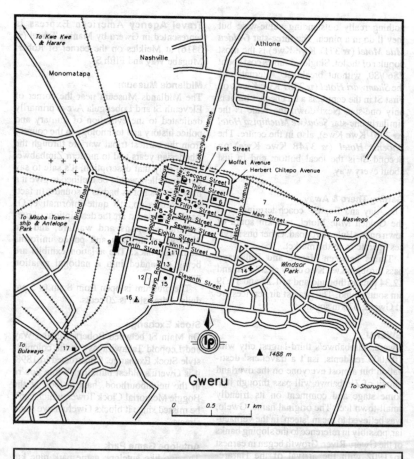

Gweru

0   0.5   1 km

1488 m

1   Bus Terminus
2   Midlands Hotel
3   Stock Exchange Building
4   Boggie Memorial Clock
    Tower
5   Police Station
6   Chitukuko Hotel
7   Showgrounds
8   Post Office
9   Railway Station
10 Granny's Restaurant
11 Town Hall & Tourist
    Office
    (Publicity Association)
12 Gweru Sports Club
13 Military Museum
14 Hospital
15 Swimming Pool
16 Caravan Park
17 Fairmile Motel

Places to Stay

Gweru's small and green camping ground and caravan park fronts up to the sports complex about 500 metres from the centre out on the Bulawayo road . They're currently in the process of building chalets on the site.

The amorphous *Midlands Hotel* (☎ 2581 Gweru) is primarily a business travellers' doss. Residents pay Z$88.40/144.80 for singles/doubles. Nonresidents, who must pay in foreign currency, are charged US$57/94.

Highway travellers caught by darkness in Gweru may prefer the *Fairmile Motel* (☎ 2581) out on the Bulawayo road which, although it enjoys the same three-star rating as the Midlands, manages to avoid the characterless pretences to luxury.

The arm-benders' venue in Gweru is the *Chitukuko Hotel* (☎ 2861) at the corner of Third St and Moffat Rd which charges around Z$45/60 for single/double rooms. As you'd expect, things can get noisy at times.

Places to Eat
Gweru has a couple of fast-food-type diners catering specifically to travellers on their way through quickly, including *The Dutch Oven* on Fifth St and *Granny's* at the Shell petrol station on the corner of Tenth St and Robert Mugabe Way. *Kollou's* serves below average African and greasy fare but their attached bakery is good. The *Polar Milk Bar* on Main St is good for quick snacks and the *Chicken Inn* at the corner of Sixth St and Robert Mugabe Way is like all Chicken Inns, with billiard tables, chicken and chips.

Entertainment
Apart from the cinema offerings and infrequent visiting performances at Gweru's flashy theatre, the Midlands Hotel's Dandaro Bar and disco, with occasional live bands at weekends, is about the extent of Gweru's entertainment scene.

If that doesn't excite you, head over to the swimming pool near the Midlands Museum for a relaxing swim. It's closed on Mondays and during the winter. Hours are 10 am to 2 pm and 3 to 6 pm Tuesday to Friday. On weekends, it's open 10 am to 12.30 pm and 2.30 to 6 pm.

Getting There & Away
The Kudzenai long-distance bus terminal is near the market on Robert Mugabe Way between Second and Third Sts, while the Express Motorways and Ajay's buses stop at the Fairmile Motel out on the Bulawayo road. All buses travelling between Harare and Bulawayo stop at one or the other.

Air Zimbabwe has six flights per week between Harare and Thornhill Air Force Base, which connect with flights to and from Masvingo.

Bulawayo to Harare rail services pass through Gweru at 1.10 and 11.30 am daily. Southbound, they stop at 3 am and 1.07 pm daily.

SHURUGWI
Shurugwi, the 'highlands of the Midlands', is interesting: a Zimbabwean country town surrounded by the Sebakwe Hills and a steep escarpment. Now dependent upon chrome mining, the town is known throughout Zimbabwe for its flowering trees and its msasa, both of which are most colourful in the late winter and spring.

On the small scale, there are still a lot of remnants of bygone days for visitors to discover in this historic place and the mountain approaches from both Zvishavane and Gweru are quite scenic.

Places to Stay & Eat
Accommodation may be a problem in Shurugwi, however. The *Ferny Creek Caravan Park* (☎ 220 Shurugwi), 2.5 km out of town, has seen better days, evinced by descriptions of it in long outdated tourist literature. For food, you'll either have to rely on basic supplies from the several small shops or visit the local booze hall three km out of town, which serves standard meals.

SOUTH-WEST OF GWERU
In the back roads near Shangani and Nsiza are some little-visited but nevertheless interesting ruins attributed to the Torwa state prior to its conquest by the Rozwi. The Torwa are thought to have risen from the declining Great Zimbabwe culture further east, improving upon its architecture and material culture. Nalatale, Danangombe, Bila and Zinjanja are all grouped within about 40 km of each other. The other Torwa

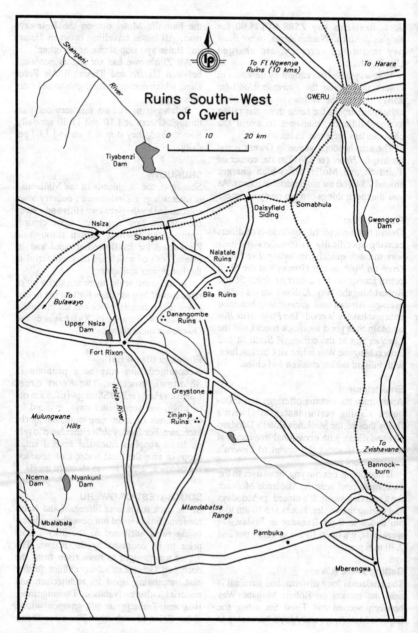

Ruins South–West of Gweru

centre, Khami, lies near Bulawayo and will be discussed in that chapter.

Unfortunately, there are no villages nearby so access is difficult. Without a car, prospective visitors will be subjected to long waits hitching. During busy periods in late September and early October, three or four vehicles may visit the sites in a day. At other times, a week may go by with no activity at all. It may help to speak with the inspector of monuments in Bulawayo (at the museum) about who may be headed in that direction. He or his crew do inspections of all the sites and may be able to steer you in the direction of a lift.

Nalatale Ruins

Although small in extent and not so elaborate or touristed as Great Zimbabwe, Nalatale rates among the nicest of all the 150 walled ruins in Zimbabwe. This simple structure on a remote granite hilltop enjoys a commanding view across the hills, plains and kopjes of Somabhula Flats. The main feature is a decorated wall which exhibits in one go all the primary decorative wall patterns found in Zimbabwe: chevron, chequer, cord, herringbone and ironstone. The original wall was topped by nine plinths but only seven haphazardly reconstructed ones remain. The plaster along the top of the wall was added in 1937 to prevent deterioration of the best preserved section.

It's possible to rough camp outside the enclosure at Nalatale but no services or facilities are available so carry your own food and water.

Getting There & Away Fortunately, the Nalatale ruins (alternatively spelt Nalatela or Nalatele) are well signposted. If you're coming from the north, turn south off the Gweru-Bulawayo road at the Daisyfield Siding. From the south, turn east from Shangani and follow the gravelled road approximately 27 km to the signposted left turning to Nalatale. From the parking area, it's a one km uphill walk to the hilltop site.

Wall patterns Nalatale ruins

Bila Ruins

Along the back road between Nalatale and Danangombe, that allows access between the two without forcing a return to Shangani, are the small, signposted Bila Ruins. They're actually just a small stone enclosure, probably little more than a kraal for animals.

Danangombe Ruins

Commonly known as Dhlo Dhlo (approximate pronunciation: 'hshlo hshlo'), Danangombe isn't as lovely or well preserved as Nalatale but it covers a larger area and has a most interesting history. It was originally designated a royal retreat under the Torwa, but after the Torwa were defeated by the Changamires it probably served as the Rozwi administrative centre. The most interesting feature is a crumbling enclosure formed partially by natural boulders. The whole thing is overgrown by wandering tree roots and sheltered by large trees. There are also some amazing cactus trees *(euphorbia ingens)* growing around these ruins.

Rough camping is possible at Danangombe but again, there are no services so you'll have to be self-sufficient.

Getting There & Away Danangombe is well signposted and 22 km from Shangani, or less from Nsiza via Fort Rixon. Lifts are extremely difficult since visitors are infrequent. Because of that, however, the site is quiet and unspoilt.

If you have a vehicle, you may also want to check out the little-known Zinjanja (Regina) Ruins 29 km south of Danangombe (via Fort Rixon and Greystone) which consist of a well-preserved three-tiered platform and lots of smaller subsidiary ruins thought to belong to the Torwa tradition. Very little is actually known about them.

MVUMA

Mvuma, an old gold-mining and railway community, is the site of the Falcon Mine, abandoned in 1925, which at the height of mining activity pioneered the oil flotation smelting process in Zimbabwe. The similar Athens Mine is still worked. Mvuma's name was taken from the Mvuma River which means 'place of magic singing' after a river pool where mysterious singing, drumming and lowing of cattle were once heard.

Today's Mvuma landmark is the crumbling Falcon Mine Stack, a 40 metre high remnant dating back to 1913. Town residents are waiting for the thing's collapse which, given its current condition, appears imminent.

SERIMA MISSION

Serima was founded in 1948 by Swiss Catholic priest and art instructor Father John Groeber who had earned a degree in architecture before beginning his work on rural missions in southern Africa in 1939. Based on the traditions of West and Central Africa where the genre reached its peak, Shona artists under his direction expressed themselves without pandering to European sensitivities. Although the church exterior is a bit worn these days, the spacious interior and all its artistic enhancements remain magnificent and are more than worth the effort of getting there.

For further information, look for *Serima* by Albert Plangger, Mambo Press, Gweru, 1974, which details the mission's history, art and architecture in words and numerous photos. It's available from the National Gallery in Harare.

Church

The Serima Mission church, designed by Father Groeber, is like a museum. On shelves above the church entrance, shepherds and wise men make their way laboriously toward a nativity scene in the centre. The bell tower is a circle of African angels gripping musical instruments. Events from the Bible are depicted in a series of frescos above the interior walls. Except for the reed-matted ceiling beams, there isn't a single piece of wood in the building that isn't carved.

Getting There & Away

Several buses a week go from Harare to Serima Mission but they're on no real schedule, so without a vehicle it's easier to hitch, cycle or walk.

Driving, turn east on Felixburg Rd from the Harare-Masvingo road 60 km north of Masvingo. After crossing the railway six km later, continue four more km and turn right again. From there, it's about 10 more km to the mission which is on the right-hand side of the road just past a small dam. The Felixburg bus from Masvingo will get you within reasonable walking distance, dropping you off at the turnoff about 10 km away.

MASVINGO

The name Masvingo (population 40,000) was adopted after Zimbabwe independence and is derived from *rusvingo*, the Shona word for walled-in enclosures, in reference to the nearby Great Zimbabwe ruins.

Historically, Masvingo prided itself on being the first White settlement in Zimbabwe. The pioneer column of the British South Africa Company, under Frederick Courteney Selous, moved through Lobengula's stronghold in Matabeleland and across the dry lowveld to the cooler plateaux. They paused at a spot now known as Clipsham Farm a few km south of present-day Masvingo to establish Fort Victoria and construct a rude mud fortification in August 1890.

During its early years, Masvingo served as a jumping-off point to the mines of Mashonaland and at one stage was the largest town in Zimbabwe. However, the Ndebele uprisings of the First Chimurenga and the subsequent defeat of Lobengula in Matabeleland opened up the Bulawayo area for White settlement and lured many of the Fort Victoria settlers toward the scent of more promising pickings. Bulawayo grew to be the country's second-largest city while Masvingo has now slid back to eighth place.

Orientation & Information

The Masvingo Publicity Association (☎ 2643 Masvingo), south of the railway crossing opposite the Chevron Hotel, is open from 8 am to 1 pm and 2 to 4 pm Monday to Friday. They're helpful with specific questions and they distribute maps, handouts and advertising for local businesses. Their monthly *Masvingo Diary*, which outlines upcoming happenings in town, is really only marginally useful and the map provided inexcusably omits Mucheke township.

Street Name Changes Recent street name changes in Masvingo include:

Old Name	New Name
Allan Wilson St	Robert Mugabe St
Brown Ave	Rekayi Tangwena Ave
Colquhoun St	Herbert Chitepo St
Dillon Ave	Leopold Takawira Ave
Fitzgerald Ave	Josiah Tongogara Ave
McLeod Ave	George Silundika Ave
Thompson Ave	Simon Mazorodze Ave
Unnamed road to	
Bus Terminus	Jairos Jiri Rd
Welby Ave	Jason Moyo Ave

Chapel of St Francis of Assisi

The interior of this Italian-style church was constructed between 1942 and 1946 by Italian POWs longing for their homeland; its chapel holds the remains of 71 of their compatriots who died as prisoners in Zimbabwe. The simulated mosaics in the apse were the work of an Italian engineer while the wall murals were completed 10 years later by Masvingo artists.

To get there, go three km east toward Mutare, take the left turn and then turn immediately left again, and yet again just in front of the military barracks entrance and you'll see the church 100 metres away.

Ecological Designs

If you're interested in Zimbabwe's contribution to global energy-saving efforts, you may enjoy a visit to Ecological Designs (☎ 3503), 'Your Appropriate Technology Workshop' at 697 Industria Rd, just north of town on a frontage to the Harare road. They'll show you around the complex and explain environmental problems and solutions pertinent in this part of the world. Notice the odd collection of machinery in their permanent display.

Shagashe Game Park

The new Shagashe Game Park is currently being developed about 10 km from Masvingo out the Harare road and should open soon. The Masvingo Publicity Association will have all the details.

Places to Stay

Masvingo's camping ground has great lawns and a riverside setting and is just a short walk

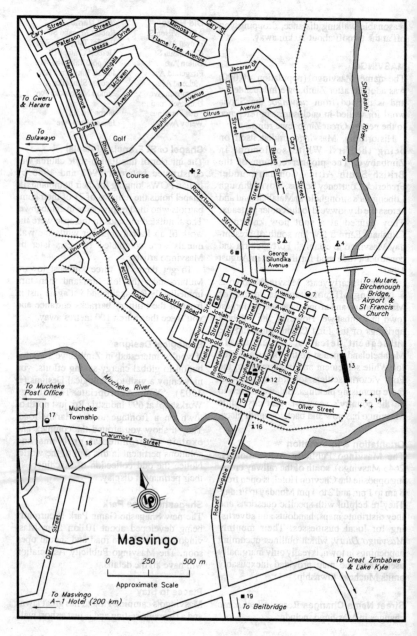

Masvingo

0   250   500 m

Approximate Scale

1	Swimming Pool	8	Riley's Shell	15	Chevron Hotel
2	Hospital	9	Apollo Restaurant	16	Masvingo Publicity
3	Weir	10	Central Police		Bureau
4	Camping Ground &	11	Main Post Office	17	Mucheke Musika (Market
	Caravan Park	12	Civic Centre & Queen		& Bus Terminal)
5	Pioneer Cottages		Elizabeth Gardens	18	Mucheke Police
6	Sports Club	13	Railway Station	19	Flamboyant Motel
7	In-Town Bus Terminus	14	Cemetery		

from the town centre. Tent sites cost Z$4.10 per night, caravan sites are Z$6.20. Day use of the park-like grounds costs Z$1 per person, and showers cost Z$2 for nonguests.

The owner of the Paw Paw Lodge in Harare is planning to open a similar establishment in Masvingo, probably at 52 Robson Manyika Ave in the centre of town. It should be ready by the time this book is published so check it out if you're interested.

Neither of the two tourist-market hotels in Masvingo, both two-star affairs, are anything special. The centrally located *Chevron Hotel* (☎ 2054 Masvingo) has a pretty high opinion of itself. Although the dining room should be avoided, the rooms are acceptable, despite the rocky beds and lack of hot water, and cost Z$61/85 for singles/doubles.

The *Flamboyant Motel* (☎ 2005 Masvingo), although nicer and more popular, is further from town on the intersection of the Beitbridge road and the Great Zimbabwe turnoff. Singles/doubles with bath cost Z$61/85. Double suites cost Z$108.

The other option is the *Masvingo A1 Hotel* (☎ 2917), set on a hilltop in Mucheke township, which has slightly cheaper rooms – Z$46/61 for singles/doubles including breakfast – but it operates at a much higher noise volume, the result of constant alcohol-induced action. Unaccompanied women may not feel comfortable.

The *Great Zimbabwe Hotel* and Mutirikwe (Kyle) Recreation Area cottages are described below in the respective discussions of those areas.

Places to Eat

Petrol stations in Masvingo cater to hungry travellers in a rush to chow down and be quickly off to somewhere else. *Riley's Shell* (famous for its loos) and the *Ace Restaurant* at the BP station are best for snacks. At the Caltex station, half a block from the BP, is the *Breadbasket Bakery*. At *Meikles* store there's a snack bar serving tea, cakes and pastries.

Although you won't have a memorable meal at the *Apollo Restaurant* on Herbert Chitepo St, it's still the best place to eat in the centre of town.

The terrace in front of the *Chevron Hotel* is great for a snack and drink on a sunny day but you may want to give their dining room a wide berth.

The *Flamboyant Motel*, however, is quite good. They offer a breakfast buffet, a la carte lunches and snacks and on weekend evenings, they put on a buffet braai.

Lots of produce, junk food and snacks are available in and around the Mucheke musika bus station. Ever had the urge to try deep-fried stink bugs? Here's your opportunity.

Getting There & Away

Long-distance buses arrive and depart from Mucheke musika just under two km from the town centre. Although hourly buses do the run and taxis are available, it's not a difficult walk unless you're carrying a lot of luggage. After entering Masvingo, all Mucheke-bound buses stop in the centre so when arriving in Masvingo, get off at the first stop unless you're specifically going to Mucheke.

Buses between Harare and Masvingo depart frequently from both Mbare (Harare) and the Mucheke terminal and there are several daily services to both Bulawayo and

Mutare. At least one daily bus leaves for Beitbridge; even though it may be delayed until 11 am, arrive at Mucheke early. The surrounding communal lands are well served and the high population density of Masvingo province makes it relatively easy to reach smaller destinations.

If you're flying into Masvingo on one of the four weekly services from Harare, you'll probably be obligated to pay UTC's Z$10 per person transfer fee from the airport into town. For information on getting to Great Zimbabwe, refer to the discussion of Great Zimbabwe below.

GREAT ZIMBABWE

The largest and most significant medieval city in sub-Saharan Africa, Great Zimbabwe provides evidence that medieval Africa reached a level of civilisation not suspected by early scholars. As a religious and temporal capital, this city of perhaps 10,000 people stood at the centre of a realm stretching across modern-day eastern Zimbabwe and into Botswana, Mozambique and South Africa. Over 150 tributary zimbabwes have been ascribed by archaeologists to the Great Zimbabwe culture and society, which actu-

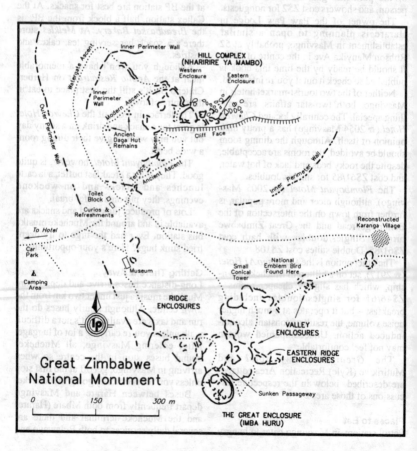

Great Zimbabwe National Monument

0   150   300 m

Top: Main Complex, Great Zimbabwe, Zimbabwe (DS)
Left: Narrow passage, Main Complex, Great Zimbabwe, Zimbabwe (TW)
Right: Rock formations, Great Zimbabwe, Zimbabwe (TW)

Top: Victoria Falls, Zimbabwe (RP)
Bottom: Kariba Dam, Zimbabwe (DS)

ally was an amalgamation of many smaller groups under a central political system.

The name Zimbabwe is believed to be derived from one of two possible Shona origins; either *dzimba dza mabwe* (great stone houses) or *dzimba woye* (esteemed houses). For many visitors, the ruins are a highlight of southern Africa.

Admission to the site, open from 8 am to 6 pm daily, is Z$1 per person. Admission to the reconstructed Karanga Village is an additional Z$1.

History

Several volumes have been written about Great Zimbabwe and the speculations about its purposes and origins have been hashed over for several centuries now. If you're keen to learn more, the most comprehensive and scholarly work on the subject is *Great Zimbabwe Described and Explained* by Peter Garlake, Zimbabwe Publishing House, Harare, 1982. It is occasionally available at Kingston's. Failing that, contact the publisher directly: Zimbabwe Publishing House (☎ 790416 Harare), 144 Union Ave, PO Box 350, Harare.

Despite nearly 100 years of effort by colonial governments to ascribe the origins of Great Zimbabwe to someone else, conclusive proof of Bantu origins was already in place in 1932 after British archaeologist Gertrude Caton-Thompson spent three years examining the ruins and their artefacts. One can almost understand the scepticism of early Whites in the area – the African peoples they encountered seemed to have no tradition of building in stone and none of the stone cities were inhabited at the time of colonisation. But even up to the time of Zimbabwe's independence, however, the Rhodesian government insisted on ignoring evidence and instead promoted far-fetched fantasies of foreign influence and habitation. Despite results based on radiocarbon dating of organic materials found at the site, many Rhodesian officials perpetuated the nonsense that Great Zimbabwe dated from the pre-Christian era. Not a scrap of proof for

Phoenician, Greek, Egyptian, Arabic, Jewish or any other origins has yet been produced.

Other outside influences did, however, play a role in the *development* of Great Zimbabwe. Swahili traders were present along the Mozambique coast from the 10th century throughout the height of Rozwi influence in the 14th and 15th centuries. Trade goods – porcelain from China, crockery from Persia and beads and other trinkets from India – have been unearthed on the site and the Africans undoubtedly adopted and adapted some of the outsiders' ways.

Fuelled by Swahili gold trade, the city grew into a powerful and prestigious religious and political capital, the heart of the Rozwi culture whose influence extended far and wide. Royal herds increased and coffers overflowed with gold and precious trade goods.

In the end, however, it seems Great Zimbabwe became a victim its own success. By the 15th century, the growing human and bovine populations and their environmental pressures had depleted local resources, necessitating emigration to more productive lands.

Hill Complex

Probably the first of the Great Zimbabwe complexes to be constructed, this hill structure was once known as the Acropolis. This clearly wasn't a fortress, though, but a series of royal and ritual enclosures. Rather than rip out the boulders to install the chambers, builders wisely followed the path of least resistance, integrating them into the structures as best they could. Evidence indicates the hill complex was occupied for at least 300 years.

Valley Enclosures

The Valley Enclosures consist of the series of 13th century enclosures and *daga* hut platforms stretching from the Sunken Passageway below the Great Enclosure toward the Karanga village reconstruction. They contain a small conical tower and have yielded some of the finest archaeological finds, including metal tools and the odd Great Zimbabwe bird with its mammal-like feet that became the national symbol.

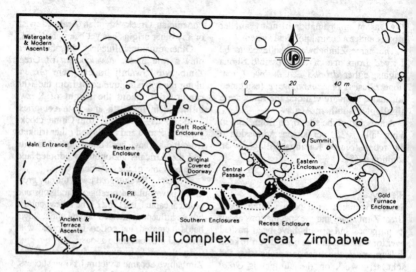

The Hill Complex — Great Zimbabwe

Great Enclosure

The elliptical Great Enclosure is the structure normally conjured up by the words 'Great Zimbabwe'. It's the most oft-photographed and perhaps the most photogenic of all the ruins. Nearly 100 metres across and 255 metres in circumference, it is the largest ancient structure in sub-Saharan Africa. The mortarless walls reach heights of 11 metres and in places are five metres thick. The most commonly accepted theory is that the Great Enclosure was used as a royal compound and a sort of cloister for the king's mother and senior wives. The object of greatest speculation is, of course, the 10 metre high, convex Conical Tower tucked away beneath overhanging trees at the south-western end. This solid and apparently ceremonial structure is almost certainly of phallic significance but no conclusive evidence of its meaning or use has been uncovered.

In the reconstructed version, the Great Enclosure has three entrances, all of which in the original were probably lintelled and covered, opening through rounded buttresses. The North Entrance, probably the main gate, is met outside by the Sunken Passageway which connects it to the Valley Enclosures.

Leading away north-east from the Conical Tower is the narrow 70 metre long Parallel Passage. It may have been a means of moving from the North Entrance to the Conical Tower without being detected by those in the living area of the Enclosure. It's also possible that the Parallel Passage's inner wall was originally intended to be an outer wall but by the time the builders had completed that far around, their construction methods had improved so dramatically they decided to rebuild all of the wall in the superior manner.

Museum

The site museum houses most of the Great Zimbabwe archaeological finds which haven't been dispersed to far corners of the earth by amateur treasure hunters. For most visitors, the seven-and-a-bit soapstone Zimbabwe birds, which were probably Rozwi dynasty totems, are the highlights. Two which were taken away to South Africa in the late 1890s were returned in 1985, exchanged for a collection of butterflies, and

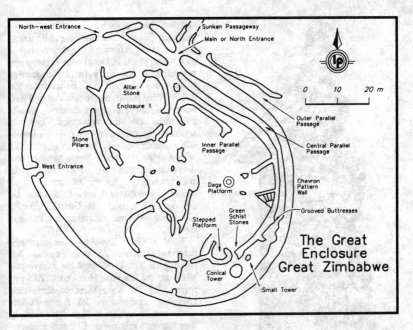

North-west Entrance

Sunken Passageway

Main or North Entrance

Altar Stone

Enclosure 1

Outer Parallel Passage

Stone Pillars

Inner Parallel Passage

Central Parallel Passage

West Entrance

Chevron Pattern Wall

Daga Platform

Green Schist Stones

Grooved Buttresses

Stepped Platform

The Great Enclosure Great Zimbabwe

Conical Tower

Small Tower

have taken their place beside the rest. Described variously as falcons, fish eagles and mythological creatures, the 40 cm high avians have come to represent Zimbabwe on its flag, stamps and official seal.

Other exhibits of interest include porcelain and glass trade goods brought by Swahili traders, which are generally considered proof of foreign contact during Great Zimbabwe's heyday. Iron relics, some of which were ritual objects and owned by the king, while others were practical and treasured by common folk, are prominently displayed along with gold, bronze and copper items, soapstone dishes and clay pottery.

The museum is open daily from 8 am to 4.30 pm.

Organised Tours

Zimtours (☎ 793666 Harare) offers daily tours of Great Zimbabwe commencing at 9.30 am from all the Masvingo hotels except the Hotel Masvingo up on the hill. After a couple of hours exploring Great Zimbabwe, you get lunch and traditional dancing at Mutirikwe Lakeshore Lodges, then a visit to Mutirikwe Dam wall and the Mutirikwe Game Park. The price including lunch is Z$65 per person. Bookings can be made directly through Zimtours, the Masvingo Publicity Bureau or the Chevron or Flamboyant Hotels in Masvingo.

Places to Stay & Eat

Campers have the best deal of all at Great Zimbabwe – the opportunity to set up housekeeping in a lovely field within sight of the Hill Complex and just over a rise from the other ruins. If you have a tent, this is an experience not to be missed. Camping costs only Z$2 per person. Cold showers are available and security guards are posted to keep an eye on your belongings while you're off exploring.

The only formal accommodation at the site is the *Great Zimbabwe Hotel* (☎ 2449 Masvingo) which charges US$55 a single

Zimbabwe bird

Getting There & Away

To reach Great Zimbabwe on public transport is straightforward in theory but a problem in practice. Despite the reassurance provided by the nifty little Morgenster Mission bus schedule you'll be handed at the publicity bureau ('three buses daily: 8 am, noon and 3.30 pm'...pure fantasy!), you'll have to be both lucky and quick – quick to squeeze through the crowds onto the normally bursting bus and lucky to connect up with it in the first place. Some days the bus runs once, sometimes it doesn't bother to run at all (as was the case the last time I tried to use it). If you do catch up with it, ask to be dropped at the turnoff to the Great Zimbabwe Hotel and walk the remaining one km into the site.

Taxis to Great Zimbabwe are currently running at about Z$30 for up to five passengers. The UTC (☎ 4054 Masvingo) bus from the Chevron Hotel costs Z$5 per person, Z$7 to Kyle View or Mutirikwe Lakeshore Lodges, and Z$12 one-way to Mutirikwe Recreational Park. The catch is they require a minimum of 10 passengers or the equivalent fares. Alternatively, you can hire a vehicle from Hertz (☎ 2131) at Founders House on Robert Mugabe St in Masvingo.

MUTIRIKWE (KYLE) RECREATIONAL PARK

A decade of drought has caused the waters of Mutirikwe Dam (still commonly called Lake Kyle) to fall to record low levels and the lake has shrunk to a fraction of its capacity. Unless the summer rains pick up soon, lowveld irrigation projects stand to suffer. The dam itself is therefore of limited recreational value at the moment but the surrounding scenic area is worthwhile and combines nicely with a visit to Great Zimbabwe.

Popoteke Gorge

The road signposted as the Popoteke Gorge access actually leads to a steep-walled gap where the Popoteke River flows through the Beza Range on its way to Mutirikwe Dam.

and US$90 a double, including a fabulous buffet breakfast offering African, English or Continental food. Foreigners must pay in foreign exchange.

The terrace restaurant at the hotel is good for drinks, coffee and snacks although you'll be constantly pestered by hordes of cheeky vervet monkeys who will stroll up to your plate and help themselves the moment you're distracted. When they're not in the act of thieving, they're sitting in the trees overhead planning the next heist. Sugar sachets seem to be their favourite spoil.

In the main dining room, you'll find more substantial meals, including the previously mentioned buffet breakfast which is also available to campers for Z$11.25.

It lies 2.5 km south of the Masvingo-Mutare road, 20 km east of Masvingo. It's a scenic stop and ideal for picnicking but camping is officially prohibited.

Rock Paintings

There are two relatively accessible rock painting sites near the lakeshore. The easiest site to reach is a small one about two km south-west of the dam wall and about 100 metres from the road. It's well signposted.

The best known site is Chamavara at Chamavara Cave, 18 km north-west of the dam wall on Murray McDougall Drive then four km east on the signposted turnoff. Most of the painted human and animal figures are confusingly dense on the cave wall and at times difficult to discern but as many of them have white faces, there has been much speculation about connections with Middle Eastern and European peoples. The cave's main figure, known as the Giant Man of Chamavara, is unique in Zimbabwe.

Mutirikwe (Kyle) Game Park

Although it seems artificial, the Mutirikwe Game Park is a good place to see white rhinos and hosts the largest variety of antelope species of any park in Zimbabwe. Animals easily observed along the park's 64 km of dirt roads include warthog, impala, giraffe, zebra, kudu, oribi, eland, baboon, tsessebe, buffalo, wildebeest and waterbuck, but there are no elephants or big cats. Game park gates close at 6 pm and entry or exit after that hour is prohibited.

Walking is permitted only around Mushagashe Arm near the National Parks lodges and camping site. Since it's outside the game fence, you won't observe much wildlife there but hippos and crocodiles are frequently seen in and around the water. The area just north of the dwala on which the parks accommodation is located has been set aside as an arboretum with over 150 species of indigenous trees identified along the tracks there.

The horse trails offer an alternative approach to game viewing as they allow participants to view wildlife at closer range than a vehicle would permit. Guided horseback trips through the game park depart at 7.45 am from park headquarters, returning at 10.30 am, for Z$6 per person.

Places to Stay

Southern Shore Most of the accommodation at Mutirikwe is along the southern shore. The beautiful National Parks camping site at Sikato Bay, just six easily walked km from Great Zimbabwe National Monument, costs Z$10 per site.

Kyle View Holiday Resort (☎ 223822 Masvingo), east of the camping site, costs Z$25 per person. On site are a restaurant and pub and it has a distinctly relaxed atmosphere. Camping is available for Z$3 per person.

The slightly more sophisticated *Mutirikwe Lakeshore Lodges* (☎ 292421 Masvingo) further east, which are large two-storey affairs beside the lake, cost Z$30 for one person and Z$20 per person for each additional occupant. Each lodge accommodates up to six people. On site there's a pub as well as a small shop and a swimming pool.

Northern Shore The only northern shore accommodation is at the National Parks headquarters where one, two and three-bedroom lodges are available for Z$20 per bedroom. The National Parks camping site has all the standard features – showers, baths and braai pits for Z$10 per site. It's a good idea to book in advance through the National Parks central booking office in Harare.

Places to Eat

Apart from the dining room at the nearby *Great Zimbabwe Hotel*, the only restaurant is at *Kyle View Chalets*. Both Mutirikwe Lakeshore Lodges and Kyle View Chalets sell basic supplies and beer (considered by some a basic supply) so campers would do well to bring their food from elsewhere.

In the game park there are two picnic sites, the Mutirikwe site on the point at the end of Ostrich Loop and the other at Popoteke where the river of the same name enters Mutirikwe Dam.

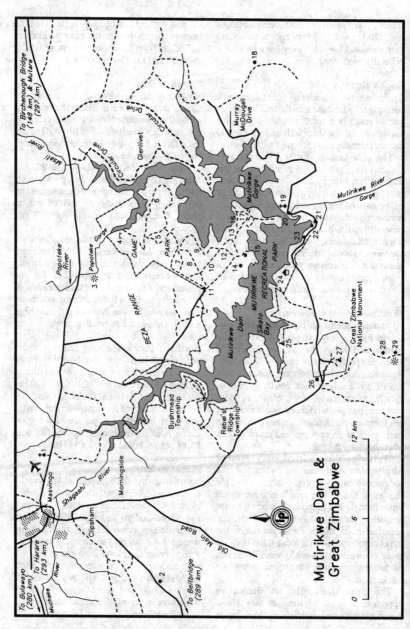

Mutirikwe Dam & Great Zimbabwe

1	St Francis of Assisi Chapel	10	Gnu Bend	21	Rock Painting
2	Pioneer Cemetery	11	Entrance Gate	22	Kyle Boat Club
3	Popoteke Gorge Lookout	12	Nyala Drive	23	Mutirikwe Lake Shore Lodges
4	Popoteke Picnic Site	13	Rhino Drive	24	Kyle View Chalets
5	Zebra Ridge	14	Fish Research Centre	25	Camping Site
6	Buffalo Loop	15	Office	26	Great Zimbabwe Hotel
7	Eland Drive	16	Ostrich Loop	27	Camping Site
8	Reedbuck Drive	17	Impala Drive	28	Finger Rock
9	Lake Shore Drive	18	Chamavara Cave	29	Morgenster Mission
		19	St Andrew's Chapel		
		20	Dam Wall		

Getting There & Away

Once you're at Great Zimbabwe, it's a fairly easy matter to walk or hitch the six km to the Mutirikwe southern shore. The main points of interest are further along, however, and require catching an infrequent bus toward Glenlivet east of the lake, or hitching along the barely travelled Murray McDougall scenic drive and Circular Drive between Great Zimbabwe and the Masvingo-Mutare road. You can also go the other way round from Great Zimbabwe via Masvingo. The northern shore is most easily accessed from the turning 13 km east of Masvingo on the Mutare road.

From the Mutirikwe Lakeshore Cottages on the southern shore, it's possible to hitch a lift to the game park with one of the rangers. From Great Zimbabwe or one of the southern shore chalets, phone the warden or the senior ranger (☎ 2913) during office hours (7 am to 6 pm daily) and ask if a boat can be sent to fetch you at a specified time.

UTC transfers are available to the chalets or the game park from Masvingo. See Getting There & Away under Great Zimbabwe for further details.

MUSHANDIKE SANCTUARY

A well-kept secret, the 13,360 hectare Mushandike (pronounced 'Moo-shan-DEE-kee') Sanctuary, lies 11 km south of the Masvingo-Bulawayo road; the turnoff is 10 km east of Mashava and 25 km west of Masvingo.

Roads through the sanctuary, a series of scenic drives through the eastern two-thirds

of the sanctuary, are quite rough and the road out from the southern boundary to the Beitbridge road is too steep to be negotiated by caravans. Before heading that way, enquire at the office whether the dam wall and southern exit are accessible since the gates along the road normally remain locked.

Although visitors are likely to have the camping ground to themselves, there's an attendant on hand to tend the boiler and chop firewood as necessary. Some of the sites provide a small patch of grassy lawn suitable for comfortable tent camping, well worth the Z$10 per site that's charged. Water and hot showers are available but the nearest shops are at Mashava and Masvingo, so carry all your food from elsewhere. You may also want to have a look at the eland research institute on the site. Day entry is Z$1 per person.

Getting There & Away

Without a vehicle, access will probably entail an 11 km walk from the Masvingo-Bulawayo road turnoff, which may be reached by hitching or by one of the frequent buses between those two centres. Lifts into the park from the turnoff will be hard to come by (when I was there, the last private car had been through 11 days earlier!) unless you're lucky enough to connect with a ranger vehicle. The friendly information office can help with enquiries.

CHIREDZI

Of very limited interest, hot and malaria-

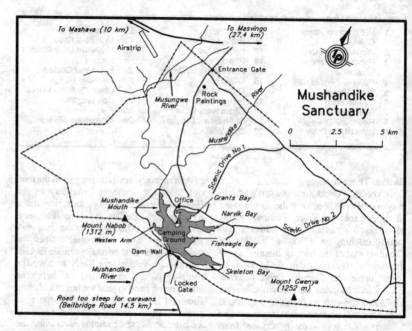

infested Chiredzi sprang up with the lowveld irrigation schemes of the mid-1960s. It's primarily a sugar town these days but not nearly as interesting as nearby Triangle.

Places to Stay & Eat

The nearest camping to be found is at Gonarezhou National Park which at the moment is guarded by the Army and closed to foreigners. (Check to see whether the situation has changed when you arrive.)

The one-star *Planter's Inn* (☎ 2281 Chiredzi) on a hill in the centre isn't bad with a raucous pub and a reasonable dining room. Single/double rooms cost Z$60/94, including bed and breakfast. Chalets which accommodate four people cost Z$120 per night, excluding breakfast.

The other option, available to those with wheels, is the two-star *Tambuti Lodge* (☎ 2575 Chiredzi) 12 km east of Chiredzi. The staff out there take a rather *laissez-faire* attitude toward the ongoing decline of this place but its setting beside the Tambuti River is quite nice. Doubles without baths cost Z$94.60, including breakfast. Add a shower and the rooms cost Z$120. Add a bath and rooms will cost a whopping Z$2 more.

Getting There & Away

Chiredzi's airport, serving mainly agricultural business traffic, is at Buffalo Range 15 km west of Chiredzi. Air Zimbabwe does three flights weekly between Buffalo Range and Bulawayo, and flies daily except Saturday to and from Harare via Masvingo.

Bus services connect Chiredzi's township bus terminal with Harare, Masvingo, Mutare, Bulawayo, Beitbridge and nearby communities like Triangle, Hippo Valley and Buffalo Range.

A goods train between Chiredzi and Bulawayo also includes economy passenger cars and leaves Bulawayo daily at 9.25 pm and Chiredzi at 5.40 pm.

GONAREZHOU NATIONAL PARK

When large-scale agriculture began encroaching on wildlife habitat in the late 1960s, the government decided to set aside a scenically interesting chunk of south-eastern Zimbabwe as a refuge from development and an as anti-poaching control corridor. The resulting Gonarezhou National Park, established in 1969, protects 5000 sq km of prime elephant territory; some of Africa's largest elephants have lived at Gonarezhou, which in Shona means 'abode of elephants'.

Poaching has long been a problem; in the 1920s, one of Africa's most notorious poachers, Stephanus Barnard, shot his way through some of the continent's largest tuskers. More recently, Mozambican guerrillas have turned the park into a butcher shop. For that reason, Gonarezhou is now closed to non-Zimbabwe residents and no facilities are available. Although that situation may change, at the moment the prospects of a reopening in the near future are slim.

Information

Gonarezhou is divided into two administrative regions: Chipinda Pools (including the Runde and Save subregions) in the north and Mabalauta (or Mwenezi region) in the south. If the park reopens, accommodation will be available at both ends although the remote southern section will remain 4WD country.

If you'd like to visit Gonarezhou, write in advance for the latest details to Gonarezhou National Park Superintendent (☎ 397 Chiredzi), PO Box 7003, Chiredzi, Zimbabwe, or contact the National Parks office in Causeway, Harare.

Fishing is permitted in several areas; at Chipinda Pools and below waterfalls on the Save and Runde rivers, bream and tiger fish and even some saltwater varieties have been caught. Permits are available through the office at Chipinda Pools.

Places to Stay & Eat

The most popular and accessible camping site is at Chipinda Pools, 59 km from Chiredzi along a badly corrugated but easily passable dirt road. Although there are no chalets or cottages available, caravans are permitted.

Several other National Parks and private camps are found throughout the park but are unlikely to be reopened soon even if the park again becomes accessible. In the past, *Swimuwini Camp*, (the 'place of baobabs') in Mabalauta, 170 km from Chiredzi, has offered both chalets and camping.

The nearest supplies are available at Chiredzi.

TRIANGLE

It won't take you long to work out that Triangle is a company town. The success of Triangle may be attributed to the persistence of one man, an unconventional Scotsman named Thomas Murray McDougall who was single-handedly responsible for initiating lowveld irrigation and turning the lowveld into a productive agricultural area. The events that led to the foundation of Triangle Sugar Estates and its takeover by the Sugar Industry Board are detailed in the museum at the site, which is now designated a National Monument.

McDougall Museum

Housed in McDougall's home, the McDougall National Monument museum sits on a hill about 1.5 km off the highway. Here you get the lowdown on Triangle, its resourceful founder and the sugar industry in general. The museum is open daily except Monday from 8.30 to 9.30 am and 3.30 to 4.30 pm. Admission is 25 cents.

BEITBRIDGE

Most people spend more time in Beitbridge than anyone would normally want to and because everyone is passing through, it must have the greatest number of petrol stations per capita of any place in Zimbabwe.

This, Zimbabwe's only border crossing to and from South Africa, is both busy and cumbersome. Long, hot waits are the norm and going through customs on both sides can become extremely tedious. Those who know this border well recommend you try to go through 15 minutes of so before the 8 pm closing when officials want nothing more than to go home.

Places to Stay

If you're caught out in Beitbridge, try *Peter's Hotel* (☎ 309 Beitbridge), the budget option which costs Z$35 per person regardless of the number of beds in the room.

The other possibility is the more upmarket but not so friendly *Beitbridge Hotel* (☎ 214 Beitbridge) where cottages cost Z$75 a single and Z$120 a double. Single/double rooms in the main building will cost Z$60/110 without bath and Z$65/130 with bath.

If you're headed north, try to reach the pleasant *Lion & Elephant Motel* at Bubi River, 78 km north of Beitbridge. They allow camping in a beautiful spot beside the river for Z$3 per person, including the use of

facilities. Singles/doubles including dinner, bed and breakfast without private bath cost Z$73/110 and Z$20 for each extra bed. For private baths, add Z$7. For campers, the buffet breakfast costs Z$8.50.

Places to Eat

The *Bird Cage Restaurant & Snack Bar* at the Beitbridge Hotel is the only real eating establishment in town. *Sunrise Takeaways* serves snacks and there's a small supermarket at the Shell station if you'd rather just pick up supplies and press on. You may want to save purchases for the South African side – it's a bit more expensive but if you've been travelling elsewhere in Africa for a while, the variety of stuff available there will knock you over!

Getting There & Away

For information on buses to and through Beitbridge, see To/From South Africa in the Zimbabwe Getting There & Away chapter.

Bulawayo

Formerly called Gu-Bulawayo or The Killing Place, Bulawayo (population 600,000) is Zimbabwe's bright and historically interesting second city. The name presumably resulted from Mzilikazi's Thabas Indunas (Hill of Chiefs) executions that accompanied the development of the Ndebele state. Because relative latecomer Harare managed to usurp the seat of government during the colonial era, however, Bulawayo has lately avoided most of the cares associated with things political.

History

In early 19th century Transvaal, newly unified Zululand suffered a series of distinctly disunifying political disturbances. After the overthrow of Zulu leader Dingiswayo by an ambitious young captain called Shaka, the realm was thrown to its knees by the ruthless new king's reign of terror. Many subordinate groups, now known as Nguni, who had experienced or feared his wrath fled northward on the mfecane, the 'forced migration'. One such refugee, Mzilikazi, who'd had a tributary dispute with King Shaka, arrived in south-western Zimbabwe with his Kumalo clan in the 1830s. The Kumalo overcame the incumbent Rozwi and established themselves at Inyati, 60 km north-west of Bulawayo, under the name Ndebele or 'those who carry long shields'.

Upon Mzilikazi's death in 1870, his son Lobengula ascended to the throne and moved his capital to Bulawayo, soon finding himself face to face with the British South Africa Company. In 1888, Cecil John Rhodes met with Lobengula and duped him into accepting the Rudd Concession, granting the foreigners mineral rights in exchange for money and weapons.

Over the following years, Bulawayo prospered. In 1898, the first leg of the proposed Cape to Cairo railway arrived from South Africa and the city grew into a commercial and industrial centre. Later, there came another railway which connected Bulawayo with Victoria Falls and the Zambia copper belt; the town's industrial base expanded and Bulawayo became the most progressive centre in the country. The nation's first Black labour unions had their roots there, with Ndebele leader Joshua Nkomo as one of their leading activists.

At Independence, the Shona took over the government and Ndebele leadership was relegated to background status. When the long-standing rivalry between ZANU and ZAPU flared up in 1983, the Mugabe government dealt brutally with the dissenters, sending the North Korean-trained Fifth Brigade to settle the matter. The Bulawayo area came under siege until Mugabe called for negotiations between the government and the Ndebele dissidents. In 1988, the miraculously successful Unity Accord was reached; Nkomo returned from exile, official amnesty was granted to the rebels and the ZAPU and ZANU forces were combined into one army.

Orientation & Information

Most of Bulawayo's population lives in the high-density suburbs west of the industrial sector and north-west of the centre, which leaves the heart of Bulawayo resembling a mid-sized town in Kansas – and by day about as exciting – with centre-strip parking, myriad takeaways and early 20th century architecture.

Central Bulawayo's African-oriented businesses and less expensive shops occupy the area south of Twelfth Ave and west of Fort St but are centred on Lobengula St near the railway station where there are many takeaways and essentials shops. The industrial sector sprawls westward from Lobengula St, centred on Khami Rd.

Street Name Changes In March 1990,

Bulawayo, like a number of other cities in Zimbabwe, changed its street names.

Old Name	New Name
Abercorn St	Jason Moyo St
Borrow St	Samuel Parirenyatwa St
Grey St/Birchenough Rd/Queens Rd	Robert Mugabe Way
Kings Ave	Masotsha Ndlovu Ave
Jameson St	Herbert Chitepo St
Johannesburg Rd	Gwanda Rd
London Rd	Josiah Chinamano Rd
Mafikeng Rd	Plumtree Rd
Rhodes St	George Silundika St
Salisbury Rd	Harare Rd
Selborne Ave	Leopold Takawira St
Wilson St	Josiah Tongogara St

Tourist Office Bulawayo's reliable Publicity Association (☎ 60867), PO Box 861, Bulawayo, is found in City Hall, set back from Fife St between Eighth and Leopold Takawira Aves. Unless you're after info about Renkini terminal buses, any questions they can't immediately answer will be enthusiastically sorted out for you as quickly as possible. Renkini advice is best sorted out at the terminal itself.

They distribute a free tourist publication, *Bulawayo This Month*, which contains a city plan (which sometimes prints up legibly) and a brief rundown of local cultural events, club meetings and even a horoscope. In addition, they distribute brochures and advertising and sell photocopies of maps of other areas around Zimbabwe for 50 cents each.

Immigration The Dept of Immigration Control (☎ 65621) can be found on the 1st floor of the Central Africa Building Society building on the corner of Jason Moyo St and Leopold Takawira Ave.

Post The GPO is at the corner of Eighth Ave and Main St. It's a good and efficient poste restante address if you're planning to receive mail or spend some time in Bulawayo. It's open normal post office hours: 8 am to 5 pm Monday to Friday (poste restante closes at 4 pm) and 8 to 11.30 am on Saturday. On public holidays, it's open between 9 and 10.30 am for general postal services. The parcel office entrance is around the other side of the building on Fort St.

Telephone Public telephone kiosks and their obligatory queues are found on the corner of Eighth Ave and Main St beside the GPO. There's no long-distance telephone office in Bulawayo.

Travel Agencies The American Express Representative is Manica Travel (☎ 62521 Bulawayo) on Tenth Ave between Main and Fort Sts. Unfortunately, American Express is no longer authorised to handle cash transactions so all legal currency exchanges must be done at the bank. This is also the place to book Ajay Motorways buses; if you're headed for Hwange or Victoria Falls, advance booking is essential.

Another option for general travel information and bookings is Sunshine Tours (☎ 67791) in the Old Mutual Arcade near the corner of Jason Moyo St and Eighth Ave.

Bookshops The main Kingston's outlet, which surprisingly offers a wider selection than its Harare counterpart, is on Jason Moyo St between Eighth and Ninth Aves. You'll also find a couple of good book exchanges, Page One and Basement Book Exchange, on Main St. One block west on Fort St is the Matopos Book Centre, a primarily Christian and school textbook shop which sells 57 cent postcards, the cheapest I found in Bulawayo.

Emergency Services The emergency services number in Bulawayo is (☎ 99). Bulawayo has no shortage of hospitals but the best equipped and most accessible is Bulawayo Central (☎ 72111) on St Lukes Ave, Kumalo suburb, not far from Ascot Race Course.

Security More laid-back than Harare, Bulawayo is also more amenable security-wise. Still, there are a couple of potential trouble spots. Lone women should avoid the more remote parts of Centenary and Central parks at any time of day. No one should walk

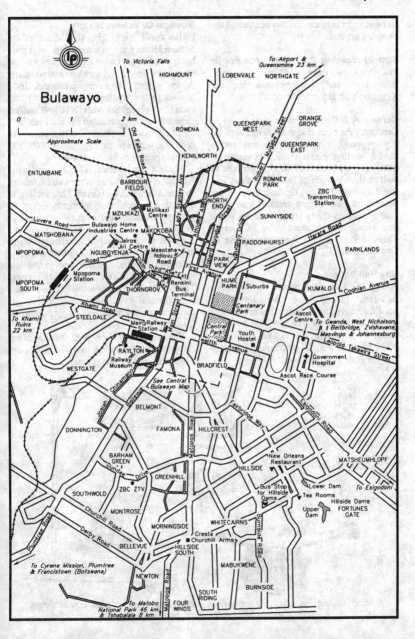

Bulawayo

0   1   2 km

Approximate Scale

alone at night between the city centre and the camping ground.

Film Processing Print film processing is available in two days – as a special concession to tourists only – at the camera shop near Kingston's on Jason Moyo St.

Centenary & Central Parks
Centenary Park caters to the younger set with a playground, a miniature railway and a model boating pond. It also contains an aviary and well-tended botanical gardens as well as the Museum of Natural History and the Bulawayo Theatre. Central Park, on the other hand, offers some areas of true bushland as well as shady lawns, benches and a few small garden areas. The Municipal Caravan Park is in a fenced enclosure of Central Park.

City Hall Square
Along the Fife St footpath at City Hall Square, street souvenir hawkers, needleworkers, artists and flower vendors display their wares. The city hall building itself houses the Bulawayo Publicity Association as well as city council chambers and the Bulawayo archives.

Museum Of Natural History
Bulawayo's highlight, the Museum of Natural History in Centenary Park, will probably require an entire day of exploration. Everything found in Zimbabwe and southern Africa – birds, antelope, predators, fish, reptiles (a few of these are still alive) and even (they claim) the world's largest stuffed elephant – is represented in well-realised displays and dioramas. One room is dedicated entirely to bugs. In all, 75,000 animal specimens are on display.

There's also historical info; pertinent African and European cultures and artefacts are described and displayed. One section is dedicated to prehistoric humanity, others to weaponry ancient and modern, mining and geology. In one corner of the museum, they've constructed an artificial mine explaining the source of Zimbabwe's considerable mineral wealth and extraction methods used down through the ages. There's also an extensive collection of rock and mineral specimens and geological explanations of Zimbabwe's most prominent features.

The museum is open from 9 am to 5 pm daily except Christmas and Good Friday. Admission is 50 cents per person.

Wooden Implements – Top right (clockwise): walking stick, headrest, ladle, cow bell, stool, umncwado, hakata, stool, wooden bowl

Railway Museum

The Railway Museum's collection of historic steam locomotives, old railway offices and buildings, passenger carriages and a model of a historic railway station with period furnishings tell the history of rail in Zimbabwe, one of only a handful of countries still using steam locomotives on scheduled routes. Although it's within walking distance of the centre, the museum's a bit hard to find. The quickest route is a circuit through the railway station and across myriad tracks.

The museum is open from 9.30 am to noon and 2 to 4 pm Tuesday to Friday and on Sunday from 3 to 5 pm. Admission is 50 cents.

If you'd like to join the engineers in the steam locomotives that chug around Bulawayo you can get a photography permit and make arrangements with the publicity officer of the National Railways of Zimbabwe on the 6th floor of the National Railways Headquarters on Fife St.

Art Gallery

The Art Gallery at City Hall Square has a permanent collection, including several excellent pieces of modern African art and Matabeleland material crafts. Many of the paintings on display are the work of Bulawayo artists. The gallery is open from 10 am to 5 pm Tuesday to Friday and Sunday, and on Saturday from 10 am to noon. Admission is 20 cents.

Mzilikazi Arts Centre & Bulawayo Home Industries

There's a significant amount of artistic talent to be found in this one institution, which in places seems more a museum than a school. The centre was originally established by the city of Bulawayo in 1963 in order to provide art training for otherwise latent talent. Their current full-time enrolment stands at about 150 with nearly 500 school-age children attending classes part-time. Proceeds from sales are ploughed back into the art school.

Free guided tours are conducted between 10 am and 12.30 pm and from 2 to 5 pm Monday to Friday. The school is divided into ceramics and stoneware, painting, iron and stone sculpting and carving classrooms, and you'll be able to watch the work emerge almost effortlessly. Pottery and stoneware seconds are available for ridiculously low prices from the shop in the office area.

Across the lawn beside the library is Bulawayo Home Industries. The centre was started and originally subsidised by the city council for widows, divorcees and abandoned and elderly women unable to support themselves. It now earns enough to pay for its own operation and offers choice items for less than curio shop prices. It's open 9 am to 4 pm weekdays.

Mzilikazi and Bulawayo Home Industries are a four km walk from the centre of Bulawayo. Otherwise, take the Mpilo suburb bus or the Barbour Fields (marked BF) bus from the Lobengula St terminus and get off at either Bulawayo Home Industries or the Mzilikazi Primary School.

Hillside Dams

Just five km from Bulawayo along Hillside Rd are Hillside Dams, the lower of which is more or less permanently dry. Around it are rock kopjes and gardens with picnic sites and braai pits. The aloe garden affords vistas of Bulawayo's most elite residences. The dams are beyond walking distance of the centre; take the Hillside Rd or Burnside bus from the City Hall terminus to the stop near Moffat Ave and walk the remaining km to the dams. The park remains open dawn to dusk and the tearoom serves tea and scones in the afternoon.

Tshabalala Wildlife Sanctuary

Tshabalala, eight km from Bulawayo, is a small wildlife reserve. There are no big predators or dangerous beasts and walking and horseback riding are both permitted and encouraged in the savanna scrub landscape. Go for the day and carry a picnic lunch; there are plenty of picnic sites with braai pits throughout.

The sanctuary is open 6 am to 6 pm in the summer and 8 am to 5 pm in winter. Admis-

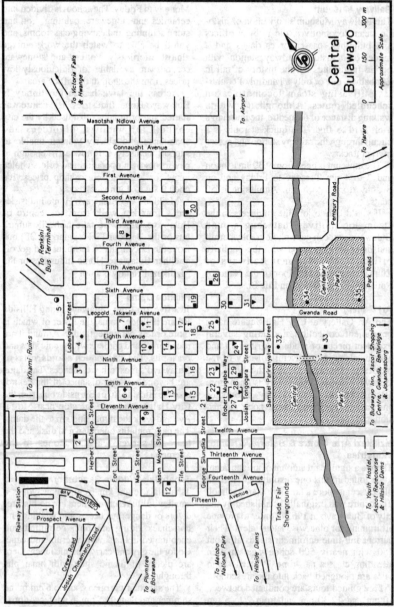

Central Bulawayo

Approximate Scale

0   150   300 m

To Victoria Falls & Hwange

Masotsha Ndlovu Avenue

Connaught Avenue

First Avenue

Second Avenue

Third Avenue

Fourth Avenue

Fifth Avenue

Sixth Avenue

Leopold Takawira Avenue

Eighth Avenue

Ninth Avenue

Tenth Avenue

Eleventh Avenue

Twelfth Avenue

Thirteenth Avenue

Fourteenth Avenue

Fifteenth Avenue

To Renkini Bus Terminal

To Khami Ruins

Lobengula Street

Herbert Chitepo Street

Fort Street

Main Street

Jason Moyo Street

File Street

George Silundika Street

Railway Station

Prospect Avenue

Customs Ave

Crewe Road

Josiah Chinamano Road

To Plumtree & Botswana

To Matobo National Park

To Hillside Dams

To Airport

To Harare

Pembury Road

Park Road

Centenary Park

Gwanda Road

Robert Mugabe Way

Josiah Tongogara Street

Samuel Parirenyatwa Street

Central Park

To Bulawayo Inn, Ascot Shopping Centre, Gwanda, Beitbridge & Johannesburg

To Youth Hostel, Ascot Racecourse & Hillside Dams

Trade Fair Showgrounds

■ PLACES TO STAY	23	Chicken Inn	11	Book Exchanges &
	24	Oriental Takeaways		British Airways Office
2 New Waverley Hotel	27	Bon Journée & La	16	Zambia Airways, South
3 YWCA		Gondola Restaurants		African Airways,
12 Plaza Hotel	28	The Cattleman Restaur-		Eurocarp/Echo Car
13 Palace Hotel		ant		Hire & National
19 Selborne Hotel	31	New Mexicana		Railways Office
20 Cecil Hotel		Restaurant	17	Bulawayo Publicity
26 New Royal Hotel				Association (City
29 Bulawayo Sun Hotel		OTHER		Hall) Tourist Informa-
30 Grey's Inn				tion
33 Caravan Park	1	Railway Museum	18	City Hall Bus Terminus
	4	High Court	22	Kine 600 & Elite 400
▼ PLACES TO EAT	5	Lobengula Street Bus		Cinemas
		Terminus	25	Art Gallery & Jairos Jiri
8 Maison Nic Restaurant	6	Manica Travel		Crafts Shop
14 Grass Hut Restaurant	7	GPO	32	Swimming Pool
15 Haefeli's Swiss Bakery	9	25c Photocopies	34	Bulawayo Theatre
21 Pizzaghetti & Capri	10	Kingston's Bookshop	35	Natural History
Restaurant				Museum

sion is Z$1 per person and horse rentals cost Z$4 per person per hour for groups of up to 11 people. Visitors are permitted to walk, cycle or drive but no motorbikes are allowed.

Hitching isn't bad but you'll have to walk away to get out of the congested area. Alternatively, catch the Kezi bus from Renkini (which passes Tshabalala) or the Matopos road bus from City Hall bus terminus, get off at Retreat and walk the remaining two km or so.

Activities

International Trade Fair Bulawayo's main annual event is the Zimbabwe International Trade Fair held the last week in April or the first week in May at the Trade Fair and Agricultural Society Show Ground where Samuel Parirenyatwa St turns into Hillside Rd. This well-attended event draws at least 200,000 visitors and 1000 exhibitors from all over the country and worldwide with displays and booths on technology and commercial ventures. A large number of peripheral events provide further entertainment.

Sport Golf is available at the Bulawayo Country Club, the Bulawayo Golf Club, and the Harry Allen Golf Club, all just a few km from the city centre.

At the corner of Ninth Ave and Fort St is a gymnasium with a weights room, aerobics classes, a sauna and squash courts, charging a very reasonable Z$5 per day, Z$12 per week or Z$24 per month for use of all equipment.

The municipal swimming pool in Central Park on Samuel Parirenyatwa St is open late August to late May between 10 am and 2 pm and from 3 to 6 pm. They charge 50 cents for as long as you'd like to swim.

Organised Tours United Touring Company or UTC (☎ 61402), at Fourteenth Ave and George Silundika St, and the highly recommended Black Rhino Safaris (☎ 41662), in the Famona suburb, conduct tours of most points of interest in and around Bulawayo, including Matobo National Park, Chipangali Wildlife Orphanage and Khami Ruins. Refer to discussion of individual sites for details.

UTC also offers half-day city tours starting daily at 9 am and 2 pm. In just a few hours, it squeezes in Centenary Park and the Natural History Museum, Mzilikazi Arts Centre and Bulawayo Home Industries for

Z$30 per person. Another tour, which operates at 9.15 Tuesday to Friday and at 2 pm Saturday, visits the Natural History and Railway Museums for Z$20 per person. A third option, which departs at 9 am and 2 pm daily, combines the Natural History Museum with Khami Ruins and costs Z$40 per person.

Places to Stay – bottom end

Camping Lauded by many as the 'finest in Africa', the *Municipal Caravan Park* on Caravan Way is in fact pretty incredible. Situated in a large grassy enclave of Central Park and landscaped with large trees and gardens, it couldn't be more ideal. It's clean and well-guarded with hot showers and baths. They charge Z$3.75 per tent and an additional Z$1.25 per person. Those with vehicles or caravans pay more. Although theft is rare it's probably best not to leave anything of value in tents. If you're concerned, the guards are happy to keep your rucksack while you're out and about.

Hostels & Crash Pads The clean *Youth Hostel* (☎ 76488) in Bulawayo, about a 20 minute walk from the centre, is in a nice old house in a predominantly White and wealthy neighbourhood. It's closed from 10 am to 5 pm. They charge Z$6 for YHA members and Z$8 for nonmembers. It's on Townsend Rd and Third St, into which Twelfth Ave unfathomably changes when it enters the Suburbs grid east of Park St. Their 10.30 pm curfew is militarily enforced.

Sheet hire costs Z$1 per night and family rooms are available. There's a TV lounge, cooking facilities and hot showers but space is limited so it may pay to book ahead or take the risk of having to sleep on the floor your first night there. It's a long walk from the railway station so if you have a lot of luggage, try catching an infrequent Waterford bus from the City Hall bus terminus. Alternatively, taxis from the railway station or the centre will cost between Z$4 and Z$5.

A cheap crash pad in Bulawayo is *Carlowick Hall* (☎ 77196) at 1 Selous Ave (near Robert Mugabe Way) in the Northend

suburb. It's a clean option with a swimming pool and they charge only Z$10 per night. Another is the honest, friendly and clean *Msafiri Guest House* at the corner of Second Ave and Fife St. It's run by the owner of the Paw Paw Lodge in Harare and costs Z$12 for a bed or Z$10 for a mattress on the floor.

Although the *YWCA* (☎ 60185) at the corner of Ninth Ave and Lobengula St is a bit more expensive – it costs Z$18 per person including bed and breakfast – it's conveniently located within easy walking distance of Renkini bus terminal and accommodates both men and women. Monthly rates for women are Z$200, for men Z$185.

Hotels The hopelessly grotty *New Waverley Hotel* (☎ 64294) at Lobengula St and Twelfth Ave charges Z$25 for a double room without bath, although rooms are just as likely to be rented by the hour. The *Palace Hotel* (☎ 64294), at Jason Moyo Ave between Tenth and Eleventh Sts, charges Z$30/40 for singles/doubles without bath or Z$2 more with bath. It's nicer than the New Waverley but not by much.

Places to Stay – middle

The *Cecil Hotel* (☎ 60295) straddles the middle and lower ranges. On the corner of Fife St and Third Ave, they charge Z$35/45 for singles/doubles with private bath, including bed and breakfast. It's comfortable enough and is one of Bulawayo's best deals.

The *Plaza Hotel* (☎ 64280) at the corner of Fourteenth Ave and Jason Moyo St offers singles/doubles without bath for Z$41/47 or with bath for Z$56/62, including breakfast. It doubles as a brothel, however, and can get noisy. The two-star *New Royal Hotel* (☎ 65764) at George Silundika St and Sixth Ave charges Z$55 a single or double.

The popular *Grey's Inn* (☎ 60121) on Robert Mugabe Way near Leopold Takawira Ave charges Z$43 for double rooms without bath whether one or two people occupy them; rooms with private bath cost Z$58 each. Triple rooms with bath cost Z$87 and family rooms are Z$116. None of these rates include breakfast.

On the corner of Leopold Takawira Ave and George Silundika St, the *Selborne Hotel* (☎ 65741) is also an old favourite and probably the nicest of the mid-range hotels. Single/double rooms cost Z$50/65, including breakfast.

Places to Stay – top end

Bulawayo's most imposing hotel, the *Bulawayo Sun* (☎ 60101), is another of those characterless towers which strive to emulate others of their ilk throughout the world. Zimbabwe residents pay Z$100/160 a single/double while foreigners pay US$100/140 in foreign currency only, a real price discrepancy.

The second upmarket hotel, convenient to Ascot Shopping Centre, is the *Bulawayo Inn* (☎ 72464), formerly the Holiday Inn, at Ascot Centre. Zimbabwe residents pay Z$95/140 for singles/doubles while visitors pay US$78/112. It's way out of town – a half-hour walk from City Hall – so it's probably not practical unless you have a vehicle or are prepared to use taxis. Buffet breakfasts, which are available to anyone, cost Z$11.50. The hotel dining room, The Pagoda Restaurant, specialises in Mongolian cuisine.

The Tudor imitation *Cresta Churchill Arms* (☎ 41016) is about five km out of town on Matopos Rd, an impractical location unless you have a vehicle. Zimbabwe residents pay Z$115/166 for singles/doubles and foreigners, who must pay in foreign exchange, are charged US$65/78.

For a real splurge, you may consider the luxurious *Nesbitt Castle* (☎ 42726), a cross between a medieval castle and an English country estate at 6 Percy Ave in the Hillside suburb. Amenities include a sauna, gymnasium, library, gardens, swimming pool and, of course, a billiard room. Breakfasts are served with champagne and each of the nine rooms has suite-like proportions. The price is US$200/300 for singles/doubles. Only advance bookings are accepted.

Places to Eat

Breakfast If you're after coffee, try the friendly and interestingly decorated *Grass Hut* on Fife St between Eighth and Ninth Aves. Their breakfast menu is also pretty good, with eggs, omelettes, bacon, sausage and several toast concoctions.

Bon Journée, on Robert Mugabe Way between Tenth and Eleventh Aves, serves up an impressive set English breakfast for Z$6.50 per person. If you're really hungry, however, visit the breakfast buffet at the *Homestead Restaurant* in the Bulawayo Sun Hotel between 7 and 10 am. All you can eat of their ample English breakfast spread costs Z$11.50. A continental breakfast will cost Z$8.75. They also serve real coffee.

Pizzaghetti near Eleventh Ave and George Silundika St serves set English breakfasts from 4 to 10 am for Z$5, not a bad option if you're leaving early on the bus to Hwange or Victoria Falls.

Lunch & Snacks *Pizzaghetti*, near the corner of Eleventh Ave and George Silundika St, is one of Bulawayo's greatest lunch venues and the food is superb. The decor is a bit odd, sort of a cross between provincial bathroom and contemporary industrial – the chairs are certainly industrial strength. But never mind – most of their pasta dishes are excellent; for a semi-nirvana experience, dig into the ravioli alfredo! Another excellent value is the salad plate which allows you to select a combination of five different salads for Z$3.50. It's a meal in itself.

There is a variety of takeaways in Bulawayo but some are definitely better than others. *AA Chicken Takeaways*, on Robert Mugabe Way between Ninth and Tenth Aves, isn't bad for chicken, samosas, soft drinks and (rather greasy) chips.

Oriental Takeaways, on Eighth Ave between Robert Mugabe Way and Josiah Tongogara St, is one of the best. Herbivores will welcome the opportunity to chow down on their vegetarian burgers, vegetable samosas and other excellent vegetarian and curry options.

Near the corner of Twelfth Ave and Fife St, the *Hot Bread Shop* serves ordinary takeaway meals as well as some creative, pseudo-Mexican concoctions. Try it for something different.

Although it's getting pretty expensive these days, the ultimate trendy takeaway is *Eskimo Hut* on Josiah Tongogara St east near the Zimbabwe International Trade Fair. This is quite a hangout but the prices limit access to the more affluent sectors of Bulawayo society.

The Portuguese-owned *Bon Journée* (also mentioned under breakfast) serves the best ice cream confections in town – thick shakes, banana splits, iced coffee – as well as meals, including steaks, burgers, chicken, omelettes and standard snacks like chips and hot dogs. Unless they're after a steak, one person can fill up here for Z$5 to Z$10. At the counter, incidentally, they sell real Cadbury chocolate. It's on Robert Mugabe Way between Tenth and Eleventh Aves, opposite the cinemas.

If you like English-style teas and light lunches, you may enjoy the *Haddon & Sly* department store's second floor tearoom. The building is on the corner of Eighth Ave and Fife St. Not to be outdone, *Meikles* department store on the corner of Jason Moyo St and Leopold Takawira Ave offers a similar, if less typically Anglo, set-up. Light pub meals are available at the *Old Vic Pub* at the Bulawayo Sun Hotel.

For traditional Zimbabwean fare, try *The Pantry* on Fifteenth Ave between Main and Fort Sts. It's a friendly little place and is open from 5 am to 3 pm.

The clean *YWCA* on Ninth Ave and Lobengula St is open to nonresidents for lunch between 12.30 and 3 pm. For around Z$1.50 you'll get a big and filling plate of sadza ladled over with the relish of the day, normally some sort of beef stew.

For other gooey treats, you can't beat *Haefeli's Swiss Bakery* on Fife St between Tenth and Eleventh Aves. They've got all sorts of doughnuts and European-style cakes, pies and pastries in addition to the excellent bread.

The *Chicken Inn* on the corner of Ninth Ave and Robert Mugabe Way serves as a hangout for local teens, with video games and billiard tables. The other fast food representative is *Wimpy*, of which there are two in Bulawayo. *Waffles*, in the arcade of the National Railways Building on Fife St, is known for its chicken curry and rice.

Dinner One of the nicest restaurants in Bulawayo is the *Capri* (☎ 68639), next door to Pizzaghetti at the corner of Eleventh Ave and George Silundika St. It's open at 6.30 pm nightly for dinner. They offer Italian dishes and serve free garlic bread and vegetable entrées while you're waiting. They also serve expensive South African wines and the best of the Zimbabwean vintages, which go for much more reasonable prices. It always appears closed – the door remains locked for security purposes – so if you want to go in, just knock through the grating and they'll open it up for you. Another Italian option is *La Gondola* (☎ 62986) between Tenth and Eleventh Ave on Robert Mugabe Way.

For Chinese, you may want to try the *Peking* (☎ 60646) on Jason Moyo St, where you'll find pretty good renditions of Sichuan and Cantonese fare. Plan on spending around Z$5 for a meat and rice dish or Z$9 for their set lunch specials which include more food than one person can comfortably polish off.

The New Mexicana (☎ 77292) is on Josiah Tongogara St between Sixth and Leopold Takawira Aves. The food is good but is only as genuinely Mexican as can be created by the Maltese and South African owners with ingredients available in Zimbabwe. The real draw is their Z$4 iceless margarita.

The *Homestead Restaurant* (☎ 60101) in the Bulawayo Sun is open from 12.30 to 2.30 pm for lunch and 6 to 10 pm for dinner.

For steak and other meals heavy on Zimbabwean beef, try *The Cattleman* opposite the Bulawayo Sun Hotel on Josiah Tongogara St and Tenth Ave, or the *Golden Spur* (☎ 70318) on Robert Mugabe Way between Eighth and Ninth Aves.

For a simple meal, try *Grey's Inn* (☎ 60121) on Robert Mugabe Way north of Leopold Takawira Ave. Their speciality seems to be chicken Kiev with salad and chips for Z$7.50, which is not a bad deal, but other standard menu items are available and the food isn't bad.

Another option is *Buffalo Bill's*, in the Selborne Hotel on the corner of Robert Mugabe Way and Leopold Takawira St, where you'll find steaks for Z$12, pizza for Z$8 or so, and salad or dessert bar for Z$1.50 each. This place is very popular with travellers.

Haute cuisine in Bulawayo comes in two forms – à la *Maison Nic* (☎ 61884) on Main St near Fourth Ave, or at *New Orleans* (☎ 43176) on Banff Rd in the Hillside suburb, which serves Cajun cuisine, inasmuch as it can be reproduced in Zimbabwe with crawfish (lobster) so difficult to come by.

Maison Nic takes the Best Restaurant Award year after year. Although its style is very upmarket, it isn't prohibitively expensive and has beautifully prepared fish dishes, including Malawi *chambo*, Kariba bream and whitebait going for Z$21 to Z$25. Antelope venison is available as well, and you can even get an entrée of crocodile tails for only Z$7. Advance bookings are necessary for either New Orleans or Maison Nic.

Self-Catering For cheap fruits and vegetables the best place is Makokoba market beyond Renkini bus terminal. The best selection of produce, however, although not so cheap, is found at *Gee's* on Eighth Ave between George Silundika and Fife Sts.

For general groceries, there's *Haddon & Sly* supermarket on the corner of Eighth Ave and Fife St or try one of the numerous small family-owned shops scattered throughout the city centre. For refined tastes, the supermarket at Ascot Centre is probably the best-stocked in town.

Wholemeal bread can be found at *Haefeli's Swiss Bakery* on Fife St between Tenth and Eleventh Aves. Get there early, however, since they're sometimes sold out by midmorning. Another bakery is *Downing's* on Leopold Takawira Ave opposite City Hall square.

Entertainment

Nightspots Bulawayo pubs and clubs are particularly sticky about their 'smart casual dress' requirements and normally interpret them rather strictly. That means (after 4.30 pm), no open-top shoes, no trainers, no denim and nothing that could remotely be construed as grubby. Men will need at least a sports jacket and probably a tie as well. If you're not equipped with that sort of wardrobe, resign yourself to drinking and dancing at the seedier places where you'll get a more representative taste of Bulawayo nightlife anyway.

The Alabama, around the side of the Bulawayo Sun Hotel, is a pleasant and normally crowded bar with live jazz music almost every evening. Smart casual dress is strictly enforced. The Top of the Sun offers live music nightly and a more upmarket atmosphere than the Alabama.

Both Italian restaurants, the Capri and La Gondola, offer disco music and dancing on weekends. Times and details will be available from the restaurants or the Bulawayo Publicity Bureau.

A popular lowlife hangout and pick-up joint is the Silver Fox, at the corner of Tenth Ave and Robert Mugabe Way, where the propositions come quickly and frequently for both men and women. An even more lively place, the New Waverley Hotel, has better music and frequent live performances, but is definitely not for lone women. A much nicer option is Talk of the Town in the Monte Carlo Building on the corner of Fife St and Twelfth Ave.

If you're interested in a glimpse of the Rhodey teen scene, check out Catch 22 at the International Trade Fair Grounds. Unaccompanied women shouldn't walk to or from this place after dark.

The hotels all have cocktail lounges – if you're up for old English atmosphere, try the Old Vic in the Bulawayo Sun Hotel or the Knight's Arms in the Bulawayo Inn. Picasso's in the Granada Spanish Restaurant on the 1st floor of the Parkade Centre at the corner of Fife St and Ninth Ave is also reputedly atmospheric.

Strewn out along Fort St between Ninth and Eleventh Aves are few more nightspots – the Las Vegas, the Top 10, and Club Tomorrow – while just a block east on Main St there are yet more – the Shumba Bar and the Zambezi Cocktail Lounge.

Cinemas Bulawayo offers good quality cinema and the widest choice to be found anywhere in Zimbabwe. The cinema at the Ascot Centre seems to have somewhat of an art following and sometimes screens more daring flicks than the general-interest cinemas in town. Of the rest, the best are the Kine 600 and Elite 400 on Robert Mugabe Way between Tenth and Eleventh Aves, the Rainbow Vistarama on Fife St between Eleventh and Twelfth Aves and the Seven-Arts on Jason Moyo St between Tenth and Eleventh Aves.

Alliance Française de Bulawayo (☎ 62797 after 5 pm) screens French films with English subtitles on the first and second Tuesday of each month. They also have a lending library open on Saturdays from 11.15 am to noon and they offer French evening classes for adults. The Art Gallery also occasionally sponsors lunchtime films – the Publicity Association keeps up with details or you could enquire at the gallery itself.

Theatre The Bulawayo Theatre (☎ 65393) in Centenary Park stages dramatic productions and hosts the occasional visiting troupe as well. Phone for information on current productions or consult the *Daily Chronicle* or the Publicity Bureau's *Bulawayo This Month*.

Sport Every sport you could imagine has some sort of following in Bulawayo and they've set up a club to accommodate it. *Bulawayo This Month* lists all the clubs; for further information on their activities and meeting times, check with the Publicity Association for contact numbers.

You can catch horse racing at Ascot on alternating Sunday afternoons.

Things to Buy
Jairos Jiri Crafts Centre The Jairos Jiri Crafts outlet beside the art gallery, which sells the work of disabled Zimbabwean artists, offers value on local Ndebele pottery and basketry. You'll also find relatively inexpensive Batonka stools from western Kariba as well as all the standard junk curios.

Camping Equipment Basic camping gear, including butane cartridges for Bleuet stoves, is available at Townshend & Butcher at 82 Jason Moyo St. If you prefer to hire camping equipment, try Iverson's (☎ 61644) on Khami Road west of town which hires everything from tents and stoves to warm clothing.

Getting There & Away
Air Air Zimbabwe connects Bulawayo to all parts of the country by air, with two or three flights daily to and from Harare, a daily service to Hwange and Victoria Falls, three-times weekly service to Buffalo Range and Masvingo, and daily flights (except Saturday) to Johannesburg. Easy connections are also available to Kariba and Lusaka, Zambia. Refer to the Zimbabwe Getting Around chapter for domestic fare information.

Bus You'll find the long distance private bus terminal at Renkini on Sixth Ave Extension west of Lobengula St about 1.5 km outside the centre. Buses to destinations in Zimbabwe – Harare, Masvingo, Beitbridge and Victoria Falls – depart daily at between 6 and 7 am or when full. Try to arrive at least one hour before you want to leave, and two hours before on holidays and weekends when everyone in town, it seems, is trying to squeeze onto the few conveyances.

Each morning three Hwange Special Express buses depart when full for Gwaai River, Hwange crossroads and Victoria Falls. The fare to the Hwange turnoff is Z$10, to Victoria Falls, Z$16.

Ajay Motorways express service uses the centrally located Bulawayo Sun Hotel as a terminal. Their service to Victoria Falls via Gwaai River and Hwange Safari Lodge departs at 7 am on Monday, Wednesday and Friday. This service must be booked in advance through Manica Travel, on Eleventh Ave between Main & Fort Sts. Ajay's express service to Harare leaves the Bulawayo Sun on Monday, Wednesday, Friday and Sunday at 8 am, arriving in Harare at 2 pm. On Tuesday, they leave at noon and arrive at 6 pm.

Ajay Motorways and Shu-Shine each depart daily (except Saturday for Shu-Shine) for Masvingo from the Renkini terminal between 6 and 7 am, arriving at Mucheke musika in Masvingo before noon. The fare is Z$10 one way. ZUPCO leaves daily except Sunday from the Lobengula St terminus at 1 pm, then continues on to the Great Zimbabwe turnoff, about one km from the Great Zimbabwe ruins, arriving at around 7 pm. The fare is Z$10.30.

There's a less-than-official bus service which operates a daily service between Bulawayo and Johannesburg, departing from the Leopold Takawira St side of City Hall Square at 8.30 am for Z$123 each way. It's a private South African company and therefore isn't officially permitted to operate in Zimbabwe (authorities appear to keep looking the other way); they're also uninsured in Zimbabwe and travel is at the passengers' own risk. Express Motorways coaches depart for Johannesburg from City Hall car park on Tuesday, Thursday and Saturday for Z$99 per person.

Zimbabwe Omnibus Company, at the Lobengula St terminus, operates twice-daily service between Bulawayo and Francistown, Botswana, departing at 8 am and 2 pm. Once weekly, the bus continues on to Gaborone, Botswana.

Train Especially if you're heading for Johannesburg, you'll need to book rail tickets well in advance and purchase them at least a week before travel, or reservations may be cancelled. Bookings and ticket sales are handled at separate windows at the railway station; if there's any sort of queue at all, settle in for a good long wait.

There are daily trains between Bulawayo and Harare departing at 8 am and 9 pm daily in either direction. To Hwange and Victoria Falls, the steam service departs at 7 pm, arriving at Dete (Hwange National Park) at 2 am and at the falls at 7.30 am. The Bulawayo-bound train chugs out of Victoria Falls at 5.30 pm daily, passes Dete at 11.13 pm and steams into Bulawayo at 7.05 am. There's also a daily goods train to Chiredzi in south-eastern Zimbabwe.

There are weekly trains to and from Johannesburg and daily service to and from Francistown, Gaborone and Lobatse in Botswana. For more specific information, timetables and fares, refer to the Zimbabwe Getting Around chapter earlier in the book. You'll require your passport to make international bookings.

Rail service enquiries should be directed to 363111 during business hours and 322284 after hours.

Getting Around

To/From the Airport The Air Zimbabwe bus runs between the Bulawayo Sun Hotel and the airport north of town for Z$2 per person but taxis will cost at least Z$20 each way.

Bus Bulawayo has two suburban bus termini. The City Hall terminus on Eighth Ave, between Fife and George Silundika Sts, serves the more affluent northern, eastern and southern suburbs. There's a published timetable but it isn't followed very closely and shouldn't be relied upon under any circumstances.

The other terminus is at the corner of Lobengula St and Sixth Ave and serves the high-density suburbs to the west and southwest of the centre. These buses are normally extremely crowded and if you're in a hurry to get somewhere in those parts, it'd probably be worth going by taxi.

City buses cost 30 cents per ride. Emergency taxis ply set routes around the city but aren't permitted outside city limits. They cost a standard 60 cents per ride, regardless of your destination.

Taxi Quite a few taxi services operate in

Bulawayo. Most vehicles are metered but on popular runs, especially from the railway station, you may be able to bargain for a lower price. For bookings, phone Rixi Taxi (☎ 60666, 61933/4/5). Other companies are available on 72454, 60154 and 60704.

Car Hire The Avis office (☎ 68571) is at 99 Robert Mugabe Way, Hertz (☎ 74701) is headquartered at the Bulawayo Sun Hotel. Transit Car & Truck Hire (☎ 76495), which also hires bicycles, is on the corner of Twelfth Ave and Fife St, and Europcar/Echo (☎ 67925) has an office in Africa House on Fife St.

Another useful option is offered by Airline Chauffeur Services (☎ 44243) at the Cresta Churchill Arms Hotel, which hires car and driver to any place within an 80 km radius of Bulawayo for around Z$200 for a 12 hour day. Alternatively, four travellers can do a half-day tour of Matobo National Park for around Z$100. Because car rental km charges rack up so quickly, this option can actually work out cheaper than hiring a car and driving it yourself.

Bicycle The level countryside in and around Bulawayo is ideal for cyclists. Bicycles may be hired for Z$10 per day plus Z$1.50 insurance against loss or theft and Z$50 deposit from Transit Hire (☎ 76495 Bulawayo) at the corner of Twelfth Ave and Fife St. Be sure to take a spin around the car park and check your bike before accepting it; most of the bikes are new but there are a few duds. If you pay by credit card, the deposit is waived.

Around Bulawayo

Bulawayo's surroundings contain some scenic and unusual landscapes, with balancing rocks and several ancient ruins and rock paintings. The highlight, of course, is Matobo National Park with its ample outdoor opportunities and rhino-rich game park. This impressive region once served as the spiritual capital of the Mwari-worshipp-ing Rozwi Empire. Later, it so impressed Cecil John Rhodes that he requested to be buried on View of the World there.

KHAMI (KAME) RUINS
Khami's nearly always deserted ruins aren't as large or impressive as those of Great Zimbabwe. At Khami, visitors can wander alone through the crumbled 40 hectare city and see it more or less as it was when its former inhabitants left as it was being destroyed by fire. Europeans first saw Khami around 1893. Until Lobengula's death in that year, the Ndebele had guarded it from the new intruders, perhaps as a royal retreat or a sacred site.

A small museum on the site explains Khami's history. Before exploring the ruins, you may want to pick up the pamphlet *A Trail Guide to the Khami National Monument* which is sold at the museum. The site is open from 8 am to 5 pm daily; admission is free. At the moment, there are no facilities but the National Museums and Monuments department is currently planning to establish a camping area at Khami, an excellent idea, as you'll probably agree once you've seen the place.

Getting There & Away
There are no buses out on Khami Rd and it's a difficult hitch since the route is very sparsely travelled. Without a vehicle, your options are pretty limited. Most travellers wind up hiring a bicycle from Transit in Bulawayo and pedalling the 22 flat km to the ruins and back, an easy half-day trip. Just head out Khami Rd (Eleventh Ave) beyond Lobengula St and follow the signposted route.

Another possibility is to pay a couple of dollars and catch a lift in the back of the inspector of monuments' pick-up truck. Check at his office in the Natural History Museum in Bulawayo and see when the next inspection tour is due.

UTC half-day tours from Bulawayo combine the Natural History Museum with Khami ruins. It departs at 9 am and 2 pm daily and costs Z$40 per person, with

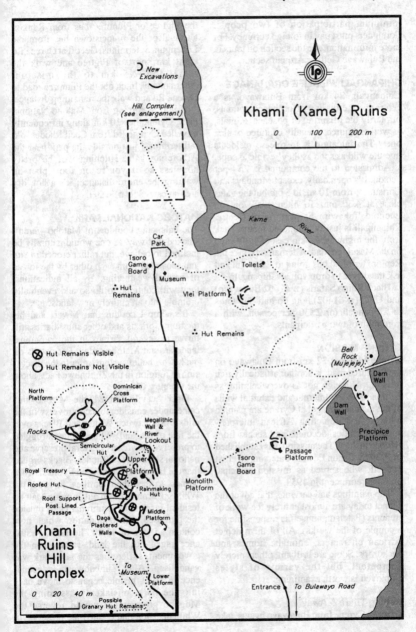

Khami (Kame) Ruins

New Excavations

Hill Complex
(see enlargement)

0   100   200 m

Kame   River

Car Park

Tsoro Game Board

Museum

Hut Remains

Toilets

Vlei Platform

Hut Remains

Bell Rock (Mujejeje)

Dam Wall

Dam Wall

Precipice Platform

Passage Platform

Tsoro Game Board

Monolith Platform

Entrance   To Bulawayo Road

⊗ Hut Remains Visible
◯ Hut Remains Not Visible

North Platform

Dominican Cross Platform

Rocks

Megalithic Wall & River Lookout

Semicircular Hut

Upper Platform

Royal Treasury

Roofed Hut

Rainmaking Hut

Roof Support Post Lined Passage

Middle Platform

Daga Plastered Walls

Khami Ruins Hill Complex

0   20   40 m

To Museum

Lower Platform

Possible Granary Hut Remains

minimum participation of two people. Foreigners must pay in foreign currency. For more information, see the section on tours in the Bulawayo Getting Around section.

CHIPANGALI WILDLIFE ORPHANAGE

Chipangali, 24 km from Bulawayo, is a centre for the rearing of orphaned animals, primarily the offspring of poached animals, as well as injured, illegally captured or sick ones. The intention is to release residents into the wild as soon as they're able to cope. Admission to the compound is Z$4 per person. It's open daily, except Mondays and Christmas, from 10 am to 5 pm but the gates close at 4.30 pm. To hitch, walk out on Leopold Takawira St past Ascot Centre. Chipangali is just two hundred metres back from the highway, 24 km east of Bulawayo on the Masvingo road. Alternatively, take the Renkini terminal bus going to Esigodini and ask the driver to drop you at Chipangali.

Black Rhino Safaris (☎ 41662 Bulawayo) and UTC (☎ 61402) both do half-day tours to Chipangali for Z$30 per person, with a minimum of two participants.

CYRENE MISSION

Cyrene Mission, 32 km from Bulawayo on the Plumtree road, is another artistically rich mission. Although not as overwhelming as Serima, both the internal and external walls of the thatched chapel at Cyrene are painted with frescos depicting African interpretations of biblical accounts and scenes from African history. The mission was established in 1939 by Canon Edward Paterson, an artist himself, who served as mission principal until his retirement in 1953.

The paintings and carvings that cover the chapel today are almost entirely the work of students (Paterson himself is responsible for a couple of the works). All of them depict African characters, animals, homes and backdrops. Some are brilliant, others merely competent, but the variety of styles employed is worth examining.

Getting There & Away

To reach Cyrene from Bulawayo by bus, take the Figtree or Plumtree bus from Renkini terminal or the Francistown bus from the Lobengula St terminus. Get off at Cyrene Rd eight km short of Figtree and walk the remaining 2.5 km to the mission. Alternatively, hitch out the Plumtree road to Cyrene Rd and walk the remaining distance.

If you're coming from Matobo National Park, Cyrene lies 10 km along infrequently travelled Cyrene Rd from Cecil Rhodes' old rail terminus, just outside the park near the Arboretum gate. Hitching will be pretty hopeless so if you're on foot, plan on walking the entire distance; it's a hot, dry area so carry lots of water.

MATOBO NATIONAL PARK

The balancing boulders of Matobo weren't stacked that way, as one would naturally be inclined to believe, but rather eroded *in situ* and separated from each other by the forces of natural weathering. By all indications, they will continue to do so and eventually crumble into an entirely new landscape.

It's almost certain that Mwari and his mediums, priests and other subsidiaries still thrive at several shrines in the communal lands around Matobo today. For details on the Mwari belief system, refer to the discussion of religion in the Zimbabwe Facts about the Country Chapter.

Once heavily farmed, the Matobo area came under considerable controversy in the mid-1900s between Whites and Blacks over the fate of the land. While Whites struggled to preserve the area as a natural preserve and national shrine to C J Rhodes, Blacks argued that the farmland was needed by subsistence farmers to feed their families. In 1962, the White government won out, moving Matobo resident farmers to communal lands outside the proposed park boundaries, which now contain an area of 43,200 hectares. Resistance raged but the land, rather than the government, suffered as the new park was vandalised. After Zimbabwean independence in 1980, people began to move back into the park, mistakenly assuming the Mugabe government would reverse the White decision that created the preserve. In

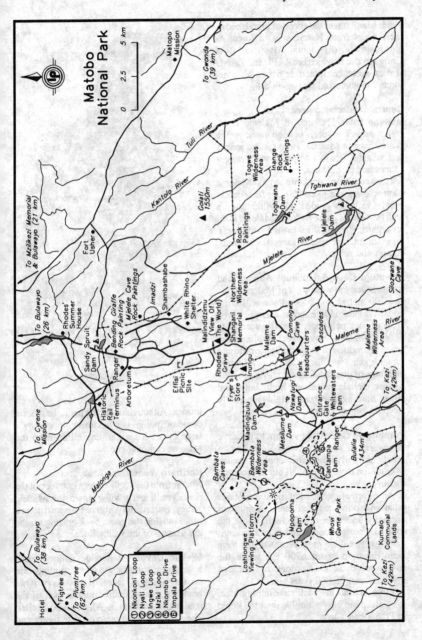

Matobo National Park

① Nkonkoni Loop
② Nyati Loop
③ Ingwe Loop
④ Mziki Loop
⑤ Nkombo Drive
⑥ Impala Drive

1983, Matobo was the scene of bloodshed as the powers from Harare sent in forces to eliminate the dissidents. After the 1988 Unity Accord in which the ZAPU and ZANU armies were combined into one national force, Matabeleland was again calm.

Central Wilderness Area

Maleme Dam The area of Maleme Dam, which serves as park headquarters, is the busiest part of Matobo. Here are the lodges and chalets, main camping area, ranger offices and picnic sites.

Horse trails are available around Maleme Dam, costing the usual Z$6 for the equally usual 1½ hours guided ride. Although it's well outside the game park, the Maleme Dam area, particularly to the west and north-west, is rich in antelope species as well as baboons, dassies and zebra.

Nswatugi Cave & Museum An easy and scenic seven km walk west of Maleme Dam and 200 metres up a steep track will bring you to Nswatugi Cave and its well-preserved array of rock paintings, an easily accessible panel in Matobo. Note especially the accuracy in the motion of the galloping giraffe and running zebra and the excellent perspective paintings of giraffes. Other well-represented figures include numerous kudu bulls and cows, hunting party and eight apparently sleeping human figures.

Pomongwe Cave In an attempt to preserve the gallery of ancient artwork from the elements, an early researcher applied shellac over all the cave figures, all but obliterating them.

An information board at the site explains what was once depicted there. A museum currently under construction will house the tools and pottery uncovered in archaeological digs here. The most recent layers have been dated to about 6500 BC while the lowest of these excavations has yielded artefacts over 35,000 years old.

From behind the Maleme camping area, it's a steep but easy scramble over the kopje to Pomongwe Cave.

Black eagle

Inungu Although not in the park, the granite dome of Inungu is a landmark, topped by a large cross. It's a half-day climb from the Maleme camping site.

Northern Wilderness Area

Not far from the north-eastern entrance of the park, you'll get a view down the Mjelele Valley. Surprisingly, it's not unusual to see rhino *outside the game park* grazing on the dry grasses of the valley floor.

Mjelele Cave Just outside national park boundaries, the Mjelele Cave paintings are on the northern faces of two very large boulders a few hundred metres east of the road eight km north of White Rhino Shelter. They contain a human/crocodile figure and some detailed ancient paintings blotted out by the amateurish work of later imitators.

Arboretum & Rhodes' Rail Terminus Not much remains of Cecil Rhodes' rail terminus two km outside the park's north-west entrance. The line was originally built so that turn-of-the-century Bulawayo socialites could have easy Sunday afternoon access to the rocky wonders of Matobo Park.

The nearby arboretum is just inside the park boundary from the rail terminus. If you're after greenness, however, the camping site there will prove pleasant.

White Rhino Shelter White Rhino Shelter lies several hundred metres along a clearly marked path from the signposted car park about five km north of the View of the World turnoff. The paintings are outline drawings rather than the polychrome paintings more commonly found in Matobo. Most prominent are the outlines of five white rhino and the head of a black rhino, with human figures visible behind them, and five well-drawn wildebeest.

Peripheral figures include a procession of human hunters and an obvious polychrome lion, which are believed to postdate the other paintings by millennia.

Malindidzimu (View of the World) The Ndebele name of this hill means Place of the Benevolent Spirits. Cecil John Rhodes didn't spend much time at his estate near Rhodes Dam just outside the northern extreme of Matobo Park but was taken with the surrounding country. When Rhodes died in South Africa six years later, on 26 March 1902, his body was carried to the spot and buried in the way he'd requested. A display at the bottom of the hill outlines highlights of Rhodes' life and career.

Rhodes' Grave The lichen-streaked boulders that surround Rhodes' grave are particularly colourful. While some of the more traditional Rhodies still make an annual pilgrimage to the site on the anniversary of his death, 26 March, most visitors just appreciate the solitude and the view.

Although the easiest access to the summit is via a road leading up from the eastern side of the hill, an alternative and more scenic walking route ascends from the picnic area directly south of it.

Other Graves Just below Rhodes' grave is that of Dr Leander Starr Jameson, a good friend of Cecil Rhodes, who commanded Ft Victoria (Masvingo) after its 1890 founding. He died in England on 26 November 1917, but because of WW I, was not brought to View of the World until 1920. Also interred at View of the World is Charles Patrick John Coghlan, the first premier of Southern Rhodesia, who was buried there on 14 August 1930.

Shangani River (Allan Wilson) Memorial The monument a little downhill from Rhodes' Grave was erected in 1904 to the memory of Allan Wilson and the 33 soldiers of his Shangani River Patrol. The troupe was massacred by the forces of General Mtjaan and 30,000 Ndebele warriors, of whom more than 400 were nevertheless slain by the patrol's superior firepower.

The bodies were brought at Rhodes' request from Great Zimbabwe, where they had previously been interred. The inscription reads simply: 'Erected in the enduring memory of Allan Wilson and his men who fell in a fight against the Matabele on the Shangani River, December 4th, 1898. There was no survivor'.

Whovi Game Park
The well-guarded white rhino population at Whovi is healthy and visitors may even spot the more elusive black rhino, which is represented here as well, but in much smaller numbers. Rhinos were reintroduced from South Africa on the basis of the rock painting in nearby White Rhino Shelter.

Besides the rhinos, Matobo also contains the world's greatest concentration of black eagle nesting sites and you may well observe them soaring above their kopje-bound nests.

As at Maleme, guided 1½ hour horseback trips are available at Whovi Game Park, costing Z$6. If you don't have a vehicle and aren't lucky with hitching, this will be your only access to this area of of the park.

At the game park entrance, women from nearby communal lands set up curio stands where you'll have the opportunity to look over some locally made Matobo basketry and carvings. Admission to Whovi is Z$1 per person. Gates open at 8 am and close at 5.45 pm.

Bambata Cave

A 40 minute walk from the Bulawayo road, Bambata Cave is in the Bambata Wilderness Area which extends westward from the main body of Matobo Park. This cave, which is full of paintings, is best known for its rendition of a cheetah with striped legs. Extensive excavations in the cave have uncovered tools and pottery from the first few centuries BC and have given the name Bambata to similar finds from the same period elsewhere in Zimbabwe.

Toghwe Wilderness Area

The remote eastern third of Matobo lies in the Toghwe Wilderness Area, the wildest of all the park wildernesses. It contains the scenic Mjelele and Toghwana valleys as well as Inange Cave and its fine collection of rock paintings. Roads are rough with some very steep bits and vehicles are infrequent; low-slung cars may encounter problems so high clearance is advised. After rains, lower-lying stretches of the rough roads may become impassable without 4WD.

Mjelele Dam This long, narrow and nearly empty dam at the far south-eastern corner of the park is becoming choked with vegetation. It's little visited at the moment but road improvements are being made and the camping site is being upgraded. It's a long walk from anywhere else in the park, so without a car, access is problematic. The road between Mjelele and Toghwana is horrid, requiring a lion-hearted and preferably high-clearance 4WD vehicle.

Togwhana Dam Toghwana Dam has a camping site, and you could make a good three day, 60 km return walk from Maleme Dam to the Inange Cave paintings, which are seven km on foot from Toghwana. Alternatively, you could walk one-way via the 27 km route through communal lands to or from Sandy Spruit at Matobo's north entrance.

The road in from either direction has some extremely steep sections and although 4WD isn't essential, you'll need a strong vehicle.

Inange Cave A four to six hour return walk from the Toghwana Dam camping site, Inange Cave is at the top of a high whale-back dome. In this remote site one encounters one of the most complex and well-executed of Zimbabwe's cave paintings.

Inange (sometimes spelt Inanke) is a rough, and at times steep, seven km walk from Toghwana Dam. If you're going, it's a good idea to get an early start, which will be facilitated if you're staying at the Toghwana camping site. For the first couple of km, the route is marked by green-painted arrows and small rock cairns. Beyond that, there are only arrows, which are not always distinct, and the way becomes frustratingly confusing as it passes over a series of nearly identical ridges and valleys.

Avoid the temptation to take shortcuts and if you do lose the marked track, retrace your steps to the previous marker and try again. Unless you're with a guide or have the appropriate topo sheet and are particularly adept at reading it, resign yourself to the possibility of becoming lost. If you're really keen to go, the Black Rhino Safaris people (see Getting There & Away) know the route well and can provide the best directions available.

Silozwane Cave This little-visited cave in the communal lands south of the park contains paintings and is more easily reached than Inange.

To reach Silozwane from Maleme, go six km east to the Mjelele and Toghwana Dam turnoff. Turn right and continue along that road for 12 km and take the signposted right fork and follow it for less than two very rough km to the car park. From there, it's a short, steep walk over the dome to the hollow. Hitching to Silozwane is probably out of the question.

Places to Stay & Eat

Since most overnight visitors to Matobo are headed for the Maleme Dam chalets and camping site, the place can become insufferably crowded on weekends and holidays – these are naturally the best times to be hitching in but not always the most pleasant to actually *be* there. In the winter and during the week, however, Maleme will only be shared by the odd traveller and the baboons, dassies and klipspringers that inhabit the surrounding bouldery hills.

Camping sites cost Z$10 per night for up to six people per site. The chalets cost Z$15 for one bedroom, Z$20 for two, and lodges cost Z$30 and Z$35 per night for one/two-bedroom units. The two-bedroom *Black Eagle* and *Fish Eagle* luxury lodges cost Z$70 and afford a boulder-packed hilltop vista of Maleme and surroundings. They're well worth the money, especially if you can muster a group of four people to share the costs. Advance bookings, which are advised, should be made through the National Parks central booking office in Harare or at the Bulawayo Booking Agency (☎ 63646 Bulawayo), 140A Fife St, Bulawayo.

Although Maleme is the most popular camping area, there are several others scattered around the park. At the northern entrance is Sandy Spruit Dam, a rather ordinary camping site too close to the highway, which is nevertheless conveniently located if you're arriving late. The site at Toghwana Dam in the Toghwe Wilderness Area is exceptionally nice but access is difficult, while Mjelele Dam, eight km south of it and equally remote, is currently undergoing improvements. Near the Arboretum entrance is a very civilised site and there's also a small but beautiful site exclusively for tent camping at Mesilume Dam.

Apart from Maleme, water in all camping sites should be boiled or purified before drinking. No toilet paper is supplied at any of the camping areas and all park waters are infected with bilharzia.

The only supplies in the vicinity are at the rudimentary Fryer's Store, just outside the park boundary, a six km walk up the Maleme River from Maleme Dam or 10 km along the road. Adjacent to Fryer's is the *Inungu Guest House*, which will accommodate one party at a time. If you want to get away from it all in the Matobo, this isn't a bad place to do it. They charge Z$80 per night for one to four adults and Z$20 per night for each additional adult up to eight. Book through Sunshine Tours (☎ 67791 Bulawayo) on the corner of Eighth Ave and Jason Moyo St in Bulawayo.

South of Matopos near Kezi is the *Omadu Maphisa Hotel* (☎ 216 Kezi), a good and recommended little place in the communal lands between the park and the Botswana border. It's accessible by southbound bus from anywhere along the Bulawayo road west of the park.

Getting There & Away

Although budget access to Matobo without a vehicle isn't easy, most travellers manage somehow and everyone assesses the effort as worthwhile. Hitching is slow, but hitchhikers always arrive eventually and since there are several camping grounds around the park perimeter, one need only reach the proximity to be within striking distance on foot.

Alternatively, you can take the Kezi bus from Renkini in Bulawayo. If you get off at the first Matobo turnoff, you can walk the six km to Sandy Spruit camping site. From the second turning at Rhodes' rail terminus, it's a five km walk into the Arboretum camping site. If you're headed for Maleme, get off at the third park access road and walk into the camping site either via the new six km shortcut or the 12 km circuit past Mesilume, Nswatugi and Madingizulu dams and Nswatugi Cave. You could also hire bicycles at Transit in Bulawayo and carry them on the bus into the park (cyclists won't be admitted to the game park).

If you have a bit more ready cash, Airline Chauffeur Services (see Getting Around under Bulawayo) hires car and driver for half-day Matobo tours (which isn't enough time for even a whirlwind pass through what's there) for up to four passengers for Z$100.

Both UTC (☎ 61402 Bulawayo) and Black Rhino Safaris (☎ 41662, fax 77300 Bulawayo) offer full and half-day tours of Matobo. The day tour with Black Rhino can't be recommended highly enough. It's apparent the work is a labour of love: the guides and owners, Russell and Adam, have probably spent more time at Matobo than anyone else, yet their enthusiasm for the place remains infectious and they'll accompany you on walks and climbs and visit areas that are overlooked by the apparently bored and bus-bound UTC drivers.

Although both UTC and Black Rhino tours both cost Z$60 per person (including lunch) and depart at 9 am, the latter are just entering the game park when UTC is already returning to Bulawayo. Black Rhino fills up quickly, however, so advance booking is essential. If you'd like to spend more than the allotted time looking around the park, Black Rhino (and sometimes UTC) will drop you at Maleme Dam when the tour is finished and allow you to return with them to Bulawayo on another day. Since tours don't run everyday, advance arrangements should be made.

If you're short of time, half-day tours are available for Z$40 with Black Rhino and Z$46 with UTC, both including lunch. They depart at 9 am and 2 pm and are available whenever there is sufficient interest.

Western Zimbabwe

GWAAI RIVER

Gwaai River, sometimes known as Dahlia Siding, is an obligatory stop for anyone, including those using public transport, travelling between Bulawayo and Hwange or Victoria Falls. They either settle in for a night at the charming *Gwaai River Hotel* (☎ 3400 Dete) or visit just long enough for tea and a snack in the garden. The primary appeal of the hotel is its owner, an exceptional fellow called Harold Brumberg, who seems to be on first-name terms with half of Zimbabwe and treats travellers like long-lost friends.

Rooms cost Z$42.50/80 for singles/doubles, including dinner, bed and breakfast. Without the brekkie, they cost Z$34/64 and for bed and breakfast only, Z$32/60. Although camping isn't officially advertised, travellers who may be short of cash for a room can normally make arrangements to camp on the grounds for a few dollars.

If you're interested in photography, *Nemba Safaris* (☎ 33 Lupane), PO Box 4, Gwaai River, does photographic tours throughout western Zimbabwe, including Hwange, Zambezi, Kazuma Pan and Chizarira national parks. Write or phone for further details.

DETE

Previously known as Dett, Dete serves as the rail terminal for Hwange National Park. Unfortunately, this access route is fraught with problems; the train from Victoria Falls arrives at 11.13 pm and from Bulawayo at 1.26 am – that is, when they're on time. Once arrived, you're still faced with a 12 km walk or hitch to the park entrance and another seven km into Hwange Main Camp, along a road upon which walking (and, officially, hitching) is prohibited. If you're booked into Hwange Safari Lodge, 18 km from Dete, you can make arrangements to be met at the station by the UTC shuttle.

The dilapidated but friendly *Game Reserve Hotel* (☎ 366) has a loud disco. When the disco isn't on, the hotel restaurant is cheap and bearable if you order sadza ne nyama. If you're arriving on the train from Bulawayo, book in advance or the hotel will be locked up. Rooms cost about Z$35/45 for singles/doubles.

In a pinch, you can crash on the concrete floor of the '1st-class' lounge at the railway station. It gets cold at night, however, so a sleeping bag is essential.

HWANGE

Hwange town, about 150 km from Victoria Falls, owes its existence to the discovery of coal. Hwange town, like the national park, was named after a local chief. For many years, it was spelt Wankie and this mispronunciation has endured to the present day, although some Black people pronounce it 'HWAN-gay'.

There's no reason to visit the town and most people hurry through. If you want to break up the trip, however, the two-star *Baobab Hotel* (☎ 323 Hwange) on the hill offers agreeable accommodation for about Z$50/70 for singles/doubles, including breakfast.

Buses and trains between Bulawayo and Victoria Falls pass through Hwange.

Hwange National Park

Although Hwange National Park is Zimbabwe's most accessible and most densely game-packed national park you will never feel crowded there and only rarely will you encounter safari vehicles beyond the short loop drives within a few km of Main Camp.

The best time to visit Hwange is during the dry season – September and October – when the animals concentrate in the vicinity

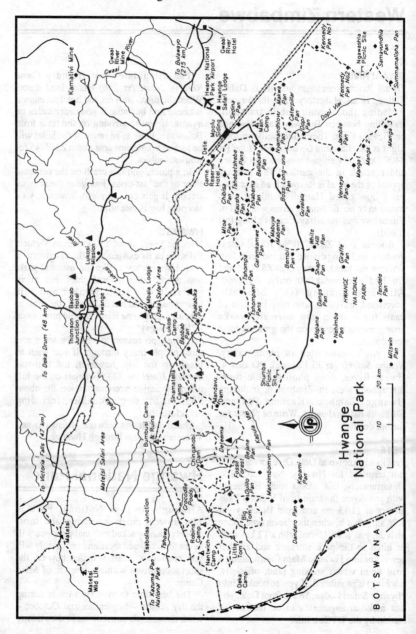

of waterholes. When the rains come and rivers are flowing, successful game viewing requires more diligence because the wildlife spreads out across the park's 14,650 sq km.

The Main Camp area is characterised by savanna and thorny acacia scrub while just south-east around Ngwethla are broad grassy *vleis*, acacia-dotted plains and game concentrations reminiscent of the great Kenyan parks – but without the crowds. Here you'll find some of the the largest herds of antelope, zebra, buffalo and elephants in Zimbabwe as well as unbelievable numbers of baboons.

Travelling west from Main Camp, around Shumba Picnic Site, the savannas dissolve into rolling thorn and *mopani*-covered hills, where the bush tends to obscure visibility. Although you won't see the staggering numbers of individual animals, there will be a good chance of observing such predators as lions, leopards, cheetahs, hyaenas and wild dogs.

Orientation & Information

Travellers using public transport will arrive at Safari Crossroads by the Hwange Special Express bus, Hwange National Park Airport by Air Zimbabwe, Dete railway station by the steam train, or Hwange Safari Lodge by Ajay Motorways. From Safari Crossroads, it's seven km to the airport turnoff and 11.5 km to the Hwange Safari Lodge. From there, it's another five km to the railway tracks marking the park entrance and six km further to Main Camp. Coming from Dete, follow the road for 12 km south-east along the railway line and turn right at the T-junction. From there, the Safari Lodge is seven km along the road to the left and Main Camp six km down the road to the right.

Maps and park information are available at the Main, Sinamatella and Robins Camp ranger offices. Park entry fees are Z$2 per person for day visits or Z$5 per day for overnight or multiday visitors.

Hwange Safari Lodge

The comfortable *Hwange Safari Lodge* (☎ 332 Dete) is one of the Sun Hotels group. Although it's not in the park proper, it serves as a transportation terminal and staging point for most organised safaris through the park. Those arriving on the Ajay Motorways service from Bulawayo or Victoria Falls will be dropped here.

Guests have access to the hotel's tennis and volleyball courts while the swimming pool may be used by nonguests as long as someone in the group appears to be busy eating at the terrace restaurant and snack bar. A massive buffet lunch is served up for Z$11 per person and the eating area overlooks the hotel's private pan where animals come to drink.

In the corner of the lawn is a museum with some basic park and wildlife information and a craft shop where you can often watch the artists at work producing wooden bowls – not indigenous crafts but works of art, nevertheless.

Single/double rooms at the Hwange Safari Lodge cost nonresidents US$80/124 for singles/doubles while Zimbabwe residents pay Z$100/170. Double suites are also available for US$200. All rooms include bed and buffet breakfast. Around the reception area you'll find representatives from Touch the Wild and UTC who offer game drives through the park.

Hwange Main Camp

Main Camp contains the majority of park services, including the ranger headquarters, petrol station, chalet, cottages, lodges, camping ground, restaurant and pub. There's also a shop which is open 8 to 10 am, noon to 2 pm and 4 to 7 pm. A small museum behind the shop displays aspects of the area's natural history.

Camping at Main Camp costs Z$10 per night for up to six people. Fully equipped one and two-bedroom lodges are available for Z$25 per bedroom per night. Cottages cost Z$20/25 for one/two bedrooms and chalets cost Z$15/20. All National Parks accommodation should be prebooked through the Harare or Bulawayo booking offices or you risk not finding a place.

Ranger Walks From the Main Camp office,

two hour ranger-guided walks to the game-viewing hide at Sedina Pan depart at 6.30 am, 10 am and 4 pm and cost only Z$2 per person. Many travellers spend several days doing the entire regimen of walks and thereby gain first-hand familiarity with the animals' chronological patterns and daily variations.

The armed guides have had extensive bush training and can draw on their wealth of knowledge to answer questions and provide a running commentary about the birds, game, vegetation and landscapes.

Nyamandhlovu Platform For those without vehicles, an excellent option is to spend a day at Nyamandhlovu Pan Viewing Platform, 10 km from Main Camp. Catch the morning UTC game drive from Main Camp to the viewing platform and sit all day under the shade watching the comings and goings, both tourist and wildlife. From this commanding perch, you'll have a view over Nyamandhlovu Pan where animals come to drink. You can then ride back in the evening with the UTC afternoon game drive, all for only Z$30 per person. See under Game Drives in Getting Around below for more information.

Moonlight Convoys For two or three nights around the full moon each month, Main Camp rangers lead a convoy of vehicles into the park for two hours to see what's brewing out there at night. Hitchhikers are normally welcome at such times – just ask the rangers or anyone with empty space in their vehicle.

Ngwethla Loop
Although Ngwethla is accessible to any car via the Kennedy Pans, the Ngwethla loop drive will require a sturdy vehicle. At dusk, herds of elephant churn the pans into mud holes. The picnic sites at Ngwethla and Jambile are available for overnight camping. For details, see the discussion of Other Camps later in this section.

Sinamatella Camp
Sinamatella Camp sits atop a 50 metre high mesa with a commanding 50 km view in all directions; the nicest of Hwange's three general camping grounds and lodge complexes. There's a ranger office and museum display, a small crafts shop, a kiosk selling basic supplies and a restaurant and pub. The petrol pumps are for park vehicles only so if you're driving, you'll have to fill up at Main Camp, Hwange Safari Lodge or in Hwange Town.

Accommodation prices at Sinamatella are the same as those at Main Camp. Ranger-escorted walks are available during the day for groups of up to six people and cost Z$10 per hour for the entire group. A recommended trip from Sinamatella is the cross-country walk to Mandavu Dam and back; it can be arranged at the ranger office at the camp. Similar overnight treks with an armed and experienced ranger guide will cost Z$100 per 24-hour day for groups of up to six trekkers, but these must be arranged in advance through the National Parks central booking office in Harare or the Bulawayo Booking Agency in Bulawayo.

Robins & Nantwich Camps
Robins and *Nantwich*, near the north-western corner of the park, lie in prime lion, cheetah and hyaena country.

The camping ground at Robins has been described as 'rough' and the rangers discourage its use due to frequent nocturnal invasion by lions and hyaenas. Even those staying in the chalets are advised not to venture to the loo at night. There is no camping area at Nantwich.

Chalets are available at Robins for Z$15/20 for one/two bedrooms. At Nantwich, there are three two-bedroom lodges each accommodating up to six people for Z$60 per night. Only outdoor cooking facilities are available at Robins and there isn't a restaurant at either camp. At Robins there is a sparsely stocked shop which is only open sporadically. Guided day walks and overnight trips similar to those described in the Sinamatella section are available from Robins as well.

Robins and Nantwich camps are closed

during the rainy season from December to March.

Other Camps

Picnic Sites At Shumba, Mandavu Dam, Ngwethla, Jambile, Kennedy Pan I and Detema Pan are enclosed picnic sites which are made available to groups of up to eight people as exclusive camps for Z$20 per night. Lions are frequently seen in the area of *Shumba* but the site itself isn't too appealing. *Mandavu* has a big expanse of water and *Kennedy Pan I* attracts large numbers of elephants at night. *Ngwethla* has a nice camping area and lies in an area of heavy game concentrations.

At *Masuma Dam*, you can camp in the beautiful hide overlooking the water and spend the night listening to hippos and elephants and, if there's a moon, watch animals coming to drink.

Exclusive Camps Exclusive camps operated by the park service rent for Z$70 per night for groups of up to 12, including the use of cutlery and cooking facilities. Each camp has a resident guide who will take you walking for as long as you'd like during your stay. *Bumbusi Camp* near Sinamatella is the nicest of the lot but for holiday periods, it's spoken for over six months in advance so book early.

Deka Camp, 25 km west of Robins Camp near the Botswana border, and *Lukosi*, in the Deka Safari Area near Mbala Camp just outside the park, offer nice amenities but there's not much game around. Deka is accessible only by 4WD vehicle. Lukosi is open only during the non-hunting season between November and April. It's possible to walk within an eight km radius of Lukosi without a guide.

Luxury Camps Touch the Wild operates three overpriced luxury camps around Hwange National Park: *Makalolo*, *Sable Valley* and *Sikumi Tree Lodge*. Makalolo, the most expensive, is the only one actually inside the park. Plan on spending between US$200 and US$300 *per person* per day. If you're still interested, book through any travel agency.

Getting There & Away

Air Air Zimbabwe flies to Hwange National Park from Harare via Kariba daily at 9 am with an extra flight on Saturday at 1.55 pm. The daily flight continues on to Victoria Falls at 11.15 am. From Victoria Falls, daily flights depart at 2.50 pm (with an extra Saturday flight at 9.55 am), continuing on to Kariba and Harare at 1.40 pm. On Saturday, they fly nonstop to Harare at 10.45 am.

UTC vehicles meet incoming flights and provide transfers to and from Hwange Safari Lodge or Main Camp for Z$10 per person, with a minimum charge of six fares.

Bus If you're coming in on the Hwange Special Express bus from Bulawayo or Victoria Falls, get off at Safari Crossroads and hitch or walk the 11.5 km to Hwange Safari Lodge. The Ajay Motorways bus will take you straight to the Safari Lodge. From there, it's another five km walk or hitch to the Dete turnoff. You can't walk or hitch beyond the railway line so you have to wait at the entrance for a lift into the park.

Alternatively, get off the Ajay or Hwange Special Express bus at the Sinamatella turnoff just east of Hwange town and try to hitch a lift along the rough 40 km road into Sinamatella Camp. Expect long waits.

For bus schedules, see Getting There & Away in the Bulawayo and Victoria Falls sections.

Train The steam train between Bulawayo and Victoria Falls passes Dete 11.13 pm eastbound and 1.26 am westbound. Refer to the discussion of Dete earlier in this chapter for further information.

Getting Around

Car The speed limit in the park is 40 km per hour so don't plan to see the whole park in a single day. Unless you're racing to reach one of the camps before closing time, there's no reason to rush. If you're booked into a camp, however, and don't turn up before the gates close, a search will be conducted and once located, you'll have to foot the bill for the rangers' time and efforts.

Petrol is available to the public at Hwange Safari Lodge and Main Camp but the pumps at Sinamatella are for park use only.

Game Drives UTC offers two hour game drives several times daily from Hwange Safari Lodge and Main Camp for Z$30 per person. Full-day game drives are available for Z$120. Another company, Touch the Wild, charges US$35 per person for two hour game drives but they take a particularly poor attitude toward nonaffluent travellers. This operation does well with package tourists who are prepared to pay. UTC and others charge half their price or less for better and more personable service. UTC is based at Main Camp but maintains an office at Hwange Safari Lodge as well.

For another option, see the discussion of Shamwari Safaris under the Safaris section that follows.

Safaris Numerous upmarket safari companies offer package trips through Hwange National Park and any travel agency can provide glossy brochures. Since most clients will be expecting higher accommodation standards than those offered by National Parks lodges, the majority will base in Hwange Safari Lodge and operate day drives through the park. Others will be based in one of the expensive luxury camps.

For those on a budget, the best option will be a safari with Roberto 'Beat' Accorsi of Shamwari Safaris (☎ 248 Dete), PO Box 53, Dete, or PO Box 2421, Bulawayo. One of the best photographic guides and naturalists around, Beat offers tailored safaris for groups of up to seven participants for around Z$145 per person per day. The price includes all meals and transfers from the airport, Dete or Hwange Safari Lodge. Participants are able to select their own routings and accommodation, whether camping or in chalets. These safaris are very popular, so advance booking is strongly advised.

Shamwari also offers day trips to Nyamandhlovu, Dopi and White Hill Pans for Z$50/80/140 for up to seven people. For the Ngwethla Loop or return trips to Shumba Picnic Site, Beat charges Z$200 for up to seven people.

Backpackers Africa runs walking safaris through the remote Shakwankie Wilderness area near the Botswana border, where buffalo and elephant gather in large numbers to drink from natural springs rising out of the Kalahari sands. These trips are not cheap but they fill up well in advance so make arrangements as early as possible. Book through Backpackers Africa (☎ 735712, fax 735716 Harare), PO Box 3961, Harare.

Hitching Officially, hitchhikers are not permitted inside the park. The rule is intended, of course, to prevent visitors being caught out among the lions and elephants without a vehicle. It is also in place to shield visitors with vehicles from the unpleasantness of having to refuse constant petitions for lifts when they'd rather enjoy a more solitary experience.

Having said that, it must be pointed out that park officials realise not everyone can afford to purchase or hire a vehicle and they do a lot of looking the other way as far as discreet hitching outside the park entrances or around Main Camp is concerned.

Victoria Falls

Victoria Falls, 1.7 km wide, drops between 90 and 107 metres into the Zambezi Gorge. An average of 550,000 cubic metres of water plummet over the edge every minute but during flood stage between March and May, about five million cubic metres per minute pass over the falls.

Humans have been living around Victoria Falls for at least hundreds of thousands of years. The first known name of the falls was Shongwe, given to it by the Tokaleya people who inhabited the area prior to the Nguni invasions. Later, the Ndebele changed the name to Amanza Thunquayo, or Water

David Livingstone

tion of which streets is known as Wimpy Corner. The bulk of Victoria Falls' population is concentrated in Chinotimba township down Pioneer Rd from the centre where you'll find lots of local shops and a rollicking beer hall.

The Victoria Falls Publicity Association (☎ 4202 Vic Falls), adjacent to the Town Council Camping and Caravan Site, distributes local advertising and sells maps and booklets about the falls area. If you're interested in background information, pick up a copy of *A Visitors Guide to Victoria Falls* by Mrs M Newman, 1987. It's full of information on local wildlife, including birds and vegetation, and contains a synopsis of the history as well.

Film isn't normally available in Victoria Falls. The Indian-run shop in the Wimpy complex sometimes has a few rolls of 110 cartridge print film. On the 1st floor of the same building is a camera and general repair shop.

Rising as Smoke. The late-arriving Makalolo, a tribe of refugees from the Nguni invasions, changed it yet again, this time to Mosi-oa-Tunya or Smoke that Thunders. On 16 November 1855, Scottish missionary David Livingstone was brought to the falls by the Makalolo in dugout canoes and, following the established procedure, promptly renamed them in honour of the queen.

VICTORIA FALLS

Victoria Falls town is gradually becoming the archetypal tourist trap. Most fortunately, the star attraction is safely cordoned off by a jungle of its own creation. To walk along the paths through the spray-generated rainforests that flank the gorge, you'd never suspect the existence of the town so close at hand.

Orientation & Information

Most visitors arrive by train, at the colonial train station which either issues them into the lawns and gardens of the Victoria Falls Hotel or along the tracks to the heart of town. The rest of the businesses are along or very near either Livingstone or Park Way, the intersec-

Safari Companies Some of the more prominent safari operators mentioned in the following text include:

Backpackers Africa represented in Victoria Falls by Safari Office Services
Kalambeza Safaris, PO Box 121 (☎ 4480, fax 4644 Vic Falls)
Safari Office Services, PO Box 125 (☎ 4471 Vic Falls)
Shearwater represented in Victoria Falls by Safari Office Services
United Touring Company (UTC), Zimbank Building, PO Box 35 (☎ 4268 Vic Falls)

Victoria Falls Park

Before setting off to view the falls, wrap cash and valuables in plastic and be sure your camera equipment is protected from the spray as well.

You can approach the park entrance from Livingstone Way east of town or down the track from the Victoria Falls Hotel, which is unfortunately lined with curio salespeople who'll certainly put a deep dent in any serenity you may have been anticipating. Admission to the park is now Z$1 per person

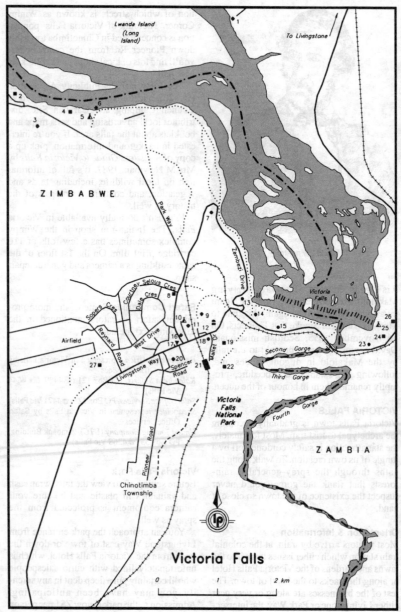

Victoria Falls

0   1   2 km

Lwanda Island
(Long
Island)

To Livingstone

ZIMBABWE

Park Way

Zambezi Drive

Courtney Selous Cres

Dale Cres

Sopers Cres

Reynard Road

West Drive

Mallet Dr

Spencer Road

Livingstone Way

Pioneer Road

Airfield

Chinotimba Township

Victoria Falls
National Park

Victoria
Falls

Second Gorge

Third Gorge

Fourth Gorge

ZAMBIA

■ PLACES TO STAY	25 Camping Area	9 Curio Row
	26 Rainbow Lodge	11 Falls Craft Village
2 Zambezi National Park	27 Sprayview Hotel	12 Post Office, Banks, UTC
Gate & Chalets		13 Livingstone Statue
4 A'Zambezi River Lodge	▼ PLACES TO EAT	14 Victoria Falls Park Entr-
5 Caravan Park		ance Gate
8 Rainbow Hotel	17 Wimpy Corner	15 Zimbabwe Border Post
10 Town Council Rest		(Immigration)
Camp (Camping	OTHER	16 Victoria Falls Publicity
Site)		Bureau
19 Makasa Sun Hotel	1 Boat Club	18 Avis & Total Petrol
22 Victoria Falls Hotel	3 Spencer Creek Crocodile	Station
24 Hotel Intercontinental	Ranch	20 Police Station & Natio-
Mosi-Oa-Tunya &	6 Booze Cruise Launch	nal Parks Office
Field Museum/Curio	Site	21 Railway Station
Stalls	7 The Big Tree	

and the daily ticket can be used for multiple visits on the same day.

Once you've reached the rim, a network of surfaced tracks – laid down to prevent tourist damage to the fragile rainforest ecosystem – takes you to a series of viewpoints. One of the most dramatic is Cataract View, the westernmost of the lot, which requires climbing down a steep stairway into (and out of!) the gorge. Another is aptly named Danger Point, where terraces of soaking and slippery moss-covered rocks combined with a sheer and unfenced 100 metre drop-off conspire to rattle your nerve as you approach the stunning and frightening view into the First Zambezi Gorge. From Danger Point, you can follow a side track for a view over the gracefully precarious Zambezi Bridge which connects Zimbabwe with Zambia.

While walking through the rainforests, note the profusion of interesting species found in this unique little enclave – ebony, ferns, fig trees and a variety of lianas and flowering plants.

The flow of water is greatest between April and June so these are the times for the misty views. When the wind is blowing, there are rainbows over the gorge. During low water from September to November, you'll get the clearest views and photos with the most rock showing between segments of the falls. During midsummer, the humidity will be at its most stifling and the rains will be hard and frequent, making viewing a generally hit-or-miss proposition. Still, air, mist and light conditions could combine to offer a variety of remarkable effects from any vantage point at any time of year.

Along the Zambezi

If you don't have a vehicle and can't afford a group tour, a free walk along the Zambezi above the falls is still an option. Although the tracks don't enter Zambezi National Park, the area has a lot of wildlife. Don't take this walk as lightly as most people are tempted to; warthogs, crocodiles, hippopotamuses, all sorts of antelope and even elephants, buffaloes and lions are frequently observed.

Along the river bank there are lots of crocodiles which can appear without warning. Although many travellers do swim in this stretch of the river, it's unwise. Bilharzia and hippos pose dangers as well.

Livingstone Statue Most Zambezi walks begin at the Livingstone statue, which overlooks Cataract View at the upper end of the Victoria Falls Park track. From there, a dirt track takes off upriver along the banks with several tributary tracks connecting it to the parallel Zambezi Drive.

The Big Tree The Big Tree provides an excuse for a walk. It's a baobab or 'upside-

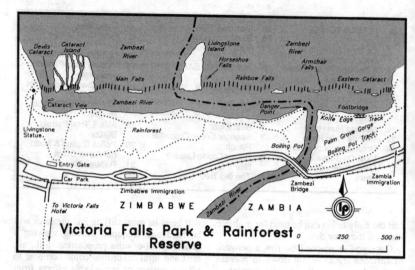

Victoria Falls Park & Rainforest Reserve

down tree', so called because a distant ancestor offended some deity or other and in punishment, was uprooted, turned over and replaced upside down. Although this specimen stands only about 25 metres high, from eye level its 20 metre circumference makes it seem much larger.

Victoria Falls Hotel

The elegant Victoria Falls Hotel, which many travellers know for its' lavish buffet breakfast, was the falls' first. The earliest tourists to Victoria Falls had to arrive overland either on foot or in wagons, travelling for days along the Pandamatenga Trail from Botswana. They originally had to sleep in railway carriages but a rudimentary hotel was built on the site in 1905, replaced by a more permanent structure in 1914. The current hotel is actually the result of several additions to the second building. The grounds are planted in lawns, with bougainvillaea, frangipani, flamboyant, palms and other tropical greenery.

Falls Craft Village

In this fortified mock-up of historical Zimbabwean ways of life, you'll have the chance to see a variety of ethnic huts, prefabricated in their area of origin and moved to the village. You can also watch craftspersons at work and consult with a couple of *nanga* (witch doctors). The main village is open from 8.30 am to 4.30 pm Monday to Saturday, and on Sunday from 9 am to 1 pm.

Curio Row & Snake Park

When you've finished browsing in the numerous kitsch curio shops, you can check out the Zambezi Taxidermy Snake Park and watch snakes being milked for Z$5. The crafts shops in the halls at the end of the street are better value than the tourist shops along the way. Here, women display local creations and will bargain over already competitive prices. Skilful bargainers can pick up great deals while contributing directly to the local economy.

Flight of the Angels

The name of this 10 to 15 minute flight over the falls is derived from an overworked quote by David Livingstone who wrote in his journal 'on sights as beautiful as this, angels in their flight must have gazed'. The flights cost Z$105 per person.

Flights depart from the old airstrip six km from town about every 15 minutes. A 30 minute option, including a game flight over Zambezi National Park, costs Z$156. Book through Safari Office Services or UTC.

Zambezi Raft Trips

Although they're expensive, white-water enthusiasts travel from all over the world to run the Zambezi rapids. The roughest rapids, which on the I to VI ratings scale are considered class V, are negotiated by well-experienced oarspeople. Rafters are always falling out of the rafts but injuries are very rare and the operators are skilled. The only negative thing is the steep and slippery walk out of the gorge afterward.

On the Zimbabwean side, raft trips are operated by Shearwater Adventures, bookable through Safari Office Services or through Shearwater's home office in Harare. High-water raft trips, which do 13 km though Batoka Gorge, normally run between 1 July and 15 August, but in low-rainfall years they may begin as early as mid-May. Rougher low-water runs, 22 km through 14 rapids, operate from around 15 August through to late December, although early rains may extend throughout the season. High-water/low-water trips cost US$90/130.

Alternatively, you can raft the Zambian side with American-run Sobek Expeditions in Livingstone. These US$85 trips, which run from March to December, begin at Boiling Pot just below the falls. Everyone who's done them reckons they're much the better option. Trips include transport and lunch and must be paid for in foreign currency. You can book them through UTC in Zimbabwe, but you'll wind up paying US$10 or so more than if you pay Sobek directly. Book through the Sobek offices (☎ 3-21432 Livingstone) on Katombora Rd in Livingstone, at the Rainbow Lodge on the Zambia shore or Sobek Expeditions USA (☎ (209) 736-2661), Angels Camp, California 95222. Sobek also runs overnight trips and rafting expeditions lasting from two to seven

days which go as far as the gorges around Moemba Falls and the Matetsi River mouth.

Breakfast, Lunch & Booze Cruises

From the boat docks upriver from Big Tree near A'Zambezi River Lodge, river cruises depart four times daily. The first is a champagne breakfast cruise which departs at 6 am and costs Z$40 per person.

Morning and lunch cruises, without the champagne, depart at 10.45 am and 12.45 pm for Z$40. At 2.15 pm, there's a lazy afternoon cruise for Z$8 more which, like the midmorning cruise, stops at Kandahar Island in midriver.

The most popular trip is the Sundowner booze cruise which costs Z$32. The smaller boat, the *Ilala*, is less crowded and includes drinks while the larger one, normally booked up by package groups, has a cash bar. Both of them depart at 5 pm.

Transport to the jetties is available from hotels 30 minutes prior to departure of the midmorning, afternoon and evening cruises. The breakfast cruise should be booked in advance so transport can be provided from town. Book through any hotel or UTC.

Kayak Trips

Victoria Falls kayak tours take place exclusively above the falls. If you want to paddle around the wide and smooth-flowing river, one day trips can be done for US$90. Book through Safari Office Services.

Spencer Creek Crocodile Ranch

With 5000 crocodiles of all sizes, Spencer Creek Crocodile Ranch offers close-up views of crocodiles for only Z$7.50. They also screen informative videos about crocodile lifestyles and there's a crocodile museum, a tearoom, a cat enclosure, a collection of farm animals and a curio shop.

The ranch is open from 8 am to 12.30 pm and 2 to 4.30 pm daily except Christmas.

Places to Stay

The following section includes accommodation in and around Victoria Falls town only. For information about lodging on the

Zambia shore, in Livingstone and in Zambezi National Park, refer to the relevant sections.

Several new hotels are in the planning stages for Victoria Falls and some may be open by the time you read this. If you're having problems booking those listed, check with a travel agent for the latest listing.

Places to Stay – bottom end

If you have a tent, the most central and inexpensive place to stay is the *Town Council Camping and Caravan Sites* and *Town Council Chalets* on Livingstone Way, smack in the centre of town. Although it's spacious, it can still get crowded. Watch for thieving monkeys. The price of tent sites here doubled in 1990 – it's now Z$11 per person – and threatens to increase again soon. Tents may be hired for Z$10 per night. Chalets cost Z$19 per person (Z$25 single occupancy) and the youth hostel-style crash pad on the premises costs Z$15 per bunk.

For those who prefer more solitude than the in-town park will allow, there's a little-used camping site in a nice setting between the boat launch site and the A'Zambezi River Lodge.

Places to Stay – middle

The only place that ranks in the middle range is the *Sprayview Hotel* (☎ 4344 Vic Falls) just out of town on Livingstone Way. Its bar and disco are popular with travellers and the terrace is a good, cheap and quiet place to enjoy drinks by the pool. Single/double rooms, including bed and breakfast, cost Z$60/100.

Places to Stay – top end

If you have the money to spend, the four-star *Victoria Falls Hotel* (☎ 4203, fax 4586 Vic Falls) is undoubtedly the loveliest of the two most expensive hotels in town. Established in 1905, this stately colonial structure and its magnificent setting above the Second Gorge of the Zambezi River ooze atmosphere. After you step off the steam train and pass through the Edwardian railway station, this place will provide a fitting climax to any grand

romantic delusions you may be suffering from.

Single/double rooms will cost Zimbabwe residents Z$185/280, while foreigners will pay US$115/170, foreign exchange only. If you're after the height of luxury, however, go for the deluxe suite which will set you back only US$520 per night.

The sheikhs and gangsters haven't yet arrived but the casino has. The *Makasa Sun Hotel* (☎ 4275 Vic Falls), which contains one of three casinos in Zimbabwe, is a two-star hotel that was somehow awarded three stars. Foreigners pay US$80/120 for singles/doubles while Zimbabwe residents pay only Z$120/180. Nonguests are permitted to use their pool but they may be charged a couple of dollars.

The three-star *Rainbow Hotel* (☎ 4585 Vic Falls), a short walk from the centre, is set in a quiet spot with nice gardens. Single/double rooms cost Z$85/131.

Out of town opposite the crocodile ranch, the *A'Zambezi River Lodge* (☎ 4561 Vic Falls) offers quiet three-star accommodation but it's quite a way from town and it would be useful to have a car for travelling back and forth. Single/double rooms cost Z$88/137 and Z$42 for extra beds. Out the back there's a spacious lawn with a pool and terrace area where they serve up a buffet braai every evening for Z$20 per person.

Places to Eat

Breakfast The buffet breakfast at the *Victoria Falls Hotel* comes highly recommended. Between 7 to 10 am you can eat enough to last the entire day for Z$9 per person but still take something to carry the leftovers. The other hotels serve both continental and English breakfasts; the one at the *Rainbow Hotel* is also good value.

Try also *Naran's Takeaways* in the Wimpy Corner complex. They do a breakfast including steak, bacon, egg, toast, chips and a glass of Mazoe orange for just Z$5.

The *Wimpy* bar also does fast-food breakfasts but Naran's is better.

Lunch & Dinner The rest of the day, *Wimpy*

serves its standard menu of burgers, chicken, chips and so on. You can eat for around Z$5 per person and if you can't afford the hotel dining rooms, it'll be your only option on Sunday.

The *A'Zambezi River Lodge* serves full meals and bar snacks all day on their pool terrace. For lunch and snacks, the Indian-run *Naran's Takeaways* does vegetarian specialities, including great vegetarian samosas. You can even get vegetarian curry sadza. Although they close sometime between 4.30 and 6 pm (depending upon afternoon business), if you have a group and make arrangements in advance, they may cook up a *thali* meal or other Indian specialties for dinner for around Z$14 per person.

If you're hungry at dinner time, the Z$28 buffet braai on the *Victoria Falls Hotel* terrace is good value. Vegetarians can opt for the tables of salads, breads, casseroles and sweets for Z$15, while others will have a choice of at least four braaied meats, sadza with various meat relishes and numerous hors d'oeuvres. The drinks are expensive, so you may want to save your beer consumption for the Sprayview.

Entertainment

Falls Craft Village At night, the Falls Craft Village stages a traditional dancing performance at dusk, around 7 pm, for Z$11. The dancing is reportedly very good, punctuated with such intriguing attractions as ominous, myth-perpetuating drumming and even a circumcision ritual.

Africa Spectacular *The* tourist show at the falls is Africa Spectacular, staged nightly at the Victoria Falls Hotel. If not completely authentic, it does appeal to short-term visitors who'd like an entertaining introduction to traditional African dancing.

The show begins nightly at 7 pm in the pavilion behind the hotel and costs Z$10 per person.

Nightlife All the big hotel bars offer toned-down live music. Beyond that and the Makasa Sun Casino, you're limited to just a couple of options.

Although it's not technically 'night' life, the beer hall in Chinotimba township is good for some local colour until early evening.

On Metcalfe Rd opposite the railway station is the All Nations Bar & Round Table #41 Shack. It offers inexpensive drinks and live or disco music on Friday and Saturday nights from 7.30 to whenever things wind down, assuming they ever get wound up.

Most travellers end up at least once at the Sprayview Lodge disco which plays reggae music as well as a lot of mundane local stuff nightly from 7.30 to 11 pm. After a few drinks, it won't matter, anyway. Locals advise visitors to beware when walking into town from the Sprayview at night. Lions frequently wander into populated areas at Victoria Falls.

Getting There & Away

Air Air Zimbabwe flies nonstop daily from Victoria Falls to Harare departing at noon on Tuesday and 5.10 pm on other days. Another daily flight to Harare, which departs at 2.50 pm, makes stops at Hwange National Park and Kariba, and an extra flight on Saturday at 9.55 am stops only at Hwange National Park.

From Harare to Victoria Falls, there are daily nonstop flights at 7.45 am, daily flights via Kariba and Hwange National Park at 9 am, and on Saturdays via Hwange National Park at 9.55 am.

For fare breakdowns, refer to the table in the Zimbabwe Getting Around chapter.

Bus The terminal for the Hwange Special Express (actually a private rather than express line) to Hwange town and Bulawayo is near the bottle return behind the Wimpy Corner shopping centre superette. The bus also makes a stop on Pioneer Rd in Chinotimba township. Normally about three buses depart daily, when full.

The Ajay Express bus departs from the Makasa Sun Hotel on Tuesday and Thursday at 7 am. It calls in at Hwange town at 8.15 am, Hwange Safari Lodge at 9.30 am, Gwaai

River at 10 am and arrives in Bulawayo at 1.15 pm. On Sunday, the departure is at 8 am and all scheduled stops are therefore one hour later. The fare between Victoria Falls and Hwange Safari Lodge is Z$28. All the way to Bulawayo costs Z$50.

There are no buses to Kazungula or Kasane from Victoria Falls so you'll have to hitch or rely on the expensive UTC Botswana transfer bus.

Train For many, the romantic highlight of a trip through Zimbabwe is riding the steam service to (or from) Victoria Falls. From Bulawayo, one-way 1st-class costs a bargain Z$41.40, 2nd-class is Z$28.80, and economy is Z$12. The former two offer sleeper service while the latter contains seats only. See the Zimbabwe Getting Around chapter for timetables.

Getting Around

To/From the Airport The Victoria Falls airport is 20 km out of town along the Bulawayo road. UTC operates an airport transfer service which meets incoming and departing flights for Z$15 per person.

Taxi Midnight Taxis (☎ 4290) is the company serving the vicinity. The taxi stand is opposite the Zambezi petrol station behind the Wimpy Corner shopping centre.

Car Rental Hire cars are available from Hertz (☎ 2203 Vic Falls) in the Zimbank Building and Avis (☎ 2532) in the petrol station complex on the corner of Mallett Dr and Livingstone Way.

Bicycle Bicycles may be rented from Avis at the Total petrol station on the corner of Mallett Rd and Livingstone Way for Z$2 per hour or Z$10 per day and a Z$20 deposit.

Slightly cheaper and much more appealing are Michael's Cycles in the curio shops between the Wimpy Corner complex and the Rainbow Hotel. Mike charges Z$2 per hour but only Z$8 per day. Wherever you hire, make sure bikes are in good working order before riding away.

VICTORIA FALLS – ZAMBIA SIDE

Most visitors either plough through Zambia as quickly as possible or venture only as far as Livingstone before retreating to Zimbabwe. That doesn't suggest the country has nothing to offer, but most will agree that it's not worth the hassle required to see it.

Don't wear anything that looks military and be wary when taking photographs. Photographing anything sensitive such as a bridge, power line, public building, dam or a military installation will invite problems.

In mid-1990, official price increases in food staples, particularly mealie meal, sent protesters into the streets. Riots and violence gripped the country and police and military forces were called in to quell the disturbances. Things have since calmed a bit but with higher prices, spiralling inflation and abysmal wages, people are finding it more and more difficult to make ends meet. Violent crime has risen dramatically (especially in Lusaka) and foreigners are obvious targets. While it's still quite safe to visit the Zambian side of Victoria Falls – it is the country's major tourist draw – things get tougher beyond Livingstone.

The unit of currency in Zambia is the kwacha, whose value falls almost daily. In late 1990, the kwacha was trading officially at kw40=US$1. The black market rate averaged nearly twice that for both cash and travellers' cheques; some street changers were offering more. You won't have to look for the black market in Zambia. All US$ prices used in this section were converted using the official rate. Only kw20 can be exported from Zambia.

Crossing the Border

From Zimbabwe's Victoria Falls town, it's an easy two km walk over the Zambezi Bridge to Zambia. Most people make a day trip of it but some opt to continue into Livingstone, 11 km further on, and stay the night before returning to Zimbabwe. If you've hired a bike in Zimbabwe, there'll be no problem taking it across the border.

The Victoria Falls border crossing is open from 6 am to 6 pm. If you're just heading into

Zambia for the day, get as early a start as possible. Once you've waited in the queues at both borders, you'll quickly realise a single day won't leave much sightseeing time before you've got to start back through the whole mess in reverse. Going in either direction, avoid late morning and early afternoon when queues are the longest and searches most thorough. Non-Commonwealth citizens will need visas for Zambia whether they're entering just for the day or for a trip through the country. These currently cost kw100 or Z$10, payable in either currency, and are issued on the spot or more accurately, whenever the typically low-energy officials get around to it. Some Lusaka-bound travellers reported being asked for consulate visas here, but normally, the border-issued visas are good for visits of up to 14 days.

Foreigners are only permitted to export Z$40 in Zimbabwean currency so if you're crossing for the day, either leave anything over that amount back at your hotel or deposit it with immigration officials at the border and collect it when you return. Any amount of Zimbabwean currency over Z$40 declared on your departure form (or discovered during a customs search) will be confiscated without reimbursement. Currency declaration forms are rarely scrutinised or distributed at this crossing. If you have a Notice to Visitor (NTV) slip in your passport (see under Visas in the Facts for the Visitor chapter), you'll be required to deposit it at the border for collection when you return.

Visiting the Falls

Once you've crossed the Zambezi Bridge, proceed up the hill to the hotels from which a jumble of tracks lead through the vegetation to various points of interest. Highlights include the track which leads back along the customs fence and gives a view over the Zambezi Bridge and into the main river gorges.

Other Points of Interest

Behind the curio stalls near the hotels is the small Field Museum, built on an archaeological site, with some displays from the excavation. The curio stalls themselves are good value, especially if you're paying in black market Zambian kwacha. Money may not be really necessary, though; a couple of years ago, travellers started swapping interesting foreign T-shirts for local arts and crafts here.

Tours through the Mosi-oa-Tunya National Park, an insignificant little game park – they used to have a few rhino but all have been poached – near the boat club north of the Maramba River, may be arranged through the Hotel Intercontinental for less than US$20 per person. If you go on your own, they'll try to overcharge for the walking safaris. Don't pay more than about 50 US cents. The hotels also arrange evening booze cruises on the Zambezi, departing from the boat club. They're about the same price as those on the Zimbabwe side and non-hotel guests are welcome to participate.

Places to Stay & Eat

The tent camping site is between the Hotel Intercontinental and the Rainbow Lodge, administered by the latter. Although it's in a good location, your belongings are not safe here and should be locked up in the hotel baggage room when you're away from your tent. Camping costs around US$5 per night, which includes the use of hotel facilities since there are none at the camping site, but watch out for hippos which wander onto the hotel lawns.

The *Hotel Intercontinental Mosi-oa-Tunya* right beside the falls offers luxury for a whopping US$160 for a double room, payable only in foreign currency. Weekend buffets are fairly good value, costing around US$12 per person.

Slightly more reasonable, the *Rainbow Lodge* offers double accommodation in rondavels for US$20.

LIVINGSTONE (ZAMBIA)

Although it's not much to look at now, Livingstone was once the object of nearly all tourist visits to Victoria Falls but that position now belongs to the Zimbabwean side.

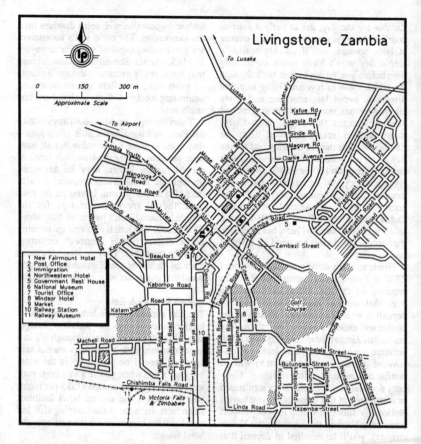

1 New Fairmount Hotel
2 Post Office
3 Immigration
4 Northwestern Hotel
5 Government Rest House
6 National Museum
7 Tourist Office
8 Windsor Hotel
9 Market
10 Railway Station
11 Railway Museum

The tourist office on Mosi-oa-Tunya Rd is good for information on happenings in Livingstone and can arrange hassle-free hotel bookings.

Railway Museum
The new Railway Museum in Livingstone lies west of Mosi-oa-Tunya road as you enter town from the south. The yards contain a collection of old engines and rolling stock while inside are lots of rail-related antiques as well as information and exhibits about general railway history. It's open daily from

10 am to 5.30 pm. Admission is the equivalent of a few US cents.

National Museum
The National Museum, adjacent to the tourist office, has an interesting collection of archaeological and anthropological relics including a copy of a Neanderthal skull estimated to be over 100,000 years old. The original was uncovered near Kabwe, Zambia (north of Lusaka), during the colonial era and is now on display in the UK. Although they may try to overcharge you by citing a non-

official 'nonresident' rate, admission is the equivalent of about 50 US cents at the official exchange rate.

Maramba Cultural Centre

Between Victoria Falls and Livingstone, about five km from the latter on Mosi-oa-Tunya Rd, is the Maramba Cultural Centre. On Saturday, Sunday and Wednesday from 3 to 5 pm, they stage live traditional dance performances, with an extra weekly performance laid on during high season from late May to October. Admission is about 50 US cents and is more authentic than Africa Spectacular on the Zimbabwean side.

Places to Stay

The cheapest accommodation in Livingstone is at the *Government Rest House,* across the tracks from the city centre. It costs only US$3 per night. Alternatively, try the much cleaner Red Cross Rest House for US$9 per person.

The cheapest hotel and the most popular with travellers is the *Northwestern* (☎ 320711 Livingstone), a pleasant but deteriorating colonial structure on Zambesi St two blocks south-east of the main street. Next up the scale is the *New Fairmount* (☎ 320726 Livingstone) right on Mosi-oa-Tunya Rd. Livingstone's other hotel, the *Windsor,* on Edward Rd down near the golf course, is currently undergoing renovations but it may have reopened by the time you read this.

Places to Eat

Eating in Zambia may present problems. There are shortages of everything and shops stock whatever is available. Sometimes this consists of only one or two items, but you'll probably be able to find produce at one of the markets.

The *Eat-Rite* serves snacks and drinks on an outdoor terrace and is very popular with travellers. Otherwise, the only alternatives are several greasy takeaways situated along Mosi-oa-Tunya Rd.

The *Rainbow Lodge* near the falls has a standard dining room or you can opt for an expensive meal in the *Hotel Intercontinental.* For alcohol, try the *Northwestern Hotel,* a local hangout, or the *New Fairmount Hotel* which both have bars. The latter stages frequent live music performances.

Getting There & Away

Only 11 km from the border, Livingstone is easily accessible by rented bicycle from the Zimbabwe side of Victoria Falls. There will be no problem taking a bicycle into Zambia but be sure to carry a rental receipt in case there are problems at the immigration posts. Hitching to or from the falls is easy.

Taxis from the Hotel Intercontinental at Victoria Falls into Livingstone will cost about US$4 while the infrequent public buses cost 25 US cents.

ZAMBEZI NATIONAL PARK

The 56,000 hectare Zambezi National Park, which is vaguely associated with Victoria Falls National Park, consists of 40 km of Zambezi River frontage and a spread of game-rich inland mopani forest and savanna. Although the tourist map shows numerous loop drives in the park, the only roads actually open at the time of writing are the Chamabondo Drive to Njoko Pan in the southern part of the park, the Liunga Loop in the north-eastern section, and the Zambezi River Drive. Entry with a private vehicle costs Z$2 per person per day or Z$5 per person for a weekly pass. The park office is open from 6 am to 6.30 pm.

Fishing Camps

There are three fishing camps – Mpala-Jena, Kandahar and Sansimba – along the river in Zambezi National Park from which you can fish for yellow bream and tiger fish. Each includes rudimentary shelters and toilets and costs Z$30 per night. Since the waters are international, no fishing licenses are required. Day use of the camps costs Z$3. Either book in advance through the National Parks central booking office in Harare, or check on availability at Zambezi National Park headquarters. No public transport is

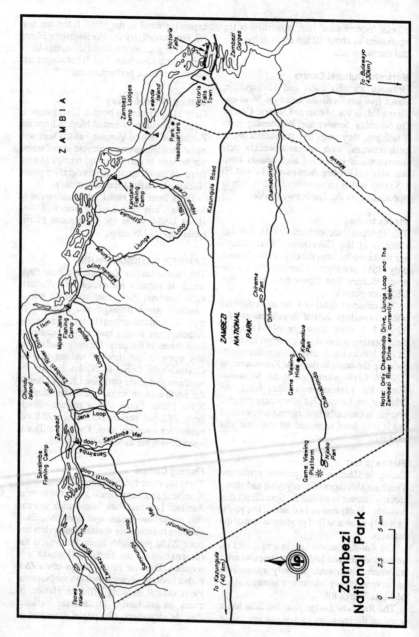

Zambezi National Park

Note: Only Chambondo Drive, Liunga Loop and The Zambezi River Drive are currently open.

0 2.5 5 km

To Bulawayo (430km)

ZAMBIA

Victoria Falls

Zambezi Gorges

Victoria Falls Town

Zambezi Camp Lodges

Lwande Island

Park Headquarters

Kandahar Fishing Camp

Hippo Loop

Liunga

Siunga

Liunga Loop

Harmony pan

Kazungula Road

Msuna

Chamabondo

Chirema Pan

Kalankua Pan

Game Viewing Hide

Chamabondo Drive

ZAMBEZI NATIONAL PARK

Game Viewing Platform

Hpko Pan

Chundu Island

Mpala–Jena Fishing Camp

Mpala–Jena River Drive 1 km

Zambezi River

Chundu Loop

Jena Loop

Sansimba Loop

Sansimba Vei

Sansimba Fishing Camp

Chamunzi Loop

Chundu River Drive

Chamunzi Vei

Simunumu Drive

Zambezi River

Tsoare Island

To Kazungula (40 km)

available, however, and hitching is naturally not permitted in the national park.

Horse Trails

Although they've received mixed reviews, two hour, half-day, full-day and overnight Zambezi Horse Trails tours offered by Shearwater are one way of seeing the park and its residents up close. Up to eight riders can be accommodated on each tour. Children under 12 must prove they've completed a riding course.

For Zimbabwe residents, the morning or evening two hour rides cost Z$60, full-day trips are Z$120 and overnight trips cost Z$190. Foreigners, who must pay in foreign currency, will pay significantly more – US$40/70/110 for two hour/full-day/overnight trips. Book through Safari Office Services in Victoria Falls.

Game Viewing

Both Kalambeza Safaris and Backpackers Africa offer one day walking safaris through Zambezi National Park. For either one, plan on spending Z$120 to Z$150 per person, including breakfast and lunch. The Backpackers Africa option includes a canoe trip on the Zambezi River as well.

A morning-only walk with Kalambeza Safaris costs about Z$45 per person, including breakfast and a transfer from Victoria Falls town. Overnight and longer trips are available but the prices seem to rise geometrically: an overnight trip will be Z$275 per person while a three-day tented camp safari costs Z$550 each; and five days, including three in Kazuma Pan National Park and two in Zambezi National Park, will cost over Z$1200 per person.

Morning, afternoon and evening game drives with Kalambeza go for Z$66 each. UTC does morning and evening game drives for Z$45 each.

Places to Stay

National Parks lodges on the Zambezi banks cost Z$60 per night. Each unit has two bedrooms, accommodating four people, a living area and a veranda. They're quite

comfortable but normally book up well in advance so it's best to make arrangements at the central booking office in Harare.

Getting Around

Without a private vehicle, visitors can't tour Zambezi National Park on their own. Although it's discouraged, it is possible to walk from Victoria Falls town to the park entrance gate and try to find a lift with someone going in.

KAZUMA PAN NATIONAL PARK

In Zimbabwe's extreme north-western corner is 31,300 hectare Kazuma Pan National Park, an unusual enclave of open savanna in otherwise teak and mopani-wooded territory. It's a good place to see such rare species as white rhino, roan antelope, wild dogs and oribi. Lions and cheetahs are fairly common, and many species of antelope, as well as buffalo and elephant, inhabit the pan area. Kazuma Pan is the only Zimbabwe park where gemsbok are seen regularly.

Only two parties of visitors are permitted in the park at any given time, probably because there are currently only two primitive camping sites without facilities of any kind. Although improvements are planned for the near future, there is no other accommodation available and the nearest services are at Victoria Falls. As at Mana Pools, walking is unrestricted but dangers still exist. For guidelines, refer to the safety discussion under Mana Pools in the Northern Zimbabwe chapter.

The park is open from March to December, due to road damage during the rainy season. The maximum length of stay is 21 days in any given month. Entry is Z$5 per person and camping sites cost Z$6 per night.

Organised Tours

Backpackers Africa and Kalambeza Safaris each operate three day (minimum) backpacking trips through Kazuma Pan between April and December but these trips are not cheap: plan on at least Z$650 per person and book early because they're extremely popular, especially during school holidays.

Booking addresses are given in the Victoria Falls section of this chapter.

Getting There & Away

Access is only by 4WD vehicle and anyone entering the park must be prebooked through the National Parks central booking office in Harare or the Bulawayo Booking Agency (☎ 63646 Bulawayo), PO Box 2283, Bulawayo.

Turn south-west off the Victoria Falls-Bulawayo road at the Matetsi turnoff and travel 25 km to Matetsi, where you check into the park and pay relevant fees. The park office is open from 7 am to 12.30 pm and 2 to 4.30 pm on weekdays. For weekend entry, phone 433526 Vic Falls or visit the warden in Victoria Falls prior to setting out. Continue for 12 more km then turn right at Tsabolisa Junction and travel 27 km to Pandamatenga on the Botswana border. Since the border post closes at 5 pm and you must pass it and register with the police there, you should try to reach Matetsi prior to 4 pm. At Pandamatenga, the road turns north-west and straddles the international boundary for 25 km before entering the park. There is no park access via Botswana.

TO BOTSWANA

You're bound to see a bit of game as you pass through Zambezi National Park along the 60 km route between Victoria Falls and the Botswana border at Kazungula/Kasane where four countries – Zimbabwe, Zambia, Namibia and Botswana meet near the confluence of the Zambezi and Chobe Rivers.

Places to Stay

Imbabala Safari Camp (☎ 4219 Vic Falls) is a luxury camp along the Zambezi near Kazungula. For US$100 per person per day, including chalet accommodation, game drives, meals, alcohol, guides, boat trips and fishing tackle, you can sit back and remove yourself from the world. It's not a bad option, really. Bookings are available through travel agencies in Victoria Falls or by writing to PO Box 110, Victoria Falls.

Getting There & Away

If you're booked into Imbabala, transfers from Victoria Falls are included.

Heading toward Zambia, Botswana or Namibia along this route there should be little problem hitching to Kasane, although traffic is sparse so prepare for waits. Otherwise, UTC does Kasane transfers daily at 6.30 am, picking up from the big hotels in Victoria Falls, for Z$65 per person. The return trip leaves Kasane between 9.30 and 10 am and, if immigration procedures go smoothly, arrives in Victoria Falls in time for the afternoon flight to Harare.

Western Kariba

The western version of Lake Kariba bears little resemblance to its eastern counterpart. In the place of hotels, safari camps, buzzing speedboats and drunken holiday-makers, the western half of the lake is better characterised by the wilderness outposts, the famous *mbanje* smoking Batonka people, rolling hills, valleys and gorges, and very keen travellers. Without a sturdy 4WD vehicle, access into most of western Kariba requires lots of time and/or money.

BINGA

The most interesting of the western Kariba settlements, Binga was constructed as a government administrative centre for the resettlement of the Batonka people. They were displaced when rising Lake Kariba waters sent them from their riverside homes to higher and less productive ground, permanently altering their culture and lifestyle.

Unless you want to fish in the lake or spend time scrounging examples of the much sought-after Batonka crafts – the decorative stools, headrests and drums as displayed in the National Gallery in Harare – there's not much to do in Binga. At the end of the road, beyond the summer houses, is Binga's Crocodile Farm which is good for a look around. It's open daily except Sunday and admission is Z$5. Up the hill between the rest camp and the 'centre' are Chibwatatata Hot Springs. Long considered a 'power place' by the Batonka, they're now used as a laundry and have become pretty polluted.

Places to Stay & Eat

It won't be difficult choosing where to stay in Binga because there's only one option – the *Binga Rest Camp* (☎ 244 Binga). You can camp and use the pool facilities for Z$5 per person. Rooms go for Z$20/35 for singles/doubles and chalets are available for families.

Although there's a restaurant serving very basic fare, it receives far less patronage than the bar, which is a local gathering place.

Getting There & Away

The roads into Binga are horrid washboard affairs but the approach from the south is currently being paved. Hitching in isn't impossible but you'll have the most luck on Saturday mornings. It is easiest to hitch out of Binga on Sunday afternoons.

One bus daily in either direction travels between Bulawayo and Siabuwa via Binga; if you want to reach Harare, you'll have to catch this bus eastbound and stay in Siabuwa, where no formal accommodation is available, and catch the bus leaving for Karoi and Harare the following morning. To reach Victoria Falls, take the Bulawayo-bound bus, get off at Dete Crossroads and either hitch or catch another bus from there.

Informal fishing trips or boat trips to Mlibizi can sometimes be arranged privately from the boat harbour down the road that turns off opposite Binga Rest Camp. For information on reaching or leaving Binga by ferry, see the Kariba section in the Northern Zimbabwe chapter.

MLIBIZI

Mlibizi is little more than a couple of fishing resort complexes: the downmarket *Mlibizi Safari and Holiday Camp*, where you can camp for Z$6.50 per person, or the relatively posh *Mlibizi Zambezi Resort*. Chalets at the latter cost Z$100 per night and may be booked through Sunshine Tours in Bulawayo. Unless they're there for the fishing, most people spend only a single night at Mlibizi after arriving on or awaiting the Kariba-bound lake ferry.

Getting There & Away

To catch up with one of the two Kariba ferries, each of which normally runs at least once weekly, first ascertain when it is running by contacting their office in Harare or Kariba or on the 1st floor of the Zimbank Building in Victoria Falls. There are normally two sailings per week with more added during peak periods.

For hitching from Bulawayo or Victoria Falls, leave notices at all hotels and camping sites well in advance of your intended departure; be sure to state whether you're willing to share petrol costs and expenses. If nothing is forthcoming, allow for a couple of days hitching via Dete Crossroads or catch the more or less daily (sometimes twice daily) Binga bus from Dete Crossroads on the Bulawayo-Victoria Falls road and get off at the Mlibizi turnoff. From there, you can walk the 15 km into Mlibizi but be sure to carry lots of water. You'll have to overnight at one of the Mlibizi resorts since the ferries normally depart around 9 am.

Those in more of a hurry may want to consult the transfer service offered by Savetime Travel Services (☎ 4631, fax 4417 Vic Falls), PO Box 216, Victoria Falls. They arrange transfers between the falls and Mlibizi for Z$150 per person, with a minimum charge of Z$400 per trip. Zimbabwe Rendezvous (☎ 729621 Harare) also provides transport between Mlibizi and Hwange Park/Victoria Falls for Z$90/150 per person with a four fare minimum. Before booking transport out, consider that the chances of hitching out of Mlibizi are pretty good, especially when you're arriving on a ferry full of outbound vehicles.

For more information on the ferries see the Kariba section in the Northern Zimbabwe chapter.

DEKA DRUM

Another fishing resort, Deka Drum, idles

beside the Deka River near that river's confluence with the Zambezi at the edge of Devils Gorge. It lacks a ferry link but there are chalets and a camping ground and caravan park where you can sit and fish the river to your heart's content. Access is via Hwange town on the Bulawayo-Victoria Falls road but there's no public transport.

CHIZARIRA NATIONAL PARK

The name of this 192,000 hectare park is derived from the Batonka word *chijalila* which means 'closed off' or 'barrier'. Chizarira has three areas, all different from the surrounding communal lands. In the north are the gorges of the Mcheni and Ruziruhuru rivers. Both drainages are accessible via walking tracks from national park headquarters at Manzituba but hikers will have to be accompanied by professional guides to get into the canyons themselves.

The easternmost extension of the Zambezi Escarpment in Chizarira rises to the 1500 metre peak Tundazi. Above the escarpment, the landscape changes to msasa-dotted upland plateau, prime wildlife country, where you may see black rhino. South of the Simagoga Hills, the land slopes gently down into the Busi Valley, smaller than but quite similar to the Mana Pools river frontage.

Chizarira lies in a heavily malarial area so take prophylaxis and carry appropriate treatments, especially if you're walking or travelling into the interior of the park. Bilharzia is also present and water should be purified or boiled before drinking. No services are available in the park so all supplies – food, spares, camping equipment, fuel and so on – must be carried from outside. Day entry into the park costs Z$2 per adult; a weekly pass, Z$5 per person.

Places to Stay

On the Busi flood plain of southern Chizarira and around Manzituba are three National Parks exclusive camps. Each may be occupied by only one party at a time and must be prebooked through the National Parks central booking office in Harare. The plushest is *Kasiswi* near the mouth of the

Ruziruhuru Gorge six km from Manzituba, a real wilderness compound with two raised sleeping huts, a cooking and dining area, hot showers and flush toilets. It costs a bargain Z$12 per night.

The other headquarters area camp is *Mobola*, which lies beside the Mcheni River six km from the Manzituba offices, which costs Z$10 per night. There are no shelters so you'll need a tent. Mobola does have a concrete cooking bench and table and pumped-in running water from the river as well as showers and flush toilets.

The third camp, *Busi Bush Camp*, is 35 km down a rough 4WD track from Manzituba on the acacia-dotted flood plain of the Busi River. It has three shelters, two for sleeping and one for dining, as well as braai pits, cooking bench, showers and flush toilets. Occupancy costs Z$8 per night but if currently planned improvements are made, the price will go up.

Getting There & Away

Without a 4WD, resign yourself to joining a tour if you want to visit Chizarira. It just doesn't see enough visitors to make hitching even marginally feasible. The best and most informative tours are with Black Rhino Safaris (☎ 41662, fax 77300 Bulawayo), PO Box FM89, Famona, Bulawayo. This option, which costs Z$160 per person per day, includes transport, meals and fees and the length and scope of the trip are left entirely up to participants. It can't be recommended highly enough.

Another far more expensive option is Backpackers Africa (☎ 735712, fax 735716 Harare), also bookable through Safari Office Services in Victoria Falls. They operate minimum five day walking safaris through the park; choose between the remote Ruziruhuru Gorge area in the park's northern section or the more popular Busi Trail in the southern area.

On public transport, the nearest you can get is the park turnoff west of Siabuwa on the Karoi-Binga track. Park headquarters at Manzituba is a 24 km game-infested road walk from there.

Getting Around

All hikers in Chizarira must be accompanied by either national parks guides or by licensed safari operators and guides. The national parks guides are licensed to escort groups of up to six hikers. They charge a very reasonable Z$10 per hour for day walks or Z$100 per night for longer wilderness treks. Participants are required to carry their own camping equipment and find their own transport into the park.

For information on organised safaris, refer to the preceding Getting There & Away discussion.

If you're driving, petrol is sporadically available at Siabuwa. Failing that, you'll have to drive 90 km to Binga to fill up so carry reserves if you'll be doing a lot of driving around. Both 4WD and high clearance are required to travel south of Manzituba and although the park is open year-round, heavy rains could render some areas inaccessible in the wet season.

Botswana

Facts about the Country

HISTORY

Early San & Bantu Groups

The original inhabitants of Botswana were San (Bushmen), who continue to inhabit the more remote regions of the Kalahari Desert of eastern Namibia and western Botswana. Their origins are unknown but they are believed to have inhabited the region for at least 30,000 years. They were followed by the Khoi-Khoi (Hottentots), who probably originated from a San group cut off from the mainstream. Sheep remains and pottery in late Stone Age diggings provide evidence that they had adopted a pastoral lifestyle.

Next arrived the agricultural and pastoral Bantu groups, who migrated from the north-western and eastern regions of the African continent – there is evidence that they originated in the area of present-day Cameroun – sometime during the 1st or 2nd century. It is likely, however, that this 'Bantu migration' bypassed or just skirted the edges of present-day Botswana, avoiding the harsh Kalahari sands and continuing on to the more amenable areas of the Transvaal and the Cape, where the newcomers inevitably encountered the San and the Khoi-Khoi. Relations between the three societies appear to have been amicable and they apparently mixed freely, trading and intermarrying.

The Bantu peoples of southern Africa have been divided into groups by anthropologists, based on similarities in their languages and social structures. The earliest such group probably arrived in Botswana during the first centuries AD, settling along the Chobe River.

Another Bantu group, the Sotho-Tswana, consisted of three distinct tribal entities: the Northern Basotho or Pedi who settled in the Transvaal, the Southern Basotho of present-day Lesotho, and the Western Basotho or Batswana who migrated northward into present-day Botswana. The Kgalagadi, the first Setswana-speaking tribe to colonise Botswana, arrived from the Transvaal around the 14th century and settled in the relatively arable and well-watered south-eastern strip of the country between present-day Francistown and Gaborone.

At that stage, north-eastern Botswana lay within Shona territory affiliated with the Torwa and later the Rozwi dynasties, but indications point to its occupation much earlier, probably by the Leopard's Kopje people, who were based in the Khami area of south-western Zimbabwe. These Shona speakers, now known as the Babirwa, were later completely absorbed into the Batswana culture, adopting the Setswana language and customs.

Between the 15th and 18th centuries the majority of the Bantu people in Botswana lived east of the Kalahari sands, but during the early 1700s peaceful fragmentation of tribal groups became the standard. Familial and power disputes were solved amicably, with the dissatisfied party gathering followers and tramping off to establish another domain elsewhere.

Fragmentation was an ideal solution to disputes as long as there remained an 'elsewhere' to set oneself up; in the case of the people living in south-eastern Botswana, it was to the vast expanses of country to the west, areas previously inhabited only by the San and Khoi-Khoi. In the north-west, where the Lozi Empire dominated, it was to the Okavango Delta region and around the shores of Lake Ngami.

Perhaps the most significant of the Tswana splits as far as Botswanan history is concerned was that of Kwena, Ngwaketse and Ngwato, the sons of a chief called Malope (or Masilo) whose domain was in the Boteti River area of central Botswana. Kwena went to Ditshegwane, Ngwaketse set himself up at Kanye in the far south-east and Ngwato settled at Serowe. The Ngwato clan split further with a quarrel between Chief Khama I and his brother Tawana, who subsequently left Serowe and established his chiefdom in

the area of Maun at the end of the 18th century. The three major modern-day Tswana groups can trace their ancestry to this three-way split of the Tswana.

Sometime during the following few years the nomadic and primarily pastoral Herero began migrating eastward from Namibia and settling in the north-western extremes of Botswana.

The Zulu

By 1800, all suitable grazing lands around the fringes of the Kalahari had been settled by pastoralists and peaceful fragmentation

was no longer a feasible solution to disputes. Furthermore, Europeans had arrived in the Cape and were expanding northward, creating an effective barrier against movement in that direction. By 1817, the first Christian mission in Botswana, Kuruman, had been founded by Robert Moffat on the Kuruman River.

In 1818 came the amalgamation of the Zulu tribes under their fierce new chief, Shaka, an event which would alter the face of southern Africa. Shaka set out with his ruthless fighting machine on a military rampage, conquering or destroying all tribes and settlements in his path. By 1830, Kwena, Ngwato and Lozi had fallen and Mzilikazi had broken away and fled northward on a similar crusade with the Kumalo clan, which would later be known as the Ndebele.

Mzilikazi stormed his way across the Transvaal, frequently sending raiding parties into the Tswana villages of Botswana and scattering them north and westward, some as far as Ghanzi and the Tshane cluster of villages in the dead heart of the Kalahari. Ngwaketse was rousted out in the process and sent fleeing into the desert, settling near Lethlakeng.

The Missionaries

As a result of all the displacement and scattering going on, the Tswana realised that fragmentation was no longer a feasible option and that their divided nation would be particularly vulnerable to subsequent attacks. They began to regroup and their society became highly structured. Each nation was ruled by a hereditary monarch and aristocracy whose economic power was based on the ownership of large herds of cattle and the use of tribute labour. In each of the Tswana nations, the king's subjects lived in centralised towns and satellite villages, one allocated to each clan under the control of village leaders. These leaders were responsible for distributing land and recruiting tribute labour for work in the monarch's fields and pastures. By the second half of the 19th century, some of these towns had grown to a considerable size. By 1860, for example, the capital of the Ngwato clan at Shoshong had an estimated population of 30,000.

The orderliness and structure of the town-based society impressed the early Christian missionaries who had set up Kuruman Mission in 1817. The primary mover behind the effort was the dogmatic and uncompromising Robert Moffat, who even after years in Africa couldn't be distracted from his purpose long enough to appreciate Africa's unique characteristics and problems, remaining uninterested in, and intolerant of, African cultures and beliefs. Nevertheless, he was responsible for the first

transliteration of the Tswana language into the Roman alphabet as well as the first translation of the Bible into written Tswana.

In 1841 arrived the inquisitive and charismatic Dr David Livingstone, who set up his base at Kuruman and married Robert Moffat's daughter, Mary. With a scientific background, Dr Livingstone found it difficult to settle down to sedentary family and missionary life. Instead, he moved away from the mission and staged a series of forays north to Lake Ngami and into the domain of the Lozi Empire. In the end, Livingstone's itchy feet got the best of him; he sent his family to England and struck out for parts unknown – Victoria Falls and beyond. It is significant that before Livingstone left, he was unjustly accused by the Boers of selling the Tswana firearms and rallying the Tswana against them. In a Boer attack on the Tswana, Livingstone's Kuruman home was destroyed and his weapons stolen.

None of the missionaries managed to convert great numbers of Tswana but they were able to advise the locals, sometimes wrongly, in their dealings with the Europeans that followed – explorers, naturalists, traders, miners and general rabble. The traders provided firearms and sent the Tswana to gun down and practically exterminate the elephant, rhino and hippopotamus populations of the country, especially around Lake Ngami. So great were the numbers killed that the European market for animal products was flooded, and prices could scarcely have justified the slaughter. At the same time, a cash economy was introduced to the Tswana who were paid for the skins and ivory they bagged.

The Boers

While Mzilikazi was wreaking havoc on the Tswana and the missionaries were busy trying to Christianise them in the north-west, the Boers, feeling pressure from the British in the Cape, began their Great Trek across the Vaal River. Confident that they had Heaven-sanctioned rights to any land they might choose to occupy in southern Africa, 20,000 Boers crossed the Vaal River into

Tswana and Zulu territory and established themselves as though the lands were unclaimed and uninhabited (indeed many were, having been cleaned out earlier by Mzilikazi).

Each male farmer staked his claim by riding out an area of 3000 *morgen* (about 2400 hectares) and set up his farm. The remaining local people were either forced to move or were pressed into working as servants and farm helps.

When Mzilikazi came up against them in 1837, the superior Boer firepower under the command of Hendrik Potgieter stalled his campaign and sent him fleeing north-eastward to settle in the Bulawayo area. Between 1844 and 1852, the Boers set up a series of fragmented little republics bent upon establishing trade links with the Dutch and Portuguese, independent of the British connection in the Cape.

At the Sand River Convention of 1852, Great Britain recognised the Transvaal's independence and the Boers immediately informed the Batswana that they were now under the control of the new South African Republic. Boer leader MW Pretorius informed the British that the Tswana were acquiring weapons from White traders and missionaries and preparing for war with the Boers, thus rendering his country unsafe for travellers, and he closed off the road through the Transvaal. Of course the Tswana were obtaining weaponry from the Whites – muzzle-loading rifles to bring down the big game they were busy decimating.

Meanwhile, the prominent Tswana leader of the Kwena clan, Sechele I, and Mosielele of the Kgatla refused to accept White rule and rebelled. The Boers, however, came back with a vengeance, embarking upon a destructive rampage in the Tswana communities. The Tswana, incurring heavy losses and rapidly decreasing territories, sent their leaders to petition the British for protection. Great Britain, however, already had its hands full in southern Africa and was in no hurry to take on and support more lands of dubious profitability; it offered only to act as arbitrator in the dispute. By 1877,

however, things had heated up so much that the British finally decided to annex the Transvaal and launched the first Boer War. It continued until the Pretoria Convention of 1881, when the British withdrew from the Transvaal in exchange for Boer allegiance to the British Crown.

The Protectorate

With the British again out of their way, the Boers looked northward into Tswana territory, pushing westward into the Molopo Basin of what had become known as Bechuanaland. They managed to subdue the towns of Taung and Mafeking (now Mafikeng) in 1882 and proclaimed them the republics of Stellaland and Goshen. The British viewed this encroachment as threatening to their 'road to the north' – the route into Zimbabwe and its supposed mineral wealth.

Meanwhile, the Tswana continued lobbying for British protection from the Boers as well as from a possible renewal of the Ndebele threat in the north-east. John Mackenzie, a close friend of the Christian Ngwato chief, Khama III of Shoshong, travelled to London and actively campaigned for British intervention to stop the erosion of Tswana territory by the expansionist Boers. Mackenzie was appointed Deputy Commissioner over the region, a post which was quickly and underhandedly taken over by Cecil Rhodes, who saw Mackenzie's opposition to the incorporation of Bechuanaland into the Cape Province as a threat to Rhodes' 'Cape to Cairo' scheme (Rhodes dreamt of British domination of Africa from the Cape to Cairo, and planned to link the two with a railway line through the heart of the continent). Cecil Rhodes also complained that Boer control was cutting off the labour supply from the north for his British South Africa Company (BSAC).

In 1885, Great Britain finally resigned itself to the inevitable. The area south of the Molopo River became the British Crown Colony of Bechuanaland, attached to the Cape Colony, while British jurisdiction and protection were extended to cover all lands north of the Cape Colony, south of 22°S latitude and east of 20°E longitude, which became the British Protectorate of Bechuanaland. This unwittingly divided Khama III's Ngwato territory in half, but Khama, grateful for protection at last, barely mentioned the issue.

The rationale behind the protectorate was to prevent Boer expansionism to the north and west and stall encroachment by other European powers, particularly the Germans in German Southwest Africa (Namibia). Only secondarily was it to provide protection for the Tswana power structures already in place there. Unfortunately, the new 'protectors' remained blase about the acquisition of Bechuanaland and tried to transfer control to the Cape Colony, which didn't really want the expense it would impose.

Rhodes Loses Ground

A new threat to the chiefs' power base came in the form of Cecil Rhodes and his British South Africa Company who remained keen to take control of the country. By 1894, the British had more or less agreed to allow him to do so.

Realising the implications of Rhodes' aspirations, three high-ranking Tswana chiefs, Bathoen, Khama III and Sebele, accompanied by a sympathetic missionary, W C Willoughby, sailed to England to appeal directly for continued British government control over Bechuanaland. Instead of taking action, Colonial Minister Joseph Chamberlain advised them to contact Rhodes directly and work things out among themselves. Chamberlain then conveniently forgot the matter and left on holiday.

Naturally, Rhodes was immovable, so they turned to the London Missionary Society who in turn took the matter to the British public. Fearing that the BSAC would allow alcohol in Bechuanaland, the LMS and other Christian groups backed the devoutly Christian Khama and his entourage. The public in general felt that the Crown had more business administering the empire than

Bathoen, Khama III & Sebele

did Cecil Rhodes with his business of questionable integrity. When Chamberlain returned from his holiday, public pressure had mounted to such a level that the government was forced to concede to the chiefs. He agreed to continue British administration of Bechuanaland, ceding only a small strip of the south-east to the BSAC to allow construction of a railway line to Rhodesia.

In 1890, the strip between 22°S latitude and the Chobe and Zambezi rivers came under British control by agreement with the Germans. Rhodes, still scheming to gain control in the protectorate, posed as an agent of Queen Victoria, tricked the Tawana king, Sekgoma, into signing a treaty of 'friendship' with Britain, and incidentally granted the BSAC mineral extraction rights. This treaty, known as the Bosman Concession, was later disallowed by the British government, which in 1896 persuaded Sekgoma to open the Ghanzi region to White settlement in exchange for the guarantee of Tawana sovereignty over the remainder of Ngamiland. Rhodes lost out again but wasn't yet defeated.

In 1895 his cohort Leander Starr Jameson launched an abortive private military foray into the Transvaal, much to the embarrassment of the British government, hoping to rein it into some sort of southern African confederation. The Boers were not impressed, Rhodes was forced to give up his prime ministership of the Cape Colony, and Jameson was imprisoned. This time, Rhodes had to admit defeat.

Colonial Years

British rule had now settled in and the chiefs more or less accepted the fact that their tribal rites, traditions and lifestyles were being forever altered by the influences of Christianity and Western technology. The cash economy had been solidly emplaced and the Tswana were actively beginning to participate. The capital of the Bechuanaland Protectorate was set up at Mafeking – which was actually outside the Protectorate, in South Africa – and taxes were established.

Each chief was granted a tribal 'reserve' in which he was given authority over all Black residents. The British assigned the chiefs, who still held some degree of autonomy over their tribes, to collect taxes, offering them a 10% commission on all moneys collected, which essentially forced everyone into the cash economy.

In 1899, Great Britain decided that a consolidation of the southern African states needed to begin and formal war was declared on the Transvaal. The Boers were finally overcome in 1902, and in 1910 the Union of South Africa, comprising the Cape, Natal, the Transvaal and the Orange Free State, was formed with provisions for the future incorporation of Bechuanaland and Rhodesia.

By selling cattle, draught oxen and grain to the Europeans streaming north in search of farming land and minerals, the protectorate enjoyed some degree of economic independence but it didn't last long. The construction of the railway through Bechuanaland to Rhodesia (built at the rate of a mile a day!) and a serious outbreak of foot-and-mouth disease in the 1890s destroyed the transit trade. By 1920 the commercial maize farmers in South Africa and Rhodesia were producing grain in such quantities that Bechuanaland no longer had a market. Furthermore, in 1924 South Africa began pressing the Tswana chiefs to vote for Bechuanaland's joining the Union of South Africa. When they refused, economic sanctions were brought against the recalcitrant protectorate and its beef market dried up completely.

This economic weakness, combined with a series of drought years and the need to raise cash to pay British taxes, sent protectorate workers migrating to South Africa for work in the farms and mines. As much as one quarter of Botswana's male population was away at any one time, accelerating the breakdown of traditional land-use patterns and eroding the powers of the chiefs, who were no longer in charge of the economy. Agriculture and domestic work were both left in the hands of women, who remained at home. Some aristocrats and cattle barons turned the situation to their advantage by increasing their areas of cultivation and the size of their herds.

In 1923, Ngwato chief Khama III died at the age of 89 and was succeeded by his son Sekgoma, who died himself after serving only two years. The heir to the throne, four-year-old Seretse Khama, wasn't ready for the job of ruling the largest of the Tswana chiefdoms so his 21-year-old uncle, Tshekedi Khama, left his studies in South Africa to become regent of the Ngwato. This intelligent and competent leader was criticised by colonial authorities for his handling of several local disputes according to tribal law, including the flogging of Phineas McIntosh, a White resident of Serowe, for the rape of a local woman. Tshekedi Khama was deposed by Resident Commissioner (well, not quite resident since he was based in Mafeking) Sir Charles Rey, but public opposition to the decision forced him to reinstate the chief.

Rey, bent on developing the territory in his charge, determined that no progress would be forthcoming as long as the people were governed by Tswana chiefs and issued a proclamation turning them into local government officials answerable to colonial magistrates. So great was the popular opposition to the decision – people feared that the decision would lead to their incorporation into South Africa – that Rey was ousted from his job and his proclamation voided.

During WW II, 10,000 Tswana volunteered for the African Pioneer Corps to defend the British Empire. At the end of the war the heir to the Ngwato throne, Seretse Khama, went to study in England where he met and married Ruth Williams, an Englishwoman.

Tshekedi Khama was furious at the breach of tribal custom – some accused him of exploiting the incident as a means to gain real power in his nephew's place – and the authorities in apartheid South Africa, still hoping to absorb Bechuanaland into the Union, were none too happy either. Seretse's chieftaincy was blocked by the British government and he was exiled from the protectorate to England. Bitterness continued until 1956, when Seretse Khama renounced his right to power in Ngwato, became reconciled with his uncle, and returned with his wife to Botswana to serve as vice-chairman of the Ngwato Council.

Independence

The first signs of nationalist thinking among the Tswana occurred as early as the late 1940s, but during the 1950s and early 1960s all Africa was experiencing political change as many former colonies gained their independence. As early as 1955 it had become apparent that Britain was preparing to release its grip on Bechuanaland. University graduates returned from South Africa with political ideas, and although the country had no real economic base, the first Batswanan political parties began to surface and started really thinking about independence.

Following the Sharpeville Massacre in 1960, South African refugees Motsamai Mpho of the African National Congress (ANC) and Philip Matante, a Johannesburg preacher affiliated with the Pan-Africanist Congress, along with K T Motsete, a teacher from Malawi, formed the Bechuanaland People's Party. Its immediate goal was independence for the protectorate.

In 1962, Seretse Khama and the Kanye farmer Quett Masire formed the more moderate Bechuanaland Democratic Party (BDP). They were soon joined by Chief Bathoen II of Ngwaketse. The BDP formulated a schedule for independence, drawing on support from local chiefs and traditional Batswana. They promoted the transfer of the capital into the country, from Mafikeng to Gaborone, drafted a new nonracial constitution and set up a countdown to independence. The British happily accepted the amazingly peaceful transfer of power. General elections were held in 1965 and Seretse Khama was elected president. On 30 September 1966 the country, now called the Republic of Botswana, was granted its independence.

Sir Seretse Khama – he was knighted shortly after independence – was certainly no revolutionary. He guaranteed continued freehold over land held by White ranchers and adopted a strictly neutral stance (at least until near the end of his presidency) towards South Africa and Rhodesia. The reason, of course, was his country's dependence upon the economic monster – Africa's largest – to

Sir Seretse Khama

Top: Female Hill, Tsodilo Hills, Botswana (DS); Aha Hills, Botswana (DS)
Bottom: San (Bushmen) paintings, Tsodilo Hills, Botswana (DS); Third Bridge,
Moremi Wildlife Reserve, Botswana (DS)

Top: Okavango Delta, Botswana (DS); Island in Okavango Delta, Botswana (DS)
Bottom: Donkey and owner, Nxainxai, Botswana (DS); Herero woman, Botswana (DS)

the south. He stood at the helm of one of the world's poorest nations and the wages of Batswana mine workers in South Africa formed an important part of the country's income. Furthermore, Botswana was heavily reliant upon South African food imports.

Nevertheless, Khama refused to exchange ambassadors with South Africa and officially disapproved of apartheid in international circles. He also had the courage to commit Botswana to the so-called 'Front Line' states of Zambia, Tanzania and Mozambique in opposing the Smith regime in Rhodesia and South African control in Namibia, but still refused to allow the Zimbabwean liberation fighters to set up training camps in Botswana. When Rhodesian armed forces performed 'hot pursuit' raids into Botswana and bombed the ferry at Kazungula to Zambia, Botswana's only frontier – a pathetic 100 metres wide – with a majority-ruled country, Botswana reacted by forming an army, the Botswana Defence Force or BDF.

Modern Developments

Economically, Botswana was catapulted into new realms with the discovery of diamonds near Orapa in 1967. The mining concession was given to De Beers with Botswana taking 75% of the profits from the mines. Although most of the population remains in the low income bracket, thanks to this mineral wealth the country now possesses enormous foreign currency reserves (US$1.2 billion in 1987). Botswana showed the world's second highest rate of economic growth in 1986 and the pula is currently the strongest currency on the African continent; in 1990, demand for black-market pula in neighbouring countries eclipsed that for the South African rand, which was in a steady decline.

Although Sir Seretse Khama died in 1980, shortly after Zimbabwean independence, his Botswana Democratic Party still commands a substantial and democratically elected majority in the Botswana parliament. Dr Quett Masire, who has served as president since then, continues along the path laid down by his predecessor while the govern-

ment in general follows similar pragmatic, cautious and pro-Western policies. There is, however, growing urban support for the BDP's rival party, the Botswana National Front, which supports redistribution of wealth and an artificial economy similar to Zimbabwe's, either of which would summarily dismantle the strengthening affluence the country currently enjoys.

During the 1980s there were accusations by South Africa that Botswana was harbouring ANC members and other political refugees from South Africa's version of 'justice'. They retaliated in the form of two helicopter raids on Gaborone in 1986 in which several innocent civilians were killed, none of them affiliated with the ANC. One hopes that recent dramatic changes in South Africa will support more sane policies and eschew future violence and aggression.

Although economic dependence on South Africa is on the wane, the two remain active trading partners and most of Botswana's food imports originate in South Africa. Currently, however, Botswana's biggest problems are unemployment, urban drift, and a rocketing birth rate – currently the third highest in the world – but thus far, economic growth has managed to keep apace.

Botswana remains a peaceful country whose overall character contrasts dramatically with the violence, repression and paranoia that exist in its southern African neighbours. In fact, it is one of exactly three African countries – the others are Namibia and Senegal – which enjoy scheduled popular elections and a fully democratic, multiparty, nonracial system of government.

GEOGRAPHY

With an area of 582,000 sq km, land-locked Botswana is about the same size as Kenya or France and somewhat smaller than Texas. It's bound on the south and south-east by South Africa, across the Limpopo and Molopo Rivers. In the north-east is Zimbabwe while Namibia wraps around the western and northern frontiers. In addition, Botswana shares exactly 100 metres of Zambezi River frontage with Zambia at

Kazungula. The country extends over 1100 km from north to south and 960 km from east to west.

Lying at an average elevation of 1000 metres, the majority of Botswana is a vast and nearly flat sand-filled basin characterised by scrub-covered desert or savanna. In the north-west, the Okavango River flows in from Angola and Namibia and disappears into the sands, forming the 15,000 sq km of convoluted channels and islands that comprise the Okavango Delta. In the north-east, where the basin reaches its lowest point, are the great salty clay deserts of the Makgadikgadi Pans. Covering nearly 85% of Botswana, including the entire central and south-western regions, is the Kalahari (Kgalagadi) Desert, a semi-arid expanse of wind-blown sand deposits and long sandy valleys (which sporadically serve as stream channels) and ridges stabilised by scrubby trees and bushes. Only in the area of Bokspits in the far south-west are the rolling, shifting dunes that to many people define the word 'desert'.

Although Botswana has no mountain ranges to speak of, the almost uniformly flat landscape is punctuated occasionally by low desert hills, especially along the south-eastern boundary and in the far north-west. Although the highest point is 1491-metre Otse Mountain near Lobatse, the most dramatic are the three peaks of the Tsodilo Hills, which lie in the country's north-western corner.

FLORA & FAUNA
Vegetation
Most of Botswana is covered by savanna – either acacia or low thorn scrub – which rolls on across the flat and almost unchanging km. In the heart of the Kalahari it reaches down through the sands to access underlying aquifers.

The country's only deciduous *mopani* forests are in the north-east, where six Chobe District forest reserves also harbour stands of commercial timber for paper and construction. Both *mongonga* and *marula* trees, whose edible nuts once served as staple foods for the San, are also found in the reserves. The soft wood of the marula is used in local wood craft and its fruit is used to make a type of beer.

In the Okavango Delta, one encounters riparian environments dominated by marsh grasses, water lilies and papyrus, alternating with well-vegetated islands thick with palms, acacias, leadwood and sausage trees.

Fauna
Although Botswana is primarily dry, much of the Kalahari, the Okavango Delta and the northern tier are prime areas for African wildlife. Most of the game reserves are vast, under-visited and, with a few exceptions, almost entirely undeveloped. In these vast spaces, wildlife enjoys among the most pristine habitats still available on the continent. Most of the major African species are present in Botswana: elephants, rhinos, lions, leopards, cheetahs, zebras, giraffes, hippos and 20 species of antelope, as well as the smaller animals such as hyaenas, baboons, monkeys and jackals.

The densest game populations are concentrated along the Chobe River frontage and Savuti Marsh areas of of Chobe National Park and in the Moremi Reserve in the Okavango Delta. Adjacent areas are also relatively rich in game while spacious reserves like Nxai Pan, Makgadikgadi Pans, Khutse, Mabuasehube, Gemsbok, and Central Kalahari have sparser but more natural densities. The small game reserves of the Tuli Block in south-eastern Botswana are largely artificial creations but are easily accessible by highway from Botswana's main population centres.

Botswana has a few unusual species of mammals as well as others which are found in greater concentrations here than elsewhere in the region. Along the Chobe and Linyanti rivers in northern Botswana one encounters puku and lechwe, small antelope species. In the Okavango lives a species of semi-aquatic antelope, the sitatunga, with odd elongated hooves which allow it to walk in mud and marsh without sinking. The brown hyaena is found in the central

Kalahari area and there have even been sightings of the rare king cheetah.

The Buffalo Fence

Anyone who's read Mark & Delia Owens' *Cry of the Kalahari* will be familiar with the 'buffalo fence', more properly known as the Veterinary Cordon Fence. It's not a single fence, but a series of high-tensile steel wire barriers which run cross-country through some of Botswana's otherwise wildest terrain. Ostensibly, they're in place to thwart the spread of foot and mouth disease from wild game populations to free-range cattle, but no one has yet produced conclusive proof that the disease is passed from species to species.

The Owens, who spent several years in the central Kalahari, researching the habits and cycles of the theretofore scarcely known brown hyaena, tell of seeing tens of thousands of migrating wildebeest as well as herds of zebra, giraffe and other animals stopped short by the Kuke fence that stretches along the northern boundary of the Central Kalahari Game Reserve. Some became entangled in it, while others died of exhaustion searching for a way around it. Still others were cut off from their seasonal grazing and watering places in the north and succumbed to thirst and starvation.

The Owens' vocal opposition to the fences and their questioning of its capacity to halt the disease, however, did nothing to change the situation. Although they brought the problem to government attention in 1980, the fences remain and the issue, at least as far as Botswana is concerned, is closed.

GOVERNMENT

The Botswanan government is one of Africa's few success stories, a stable and functioning multiparty democracy which oversees the affairs of a peaceful and marginally neutral state. Freedom of speech, press and religion are constitutionally supported.

The constitution, which was drafted prior to independence in 1966, provides for three governmental divisions. The executive branch consists of the president, who is the head of state, as well as 11 cabinet ministers and three assistant ministers. The ministers are selected by the parliament while the president is elected by noncompulsory vote of all citizens over 21 years of age. The presidential term coincides with that of the National Assembly.

The legislative branch is made up of the aforementioned parliament which in turn is composed of the 41-seat National Assembly and the executive president. Assembly members are elected by voters every five years unless the body is dissolved by an interim popular election. Before acting on issues of land tenure, local government and traditional law, parliament must first consult the House of Chiefs, an eight-member advisory body comprising chiefs from the eight major tribes of Botswana.

Judicial responsibilities are divided between the national and local governments with the *dikgotla* or town councils handling local civil and domestic disputes. Rural issues and services are overseen by district councils.

Botswana was a founding member of the Front Line states, a loose organisation of southern African countries – including Mozambique, Angola, Zambia, Tanzania, Zimbabwe and Namibia – which support the current independence and majority rule movements in South Africa, the final 'colonial' stronghold.

ECONOMY

Botswana's economy is one of the world's fastest growing. Aided by a stable political climate and the presence of natural resources, the pula is Africa's strongest currency and Botswana's current economic outlook is bright. In 1988, the gross domestic product, for a population of just over one million, was nearly US$2 billion for an average per capita income of over US$1000. It may not sound like much, but when one considers that the majority of the country's population still exists at subsistence level and generates very little income at all, one realises that urban dwellers working at the vocational and professional levels aren't doing too badly.

Mineral Resources

The recent booming of Botswana's economy rests to some extent upon the stability of its government but otherwise the wealth is geologic, derived from terrestrial heat, pressure and time working on carbon deposits laid down up to 300 million years ago. The diamond-bearing geologic formation in Botswana is known as the Karoo, a layer of sediments which underlies the entire Kalahari desert. The diamonds are found around intrusions known as kimberlites, igneous dykes that have pushed through the Karoo rocks, providing sufficient heat and pressure to form diamonds.

Botswana's diamond interests, which represent 80% of the nation's GNP, are overseen by the De Beers Botswana Mining Company Ltd (Debswana) which mines, sorts and markets the diamonds. The country's greatest known deposits lie around Orapa, Lethlakane and Jwaneng which between them produced 13.2 million carats and a net profit of P1 billion in 1987. During 1989, they brought in over P2 billion.

Other mineral resources, although not as economically important as the shiny rocks, provide further foreign exchange income. Copper and nickel are mined in great quantities from two major deposits near Selebi-Phikwe (oddly enough, the mines are known as Selebi and Phikwe!).

Some gold is mined around Francistown and limited amounts of coal are being taken from eastern Botswana. The most recent large-scale project is the soda ash (sodium carbonate) and salt extraction plant just swinging into operation on Sua (sometimes spelt 'Sowa') Pan. This has been set up as a joint Botswanan-South African venture to diversify Botswana's current diamond-dependent economy. It will involve pumping over 16 million cubic metres of brine per year from 40 wells into 25 sq km of solar evaporation ponds. The expected annual yield will be 300,000 tonnes of soda ash and 700,000 tonnes of sodium chloride.

Agriculture

Because of the extent of the desert, beyond cattle ranching, commercial agriculture doesn't play a major role in Botswana's economic scene. It is significant, however, that 80% of the country's population is to some extent dependent upon it. In addition to herding cattle, sheep and goats, they grow maize, sorghum, beans, peanuts, cottonseed and other dry land crops on a subsistence scale.

Larger cotton and citrus projects are evolving in the irrigated Tuli Block along the Limpopo River and dry land farming methods are being tested at Pandamatenga near the Zimbabwe border.

POPULATION & PEOPLE

Botswana's population is currently around 1.2 million, with around 60% claiming Tswana heritage. It currently has one of the world's highest birth rates – about 3.5% – and is one of the world's most predominantly urban societies. Thanks to the adoption of Christianity and an essentially European form of central government, most traditional practices have been phased out and rural villages are shrinking as people migrate into urban areas for cash-yielding vocational and professional jobs.

The increasingly urban population is concentrated in the south-eastern strip of the country between Lobatse and Francistown. The small percentage of Europeans and Asians live primarily in the larger cities, and such groups as the Herero, Mbukushu, Yei, San, Kalanga and Kgalagadi are distributed mostly through the remote hinterlands of the west and north-west.

In Setswana, the predominant language, tribal groups are denoted by the addition of the prefix 'Ba' at the beginning of the word. Therefore, the Herero are sometimes referred to as 'Baherero' and the Kgalagadi as 'Bakgalagadi'. The San people are occasionally known as 'Basarwa', a Tswana word meaning 'people of the bush', or, more colloquially, 'Bushmen'.

The Tswana

It should first be pointed out that the word 'Batswana' denotes not only those of Tswana lineage but also refers to anyone of Botswanan nationality. Therefore, all the nation's citizens, regardless of tribe or colour, are known as Batswana, but for the purposes of this discussion the name refers to those of Tswana lineage.

The Tswana are divided into a number of lineages, the three most prominent having descended from the three sons of 14th century Tswana chief Malope. The Ngwato are centred on the Serowe area, the Kwena west of Molepolole, and the Ngwaketse in the south-east. An early split in the Ngwato resulted in a fourth group, the Tawana, who are concentrated around Maun in the north-west. Another group, the Kgalagadi, are probably an offshoot of the Tswana that broke away sometime around the 15th century. Since then they've mixed with the San and other peoples to form a new group, generally considered separate from the Tswana.

Tswana villages are large, sprawling and densely populated affairs, comprised mainly of pole and *daga* huts revolving around some commercial venture such as a food and bottle store and a *kgotla*, a traditionally constructed community affairs hall. Historically, the village chief lived at the village centre with the hierarchy of *wards* or family groupings situated in concentric circles around him. Although he had councillors and advisers, the chief was considered the ultimate authority in all matters and the nearer one lived to him, the higher the family's community status.

Family units typically had – and still have – three homes each: one in the village, one at their fields and one at their cattle post where village boys or San men look after the herds. As in many African societies, family wealth was, and in some cases still is, measured by the number of cattle it owned. Land, however, was not owned but rather held in a village trust and used by individual families, allocated at the discretion of the chief.

The San

Much has been written about and attributed

Two San hunters

to the San of the Kalahari. The San have probably inhabited southern Africa for at least 30,000 years but their tenure hasn't really yielded any benefits in the modern scheme of things. Although they're rapidly being dragged into the modern world, they're treated as second-class citizens in nearly every respect. One of the most fascinating peoples on earth, they have now sadly resigned themselves to the changes that have ended forever their Utopian historical existence in which integration with their harsh desert domain was complete.

'San' is actually a collective term for the various groups of non-Negroid peoples of southern Africa (or 'Khoisan' if the Khoi-Khoi are included). Although their characteristics and languages are distinct, all their languages share the dental and palatal clicks that have been adopted even by some Bantu groups like the Ndebele (see the Language section in the Zimbabwe Facts about the Country chapter). As a matter of interest, the San clicks are of three types: '!' is the palatal click made by pulling the tongue away from the roof of the mouth. 'X' or '/' is the lateral click, formed by pulling the tongue away from the upper right teeth. 'C' or '//' is a dental click, made when the tongue is pulled from the upper front teeth.

Early San encounters with other groups were probably happy ones. It's generally believed that they peacefully coexisted, intermarried and traded with early community-minded Bantu groups moving into the area. Although they would have had every opportunity to learn agriculture and herding, it remains a mystery why they chose to continue their nomadic ways.

The Europeans who arrived at the Cape in the mid-17th century, however, saw the San and Khoi-Khoi as little more than wild animals and potential cattle raiders. The early Boers set about an extermination campaign that would last 200 years and kill as many as 200,000 San.

The traditional San were nomadic hunters and gatherers who travelled in small family bands. They had no chiefs or system of leadership and individualism was respected. Personal decisions were made individually and group decisions by the group. In fact, there was no pressure to conform to any predetermined ideals and anyone with itchy feet could leave the group without placing stress on the whole. During times of plenty, groups could contain as many as 120 people, while during hard times when people had to spread out to survive they diminished to family units of 10 or fewer people.

A thoroughly mobile society, the San followed the water, the game and the edible plants. They had no animals, no crops and no possessions. Everything needed for daily existence was carried with them. Women spent much of their time caring for children and gathering edible or water-yielding plants while the men either hunted or helped with the food gathering.

One myth has it that the San are unable to distinguish colour because most San languages contain few colour-related words. In fact, the languages are more concerned with tangibles than abstracts. It's just considered unnecessary to linguistically separate an object from its attributes. Another myth is that the San people possess extremely keen senses of hearing, eyesight and direction. Although their awareness of surroundings certainly seems phenomenal to the technology-dependent world, anthropological studies have determined that it's been learned as a result of necessity rather than a physiological adaptation. It's generally agreed that anyone, given the right circumstances and healthy faculties, can develop a similar awareness.

Of the remaining 55,000 or so individuals, approximately 60% live in Botswana, 35% are in Namibia and the remainder are scattered through South Africa, Angola, Zimbabwe and Zambia. Of these, perhaps 2000 still live by hunting and gathering. The remainder work on farms and cattle posts or languish in squalid, handout-dependent and alcohol-plagued settlements centred on bore holes in western Botswana. Among other Batswana, they are currently gaining a reputation as cattle rustlers and undesirables.

It would be pleasant to end this discussion on a more hopeful note, but it would require grasping at straws. The pattern, already in place among Australian Aborigines and native Americans, is summed up in the San word *shita*, the concept of life as a burden. The Botswanan government still allows use of the Central Kalahari Game Reserve by the few remaining traditional San but the majority express the desire to join the Batswana mainstream. May they succeed.

The Kalanga

The majority of the Kalanga people, related to the Shona, now live in western Zimbabwe but they still comprise the second-largest group in sparsely populated Botswana. They are generally considered to be descendants of the people of the Rozwi Empire, who were responsible for building Great Zimbabwe and what are now the series of ruins centred on Bulawayo. The Rozwi were overcome and scattered by the Ndebele in the 1830s, spreading as far west as the Thamalakane

River in northern Botswana and south to the Boteti River where some were partially absorbed by the Ngwato branch of the Tswana.

The Mbukushu & Yei

The Mbukushu, who now inhabit the Okavango Delta area of Ngamiland, were originally refugees from the Caprivi area of north-eastern Namibia, forced to flee in the late 1700s when they were dislodged by the forces of Chief Ngombela's Lozi Empire. Next down the line of dominoes were the Yei, settled in the Chobe and Linyanti Valleys of north-western Botswana and in turn displaced by the fleeing Mbukushu.

The Mbukushu carried on to the south-eastern corner of Angola, just north of present-day Andara, Namibia. There they encountered more difficulties, this time in the form of Portuguese and African traders who began purchasing Mbukushu slaves from the tribal leadership. The local rainmaking deity also seemed to have a taste for Mbukushu infants and many people decided it was in their best interest to depart. Essentially a riverine tribe, some of the Mbukushu headed down the Okavango to settle into farming maize and sorghum in the Panhandle area of the delta. At that stage their running days were apparently over and, now mixed with later arriving Tswana, many remain in villages like Shakawe and Sepopa.

Meanwhile the Yei scattered down the Panhandle, roaming as far south as Lake Ngami. Essentially a matrilineal society, they never settled in large groups and eventually melted into the islands and channels of the Okavango Delta where they travelled by *mokoro*, or pole boat, through the shallow waters.

Like the Mbukushu, many have now mixed with Tawana who arrived in the mid-1800s. The Yei were conquered by the more powerful group and forced into clientship, a sophisticated form of enslavement in which the clients had a lot similar to that of serfs in a fiefdom. Interestingly, the Yei, who were second-class citizens in Tawana society, themselves took clients among the San, who wound up at the bottom of the heap. Many Yei still inhabit the delta region and depend primarily upon fishing and hunting.

The Herero

Those visiting Maun and western Botswana will undoubtedly notice the colourfully dressed Herero women, attired in their full-length Victorian-style finery on even the most stifling days. The unusual dress, which is now a tribal trademark, was initially forced upon them by the prudish German missionaries in the late 1800s.

The Herero people probably originated in eastern or central Africa and migrated across the Okavango River into north-eastern Namibia around the early 16th century. There, the group apparently split: the Ovambo settled down to farming along the Kunene River in northern Namibia and the Herero moved on into the Kaokoveld of extreme north-western Namibia. Disputes there sent one contingent, the Mbanderu, eastward where they turned to a pastoral lifestyle in the western Kalahari.

The nomadic Herero never practised farming so they were utterly dependent upon their cattle, which took on a religious significance as the source of Herero life. Their dietary staple was *omaeru* or sour milk.

In 1884 the Germans took possession of German Southwest Africa (Namibia) and summarily took over the Herero grazing lands in that country. While the Germans were engaged in a war with the Nama people further west, the Herero, hardened by their own years of war with the Nama, seized the opportunity to take revenge for injustices meted out by the colonials and attacked a German settlement, killing about 150 people. The Germans, however, came back with a vengeance and the remaining Herero were forced to abandon their herds and flee into Botswana.

The refugees settled among the Tawana and were initially subjugated to clientship, but eventually regained their herds and independence. Today they are among the wealthiest herders in Botswana and, now that

Namibia is independent, many speak of returning to the 'old country' with which they still seem to feel strong kinship.

ARTS

The original Batswana artists were everyday people who felt the need to inject individuality, aesthetics and aspects of Batswana life into their utilitarian implements. Baskets, pottery, fabrics and tools were decorated with meaningful designs derived from tradition. Europeans introduced a new sort of art, some of which was integrated and adapted to local interpretation, particularly in weavings and tapestries. The result is some of the finest and most meticulously executed work in southern Africa.

In an attempt to provide a cash income for rural Batswana, the Botswanacraft Marketing Company (☎ 312471, fax 313189 Gaborone) was set up to search out the best of cottage creativity and purchase it for resale in retail shops or export. The company ensures that the bulk of the profit goes to the producer. In addition, it holds an annual basketry competition and awards bonuses for higher quality work. For more information on Botswanacraft or a look at a catalogue of its offerings, write to the company at PO Box 486, Gaborone, Botswana.

Visitors travelling in rural areas have the opportunity to purchase crafts directly from the producers. Alternatively you can visit one of the several weavings and crafts cooperatives in operation around the country. Whether you're buying or just appreciating the artisans' skill, few will fail to be impressed at the quality of what's available.

Botswana Baskets

Botswana baskets are the most lauded of the country's material products. Interestingly, the designs generally considered to be the most beautiful aren't indigenous, having been brought to north-western Botswana by Angolan Mbukushu refugees in the last century. Although the baskets still get practical use – the storage of seeds, grains and

bojalwa mash for sorghum beer – the art has since been finely tuned and some of the work is unbelievably exquisite. The baskets are made from fibrous strands of the *mokolane* palm (*Hyphaene petersiana*) and coloured with natural earth-tone dyes in swirls and designs with such evocative names as Flight of the Swallow, Tears of the Giraffe, Urine Trail of the Bull, Forehead of the Zebra, Back of the Python and The Running Ostrich.

Although the finest and most expensive work comes from Ngamiland, more loosely woven but still beautiful Shashe baskets are available in Francistown.

Weavings

Contemporary weavings – tapestries, rugs, bed covers and the like made from *karakul* wool – combine African themes with formats adopted from European art to produce work that appeals to both cultures. Most of the country's output is produced at two weaving cooperatives in south-eastern Botswana: the Lentswe-la-Odi Weavers in Odi village and the newer Tiro ya Diatla in Lobatse where artists are given free reign to choose their own themes, colours and presentation. Some of the results are truly inspired.

Woodcarving

Woodcarving has been used traditionally in the production of such practical items as tools, spoons, bowls and containers from the densely grained wood of the mopani tree. Artists are now utilising the mopani to produce jewellery, as well as both realistic and fantastic figurines of animals and renditions of more modern innovations such as tractors and aeroplanes.

Pottery

The original pottery used in Botswana was constructed of smoothed coils and fired slowly, leaving it porous. Therefore, evaporation through the pot worked as a sort of refrigeration system, keeping the liquid inside cool and drinkable on even the hottest days. Although more modern pottery is being produced today, traditional patterns and designs are still used at several pottery workshops around the country. The most accessible are Moratwa Pottery in Lobatse, Thamaga Pottery in Thamaga and Pelegano Pottery in Gabane. Thamaga and Gabane are villages west of Gaborone.

Other Material Arts

The San people of western Botswana are adept at creating seed-and-bead bracelets and necklaces and beaded leather bags and aprons. The beads are traditionally hand-made from ostrich egg shells, but nowadays plastic beads are creeping into the work. It's just as well; the ostriches will appreciate it, and some foreign governments don't allow the import of ostrich egg products, anyway.

The Herero people, who emigrated to Botswana from Namibia, dress in a unique style introduced by German missionaries during the last century – the women habitually wear billowing Victorian-style skirts and the men, when traditionally dressed, wear a variation on the Scottish tartan kilt. The Herero women are skilled at making similarly dressed dolls of fabric and natural materials, which are much in demand and may be found around Maun and Ghanzi.

Literature

Since the indigenous languages have only been written since the coming of the Christian missionaries, Botswana doesn't have much of a literary tradition. What survives of the ancient myths and praise poetry of the San, Tswana, Herero and other groups has been handed down orally and only recently written down.

Botswana's most famous modern literary figure was South African-born Bessie Head who settled in Sir Seretse Khama's village of Serowe. Her writings, many of which are set in Serowe, reflect the harshness and the beauty of African village life and indeed of the physical attributes of Botswana itself. Her most widely read works include *Serowe – Village of the Rain Wind, When Rain Clouds Gather, Maru, A Question of Power, A Bewitched Crossroad* and *The Collector of Treasures*, the last an anthology of short stories. Bessie Head died in 1988.

RELIGION

The early tribal religions were primarily ancestor-worshipping cults, in which ancestors directed family matters from their underworld domain and were contactable only through the heads of family groups. Religious rites included the *bogwera* and *bojale* or male and female initiation ceremonies and the *gofethla pula* or rainmaking rites. The supreme being and creator, who was more or less incidental in the scheme of things, was known as Modimo.

Polygamy was practised. The children of the head wife inherited the man's estate, while the man's cattle were typically passed to that woman's family, thus securing her children's inheritance. The head wife wasn't necessarily the first wife, but rather the one with whom an inheritance agreement had been made prior to marriage.

San folklore is rich with supernatural explanations of natural events that pervade all cultures. Their traditional religious beliefs are quite simple and not at all burdened with dogma or ritual. Their two supernatural beings represent good and evil, order and entropy. N!odima, the good, is the omnipotent creator who seems to have little time to meddle in the affairs of mortals. His opponent, Gcawama, is a mischievous trickster who spends his time trying to create disorder of the perfect natural organisation laid down by N!odima. Gcawama, unfortunately, seems to take a bothersome amount of interest in the lives of humans.

Like most Africans, the religion of the Herero was based upon ancestor worship. In their estimation the first ancestor, Mukuru, surpassed even Ndjambi, their supreme deity. So revered were the ancestors that Herero men set aside up to 200 head of cattle for them. When the man died the selected beasts were suffocated as sacrifices to keep the ancestors in a pleasant mood lest the man's family suffered.

When the first Christian missionaries

arrived in the early 1800s, they brought with them an entirely new set of ideas which derailed nearly all the Tswana traditions and practices. They naturally forbade ancestor veneration and the rites associated with it as well as polygamy, inheritance practices and the consumption of alcohol.

Christianity is currently the prevailing belief system in Botswana, with the largest number of Christians belonging to the United Congregational Church of Southern Africa. The Lutheran, Roman Catholic, Anglican and Methodist churches also have significant membership in the country.

LANGUAGE

English is the official language of Botswana and the medium of instruction from the fifth year of primary school on. The most common language, however, is Setswana, a Bantu language in the Sotho-Tswana group, which is understood by over 90% of the population. It is the language of the dominant population group, the Tswana, and is used as a medium of instruction in early primary school. The second most widely used Bantu language is Sekalanga, a Shona derivative spoken by the Kalanga people who live around Francistown.

It is interesting to note that the name of most of Botswana's population is of Tswana heritage. The Tswana people are known as Batswana (although the word has also come to apply to any citizen of Botswana) just as the Yei people are known as Bayei. By the same token, a Tswana individual (or individual citizen of Botswana) is called Motswana. The language of the Tswana people is Setswana, while that of the Kalanga is Sekalanga and that of the English is Seenglish! The land of the Tswana is, of course, Botswana.

The language is spelt more or less phonetically except the 'g' which is pronounced as an 'h' or, more accurately, a strongly aspirated 'g'. 'Th' is pronounced simply as a slightly aspirated 't'.

The greetings *dumêla rra* when speaking to men and *dumêla mma* to women are considered compliments and Batswana

appreciate their liberal usage. When addressing a group, say *dumêlang*.

When accepting a gift or anything for which you're grateful, receive it with both hands or take hold of it with your right hand and hold your right arm with your left. Another useful phrase, which is normally placed at the end of a sentence or conversation, is *go siame* meaning the equivalent of 'all right, no problem'.

The book *First Steps in Spoken Setswana* is useful; it's available from the Botswana Book Centre in Gaborone.

The list of words and phrases below should help you get started with Setswana pleasantries.

Greetings & Civilities

Hello (to a woman/man)
  Dumêla mma/rra
Hello (to a group)
  Dumêlang
Hello! (hailing someone from your door)
  Ko ko!
Come on in!
  Tsena!
How's it going?
  O kae?
I'm fine. (informal)
  Ke teng.
How are you? (lit. 'how did you wake up?')
  A o tsogile?
Did you get up well?
  A o sa tsogile sentlê?
Yes, I woke up well.
  Ee, ke tsogile sentlê
How are you?(afternoon)
  O tlhotse jang?
I'm fine. (response)
  Ke tlhotse sentlê.
Goodbye. (to person leaving)
  Tsamayo sentlê.
Goodbye. (to person staying)
  Sala sentlê.
OK/all right/no problem/
  Go siame
Please
  Tsweetswee
Thank you
  Kea itumêla

Useful Phrases

yes/no
ee/nnyaa
Do you speak...?
A o bua Se...
Where are you from? (birthplace)
O tswa kae?
I'm from Australia.
Ke tswa kwa Australia.
Where do you live?
O nna kae?
I live in Maun.
Ke nna kwa Maun.
Where are you going?
O ya kae?
What is your name?
Leina la gago ke mang?
My name is...
Leina la me ke...
Where is the way to...
Tsela...e kae?
Where is the railway station/hotel?
Seteseine/hotele se kai?

Is it far?
A go kgala?
What would you like?
O batla eng?
I would like...
Ke batla...

Food & Drink

bread
borotho
milk
mashi
meat
nama
food
dijo
mealies
bogobe
water
metsi
How much is it?
Ke bokai?

Facts for the Visitor

VISAS & EMBASSIES

Everyone entering Botswana must have a valid passport from their home country. For tourist visits of up to three months – although on entry you'll only be granted an extendible 30 days – no visas are required by citizens of the following countries: all Commonwealth countries (except Ghana, India, Mauritius, Nigeria and Sri Lanka), Austria, Belgium, Denmark, Republic of Ireland, Finland, France, Germany, Greece, Iceland, Israel, Italy, Liechtenstein, Luxembourg, Netherlands, Norway, San Marino, South Africa, Sweden, Switzerland, USA, Uruguay and Yugoslavia. All others must apply for a visa through a Botswanan diplomatic mission or a British High Commission abroad, or by post to the Immigration and Passport Control Officer (☎ 374545 Gaborone), off Khama Crescent, PO Box 942, Gaborone, Botswana.

Those wishing to stay more than three months for tourism purposes must also apply in advance to the Immigration Office. Otherwise, a maximum of 90 days in any calendar year is permitted. Renewable three year residence permits are generally available to those with skills in demand in Botswana. Refer also to the discussion of Work later in this chapter.

Botswanan Diplomatic Missions

In countries where Botswana has no diplomatic representation, information and visas are available through the British High Commission.

EC (European Community)
Botswana Embassy to the EC, 189 Ave de Tervueren, 1150 Brussels, Belgium
UK
High Commission of the Republic of Botswana, 6 Stratford Place, London W1
UN
Permanent Mission of the Republic of Botswana to the UN, 866 Second Ave, New York, New York 10017, USA

USA
Embassy of the Republic of Botswana, Suite 404 Van Ness Center, 4301 Connecticut Ave NW, Washington, DC 20008
Zambia
High Commission of the Republic of Botswana, PO Box 1910, Lusaka
Zimbabwe
High Commission of the Republic of Botswana, Southern Life Building, Jason Moyo Ave, Harare

Foreign Embassies & Consulates in Botswana

The following is a list of foreign diplomatic missions in Botswana. South Africa has no representation in Botswana. To secure a visa for South Africa, you'll have to go to the South African Trade Mission in Harare, Zimbabwe. Alternatively, write to their representative in Bophuthatswana: South African Embassy, Private Bag x2110, Mafikeng, South Africa.

Denmark
Danish Consulate Royal, 142 Mengwe Close, PO Box 367, Gaborone (☎ 353770)
EC
Delegation of the EC to Botswana, PO Box 1253, Gaborone (☎ 314455)
France
French Embassy, 761 Robinson Rd, PO Box 1424, Gaborone (☎ 353683)
Germany
Embassy of the Federal Republic of Germany, 2nd Floor IGI House, The Mall, PO Box 315, Gaborone (☎ 353143)
Namibia
UN Commission for Namibia, BCC Building, 1278 Lobatse Rd, PO Box 1586, Gaborone (☎ 314227) note: The UN Commission exists in place of an embassy and will change as soon as Namibia sets up diplomatic representation in Botswana. Those requiring Namibian visas should currently apply through the Zambian consulate.
Netherlands
Netherlands Consulate, Haile Selassie Rd, PO Box 10055, Gaborone (☎ 357224)
Sweden
Royal Swedish Embassy, Development House, The Mall, Private Bag 0017, Gaborone (☎ 353912)

UK

    British High Commission, Queens Road, The Mall, Private Bag 0023, Gaborone (☎ 352841)

USA

    US Embassy, Badiredi House, The Mall, PO Box 90, Gaborone (☎ 353982)

Zambia

    Zambia High Commission, Zambia House, The Mall, PO Box 362, Gaborone (☎ 351951)

Zimbabwe

    Zimbabwe High Commission, 1st Floor, IGI House, The Mall, PO Box 1232, Gaborone (☎ 314495)

DOCUMENTS

If you're entering from a yellow fever infected area, you'll need a yellow fever vaccination certificate, but otherwise no vaccinations are required.

Visitors are permitted to drive on a home licence for up to six months (non-English licences must be accompanied by an English translation), after which they'll have to apply for a Botswanan licence. There won't be any driving test involved; just present your old licence and pick up the local one.

If you're entering by vehicle, you must be able to prove current registration in your home country and provide evidence of third-party insurance from somewhere in the Southern African Customs Union (South Africa, Botswana, Lesotho, Swaziland). Otherwise, you'll have to purchase insurance at the border. All vehicles are subject to a road tax of P1 upon entry.

CUSTOMS

Botswana, along with South Africa, Swaziland and Lesotho, is a member of the Southern African Customs Union which means that unrestricted and uncontrolled items may be carried between them duty-free. If you're entering Botswana from any other country, you'll be subject to normal Botswanan duties on any items that aren't to be re-exported.

Visitors are allowed to import 400 cigarettes, 50 cigars and 250 grams of tobacco duty-free. Extra petrol and South African alcohol are always subject to duty, but otherwise you may import up to two litres of wine and one litre of beer or spirits duty-free. Cameras, film and firearms must be declared upon entry but aren't subject to duty. If you're carrying any animal products, including meat, milk and eggs, finish them off before you arrive at the border or they'll be confiscated.

Special regulations apply to importing items such as unworked metals and precious stones, live plants, game trophies, pets, and firearms. If you're bringing an animal or bird, information and applications are available from the Director of Veterinary Services, Private Bag 0032, Gaborone, Botswana.

MONEY

The first thing to remember about money in

Botswana is to bring a lot of it; otherwise it's a safe bet to say you won't enjoy your visit much because none of the places of interest will be available to budget travellers. For a rough idea of the amounts we're talking about here, see Costs later in this chapter.

Travellers entering the country are required to declare their currency upon entry. When leaving, they must estimate the amount of money spent in Botswana. There are no currency controls in place – this is just so they'll know whether you're taking more money out than you brought in, a bad idea unless you have a work permit. I've heard tales of meticulous scrutiny, but in the nine or so times I've entered Botswana no one has ever asked to see either my declared currency or travellers' cheques. Foreigners may only export up to P500 in cash.

Currency

Botswana's unit of currency is the pula, which is divided into 100 thebe. 'Pula' is also the national motto of Botswana and appears on the national coat of arms. That doesn't, however, signify inordinate financial preoccupations. Rather, 'pula' means 'rain', in reference to something very precious in a desert environment like Botswana. Almost predictably, 'thebe' means 'raindrop'. Bank notes come in denominations of P1, 2, 5, 10, 20 and 50, coins in denominations of 1t, 2t, 5t, 10t, 25t, 50t and P1.

Banking

Full banking services are available in Gaborone, Francistown, Mahalapye, Palapye, Selebi-Phikwe, Serowe, Jwaneng, Kanye, Maun, Mochudi, Ghanzi and Molepolole, and in Kasane on weekdays except Thursday. Standard banking hours in major towns are from 9 am to 2.30 pm on Monday, Tuesday, Thursday and Friday, from 8.15 am to noon on Wednesday, and from 8.15 to 10.45 am on Saturday. If you're exchanging money at one of the main bank branches in Francistown or Gaborone, it is vital that you queue up well before the bank opens and set aside the entire morning for the task. The exchange process is excruciatingly

slow, with lots of form-filling compounded by the sinuous queues of newly arrived Zimbabwean shoppers waiting to exchange their Zimbabwe dollar travellers' cheques for precious pula.

No foreign exchange is transacted on Saturdays except at the Gaborone Sun Hotel branch of Barclays Bank. This branch is open from 8.30 am to 2 pm daily, except Wednesday when it closes at 1.30 pm. The Sir Seretse Khama International Airport branch is open for foreign exchange from 9.30 am to 5 pm on weekdays.

It isn't possible to purchase Zimbabwean dollars or Zambian kwacha in Botswanan banks, but pula are so much in demand elsewhere in Africa that high black market rates are available from just about anyone travelling on the trains or in border areas; particularly Zimbabweans who've come over to immerse themselves in Botswana's cornucopia of South African imports. Keep in mind, however, that currency restrictions prevent the import of more than Z$40 into Zimbabwe or kw20 into Zambia per visit and that such currency is next to worthless outside those two countries.

The pula is currently stronger and more in demand than the South African rand. South African imports are priced the same in pula as they are in rand across the border, making them approximately 50% dearer in Botswana.

Most major credit cards – they really like Barclays Visa – are accepted at hotels and restaurants in the larger cities and towns although they may not be used to purchase petrol. Barclays Visa may be used to purchase Barclays US$ or £sterling travellers' cheques with little or no commission taken. Credit card cash advances are available in Gaborone, Lobatse, Maun and Francistown through Barclays Bank or Standard Chartered Bank. In smaller towns, you can apply at the banks for cash advances but may have to wait hours or days before authorisation is forthcoming.

Cash transfers from foreign banks are most conveniently done through Barclays where it will be received by the Barclay

House Branch on Khama Crescent, Gaborone. If the money isn't sent through a Barclays branch overseas, allow seven to 10 working days for the process to sort itself out. All monies will be converted to pula on receipt (with a commission plus a transfer fee deducted), and if you want to convert it into US$ or UK£ to purchase travellers' cheques, yet another commission will be taken.

In remote towns and villages where there are no established banks, travelling banks are available at regular intervals. In many cases the service arrives once monthly and conducts transactions for just an hour or two. In such places as Lethlakane, the bank arrives on the Debswana (the De Beers of Botswana) payday, from where all the town's money is derived anyway! In Shakawe and Gumare it comes on the government payday. Some other villages offer banking services once or twice weekly. For specific days and hours, which change periodically, enquire at branches in larger towns. These rural banking services will normally change foreign travellers' cheques but not cash.

Exchange Rates

At the time of writing the pula was worth:

A$1	=	P1.72
US$1	=	P2.18
UK£1	=	P3.82
¥100	=	P1.69
DM1	=	P1.30
SFr1	=	P1.50
FFr1	=	P0.38
NZ$	=	P1.24
C$1	=	P1.94
SAfR1	=	P0.78
Z$1	=	P0.43

Costs

Botswana's recent policy of discouraging all but high cost, organised tourism essentially places it out of reach for those on shoestring budgets. Travelling cheaply in Botswana, while not completely impossible as long as hitchhiking is permitted, will prove a frustrating uphill battle. Those who simply

can't afford the occasional blowout – a flight into the Okavango, a day or two at Moremi Reserve or Chobe National Park, or a 4WD trip through the Kalahari – probably won't think much of the country.

Accommodation, particularly in Gaborone, operates on the principle of supply and demand, and while demand is very high thanks to the housing shortage, the supply is minimal. A couple of new hotels have sprung up recently in Gaborone but the least expensive is still about P100 per night for a double. Currently, no licences are being granted for youth hostels, backpackers' lodges, camping grounds or any other budget options. Outside Gaborone there are a few relatively inexpensive camping sites, but none are convenient to towns.

Supermarket, fast-food and restaurant prices will be comparable or slightly less than those in Europe, North America or Australasia. Small local food halls are normally a cheap option but don't expect much variety beyond *mealies* and relish.

Hitchhiking, buses and trains are all relatively cheap but they won't get you to the interesting parts of the country. The least expensive vehicle rental currently runs around P50 per day plus 55t per km, but if you want to get out into the western part of the country you'll need to pay P105 per day and 95t per km for a 4WD vehicle. Businesses proposing bicycle rentals around Gaborone have been refused licences. For more information on transport costs in Botswana, refer to the Botswana Getting Around chapter.

National park and reserve entrance fees will be the independent travellers' biggest thorn in the side. While those on organised tours pay only P30 per day entry, with luxury accommodation normally prepaid through the tour companies, those doing it on their own will pay P50 per person per day park entry fee and an additional P20 per person for camping. Botswanan residents pay only P10 per day entry and P5 camping while citizens pay P2 entry and P5 camping.

The rationale behind this seems at least partially sound: the Botswanan government wants to extract as much revenue as possible while limiting expenditures on infrastructure and maintenance and minimising the effects of mass tourism. On the other hand, since most Botswana citizens don't have long holidays or the ready cash to spend on them and most independent foreign travellers can't foot the entry fees, the national parks and reserves have essentially become private playgrounds for tour companies, expatriate workers and overseas volunteers.

Tipping

While tipping isn't exactly required, thanks to the official policy of promoting only upmarket tourism, it's becoming more and more expected in hotels, taxis and nicer restaurants. In most places a service charge is added as a matter of course, so if you're feeling the urge to augment that, about 10% should suffice.

CLIMATE & WHEN TO GO

Despite straddling the tropic of Capricorn, Botswana experiences extremes in both temperature and weather. Although it is primarily a dry country, Botswana experiences a pronounced rainy season during the summer months which runs roughly from November to March. Afternoon showers and thunderstorms are the most frequent manifestations of *pula*, the commodity so precious that Botswana's currency was named for it.

For visitors hoping to hit the back roads, enjoy game viewing or go exploring in the Okavango, summer is definitely not the best time. Prolonged rains may render sandy roads impassable and rivers uncrossable, and during periods of high water Chobe National Park and Moremi Wildlife Reserve may be closed. Unless you're after flamingos in the salt pans, the wildlife will be harder to spot anyway. Game disperses when water is abundant and it's not necessary to stay close to perennial water sources. Summer is also the time of the highest humidity and the most stifling heat; daytime temperatures of over 40°C are usual.

In the winter, the period from late May to August, rain is rare anywhere in the country. Days are normally clear, warm and sunny and nights are cool to bitterly cold. In the Kalahari, subfreezing night-time temperatures are normal in June and July and, where there's enough humidity, frosts are common. Wildlife never wanders far from water sources so game viewing is more predictable than during the summer.

The in-between periods – April/early May and September/October – still tend to be dry, but the days are cooler than in summer and the nights are warmer than in winter.

TOURIST OFFICES
Local Tourist Offices

The national tourism office in Gaborone (☎ 353024, fax 371539 Gaborone) is inconveniently located a long way from the centre, on the 1st floor of the Botswana Building Society building, one block from Broadhurst shopping centre. It has all the maps, pamphlets and brochures you're likely to find and the staff are pretty helpful with queries, but don't expect miracles, especially as regards an inexpensive place to stay in Gaborone! Their address is: Tourism Development Unit, Ministry of Commerce and Industry, Private Bag 0047, Gaborone, Botswana.

Maun's tourist office (☎ 260492 Maun) is adjacent to the world-famous Duck Inn near the Maun airport. It doesn't have any brochures and there's precious little information on offer; you'll get more from any of the private travel agencies around town. For what it's worth, the office's mailing address is PO Box 439, Maun.

A bit more helpful is the office in Kasane (☎ 250327 Kasane) which sells some beautiful posters of the Okavango and Chobe for a pittance and dispenses Chobe-related information and advertising. The mailing address is PO Box 66, Kasane.

BUSINESS HOURS & HOLIDAYS
Business Hours

Normal business hours in Botswana are from around 8 am to 5 pm, often with a one or two hour closure for lunch, which is normally from 1 to 2 pm. On Saturday shops open early and close at noon or 1 pm, while on Sunday there's scarcely a whisper of activity anywhere.

In the major towns, banking hours are from 9 am to 2.30 pm Monday, Tuesday, Thursday and Friday, from 8.15 am to noon on Wednesday and from 8.15 am to 10.45 am on Saturday. For special banking hours, see under 'Money' earlier in this chapter. Major post offices are open from 8.15 am to 4 pm with a lunchtime closing between 12.45 and 2 pm. On Saturday they're open between 8 and 11 am. Government offices remain open from 7.30 am to 12.30 pm and 1.45 to 4.30 pm, Monday to Friday.

Bottle stores generally open midmorning and close at precisely 7 pm. If you want to purchase alcohol after that hour anywhere in Botswana, you'll have to resort to hotel and restaurant bars.

Public Holidays

1 January
  New Year's Day
2 January
  Day After New Year's Day
March or April
  Good Friday, Easter Saturday, Sunday & Monday
April or May
  Ascension Day
10 July
  President's Day
11 July
  Day After President's Day
30 September
  Botswana Day
1 October
  Day After Botswana Day
25 December
  Christmas Day
26 December
  Boxing Day

POST & TELECOMMUNICATIONS
Post

In major towns, post offices are open between 8.15 am and 4 pm, closing for lunch from 12.45 to 2 pm. Expect long slow-moving queues while the lackadaisical postal employees chat on the phone or among themselves between customers. Similarly, although it's generally reliable, the post can be painfully slow. Plan on two weeks to a month for delivery to or from an overseas address.

Poste restante is available in major towns but if you want to receive anything within the 30 days normally allowed tourists by Botswana immigration, you'd be safest

sticking with poste restante at the GPO on The Mall in Gaborone. A new GPO near the southern end of Khama Crescent is scheduled to take over most Gaborone postal services in the near future but it remains to be seen whether poste restante will move to the new location.

If you're staying in Botswana for a while and would like a post office box, get your name on the waiting list as soon as possible. Until something becomes available, which is currently taking years, you'll have to rely on poste restante or receive mail via your employer's private bag.

To post or receive a parcel, go to the parcel office round the side of the GPO, fill out the relevant customs forms and/or pay duties. Parcels may be plastered with all the sticky tape you like, but in the end they must be tied up with string or they won't be accepted. You must present your passport or other photo ID to pick up parcels.

Aerogrammes, which are available at post offices, or postcards are the least expensive items to send, followed by 2nd-class airmail letters, which are designated by clipping the corners off the envelope.

Telephone
Reliable call boxes may be found around post offices in all major towns and cities. Direct dialling is available to most locations within Botswana, but for international calls you'll have to go through the operator and have pockets full of pula and thebe coins to plug into the box.

In Gaborone there's a telephone office in the Standard Bank Building on The Mall where you can book and pay for long-distance calls, but expect to spend lots of time waiting for the procedure to work. In Francistown there's a similar setup at the telecommunications office. The office is unfortunately only open during normal business hours, so if you're phoning Australia or North America you'll probably be dragging someone out of bed.

Few if any countries have reciprocal reverse charges agreements with Botswana, but time and charges information is available for private telephones immediately after you hang up if you request it when booking the call.

For calls from abroad, Botswana's direct dialling code is 267.

LAUNDRY
As far as I'm aware, there are no self-service laundries in Botswana. One commercial dry-cleaning and laundry service is available at No Mathatha shopping centre in Gaborone, but that's the extent of it. Large hotels all offer laundry services, but at a premium, while in smaller villages there will always be local women happy to fill the laundry gap for a few pula. Failing all that, you'll just have to wash clothing by hand and hang it out to dry, which in Botswana's desert climate will occur in record time.

BOOKS & MAPS
Outside South Africa, the Botswana Book Centre on The Mall in Gaborone is the region's best stocked bookshop, with row after row of international literature, novels, reference books, school texts and souvenir publications. Smaller and more limited selections are available at the bookshop opposite the railway station in Francistown and on the Mall in Selebi-Phikwe. Most tourist hotels also stock souvenir and coffee table books as well as limited selections of pulp novels.

Literature & Fiction
Apart from the recent writings of Bessie Head (listed under Literature in the Arts section of Botswana Facts About the Country) and the 19th and early 20th century works by Sol Plaatje, there's really very little Botswanan literature to recommend. The country simply hasn't had the sort of tumultuous history that normally inspires the creative outpouring of social statement. It may pay off to keep watch on the African Literature shelves at the Botswana Book Centre in case something turns up.

Nor is there much straight fiction dealing with Botswana. For light reading, try Wilbur Smith's *The Sunbird*, a fanciful but well-told tale about the mythical 'Lost City of the Kalahari'.

Natural & Political History

For more in-depth reading the following books are recommended:

The History of Southern Africa by Kevin Shillington, Longman Group UK, Ltd, Essex, 1987. Good overall historical discussion of Botswana, Namibia, South Africa, Lesotho and Swaziland in textbook form. It objectively and sensitively covers prehistory as well as African and colonial history.

History of Botswana by T Tlou and Alec Campbell, MacMillan Botswana, Gaborone, 1984. The best history devoted exclusively to Botswana, this work takes a similar approach to the previous book.

The Lost World of the Kalahari by Laurens van der Post, Penguin, Harmondsworth, UK, 1962. This well-written work about the San of the Kalahari has become an anthropological classic and is essential reading for anyone interested in their traditional lifestyles. The author's quest for an understanding of their religion and folklore is continued in his subsequent work, *Heart of the Hunter*.

Monarch of All I Survey: Bechuanaland Diaries 1929-1937 by Sir Charles Rey, Botswana Society, Gaborone, 1988. These colourfully insightful diaries by the eight-year Resident Commissioner of Bechuanaland reveal the overall ho-hum attitude of the British toward the Protectorate.

Serowe – Village of the Rain Wind by Bessie Head, Heinemann African Writers' Series, Oxford, UK, 1981. This account of Serowe told by Bessie Head through interviews with its residents straddles the division between history and literature. It's marvellous reading for its insight into modern Botswanan village life, especially for intending visitors to Serowe.

A Marriage of Inconvenience: The Persecution of Seretse and Ruth Khama by Michael Dutfield, Unwin Hyman, London, 1990. Another highly recommended account, this about the largely negative responses, both African and colonial, to the marriage of Ngwato heir Seretse Khama and Englishwoman Ruth Williams in the 1950s.

Cry of the Kalahari by Mark and Delia Owen, Fontana/Collins, Glasgow, 1986. Entertaining and readable account of an American couple's seven years studying brown hyaenas in Deception Valley in the Central Kalahari. This book is to Botswana what *The Snow Leopard* is to Nepal and *Gorillas in the Mist* is to Rwanda.

Kalahari – Life's Variety in Dune and Delta by Michael Main, Southern Book Publishers, Johannesburg, 1987. A study of the many faces of the Kalahari from its vegetation and wildlife to its geological and cultural history. Good colour photos and extra helpings of personality are thrown in to keep it moving along smoothly.

Travel Guides

Guide to Botswana by Alec Campbell, Winchester Press, Gaborone, 1980. This thoroughly researched but long outdated guide is still the best source of background information on the land and people of Botswana.

Zimbabwe & Botswana – the Rough Guide by Tony Pinchuck and Barbara McRae, Harrap Columbus, Bromley, UK, 1990. If you want lots of background information, this good all-round guide is where to find it.

Visitors Guide to Botswana by Mike Main and John & Sandra Fowkes, Southern Book Publishers, Johannesburg, 1987. While this book will be quite useful for those travelling with their own vehicles into the wilder regions of the country, its lack of general practical and background information makes it of limited use to other travellers.

Wüsten, Sümpfe und Savannen: Reise-Handbuch Botswana by Michael Iwanowski, Herausgeber Verlag u. Vertrieb, Ettenheim, Germany, 1987. One of the best guidebooks dealing exclusively with Botswana but unfortunately it's available only in German. It contains concise history and background information but is quite weak on coverage of the cities.

Welcome to Botswana by the American Women's International Association. The limited intended audience of this pamphlet-size book is the American female expatriate in Gaborone. It does, however, contain some useful general interest tidbits.

Language

There are a couple of English-Setswana dictionaries as well as the useful *First Steps in Spoken Setswana*, available at the Botswana Book Centre in Gaborone; but given the number of expatriates living in Botswana there's currently a need for a good up-to-date English-Setswana phrasebook. The *Setswana-English Phrasebook* by 19th century Molepolole missionary A J Wookey is amusing but otherwise a complete waste of time.

Maps

The Department of Surveys and Lands in Gaborone publishes topographic sheets, city and town plans, aerial photographs, geological maps and Landsat images. Regional and national maps of various scales are available to the public for P4 to P7.50 per sheet from their office in Gaborone. For a catalogue, write to the Department of Surveys and Lands, Private Bag 0037, Gaborone, Botswana.

The best and most accurate overall map of the entire country is the 1:1,750,000 *Republic of Botswana* published by the Cartographic Department, Macmillan UK. It contains several good inset maps, including the tourist areas and central Gaborone.

Also useful is the *Shell Road Map* which shows major roads and includes insets of several tourist areas. It's available from Shell Oil Botswana, Shell House, The Mall, Gaborone.

A similarly useful production is the *Botswana Mini-Map*, published by B&T Directories (☎ 371444, fax 373462 Gaborone), PO Box 1549, Gaborone. This map includes insets of the Okavango and Chobe National Park as well as a city plan of Gaborone. It costs P4 and can be found in bookshops and hotels around the country. B&T also publishes town plans of Francistown, Selebi-Phikwe and Lobatse on one sheet. A second sheet is devoted to Gaborone and its suburbs.

MEDIA

Newspapers & Magazines

The government-owned *Daily News*, published by the Ministry of Information and Broadcasting, is distributed free in Gaborone but includes little more than news pertaining to the Botswanan government. In addition, there are three weekly independent papers. The *Gazette*, which comes out on Thursday, and the *Botswana Guardian*, published on Friday, take a middle-of-the-road political stance and are good for general national news. Those who prefer their news more politically vocal should check out the loudly left-wing *Mmegi* (Reporter), the Saturday paper whose relentless criticism of the Botswanan government is a tribute to official tolerance for dissenting opinion.

Several South African dailies are available and provide an array of voices and coverage. In the Gaborone Sun and the Botswana Book Centre in Gaborone you can often pick up the *International Herald Tribune*, but sometimes a week after it's published. In large hotels and bookshops in Gaborone, Francistown and Selebi-Phikwe, you'll find up-to-date editions of *Time* and *Newsweek*. The *New African*, an Africa-oriented news magazine, has wider availability.

To keep up with local events, pick up a copy of the *Botswana Advertiser* in Gaborone or the *Northern Advertiser* in Francistown. They're both published weekly on Friday.

Radio & TV

Nationwide programming is provided by Radio Botswana, broadcasting in both English and Setswana. With a short-wave set, you'll be able to pick up the BBC World Service three times daily as well as Voice of America, the quirky American Armed Forces Radio, and Radio Australia.

Botswana has one television station, the Gaborone Broadcasting Corporation (GBC), which transmits nightly for a few hours beginning at 7 pm and provides an interesting blend of foreign programming – primarily British – and occasional local productions. It can be picked up only in the capital.

In addition, four South African stations are boosted in for Botswanan consumption. The clearest reception is on BOP-TV, the Bophuthatswana station, which originates in Mafikeng. The other three come from Johannesburg and broadcast typically inane White South African game shows, news programs and sitcoms in English and Afrikaans on alternating evenings.

DANGERS & ANNOYANCES

The greatest dangers in Botswana are posed by the natural elements combined with a lack of preparedness on the part of visitors. Some of these are covered under Dangers & Annoyances in the Regional Facts for the Visitor chapter. Others are dealt with in the Getting Around chapter.

Police & Military

Although police and veterinary roadblocks, bureaucracy and bored officials may become tiresome after a while, they're more a harmless inconvenience than anything else. Although careful scrutiny is rare, they may ask you to unpack your luggage – or your entire vehicle, should you have one – and go over your belongings with a fine-tooth comb.

The Botswana Defence Force (BDF), on the other hand, takes its duties quite seriously and is best not crossed. Avoid the State House in Gaborone at all times, but after dark don't even walk past it. If you're using an old map, be especially careful to avoid the airstrip marked as the Gaborone airport. This is now a BDF base; after dark, even to drive down Notwane Rd is extremely risky. You'll undoubtedly hear tales which are unfortunately true; trespassers won't be asked any questions before it's made certain they never trespass again.

Theft

Although theft occurs, Botswana enjoys a very low crime rate compared to other African (and most Western) countries. Set aside a good block of time if you do have something stolen and have to report it to the police for insurance purposes.

WORK

Botswana is developing rapidly and the educational system can't seem to keep up with the growing demand for skilled professionals in several fields, so if you have a skill which is in demand the country will probably welcome you with open arms. Those with background, training and experience in a variety of professions – medical doctors, secondary school teachers, professors, engineers, computer professionals and so on – will have the best chances. At the present time there is no shortage of primary school teachers or nurses; but the situation may change, so if you're keen on staying, it wouldn't hurt to try, anyway. Most people want to remain around Gaborone or Francistown but if you're willing to work in the back of beyond your chances will probably improve considerably.

Those accepted will normally be granted a three-year renewable residency permit. Applications and information are available from the Immigration and Passport Control Officer (☎ 374545 Gaborone), off Khama Crescent, PO Box 942, Gaborone, Botswana.

Prospective residents of Gaborone should be warned that the city is the world's fastest growing capital and is experiencing a chronic housing shortage. Construction cannot begin to keep up with demand and numerous expatriate professionals are being housed in P200 per day hotels at government or business expense while languishing on a volume-size waiting list for long-term housing. The hotels are overflowing with permanents and the system is being taxed beyond all reason.

International volunteer organisations – Danish, German, Swedish and Norwegian volunteers and the American Peace Corps – are very active in Botswana and may provide an alternative for those suitably disposed.

HIGHLIGHTS

There's little that's artificial or pretentious about Botswana. What it lacks in diversity, it happily makes up in inspiration. Although it's missing the diverse attractions to be found in neighbouring countries, its appeal lies in the pristine wildness of its empty spaces, the friendly unhurried pace of its rural villages and the stability and security provided by its peaceful nature. The top 10 attractions are:

Okavango Delta Botswana's watery number one tourist destination is one of the highlights of Africa – a maze of beautiful channels and islands teeming with wildlife and inviting exploration. Moremi Wildlife Reserve in the eastern Delta teems with African wildlife and pristine landscapes.

Chobe National Park Actually several parks in one, the game-rich and elephant-ravaged river front and the inland marshes and savannas make Botswana's most accessible game park the country's second most visited area.

Tsodilo Hills Brought to world attention by Laurens van der Post in *The Lost World of the Kalahari*, the remote Tsodilo Hills are an incredible gallery of ancient San paintings. They're not only the country's most impressive peaks, but also one of its best hiking areas.

Sua Pan The vast and featureless expanses of Sua Pan have been immortalised in the popular film *The Gods Must be Crazy* and in the more recent spectacular film *The Flame Birds of Makgadikgadi*. Sua Pan is also the site of Botswana's newest economic diversification – the mining of soda ash on Sua Spit.

Tuli Block Lying along the Limpopo River, the private game reserves, rustic settlements and walking and camping opportunities of the Tuli Block make it a largely neglected option for budget travellers.

Nxai Pan National Park The grassy expanses of Nxai Pan, an ancient lake bed, is used as a unique rainy season gathering place for migrating wildlife. Nearby, Baines' Baobabs offer an interesting stand of misanthropic trees.

Makgadikgadi Pans Game Reserve This beautiful and almost undeveloped region of grasslands and palms provide habitat for most game species found in Botswana.

Gcwihaba Caverns Remote and forgotten, the Gcwihaba Caverns, or Drotsky's Cave, in the heart of the Kalahari offer an entirely undeveloped underground experience, but only for the most adventurous...and those with a bit of luck or cash to arrange transport.

Serowe Sprawling Serowe, the village of Sir Seretse Khama and his forebears, is said to be the largest village in Africa and the museum devoted to the history of the Khama clan is definitely worth a look.

The Kalahari Although several of the other Top 10 attractions are within the Kalahari, the desert itself offers the opportunity to experience a spectacular solitude all its own. If at all possible, don't miss a starry night camping in its wild expanses.

ACCOMMODATION
Camping

There are several types of camping available in Botswana, the most common being the practical type. Several hotels and lodges around the country offer camping areas with varying amenities for campers. Most will offer some sort of shower as well as a cooking and washing area. Campers will have access to hotel bars and restaurants but few of these, with the exception of the Kalahari Arms in Ghanzi and the Chobe Safari Lodge at Kasane, are easily accessible to shopping areas without a vehicle. These camps will average around P10 per person per night.

The next variety of camp is found in the national parks; these camps are normally very rudimentary. Foreigners, who are paying P50 just to *be* in the park, will have to shell out another P20 to set up a tent and use the loos, if they exist. There are a couple of reasonably comfortable camping sites with *braai* pits and flush toilets in Moremi Reserve and Chobe National Park, but the rest are basically just clear spots in the dust. For your money, expect a lot of wildlife activity in the night.

The third type of camping is the unofficial sort. Basically, if you can get out of sight – as you can throughout most of Botswana – and are self-sufficient in food, water, transport, petrol and so on, you can set up camp just about anywhere, cook over an open fire and soak up the unbelievable Kalahari night skies, sounds and smells; this could well be Botswana's primary appeal. If you're caught out near a village, however, and can't escape local scrutiny, enquire after the local chief or visit the police station to request permission to camp and directions to a suitable site.

Camps & Lodges

This designation is normally reserved only for tourists and is found exclusively in Chobe National Park, Tuli Block, and the Moremi/Okavango Delta areas. They're difficult to generalise; some lie along the road system and others are in remote wilderness areas. They range from tenting sites to established tent camps to chalets to luxury lodges or any combination of these. Prices also range accordingly from approximately P15 per night for camping at Oddball's in the Okavango to more than 100 times that for a double room at the exclusive Chobe Game

Lodge with all its Taylor-Burton honeymoon frills.

Most of the upmarket ones are normally prebooked overseas in conjunction with an organised tour or through a local travel agency or company representative. The main exceptions are the camps in the immediate vicinity of Maun and Kasane where travellers may turn up whenever they can find transport.

Many lodges and camps, especially those in the Okavango Delta, are in remote areas and access will be arranged by the booking agency or tour organiser and included in the package price. Others are readily accessible from the road system, such as it is, and will be open to those with their own (in some cases 4WD) vehicle.

Hotels

Hotels in Botswana are much like hotels anywhere. All the towns have at least one and the larger centres will offer several price ranges. Although you won't find anything as cheap as the lower end in other African countries, the least expensive hotels in Botswana are still likely to double as brothels.

Gaborone, as was mentioned previously, is in a unique situation. Since its upmarket hotels serve as temporary housing for expatriate residents awaiting construction of more permanent accommodation, vacancies are few. Whenever a convention or special entourage arrives in town, there's a lot of shuffling and scuffling; the hotel residents are given notice to find other quarters for a few days and the visiting delegations are moved in until the event is over. This leaves ordinary tourists at the bottom of the heap. Unless they've organised their trip through a tour operator who's booked up blocks of rooms, their chances of finding a 1st-class hotel room in Gaborone are not good. In other quality ranges, however, the pickings will be better unless you're in town during some special event.

FOOD

While eating in Botswana isn't particularly exciting – there's no delectably refined national cuisine to knock your socks off – self-caterers will find the pickings among the best in Africa and the restaurants, however expensive, normally serve quality fare.

Snacks & Meals

Both takeaways and fast food figure prominently in Botswana's cities and towns; cheap eating in Gaborone and Francistown revolves around quick chicken and burger fixes.

To my knowledge, there's exactly one health-food-cum-vegetarian restaurant in Botswana – in Gaborone. The normally pretentious and expensive hotel dining rooms and finer restaurants tend to concentrate heavily on the beef end of the scale, although fish, lamb and chicken dishes are normally served as well.

International cuisine is available only in Gaborone, where you'll find Chinese and Indian restaurants. In the smaller towns and villages, however, expect little menu variation. Chicken, chips, beef and greasy fried snacks will normally be included as well as *mabele* (sorghum porridge) and *bogobe* (mealies, sometimes known by the Afrikaans name, *mielie pap*), served with some sort of meat relish. Beyond the staples, you'll probably want to try *vetkoek* (both pronounced and meaning 'fat cake' in Afrikaans), the southern African version of the doughnut, available nearly everywhere.

Self-Catering

Visitors entering Botswana from Zimbabwe and points north may well be overwhelmed at the quantity and variety of food available in Gaborone and Francistown supermarkets; you can buy anything from Marmite to taco shells, corn chips to freshly ground coffee, fresh prawns to grapefruit. If you've been haunted by food fantasies while travelling across Africa, Botswana is where they can be fulfilled.

The reason for the abundance, of course, is Botswana's open trading with South Africa. Those with aversions to consuming products originating in South Africa should stick with the beef, mealies, bitter melons and ground nuts. In the right season, it's possible to find citrus, primarily oranges, grown in the Tuli Block.

Prices in Botswanan supermarkets and bush shops are comparable to or slightly lower than those in the USA, Australia and the UK. The open market isn't as prevalent an institution in Botswana as in Zimbabwe and other countries but you will occasionally find informal sales stands set up, especially around bus terminals and railway stations. In Gaborone, there's a small impromptu produce market between Broadhurst Mall and the BBS building. In Francistown, the fruit and vegetable stands are strung along Baines St east of its intersection with Blue Jacket St.

Traditional Foods

Historically, men were responsible for tending the herds and subsisted primarily on meat and milk while women were left to gather and eat wild fruits and vegetables. The Tswana staple was mainly beef, but each of the several Tswana groups had its own food taboos; no one ate fish or crocodile, the latter being the totem of the tribe as a whole, while other groups were forbidden to eat their individual totems. Other tribes relied upon different foods: the Yei of the Okavango were dependent upon fish, the Kalanga ate mainly sorghum, millet and maize, and the Herero subsisted primarily on thickened, soured milk. More recently, mabele or bogobe has formed the centre of most Batswanan meals but is rapidly being replaced by imported maize mealie meal.

Before South African imports reached the nethermost corners of the Kalahari, the desert was dishing up an amazingly diverse array of wild edibles to augment the staple foods. Although most of modern-day Botswana derives its food from agriculture or the supermarket, people in remote areas still supplement their diets with a variety of natural wild foods.

One of the most useful desert plants is the *morama*, an immense underground tuber whose pulp contains large quantities of water and served as a primary source for desert dwellers. Above ground, the morama grows the leguminous pods which contain edible beans. Other desert delectables include marula fruit, wild plums, berries, tubers and roots, *tsama* melons, wild cucumbers, honey and a type of edible fungus related to the European truffle. The nutritious and protein-rich *mongongo* nut, similar to the cashew, is eaten raw or roasted, and has historically been a staple for some San groups. People also gather wild animal products when available: birds and their eggs, small mammals and reptiles, and even ant eggs!

One interesting item you may encounter in your Botswanan travels is mopani worm, a caterpillar-like inhabitant of the mopani tree which may remind Aussies of their own dear witchetty grub. They're normally gutted and cooked in hot ash for about 15 minutes. Alternatively, they're boiled in salt water or dried in the sun for several days, to be later deep-fried in fat, roasted or ground up and eaten raw.

Apart from herding, desert agriculture is limited by the scanty water supply to *monoko* (ground nuts or peanuts), *mabele*, *digwana* (gourds), *magapu* (melons), *dinawa* (beans) and *mabelebele* (millet).

DRINKS

A range of 100% natural fruit juices from South Africa are sold in casks in supermarkets in the major cities and towns. You'll also find a variety of teas, coffees and sugary soft drinks.

Beer is the extent of Botswana's alcohol production, with Castle, Lion and Black Label being the three domestic options. Otherwise, bottle shops are well stocked with imported beer, wine and spirits at prices comparable to those in Europe or North America. You may want to sample some of the superb red and white wines produced in the Cape which are available for very reasonable prices.

Traditional drinks are many. Several of the more popular ones are less than legal, including mokolane or palm wine, an extremely potent swill made from distilled palm sap. Another is *kgadi*, made from distilled brown sugar and berries or fungus, and flavour-enhanced with any of a variety of additives.

Legal home brews include the common bojalwa, an inexpensive, sprouted sorghum beer which is brewed commercially as Chibuku. Another serious drink is made from fermented marula fruit (which fall from the trees and provide some light moments for wildlife, as well!). Light and nonintoxicating mageu is made from mealies or sorghum mash. Another is madila, a thickened sour milk which is used as a relish or drunk (normally 'eaten' would be a more appropriate term) plain.

THINGS TO BUY
The standard of Botswanan handicrafts is generally very high, particularly the beautifully decorative Botswana baskets which were originally produced in Ngamiland. If you think they're too nice to use as bins, laundry hampers or magazine holders, they make lovely wall decorations and quite a few establishments around Botswana use them for just that purpose.

In Gaborone, they're available at Botswanacraft on The Mall and at several other cooperatives, including an excellent one in the Naledi Industrial Site on Old Lobatse Rd, run by a school for disabled Batswana. If you're headed toward Ngamiland, particularly to the village of Gumare or the Etshas, save your purchases for the source where you'll pay less and contribute directly to the local economy. There is also a wide range of basketry available in Maun.

In the remote western regions, beaded San jewellery and leatherwork are normally of excellent quality and you'll be deluged with offers. The genuine articles, however, will grow scarcer as tourism pushes further into the desert areas and demand for mass-produced items increases.

Beautiful weavings and textiles are also available. Although the most inspired pieces will be quite pricey, they'll still probably cost a lot less than you'd pay at home and the handmade quality and individuality easily justify the prices. The best and least expensive work will be found right at its source at the several weavings cooperatives around Gaborone and Francistown.

For further information about Botswanan material crafts, refer to the discussion in the Arts section of the Botswana Facts about the Country chapter.

Getting There & Away

BORDER CROSSINGS

Overland entry into Botswana is normally straightforward and if you respond respectfully to the officers and comply meticulously with instructions, few hassles will be encountered. When entering Botswana overland, visitors will have to wipe all their shoes, even those packed away in luggage, in a disinfectant dip to prevent carrying foot and mouth disease into the country. Vehicles will have to pass through a pit filled with the same disinfectant.

There are currently no immigration posts on the Botswanan side of the Werda, Bokspits, Shakawe, Ngoma Bridge, Baines Drift, Pilane, Kazungula or Mpandamatenga borders, so immigration formalities must be completed at the applicable police station. In the case of Ngoma Bridge and Kazungula, formalities are handled at the immigration office in Kasane. An immigration post should soon be set up at Ngoma Bridge and Shakawe/Mohembo on the Namibian border, so check locally for updated information. Passengers travelling by train from Ramatlhabama in Botswana to Mmambatho (Bophuthatswana) in South Africa are still required to disembark and walk between the immigration posts, although this is due to change in the near future.

The Kazungula ferry between Botswana and Zambia has a reputation for flipping in mid-Zambezi, so be warned. There's just enough room on the ferry for one cargo truck and one car per crossing so prepare for long waits if there's any traffic at all.

Border Opening Hours

Border opening hours are subject to frequent changes so use these opening times as general guidelines only and check locally for the latest information before turning up at remote posts, especially on weekends. Some border posts are closed for lunch between 12.30 and 1.45 pm. The international airport immigration offices at Gaborone, Francistown and Maun open whenever scheduled flights arrive or depart.

To/From Namibia
Mamuno 8 am to 4 pm
Ngoma Bridge 8 am to 4 pm
Shakawe 8 am to 4 pm

To/From South Africa
(note: Molopo River crossings are closed when the water is high.)
Baines Drift (Limpopo River) 8 am to 4 pm
Bokspits (Molopo River) 8 am to 4 pm
Bray (Molopo River) 8 am to 4 pm
Martin's Drift (Limpopo River) 8 am to 6 pm
McCarthysrus (Molopo River) 8 am to 4 pm
Parr's Halt (Limpopo River) 8 am to 4 pm
Pioneer Gate (Lobatse) 7 am to 8 pm
Pitsane (Molopo River) 7.30 am to 4.30 pm
Platjanbridge (Limpopo River) 8 am to 4 pm
Pont Drift (Limpopo River) 8 am to 4 pm
Ramatlhabama (road and railway) 7 am to 8 pm
Ramotswa 8 am to 4 pm
Sikwane 6 am to 7 pm
Tlokweng (Gaborone) 7 am to 8 pm
Werda (Molopo River) 8 am to 4 pm
Zanzibar (Limpopo River) 8 am to 4 pm

To/From Zambia
Kazungula Ferry (Zambezi River) 6 am to 6 pm

To/From Zimbabwe
Kazungula road weekdays 6 am to 6 pm
Kasane/Victoria Falls weekends 8 am to noon
Mpandamatenga weekdays 8 am to 5 pm
Ramokgwebana (road & rail) 6 am to 6 pm

TO/FROM ZIMBABWE

There are two well-used border crossings between Zimbabwe and Botswana: the road and rail link at Plumtree/Ramokgwebana and the Kazungula/Kasane border west of Victoria Falls. There's also a lesser-used back road crossing at Mpandamatenga-Kazuma Pan National Park in Zimbabwe and Kazuma Forest Reserve in north-eastern Botswana. If you're driving, fuel is considerably cheaper on the Zimbabwe side.

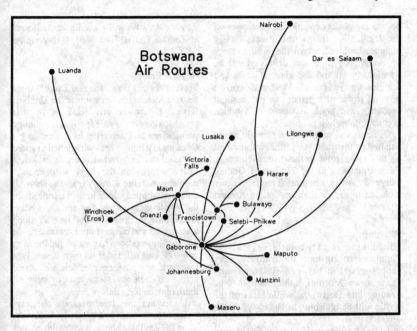

Botswana Air Routes

Air

Air Botswana and Air Zimbabwe each fly nonstop between Harare and Gaborone three times weekly. Air Botswana flies between Bulawayo and Gaborone with a stop in Francistown in either direction on Tuesday and Thursday.

The Air Botswana office in Zimbabwe is at Suite 501, Cresta Jameson Hotel, Harare, (☎ 703132). The Air Botswana office in the IGI Building, The Mall, Gaborone, is also an agent for Air India, Air Mauritius, Air Zimbabwe, Lufthansa, Royal Swazi Airlines, South African Airways, SAS, Swissair, Zambia Airways, Air Tanzania, Air Malawi and KLM.

Bus

The Zimbabwe Omnibus Company operates a twice-daily bus service between Bulawayo and Francistown, departing at 8 am and 2 pm from the Lobengula St terminus in Bulawayo and the railway line bus terminal in Francis-

town. Prepare for lengthy delays at the border, especially northbound, while Zimbabwe customs officials closely scrutinise passengers' Botswanan purchases. Once weekly, the southbound service continues on to Gaborone.

Train

From Bulawayo to Lobatse there's a train daily (except Thursday) which pulls out of Bulawayo at 2 pm and arrives in Lobatse at 10.10 am the following morning. On Thursday, the service departs at 11.10 am, stopping at Gaborone at 1.30 am and Lobatse at 3.25 am, and continues on to Johannesburg, arriving at 12.45 pm on Friday. The train from Lobatse to Bulawayo departs daily except Tuesday at 4 pm, stopping at Gaborone at 6 pm and Francistown at 6 am and arriving in Bulawayo at 12.10 pm. On Tuesday it departs from Johannesburg at 1.30 pm and arrives in Bulawayo at 2.45 pm Wednesday.

It's significant to note that Zimbabwe

dollars are not acceptable for purchases on the train. The trains only occasionally include a buffet car so you may want to stock up on all the food and drinks you'll be wanting. In 1st and 2nd classes, males and females are separated. Men and women wishing to travel together can pay a slight surcharge and book a coupé cabin which accommodates two people.

Customs and immigration formalities are handled on the train. For further information on this route, refer to the discussion under From Botswana in the Zimbabwe Getting There & Away chapter. Timetables are included in the Zimbabwe Getting Around chapter.

Hitching

Hitchhiking is particularly easy at the Plumtree crossing due to the relatively heavy shopping traffic between Bulawayo and Francistown. Morning is the best time to be heading into Botswana, while most of the traffic will be returning to Bulawayo in the afternoon.

Lifts between Victoria Falls and Kazungula/Kasane may require some waiting but you'll eventually get something. From Kasane, the direct route to Maun across Chobe National Park should essentially be considered unhitchable. The 4WD road is horrid much of the way and although people have gotten lucky, this is certainly the exception to the rule. Although it's laboriously roundabout, the route from Kasane to Maun via Nata will normally prove far quicker.

TO/FROM ZAMBIA

Apart from the air route, your only straight-through option between Zambia and Botswana is the Kazungula ferry, which is an experience unto itself.

Air

Air Botswana flies nonstop between Lusaka and Gaborone on Tuesday and Saturday, departing from Lusaka at 9 am and Gaborone at 6 pm.

Zambia Airways in Botswana can be found at Zambia House, The Mall, Gaborone (☎ 312027).

Road & Ferry

Travel between Botswana and Zambia is via the free Kazungula ferry across the Zambezi River. However you look at it, this ramshackle setup is an experience, although perhaps not as interesting as it used to be. Once upon a time, a heavy truck had to speed on board the ferry and slam on the brakes in order to provide the ferry with enough momentum to break away from the shore. If the truck stopped a little long or a little short, the whole mess would flip and the system would have to close down while everything was righted and cleaned up. Fortunately, the whole thing has been renovated and the ferry can now cast off under its own steam. One truck and one passenger vehicle are carried across on each run, so as you can imagine, there may be long delays.

Under normal circumstances, the ferry operates from 6 am to 6 pm daily. In Kasane or on the Zambian shore, it's possible to pick up trucks going through to Livingstone, Lusaka and points beyond. Alternatively, from Livingstone it's fairly straightforward finding a bus to Lusaka.

If the delays are too long – and they frequently are – or if for some reason the ferry isn't operating when you arrive, it's possible to cross into Zimbabwe at Kazungula, hitchhike to Victoria Falls, and enter Zambia at Livingstone, but you may have to show an onward ticket from Zimbabwe; officials have been getting very sticky about this requirement lately. Naturally, all this applies in the opposite direction as well.

TO/FROM SOUTH AFRICA

Although there are numerous border posts between Botswana and South Africa, most of the traffic passes through the road and rail crossing at Ramatlhabama/Mmambatho on the Bulawayo to Johannesburg railway line, the Tlokweng gate less than 20 km from Gaborone, or the Lobatse/Zeerust post further south. The other posts are primarily on back roads across the Limpopo in the Tuli Block or across the Molopo in southern Botswana.

Most of the time, South African officials will place their stamps on a looseleaf sheet rather than in your passport, but there are an obstinate few who will insist on stamping the book, thereby invalidating it for travel to much of Africa and the Middle East. As reforms come to South Africa, this problem should become less relevant. Because of the Southern African Customs Union and the normally good attitude of Botswanan immigration officials, travellers entering Botswana from South Africa should encounter a minimum of ado.

Air

Air links between South Africa and Botswana are good. In fact, until Gaborone's Sir Seretse Khama International Airport was opened in September 1984, Johannesburg served as Botswana's international air link. Between them, Air Botswana and South African Airways connect Gaborone and Johannesburg at least twice daily with connections to and from Durban and Cape Town. Namib Air also flies from Gaborone to Johannesburg on Thursday at 8.30 pm and in the opposite direction on Saturday at 7.30 am.

Air Botswana is located at 1627 Jan Smuts, Johannesburg, South Africa (☎ 975-3614).

Train

The express train between Bulawayo and Johannesburg runs northwards on Tuesday and southwards on Thursday, requiring an overnight trip. Entering South Africa at Ramatlhabama/Mmambatho, you'll have to get off the train and pass through ludicrous double immigration formalities, one set for Bophuthatswana, the artificial 'homeland' or Bantustan set up by the South African government as a reserve for Tswana people, and another for South Africa itself. The Bophuthatswana post will require you to fill out forms for a transit visa while the latter

will normally demand that you have sufficient funds and an onward ticket.

Further information about this route will be found in the Zimbabwe Getting Around chapter.

Hitching

Hitchhiking between South Africa and Gaborone is easy and straightforward if you stick to the Tlokweng, Lobatse and Ramatlhabama border posts. Due to the dual border formalities at Ramatlhabama, the Tlokweng and Lobatse gates involve the least potential hassles. Tlokweng is reportedly the most relaxed border crossing into South Africa, having minimal searches and generally well-disposed officials.

TO/FROM NAMIBIA

There are three land crossings between Botswana and Namibia – Ngoma Bridge between the eastern Caprivi Strip and Chobe National Park, Mohembo-Shakawe in the upper Okavango panhandle and Buitepos-Mamuno, west of Ghanzi in the Kalahari.

Although they're currently being set up, there were no Botswanan border posts at Ngoma Bridge and Shakawe at the time of writing. At the former, you'll have to check in and out of Botswana at the immigration office in Kasane. In Shakawe, immigration formalities are handled at the police station.

Contrary to what you may hear, there is no longer guerrilla activity in the Caprivi – Namibia gained its independence on 21 March 1990 – and there are no longer any travel restrictions or permit requirements. The worst you can expect is the occasional roadside passport check.

Air

Namib Air serves both Windhoek airports – Eros in the centre of town and Windhoek International about 40 km east of the city. It has a direct flight on Thursday from Windhoek International to Gaborone, returning to Windhoek on Saturday. On Friday Namib Air flies in either direction between Katima Mulilo (in the Caprivi) and Maun, and on Wednesday, Friday and Sunday it flies between Windhoek Eros and Maun, connecting to Air Botswana flights to and from Gaborone.

Between Gaborone and Windhoek, the cheapest fares are 14 day advance purchase for about P700 return. The one-way fare is only slightly less at around P570.

Road

There is no public transport between Namibia and Botswana through any of the three land border crossings. If you're driving, the Ngoma Bridge border is the only one consistently open to non-4WD vehicles. Roads on the Namibian side of the Mohembo-Shakawe and the Buitepos-Mamuno crossings are good gravel until the tar begins at Rundu and Gobabis respectively. In Botswana they deteriorate into very rough tracks covered in places with mud or drifted sand which will bog most conventional low-clearance vehicles.

On the Botswana side, fuel is available at Kasane, Ghanzi and Maun, but on the Shakawe route there is no petrol available between Maun and Andara, which is 64 km into Namibia, so a reserve tank will be essential. In a pinch, you can sometimes get a few litres at Etsha 6 (but only if the barge has come in recently) or at Shakawe Fishing Camp just south of Shakawe, but don't count on either source.

Hitching

The easiest and most frequently used cross-ing for hitchhikers between Botswana and Namibia is the Ngoma Bridge at Chobe National Park. The 54 km transit route through the park is relatively well travelled, and if you avoid the Chobe riverfront tourist drives you won't be subject to the P50 per day national park fee.

There's no border post on the Botswana side so you'll get a cursory check by park personnel at the park entrance and be instructed to check in at the immigration office, which is in the same building as the tourist office in Kasane. Leaving Botswana, you'll also have to check out here before proceeding to Ngoma Bridge. Since nearly everyone stops to refuel before heading toward Namibia (or in any direction), it may be better to wait for a lift at the petrol station near Chobe Safari Lodge rather than the Ngoma Bridge transit route turnoff near Kazungula.

The route between Gobabis and Ghanzi is difficult; hot and dry conditions are normal and only a couple of vehicles pass daily. If you're heading west from Ghanzi, enquire about lifts at the petrol station or the Weilbacher & Weilbacher Hardware. Both are normally obligatory stops for through traffic. Alternatively, you can arrange a shared taxi as far as the border but you'll have to make your own way from there along the desolate but smooth high-speed gravel road to Gobabis.

Getting Around

Botswana's surface public transport network can be summed up in a couple of words: very limited. Although the air services are good, domestic Air Botswana routings and air charters are pricey and the small population dictates that only a few locations are regularly served. The country's single railway line offers reliable but rather slow service, and the extent of bus services is constrained by the highway systems – roads deserving to be called such are thin on the ground.

AIR

The only scheduled domestic flights are available on the national carrier, Air Botswana, which serves larger communities around the country. There is at least one flight daily from Monday to Saturday between Francistown and Gaborone, and on Wednesday and Friday direct between Francistown and Maun. Between Gaborone and Maun there are flights daily. On Monday and Wednesday, the Maun flights connect with flights to and from Ghanzi. Selebi-Phikwe is served from Gaborone on Wednesday and Friday and via Francistown on Monday, Wednesday and Friday.

Although there are occasional air fare package deals, especially between Maun and Gaborone in conjunction with hotel accommodation and sightseeing, prices change frequently and are generally quite high. You'll get some relief with 14 day advance purchase, but the one hour flight one way between Gaborone and Maun, for example, normally works out to around P300.

Air Botswana Offices

Thapama Lodge, PO Box 222, Francistown (☎ 212393)
IGI Bldg, The Mall, PO Box 92, Gaborone (☎ 351921)
Kalahari Arms Hotel, Ghanzi (☎ 296311)
Hillcrest Mansions, Main St, PO Box 392, Lobatse (☎ 330502)

Airport Rd, PO Box 191, Maun (☎ 360391)
The Mall, PO Box 2, Selebi-Phikwe (☎ 810654)

Air Charters

Several air charter companies operate from Gaborone and in the tourist areas to provide transport to and from remote lodges and villages. Most aren't cheap, but if you join a trip organised by a travel agency or safari company rather than charter individually you'll pay a set ticket price, rather than by the km for a *return* trip from the airfield to your destination (charter companies justifiably point out that someone has to pay for their return to home base once they've dropped you off).

The company most often used to access the inner Okavango Delta is Aer Kavango (☎ 260390 Maun), PO Box 169, Maun Airport. Normally, if there are seats available you can join these flights at the last minute and may sometimes pay less than when booking through an agency. Agency-arranged charter flights from Maun into the Chief's Island area of the Okavango Delta are currently running between P80 and P120 each way. Access to more remote camps will cost more. Ngami Air (☎ 260383) and Delta Air (☎ 260220) are also based in Maun and serve primarily the Okavango Delta area.

Northern Air (☎ 250234 Kasane), PO Box 40, Kasane, operates flights between Kasane and Maun. Air Botswana doesn't operate out of Kasane and demand for agency-organised flights is sporadic, so you'd probably end up chartering a whole plane for the very expensive return trip. Northern Air also maintains an office at the Maun Airport (☎ 260385 Maun), PO Box 40, Maun.

Similar arrangements are available through Okavango Air Services (☎ 810273), PO Box 54, Selebi-Phikwe, and a couple of charter companies operating out of Sir Seretse Khama International Airport in Gaborone. Western Air (☎ 373386 Gaborone), PO Box 40763, Gaborone, and

Kalahari Air (☎ 351804) PO Box 41278, Broadhurst, Gaborone, concentrate primarily on freight and business charters to villages in the central, western and southwestern areas of the country. Normally, no agency bookings are available, but if seats are available you may be able to arrange an air lift by turning up just prior to departure.

BUS

Bus and minibus services operate almost exclusively through the eastern part of the country. Schedules are erratic at best and buses run according to demand, departing when full, and intending passengers must haunt the bus terminals enquiring and waiting for something to happen. Most travellers find the procedure too time-consuming and, especially along the Lobatse to Francistown route, opt to hitchhike or take the slow but scheduled train.

The most frequently served bus routes follow the highway corridor between Ramatlhabama and Francistown, often doing only part of the route. Buses may connect Gaborone and Mahalapye six times a day, but perhaps only three of these may continue onto Palapye and two finish up in Francistown. Other services operate between Francistown and Bulawayo (Zimbabwe); Francistown and Lusaka (Zambia); Serule and Selebi-Phikwe; Palapye, Serowe and Orapa; Francistown, Nata and Kasane and occasionally between Nata and Maun. Once the highway to Maun is smoothed and tarred, the subsequent growth in Botswana's west will undoubtedly result in more reliable public transport connections to Maun.

Some major bus companies include Sesennye (☎ 212112 Gaborone) and Mahube Express (☎ 352660 Gaborone), which operate between Gaborone and Francistown. KB Transport (☎ 410202 Mahalapye) serves the Gaborone to Mahalapye route. Between Palapye and Selebi-Phikwe, the main operator is Loedza (☎ 810025 Selebi-Phikwe).

Between Kasane and Victoria Falls, there's an expensive transfer service operated by Zimbabwe's United Touring Company. Although there's no bus service through Chobe National Park between Kasane and Maun, several safari companies offer three day mini-safaris between Maun and Kasane via Moremi for around P600, excluding park fees. You pay separately – fortunately at the P30 per day safari rate – for Moremi and Chobe.

TRAIN

Botswana's only train line is part of the Bulawayo to Johannesburg route running through the country between Ramatlhabama on the South African border and Ramokgwebana on the Zimbabwe border. Though slow, the train is reliable and the trip is a relaxing and effortless way to pass through the less-than-interesting stretches of dusty and nearly featureless scrub between the Zimbabwean and South African borders. If such landscapes appeal, you can gaze out the window at the passing scene. If not, pull out a book or while away the hours with a snooze.

The timetable, some sample fares and suggestions for this route are found in the Zimbabwe Getting Around chapter. Other information about the route is under To/From Zimbabwe and To/From South Africa in the Botswana Getting There & Away chapter and under To/From Botswana in the Zimbabwe Getting There & Away chapter.

Reservations

Information, reservations and tickets are available at the Gaborone station on weekdays from 7 am to 1 pm and 1.45 to 4.30 pm. In Francistown, the windows are open on weekdays from 8 am to noon and 1 to 4 pm. For 1st and 2nd-class sleepers, advance bookings are essential.

Classes & Costs

By all accounts, the train is an inexpensive way to travel through Botswana. Economy class, which will be crowded and rather uncomfortable, is only P20 for the entire route from Francistown to Lobatse. In 2nd

Top: Odi, Botswana (DS)
Bottom: Hippo, Chobe National Park, Botswana (DS)

Top: Museum, Mochudi, Botswana (DS)
Middle: Gcwihaba Caverns (Drotsky's Cave), Botswana (DS)
Bottom: Crossing Sua Pan, Botswana (DS)

class, which features six-passenger sleeper compartments, that trip costs P67.20. In 1st-class carriages with four-passenger compartments it is P96. Bedding will cost an additional P5 per night in either 1st or 2nd class.

CAR & MOTORBIKE

Travelling by vehicle in Botswana comes in three varieties: a high-speed pass along the excellent tarred road system, the hit-or-miss affair of avoiding bogging along horrid secondary roads, or exploration of the wildest wilds in a sturdy, high-clearance 4WD passenger vehicle or truck. Travellers who want to get the most out of Botswana's offerings will probably need a vehicle or have plenty of time to wait for hitchhiking luck.

Conventional motorbikes will perform excellently on the tarred roads and high-powered dirt bikes will be great fun on back country desert tracks, but in-between are roads where clouds of dust and sand kicked up by high-speed vehicles will make for a miserable experience on a motorbike. Furthermore, motorbikes aren't permitted in national parks or reserves.

Roads

The number of tarred km is increasing, but away from the eastern corridor where a flat, nearly straight, dashed white line connects the South African border with Plumtree and Kasane, most roads are difficult and change-able. Many are impassable without 4WD and some are difficult even with it. Even long stretches of the new tarred road from Sehitwa to Gumare in the north-west already lie buried beneath drifted sand! This may go a long way to explaining why this country of vast distances and roads carved from shifting sand doesn't lend itself to an extensive, reli-able and organised transport system.

At the time of independence in 1966, Botswana's only tarred road, completed in 1947 in preparation for the visit by King George VI, extended for five km from Lobatse station to the High Court in Lobatse.

Currently tarred sections include: Francis-town-Orapa; Francistown-Ramokgwebana; Mopipi-Rakops; Palapye-Orapa; Gaborone-Molepolole-Lethlakeng; Sehitwa-Gumare (normally buried in sand); Kazungula-Nata-Francistown-Gaborone-Ramatlhabama; Tshabong-Werda; Serule-Selebi-Phikwe-Bobonong; and Lobatse-Kanye-Jwaneng.

The surfacing of the very rough but frequently travelled route between Nata and Maun has recently been given the green light but it will be quite a while before much comes of it. The completion of a road from Rakops to connect with the Nata-Maun road has also been considered but no decision has been made as yet.

Road Rules

Like the rest of southern Africa, Botswana keeps to the left. The national speed limit on tarred roads in 110 km/h, while through towns and villages it will normally be posted lower. In the absence of a sign, assume a speed limit of 60 km/h through towns. Seatbelt usage is compulsory, as is proof of no-fault insurance. If an accident causing injuries occurs, it must be reported to authorities within 48 hours. If only minor vehicular damage has been sustained and all parties agree, names and addresses may be exchanged and the matter sorted out later through insurance companies.

When driving through open range, especi-ally at night, be particularly mindful of animals wandering onto the road. In theory, stock owners are responsible for keeping their charges off the roads, but it's much better not to hit the beasts in the first place. All the red tape involved in finding and filing a claim against the owner will probably come to nought, anyway, and may backfire if the owner can prove driver negligence in the matter.

Especially if you're heading into the pans or the Kalahari, it is important to leave your intended itinerary and estimated time of return with someone who will sound an alarm if you're not back or in touch at the specified time.

Bush Driving & Wilderness Travel

The maze of tracks and ruts crisscrossing the Botswanan bush will utterly confound most drivers. They'll usher you into sandy villages from which tracks radiate in all directions, without a clue which leads where. Some provide access to remote cattle posts, others lead to villages. Still others will carry you to larger roads or water sources. The Department of Surveys and Lands has given up trying to keep up with these spontaneously created tracks which are maintained only by use. Once they become too rutted to pass or flood with water, a new route is created. Indicative of changing surface conditions, multiple parallel tracks split and join, cross, wander off and back and even disappear altogether on occasion.

The following points about bush driving on Botswana back tracks should at least get you started. For the best rundown on tips and techniques as well as remote routes, pick up a copy of *The Visitors' Guide to Botswana* by Mike Main and John & Sandra Fowkes, which is available at the Botswana Book Centre in Gaborone and at hotels and tourist shops elsewhere.

1. Take the best set of maps you can find. The Department of Surveys and Lands in Gaborone has reasonably accurate and up-to-date maps of remote areas. Tracks change frequently, however, so you'll still need to ask directions locally whenever possible.

2. Carry a compass and take readings periodically to make sure you're still travelling in the right direction. You'll need to be at least three metres from the vehicle to get an accurate reading since vehicular mechanisms create their own magnetic fields.

3. A minimum 150 litre reserve fuel tank will be essential for off-road travel through central or western Botswana. Fuel is available consistently only in Maun and Ghanzi or across the borders in South Africa and Namibia.

4. Carry at least five litres of water per person per day (allowing for delays and breakdowns when calculating the length of the trip). It will travel best in a reserve tank or an indestructible metal container. Plastic will not stand up to the constant bumping the roads will mete out.

5. Even if you're travelling along reasonably well-travelled routes, make sure your 4WD and other vehicle functions are working properly before setting off. Although the ingenuity of some villagers will astound you when it comes to jury-rigging repairs, when you must have a particular spare and it isn't locally available (it almost never will be!) you'll spend a lot of time and money awaiting delivery from a larger centre.

6. If you'll be driving across the remotest never-never, you'll need to be self-sufficient in everything, including vehicle spares, tools and the expertise to repair problems that may arise. The following should be considered essential: a towrope, torch, shovel, extra fan belt, vehicle fluids, spark plugs, baling wire, jumper leads, fuses, hoses, a good jack (and a wooden plank to act as a base in sand or salt!), several spare tyres (or a tyre lever and a puncture repair kit) and a pump. A winch would also be a valuable asset but most rental vehicles aren't so equipped.

7. Wrap tools and heavy or solid objects in blankets or other soft packing materials and place them in the bottom of the boot or truck bed. Food should be wrapped and packed tightly in solid unbreakable containers – cardboard boxes will disintegrate on back roads. Aluminium packing boxes are available in Gaborone for about P35 each. Once packed, the whole thing should be strapped down tightly. Keep plastic drink bottles, fragile snacks and poorly packaged items in the cab if possible.

8. The minimum camping equipment will include a tent and a warm sleeping bag – Kalahari nights can get very cold, especially in the winter. Camp beds will normally be unnecessary since the soft Kalahari sand normally works adequately. For fire cooking, follow the locals' example and buy a three-legged cast-iron *potjie* (most often pronounced 'POY-kee') pot, available just about anywhere in Botswana. A plastic basin and soap for washing up will be essential to preserve water supplies. And don't forget a few pots and pans, eating implements, a tin opener and lots of waterproof matches.

9. When driving on the sand which makes up most of Botswana's bush roads and tracks, keep in mind that it's more easily negotiated and less likely to bog vehicles in the cool of the morning or evening when air spaces between sand grains will be smaller. To further prevent bogging or stalling, avoid suddenly jamming on the accelerator. Drive quickly where possible and keep the rpm up; shift down in advance of deep sandy patches or the vehicle may stall and bog. When negotiating a straight course through rutted sand, allow the vehicle to wander along the path of least resistance. Anticipate corners and turn the wheel slightly earlier than you would on a solid surface – this will allow the vehicle to ski smoothly around – then accelerate gently out of the turn.

10. Much Kalahari driving will be through high grass and the seeds it scatters will soon foul radiators and cause vehicle overheating. If the temperature gauge begins to climb, stop and remove as much of the plant material from the grille as possible.

11. Unbogging or driving on loose sand may be facilitated by lowering the air pressure in the tyres and thereby increasing the gripping area of the tyres.

12. When driving on the saltpans, carry a compass and map and keep to the tracks of vehicles that have gone before, or stick to within a couple of hundred metres of the edge of the pan. The tempting flat, grey expanses easily become graveyards for vehicles which stick, sink and even break through into hidden subsurface cavities.

13. For information about dealing with the wildlife in Botswana, refer to the Dangers & Annoyances discussion in the regional Facts for the Visitor chapter at the beginning of the book.

Rental

Renting a vehicle in Botswana, particularly of the 4WD variety, will necessarily require a lot of cash, but it will allow you the freedom to wander and explore the country, especially the Kalahari, which is one of Africa's most pristine wilderness areas.

To hire a vehicle, you must be at least 25 years of age and must have a valid driving licence from your home country. If it isn't in English, a translation must be provided.

Standard vehicle hire prices are quite high, and with the distances involved the per km charges rack up frightfully quickly. Of the two car-hire firms operating in Botswana (Avis and Holiday), I found Holiday to be cheaper and friendlier. With all car hire, be wary of add-on charges, and check the paperwork carefully. Whichever you go with, check the vehicle carefully before accepting it, especially if you're taking a 4WD. Make sure the 4WD engages properly and that you understand how it works. Also check the vehicle fluids, brakes, battery and so on. The Kalahari is a harsh place in which to find out that the rental agency has overlooked something important!

As a general price guide, for a standard Toyota Corolla, Avis charges P50 per day and 55t per km, or P110 per day unlimited km with a minimum rental of six days. To rent a 4WD vehicle, you'll pay P105 per day and 95t per km or P245 per day with

unlimited km, again with a minimum six day rental period. Holiday, on the other hand, charges P48 per day for the Corolla and 55t per km, or P95 per day unlimited km with a minimum rental period of seven days. A Toyota Hilux 4WD vehicle, which includes a 150 litre reserve fuel tank, will cost P98 per day and 98t per km, or P225 per day for unlimited km, with a minimum of seven days rental.

The following is a list of the Avis and Holiday offices in Botswana:

Avis
    Sir Seretse Khama Airport, PO Box 790, Gaborone (☎ 313093, fax 312205 Gaborone)
    Francistown Airport, PO Box 222, Francistown (☎ 213901, fax 212867 Francistown)
    Maun Airport, Maun (☎ 260258, fax 260268 Maun)
    Kubu Lodge, Kasane (☎ 250312 Kasane)
Holiday Car Hire
    Gaborone Sun Hotel, Gaborone (☎ 353970, fax 312280 Gaborone)
    Chobe Safari Lodge, Kasane (☎ 250226, fax 250223 Kasane)
    Merlin Services & Travel, Maun Airport, Private Bag 0013, Maun (☎ 250351, fax 250571 Maun)
    Pan African Travel Bureau, PO Box 82, Francistown (☎ 213908 Francistown)

Purchase

Unless you're going to spend some time in Botswana, it's probably not worth purchasing a vehicle there. Even used vehicles are extremely expensive and a 4WD, which you'll need to get around the most interesting parts of the country, will be out of the question for most people. A used Botswana-standard Toyota Hilux, for example, will cost around P60,000. Even if you intend selling the vehicle after your visit, you'll have to come up with the cash for the initial purchase.

An alternative would be to buy a used vehicle in South Africa, where prices are considerably lower, then return to South Africa and sell it when you've finished with it. Naturally, you wouldn't be able to sell it in Botswana without paying heavy import duties.

BICYCLE

Botswana is largely flat but that's the only concession it makes to cyclists. That doesn't mean that a fair number of travellers don't try to avoid the uncertainties inherent with reliance on the public transport system, but unless they really know what they're doing, prospective cyclists should probably abandon any ideas they may have of setting off on a Botswanan bicycle adventure.

A major concern will be the hot, dry nature of the landscape; distances are great, horizons are vast and villages are few and far between, even along major routes. Water is scarce or nonexistent along some stretches. Furthermore, the sun is intense through the clear and semitropical desert air and prolonged exposure to the dry heat and burning ultraviolet rays will naturally be potentially hazardous.

It will also be necessary to consider your objectives. Neither bicycles nor motorbikes are permitted in Botswana's game reserves. If you want to allow yourself access to areas off the beaten tourist track, bicycles are also unsuitable. Experienced cyclists have pronounced most of Botswana's roads and tracks uncyclable. Along the Nata to Maun and Maun to Ghanzi routes, vehicles howl past in billowing clouds of sand and dust, and anywhere off the tarred roads you'll encounter deep drifted sand, so only those prepared to carry their bike and luggage over long, uninhabited distances should venture off the main routes.

Botswana's tarred highways are largely flat and straight and the national speed limit of 110 km/h doesn't stop traffic from cranking up the rpm and topping 150 or even 160 km/h on remote and open stretches. When a semitrailer passes at such speeds, cyclists can be blown off the road unwittingly.

Sorry to be so discouraging. If you choose to have a go anyway, let us know what you think!

HITCHING

With such erratic public transport systems in Botswana, nearly all the locals and most of the travellers without vehicles must rely on hitchhiking as their primary means of getting around. Along the main routes, which includes the horrid but well-travelled road between Nata and Maun, you'll have little problem finding a lift. Recognising a business opportunity in the country's limited transport system, most Blacks will ask the equivalent of bus fare, but Whites and expats rarely charge for lifts. Ascertain a price or negotiate a fare before climbing aboard, however, to prevent uncomfortable situations at the end of the ride.

Hitchhiking the back roads will be another issue. If you're travelling through the remoter regions of the Tuli Block or trying to reach Ghanzi and the Namibian border, Chobe, Moremi or the Okavango Delta Panhandle from Maun, you could be faced with waits of several days. Carry camping equipment, a couple of good books and plenty of food and water, and leave yourself lots of time. For trips into such places as Makgadikgadi Pans Game Reserve, Sua Pan, Nxai Pan, Gcwihaba Caverns, Khutse Game Reserve, Mabuasehube Game Reserve and other extremely remote areas, hitchhikers need to arrange for lifts in advance. The best places to make enquiries are the lodges at Maun, Nata, Gweta and Ghanzi.

LOCAL TRANSPORT

Only Gaborone has any sort of a local public transport system and, sadly, it is far from adequate for the city's growing population. Solidly packed little white minibuses, recognisable by their blue number plates, start from the ranks just off Botswana Rd opposite the President Hotel and circulate according to set routes. The standard city route passes all the major shopping centres. Other Gaborone minibuses leave for surrounding villages, departing from the railway station terminus.

Botswana's cities and towns either lack taxis or have next to none so it's hardly worth searching for one. Without your own vehicle, plan on hiring one or walking, hitchhiking and using the minibuses.

To/From the Airport

The only reliable transport between the airports and towns of Gaborone, Francistown and Selebi-Phikwe are the minibuses operated by the big hotels for their guests. If you're not a guest, you can sometimes talk the driver into a lift to or from the centre if there's space, but you'll have to tip at least several pula. In Gaborone, only occasionally does a taxi turn up at the airport; so rarely, in fact, that they can scarcely be considered an option.

Taxi

Although the collective public transport minibuses in Gaborone are known as 'taxis', conventional taxis are thin on the ground in Botswana and when they are available,

prices are left up to the whims of the driver. Taxis are recognisable by their blue number plates.

TOURS

The Botswanan government actively encourages tourist participation in organised tours and offers discounts on national park entry fees. The majority of tours available in Botswana will centre on either Maun or the Okavango Delta, but a few operate elsewhere as well. If you'd like to join a safari tour, it will normally be more economically arranged through Botswanan companies than through overseas agents.

A rundown of what's available in the various regions of the country is included in the respective chapters.

Gaborone

Gaborone is a sprawling village suffering from the growing pains and lack of colour or definition that accompany an abrupt transition from rural settlement to modern city. Although Gaborone has a few interesting sights to keep visitors occupied if they're in town anyway, it is one of the continent's most expensive cities and is certainly nothing to go out of one's way for.

In 1962, because of its proximity to water and the railway line, this otherwise unlikely spot was selected as the future capital of Botswana. The task of designing the new city, which was intended to accommodate a population of no more than 20,000 inhabitants, was assigned to the Department of Public Works. By 1990 it had exceeded that figure by over 100,000 and continues to grow at an astonishing rate. Gaborone is in fact suspected to be the world's fastest growing city.

Orientation

Gaborone lacks any definite central business district; urban action focuses on the city's dispersed shopping malls. The main one, The Mall, is between the town hall and the government complex of ministries and offices on Khama Crescent.

Several blocks south is the African Mall, which has several good restaurants and some inexpensive shops. Everything north of Nyerere Drive is known as Broadhurst, where there are several other shopping centres. The most prominent is Broadhurst North Mall, which contains more upmarket shops.

Information

Tourist Office The tourist office used to be on The Mall but recently moved to the 1st floor of the BBS building near Broadhurst North Mall. The office has a few brochures but doesn't distribute a city map. It's probably only worthwhile if you're headed out there, anyway.

Money The best and quickest place to exchange cash or travellers' cheques is the Gaborone Sun branch of Barclays Bank. If you're changing money at any of the banks on The Mall, queue up before the bank opens and prepare to settle in for a wait while crowds of Zimbabweans flog their annual export allotment of Zimbabwe dollar travellers' cheques for hard currency pula.

Cash transfers should be directed to the Barclay House branch of Barclays Bank.

Post The GPO on The Mall is open from 8.15 am to 1 pm and 2 to 4 pm Monday to Friday, and from 8.30 to 11.30 am on Saturday. Expect queues and generally lethargic service at any time of day.

Telephone The telecommunications office is in the Standard Chartered Bank building on The Mall. There you can book calls to anywhere in the world, but don't be in too much of a hurry. The office is only open Monday to Friday from 9.15 am to 1 pm and 2.15 to 4.30 pm and on Saturday from 8.15 to 11.30 am. No reverse charge calls are accepted. Overseas call bookings cost a standard P10 and an average of P10 for each minute on the line.

Visa Extensions The immigration office (☎ 374545) near the corner of State Drive and Khama Crescent handles visa extensions and enquiries.

Travel Agencies There are several travel agencies on The Mall, all about equally useful. Kudu Travel (☎ 372224, fax 374224) in Shell House also hires conventional cars for P45 per day and 45t per km, but no 4WD is available. The efficient and reliable travel agency in the arcade at the African Mall is recommended. The American Express representative is Manica Travel Services (☎ 352021) in Botsolano House in The Mall.

1 Woolworths Metro Shopping Centre
2 Broadhurst Shopping Centre
3 Old Spar Shopping Centre
4 No Mathatha Shopping Centre
5 Maru–a–Pula School & Maitisong Cultural Centre
6 Gaborone Game Reserve
7 Grace Kgari Nurses' Association Hostel
8 Gaborone Sun Hotel
9 Gaborone West Shopping Centre
10 Peace Corps Botswana Headquarters
11 National Stadium
12 University of Botswana
13 Botswana Defence Force Base
14 Gaborone Club
15 The Lodge

To Francistown (433 km)

To Sir Seretse Khama Airport

Segoditshane Way

Limpopo Drive

Lemmenyane Dve

Phase 3 Broadhurst Industrial Estate

Broadhurst Industrial Estate

Francistown Road

Broadhurst Drive

Gaborone

0   0.5   1 km

see Central Gaborone map

To Sheraton & Mogo Hotel

Molepolole Road

Lobatse Road

Madibeng

Sobhuza Rd

Nyerere Drive

Old Spar Shopping Centre

Nyerere Drive

Segoditshane Way

Maru–a–Pula

Badiri

Pholo golo

Mobutu Drive

The Mall

Borakanelo

Notwane Road

Gaborone West

Gaborone West Industrial Estate

Madirelo

Lobatse Road

Village

Phase 4 Gaborone West Industrial Estate

Babusi

Machel Drive

To Tlokweng Border Gate, Oasis Hotel & Morning Star Hotel

Tlokweng Road

Ngotwane Road

Bookshops The Botswana Book Centre on The Mall is one of the continent's best stocked bookshops. Also in The Mall is the left-of-centre Via Africa bookshop. You'll find other bookshops at the Metro Shopping Centre. Gift shops at the big hotels sell souvenir books and a few novels for passing the time in Gaborone.

Those with access to a vehicle who'll be spending some time around Gaborone may want to enquire about the availability of the booklet *Sites of Historic and Natural Interest in and Around Gaborone*, published by the National Museum in 1978. It lists numerous rock paintings, caves, abandoned mine workings and ruined villages.

Libraries The University of Botswana library has a Botswana Room with books and periodicals dealing exclusively with Botswana and related topics. The Botswana National Library, just east of The Mall on Independence Ave, is open Monday to Friday from 9 am to 6 pm and on Saturday from 9 am to noon. On the same premises is a reference room with publications dealing only with Botswana.

The British High Commission on The Mall has a comfortable reading room with British periodicals. At the American Library, also on The Mall, you can read the latest editions of *Time* and *Newsweek* and other US periodicals and newspapers. Alliance Française (☎ 351650), on Independence Ave near The Mall, offers French films and language courses and has a library of French-language books and periodicals.

Maps The maps in this book probably provide most of the information necessary for a casual visit but several other publications are available. B&T Directories (☎ 371444, fax 373462), PO Box 1549, Gaborone, publishes the best overall town plan of Gaborone and its inner suburbs.

The 1:1,750,000 map *Republic of Botswana* (Macmillan UK) contains several good inset maps, including a very good map of The Mall area of Gaborone.

Some of the P4 *Botswana Mini-Map* versions published by B&T Directories contain good inset city plans of Gaborone. They're available at the Botswana Book Centre on The Mall and normally also at the big hotel gift shops.

The Department of Surveys and Lands, at the corner of Station and Lobatse Rds, publishes a large-scale city plan in several sheets. It's available to the public for P7.50 per sheet, but unless you're surveying for a new building site it'll be too bulky and contain far more detail than most tourists want or need.

Left Luggage There's a left luggage service at the railway station but it's open at rather inconvenient hours: 8 am to 1 pm and 2 to 4 pm, on weekdays only. If you may need to pick up your things at any other times, think twice before depositing them there!

Laundry Laundry and drycleaning services are available next door to No Mathatha supermarket in South Broadhurst. All the hotels offer laundry service as well.

Film Although film is readily available in Gaborone, it's expensive, and you'd be lucky to find a roll of good slide film. There's a one hour photo developing service at Photolab on The Mall, but quality varies.

Camping Equipment The best place to find camping equipment, including butane cartridges, is Woolworths – unlike any Woolworths you've ever seen – in the Broadhurst Industrial Estate. Another more conveniently located option is the appropriately named Explosions guns and ammo shop in the African Mall. Gaborone Hardware on The Mall also sells basic outdoor supplies.

Emergency Services The Princess Marina Hospital (☎ 353221), on North Ring Rd at Hospital Way two blocks east of The Mall, is equipped to handle standard medical treatments and emergencies. For anything serious, however, you'll probably have to go to Johannesburg.

The police (☎ 351161) are based on Botswana Rd opposite the President Hotel.

National Museum & Art Gallery

The museum complex in Gaborone, with its stuffed wildlife and cultural displays, is good for a morning looking around Botswana's past and artistic present. The small National Gallery is a repository for both traditional and modern African and European art. Besides the permanent collection, visiting exhibitions are staged.

The complex is on Independence Ave just north-east of The Mall. The museums are open Tuesday to Friday from 9 am to 6 pm, and on weekends and holidays (except Easter weekend, Christmas and Boxing Day) from 9 am to 5 pm. Admission is free. The museum shop sells artwork, crafts and books and is open Tuesday to Friday from 9 am to 4.30 pm. Occasional lectures and presentations are given at the museum lecture hall.

Gaborone Game Park

On 1 March 1988, the Gaborone Game Park was opened to give the Gaborone public the opportunity to view Botswana's wildlife in a natural setting just one km east of Broadhurst. Access is by vehicle only. The park offers mainly a variety of antelopes, although there's also a well-guarded rhino in a separate enclosure. It's open from 6.30 am to 6.30 pm daily and costs P1 per person and an additional P2 per vehicle. Access is from Limpopo Drive; turn east on the back road just south of the Segoditshane River.

Activities

Sports The club scene carries over into the athletic end of the spectrum, with clubs devoted to tennis, cycling, running, golf, squash, cricket, riding, yachting and so on. The best established all-purpose sports centre is the Gaborone Club (☎ 356333) in Village which offers swimming, tennis, squash, rugby and bowls. Membership is required if you're living in Gaborone, but once-only visitors are welcome if invited by a member.

The Oasis Motel in Tlokweng offers individual memberships for the use of its miniature golf and swimming pool facilities. The Gaborone Sun allows the use of its pool and squash and tennis courts for P200 annually. The Notwane Club (☎ 352399) offers tennis and squash, and the Gaborone Squash Racquets Centre (☎ 314620) beside the National Stadium on Notwane Rd offers memberships for around P150. Information about other participatory sports clubs is available weekly in the *Botswana Advertiser*.

Places to Stay

The biggest headache in Gaborone is finding a place to stay. If you're on a tight budget, your success will amount to the sum of your creativity. There are no official camping areas, no reliable hostels and not even a reasonably priced dump of a hotel to fall back on. Not even the YWCA accepts guests; and foreign missions refuse to accommodate non-affiliates. Sleeping at the railway station is also a nonstarter since they began requiring platform passes.

Camping Wild camping isn't permitted in Gaborone either, but if you're willing to put up with a bit of inconvenience and maintain a low profile you can unofficially set up a tent somewhere in the low hills out on the Molepolole or Lobatse roads; just hitch or take the bus to and from the city. Alternatively, it's sometimes possible to camp in the dusty and gravelly courtyard of the *Mogo Hotel* in Mogoditshane for about P10 per person.

Another option (which many travellers wind up taking!) is to offer ex-pats and foreign workers a few pula for space to set up a tent in their garden. They understand the predicament travellers are in – many have been there themselves – and are normally pleased to help. Try the neighbourhoods of Maru-a-Pula, Broadhurst, Village or Gaborone West.

Some travellers were recently permitted to camp at the golf course behind the Gaborone Sun (they enquired at the golf course, *not* the Sun), but only for one night and only because

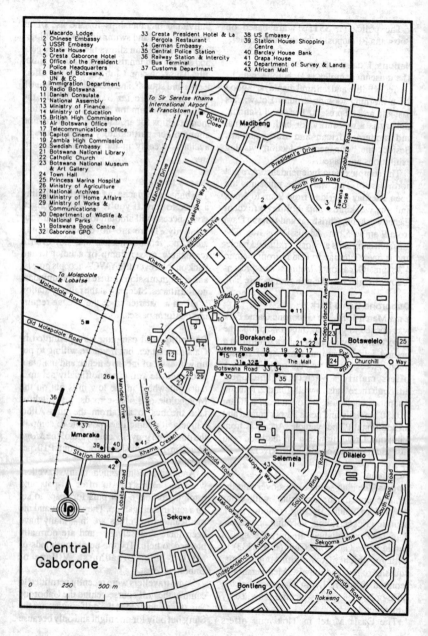

Central Gaborone

they'd arrived late and all the hotels were booked up.

Hostels The Norwegian, Swedish, Danish, Peace Corps and German *Volunteer Hostels* are concentrated in the vicinity of The Mall, but have long ago stopped extending hospitality to travellers. While the Peace Corps is typically immovable and accepts no one, the other hostels welcome guests for P15 per night in the following order: volunteers in Botswana from the country sponsoring the hostel, volunteers from the sponsoring country working in neighbouring countries, families of volunteers, friends of volunteers, citizens of the sponsoring country, and lastly, everyone else. Your chances of getting in without at least a volunteer contact are slim to none, so it isn't even worth trying.

If there's space, the *Grace Kgari Nurse's Association Hostel*, at 2684 Phiri Crescent near the Gaborone Sun, will accept travellers for P25 per night, but it's normally filled up with live-ins from outside the city.

Sleepers When all the hotels are booked up, some travellers have become desperate and resorted to the P55 2nd-class sleepers in the overnight train to Francistown. They can visit Gaborone one day, Francistown the next, then Gaborone the next day...Once you've left Gaborone, however, you may not be all that excited about returning so quickly.

Hotels The new *Cresta Gaborone* (☎ 375200, fax 375201) at the railway station fills the gap left by the historic but recently demolished Gaborone Hotel. In addition to a great bar and live music every weekend, it offers snacks and takeaway meals. Rooms, including private baths and television, cost P70 a single and P90 a double. This place is understandably popular and advance bookings are essential. The central reservations number is 312431, fax 375376.

A second new mid-range hotel, called simply *The Lodge*, was just being completed at the time of writing. It's on the south side of Machel Drive just off the Lobatse road.

Single/double rooms cost P99/119. Their restaurant, Chatters, is reportedly good but quite upmarket.

Another conveniently located mid-range option is *Macardo Lodge* (☎ 373980) at 4863 Dinatla Close on the corner of Morupule Drive, just off the Francistown road. Rooms cost P100 a single and P120 a double, including a superb English breakfast and use of the swimming pool. Since guests have access to the kitchen and fridge, the Macardo will actually prove more economical than it initially sounds. You can also get beer and snacks at reasonable prices.

Out on Tlokweng Rd, seven km from town, is the slightly seedy *Morning Star Hotel* (☎ 352301) which costs P70 a single and P100 for a double room. There's unfortunately no public transport available so you'll have to hitch back and forth.

Equally distant but erratically accessible by minibus from the railway station is the *Mogo Hotel* (☎ 372228) in Mogoditshane village on the Molepolole road. They can also be persuaded to let you camp in their less-than-amenable courtyard for around P10 per person. Rooms cost P45/65 for singles/doubles. A full English breakfast costs P9 while continental is only P4. For just coffee and toast you'll pay P3.

The *Oasis Motel* (☎ 53671 Tlokweng) in Tlokweng costs P150/175 for single/double chalets, but rooms are only P125/140. There's no public transport available in that direction.

Once known for its haughtiness, the *Gaborone Sun* (☎ 351111) on Nyerere Drive has recently been humbled by competition in its market range. It's frequently booked up by business travellers and residents awaiting permanent accommodation in Gaborone. In the old wing, singles/doubles cost P162/200, while in the newer wing they cost P185/220. Although the coming of the Sheraton may whip them into shape, both the grill and dining room are frightfully expensive and service is marginal at best. If you're spending time in Gaborone, an annual membership fee of about P200 will provide access to the Sun's swimming pool and squash and tennis courts. Itinerant travellers have successfully gained access to the pool by going for a bite at the terrace snack bar.

Right on The Mall, the *Cresta President* (☎ 353631, fax 351840) offers friendlier, cheaper and more central accommodation than the Sun. Standard single/double rooms cost P130/150. A buffet English breakfast costs an additional P14.50, while continental breakfasts are only P9.50. The President's La Pergola terrace restaurant overlooking The Mall offers healthy European-style cuisine, including vegetable-rich lunches, cappuccino and sweets.

The new *Sheraton Hotel*, near the Mogo Hotel between Gaborone West and Mogoditshane, offers five-star international standards at P160/180 for singles/doubles.

Places to Eat

Snacks & Lunches For a cheap food fix, visit the dining hall at *Food Town* on The Mall which is very popular with the lunchtime crowds. There you'll find an adequate and filling dose of stew or mealies and relish for just P2.50.

Fast food and takeaways figure prominently in Gaborone. At Broadhurst, the African Mall, Tlokweng and the Metro Mall you'll find *Snack Shack* takeaways which sell burgers, chips and other quick items. Similar fare is available at *King's Takeaways* on The Mall. It's a favourite office workers' lunch spot so expect long queues between noon and 1 pm.

If you want chicken, there's an authentic *Kentucky Fried Chicken* in the African Mall where you'll get a standard lunch box for around P7. Providing the Colonel with a bit of competition is the new *Chicken Lick'n*, also in the African Mall.

The *Gourmet 2000 Dial-a-Meal* (☎ 313474) at No Mathatha Shopping Centre does walk-in or phone-in takeaway pizza, burgers, pies and sweets. It's open daily from 11 am to 9 pm and until 10 pm on Friday and Saturday nights.

At the Cresta President Hotel, *La Pergola* on the terrace serves such wonderful lunchtime concoctions as spinach quiche, cream

of asparagus soup and vegetable curries. At other times of the day you can sit there in the shade, drink a rich and frothy cappuccino, eat a crème éclair and survey the passing scene in The Mall below.

An unexpected pleasure, and a highly recommended option, is the *Kgotla* in the Broadhurst North Mall, down the side road toward the BBS building. There's a creative and exhaustive menu of vegetarian options and just about everything else from healthy and tasty to rich and tasty. The salads, desserts, cappuccino and iced coffee are particularly appealing. It's open from 9 am to 9 pm daily.

For tempting snacks, try one of Gaborone's two speciality bakeries. *Hot & Crusty* in Broadhurst North Mall sells great personal-size pizzas for P3 as well as a variety of breads and sweets. *Sugar & Spicy* in the Old Spar Shopping Centre offers tarts, meat pies, pastries, cakes, scones, biscuits, rolls and other assorted gooey and delectable sweets.

Dinners In the Oasis Motel itself is the more upmarket *Reflections* (☎ 356396) which specialises in an amazing variety of seafood; your meal will be rounded off with a free glass of sherry and chocolates. It's an extremely popular dinner spot, so advance bookings are necessary.

The African Mall has several good options. Most popular is the *Park*, with its folksy atmosphere and standard, inexpensive offerings: curries, beef, chicken, lamb and salad bar. For dessert don't miss the chocolate banana crepes. Next door is the *Taj* (☎ 313569) which serves Indian, Chinese and Mauritian foods. It's also known for its salads. The *Mandarin* nearby serves only Chinese food. The fourth African Mall restaurant is the Swiss-owned *Le Bougainville*, an expensive haunt specialising in French and Continental cuisine.

For Italian food, there's the recommended *Mama's Kitchen* at Broadhurst North Mall. The Hungarian-owned *Crazy Bull* near the railway station serves excellent pizza but their pasta leaves some room for improvement. Inexpensive Chinese food is available at the popular *China Restaurant* (☎ 357254) in the No Mathatha Shopping Centre, open from noon to 2 pm for lunch and for dinner from 6.30 to 11 pm. At the Old Spar Shopping Centre is *The Moghul*, a newly opened Indian restaurant which I haven't tried but it's reportedly quite good.

The big hotels all have dining rooms as well as more casual grill restaurants. They cater primarily to business travellers on expense accounts or a captive audience of live-ins with government or private meal subsidies. Most menus are typically heavy on the beef dishes, if that's where your interests lie.

Self-Catering There's really no such thing as an open market in Gaborone, but you will find impromptu stalls set up around the railway station and east of the Broadhurst North Mall. The best stocked supermarkets are the *Spar Markets* at the Old Spar Shopping Centre and the North Broadhurst Mall. Other options include the *Fairways* in the Station House Shopping Centre near the railway station, the *Corner Market* on The Mall and *Woolworths Market* at the Metro Shopping Centre.

At *Tony's* in the African Mall you can stock up on fruit and cheap fresh vegies for bargain prices, but you'll need to muster a group to share them with; 50 oranges cost only P6! Also in the African Mall is the cheapest butchery, the *Gaborone Meat Centre*, where you'll also find Oriental groceries.

Entertainment

Theatre & Cinema The 450-seat theatre in the Maitisong Cultural Centre (☎ 371809) at Maru-a-Pula (Rain Cloud) Secondary School was opened in 1987 as a venue for cultural events in Gaborone. Anything staged here is well attended, so book in advance if you're interested. The schedule of coming events is posted on a bulletin board outside, and listed in the *Botswana Advertiser* which is published on Friday.

The local amateur group Capital Players

(☎ 372120) is good fun. Performances are held at the Memorable Order of Tin Hats (MOTHS) Hall just off the Molepolole road. For information on productions, check the *Botswana Advertiser* or write to Capital Players, PO Box 65, Gaborone. More serious local theatre groups, including some excellent new African troupes, perform exclusively at Maitisong.

Gaborone's only cinema, the Capitol in The Mall, provides predominantly escapist American entertainment. The Gaborone Film Society and Alliance Française frequently screen classic films as well. Again, refer to the *Botswana Advertiser* for information.

Nightspots The most popular live music venues are the Club Status at the Oasis Motel in Tlokweng and Night Shift in the Broadhurst North Mall. African disco music and dancing are popular at the Platform in the Gaborone Sun Hotel and at Club 585 in No Mathatha Shopping Centre, just around the corner from the Sun. If you're staying at the Mogo Hotel, try the Blue Note in Mogoditshane. The formerly popular Bull & Bush pub has recently changed hands. There's now a cover charge of P7 on the weekends and a glass of beer costs P2.50.

Folk music performances are given at 7.30 pm on the first Saturday of the month at the Gaborone Club on Okwa Rd in Village.

Getting There & Away

Air Air Botswana, British Airways, Zambia Airways, Air Zimbabwe, Namib Air and South African Airways all serve Gaborone from abroad, and Air Botswana operates scheduled domestic flights from Maun, Francistown, Selebi-Phikwe and Ghanzi. The Sir Seretse Khama International Airport is 14 km from town. The more central airport, marked on older maps as Gaborone Airport, belongs to the Botswana Defence Force and should be given an extremely wide berth.

An interesting transport possibility from Gaborone is sometimes available from the Flying Mission which frequently sends planes to Zimbabwe and to bush locations around Botswana. When there are extra seats available, the mission will take on passengers for minimal fares – as little as P100 one way to Harare. If you're interested, make enquiries with the mission.

Bus You'll find the intercity bus terminal, such as it is, at the Gaborone railway station where minibuses arrive from and depart for outlying villages. The larger buses which ply Botswana's tarred highways (making the occasional foray out to Maun as well) operate according to no fixed schedules. Service is available (although not always directly or when you'd like to go) to Lobatse, Ramatlhabama, Mahalapye, Palapye, Serowe, Selebi-Phikwe, Francistown, Nata, Kasane and Maun. The last three destinations are accessible only occasionally, and all bus trips begin with a visit to – and at least one night in – Francistown. There's a more regular service to Mochudi.

Train Gaborone, which lies on Botswana's eastern corridor railway line, is accessible by train from Bulawayo, Francistown and Lobatse daily. Once a week there is a service to and from Johannesburg. The northbound train arrives at 6.30 pm daily, except Thursday when it comes at 1.04 am. The southbound train arrives at 6.10 am, except on Tuesday when it gets in at 1.30 am.

If advance arrangements are made, the big hotels will send their minibuses to meet their guests arriving at the station.

Getting Around

Gaborone's local public transport system is scarcely adequate for the city's growing population.

To/From the Airport The only reliable transport between the airport and town are the minibuses operated by the top-end hotels for their guests. If there's space, nonguests can sometimes talk the driver into a lift to or from the centre, but you'll have to tip at least several pula. Only very occasionally does a taxi turn up at the airport; so rarely, in fact,

that taking a taxi can scarcely be considered an option. If you somehow do connect up with a taxi, expect to pay anywhere from P10 to P30 per person for the 14 km trip to the centre. Alternatively, walk down the road a few hundred metres and try hitching a lift.

Minibuses The crowded little white minibuses, recognisable by their blue number plates, are based at the ranks just off Botswana Rd opposite the President Hotel. They circulate according to set routes and cost 50t per ride, but if you pass the terminus you'll have to pay twice. The standard city route passes all the major shopping centres. Minibuses to surrounding villages depart from the railway station terminus, following erratic schedules. Their routes can only be sorted out by visiting the station and enquiring of drivers or other prospective passengers.

Taxi Although the public transport minibuses in Gaborone are sometimes known as 'taxis', Gaborone has next to no conventional taxis, so it's hardly worth searching for one. Not even the Gaborone Sun can get you a taxi. On the rare occasion one is available, it will be recognisable by its blue number plates; prices are left up to the whims of the driver. Without a vehicle, resign yourself to walking, hitching, using the minibuses, or hiring a vehicle.

Around Gaborone

MOCHUDI

The most interesting village in south-eastern Botswana, Mochudi was first settled by the Kwena in the mid-1500s, as evinced by a few remaining stone walls in the surrounding hills. In 1871 it was settled by the Kgatla people, forced from their lands by northward-trekking Boers. Today's village has some interesting mud-walled architecture and a prominent kgotla, used as a meeting house and village court. Opposite

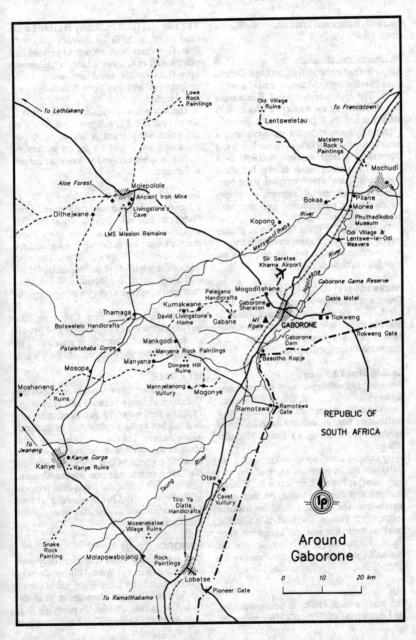

To Lethlakeng

Lowe Rock Paintings

Old Village Ruins

To Francistown

Lentsweletau

Matsieng Rock Paintings

Mochudi

Aloe Forest

Ancient Iron Mine

Molepolole

Livingstone's Cave

Dithejwane

LMS Mission Remains

Bokaa

River

Pilane
Morwa

Phuthadikobo Museum

Odi Village & Lentswe-la-Odi Weavers

Kopong

Metsemotlhaba

River

Sir Seretse Khama Airport

Nooetlane

Gaborone Game Reserve

Pelegano Handicrafts

Mogoditshane

Oasis Motel

Kumakwane

Gaborone Sheraton

Thamaga

David Livingstone's Home

Gabane

Mt Kgale

GABORONE

Tlokweng

Botswelelo Handicrafts

Mankgodi

Tlokweng Gate

Pataletshaba Gorge

Manyana Rock Paintings

Gaborone Dam

Mosopa

Manyana

Dimawe Hill Ruins

Basotho Kopje

Moshaneng

Mannyelanong Vultury

Mogonye

Ruins

Ramotswa

Ramotswa Gate

REPUBLIC OF
SOUTH AFRICA

To Jwaneng

Kanye Gorge

Kanye

Kanye Ruins

Taung

River

Otse

Cavet Vultury

Tiro Ya Diatla Handicrafts

Snake Rock Painting

Mosenekatse Village Ruins

Molapowabojang

Rock Paintings

Around Gaborone

0   10   20 km

Lobatse

Pioneer Gate

To Ramatlhabama

the kgotla is the royal kraal where two Kgatla chiefs are buried.

Phuthadikobo Museum

Atop Phuthadikobo Hill is the Cape Dutch-style Phuthadikobo Museum, established in 1976. The museum is one of Botswana's best, focusing on the history of Mochudi in particular and the Kgatla people in general.

During museum hours on weekdays a screenprinting workshop, founded by a German volunteer worker in 1980 as a source of dressmaking fabric for local women, operates in the courtyard. It has been turned into a successful commercial enterprise producing silkscreened curtains, wall hangings and clothing.

The museum is open Monday to Friday from 8 am to 5 pm and on weekends from 2 to 5 pm. Admission is free but donations are gratefully accepted.

Places to Stay

There's no accommodation in Mochudi itself, but the seen-better-days *Sedibelo Hotel* in Pilane offers mid-range accommodation just six km away on the main Gaborone-Francistown road.

Getting There & Away

Buses to Mochudi depart from the Gaborone railway station when full, at least six or seven times daily. Alternatively, catch any northbound bus, get off at Pilane and hitch or walk the remaining six km to Mochudi village.

By vehicle, travel about 35 km north from Gaborone on the Francistown road and turn right (east) at Pilane. Turn left at the T-intersection about three km further on, then right just before the hospital into the historic centre of the village. The road ends with the kraal on your left and the kgotla on your right. From there, a track winds up Phuthadikobo Hill to the museum on its summit.

ODI

The small village of Odi is best known for the Lentswe la Odi (Hills of Odi) weavers (☎

312368 Odi). The cooperative was established in 1973 by Swedes Ulla and Peter Gowenius in an attempt to provide the village with an economic base. It has grown into Botswana's most renowned such cooperative and has been internationally acclaimed.

The workshop is open to visitors from 8 am to 1 pm and 2 to 4.30 pm weekdays, and the sales shop from 8 am to 5.30 pm weekdays and 2 to 5.30 pm on weekends. Coffee, tea, biscuits and vetkoek are served at the shop.

Getting There & Away

Follow the Francistown road north from Gaborone and turn right (east) at the Odi signpost about 18 km out from town. From there it's eight km to the railway line and the bridge over the Notwane River. The road takes a sharp left turn at the 'two hills of Odi', and from there it's about 1500 metres through the village to the weaving cooperative.

By public transport from Gaborone, take any northbound bus or minibus and get off at the Odi turnoff. From there, either walk or hitch the remaining distance into the village.

MT KGALE

The 'sleeping giant' peak overlooking Gaborone is easily climbed and affords the capital's best view. To get there, take any Lobatse bus to the Kgale siding or hitch out along the new Lobatse road eight km from town to the satellite dish. Just a couple of hundred metres towards town, opposite the dish, is a concrete stile over a fence. Cross it, turn left, and follow the fence until it enters a shallow gully. From there a set of whitewashed stones lead the way up the hillside to the summit.

GABORONE DAM

Access to the dam wall is allowed only with permission from the Water Utilities Corporation, which is on Luthuli Rd just south of the Khama Crescent roundabout near the Gaborone railway station. To reach the dam wall, go down Mobutu Drive and then, just north of The Lodge, turn left at the Sanitas sign and continue five km along that road.

OTSE

Otse ('OOT-see') village, a former manganese-mining and forestry village 45 km south of Gaborone, is best known for its vultury on Mannyelanong Hill, one of only two Cape vulture nesting sites in Botswana.

Just a short distance north along the western side of the same hill is Refuge Cave, a large fault in the cliff face 50 metres above the base. Pottery has been found inside and the cave was probably used as a hiding place during the Boer invasions of the 1870s.

LOBATSE

Despite its nice setting 68 km south of Gaborone, Lobatse is one Botswana's dullest places, known primarily as the site of the country's largest abattoir and the national

mental hospital. The original Lobatse was established by the Ngwaketse in the late 18th century. It served as the site of the High Court of Bechuanaland Protectorate while the seat of government was Mafikeng. Due to a lack of permanent water, it just missed out becoming the national capital when Gaborone was selected in the early 1960s.

Arts Cooperatives

Tiro Afrique Knitwear in Lobatse creates designer woollen knitwear from Accorda wool. The quality clothing is available for reasonable prices, and the women will serve refreshments and show you around the work area.

The Tiro ya Diatla Weavers opposite the Botswana Meat Commission started out producing heavy and durable rugs of high quality karakul wool. They now weave artistic tapestries and clothing from the same materials and sell the finished product for

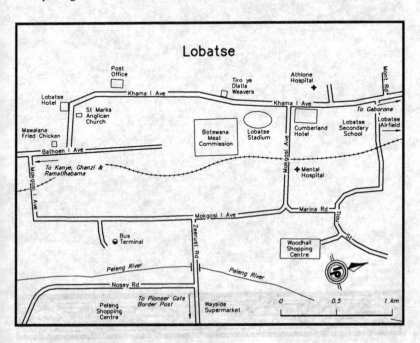

better prices than are available in shops. The weavers also give tours of the site.

Anglican Church

St Mark's Anglican Church, a thatch-roofed stone building in the centre, is quite nice. When it's open, visitors are welcome to have a look at the tiny chapel, which would be more at home in a damp, rural English village.

Places to Stay & Eat

If you're stuck in Lobatse while trying to hitch to Ghanzi or South Africa, the hills behind town provide suitable unofficial camping sites. The least expensive place to crash in Lobatse is the *Lobatse Hotel* (☎ 330157 Lobatse), opposite the Standard Bank in the centre, an African hotel. Spartan single/double rooms cost P50/80. There's no sign out the front but you shouldn't have any trouble finding it.

More upmarket is the *Cresta Cumberland* (☎ 330281, fax 332106) on the road in from Gaborone. Single/double rooms, including en suite baths and breakfast, cost P110/130. If you're not staying at the Cumberland you can still buy meals there. There's a buffet English breakfast for P10.50 or a continental breakfast for P7, while dinner in the grill cost about P15 to P20 per person.

There are several greasy restaurants and fast food takeaways, including *Mawalana Fried Chicken*, along the street parallel to the railway line.

Eastern Botswana

Although it looks like a desert, the scrubland strip along the South African border and part of the Zimbabwean border is the part of Botswana most amenable to agriculture, and therefore human habitation. Few people could imagine referring to it as lush, but it still receives Botswana's highest rainfall.

FRANCISTOWN

As a settlement, Francistown was originally conceived as a goldmining centre, but industry and commerce have now taken over the economy. The town's current population of about 60,000 is double what it was in 1980; the growth is primarily due to economic expansion combined with seven years of drought in the rural hinterlands.

Although gold is still mined in small quantities, the primary base of Francistown's current industrial boom was laid down in the late '70s. In order to avoid closure under economic sanctions prior to Zimbabwean independence, numerous Rhodesian firms escaped to Botswana and established themselves in Francistown, two hours' driving from Bulawayo. The growth trend continues unabated; rapid expansion has taken place with little reason or planning, and the town has grown into the economic hub of eastern Botswana.

Orientation & Information

Most of Francistown's shopping is concentrated in the few blocks between the railway line on the west, Khama St on the east, Selous Ave on the north and Guy St on the south. The main street is Blue Jacket St. Beyond this small central enclave, Francistown is mainly a dusty, unconsolidated settlement. There are two hotels in centre, the Tati Lodge and the Grand Hotel. The Cresta Thapama Lodge lies immediately south of the core area on Blue Jacket St and the Marang Hotel is 4.5 km from the Thapama Lodge on Old Gaborone Rd, east of the roundabout.

Tourist Office As it has no tourist attractions, Francistown doesn't bother with a tourist information office. Queries may be directed either to the hotel reception desks or to Pan African Travel in Blue Jacket St.

Money Francistown's two banks are the Standard Bank, on Haskins St opposite the railway station, and Barclays Bank, on the corner of Blue Jacket St and Lobengula Ave. If you need to exchange foreign currency for pula, join the queue early and plan on a few hours there. Those making foreign exchange transactions have to wait in one queue to pick up the forms and a second one to make the transaction.

Post & Telephone The GPO is on Blue Jacket St. Telephone calls may be made from the Teletswana Office on Lobengula Ave near Blue Jacket St. Hours are Monday to Friday from 7.45 am to 12.30 pm and 1.45 to 4 pm, and Saturday from 8 to 11 am.

Travel Agencies Pan African Travel (☎ 213909), at the corner of Lobengula Ave and Blue Jacket St, is Francistown's largest agency and is a good bet. The staff there can arrange lodging, transport or car hire around Botswana and also handle international airline bookings with amazing efficiency. In the same office is the Francistown branch of Holiday Car Hire.

Bookshops The Francistown Stationers & Bookshop on Haskins St, opposite the railway line, offers a surprisingly limited selection of light novels and magazines. Several tourist publications and coffee table books are available at the gift shop in the Thapama Lodge.

Left Luggage The left luggage service at the railway station is open between 8 am and 4 pm on weekdays and from 7.30 to 11 am on Saturday.

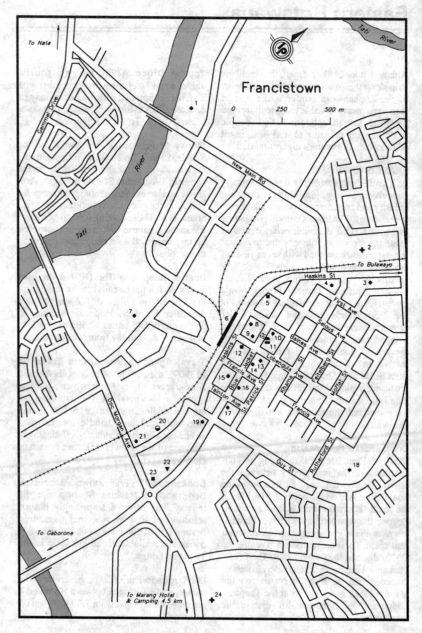

Francistown

0   250   500 m

To Nata

Gemmel Dyke

Tati River

New Main Rd

To Bulawayo

Haskins St

Tati

Doc Morgan Ave

Haskins St

First Ave

Selous Ave

Baines Ave

Fetterberg St

Moffat St

Lobengula Ave

Khama Ave

Francis Ave St

Blue Jacket St

St Patrick St

Tainton Ave

Guy St

Rutherford St

Francis Ave

To Gaborone

To Marang Hotel
& Camping 4.5 km

1	Stadium	10	Fruit & Vegetable Market	17	The Mall Shopping Centre
2	Jubilee Hospital			18	Sports Field
3	Police Station	11	Post Office	19	Bottle Store
4	Children's Playground	12	Tati Hotel	20	Bus Terminal
5	Grand Hotel	13	Teletswana Communications Office	21	Towngardens
6	Railway Station			22	Sizzler Restaurant
7	Catholic Mission	14	Civic Centre	23	Thapama Lodge
8	Standard Bank & Bookshop	15	Pan African Travel	24	New Hospital & National Health Unit
9	Barclay's Bank	16	Cine 2000		

Emergency Services Francistown's Jubilee Hospital (☎ 212333) lies across the railway line from Haskins St, immediately north of the central area. A new hospital is opening a few hundred metres east of the roundabout near the Thapama Lodge. For emergency medical services telephone 997. The police station is on Haskins St, north of the central area; their emergency telephone number is 999.

Places to Stay – bottom end

The *Marang Hotel* (☎ 213991), on the old Gaborone road 4.5 km from the business district, has a nice and secluded grassy area for tent and caravan camping on the bank of the Tati River for P10 per person, including access to the hotel washing facilities, showers and swimming pool. There are occasionally 50t minibuses doing the run as well as the odd taxi minibus for 70t per person. Alternatively, you can walk or hitch. Coming from the centre, turn left at the Thapama Lodge roundabout ('Matsiloje' on the sign) and continue until the Marang Hotel comes up on your left.

Places to Stay – middle

Two hotels in town offer reasonable midrange accommodation. For P48/60 you can get single/double rooms with communal baths and toilets at the *Grand Hotel* (☎ 212300) on the corner of Haskins St and Selous Ave. Lone women may want to avoid this one.

Even further down the scale is the popular *Tati Lodge* (☎ 212321) on Lobengula St, between Haskins St and Blue Jacket St,

where rooms with shared baths and facilities will cost P45/55 for singles/doubles.

The *Marang Hotel* (see bottom end) offers 'budget rooms' without telephones for P85 a single, a viable alternative to its more expensive chalet accommodation.

Places to Stay – top end

The *Marang Hotel* (see bottom end) has single/double rooms for P125/145 and single/double raised-thatch chalets for P150/170.

Francistown's most upmarket hotel is the recently expanded *Cresta Thapama Lodge* (☎ 213872) at the corner of Doc Morgan Ave and Blue Jacket St. It caters mainly to business travellers. Single/double rooms with breakfast cost P142/173; extra beds cost P20 each. A suite will cost a whopping P250.

Places to Eat

Hotels & Restaurants The English breakfasts at the *Marang Hotel* are quite good. In the evenings, the thatched restaurant at the Marang offers a salad bar and a standard menu for approximately P15 to P20 per person.

The buffet breakfast at the *Thapama Lodge* costs P14 per person. Other Thapama Lodge offerings include the Ivory Grill where you'll find carvery and curry dishes. Light snacks are available at the pool terrace in the afternoon and the cocktail bar serves light meals and snacks as well.

For steaks, there's the *Sizzler* behind the Thapama Lodge. The *Hornbill Restaurant* beside the Grand Hotel offers basic African meals.

Takeaways In The Mall Shopping Centre on Blue Jacket St is *Fast Burger*, a burger, hot dog and soft drink joint.

For Greek-style takeaway try *Donna's*, opposite the Grand Hotel in the centre area.

The *Hot & Crusty Bakery* in The Mall Shopping Centre offers sweets, bread and biscuits. Further north on Blue Jacket St is *Chicken Run*, which of course serves chicken.

Self-Catering Besides the well-stocked supermarkets, Francistown has a small outdoor market at the corner of Blue Jacket St and Baines Ave where you'll find a good variety of fruits and vegetables as well as light hot snacks. Other informal food stalls may be found around the bus terminal.

Entertainment

The bar at the Marang Hotel is always crowded, while the more elegant pub at the Thapama Lodge attracts primarily business travellers. The most raucous African pub is the Grand Hotel, with drinking at all hours. On weekends, the New Yorker in Blue Jacket St is popular with the younger disco crowd.

Francistown's only cinema, Cine 2000 in Blue Jacket St, has one or two showings nightly. The swimming pool behind the Civic Centre is another option when you get desperate for something to do.

Things to Buy

Handicrafts The BGI Crafts outlet across the railway line from the end of Francis Ave is good for Shashe baskets, more loosely woven than their Ngamiland counterparts.

Tswana Weaving (☎ 213037) in the Tswelelo Industrial complex sells a variety of original design tapestries hand-woven on site from karakul wool. It's open during shopping hours on weekdays and by telephone appointment on weekends.

Getting There & Away

Air The Air Botswana office (☎ 212393) is at the Thapama Lodge. You can fly from Francistown to Gaborone at least once daily; most flights depart between 8 am and 1 pm,

but on Wednesday and Friday there's an evening flight at 6.15 pm. There's a service to Selebi-Phikwe in the morning on Monday, Wednesday and Friday.

From Gaborone to Francistown, there are one or two flights daily in the morning and also an afternoon flight at 4 pm on Wednesday and Friday. From Selebi-Phikwe, there are flights on Wednesday and Friday at 5.20 pm.

Bus Because it lies at the intersection of the Gaborone, Nata/Kasane, Bulawayo and Orapa roads, Francistown is a real terrestrial transportation hub. The bus terminal is wedged between the railway line and the small frontage road connecting Haskins St to Doc Morgan St. There you'll find bus services south along the tarred road to Gaborone at least twice daily. Although there is meant to be at least a once-daily service to Kasane via Nata, it isn't a foregone conclusion. The service to Maun is best described as 'once in a while'; at last notice the Maun bus was leaving Francistown only once or twice a week.

Twice daily, the Zimbabwe Omnibus Company operates a direct service between Francistown and Bulawayo. Depending on the time spent at the border, the trip will take anywhere from three to six hours. A weekly service to Lusaka, Zambia, via Kasane and the Kazungula ferry should have started up by the time you read this. Check at the bus terminal for the best details you're likely to find.

Train The Bulawayo to Johannesburg railway runs through Francistown. The ticket office at the Haskins St railway station is open on weekdays from 8 am to noon and 1 to 4 pm.

Every day except Tuesday, the southbound train (which only goes as far as Lobatse) arrives at Francistown at 6.26 pm; on Tuesday, when it continues on to Johannesburg, it arrives at 3.51 pm. The northbound train is meant to depart from Francistown at 6 am daily except Thursday, but normally sits for a while instead. On

Thursday, when it's coming from Johannesburg, it departs from Francistown at 9.56 am. For further timetable information, refer to the train timetables in the Zimbabwe Getting Around chapter.

Getting Around

When driving in Francistown's centre, be particularly mindful of the one-way streets between Haskins St and Blue Jacket St.

As well as the ubiquitous minibuses, Francistown has a few taxis (☎ 212260) which look more like minibuses and operate much like Zimbabwe's emergency taxis. They can be found most easily at the railway station. For the ride out to the Marang Hotel they charge 70t, while the normal minibuses cost 50t. As in Gaborone, the taxis and minibuses are recognisable by their blue number plates.

SELEBI-PHIKWE

Prior to 1967, Selebi-Phikwe, now Botswana's third largest community, was nothing but a cattle post. In the early 1960s, however, the twin copper/nickel/cobalt deposits of Selebi and Phikwe, 14 km apart, were discovered and taken over by the BCL (Bamangwato Concessions Ltd). Production commenced in 1973 and has worked up to a combined annual total of 2.5 million tonnes.

As in Gaborone, the town is centred on The Mall and there seems to be a concerted community effort to keep the business district planted in flowering trees and plants. There you'll find the police, Teletswana office, hotel, post office and a couple of eating places, as well as a very good bookshop with a wide variety of novels, magazines and other books.

Places to Stay & Eat

The *Bosele Hotel* (☎ 810675) on Tshekedi Rd beside The Mall exists primarily for visitors on mining business. It has a standard dining room. If you're booked in, you can arrange to have them fetch you from the airport.

On the Mall are the *Pioneer Restaurant* and *Pioneer Takeaways* – just about the extent of the town's non-hotel dining possibilities. The market just north of The Mall is a good source of cheap produce and hot snacks, and out on the Francistown road are a couple of small takeaways.

Getting There & Away

The only reason for non-business travellers to visit Selebi-Phikwe would be to visit someone or to look for a lift into the Tuli Block, and for that it should serve you well since there's a bit of commercial traffic passing through.

Buses normally run between Selebi-Phikwe, Serule and Francistown a couple of times a day. An air service is available three times weekly to and from Francistown or Gaborone.

TULI BLOCK

The Tuli Block is a strip of freehold farmland 350 km long and 10 to 20 km wide stretching along the northern bank of the Limpopo River. Originally Ngwato tribal lands, it was ceded to the BSAC for the railway shortly after the Bechuanaland Protectorate was declared. The cost of bridging the numerous intermittent streams, however, made the project unfeasible; the land was opened to White settlement and the railway route was shifted north-west to its present location.

The private Tuli Block game reserves provide both a sampling of Botswana's wildlife and an accessible alternative to prohibitive national parks fees charged in the big northern reserves.

Sherwood Ranch & Zanzibar

If you're into rustic, decomposing villages, the two near-ghost-towns of Sherwood Ranch and Zanzibar will have something to offer apart from border crossings between Botswana and South Africa. There's no accommodation in either place, but Sherwood Ranch, eight km from the Martin's Drift border post (open 8 am to 6 pm), does have a very basic shop, a petrol station and a bottle store.

Along the road between Zanzibar and Pont Drift are three insignificant border

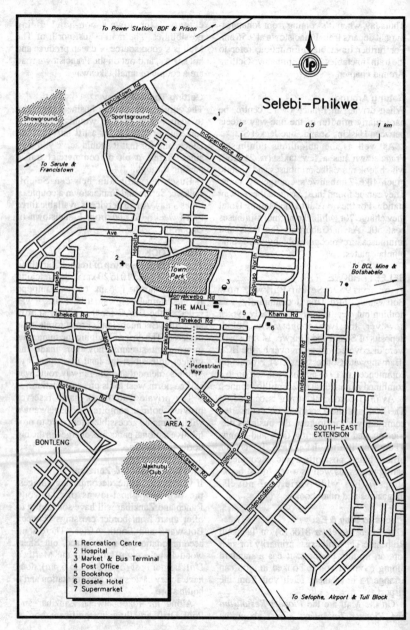

Selebi-Phikwe

To Power Station, BDF & Prison

To Serule & Francistown

To BCL Mine & Botshabelo

To Sefophe, Airport & Tuli Block

Showground

Sportsground

Town Park

THE MALL

Makhubu Club

BONTLENG

AREA 2

SOUTH-EAST EXTENSION

Francistown Rd

Independence Rd

Hospital

Ave

Ave

Thapelo

Thapelo Rd

Tshekedi Rd

Botswana Rd

Borkanelo Rd

Ikgwane Rd

Monyakwebo Rd

Tshekedi Rd

Pedestrian Way

Lopano Rd

Boipuso South Rd

Boipuso North Rd

Khama Rd

Independence Rd

Boipuso Rd

Botswana Rd

1 Recreation Centre
2 Hospital
3 Market & Bus Terminal
4 Post Office
5 Bookshop
6 Bosele Hotel
7 Supermarket

0   0.5   1 km

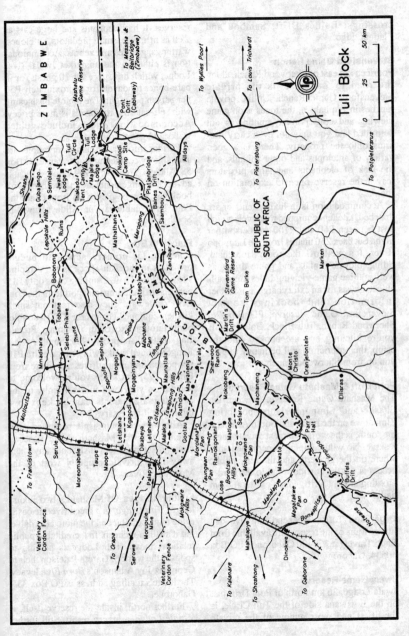

Tuli Block

crossings: Baines Drift, Sambou and Platjanbridge.

Stevensford Game Ranch

Fourteen km east of Sherwood Ranch, along the road to Zanzibar, is the private Stevensford Game Ranch. Unlike private ranches in Zimbabwe, the focus is on game viewing and conservation; hunting is not permitted and you may not even carry firearms onto the property. There is a good variety of antelopes and other animals, and the lack of elephants and large predators leaves the reserve open to exploration on foot.

Accommodation is in luxury tents or six thatched, kitchen-equipped rondavels which cost between P60 and P100 per person per night. Set back 250 metres from the Limpopo River, it's well off the road. Horseback riding, bicycle rentals and game drives as well as three game-viewing hides are available to guests for an extra charge. For further information and bookings contact Stevensford Game Reserve, PO Box 26, Sherwood Ranch, Tuli Block, Botswana. If you're hitching and are booked into the camp, the proprietors will be happy to pick you up from Sherwood Ranch.

Pont Drift & Mashatu Game Reserve

The Mashatu Game Reserve, between the Shashe and Limpopo rivers, bordering Zimbabwe on the north and South Africa on the south, is the world's largest private game reserve. No wild camping is permitted anywhere on the property and the only public access is via the corridor road to the border crossing at Pont Drift, which closes at 4 pm daily.

Organised Tours Weekend and five day luxury tours of the reserve are available from Phuti Travel (☎ 371400 Gaborone), PO Box 40534, Gaborone.

Jwala Game Reserve

Jwala Lodge, 26 km north of Pont Drift just on the Botswana side of the Tuli Circle, is the driest and most remote of the private reserves. It has elephants and large cats as well as primates, small predators, antelopes, warthogs, giraffes and zebras. Accommodation is either in the upmarket Jwala River Lodge, which has space for 10 guests, or in bare-bones rondavels for approximately P50 per person per night. The remote bush camp with self-catering rondavels is more pricey. Accommodation prices include guided walks and game drives.

Further information and reservations are available by contacting Roger Petty, PO Box 58, Alldays, Transvaal 0909, South Africa. If advance arrangements are made, those with bookings may be picked up from either the Pont Drift cableway or Alldays town in South Africa.

Places to Stay

Camping Of primary appeal to budget travellers in the Tuli Block is the camping site near Pont Drift. Camping costs only P15 per person, including transport from the Pont Drift cableway. They also rent out small kitchen-equipped chalets for P120 a double; book through Nokolodi Camping, Private Bag 1040, Waterpoort 0905, South Africa. Ranger-guided walks will cost an extra P10 per person and game drives anywhere from P15 to P25, but since you're welcome to wander on your own in the vicinity of the camping area, costs can be kept to a minimum if necessary.

Although camping isn't permitted anywhere inside the Mashatu Game Reserve, you can set up a tent just about anywhere away from private property west of the Motloutse River.

Luxury Lodges Of Mashatu's two luxury lodges, *Tuli Lodge*, in a green riverine oasis, is the more popular and the more affordable, but it's still not cheap. In a creditable public relations move, Tuli Lodge is helping to sponsor the work of Gareth Paterson, heir to George & Joy Adamson's *Born Free* legacy. The lodge's mailing address is PO Box 335, Gaborone.

Further north, inside the reserve itself, is *Majale Lodge*, a luxury resort. Still further out in the park is the *Thakadu Tent Camp*, a 'rustic' luxury alternative. Each tent is furnished like a hotel room and has en suite flush toilets and shower facilities. There's a swimming pool and bar, naturally, and game drives are included in the price.

Reservations and information may be made through Mashatu Game Reserve, Suite 4, Tulbaugh, 360 Oak Ave, Ferndale (PO Box 2575, Randburg 2125), South Africa.

Getting There & Away

Although 4WD won't be necessary to get around, you will need a vehicle of some sort to get the most out of the Tuli Block. On the Botswana side, roads are relatively well-graded and well-defined gravel or dirt, passable to even low-clearance vehicles. The easiest access from Gaborone, however, is via tarred South African highways through one of the several Limpopo border crossings. A South African visa will be required. If you're entering at Pont Drift during periods of high water when the river can't be forded, you'll have to leave the vehicle in South Africa and cross into Botswana on the rope cableway. With advance notice, any of the game lodges will pick up guests from the Botswana shore. Keep in mind that the border closes at 4 pm.

From the Botswana side of the border, six access routes lead into the Tuli Block from the Gaborone-Francistown road: Artesia (just 53 km north of Gaborone); Dinokwe; Mahalapye (if you're coming from the north, there's a rough shortcut from Lose); 10 km south or 20 km north of Palapye; and the most-travelled – and therefore easiest to hitch – from Serule via Selebi-Phikwe to Zanzibar.

While hitching is a viable option, hitchhikers can expect substantial waits along the Tuli Block's infrequently travelled byways. The only public transport venturing into the area is the occasional bus from Selebi-Phikwe to the villages of Bobonong and Molalatau. Sometimes it continues on as far as Mathathane, just over 20 km from Platjanbridge. Naturally, the service is erratic; the best up-to-date information will be available at the bus terminal in Selebi-Phikwe.

PALAPYE

The real name of this town is Phalatswe, meaning either 'many impala' in Sekgalagadi or 'large impala' in Setswana. The current spelling is the result of mis-transliteration by early colonials.

Old Phalatswe Church Ruin

If you have a car you can visit the site of the Old Phalatswe Church. It stands at the former Ngwato capital of Phalatswe, at the foot of the Tswapong Hills near present-day Malaka, 20 km east of Palapye. The simple Gothic church, now in ruins, was completed in 1892 at a cost of P3000, funded by the people themselves. If you explore around the area, you may find the remaining poles of King Khama's kgotla and stone remnants of other early Phalatswe buildings. Of course, Botswanan law requires that everything be left intact.

Places to Stay & Eat

Palapye has two hotels. The upmarket *Cresta Botsalo* (☎ 420245) on the Gaborone-Francistown road, complete with swimming pool, is used primarily by drivers on the long and uninteresting trip between the country's two largest cities. Its dining room is probably the best restaurant in town and the hotel bar is predictably popular.

The *Palapye Hotel* (☎ 420277) is right in town, five km off the highway. It's looking very tatty around the edges these days but singles/doubles still cost P60/70 with shared facilities. Expect sustenance but a limited menu at the hotel restaurant. If you're headed south, it would be preferable to drive on to Mahalapye where the inexpensive hotel is a much nicer option.

Getting There & Away

Buses along the main Gaborone-Francistown road pass through Palapye, as does the railway line; the train arrives in the wee hours in either direction.

MAHALAPYE

Although it's nothing to look at, Mahalapye is actually one of Botswana's nicer small towns, with a friendly demeanour and a shabby but relaxed appearance. With good reason, Mahalapye is frequently confused with Palapye, 69 km to the north. The original name, Mhalatswe, was probably derived from the Sekgalagadi word for 'a large herd of impala'. Since Mahalapye primarily serves as a refuelling stop for both vehicles and travellers, there are lots of petrol stations, shops and takeaways.

Places to Stay & Eat

To reach the *Mahalapye Hotel* (☎ 410200), which according to the Peace Corps was formerly known as the Chase-Me-Inn, turn east at the post office, left at the roundabout and follow the road around until you see the hotel signpost, about 1.5 km further along. Single/double rooms cost P60/75 without breakfast. Camping is permitted on the site for P10 per person and a laundry service is available. A set English-style breakfast at the hotel will cost P7.80. The hotel dining room is good for other meals as well, and isn't too expensive.

Most travellers stop at *Kaytee's*, which arguably serves up the best fare anywhere along the highway, at the southern entrance to town. Not far off is *Theo's Fried Chicken & Takeaways*. For its size, Mahalapye has a surprisingly well-stocked supermarket with an array of imported grocery items.

Entertainment

At Madiba, four km west of Mahalapye, is a marginal disco that for some unfathomable reason operates only on Thursdays. On Fridays the Railway Club offers a cinema in town, but guests must be invited by a club member. It was started by Zimbabwe Railway employees when Zimbabwe ran the railway. If you're interested, membership in the Railway Club, which includes access to the cinema as well as the basketball, tennis and squash courts, the swimming pool, ping-pong tables and the cheapest bar in Mahalapye, costs P60 per family per year!

Getting There & Away

Getting to and from Mahalapye is the same as for Palapye, but with more frequent buses running between the former and Gaborone.

SEROWE

With a population of around 60,000, sprawling Serowe, the Ngwato capital, is generally considered sub-Saharan Africa's largest village. It is the capital of Botswana's largest political district, the Central District, and has served as the Ngwato capital since King Khama III moved it from Phalatswe in 1902. Serowe, like Mochudi, is historically one of Botswana's most interesting villages. So taken was writer Bessie Head, a South African immigrant, that she immortalised it in her classic treatise *Serowe – Village of the Rain Wind* and used it as the setting for several other works.

History

In 1948, Seretse Khama, nephew of Tshekedi Khama and heir to the Ngwato throne, met and married an Englishwoman, Ruth Williams, while studying law in London. As a royal, Seretse was expected to take a wife from a Tswana royal family. Indignant at such a breach of tribal custom, Tshekedi Khama had his nephew stripped of his inheritance; and the Whites in the protectorate government were also unhappy. He was exiled from Serowe by the Ngwato government and from the protectorate by the British, who assured him that he'd be better off remaining in London than in Bechuanaland.

It wasn't until 1956, when he renounced his rights to the Ngwato throne, that he was permitted to return to Serowe with Ruth and take up residence. There they began campaigning for Botswana's independence, which came 10 years later. As a result, Seretse Khama was knighted and became the country's first president, a post which he held until his death 14 years later.

For a thorough treatment of this amazing saga, which reads like a well-conceived novel, check out the new account, *A Marriage of Inconvenience: The Persecution of*

Seretse and Ruth Khama by Michael Dutfield. For details, refer to the section on Books in the Botswana Facts for the Visitor chapter.

Khama III Memorial Museum

Over (or around) the mountain from The Mall is the Khama III Memorial Museum. It was opened in October 1985 after a concerted effort by local citizens, including Leapeetswe Khama, who donated his home, the Red House, for the museum premises.

The museum contains the history of the Khama family both in and away from Serowe, including personal effects of Khama III and his descendants as well as artefacts outlining the history of Serowe. There is also a growing natural history display, including a large collection of African insects and a display on snakes of the region.

Cemetery

Atop Thathaganyana Hill in the village centre are the ruins of an 11th century village, evidence of habitation long before the arrival of the Ngwato and the Khama dynasty in 1902. The royal graves lie atop the hill overlooking the kgotla, with the grave of Khama III marked by a bronze duiker, the Ngwato totem.

Woodcarvings

Produced at Marulamans in the outskirts of Serowe, the uniquely intricate Serowe woodcarving is easily recognisable. If you just want to have a look at it, the Serowe Woodcarvers outlet is near the Cash Bazaar in The Mall. The workshop is an unfortunately complicated trip from the centre and will take a little more effort. For

directions, enquire at the Roman Catholic mission, which sponsors the artists.

Places to Stay & Eat

The friendly *Tshwaragano Hotel* (☎ 430377) which sits on the hillside overlooking the Mall has single/double/triple rooms for P50/60/90. In a pinch, you may be able to persuade the proprietors to allow you to camp on the grounds, but finding a flat space large enough for a tent may prove problematic. The nice little hotel restaurant serves basic meals for P5 to P8. You'll also find good cheap beer and a good view.

The *Serowe Hotel* (☎ 430234) on the Palapye side of town charges P60 a single and P75 a double. An English breakfast in the restaurant costs P7.80 while continental costs only P3.75.

The action spot in Serowe is *Chick's*, a restaurant, disco and bar that often offers live music.

Getting There & Away

Getting to Serowe on public transport first entails getting to Palapye, then catching one of the several daily buses for the remaining 46 km into the village. Some of the buses continue on to Orapa while others just return to Palapye. Hitching the route from Palapye is fairly straightforward since there's a fair amount of traffic to and from the Orapa diamond mine further up the road.

If you're driving and are tempted to try the shortcut to Maun via Orapa and Rakops, be warned that the road effectively ends at Rakops and 4WD is necessary for the very rugged trip through to the Nata-Maun road. It isn't at all feasible to try hitching this way.

North-Eastern Botswana

Because it has the bulk of Botswana's national parks and game reserves, north-eastern Botswana holds a strong appeal for visitors. Although Nxai Pan and Makgadikgadi Pans offer an almost pristine vision of Africa, access is difficult and facilities are absent, leaving Chobe National Park as the major draw. Indeed, many of Botswana's visitors get their only taste of the country on a one or two-day foray to the Chobe riverfront from nearby Victoria Falls in Zimbabwe.

The Pans

NATA

Dusty Nata is an obligatory refuelling stop for anyone travelling between Kasane, Francistown and Maun. If you're counting km, Nata is 180 smooth km to Francistown, 280 km to Kasane, and a rough and dusty 304 km to Maun. Many travellers find themselves hitching through here en route between Francistown and Maun or Kasane; most wind up at the Nata Lodge, which offers inexpensive camping options.

Organised Tours

If you have a group of four to 10 people, Nata Lodge does organised trips to the edge of Sua Pan and runs custom safaris onto the salt, to the game reserves at Makgadikgadi or Nxai Pan, and even as far afield as Chobe and the Okavango.

Places to Stay & Eat

All the action in Nata centres on the *Sua Pan Lodge* with its fuel pumps, water tap, bar, restaurant, hotel, swimming pool (albeit dust-corrupted) and camping ground. Single/double rondavels cost P50/70 while camping is P6 per person. The camp site, at the intersection of the Kasane, Maun and Francistown roads, is dusty and noisy since the public bar is less than 50 metres from the camp.

Friendly *Nata Lodge* (☎ 611210), complete with a camping ground, an excellent and affordable restaurant, an outdoor bar and swimming pool, is normally a welcome sight for travellers. Three-bed chalets cost P100 and extra beds are P10 each. Preset four-bed tents with bedding included cost P70 each – a good deal if you have a group. Camping in your own tent or caravan costs P8 per adult and P4 per child, including use of the pool. Hitching is easy both ways between the lodge and town.

Getting There & Away

All the buses travelling between Kasane, Francistown and Maun pass through Nata. Since the petrol station at the Sua Pan Lodge is a natural stop for everyone travelling through Nata, it's the best place to wait for a lift. It is also not too difficult to arrange lifts around the bar at Nata Lodge.

MAKGADIKGADI PANS

Covering more than 12,000 sq km, Botswana's great salt pans, Sua (or Sowa) and Ntwetwe, collectively comprise the Makgadikgadi Pans. They shouldn't be confused, however, with the grassy game reserve of the same name which encompasses only small a corner of Ntwetwe Pan. It was here that Tim Liversedge made his award-winning film *The Flame Birds of Makgadikgadi*.

The pans are the residue of a great lake which once covered much of northern Botswana, fed by rivers carrying salts leached from the lake's catchment. Less than 10,000 years ago, climatic changes caused the lake to evaporate, leaving the salt deposits. When there's water in the pans, millions of flamingos, pelicans, ducks, geese and other water birds arrive to build their nests along the shorelines, feeding on the

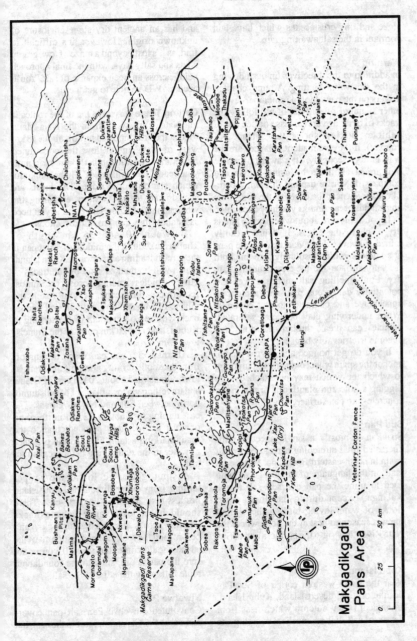

Makgadikgadi
Pans Area

0   25   50 km

algae and tiny crustaceans which have lain dormant in the salt awaiting rain.

Warning

In addition to the directives on bush driving in the Botswana Getting Around chapter, drivers on the pans should remember several other standard rules. First of all, follow the tracks of other drivers (unless you see bits of vehicles poking above the surface, of course!). If they've made it, chances are the way is dry. Secondly, stay aware of where you are at all times by using a map and compass. If you're driving through a complicated area near the edges of the pans, note any islands or landmarks you may encounter.

If you're unsure about whether the pan is dry, stick to the edges. If it has recently rained, however, don't venture onto the pans at all unless you're absolutely sure that both the salty surface and the clay beneath it are dry. Foul-smelling salt means a wet and potentially dangerous pan, very similar in appearance and character to wet concrete. When underlying clay becomes saturated, vehicles can break through the crust and become irretrievably bogged.

If you do get bogged and have a winch, anchor the spare wheel or the jack – anything to which the winch may be attached – by digging a hole and planting it firmly in the concrete-like pan surface.

Sua Pan

Sua Pan is mostly a single sheet of salt-encrusted mud stretching across the lowest basin in north-eastern Botswana. *Sua* means 'salt' in the language of the local San, who used to mine the pan and sell salt to the Kalanga. Except during the driest years, flocks of water-loving birds gather during the wet season to nest at the delta where the Nata River flows into the northern end of Sua Pan.

Kubu Island

Near the south-western corner of Sua Pan lies the original desert island, Kubu Island, an ancient rocky outcrop which rises from the sea of salt. It is an excellent camping site and has an ancient dry stone enclosure of unknown origin. However, it's difficult to find, as it's lost beyond a maze of low, grassy islets and salty bays, with the final approach being across an open expanse of salt. You'll need a 4WD vehicle to get there.

Getting There & Away One of the routes is via Nata. Turn south from the Nata-Maun road at the unsignposted turnoff about 18 km west of Nata and follow the convoluted tracks in a general southerly direction until you reach the village of Thabatshukudu, which sits on a low ridge. The locals are accustomed to lost visitors enquiring the whereabouts of Kubu Island, so if you need assistance, they can provide directions.

Between 30 and 35 km south of Thabatshukudu in the middle of a flat pan is the turnoff leading east towards Kubu Island, which will be marked only by the tracks of other vehicles leading across the almost featureless landscape. If you reach the village of Mmatshumo, turn around and go back; you're 26 km south of the turning to Kubu Island and 20 km north of the Francistown-Orapa road.

Alternatively, you can reach the turnoff from the south, turning north off the Francistown-Orapa road about 20 km east of Orapa, and travelling via the village of Mmatshumo, north between Sua and Ntwetwe pans. The east turning to Kubu is 12 km north of an obvious line of trees perpendicular to the road, marking a fault line and the presence of water in the underlying geological structure.

Assuming you've found the proper turning from either direction, Kubu Island lies less than 20 km to the north-east. There should be at least vague vehicle tracks leading across the grassy tussocks, and before long the rocky 20 metre summit of the island should come into view. If you're not sure the pan is dry, stick to the roundabout route following the edge of the salt.

Ntwetwe Pan

Convoluted Ntwetwe Pan salt pan covers more area than its counterpart to the east, but since the waters of the Boteti River which once fed it have been diverted at Mopipi Dam to provide water for the Orapa diamond mine, it's almost permanently dry.

The western shore of Ntwetwe Pan is probably the most interesting landscape in the Makgadikgadi area, with mazes of rocky outcrops, dunes, islets, channels and spits.

Getting There & Away

Of the two big pans, Sua Pan is the more accessible, but unless you're on an organised tour you'll need a 4WD vehicle, a lot of common sense, and confidence in your driving and directional skills (aided by a good map and compass, naturally!) to explore it at length. Drive only in the tracks of vehicles that have gone before and stay near the edges of the pan.

There's no problem camping anywhere around the edges of the salt, but carry food, fuel and all the water and other supplies you'll be needing.

Nata Lodge, 10 km south-east of Nata, arranges custom mobile safaris into the pan. They're not cheap, but you will save the considerable time and expense of arranging equipment for a private expedition. Alternatively, you can join one of the lodge's trips to the edge of Sua Pan for P30 per person (minimum of four people).

Car & Motorbike Although the pan area is crisscrossed with mazes of tracks, they are changeable and unreliable, so local advice should always be sought before venturing into remote areas. Three north-south networks of tracks connect the Nata-Maun road with the Francistown-Orapa road, one on either side of the pans and one down the strip between them (which passes within striking distance of Kubu Island). Any of these routes, however, amounts more to an expedition than a casual drive.

During the dry season there are several places where you can approach Sua Pan for a cursory look without 4WD. The easiest and quickest access is an unmarked turnoff just 18 km south-east of Nata along the Francistown road. Once you've passed Nata Lodge,

count off eight km. On the right (south) side of the road, opposite a radio tower, there's gate, an anthill and a large baobab beyond. Pass through the gate and drive eight more km along the white sand track over featureless grassland to the edge of Sua Pan.

Another access route is via the signposted turnoff to Sua Spit, about a 10 minute drive north of the Dukwe buffalo fence. The spit, a long slender protrusion extending into the heart of Sua Pan, is the nexus of Botswana's nascent soda ash industry. Security measures will prevent public access to the plant once it's in operation but private vehicles should still be permitted at least as far as Sua, which sits at the pan's edge.

Hitching The best way to get a lift to the pan is to ask around Nata Lodge to see who's going, or just hitch to the gate near the radio tower mentioned previously and wait for someone going in. It's worth it!

GWETA

Gweta is about 100 km west of Nata. The main attraction in the picturesque village is the Gweta Rest Camp, which provides an affordable respite along the dusty trek between Nata and Maun. The rest camp bar with its popular dartboard is the focus of activity – a beer is only P1.50 and a serve of fish & chips is P5.50. Camping costs only P7.50 per person; a thatched rondavel costs P50 a double.

At last notice, fuel was not available at Gweta.

MAKGADIKGADI PANS GAME RESERVE

West of Gweta, the road follows the northern boundary of Makgadikgadi Pans Game Reserve, a 3900 sq km tract of pans, grasslands and savanna country.

Because they are complementary as far as game migrations are concerned, Makgadikgadi Pans and nearby Nxai Pan were simultaneously set aside as parks and reserves in the early 1970s. Since the park is unfenced, animals can wander in and out at will.

During the winter dry season, game concentrates around the Boteti River, but between February and April herds of zebras and wildebeests migrate north to Nxai Pan, returning to the Boteti with the end of the rains in early May.

Places to Stay

At the *Game Scout Camp* near Xhumaga, on the park's western boundary, there's a public camping site with a loo and a sometimes operable cold shower. Drinking water is available but it's quite sulphurous. For these amenities you'll pay P20 per person per day, but the setting is so pristine it's almost worth it until you consider that they'll also want P50 per person per day park fees and an additional P5 for the vehicle. Wild camping is prohibited in the park. Many people do anyway, but if you're discovered by a game scout, penalties are stiff.

Getting There & Away

To visit the park, 4WD is necessary. The easiest access is via the well-worn turnoff south from the Nata-Maun road, about eight km east of Phuduhudu. From that point it's a beautiful 30 km trip through deep sands, stands of palms and vast grassy savanna to the Game Scout Camp on the Boteti where you pay the park fees.

NXAI PAN NATIONAL PARK

Nxai Pan National Park, covering 2100 sq km, is one of the few places in Botswana which are more interesting in the rainy season than during the dry. Although your movements may be restricted by flooding in some of the pans, February to April is the best season to see large herds of wildebeests, zebras and gemsboks in Nxai's grassy pans. Nxai Pan itself is part of the same ancient lake bed as Sua and Ntwetwe Pans, but because it's not so low it escaped deep encrustations of leached salts when the lake evaporated. Visitors to Nxai Pan are subject to the usual P50 per person per day and P5 per vehicle, payable at the Game Scout Camp gate near the park's southern entrance.

Places to Stay

Apart from the two public camping sites, there are no facilities at Nxai Pan National Park and visitors must be self-sufficient. The camping site east of *Game Scout Camp* has toilets, and most of the time water is available. Both sites are 10 km from the Game Scout Camp where the P20 per person camping fees must be paid.

An alternative (and free) camping site is at Baines' Baobabs outside the park, but ablutions are not available (see description under Baines' Baobabs).

Getting There & Away

As with Makgadikgadi, you'll need a 4WD vehicle to visit Nxai Pan. Turn north from the Nata-Maun road 170 km west of Francistown and continue along that track for about 35 km to the Game Scout Camp at the edge of Nxai Pan. There's one public camping site 10 km across the pan (which may be inaccessible during the wet) and another 10 km east. From the eastern camp it's a further 15 km to the eastern pan complex, also rich in game, and another nine km to the southern end of Kgama-Kgama Pan where King Khama III of the Ngwato once had a cattle post.

Without your own vehicle, access is either extremely expensive or nigh impossible. Customised mobile safaris into Nxai Pan and Baines' Baobabs can be arranged through travel agencies in Maun, but prices are steep. Otherwise, you're probably out of luck unless you can find that golden lift that seems to pervade Botswanan hitchhikers' dreams.

BAINES' BAOBABS

Originally known as the Sleeping Sisters, this hardy clump of large baobabs was immortalised by artist and adventurer Thomas Baines on 22 May 1862, when he painted them for posterity.

There's nothing out of the ordinary about this stately group of trees, but when the pan contains water they stand out from their surroundings. Bush camping is possible at the baobabs but there are no facilities.

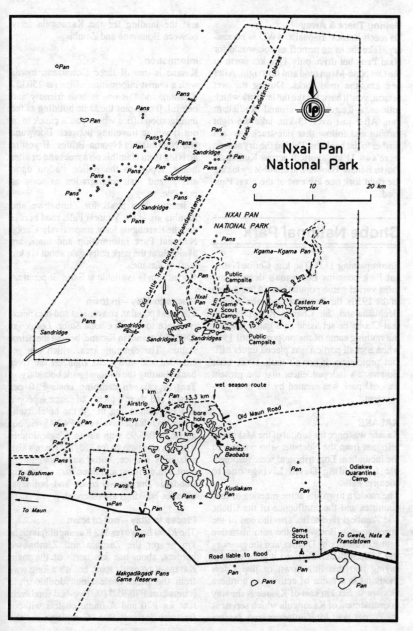

Getting There & Away

To reach Baines' Baobabs, 4WD is necessary. Take the same turnoff as you would for Nxai Pans but drive only 17.4 km north to the Old Nata-Maun road and turn right. After one km, the road forks. During the wet season, you'll have to take the left fork which follows a longer route around Kudiakam Pan. After just over 13 km, take the right turning and follow that side track five km further to the baobabs. During the dry season there's an 11 km shortcut across Kudiakam Pan to Baines' Baobabs, accessible by taking the right fork one km east of the Nxai Pans road.

Chobe National Park

Encompassing 11,000 sq km, Chobe National Park contains Botswana's densest and most varied game populations. After a visit in the 1930s, the Resident Commissioner of Bechuanaland, Sir Charles Rey, proposed that Chobe be set aside as a game reserve, but nothing came of the proposal until 1960 when a small portion was placed under official protection. It wasn't until 1968, after Botswana's independence, that the present national park was created by the new government.

KASANE

Kasane was once the capital of the Makololo, refugees from the Ndebele, who conquered the incumbent Lozi tribe and were responsible for guiding David Livingstone to Victoria Falls.

The modern town sits at the meeting of four countries and the confluence of the Chobe and Zambezi rivers. It's also the end of the tarred road in Botswana, the administrative centre of the Chobe District, and the gateway to Chobe National Park, so it goes without saying that this little town of just a few thousand is a focus of activity in northern Botswana. Six km east of Kasane is the tiny nonsettlement of Kazungula which serves as the border post for Zimbabwe and Zambia

and the landing for the Kazungula ferry between Botswana and Zambia.

Information

Kasane is one of three Botswanan towns with a tourist information office (☎ 250327 Kasane), and this one is both friendly and helpful. It occupies the same building as the immigration office where you'll check in or out if you're travelling between Botswana and Namibia via Ngoma Bridge. If you're arriving from Namibia on a weekend or after hours, report to the police station upon arrival and visit immigration as soon as possible.

Immigration posts for Zimbabwe and Zambia are at the Victoria Falls road border and the Kazungula ferry, respectively. Chobe National Park information and maps are available at the park entry gate about six km west of Kasane.

Kodak film is available at Saras Superette.

Places to Stay – in town

The most popular, convenient and inexpensive place to stay is *Chobe Safari Lodge* (☎ 250336 Kasane) in Kasane, behind the petrol station. The camping area, which can get crowded and noisy, sits right on the river bank abutting the national park boundary. Tent or caravan camping costs P10 per person and there's plenty of space – people just keep squeezing in. At the hotel itself, single/double rondavels cost P40/45 without a bath or P85/95 with a bath. Single/double rooms with a bath go for P65/75. There's also a laundry service, bottle store, swimming pool, dining room and three bars of varying standard. During weekends and holidays, advance bookings are essential.

Places to Stay – out of town

The *Kubu Lodge* (☎ 312 Kazungula) is eight km nearer the Zambia and Zimbabwe borders, about one km north of the main Kasane-Kazungula road, but it's a long way from the park. Basic single/double/triple rooms cost P70/95/120. Two-bed rondavels rent for P70 and A-frame chalets without facilities for just P25. Camping near the

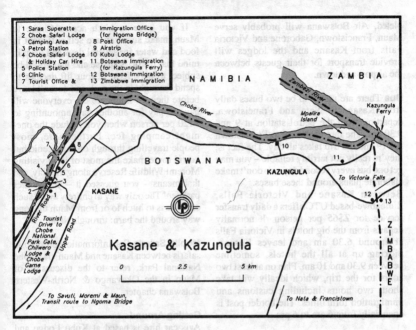

1 Saras Superette
2 Chobe Safari Lodge
  Camping Area
3 Petrol Station
4 Chobe Safari Lodge
  & Holiday Car Hire
5 Police Station
6 Clinic
7 Tourist Office &

Immigration Office
  (for Ngoma Bridge)
8 Post Office
9 Airstrip
10 Kubu Lodge
11 Botswana Immigration
   (for Kazungula Ferry)
12 Botswana Immigration
13 Zimbabwe Immigration

Kasane & Kazungula

0   2.5   5 km

riverbank in less appealing surroundings than at Chobe Safari Lodge costs P10 per person.

A more upmarket option is the semi-luxurious *Chobe Chilwero Lodge* (☎ 250234 Kasane) which sits on the hill about three km from the Chobe entrance gate. Its thatched bungalow accommodation affords a fantastic view over the park and the river. Singles/doubles cost P265/450 including meals, game drives and river trips.

Another option, albeit an expensive one, is the *Chobe Game Lodge*, which is described in the Chobe Riverfront part of the this section.

Places to Eat

A buffet English breakfast at *Chobe Safari Lodge* costs P12 per person. Lunches and dinners cost P16 and P22 respectively for quite good fare. They sometimes offer bream, but otherwise the menu is nothing out of the ordinary.

At *Kubu Lodge* the full buffet breakfast costs P12 while an average dinner is around P22.

For self-catering you're pretty much limited to *Saras Superette*, diagonally opposite the petrol station. It has a good variety of freeze-dried food and packaged groceries for trips into Chobe National Park and beyond. Between Kasane and Maun there are only sparsely stocked bush shops and well-stocked bottle stores, so if you're travelling on you may want to stock up here.

Getting There & Away

Air Northern Air and Air Chobe currently do charter flights between Kasane and Maun as well as other northern Botswana destinations from the small airstrip in Kasane, but there is no scheduled air service. Single-engine five-passenger planes charter for P1.70 per km but you'll have to pay for the plane to return to base, hence double the mileage.

If the proposed airport project is ever completed, Air Botswana will probably serve Maun, Francistown, Gaborone and Victoria Falls from Kasane and the lodges will provide transport for their guests between the airport and town.

Bus There are meant to be two buses daily from Kasane to Nata and Francistown, departing from the petrol station at 9 and 9.30 am. The fare each way to Francistown is P19 and the trip takes all day. The fact is, they're really not terribly reliable – you may get one bus every second day – so don't make elaborate plans around these buses.

Between Kasane and Victoria Falls, Zimbabwe-based UTC offers a daily transfer service for Z$65 per person. It normally departs from the big hotels in Victoria Falls at around 6.30 am and leaves Kasane, picking up at all the hotels, sometime between 9.30 and 10 am. Plan on at least two hours for the trip, which ideally will take about two hours including customs and immigration formalities. The border post is open daily from 6 am to 6 pm.

Road The Kazungula ferry across the Zambezi to Zambia operates from 6 am to 6 pm, but if you're driving, arrive early to queue up at the border post for the free trip.

See the Botswana Getting There & Away chapter for more information on this ferry.

Hitching Hitching will normally prove more convenient than the bus for reaching Nata or Francistown. In the morning, when most people are starting out, hitchhikers have lots of company at the intersection of the Kasane-Kazungula road and the Kasane-Francistown road. You can sometimes increase your chances of a lift by hanging around the petrol station and chatting with drivers as they fill the tank. For lifts into Chobe or to Ngoma Bridge, routes on which there are no buses operating, this normally proves relatively fruitful. If you're heading for Ngoma Bridge, ascertain whether your driver intends to travel via the transit route or the riverfront tourist drives. For the latter, you'll have to pay park fees.

If you hope to hitch across Chobe to Maun, make sure you are self-sufficient in food and water for several days and keep in mind that traffic is sparse and that you'll be subject to park fees. If your lift decides to spend the night in the park and doesn't leave before their 24 hours are up, everyone will have to pay for another day, amounting to P120 per person when you include the one-night camping fee. Furthermore, most people travelling through on this scenic but horrid route make the most of it by visiting Moremi Wildlife Reserve along the way, and that means – you guessed it – yet another park fee! The only way to entirely avoid such expense is to hitch to or from Maun the long way around the barn: through Nata!

Mobile Safaris For information on mobile safaris between Kasane and Maun via Chobe National Park, refer to the discussion of Maun in the Okavango & North-Western Botswana chapter.

Getting Around
Avis car hire is based at Kubu Lodge and Holiday is at Chobe Safari Lodge. For approximate rates, refer to the Botswana Getting Around chapter.

Go Wild Safaris, operated by Denis Vanessen at Chobe Safari Lodge, does expensive transfers to Savuti and occasionally to or from Maun. With a group, this is a logical way to go and you'll qualify for the P30 park fee. Chobe Game Lodge, Kubu Lodge and Chobe Safari Lodge offer transfers to and from Serondella Camp for P15 per person, but if you're camping at Serondella you'll still have to pay the P50 park fee and P20 for camping.

For information on getting around in the park, see River Trips and Game Drives in the next section.

CHOBE RIVERFRONT
Unless you're a Botswanan resident or have a bit of money, a trip to Chobe will probably mean a quick pass through along the riverfront. While organised river trips and game drives are reasonably priced, park fees must

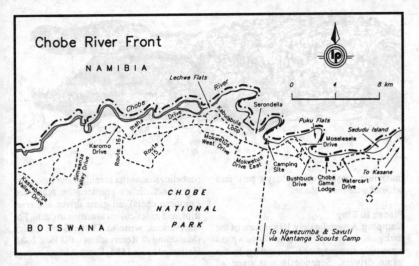

be added for each day or partial day spent in the park. Most visitors therefore join an organised river trip and game drive, qualifying them for the one-day reduced park fee of P30 per person, and try to make the most of the experience in the time available.

The Chobe riverfront is the part of the park most densely packed with game, particularly elephants. An estimated 73,000 elephants inhabit Chobe National Park and herds of up to 500 individuals have been wreaking havoc along the river, as evinced by decimated bush.

River Trips

One way to enjoy the riverfront is to take one of the river trips offered by lodges in the Kasane area, but since the majority enter the park you'll have to pay the fees as well as the price of the cruises. The best time to go is in the late afternoon, when the hippos amble onto dry land and the riverfront fills with elephants heading down for a drink and a romp in the water.

Chobe Safari Lodge offers a three-hour afternoon 'booze cruise' up the river on the multi-level boat *Fish Eagle*. Lodge guests (including campers) pay P15 per person while others pay P20. The lodge also hires out small outboard-powered fishing boats for P35 per hour, including driver and fuel.

The Chobe Game Lodge offers an afternoon cruise on the *Mosi-oa-Tunya*, a pretty good replica of the *African Queen*, for P28 per person. During the day, the game lodge operates small motorboat tours of the river whenever anyone turns up ready to go. Those who are not staying at the lodge pay P30 per person for the two-hour trip. The small boats are preferable to the larger because the trips are individualised and they can move in closer to the animals without alarming or endangering them.

Game Drives

Morning and evening game drives from Chobe Safari Lodge, Kubu Lodge and Chobe Game Lodge ply the riverfront routes beginning at 6.15 am and 4 pm. Both are worthwhile, but if you can only pay one day's park fees and want to take a booze cruise as well, you'll be limited to the morning game drive. Those who want to do both game drives can opt for a small boat trip at midday instead of the booze cruise, the

Crocodile

maximum possible on one day's park fees without your own vehicle.

Places to Stay

Camping Approximately 10 km west of the park gate, *Serondella Camp* is Chobe's most accessible camping site. According to the game drivers, Serondella was once an inhabited village which was uprooted and shifted to Kasane when Chobe became a national park.

Camping at Serondella costs P20 per person, but although it's a lovely spot with toilets and cold water showers and has incredible close-up game-viewing opportunities, don't plan on a lot of sleep with all the animal noises that will be going on outside.

Transfers to Serondella are available from Kasane for P15 per person in conjunction with the morning or afternoon game drives and you can ask to be picked up the following day. Since this doesn't constitute an organised tour, however, foreigners still have to pay the P50 park fees.

Lodges Botswana's most expensive accommodation is at the tasteful *Chobe Game Lodge* (☎ 250340 Kasane), just inside the national park boundary overlooking the Chobe River. Richard Burton and Elizabeth Taylor spent one of their honeymoons in a plush suite, complete with a private swimming pool, which now rents for P1080 per night. More realistic accommodation costs P500/880 for singles/doubles but that includes park fees, three meals per day

(unbelievable buffet breakfast and lunch and a gourmet dinner prepared by renowned European chefs), all game drives and river trips, and a meticulous attention to detail. For reservations, write to Chobe Game Lodge (Marketing & Reservations), PO Box 2602, Halfway House 1685, South Africa.

Getting There & Away

Northern Entrance The northern entrance of the park lies eight km west of Kasane and is accessible with conventional vehicles. To approach from Maun or proceed across the park, visitors will need a high-clearance 4WD vehicle. Due to high water, Savuti is normally closed (and inaccessible anyway) between January and March.

Transit Route Driving or hitching the transit route across Chobe National Park to Ngoma Bridge on the Namibian border won't cost anything, but it shouldn't be considered a cheap way of seeing the park. The scenery is decidedly uninteresting along this wide, straight thoroughfare and what little game there is will be hidden by trees. Your best chances of finding a lift to Ngoma Bridge are from the petrol station in Kasane or somewhere along the transit road, a two km walk (via the shortcut) from Chobe Safari Lodge.

SAVUTI & THE MABABE DEPRESSION

The Mababe Depression, like the Makgadikgadi Pans and Nxai Pan, is actually a remnant of the large lake that once covered much of northern Botswana. It takes

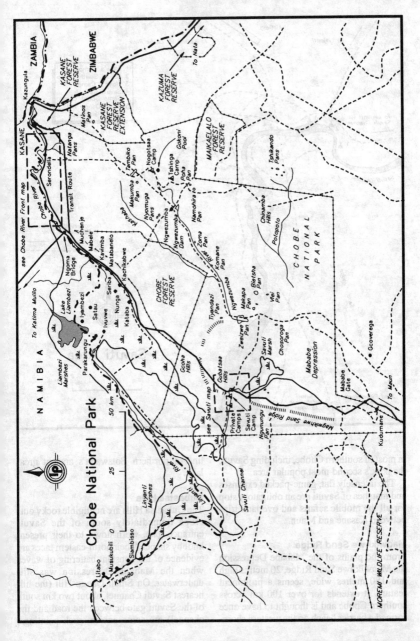

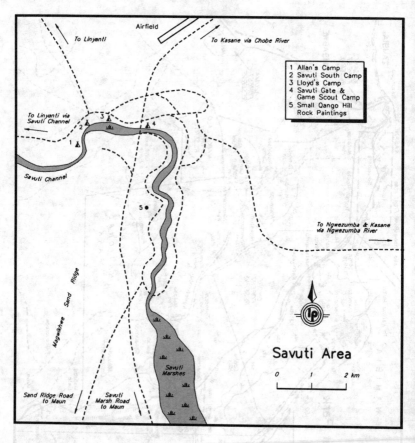

Savuti Area

0   1   2 km

1 Allan's Camp
2 Savuti South Camp
3 Lloyd's Camp
4 Savuti Gate &
   Game Scout Camp
5 Small Qango Hill
   Rock Paintings

in most of southern Chobe, including Savuti, the park's second most popular area.

The intensely flat, game-packed expanses and marshes of Savuti are an obligatory stop for all the mobile safaris and overland trips between Kasane and Maun.

Magwikhwe Sand Ridge

From the plains of the Mababe Depression the Magwikhwe Sand Ridge, 20 metres high and 180 metres wide, seems a prominent feature. It extends for over 100 km across southern Chobe and is thought to have once formed a barrier beach on the western shore-line of northern Botswana's ancient great lake.

Gubaatsa Hills

The Gubaatsa Hills are negligible rocky outcrops immediately south of the Savuti entrance gate, worn down to their present knobby shapes. Their north-eastern faces are evidence of the constant battering of waves when the Mababe Depression was still underwater. On Small Qango Hill (the hill nearest Savuti Channel, about two km south of the Savuti gate between the road and the channel) are some ancient rock paintings, probably of San origin. They're accessible by a short walk from the road. Some of the paintings are on the north side of the hill near the base, while the best are about halfway to the summit, facing east.

Places to Stay

Camping Sites Like all national park camps in Botswana, the Savuti public camping site on the Savuti Channel costs P20 per person per night. Drinking and washing water is available and there are toilets and cold showers. Book in at the Savuti entry gate just south-east of the camping area.

Private Camps About one km north-west of the public camping site are three private camps, all of which must be booked in advance. All-inclusive accommodation, including meals and game drives, costs around P250 per person per day.

The most interesting is *Lloyd's Camp* (☎ 260351 Maun), PO Box 37, Maun. Lloyd emphasises that his camp must not be considered 'luxury accommodation', but it seems pretty upmarket nevertheless. Expect lots of wildlife.

Nearby is *Allan's Camp* (☎ 312431), c/o Gametrackers, Private Bag 0077, Gaborone, very much a Botswana 'insiders' venue with accommodation in thatched A-frame chalets. Its less xenophobic neighbour, *Savuti South* (☎ 260302 Maun), may be booked through Gametrackers, PO Box 100, Maun.

Getting There & Away

Under optimum conditions you'll need four hours to drive between the riverfront park gate and Savuti via either of the two routes. The more travelled route leads out of the national park south of Ngoma Bridge, skirting a broad marshy area south of the Chobe-Linyanti river system and passing through the Chobe Forest Reserve before re-entering the park and continuing on to Savuti. This way is rough, much of it through deep sand. Except in the immediate area of Savuti and through the small villages above the river flats, it isn't terribly interesting. When it's dry, the less popular but more

scenic route through the Ngwezumba Pans is more easily passable to vehicles, but 4WD is necessary for either option.

The route to or from Maun is all sand, and some places, especially the southernmost extension of Chobe National Park, are exceptionally rough and slow going. There is no fuel available along the route and 4WD is essential.

NGWEZUMBA DAM & PANS

Just over halfway from Savuti to Serondella on the eastern route is the Ngwezumba area, which has an artificial dam and a series of pans set amid mopani forest. There you won't get the overwhelming numbers of animals that occur along the riverfront or at Savuti, but the geography and vegetation are different, with herds of buffalos and elephants as well as reedbucks, gemsboks and roan antelopes. There'll also be the opportunity to see the rare oribi antelope in its only Botswanan habitat.

Places to Stay

The Ngwezumba area has two public camping sites, Tshinga and Nogatsaa. If Serondella's full, you can head for *Nogatsaa Camp* which is only 70 (albeit somewhat rough) km away. This pleasant and secluded camp has cold showers and toilets and there's a game hide overlooking the dam.

After 22 more km you'll come to *Tshinga* (also spelt Tjinga or Tchinga). This rudimentary camp has no facilities except a water tank with an erratic pump. You'll need some mechanical expertise to get it started, so it may be wise to carry your own water. Camping costs P20 per person per night.

Getting There & Away

From either the transit road or Serondella, near the riverfront, the main route to the dam and pans runs south to Nogatsaa and past a series of pans to Ngwezumba Dam before turning west along the intermittent Ngwezumba River and making for Savuti. To reach Tshinga from Nogatsaa, take the south-east turning about five km south-west of Nogatsaa.

Okavango Delta & North-Western Botswana

Most people who've heard of Botswana have heard of the Okavango Delta. Southern Africa's third largest river, the 1300 km long Okavango rises near the village of Nova Lisboa in central Angola, flows southeastward across Namibia's Caprivi Strip, and enters Botswana near Shakawe. There the river spreads, evaporates and seeps into the Kalahari sand. Described as 'the river which never finds the sea', the Okavango disappears into a 15,000 sq km maze of lagoons, channels and islands.

Okavango Delta

Visiting the Delta

The Okavango water levels are at their lowest during the rainy season between November and March, when channels are constricted and water access to the most interesting areas is limited. In the Panhandle the flow peaks in April and May, while well-visited Chiefs Island and the Inner Delta are at optimum levels from late May to late June but are ideal for visits until late September. The Eastern Delta has the best chance of high water from late June to late July, but the increase in flow will probably be negligible this far along, especially during poor years. The best months to visit are July to September.

Before you go to the effort of reaching Maun, you have to realise that there's virtually no way to see the Okavango Delta on a shoestring. Without a lot of creative organisation, you'll have to do it through some sort of outfitter, be it a wilderness camp, travel agency, tour company or even a freelance boat owner. A bewildering number of options are available so it's a good idea to shop around before deciding on something.

The average Okavango visit will include at least some time travelling by *mokoro* (plural *mekoro*), a shallow-draught dugout canoe hewn from an ebony or sausage tree log, which accommodates up to four people (including the pilot). The mekoro are poled from a standing position rather than paddled and you'll be surprised to find that their precarious appearance belies their amazing stability.

On most mokoro trips, travellers ride for several days with the same poler, breaking the journey with walks on the palm islands and moving between established camps or wild camping along the way. The quality of the experience for all depends largely upon the skill of the poler, the meshing of personalities and the degree of enthusiasm of those being poled. In order to avoid uncomfortable situations, ask when booking a delta trip whether the poler will carry his own food or the travellers will be expected to provide his meals.

The primary tourist destinations lie within Moremi Wildlife Reserve, the region of wetland bordered on the west by Chiefs Island and on the east by the Moremi Peninsula (sometimes called Moremi Tongue). This is where the wildlife and best protected delta environments are to be found, but it's also the domain of park fees and upmarket safari camps with high prices; some of the lodges offer five-star accommodation.

Next down the scale is the Inner Delta, the area west and north of Chiefs Island, where one finds the classic delta scenery. Accommodation is available in nearly every price range, but travellers still have to arrange a plane ride to get there. Some camps are as much as an hour's flying time from Maun. Ventures into Moremi Reserve are optional. Those who'd rather not pay park fees can instruct their poler to steer clear of it. Outside the reserve there's still a bit of game and most visitors encounter at least hippos and some antelopes.

The lowest-budget destination is the Eastern Delta which is accessible by a combination of 4WD vehicle, motorboat and mokoro. There aren't yet any controls on operations here, the majority of which are run by Maun area lodges, and the polers are normally unlicensed freelancers hoping for enough experience to move up to the bigger camps. If you're truly short of cash, however, the Eastern Delta will provide some idea of what the place is about. Those opting for this route would do well to talk with travellers who've gone before and search out recommendations on operators, polers and the best areas to visit.

In the Panhandle, the final area, there are a few fishing camps strung out along the river, but they're accessible only by air or the long way around on the highway. The area is culturally interesting but the camps are aimed at the fishing crowd and don't pretend to provide a classic delta experience. These are discussed in the North-Western Botswana section.

During parts of the rainy season, particularly between January and March when tourism is especially low, some of the lodges close down. Some do stay open, however, so if you don't mind rain, heat and humidity, this time of year will provide an experience of the place with few tourists about.

MAUN

With a variety of colourful characters from all sectors of Batswana society, Maun, at the edge of the Okavango Delta, takes on a rather frontier-like aspect. Unfortunately, Maun's distinction as merely an outpost in Botswana's back of beyond promises to be short-lived. Upon completion of the tarred road from Nata, the outside world will be able to reach Maun in any vehicle. With easy accessibility will come growth as well as more tourist money and it's a safe bet that Maun will never be the same again.

The village got its start in 1915 as the capital of the Tawana tribe and is now occupied by people of numerous groups: Herero, Yei, Mbukushu and Europeans.

Orientation

Like most Botswanan towns, Maun lacks any definite centre; the town is strung out for several km along the tarred road that parallels the Thamalakane River. The only semblance of commercial concentration is the shopping area called The Mall, while the real centre of Maun is the tourism-oriented airport area.

Information

Tourist Office The tourist information office (☎ 260492 Maun), beside the Duck Inn at the airport, is open from 7.30 am to 12.30 pm and 1.45 to 4.30 pm Monday to Friday. It's next to worthless, but since you'll probably be headed into the delta anyway there shouldn't be any problems shopping around for the best prices and making enquiries at the many travel agencies in town. Similarly, the friendly Matlapaneng Lodges, particularly Island Safari Lodge, will be happy to answer your questions and provide information and advertising to point you in the right direction.

Money Branches of both Barclays Bank and Standard Chartered Bank are near the post office.

Post The post office on the tarred road near The Mall is open from 8.15 am to 1 pm and 2.15 to 4 pm on weekdays and from 8.30 to 11.30 am on Saturday.

Immigration The immigration office is behind the labour office, on the river side of the tarred road between Riley's Hotel and the airport road.

Travel Agencies & Safari Companies

Travel agencies and safari companies are Maun's mainstays and are responsible for Moremi and Inner Delta bookings. Each agency has affiliations with certain camps, however, so for information on the variety of accommodation available in the delta you'll

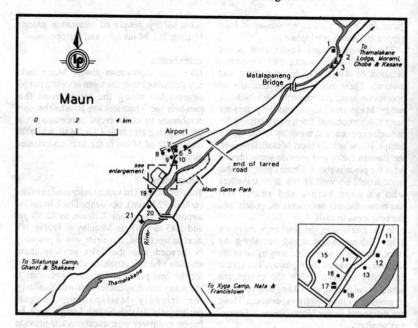

have to visit several agencies. All of the companies in the following list sell or operate trips into the delta and are referred to later in the text without addresses or telephone numbers.

Bonaventures Botswana
    PO Box 201, Maun (☎ 260502 Maun)
Crocodile Camp Safaris
    PO Box 46, Maun (☎ 260265 Maun)
Desert & Delta Safaris
    Private Bag 0010, Maun (☎ 260569 Maun)
Gametrackers
    PO Box 100, Maun (☎ 260351 Maun)
Island Safari Lodge
    PO Box 116, Maun (☎ 260300 Maun)
Ker, Downey & Selby Safaris
    PO Box 40, Maun (☎ 260211 Maun)
Merlin Services
    PO Box 13, Maun (☎ 260351 Maun)
Okavango Explorations
    Private Bag 0048, Maun (☎ 260528 Maun)
Okavango River Lodge
    PO Box 32, Maun (☎ 260298 Maun)
Okavango Tours & Safaris
    PO Box 39, Maun (☎ 260220 Maun)

Okuti Safaris
    Private Bag 0049, Maun (☎ 260307 Maun)
Riley's Hotel
    PO Box 1, Maun (☎ 260204 Maun)
Sitatunga Safaris
    PO Box 47, Maun (☎ 260307 Maun)
Thamalakane Lodge
    Private Bag 0011, Maun (no phone)
Travel Wild
    PO Box 236, Maun (☎ 260493 Maun)
Tsaro Safari
    PO Box 448, Maun (☎ 260205 Maun)

Camping Equipment Lanterns, butane cartridges and minimal camping gear are available at Northern Building Supplies on the corner of the main Maun road and the Nata road. Camping equipment can be hired from Kalahari Canvas on the main road, east of the airport road. If you're booked onto one of its safaris, Island Safari Lodge also hires tents for P7.50 and sleeping bags for P6 per night. Several of the inexpensive lodges in the delta also hire equipment on site, so if you need it make enquiries when booking.

Mobile Safaris
A number of mobile safaris operate between Maun and Kasane, travelling via Moremi Wildlife Reserve and Chobe National Park. They're not cheap, but if you've given up on hitching directly to or from Kasane and are put off by the long, rough detour through Nata, they're an option. Furthermore, they'll allow you to see Third Bridge and the Moremi Peninsula as well as the Savuti area of Chobe National Park with a minimum of effort and at the reduced park fees available to organised safari participants.

The least expensive safaris cost approximately P150 per day, with an additional P30 for each day spent in either Moremi or Chobe, and they require participants to help with cooking, washing up and erecting tents. The luxury versions will cost upwards of P350 per day, including park fees, with all the work done by camp staff.

For further information contact Okavango Tours & Safaris in Maun or, if you're coming from the north, Safari Office Services in Victoria Falls, Zimbabwe. Alternatively,

check with one of the big overland trucks which stay at Island Safari Lodge. Although most are heading the opposite direction, some do go north and if they have space you may be able to join in for minimal cost plus food and park fees.

Crocodile Camp does mobile safaris into Moremi for P275 per person per day, but if you can organise a group, the rock-bottom cheapest way to visit Moremi is with Island Safari Lodge's two night, three day trip for up to six people. It costs P500, including driver, guide, transport and two nights at Island Safari lodge on either end of the trip. Camping and park fees (P10 and P30 per person respectively) are extra and you'll have to organise your own food. This trip takes in Third Bridge and the Moremi Peninsula but doesn't visit Chiefs Island.

Department of Wildlife Game Park
The Department of Wildlife Game Park is on the eastern bank of the Thamalakane River, almost directly opposite Riley's Hotel. From the Wildlife Training Centre at the park entrance you can organise a guide to take you around. Admission is free and the rangers are quite friendly, often arranging a vehicle to take you around. There are antelopes, giraffes, zebras and other creatures. Carry lots of water.

To get there from town, cross the Thamalakane bridge on the Francistown road, turn left at the first turning east of the river and continue just over two km to the Wildlife Training Centre.

Organised Tours
Riley's Hotel operates boat tours and flightseeing air charters (nine-passenger Islanders charter for P675 per hour and five-passenger Cessnas for P470 per hour) as well as a two hour afternoon booze cruise for P30 per person with a minimum of six people. Further information on the boat tours is included in the Eastern Delta area discussion.

Places to Stay
Maun The only accommodation in Maun is

Riley's Hotel (☎ 260204 Maun). It charges like an upmarket hotel but falls well short of that mark. Single/double rooms start at P120/150 including B&B, while suites costs P140/170. On Saturday there is a braai lunch.

If you're on a tight budget and arrive in Maun too late to get out to the Matlapaneng Lodges, ask at the police station where the friendly officers will sometimes allow you to camp in their compound.

Matlapaneng Lodges The five lodges and camps known collectively as the Matlapaneng Lodges lie north-east of Maun either on or near the Chobe road; four are between nine and 11 km from Maun and the fifth is another nine km up the Chobe road. For information about delta trips originating at the Matlapaneng Lodges, refer to the Eastern Delta discussion later in this section. To reach any of the lodges you can either hitch from Maun or phone the individual lodges for the P15 per person transfer system to and from the airport.

The most popular of the lot is *Island Safari Lodge* (☎ 260300 Maun), known for its social life. It is good fun and the river view setting is nice. Camping costs P5 per night including hot showers, while the single/double chalets with B&B are P80/95 and P27.50 for each additional person. The lodge has a cinema four nights a week and there's a reasonably priced laundry service as well as a do-it-yourself washing up area. The bar and restaurant offer both snacks and meals as well as a buffet breakfast. The shop in the reception area sells film and postcards.

To get there from Maun, turn left just before the Matlapaneng Bridge and follow your nose through the plethora of tracks to the lodge, asking directions at any opportunity. If you reach an agricultural research station or don't arrive at the safari lodge within four km of the bridge, turn around, go back the way you came and try again.

The next three camps and lodges are clustered together between nine and 11 km from Maun. The nearest to town, Kubu Camp, is approximately two km beyond the Matlapaneng Bridge.

The *Okavango River Lodge* (☎ 260298 Maun), which also has a nice bar, is just across the river from the Island Safari Lodge, and the latter runs a ferry between the two. It has the nicest camping area of the lot with good riverfront sites, but beware of hippos and crocodiles which also like the setting. Backpackers pay P3.50 per person to camp but those with vehicles are charged P5. Single/double chalet accommodation including B&B costs P77/88.

The cheapest and friendliest place to stay is *Kubu Camp* (☎ 260307 Maun), where you can camp for P2 per night near a less-than-lovely stretch of river bank. They're currently building chalets which promise to be fairly nice, but until then you'll be camping in a sand trap surrounded by a veritable junk yard.

Beside Okavango River Lodge is *Crocodile Camp* (☎ 260265 Maun) started by the crocodile hunter Bobby Wilmot. It has the least appealing camping site of the lot inside a claustrophobic fenced enclosure far from the river. Camping costs P5 per person while the more pleasant chalets, probably the quietest of the Matlapaneng Lodges save Thamalakane, cost P65/75 for singles/doubles.

The *Thamalakane Lodge* (☎ 260307 Maun), 20 km from Maun, enjoys a great remote setting with lots of hippos and a beautiful stretch of river at its doorstep. The P5 per person camping site is marginal but the chalets, which cost P75/85 for singles/doubles, are quite nice. The owners commute into town frequently, so if you're looking for a lift out, check with Okavango Tours & Safaris or ask around at the Duck Inn.

Other Lodges One of the nicest camps in the vicinity of Maun is *Xyga Camp*, 35 km east of town along the Nata road. Chalets cost P45 and camping along a lovely papyrus-filled stretch of the Boteti River costs P5 per person. Boat hire for fishing or exploring the river is P20/100 per hour/day.

South-west along the rough road toward Toteng and the Panhandle, 14 km from

Maun, is the spartan and charming *Sitatunga Camp* (☎ 260307 Maun). The secluded camping area costs P6 per person, chalets cost P50 double. There's a small restaurant as well, if you're not keen on the rough trip back into Maun for meals. Sitatunga Camp is adjacent to its well-signposted Crocodile Farm.

Places to Eat

Hotels Apart from *Riley's Hotel* dining room, the only real restaurant in Maun is the local watering hole, *Duck Inn*, which has a standard menu of chicken and beef dishes, curries, salads (including a wonderful Greek salad) and various snacks. The relaxed atmosphere and thatched veranda make it a nice place to spend an afternoon.

The *Island Safari Lodge* at Matlapaneng serves pizza, chicken & chips, meat pies and other inexpensive snacks at the bar, while their dining room offers full meals. Lunches and dinners will cost P15 to P20 while the breakfast is P11. *Crocodile Camp* charges P12 for an English breakfast and P12/30 for lunch and dinner respectively.

At *Thamalakane Lodge*, breakfast is P10, lunch P15, and the very nice dinner P30.

The restaurant at *Sitatunga Camp* is handy if you're staying there, as it saves you the trip back into Maun for meals.

Takeaways In the shopping area of Maun, *Root's* is popular for pizza and takeaways but there's unfortunately no place to sit around and chat while eating. *Meet & Eat*, just a stone's throw away, is a similar operation.

Self-Catering For fruit and vegetables, *Maun Fresh Produce* near Okavango Tours & Safaris has a small but varied selection of groceries, breads, and of course great greens, fruit and vegetables.

Maun has two supermarkets which stock the basics. If you're flying into the delta, keep in mind you'll be allowed only 10 kg of baggage, including camping equipment, so go light on the food!

Next door to the more central supermarket is a butchery which sells reasonable *biltong*,

which is great for camping in the delta and mixing with the tinned food you'll be eating on mokoro trips.

Entertainment

The entertainment scenes in Maun are the Duck Inn at the airport and the Island Safari Lodge in Matlapaneng. The former is *the* venue for ex-pats and White Batswana. Island Safari Lodge, on the other hand, caters to independent backpackers and organised overland truck drivers, neither of whom much approve of the other, but it's still good fun. In the thatched bar the booze normally starts flowing around 6 pm, and by 9 pm participants are dancing, performing acrobatics and drinking feats, and staging climbing competitions up the roof support pole.

Island Safari Lodge has a cinema which shows films on Tuesday, Wednesday, Friday and Saturday. Guests (including campers) pay P3 admission while outsiders pay P5.

Getting There & Away

Air The airport is a centre of Maun activity, especially with the Duck Inn nearby and all the tourists, freight and safari operators buzzing back and forth between Maun and the myriad delta camps.

On Wednesday and Friday Air Botswana flies direct between Francistown and Maun. Between Maun and Gaborone there are flights daily, and on Monday and Wednesday one can fly to or from Ghanzi.

Most of the short-haul air travel in the Maun area is done by air charter companies like Aer Kavango, Northern Air, Delta Air and Ngami Air. In addition to doing flightseeing trips and providing transport into the delta camps, either of which are easily organised by travel agencies, they'll also wander further afield. For example, five or fewer people can fly to the Tsodilo Hills for under P1000 return.

Addresses and further information about air charter companies will be found in the Botswana Getting Around chapter.

Bus At last report, the bus from Maun to

Francistown was running twice weekly according to no particular schedule. It supposedly departs around 8 am from in front of the post office and arrives in Francistown at night. It's best not to count on this bus.

Hitching Most travellers who've hitched to or from Maun have a story to tell about the experience, but everyone does arrive eventually. If you're relegated to the back of a Hilux or other open truck, however, plan on a rough and dusty ride.

Getting Around

Car Hire For driving around the Maun area only, Island Safari Lodge rents Toyota Hilux 4WD vehicles for P75 with 100 free km per day and 75t for each additional km. With a driver, it's P190 per day.

Holiday Car Hire is based at Merlin Services near the airport while Avis is just down the road that parallels the airport tarmac. For rates, refer to the Botswana Getting Around chapter.

Hitching Hitching is normally easy between town and the Matlapaneng Lodges, but transfers between the airport and the four nearest lodges are available for P15 per person if you phone the lodges in advance.

EASTERN DELTA

The area normally defined as the Eastern Delta takes in the wetlands lying between the southern boundary of Moremi Wildlife Reserve and the buffalo fence north-west of the Matlapaneng Lodges.

Many of those who can't afford the airfare into the Inner Delta opt for a mokoro trip into the Eastern Delta starting from Maun. The cheapest delta trips operate in this area, most of them offered by the lodges themselves. Although they provide an affordable glimpse of the delta's fringes, the majority of the polers are unlicensed and therefore haven't completed the studies in natural history and delta knowledge required by the government, so patrons risk getting what they pay for.

Nevertheless, there are some good ones out there, especially those who've grown up in the delta and learned its ways from practical experience. Mostly it's just a matter of luck; some travellers have seen more wildlife or received better service from these operations than others who've paid for the Inner Delta experience. Generally, the further north you travel, the better your chances of seeing game.

Mokoro & Canoe Trips

All the camps offer reasonably priced mokoro trips. For P60, Kubu Lodge will take you by motorboat for one to 1½ hours up the Boro River to Mporota Island, beyond the buffalo fence. There you travel by mokoro for P40 per person per day for as long as you like.

From the Island Safari Lodge and Okavango River Lodge, delta trips start with a P50, 4WD trip to the buffalo fence, and then it's P40 per person per day for travel by mokoro up the Boro River. Alternatively, you can travel by motorboat for 45 minutes up the Boro for P95 per person return and then embark on the mokoro trip.

At the time of writing, Crocodile Camp was only offering mokoro trips from the camp itself for P30 per day. Unless you have 10 days to get up into the delta, this would be a very marginal experience indeed and interesting only as an afternoon jaunt to while away a few hours.

Thamalakane Lodge offers another variation, travelling up the Santantadibe River rather than the Boro. There's no commercial traffic and you won't find any motorboats buzzing around to disturb the peace, but it's also a bit more expensive. The lodge provides transport to the buffalo fence and then charges P100 per person per day – P50 for the mokoro and an additional P50 for the licensed guide.

It's also possible to forego the tour operators and lodges, travelling with them only as far as the buffalo fence for P50 to P70 per person. There you can hire from the pool of freelance mokoro polers who wait there for clients. By avoiding the commercial commissions, you can get the daily rate down to around P25 or P30. Keep in mind that you'll be expected to provide food for your poler on these trips.

Another option is to check with Mike Bullock at the Yamaha dealer (☎ 260536 Maun) in Maun. He rents out mekoro and canoes for P30 per day and you're permitted to paddle around on your own, but you will be required to hire a guide. He also takes canoes back and forth to camps, so if he needs a shuttle you can offer your services paddling them into or out of the delta. But be warned: the trip upstream is not easy work.

The yet more adventurous can organise their own trip either in Matlapaneng village or in Maun by enquiring around for freelance mokoro owners who may be interested in doing a trip. Close scrutiny is in order, however. The delta is a convoluted complex of waterways and not everyone knows it as well as they may want to believe.

Canoes and guides may be hired at Island Safari Lodge for P35/40 per day for two or three-seat canoes.

Motorboat Trips

For environmental reasons, you may want to avoid the motorboat trips. In the tranquillity of the delta their buzzing engines sound like 747s and disturb wildlife, to say nothing of their effect on the relaxation factor. Furthermore, their wake creates ripples in the nearly still waters, disturbing and altering sand islands and delta vegetation, and there is a constant risk of fuel spilling into the water from the engines.

For those in a hurry, however, this may be the only opportunity to see the delta. With a minimum of three people, Riley's Hotel does motorboat trips around the Eastern Delta for P60 per person while Island Safari Lodge will take you on a day trip into the Mporota Island area for P95 per person return.

INNER DELTA

Roughly defined, the Inner Delta is a catch-all name for the area west of Chiefs Island and between Moremi Wildlife Reserve and the base of the Panhandle. It contains lodges and camps catering to most budget ranges and provides some of the most magnificent delta scenery and experiences. For convenience, this section also includes lodges and camps lying on the western shore of Chiefs Island within Moremi Wildlife Reserve.

Mokoro Trips

Mokoro trips through the Inner Delta will invariably be arranged through the camps, each of which has its own pool of licensed guides/polers. Ask people around your camp who've already returned from their mokoro trips for poler assessments and recommendations, and if you hear of a good one, request his services. The keenest ones will recognise and identify the plants, birds and animals along the way, explain the cultures of the delta, and perhaps even teach you how to fish using the local methods.

Enquire in advance whether you're expected to provide food for your poler. Even if he does bring his own food, many travellers who are wild camping prefer to share meals, but that should be established before setting out. The poler will most likely provide a sack of mealies and the cooking implements while the travellers will come up with the relishes – tins of curries, stews and vegetables.

Most of the camps and polers will assume you'll want to enter Moremi Wildlife Reserve and do so as a matter of course, but if you'd rather avoid paying the P50 per day combined park and camping fees (they're reduced because mokoro trips qualify as organised tours), inform your poler at the outset and he'll follow an alternative route. You won't see as much game as you would in the reserve – and no elephants or lions – but the natural element is just as lovely and there will normally be a few antelopes as well as baboons, warthogs, hippos and even the occasional leopard to liven the scene. Also advise the poler if you'd like to break up your trip with bushwalks around some of the palm islands.

The cheapest Inner Delta mokoro trips will cost from P50 to P60 per person per day for the boat and poler. A mokoro normally

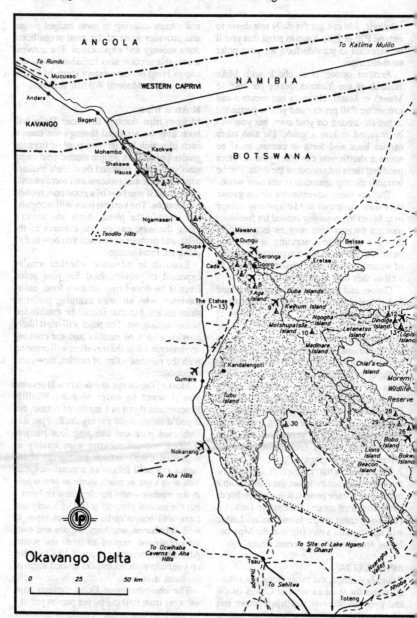

Okavango Delta

0   25   50 km

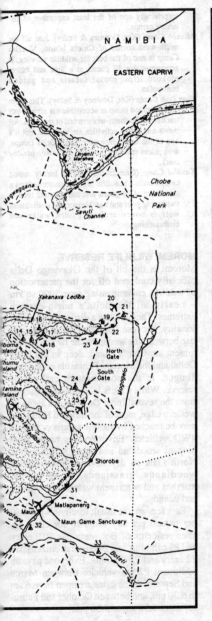

1	Drotsky's Cabins
2	Shakawe Fishing Camp
3	Xaro Lodge
4	Nxamaseri Fishing Camp
5	Akukwe Fishing Camp
6	Etsatsa Camp
7	Qhaaxwa Camp
8	Guma Lagoon Camp
9	Jedibe Camp
10	Mombo Camp
11	Xugana Camp
12	Shindi Camp
13	Camp Okavango
14	Third Bridge Camping Site
15	Camp Moremi
16	Xakanaxa Lediba Camping Site
17	Xakanaxa Camp
18	Camp Okuti
19	Tsapo Lodge
20	Khwai River Airstrip
21	Machaba Camp
22	Khwai River Lodge
23	North Gate Camping Site
24	South Gate Camping Site
25	San-ta-wani Lodge
26	Gunn's Camp
27	Oddball's Camp
28	Delta Camp
29	Xaxaba Camp
30	Pom-Pom Camp
31	Thamalakane Lodge
32	Sitatunga Camp
33	Xyga Camp

accommodates a poler and up to three passengers and their camping equipment. Some mokoro trips, however, travel between established camps and although you won't need to carry equipment, the prices will be considerably higher. If you do enter Moremi Wildlife Reserve you'll be charged the appropriate fee after your trip.

Other Trips

Most of the upmarket lodges offer motorboat trips and booze cruises to those clients who prefer to avoid the mekoro. Prices and offerings vary according to the lodge. Maun travel agencies can fill you in on options but will probably only provide information on lodges for which they serve as agents.

Camps – bottom end

Oddball's Camp (Okavango Tours & Safaris). Oddball's is the Okavango's only real concession to backpackers, offering camping for P15 per person per night, a rustic bar, showers and food shop and an overall friendly and relaxed attitude. It's highly recommended, but allow yourself a couple of days of relaxation and bushwalking around the camp as well as time for your mokoro trip. Air transfers are only P80 each way. Five and eight day specials are available for P499 and P650 per person, including transfers, two nights at the camp, and the remainder travelling by mokoro and camping on remote islands but they don't cover park fees if you enter Moremi Reserve.

Gunn's Camp (Merlin Services). Only slightly more upmarket than Oddball's, Gunn's Camp (also called Ntswi Camp) on Ntswi Island offers camping for P15 per person. If you have a group of four, self-contained bungalows cost P180 per person per day, but with only two people they'll cost P240 per person. Package deals including camping, mokoro trips, meals (only when in camp) and a poler/guide will cost P120 per person per day if you have a minimum of two people. Return flights from Maun cost P215 or you can opt to fly one way and travel by motor-boat back to Maun. Both Gunn's and Oddball's lie just across the channel from Chiefs Island and Moremi Reserve. Food and supplies should be brought from outside.

Camps – middle & top end

The middle and top end camps in the Inner Delta don't vary much. Most charge between P250 and P300 per person per day (based on double occupancy) including meals and all safari activities.

Delta Camp (Okavango Tours & Safaris). Accommodation is in thatched chalets with all the amenities en suite. All-inclusive catered mokoro trips are optional and guided walks are available on the island. The rate includes drinks and three gourmet meals per day.

Jedibe Camp (Okavango Explorations). Accommodating 16 guests, Jedibe is the most remote camp in the Inner Delta. No motor vehicles are permitted and you're a long way from anywhere here, so the peace and seclusion factors will be nearly complete. Look for Pel's fishing owls, red lechwe and the rare sitatunga which are commonly seen in the area. Luxury mokoro trips, fishing and nature walks are available. Although air transfers from Maun are quite dear, Jedibe is surprisingly one of the least expensive of the luxury camps.

Mombo Camp (Ker, Downey & Selby). Just off the north-west corner of Chiefs Island, Mombo Camp is one of the best for wildlife viewing. It accommodates 12 guests at a time and offers mokoro trips, motor safaris and guided bushwalks.

Pom Pom Camp (Ker, Downey & Selby). This quite remote tented camp is accessible via air or bush track from the south-western end of the delta. All meals and safari activities are included, but it's one of the more expensive Inner Delta camps, with prices cracking the P300 per person per day mark.

Xaxaba Camp (Gametrackers). This luxury tented camp beside a beautiful lagoon accommodates a maximum of 24 guests and has gourmet food, a swimming pool and bar. Mekoro are available as well as booze cruises, guided walks and birdwatching.

MOREMI WILDLIFE RESERVE

Moremi is the bit of the Okavango Delta officially cordoned off for the preservation of wildlife, encompassing over 3000 sq km – nearly all the delta's north-eastern extremes. The park has a distinctly dual personality, because large chunks of dry land rise between the wetlands; the two most prominent are Chiefs Island, deep in the Inner Delta, and the Moremi Peninsula or Moremi Tongue, in the north-eastern end of the reserve. While Chiefs Island is best reached from the several Inner Delta camps along its western edge, most of the Moremi Peninsula may be reached by mobile safaris or private 4WD vehicles. Environments range from mopani woodland and thorn scrub around North Gate to dry savanna and riparian woodlands, grasslands, flood plains, marshes and permanent waterways, lagoons and islands.

Park fees are the usual: foreigners pay P50 per person per day and P20 for camping, alien residents of Botswana pay P10 entry and P5 camping, and Botswanan citizens pay P2 entry and P2 camping. Everyone pays an additional P2 per vehicle. Between March and September the gates are open from 6 am to 6.30 pm, and between October and February from 5.30 am to 5.30 pm.

South Gate

The more southerly of the two Moremi road entrances is aptly known as South Gate, 54 km north of Maun. Here visitors pay park fees. There's a clean, developed camping site at South Gate with showers and a shady picnic area.

Third Bridge

Moremi's most interesting camping site is Third Bridge, literally the third log bridge one crosses after entering the reserve at South Gate, 48 km away.

Everyone swims there, but do so only in broad daylight, keeping close watch in the reeds – there are crocodiles. And don't camp on the bridge itself or sleep in the open, since there are a lot of lions in the area. Camping sites are strung along the road on either end but there are no facilities, so use common sense when cooking and performing ablutions: burn rubbish, bury solid waste well away from the water and use a basin rather than the river when washing up.

Mboma Island

The grassy savannas of Mboma Island – actually just a subpeninsula of the Moremi Peninsula – contrast sharply with surrounding areas. The turnoff to Mboma is approximately two km west of Third Bridge and makes a nice side trip if you have the time, but you'll have a good idea what the area looks like from the turnoff itself.

Xakanaxa Lediba

The third Moremi camping site is at Xakanaxa Lediba on a narrow strip of dry land surrounded by marsh and lagoon. With one of the largest heronries in Africa, the area offers good birdwatching.

North Gate

North Gate, with a less-than-appealing developed camping site, is the Moremi entrance for traffic coming from Chobe. The trip between North Gate and Xakanaxa has its scenic moments, but if you're driving, the network of unmarked tracks through the mopani forest may well cause disorientation, especially around the Khwai River Lodge airstrip.

Moremi Area Private Camps

This section includes camps within Moremi Wildlife Reserve as well as those camps in the delta north of the reserve. All of the following are in the middle to top price range, with the average being around P270 per person per day. The only relatively low-cost accommodation available in Moremi are national park camping sites.

African Skimmer Riverboat (Okavango Explorations). Departing from Xugana Camp, the African Skimmer Riverboat offers a 'floating hotel' view of the wild country north-west of Moremi Reserve. At night, the boat moors alongside islands.

Camp Moremi (Desert & Delta). With its famous treehouse dining room, Camp Moremi is just as elegant as its sibling, Camp Okavango. Further east, it enjoys more of a savanna than a swamp environment but it also offers birdwatching trips and a sundowner cruise – too elegant to be called a booze cruise – on the delta. Both Camp Moremi and Camp Okavango should be booked well in advance.

Camp Okavango (Desert & Delta). If you want the Okavango with silver tea service, candelabras and fine china, this is the place to go. The tent accommodation includes gourmet dining and meticulous attention to detail in addition to the standard game-viewing canoe trips, but we're

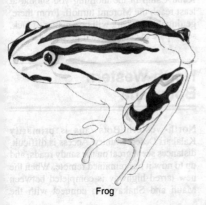

Frog

talking approximately P500 per person per day here, so stuff your wallet well before setting out!

Camp Okuti (Okavango Tours & Safaris). Camp Okuti on Xakanaxa Lediba offers accommodation for 14 guests in thatch-roofed brick bungalows. The daily rates include all meals, game drives, motorboat trips and guided walks.

Khwai River Lodge (Gametrackers). Although Khwai River Lodge, at the very edge of the Okavango, allies itself more with the dryland aspects of Moremi than the water world of the Okavango, both elephants and hippos abound. There's a swimming pool and bar, and game drives, foot safaris and guided birdwatching trips are included in the price. One of the delta's largest lodges, it has friendly staff and space for 24 guests in thatch-roofed brick bungalows.

Machaba Camp (Ker, Downey & Selby). Along the Khwai River just outside Moremi Reserve, the waters around Machaba Camp are an evening drinking venue for hundreds of animals, including elephants, antelopes, zebras and so on. The camp accommodates up to 10 guests in luxury tents and the price includes game drives and photographic safaris in Moremi. Park fees are extra.

San-ta-Wani Lodge (Gametrackers). On an island near the South Gate of Moremi Reserve on the fringe of the Okavango, San-ta-Wani Lodge offers gourmet meals, a bar and superb game viewing and motorboat trips.

Shindi Camp (Ker, Downey & Selby). Between the savanna and the delta, Shindi offers both 4WD game drives and mokoro trips to the fabulous heronries and the nesting sites of numerous other water birds in the remote Moremi Madiba. Mokoro trips and photographic expeditions are available. Access is by air to Xugana airstrip and then 30 minutes by motorboat.

Tsaro Lodge (Okavango Explorations). Tsaro Lodge overlooks the Moremi flood plains, with their diversity of wildlife, near the Khwai River at the reserve's North Gate. There's 24 hour electricity and a bar and swimming pool. Meals and twice-daily game drives are included in the price of accommodation, but P30 per day park fees are not.

Xakanaxa Camp (Okavango Explorations). In the heart of Moremi, Xakanaxa is probably the best option for those wanting to max out on the game-viewing and birdwatching. In a pleasant mix of delta and savanna, the area is teeming with elephants and other wildlife as well as three of the delta's largest heronries at Xakanaxa, Gadikwe and Xobega Madiba lagoons. Accommodation is in luxury tents and the price includes meals, game drives, boat trips, fishing and birdwatching. Park fees are extra.

Xugana Camp (Okavango Explorations). Originally inhabited by San hunters, the name Xugana means 'kneel down to drink', in reference to the welcome sight of perennial water after a long hunt. The only access to this remotest of the Moremi area camps is by air. Accommodation is in luxury tents under big shady trees, and there's a bar, gourmet dining room and swimming pool to add to the overall wilderness opulence. Xugana Camp still gets considerable mileage out of the fact that Prince Charles stayed there for a few days in 1984.

Getting There & Away

If you're booked into one of the camps, air, road or boat transport will be arranged by the camp, but prices will vary considerably. For wild camping, you'll have to join a mobile safari (refer to the Maun discussion for details) or have access to a 4WD vehicle.

To reach Moremi from Maun, head northeast from Maun along the deep sand road past the Matlapaneng Lodges. After 44 km you'll pass the buffalo fence, and 10 km later is the signposted turnoff to Moremi. At 84 km from Maun you'll reach the entrance at South Gate. South Gate to Third Bridge is 48 km, about a two hour drive over an intermittently horrid road through glorious, game-rich country. It's only 25 km from Third Bridge to Xakanaxa and from there approximately 60 km to the park entrance at North Gate.

Hitching from Maun will be slow, but if you stand on the road anywhere north of Kubu Camp in the morning you should at least reach the Moremi turnoff. From there, getting into the park will be a matter of luck, so prepare to camp there if necessary.

North-Western Botswana

North-western Botswana is primarily Kalahari Desert country. Access is difficult, distances seem great on the sandy roads, and up to now it has remained remote. When the new tarred highway is completed between Maun and Shakawe to connect with the superb Namibian highway system at Mohembo, everything will change.

A major problem will be fuel. Although Shakawe has been granted a petrol station permit, as yet there is no reliable source of fuel in north-western Botswana. If you're in dire straits, try the cooperative shop in Etsha 6 which has a supply whenever the truck has made a recent trip to Maun. In an emergency you may be able to purchase a few litres at Shakawe Fishing Camp, south of Shakawe. Failing that, the nearest source will be at Mukwe (near Andara) on the Namibia/Angola border 66 km north of Shakawe, but try to get hold of some South African rand before you go. Unless you can make some sort of exchange deal with the Portuguese management at the Mukwe Wholesalers, you'll be forced to exchange pula for rand at the poor rate of 1:1.

LAKE NGAMI

Lake Ngami has no outflow and is filled only by Okavango overflow down the Nhabe River. When that happens, the water lures hundreds of thousands of flamingos, ibis, pelicans, eagles, storks, terns, gulls, kingfishers, ducks and geese to its shallows to feed on crustaceans which lie dormant in the lake bed awaiting water. It's been dry since 1982, so don't be fooled by the blue swathe on Botswana maps or the lovely photos of pelicans and Egyptian geese splashing in the water. By the time you read this Lake Ngami may be worth visiting, but at the moment it's just another nondescript spread of bush.

There's no accommodation in either Toteng or Sehitwa but you'll be able to camp anywhere in the bush away from the main road and the villages.

Getting There & Away

There's no public transport anywhere around Lake Ngami, but if the lake does refill it won't be too difficult to hitch to nearby Sehitwa from Maun.

Despite what you may read elsewhere, there's one deep sandy stretch along the Maun-Sehitwa road which will require 4WD. Head south from Maun along the Sehitwa road, and about 15 km beyond Toteng begin looking for tracks leading into the bush south-east of the road. The best route to the northern end of the lake turns off just north of a place where the road passes through a strip of reddish sand as it rounds a bend.

Another access route leaves the road about two km north of Sehitwa. Don't let anyone tell you to look for a sign reading 'fishing camp' – that sign hasn't been there for years. Just take the first prominent track north-east of Sehitwa, and if there's water in the lake it'll be obvious just two km or so from the turning.

GCWIHABA CAVERNS (DROTSKY'S CAVE)

The name of this impressively decorated cavern system in the Gcwihaba Hills near the Namibian border means Hyaena's Hole in the !Kung language. The caverns and their stalagmites and stalactites, which reach lengths of up to 10 metres, were formed by water seeping through and dissolving the dolomite rock; the dripping water deposited minerals and built up the cavern decorations from the ceiling and floor.

The caverns probably weren't brought to European attention until the mid-1930s when the !Kung showed them to a Ghanzi farmer, Martinus Drotsky, and for years they were known as Drotsky's Cave.

There are two entrances 300 metres apart and it's possible to make your way between them, but there are no guides, no lighting, and little indication of which route to take. Some visitors have left lengths of string marking the route but there's no guarantee they'll still be there when you arrive. You must have strong torches and carry an emergency light source such as matches or a cigarette lighter.

There is no water available at the caverns and no facilities, but you'll find lots of camping sites beneath the thorn trees around the cave entrances.

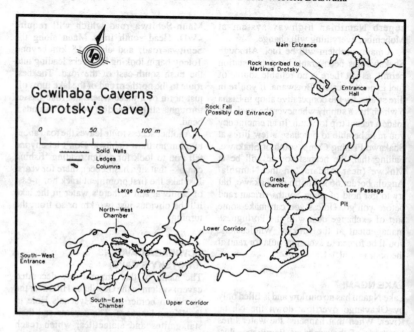

Gcwihaba Caverns
(Drotsky's Cave)

Getting There & Away

There's very little traffic to Gcwihaba Caverns – perhaps one vehicle in a week – so hitching will almost certainly be fruitless. Your only chance will be to ask around Maun or the Matlapaneng Lodges for someone headed that way. If they have space, they'll probably be happy to share expenses and the difficult driving. Be sure to ascertain whether the vehicle carries sufficient water for everyone; if not, you'll have to carry your own *durable* containers.

If you're driving, you'll need not only 4WD and high clearance but also long-range petrol tanks, a reserve water tank and camping equipment. There are no facilities between Maun and the Gcwihaba Caverns.

From Maun to Tsau the road is reasonable sand and gravel, but on one stretch 4WD will be necessary to prevent bogging in deep sand. At Tsau the tarred road begins, but you only get to enjoy it for the 1.5 km to the caverns turnoff. There's no signpost but it's initially a fairly clear track that deteriorates as you head over dunes, ruts and deep sand. After 86 km you'll reach the turning to Xhaba bore hole, which is 27 km south of the caverns road, but continue straight on unless you're in need of water. At 144 km, take the left turning to the caverns. From there it's 27 km down the fossil valley to the Gcwihaba Hills, where the caverns are found.

GUMARE

Although the road between Tsau and Gumare is tarred, it is often covered with drifted sand which acts like millions of ball bearings on the hard surface and makes for some tedious driving. Gumare is currently the end of the tar headed north, and you're diverted through this clean and pleasant village on a roundabout detour. The only services available are a bakery and a couple of bush shops, but if you have time, Gumare is worth an hour or two of exploration.

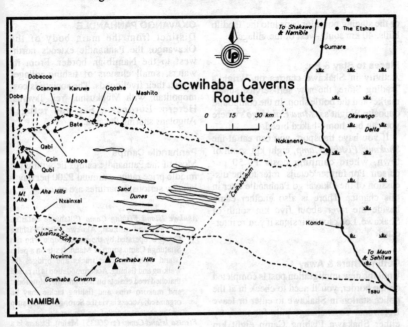

Gcwihaba Caverns Route

THE ETSHAS
In the late 1700s the Mbukushu people were forced by Lozi aggression from their homes along the Chobe and Linyanti valleys of north-eastern Namibia to the banks of the Okavango in southern Angola, in turn displacing the peaceful Yei. Over the following decades their settlements spread slowly down the Okavango River into present-day Botswana.

In the late 1960s Angola was experiencing civil war, and many of the remaining Mbukushu fled southward and were granted refugee status in Botswana. Initially they waited in Shakawe while a new settlement, Etsha, was completed for them. In the shift to Etsha in 1969, they naturally organised into 13 groups based on clan and social structure carried from Angola, with each group settling a km or so from the next. To facilitate their accounting system, the government bestowed the villages with numerical names – Etsha 1 to Etsha 13.

There's no accommodation at the Etshas. Apart from the chance of finding fuel out the back of the well-stocked bush store at Etsha 6, there's not much reason to visit unless you're looking for original Mbukushu basketry. The government is building a new multimillion pula secondary school at the Etshas to accommodate the growing population.

Getting There & Away
To get there, turn east off the highway – there's no signpost – approximately 15 km north of Gumare. From there, it's 13 more km to the Etshas.

SHAKAWE
Until the tarred road arrives, the desultory but picturesque village of Shakawe will remain a sleepy little outpost on the Okavango. For travellers it's either a Botswana entry or exit stamp, a transit site for a fishing holiday in the Okavango Panhandle,

or the staging point for trips into the Tsodilo Hills, 40 km south-west of the village.

Places to Stay & Eat

Activity in Shakawe centres on Wright's Trading Store, the new self-service supermarket and the bottle shop. In the compound opposite Wright's is *Mma Haidongo's* where you can buy home-baked bread.

If you have transport, you can eat at the *Shakawe Fishing Camp*, eight km south of town, where camping costs P9.50 per person. For further details, refer to the discussion of the Okavango Panhandle later in this chapter. There is also another camp beside the river about five km south of Shakawe. Look for their signs if you're interested.

Getting There & Away

Until the new immigration post is completed on the border, you'll need to check in at the police station in Shakawe to enter or leave Botswana. To exchange pula for rand, try either Shakawe Fishing Camp eight km south of Shakawe or Wright's Trading Store in town. At the time of writing, P1 was trading for R1.40 here.

The road from Shakawe north to Mohembo and the Namibian border is poor in places, but once you're through the booms and fences that separate the two countries it's good gravel. Once inside Namibia you'll have to stop at the gate of Mahango Game Reserve to secure an entry permit. Transit through the park is free, but if you want to look around it costs R5 per person and an additional R5 for the vehicle. Just beyond the northern boundary of Mahango is Popavalle, a series of cascades in the Okavango River, and its national park camping site. Day entry is R5 per person while camping costs R25 per site.

From just north of Popavalle, you may turn west at the fork toward Andara, Mukwe, Rundu and Windhoek (refer to the Namibia section of the book) or east toward Katima Mulilo, Kasane, Kazungula and Victoria Falls.

OKAVANGO PANHANDLE

Distinct from the main body of the Okavango, the Panhandle extends north-west to the Namibian border. From its waters, small clusters of fishing villages extract their livelihoods. The society is cosmopolitan, with Mbukushu, Yei, Tswana, Herero, European, San and refugee Angolans sharing the area.

Panhandle Camps

Most of the Panhandle camps lie within the middle price range – around P200 per day – but any serious departures are noted.

Akukwe Island Fishing Camp (Sitatunga Safaris). Friendly and unusual, Akukwe Island Fishing Camp is operated by the same people who run Sitatunga Camp south of Maun. It sits on a palm island with numerous tracks and bridges for walking and fishing. Accommodation is in raised thatched reed chalets built on anthills. Motorboat and mokoro trips and fishing tackle may be organised. Access is via the Seronga landing strip on the eastern shore of the Panhandle.

Etsatsa Island Camp (☎ 260351 Maun). Etsatsa is a luxury tented camp which offers bream and tiger fishing, birdwatching and photographic opportunities. Birdwatching boat trips are available. Etsatsa is reached by boat via the airstrip at Seronga.

Guma Lagoon Camp. Guma Lagoon Camp lies just north-east of the Etshas, on the Thaoge River at the base of the Panhandle. It accommodates 10 guests in thatched reed bungalows. Its focus is the excellent tiger and bream fishing available in the area.

Nxamaseri Camp. The highest priced Panhandle Camp, Nxamaseri provides luxury accommodation for the fishing crowd in five-star chalets. Birdwatching excursions and fishing trips are the highlights. The camp is about midway between Shakawe and Sepopa and is accessible by 4WD from either place, or by air from Maun to Shakawe and then by 4WD vehicle to the camp.

Qhaaxwa Camp (Gametrackers). At the base of the Panhandle, Qhaaxwa Camp lies just east of the Etshas and is the most 'Okavango' of the Panhandle camps. There are good chances of seeing red lechwe and the rare sitatunga as well as a variety of waterbirds and birds of prey. Accommodation is in reed chalets; meals, motorboat trips, fishing, mokoro trips and birdwatching excursions are included in the price.

Shakawe Fishing Camp (Travel Wild). This slightly quirky tented camp is in the northernmost part of the Panhandle, easily accessible by 4WD vehicle from Shakawe or by a combination of air and vehicle from Maun to Shakawe airstrip. Chalets cost P100 a double; flights and 4WD trips to the Tsodilo Hills are offered as add-ons, but they're quite expensive. Adjacent to the chalet camp, which has a swimming pool and bar, is a camping site where you can pitch a tent for P9.50 per person and enjoy the good fishing and lovely river view. Motorboat rentals are available for P20 per hour and P2 per litre for fuel.

Xaro Lodge (Okavango Explorations). This luxury tented camp lies on the Panhandle just south of Shakawe Fishing Camp and is accessible by 4WD vehicle. Especially during the dry season, the sandy river banks serve as a nesting site for numerous species of water birds. Pel's fishing owl is also common here as are herons, fish eagles and several types of bee-eaters. The tented lodge is open between March and September and offers motorboat excursions, fishing, guided nature walks and add-on trips into the remote Tsodilo Hills.

TSODILO HILLS

Like Australia's Ayers Rock, the Tsodilo Hills rise abruptly from a rippled, ocean-like expanse of desert and are threaded with myth, legend and spiritual significance for both the Makoko and Dzucwa San and the Mbukushu people. The Mbukushu believe that the gods lowered themselves and their cattle down a rope onto the summits, while the San see the Tsodilo Hills as the site of the creation itself. These four masses of rock were the 'Slippery Hills' of Sir Laurens van der Post. The name Tsodilo is derived from the Mbukushu word *sorile*, meaning 'sheer'.

There is evidence that the area of the Tsodilo Hills has been inhabited by ancestors of the present-day San for nearly 35,000 years. Numerous flaked stone tools have been excavated, and Bantu sites have been dated back as early as 500 AD. In addition, 2750 individual outline-style paintings at over 200 sites have been discovered and catalogued. Although no date can be fixed on most of the rock paintings, some are clearly fairly recent – later than 700 AD – because of their degree of preservation and their depiction of cattle which were brought in around that time.

Orientation & Information

Although there are four main hills at the Tsodilo – the Male, the Female, the Child and the Nameless Infant – the latter two require a bit of effort to reach and only the Male and Female are normally visited. The Male Hill, the highest of them, is a single peak and rises a sheer 300 metres from its south-western base. The Female Hill, on the other hand, is an irregular series of valleys and summits where the majority of the most impressive rock paintings have been rendered. The cliffs and walls of both hills are streaked with incredible natural pastels – mauve, orange, yellow, turquoise and lavender – which are so vivid they appear artificial.

Several hundred metres west of the Male Hill is the collection of huts known as the Bushman Village, but don't go expecting to find the utopian San so esteemed by Laurens van der Post or irreverently portrayed in *The Gods Must be Crazy*. Tourism and other outside influences have so tragically affected these people that they've lost interest in nearly everything except flogging trinkets and awaiting handouts.

Further south is the Mbukushu village, where visitors are meant to report upon arrival to make their presence known to the chief and sign his guest book.

There are no shops or services in either village. Water is available at the bore hole for cattle about 600 metres south-west of the airstrip.

Guides

The best way to get around is to walk, naturally, but to see the site thoroughly will require several days on foot, and even then you're unlikely to find some of the best paintings. Most people wind up hiring Benjamin, the English-speaking guide who lives in the nearby Mbukushu village. Benjamin is well on in years, so unless you have a vehicle to drive him around you'll

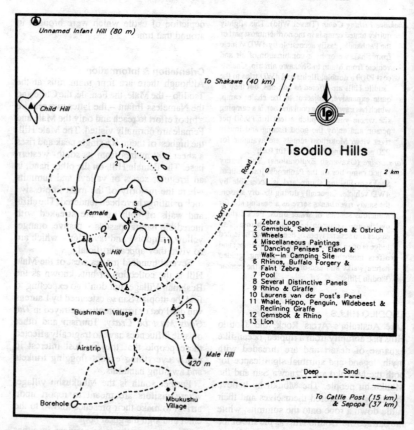

Unnamed Infant Hill (80 m)

Child Hill

To Shakawe (40 km)

Horrid Road

Tsodilo Hills

0   1   2 km

Female Hill

Hill

"Bushman" Village

Airstrip

Male Hill
420 m

Borehole

Mbukushu Village

Deep   Sand

To Cattle Post (15 km)
& Sepopa (37 km)

1 Zebra Logo
2 Gemsbok, Sable Antelope & Ostrich
3 Wheels
4 Miscellaneous Paintings
5 "Dancing Penises", Eland &
  Walk-in Camping Site
6 Rhinos, Buffalo Forgery &
  Faint Zebra
7 Pool
8 Several Distinctive Panels
9 Rhino & Giraffe
10 Laurens van der Post's Panel
11 Whale, Hippo, Penguin, Wildebeest &
   Reclining Giraffe
12 Gemsbok & Rhino
13 Lion

miss the best of the paintings. Even with a vehicle, he won't be able to accompany you to any of the higher sites. At any rate, you won't have to go looking for him; he keeps an eye out for visitors and offers his services immediately anyone happens along.

Alternatively, you can hire one of the San guides from the Bushman Village who are knowledgeable about the flora and fauna and well-versed in local lore, but there could be language difficulties. None of the guides have set rates but most groups pay about P6 to P10 for a day clambering around the hills – a real bargain for Botswana.

Organised Tours

Several of the Maun travel agencies organise tours to the Tsodilo Hills, but they invariably allow only a day or two of sightseeing and cover only the major paintings, with little time available for climbing or individual exploration. Merlin Services, near the Maun airport, offers custom tours for P650 per day for groups of up to eight people, but that doesn't include the charter flight between Maun and the Tsodilo Hills.

Places to Stay

There are no facilities in the Tsodilo Hills but

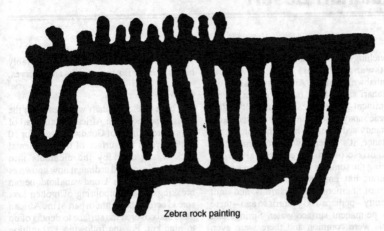

Zebra rock painting

you're free to camp anywhere on or around them. Several ideal camping sites may be found around the bases of the hills. The established site is at the prominent crevice along the western base of the Female Hill, but this is the first one occupied by tour groups so independent visitors may want to avoid it.

There's another site further south near the Rhino and Giraffe painting, and at the southern tip of the Female Hill is a sheltered but very public space behind the sign reading 'Tsodilo Hills'. In a hollow around the eastern side of the Female Hill near the Rhinos painting is a site amid shady trees, but since it's quite popular you may have to share it with other parties.

At the Lion on the Male Hill there's also a fairly nice camping spot. It's a good place to come home to, once you've climbed to that summit and down.

Getting There & Away
Car & Motorbike Shakawe Fishing Camp in Shakawe hires out vehicles for the trip for around P245 per day including fuel, which is a really good deal considering how much abuse the vehicle will be exposed to. If you'd

rather not tackle the decidedly difficult driving yourself, ask whether they can provide a driver/guide to help out.

There are two vehicle routes, one from the east which is signposted and turns off about seven km south of Sepopa, and another from the north-east which leaves the main road just south of Shakawe (bear left at the fork immediately west of the turning). The former route is very poor; the first 22 km are fine, but at the cattle post it deteriorates into a particularly deep dune and the 15 remaining km will be a difficult battle through in low-ratio 4WD. The alternative route, however, is even worse.

Hitching Since it is only 40 km from the main road, travellers have also been known to try walking in, assuming that if someone comes along they'll be given a lift. The only advice offered is to let someone in Shakawe or Sepopa know what you're doing and be sure the majority of the weight you're carrying is water. To spend two days walking in the dry Kalahari heat, you'll need a minimum of six litres per person, and perhaps more.

Kalahari Desert

Stretching across parts of seven countries – Botswana, Zambia, South Africa, Zimbabwe, Namibia, Angola and Zaïre – the Kalahari sands form one of Africa's most prominent geographical features. It isn't a classic sandy desert, but rather a vast deposit of sandy sediments. Unlike the Sahara, for instance, it's covered with trees and scrub and crisscrossed by ephemeral rivers. During the summer the Kalahari can receive copious but unpredictable rainfall in the form of afternoon thunderstorms, and until recently – perhaps 100 years or so ago – there was permanent surface water. Springs and pools were common and there were even marshes and reedbeds, but overuse by humans and overgrazing have changed all that.

Visiting the Kalahari – or more accurately the Kgalagadi, as it's known to the Tswana – isn't an easy prospect. Distances are vast, roads are rudimentary, transport is thin to nonexistent, facilities are few, and the scant villages, such as they are, huddle around bore holes. There are plans afoot, however, to tar the road from Gaborone to Ghanzi and on into Namibia. When that project is complete, expect a dramatic change as the Kalahari opens up to just about everyone.

While the open skies and spaces of the Kalahari hold undeniable appeal, there are few attractions to speak of and no real population centres. The only towns are the diamond-mining centre of Jwaneng on the ragged eastern edge of the region, and Ghanzi, the drowsy 'metropolis' of the western Kalahari which is visited primarily in transit to or from Namibia. Further south is a destination of sorts, a cluster of tiny villages which comprise one of Botswana's most remote populations. The four vast game reserves which dominate the map of western Botswana – Khutse, Central Kalahari, Mabuasehube and Gemsbok – enjoy only sparse concentrations of game. They're ideal if you're after solitude, but if it's game you're after the numbers are considerably higher in other Botswana parks and reserves.

Geology

The base of the Kalahari was created in the Triassic period when Africa was still part of the supercontinent of Gondwanaland. For 10 million years the surface of the continental rock was ground by the elements into deposits of sand and sediment now known as the Karoo. When Gondwanaland began breaking up, an outpouring of molten lava spread across the southern part of the African plate and covered the surface to depths of up to nine km. For the following 120 million years these lavas also eroded and formed the near-level plateau that characterises most of southern Africa today.

Between 65 and two million years ago the climate grew more arid and continuing erosion caused sandy sedimentation which was spread over vast areas by wind and ephemeral streams and tossed about by increasing tectonic activity. To the north-east the Great Rift was forming, causing Africa itself to split apart. The rift, which ended in a maze of faults across Zimbabwe and northern Botswana, caused a stretching of the land mass and resulted in an immense, shallow basin across the southern African plateau. Uplifting around the edges diverted rivers away from the basin while the sand deposits continued to shift and consolidate, settling finally into its lowermost parts.

In recent times – between 25,000 and 10,000 years ago – rainfall was much higher than it is now and the lowest parts of this basin were filled with the great lake whose remnants include the Makgadikgadi Pans, the Okavango, the Mababe Depression and Lake Ngami. It was eventually lost to increasing aridity and tectonic uplifting.

LETHLAKENG

Practically in Gaborone's backyard, this eastern outpost of the Kalahari is the gateway

to the Khutse Game Reserve, the nearest wildlife area to the capital city. The Kwena name of this village means 'the place of reeds' and tradition has it that there were once springs which attracted large numbers of elephants, rhinoceroses and buffaloes.

Lethlakeng, the end of the tarred road from Gaborone, lies 116 km from Gaborone and 124 rough and sandy km from the Khutse Game Reserve gate.

KHUTSE GAME RESERVE

The smallish (2500 sq km) Khutse Game Reserve is a popular weekend excursion for Gaborone dwellers. Due to prolonged drought in recent years there aren't the concentrations of game which can be expected in the northern Botswana reserves, but the solitude of the pans and savanna scrub can be almost complete. Expect to see a variety of antelopes – wildebeests, elands, duikers, steenboks, hartebeests, kudus, gemsboks and springboks – but not in large numbers. There'll also be the odd predator, including the big cats and brown or spotted hyaenas, jackals, caracals and even hunting dogs.

Ostriches are common and the Botswana Parks & Reserves literature recommends

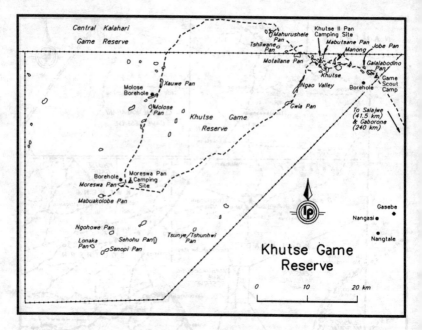

Central Kalahari Game Reserve

Khutse Game Reserve

0   10   20 km

that, especially around pans, visitors watch out for smaller creatures such as ground squirrels, bush squirrels, three species of hares, bat-eared foxes, black-footed cats, pangolins, ant bears (aardvarks), aard-wolves, hedgehogs and warthogs. Furthermore, the bird life is varied and profuse, and they say that if you leave fruit or sliced tsama melons (which look a bit like tennis balls and grow all over the Kalahari) near your camp, the moisture will attract numerous species of birds. I haven't tested the advice but it sounds logical enough.

Unfortunately, the usual park fees apply at Khutse; foreigners will have to fork over P50 per person per day to be in the park and a further P2 for their vehicle.

Places to Stay

There are two camping sites at Khutse but no facilities. The first you come to is at Khutse II Pan, 14 km from the entry gate and Game Scout Camp, where slightly saline water is available. Moreswa Pan, which is deep in the reserve, lies 67 km beyond the gate and is the nicer of the two sites. Camping at either site costs P20 per person.

Getting There & Away

Although some sources claim that Khutse has been reached by conventional vehicles, 4WD is strongly recommended; the road between Lethlakeng and the park gate is quite sandy and anyone wanting to drive inside the reserve will appreciate the sense of security it offers. Plan on at least five hours from Gaborone to the entry gate and carry all the fuel, food and water you'll be needing for the journey.

Hitchhikers should have relatively little difficulty finding lifts as far as Lethlakeng, but to get into the reserve the most luck will be forthcoming on weekends.

CENTRAL KALAHARI GAME RESERVE

The Central Kalahari Game Reserve is

The 'creche'

perhaps best known for Deception Valley, the site of Mark & Delia Owens' brown hyaena study in *Cry of the Kalahari*. Until recently, public entry has been by permit only. In addition to providing a reserve for wildlife, the dunes and fossil valleys of this vast and virtually undisturbed expanse have served as home for the few remaining San – perhaps 800 people – who choose to pursue their traditional hunting and gathering lifestyle.

Getting There & Away

There are no facilities anywhere within its boundaries and the only nonpermit public access road is a sidetrack from the Khutse Game Reserve road which leads to Mahurushele Pans, just within the Central Kalahari's southern boundary.

Afro Ventures Safaris (☎ 260351 Maun) in Maun offers eight-day Kalahari safaris which include a four-day camping foray into Deception Valley. You'll need quite a lot of cash for this unusual trip but it is currently the only nonpermit access into the Central Kalahari Game Reserve. For further information, telephone Afro Ventures or write to them at Private Bag 13, Maun, Botswana.

If you'd like to have a go at independent 4WD access and feel you have a good reason to visit, entry permit applications are available by writing to the Ghanzi District Commissioner, Ghanzi, Botswana.

JWANENG

During the late Cretaceous period – some 85 million years ago – a weakness in the earth's crust caused the immense pressures in the mantle of the earth to build up against the carboniferous seams deep in the crust. Eventually molten rock was forced toward the surface, penetrating the overlying solid rock. With these intrusions – known in southern Africa as kimberlite pipes – came bits of carbon metamorphosed by pressure into the diamonds which now provide 85% of Botswana's export income.

The world's largest gem deposit was discovered at Jwaneng (then called Jwana) in 1978. By 1981, the village of just a few huts had grown to a town of over 5500 people. The mine opened in 1982, and by the end of the decade the population of the Debswana-planned town had swelled to 14,000 and the mine was producing nearly nine million carats annually! Unlike Orapa, Jwaneng is an open town, with non-Debswana employees permitted to settle and establish businesses. Unfortunately, security is such that mine tours aren't currently an option.

Places to Stay & Eat

For travellers heading north-west, Jwaneng is the last hotel, restaurant, shop and reliable petrol station before Ghanzi. At the *Mokala Hotel* (☎ 380614 Jwaneng), double rooms cost P90. The hotel also has an à la carte restaurant and bar. Alternatively, try *KRM Takeaways* in the Mall for inexpensive snacks, ice cream and soft drinks.

JWANENG TO GHANZI

The 750 km road between the cowboy town of Ghanzi and Jwaneng follows the cattle route from the Ghanzi Block freehold ranches to the BMC abattoir in Lobatse. Although the overland cattle drovers are being phased out in favour of semitrailers, the occasional cattle drive still passes along the route. Anyone interested in experiencing a taste of the Old West, Botswana-style, however, had better get there before the road is tarred or it'll be too late.

This route is a rough and tumble ride along less-than-optimum roads but it's relatively well travelled and quite a few hitchhikers have eventually been successful with it. There's normally no fuel available between Jwaneng and Ghanzi so you'll need a reserve tank. With a good 4WD vehicle, the entire journey will take between 11 and 14 hours, depending on conditions.

Travelling from Jwaneng to Ghanzi, opposing the cattle traffic, the tar ends just outside Jwaneng and launches onto a patience-wearing corrugated gravel surface to Sekoma, where the road to Tshabong and Bokspits heads south. West of there you get into rutted sand, and after 170 km or so you'll reach the sandy but friendly and picturesque village of Kang. The petrol pump in Kang dispenses blue-dyed petrol, signifying that it's for government vehicles only, so don't

count on being able to buy any. Along the main route there's a general store run by a lovely Afrikaner couple. Everyone stops there so it's a good place to wait for a lift. You'll also find a garage, a bakery and a welding station run by the Brigades.

If you're heading for the Kgalagadi Village Cluster or Tshabong, which is 360 km from Kang via Mabuasehube Game Reserve, turn south at Kang. Otherwise, continue north-west along the main Ghanzi road which heads out into deep sand for the 150 km to the San village of Takatswaane. From there it's approximately 125 km in to Ghanzi.

KGALAGADI VILLAGE CLUSTER

The four villages of Tshane, Hukuntsi, Lokgwabe and Lehututu make up the Kgalagadi Village Cluster, an unlikely population centre in the remotest Kalahari beginning 104 km west of Kang. The road into the village travels through extremely deep sand, so 4WD will be essential. Although Hukuntsi does have blue-dyed petrol available for government vehicles, there is no fuel available to the public in any of the villages.

Hukuntsi, the largest of the villages, sprawls sparsely over a wide area. It has overtaken Lehututu, 12 km to the north, as the commercial centre of the cluster and serves as the government administration centre as well. Although the surrounding landscape is sandy and desolate, it has the most reliable bore hole in the area and there's a bush shop where you'll find a variety of supplies.

In Tshane, 12 km east of Hukuntsi, take a look at the colonial police station which dates back to the early 1900s. It overlooks Tshane Pan where, due to the shortage of water, cattle drink from hand-dug wells around its perimeter. The other village, Lokgwabe, lies 11 km south-west of Hukuntsi. Its only claim to fame is that it was settled by Simon Cooper, who sought British protection in Bechuanaland after leading the 1904 Nama rebellion in German Southwest Africa.

About 60 km south-west of Hukuntsi is

Tshatswa, a small San village of 277 people. If you're going this way, be sure to carry your own water. There's a serious shortage in Tshatswa; their bore hole yields only about 150 litres of saline water daily, which must be condensed and desalinated before it's potable. The extracted salt is then sold to earn a bit of money for the village.

Along the way between Hukuntsi and Tshatswa you'll pass a lot of sparkling white salt pans and, as desolate as the area seems, there are good populations of gemsbok, ostriches and hartebeests.

Places to Stay
In Hukuntsi there's a government hostel, but it is only available to the public in an emergency, so visitors must either know someone to stay with in the villages or carry a tent. Before setting up camp, ask permission of the village chief and perhaps ask him to suggest a suitable site where you won't disrupt village activities.

Getting There & Away
We're talking remote here. The Kgalagadi Village Cluster lies 104 km west of Kang and about 255 km north of Tshabong, neither of which are much to speak of in their own right. Without a 4WD vehicle, the only chance of reaching this area would be to hitch to Kang and wait around the general store until a vehicle headed in the right direction happens along. Finding a lift back may be another story altogether.

MABUASEHUBE GAME RESERVE
Remote Mabuasehube Reserve, a small 1800 sq km appendage to Gemsbok National Park, focuses on three major pans and a number of minor ones with beautiful red dunes up to 30 metres high on their southern and western edges. In Segologa the name of the reserve is Mabuashegube, appropriately meaning Red Earth.

The largest and northernmost of the pans, Mabuasehube Pan, is used as a salt lick by itinerant eland and gemsbok. At the western end of the pan are wells artificially deepened by Gologa herdsmen for their cattle; the

wells often hold water even when the rest of the pan is dry. Further south is the grassy Bosobogolo Pan, which has large herds of springboks and is also popular with such predators as lions, cheetahs, brown hyaenas and hunting dogs.

The reserve is best visited in late winter and early spring when herds of eland and gemsbok are migrating out of the Gemsbok Park immediately west.

Places to Stay
There's a rudimentary camping site at Mabuasehube Pan, and although there are no facilities you'll be required to pay the standard park fees if there are parks personnel around. Water isn't always available at the Mabuasehube Pan bore hole, so carry all you'll be needing.

Getting There & Away
The roads into Mabuasehube are very bad and will require a strong 4WD vehicle. There are two access routes into the reserve, one from Tshabong, the Kgalagadi District headquarters, which is reached via Jwaneng and Sekoma (see Jwaneng to Ghanzi earlier in this chapter) and the other via Kang and the Kgalagadi Village Cluster. Traffic is thin to nonexistent so hitching will be a nonstarter. Drivers through this extremely remote area must be self-sufficient in all respects and be very familiar with bush driving techniques.

The nearest reliable fuel pumps are at Ghanzi and Jwaneng, while Tshabong, 100 km south of the reserve, has a sporadic supply. Failing that, you'll have to travel into South Africa for fuel.

BOKSPITS
On the intermittent Molopo River in the extreme south-western corner of Botswana, the picturesque frontier settlement of Bokspits sits amid ruddy sand dunes. It's a centre of karakul wool production, but unless you're in the area it isn't worth going out of your way for. There's no accommodation and most vehicles passing through are using the border crossing between Botswana and South Africa en route to or from the

latter's Kalahari Gemsbok National Park. Bokspits is accessible via South Africa or down the dry Molopo riverbed from McCarthysrus near Tshabong.

GEMSBOK NATIONAL PARK

In Botswana's remote south-western corner, the immense 11,000 sq km Gemsbok National Park abuts South Africa's Kalahari Gemsbok National Park on the west. This is the one area of Botswana where you'll see the shifting sand dunes that many mistakenly believe to be typical of the Kalahari.

The gemsbok for which the park is named are best observed between March and early May when the rains have brought a splash of green to the overwhelmingly red landscape. Springboks, elands and red and blue hartebeests may also be seen in relatively large numbers at these times, but during the rest of the year you may be lucky to see anything at all.

Since the Botswana side of the park isn't really accessible by road – it's reached only by unofficially crossing the normally dry Nossob River – Botswana park fees aren't applicable.

Places to Stay

All park camping sites and cottages are on the South African side of the Nossob River. Bookings are necessary for weekends and public holidays and may be made by writing to the Chief Director of Parks, PO Box 787, Pretoria 1000, South Africa.

Getting There & Away

The only access is via Bokspits, from which a road passable to conventional vehicles follows the border north to the park entrance at Twee Rivieren where you'll have to pass through South African immigration. A dirt track then follows the intermittent Nossob River – the western boundary of both Botswana and Gemsbok National Park – for 160 km to Nossob Camp. From there, the track continues for another 130 km to the locked gate at Union's End where Botswana, Namibia and South Africa meet. It's not possible to enter either Namibia or South

Africa here; the nearest access to Namibia is via the Aoub River road from Twee Rivieren across the South African 'panhandle'.

GHANZI

The name Ghanzi is derived from the San for a one-stringed musical instrument with a gourd soundbox, and oddly enough not from the Tswana word *gantsi* ('the flies') which coincidentally would be quite appropriate.

Ghanzi sits atop a 500-km-long limestone ridge that curves from Lake Ngami in the north-east to Windhoek, Namibia's capital, in the west. Although it's not visible from the ground, it contains great stores of artesian water which render agriculture and cattle ranching feasible and even profitable activities.

History

For such a small and remote little place, Ghanzi has enjoyed quite a colourful history. Although a number of itinerant travellers passed through earlier, the man who made Ghanzi, Hendrik Matthys Van Zyl, arrived in 1868. A rather ruthless character, this former Transvaal MP wandered the Botswana wilderness trading munitions, knocking over elephants, killing San and gaining the respect of local Bantu chiefs. In 1874 he settled at Lake Ngami, briefly usurping the leadership of dissident factions in Chief Moremi's Tawana tribe. At one stage he avenged the San murder of a Boer, William Frederick Prinsloo, by luring 33 San with tobacco and brandy and murdering them in cold blood.

By 1877, after a profitable trip to Cape Town, he had returned to Ghanzi and established his residence. During his first year there it's estimated that he shot over 400 elephants which yielded at least four tonnes of ivory. With the proceeds of these exploits, Van Zyl built himself a two-storey mansion with stained-glass windows, filled it with opulent imported furniture and lived the life of a maharajah in the Botswana wilderness. Tales of his power and generally disagreeable nature prevented many Boer Dorsland Trekkers settling in the area of Ghanzi.

The manner of Van Zyl's death is

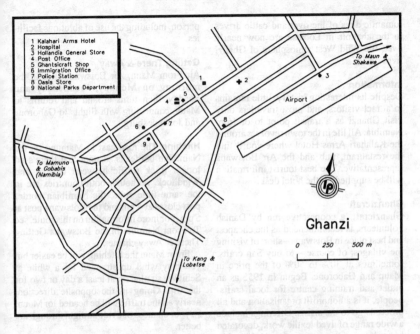

1 Kalahari Arms Hotel
2 Hospital
3 Hollandia General Store
4 Post Office
5 Ghantsicraft Shop
6 Immigration Office
7 Police Station
8 Oasis Store
9 National Parks Department

To Maun & Shakawe

Airport

Ghanzi

0   250   500 m

To Kang & Lobatse

To Mamuno & Gobabis (Namibia)

unknown, but a number of colourful tales have arisen, none of which is terribly credible. Some have him being struck down by vengeful San, others by a wily San servant in his household. One tale has him angering the Damara to the point of murder, another credits the Khoi-Khoi. All that's certain is that after his death his wife, three sons and daughter escaped to the Transvaal and were never heard from again.

Without Van Zyl, Ghanzi plodded on into the late 19th century. That the town survived at all is probably due to Cecil Rhodes' designs on its potential as a foot in the Bechuanaland door for his British South Africa Company. Although some consider the takeover and usurpation of the Ghanzi Block to have been a British attempt to thwart German aggression from Namibia, it was almost certainly for commercial rather than strategic aims. Rhodes was able to fraudulently secure Tawana concessions to the land and, by offering free land and equip-

ment and promoting it as a paradise on earth, divert a contingency of Voortrekkers into Ghanzi. Rhodes' commercial ambitions were stalled, however, by the ill-conceived and abortive Jameson Raid which had been intended to destabilise the Boer republics in the Transvaal and force their annexation to the Cape Colony, an unauthorised assumption of military power. Rhodes was forced to resign as prime minister of Cape Colony, Jameson was imprisoned and the Boer settlers at Ghanzi were left to fend for themselves.

Although the area was prime cattle country, by 1908 the majority of the freehold farmers had abandoned ship and again Ghanzi was in danger of becoming a ghost town. In 1913, however, nearly all the farms were sold at auction to bidders committed to making a go of cattle ranching, and through a series of fits and starts during the following 50 years the settlement grew into Botswana's most productive ranching area. Although the romantic days of the overland cattle drives to the abattoir in Lobatse are now nearly over, the Wild West atmosphere of Ghanzi lives on.

Information

Despite its interesting history, little remains to attract visitors, and most travellers only visit Ghanzi as a transit point to or from Namibia. All life in the town revolves around the Kalahari Arms Hotel where you'll find the restaurant, pub and the Air Botswana representative. The best tourist information will be supplied by the hotel desk.

Ghanzicraft

Ghanzicraft, a cooperative run by Danish volunteers, is recommended as the cheapest and best place in Botswana – short of visiting the villages, of course – to buy San crafts, sometimes at 30% to 50% of the price in Maun and Gaborone. Begun in 1953 as an outlet and training centre for local craftspeople, it is a nonprofit organisation and all proceeds go to the artists. Offerings include a wide range of dyed textile work, decorated bags, bow and arrow sets, springbok-skin dancing skirts, leather aprons, musical bows, plastic bead or hatched ostrich eggshell necklaces, woven mats, hats, and ingenious dancing dolls. To cover administrative costs, a 10% surcharge is levied on articles under P20 and P2 is added to higher priced items.

Places to Stay & Eat

There isn't much option. The *Kalahari Arms Hotel* (☎ 296311) is the centre of town in nearly every respect. Standard rooms are available but budget travellers will welcome the option of camping out the back for P4 per person, including the use of ablutions facilities.

Getting There & Away

Air From Maun, Air Botswana flies in the morning on Monday, Wednesday and Sunday, then turns around and returns to Maun, connecting with flights to Gaborone and Johannesburg.

Hitching The road east to Mamuno on the Namibian border is so poor that there's no longer truck traffic between Ghanzi and Windhoek. Although both countries are in the same time zone, the Namibian border post closes at 4 pm and the Botswana post at 5 pm. For more information on this route, see To/From Namibia in the Botswana Getting There & Away chapter.

From Maun the hitching will be easier but you may wind up stranded for a while at Sehitwa, so plan on at least a day or two for the trip. Going in the opposite direction, nearly all the traffic will be headed for Maun, so your chances of a ride straight through are better.

There's a lot of cattle traffic to and from Jwaneng and Lobatse, so hitchhikers will eventually get a lift if they wait long enough.

D'KAR

If you're passing through D'kar, 38 km north of Ghanzi on the Maun road, you may want to visit the successful mission which, in addition to providing religious instruction, gives the San practical agricultural training and organises leather-working and material crafts industries. There's a crafts shop where visitors can purchase the fruits of the San efforts.

Namibia

Facts about the Country

HISTORY
Pre-Colonial History
San & Khoi-Khoi It is generally accepted that the earliest named inhabitants of Namibia and Botswana were San (Bushmen), nomadic people organised in extended family groups who were able to adapt to even the severest terrain. Population densities were very low and much movement took place.

San communities seem to have come under pressure from Khoi-Khoi (Hottentot) groups, the ancestors of the modern Nama, with whom they share a language group. The Khoi-Khoi were a partially tribally organised people who raised stock rather than hunted and who were probably responsible for the first pottery-making in the archaeological record. They seem to have come from the south, gradually displacing the San in Namibia, and remained in control of the country until around 1500 AD.

The descendants of the Khoisan can still be seen in Namibia today, but few have retained their original lifestyles. The Topnaar Hottentots of the Kuiseb River area in Namibia are an exception, maintaining a lifestyle not very different from that of their predecessors based on the raising of goats.

Bantus Between 2300 and 2400 years ago, the first Bantus appeared on the plateaux of south-central Africa. Their arrival marked the arrival of the first tribal structures in southern African societies. Khoisan groups gradually disappeared from the scene, either retreating to the desert or the swamps of the Okavango Delta or being enslaved into Bantu society, a process which has continued right up to today.

Around 1600 AD in Namibia the Herero people, who were Bantu-speaking cattle raisers, arrived from the Zambezi area and occupied the north and west of the country, causing conflicts with Khoi-Khoi with whom they were competing for the best grazing lands and waterholes. The aggressive Herero displaced not only Khoi-Khoi but also the remaining San, and the Damara people (whose origin is unclear).

It is thought that the Nama people of present day Namibia are descended from Khoi-Khoi groups who held out against the Herero despite violent clashes in the 1870s and 1880s. In addition, by then a new Bantu group, the Wambo, had settled in the north along the Okavango and Kunene rivers, and were probably descended from people who migrated from eastern Africa more than 500 years before.

European Exploration
Against this background of tribal conflicts, Namibia was beginning to receive its first European visitors as a result of increased activity by traders and missionaries. The Portuguese had an extensive trading fleet in the 15th century and in 1486 one of their ships, captained by Diego Cão, sailed as far south as Cape Cross, where he erected a limestone *padrao* (cross) to mark the event. Today, a modern replica stands on the spot.

Two years later Bartholomew Diaz sailed round the Cape of Good Hope, on the way reaching the site of present-day Lüderitz on Christmas Day 1488. Diaz Point, just south of the modern town, has another cross marking the event. During the early 1600s more voyages of exploration along the coast of Namibia were undertaken, this time based at Dutch colonies in the Cape, but no formal settlements were started.

The next major period of activity started in 1750 with several major events. First, a Dutch elephant hunter called Jacobus Coetse became the first White to travel from the Dutch Cape Colony in the south across the Orange River into Namibia. He was followed by a progression of traders, hunters and missionaries who gradually opened up the interior. On the coast, the Cape Colony government decided to put the ports of Angra Pequena and Walvis Bay under Dutch protection against a perceived threat from the British, the Americans and the French.

Serious missionary activity in Namibia began in 1805, and mission stations were founded at Windhoek (1842), Rehoboth (1845) and Keetmanshoop (1866), along with others. German missionaries from the Rhenish Missionary Society began living among the Herero in the 1840s.

The rich guano resources off the coast had begun to attract attention in 1843, and in 1867 Britain annexed the guano islands. Walvis Bay and the surrounding hinterland was taken over by Great Britain in 1878, and the British also assumed a major role in maintaining law and order in the Khoisan-Herero wars. Meanwhile, Adolf Lüderitz had bought the port of Angra Pequena (now Lüderitz) and its hinterland from a Nama chief in 1883, and a year later the whole of Namibia was taken under German 'protection', becoming a fully fledged German Protectorate (called German Southwest Africa) in 1890 and initiating the colonial era.

Colonial History

Territorial conflicts between Germany and Great Britain within what is now Namibia resulted in Adolf Lüderitz persuading the German chancellor Bismarck to take over the country, although it is a matter of record that between 1885 and 1890 the German colonial administration was a little on the small side, with only three civil servants in the entire country!

The boundaries of Namibia were finally agreed in the late 1890s between the Portuguese in Angola, the British in Bechuanaland (Botswana), and the Germans, who were acting through a colonial company, much like the British East India Company in India in the days before the Raj. This organisation was incapable of maintaining law and order, and in the 1890s Namibia saw the arrival of the first German troops, the Deutsche Schutztruppe, whose forts can still be seen all over the country. A famous name from this period is their general, Curt von François, who had a leading role in the wars between Herero and Khoi-Khoi and, later, Herero and Khoi-Khoi versus German.

The colonial era extended up until WW I, by which time the German Reich had taken over all Khoi-Khoi and Herero land and virtually demolished the old tribal structures, at least among the Herero. Extensive colonisation and the development of a White farm network dates from this period, and there are many architectural relics of the colonial past throughout Namibia.

During WW I, South Africa was pressured by Great Britain until it eventually agreed to invade Namibia, and in 1914 the German troops were pushed gradually northwards until their final defeat, with subsequent internment of the survivors, at Khorab near Tsumeb in 1915. In 1921 South Africa gained a formal League of Nations mandate to take over the administration of Namibia, and a large number of former German farms were sold to Afrikaans-speaking settlers.

The Bantu peoples became subject to territorial demarcations like the South African 'homelands' policy, and this network of tribal areas was retained until independence in 1990. The original intention was to channel economic development into these predominantly poor rural areas, but the inevitable result was the growth of a demarcation line between the rich, predominantly White-owned farms in the south of the country and the poorer tribal areas to the north.

Independence

From 1950 all sorts of international pressure was piled on South Africa to release its hold on Namibia, but the rich mineral resources of the country and its strategic importance made South Africa reluctant to do so. However, during the 1970s the independence movement gathered momentum, and the first conference involving all Namibia's 11 ethnic groups took place. Unfortunately this excluded the opposition independence movements, especially the powerful

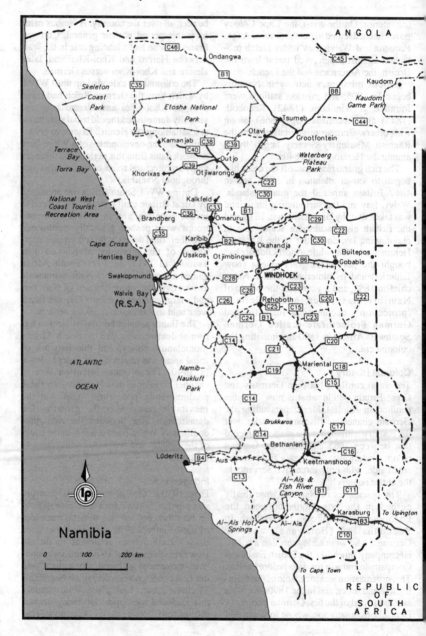

ANGOLA

Skeleton Coast Park

Etosha National Park

Kaudom Game Park

Terrace Bay

Torra Bay

National West Coast Tourist Recreation Area

Cape Cross

Henties Bay

Swakopmund

Walvis Bay (R.S.A.)

ATLANTIC OCEAN

Waterberg Plateau Park

Namib-Naukluft Park

Brukkaros

Ai-Ais & Fish River Canyon

Ai-Ais Hot Springs

Ai-Ais

Ondangwa

Kaudom

Tsumeb

Grootfontein

Kamanjab

Otavi

Khorixas

Otjiwarongo

Kalkfeld

Brandberg

Omaruru

Karibib

Usakos

Otjimbingwe

Okahandja

WINDHOEK

Buitepos

Gobabis

Rehoboth

Mariental

Bethanien

Lüderitz

Aus

Keetmanshoop

Karasburg

To Upington

To Cape Town

REPUBLIC OF SOUTH AFRICA

Namibia

0   100   200 km

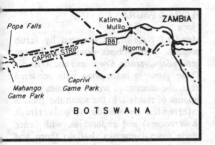

SWAPO (South West African People's Organization), ostensibly because of its Soviet support. The UN Security Council then put some pressure on South Africa with the result that SWAPO began to be included in talks and conferences. Various attempts at self-government were made during the early 1980s resulting in the establishment of a Multiparty Conference and the Transitional Government of National Unity in 1985.

The South African government remained responsible for foreign affairs and defence, with a huge military presence operating against SWAPO 'terrorists' during the so-called 'bush war' from bases in Angola. The highly complex political situation involved the activities of Marxist-backed rebels in Angola with ample Cuban interference, but eventually South Africa, Angola and Cuba agreed on 1 April 1989 to grant independence to Namibia by implementing UN Resolution 435. Cuban forces were to withdraw from Angola and stop supporting SWAPO, and South Africa was to pull its troops out of Namibia. Namibia finally became independent on 21 March 1990, under UN supervision. The first election provided a stable SWAPO-dominated government. The country is now settling down and finding its feet under the new political regime with high hopes for the future.

GEOGRAPHY

Namibia is an arid country but one which includes immense geographical variations. Broadly speaking, its topography can be divided into four sections. The first of these includes the dunes and desert coastal plains of the Namib itself, together with the surrounding pro-Namib farmland and the Skeleton Coast in the north. Secondly, there is the Central Escarpment which surrounds the capital, Windhoek, and extends northwards into the Kaokoveld near the Angolan border, westwards into the Khomas-Hochland range which forms the border with the Namib, and south-east into the mountains of Namaland which make a central spine for the country sloping off gradually towards the east.

The third section is the southern and eastern part of the country which is effectively an extension of the Kalahari Basin and forms the border country between Namibia and its neighbours Botswana and South Africa. The fourth geographical segment is the densely wooded bushveld of the north in the regions of Kavango and Caprivi, forming the northern border of the country fringing the Okavango River. This leads east along the narrow strip of land known as the Caprivi Strip, linking Namibia to Zambia and the Okavango delta area of Botswana.

The coast is extremely dry, having between 15 and 100 mm of rain per year. The narrow band of the Namib Desert stretches the full length of the coast from the Orange River in the south to the Kunene River in the north. The Namib is distinguished by some of the strangest fauna and flora in the world, with plant and animal communities adapted specifically to the unique climatic conditions.

It is often claimed that the Namib is the world's oldest desert, having been around for more than 80 million years even by the most conservative estimate. It owes its existence partly to the offshore Benguela Current, which flows south to north and is extremely cold. Warm onshore winds flowing over the current create a belt of fog over the coast, and the condensed moisture gives life to the lichens and other specialised vegetation which form the basis of the desert food chain.

Landscapes include the mountainous, linear field of red dunes in the southern

Namib, the interior plains and inselbergs (flat-topped, steep-sided and isolated mountains) of the central Namib and the bare scorched dunes of the Skeleton Coast in the north.

The coastal dunes gradually give way to gravel plains as they rise in altitude inland, the plains in turn becoming savanna grassland at the edge of the farming country near the Central Escarpment. The Namib Desert itself is crossed by a number of rivers which very seldom carry water. Some, like the Tsauchab, once reached the sea but now end at a *vlei*, a flat calcrete pan which may hold water for a few short weeks a year. Others, like the Kuiseb, may run for a few weeks in summer, but at one time many millions of years ago carried huge volumes of water and thus carved out spectacular rocky canyons in their upper courses.

The rivers rise in the Central Escarpment. Their canyons, particularly the Fish River Canyon in the south and to a lesser extent the Kuiseb Canyon in the centre, are some of the most scenic parts of the country.

The width of the coastal plains varies with locality – at Lüderitz, for example, the plains are nearly 300 km wide, whereas in the northern Kaokoveld the mountains almost reach the sea. Inland from the desert coast the landscape of the coastal plain is punctuated by chains of dramatic mountains and inselbergs, some volcanic in origin and all honeycombed with the caves and rock shelters which provided homes for early humans. The Brandberg and Erongo mountains north of Karibib have some of the best known scenery, but all the roads from the desert to the centre of the country climb from plains through the mountains via spectacular passes.

The Central Escarpment is dissected by old river courses and is often covered in forests of aloes, thorn trees and scrub. In the south-east of the country the land slopes gently away from the escarpment, joining the savanna plains at the edge of the Kalahari, steppe vegetation quite different from that of the Namib Desert, and a rolling, dusty, typically African landscape.

FLORA & FAUNA
Flora

Much of Namibia is covered by scrub savanna, with grasses dominated by the genera *Stipagrostis*, *Eragrostis* and *Aristida*. These grow in association with scattered trees, the amount of which depends on the amount of rainfall. In the south the grass is interrupted by stands of quivertrees (*kokerbooms*) and euphorbias, with dense shade from tamarisks, buffalo thorn and camel thorn trees along the watercourses.

In the plains of the east, sloping towards the Kalahari Gemsbok Park, raisin bushes (*Grewia* species) and candle thorn appear among the trees, and around Windhoek the hillsides are covered with green-flowered *Aloe viridiflora* and wild camphorbush. In central Namibia, especially around Omaruru, citrus fruits are grown, and many Windhoek gardens contain orange and lemon trees.

The western fringes of the Namib and the Naukluft have a classic semidesert scrub savanna vegetation, with some rare aloe species (*Aloe karasbergensis* and *Aloe sladeniana*), and the strange *Welwitschia mirabilis* may be found in the rocky parts of the Namib Desert itself.

In areas with higher rainfall (such as the Waterberg Plateau Park) the characteristic grass savanna gives way to acacia woodlands, and in Etosha there are two subtypes: a tree savanna in the east around Namutoni and a thorn tree savanna in the west. The higher rainfall of Caprivi and Kavango has produced extensive *mopane* woodland with reedbeds, acacia belts and grasslands near the rivers. River fringe vegetation near Katima Mulilo is a mixed woodland of copalwood, Zambezi teak, leadwood and silver cluster leaf.

Fauna

Reptiles Namibia has a full complement of more than 70 snake species including three types of spitting cobra. Here again it is the African puff adder which causes the most problems, particularly since it is common in dry, sandy, harmless-looking riverbeds.

Boomslangs and vine snakes are common in Kavango but there are few cases of reported bites. Horned adders and sandsnakes may be seen in the gravel plains of the Namib, and the sidewinder adder lives in the Namib dune sea.

The Namib also has a fine range of lizards, including a large vegetarian species, *Angolosaurus skoogi*, and a sand-diving lizard, *Aprosaura achietae*, famous for its 'thermal dance' in which it lifts each leg in turn to get some relief from the heat of the sand. There are also some wonderfully camouflaged chameleons and the surreal bug-eyed palmatto gecko which lives in the dunes. Crocodiles are farmed commercially near Otjiwarongo in Namibia.

Birds Namibia also has a series of bird species found nowhere else, including the Namaqua sandgrouse and Grey's lark. The harbours and coastal wildfowl reserves also shelter white pelicans, grebes, herons, cormorants, ducks, and several hundred other species of wetland birds. The sheer quantity of birdlife there, making a living on the ample fish stocks of the Benguela Current, has contributed to Namibia's lucrative guano industry – artificial islands near Walvis Bay have been constructed offshore to stimulate production.

The riverbeds and canyons crossing the central Namib also have a rich variety of birdlife, including nine species of birds of prey, the hoopoe, the cheerfully surreal red-eyed bulbul and a small bird called the familiar chat. Near the Western Escarpment you can see sunbirds and the occasional flash of an emerald cuckoo. Lüderitz is also a wonderful place to watch penguins.

Fish The entire Namib coast from Swakopmund to the mouth of the Ugab River is a sea angler's paradise. No licence is required but there are restrictions on sizes and numbers of fish which can be taken. You need a licence for freshwater fishing in Namibia, which can be obtained from the local tourist office. The most popular species caught are black bass, carp, yellowfish, bream and barbel. Crayfish can be caught in the Lüderitz area.

Spiders & Insects The Namib has some wonderful spiders, the white, hairy tarantula-like 'white lady of the dunes' being the most famous. These disgusting creatures also 'dance', raising one hairy foot at a time, and are attracted to light. This is worth noting if you have a sudden nocturnal need to venture outside the tent when camping out. There is also a large, grotesque, false spider (also called a solifluge or sun spider) which is white and semitransparent, enabling you to see its blood circulating. Fortunately they are usually buried in the sand. Rumour has it that a black sun spider was once seen in the vicinity of Spitzkoppe and scientists have been looking for another ever since, though I can't imagine why.

The Namib dunes are also famed for an extraordinary variety of beetles of all shapes and sizes, scurrying round the sandy slopes. All are carefully adapted to their desert habitat and rely on fog moisture. Some are clearly sex-mad; one species nicknamed *toktokkies* seems to spend its entire life in pursuit of the opposite sex. Nuisance insects in the gravel plains of the pro-Namib include ticks, which favour shady thorn trees. They are especially prevalent where there is a lot of stock or wild animals, and a bite can be very bad news.

National Parks
Namibia has a superb system of national parks (sometimes known as game parks), operated by the Division of Nature Conservation (commonly called just Nature Conservation). The largest and best known is the Etosha National Park in the north of the country, a huge area of arid bushveld (grass and thorn trees) and savanna some 200 km wide surrounding a dry calcrete pan or shallow lake. The pan occasionally retains water for a few days in the rainy season, when it becomes covered with flamingos.

It is possible to stay in the park in one of the three official rest camps or go as a day visitor, but there is no public transport and it is necessary either to have your own vehicle or to take an arranged tour. The roads, though gravel, are well maintained and the park is never crowded. During the dry season (May-September) you can see huge herds of gemsboks, springboks, wildebeests and zebras with impressive numbers of lions, elephants and rhinos as well.

The other main park in Namibia includes part of the Namib Desert and its surrounding plains, and is divided into the Namib-Naukluft Park, the Skeleton Coast Park, the Sesriem/Sossusvlei area and Sandwich Harbour. Sandwich, a famous bird sanctuary just south of Walvis Bay, can only be reached with a 4WD vehicle.

You can drive along most of the Skeleton Coast (except for the most northerly area) and stop off at Cape Cross Seal Reserve, where more than 100,000 Cape fur seals can be seen.

The Namib-Naukluft section of the park is divided into the central Namib Desert (centered around the dry Kuiseb River), through which you can walk and camp, and the Naukluft Park (formerly the Naukluft Mountain Zebra Park), a mountainous area famous for its hiking trails, mountain zebra and dramatic scenery. At Sossusvlei you can reach the interior of the great Namib dunefield, where the dunes reach 300 metres and more in height.

Although not technically national parks, it is worth mentioning the game reserves: the Waterberg Plateau Park in central Namibia, the Caprivi, Khaudum and Popa Falls game reserves in Caprivi, and the magnificent Fish River Canyon in the south of the country, next in size to the Grand Canyon but with fewer people about. All these parks are operated by Nature Conservation and can be easily visited.

GOVERNMENT

Since independence in March 1990, Namibia has been governed by a SWAPO-dominated National Assembly, although the principal opposition party, the Democratic

Stamp comemmorating independence

Turnhalle Alliance (DTA), a moderate 11-party alliance, came very near to winning the election. The president, Sam Nujoma, a former SWAPO leader, is widely respected; with the exception of a few incidents involv-

Sam Nujoma

ing his over-zealous personal bodyguards, the country has been remarkably quiet since independence. Minority parties such as the Hersigte Nationale Party (HNP), which advocates apartheid and Namibia becoming a province of South Africa, do still exist but are politically powerless. The Action Front for the Retention of the Turnhalle Principles (AKTUR), a White-dominated party to the right of the DTA, still retains some influence.

Members of the White community were agreeably surprised to find that a SWAPO-dominated government did not lead to the predicted Armageddon, although there are still widespread accusations of corruption and less-than-ethical government practices. The country is now stable and there is an air of optimism for the future, engendered perhaps by the fact that, unlike many newly independent African states, Namibia does not seem to be inclined to left-wing political extremism, despite its Marxist affiliations. However, it is still early days.

ECONOMY

Despite a number of disadvantages, including a lack of water and local fuel sources, a small and scattered population, and the vast distances between settlements, Namibia is already a prosperous country by African standards, with a gross domestic product twice the average for Africa and no shortage of land or food. However, it still imports more than 80% of its food and manufactured goods from South Africa, creating an unhealthy degree of economic dependence. The development of the Namibian economy rests on its ability to attract foreign investment, and develop (via education and training) its own human resources to exploit the many natural resources of the country.

The economy is based chiefly on mining (diamonds and uranium), agriculture (cattle and karakul sheep) and fishing; although tourism is now widely thought to be the third most important sector, having overtaken fishing (at least this was the case before independence – no later figures are available).

Mining

The country is the fourth-largest mining country in Africa and the 17th-largest in the world, with the world's richest diamond fields and largest uranium mine. This mine, at Rössing near Swakopmund, produces over 60 million tonnes of ore a year. Namibia also has large deposits of lithium, germanium, silver, vanadium, tin, copper, lead, zinc and tantalum. The diamonds are found in the alluvial sands and gravels north of the Orange River and in the southern Namib, and are mostly extracted by strip mining. The major company operating is Consolidated Diamond Mines (CDM), one of Namibia's largest employers, which searches 20 million tonnes of dirt a year, recovering 200 kg (one million carats) of diamonds.

Another major mining operator is the Tsumeb Corporation Ltd which produces about 70% of the other minerals in the mining area around Tsumeb, Grootfontein and Otavi in north-central Namibia. Other major mining areas are around Rosh Pinah south of Lüderitz (zinc, lead, silver), Uis (tin) and Karibib (quartz, lithium and beryllium).

Agriculture

Around 16% of the active labour force of Namibia work in commercial agriculture, but at least 70% of the population depend on agriculture for their living. The farms are often of the subsistence type in so-called communal (formerly tribal) land areas, mostly in the high rainfall zones of Owamboland, Kavango and Caprivi. The commercial farming sector produces about 80% of the total agricultural yield and is dominated by White farmers (who generally speak German or Afrikaans) in the southern and central parts of the country, with economies based around raising stock, especially beef cattle and sheep.

The lack of water and sporadic droughts make this kind of farming a high-risk occupation, but the farms are well managed and have evolved strategies for coping, including an increase in such activities as game (rather than cattle) farming. It is now common for farmers to raise gemsboks, zebras and springboks for meat and hides, and there is a small but growing ostrich-farming industry.

In the drier southern area of the country the karakul sheep is becoming an increasingly common sight. Although unlovely animals sometimes bearing a strong resemblance to scraggy goats, karakuls are well suited to the dry conditions and produce high-quality meat and wool. Karakul wool forms the basis of an expanding weaving industry and karakul pelts dominate the export market for luxury leather and skin goods.

Some crop farming is carried out, mainly around Grootfontein, Otavi and Tsumeb, with maize as the principal crop. There are also many small arable farms, some specialising in fruit and vegetable growing, in communal areas such as Owamboland.

Fishing

The waters off the Namibian coasts are thought to be some of the richest fishing grounds in the world, due to the presence of the cold offshore Benguela Current which flows northwards along the coast from the south polar region. The current is exceptionally rich in plankton, which accounts for the plentiful anchovy, pilchard, mackerel and other whitefish resources. But there are many problems with the narrow offshore fishing limit, and resentment that other nations, especially the USSR and Spain, can exploit Namibian fish stocks. Efforts are being made to extend the fishing zone to 200 nautical miles in order to make Namibian fisheries more competitive.

Tonnes of rock lobsters from the Lüderitz area are exported every year, along with canned fish, fishmeal and oil. However, the modern fishing industry is but a shadow of its former self; of the 11 fish-processing factories in Walvis Bay and Lüderitz which were active 20 years ago, fewer than half survive today. The rock lobster industry, which employs around 1000 people, exports most of the catch to Japan. Oysters are also cultivated and marketed in the Swakopmund area and a new oyster farm has now started near Lüderitz.

Manufacturing

Manufacturing contributes less than 5% of Namibia's gross national product, emphasising the heavy reliance on South African imports. The manufacturing sector is dominated by meat processing and the supply of goods and materials for the mining industry.

It is vital that Namibia develops this sector, but lack of training, the high cost of raw materials and a measure of political uncertainty do not make this easy. Namibia is desperate to encourage investment in manufacturing since to a certain extent this will determine the economic future of the country.

Other Industries

Tourist travel to Namibia has declined very substantially since independence, primarily because of the lack of visitors from South Africa who formerly constituted at least 75% of incoming tourists. Moreover, although the country is cheap to get around, the incoming flight capacity is low and Namibia Tourism aims to develop a high-cost, low-volume product. The aim is to attract wealthier European visitors interested in wildlife, who may perhaps have already become tired of the crowded national parks of East Africa.

The retail sector in Namibia is still flourishing, with many people depending on small market and street trading stalls. The network of small bush *cuca* shops in Owamboland is an important economic sector.

POPULATION & PEOPLE

Namibia has an estimated population of 1.3 million, an annual population growth of 3%, and one of the lowest population densities in Africa at 1.5 persons per sq km.

The inhabitants of the country include more than 11 major ethnic groups, derived from stock herders, nomadic hunter-gatherers, rural farming communities and people living in small industrial towns.

There is a strong German and South African colonial legacy. Since independence in March 1990, much effort has been made to emphasise the history and traditions of the different tribal groups.

The largest population group is the Wambo (641,000), who live mainly in the north of the country and divided into eight different tribal groups. They are tall, elegant people whose men often have a bushy beard and who pride themselves on their commercial abilities. Many of the leaders of the present government come from Wambo tribes. Wambo people are famous for their skilled basketry.

Kavango people (120,000) live in the north of the country in a woodland environment, traditionally depending on fishing and small farms as a subsistence base. They are also highly skilled woodcarvers.

The Herero (97,000), who have two main tribal groups, live north of the central plateau near Okahandja, Otjimgwe and the Waterberg Plateau. Another group lives in the east, around Gobabis. The Herero are primarily stock farmers, and Herero women are tall and stately and famous for their dress, an immaculate Victorian-style crinoline of enormous proportions worn over a series of petticoats, with a matching hat or headdress.

The Damara (97,000), who live on the western side of the country between the escarpment and the desert, were originally miners and traders in tobacco and copper until they settled in what is now Damaraland at the end of the 19th century and began to farm. They share a language, but not an ethnic derivation, with the Nama people, who are descended from Khoisan hunter-gatherers who later became stock farmers. Other Khoisan descendants, called Topnaar Hottentots, live around the Walvis Bay and Kuiseb River area of central Namibia, where they farm goats, harvest !nara (a desert melon) and work in the fish-canning factories.

Whites (82,000) are concentrated in the urban, central and south of the country and are primarily of German and Afrikaner stock. Europeans first came to Namibia in 1760; after 1780, traders, hunters and missionaries arrived. People descended from the inter-mixing of local people with settlers from Cape Province in South Africa (sometimes called Coloureds) number 52,000. Many live in urban areas.

In the extreme north-east are the Caprivians (48,000), consisting of five complex tribal groups of subsistence farmers on the banks of the Zambezi and Kwando rivers.

The San (37,000), who were the earliest inhabitants of the country, still live in these areas as well. They are divided into three groups: the Haixom in the northern districts of Otavi, Tsumeb and Grootfontein; the Qgu (!Kung) in Bushmanland; and the Mbarakwengo in west Caprivi. Few San still maintain their traditional way of life, and many work as servants in Kavango and Caprivi.

The Basters (32,000) have their origins in the intermixing between the Oorlams and White stock farmers from Cape Colony. They live mostly around Rehoboth and practise small stock farming, priding themselves on their origins.

The Tswana (8000) form the smallest ethnic group, and are related to the Tswana of South Africa and Botswana. They are found mainly in the Aminius and Epukiro areas.

EDUCATION

Education is compulsory for all children. The percentage of Namibians in primary education is steadily increasing and now stands at nearly 75% of the population. Teaching is carried out in both English and Afrikaans, although there are a number of private schools, many dating from colonial times, where German is the language of instruction. It is SWAPO policy to have English as the dominant teaching language.

Like many other African countries, less than 75% of children complete five years of schooling (Standard 5), and less than 8% of the population goes on to secondary education. Current estimates suggest that less than

1% reach higher education or professional training. There is a shortage of qualified teachers, who are paid extremely badly, and a disparity between the educational achievements of Whites and other ethnic groups.

Few non-Whites have sufficient educational qualifications to enter teacher training, although there are training colleges in Owamboland and Windhoek which are heavily subsidised. Non-White children often perform badly in matriculation examinations and are educationally disadvantaged, though since independence great efforts have been made to even out this imbalance.

There are two institutes of higher education in Namibia: the Academy (equivalent to a university) which offers degree-level courses in arts, economics, education and medicine, and the Technikon (like a Polytechnic) with career-orientated courses in business, agriculture, nature conservation, nursing and secretarial studies.

The College for Out-of-School Training offers theoretical and practical courses in crafts and nursing, including some by external study. Some Namibians (generally White) still leave the country to attend university in South Africa (often Stellenbosch or the University of Cape Town) or in Europe via UN or Commonwealth scholarships.

RELIGION

Perhaps 75% of the population of Namibia are Christians. Of those, most are Protestants of various denominations, German Lutheran being the dominant sect. However, as a result of early missionary activity there is also a substantial Roman Catholic population, mainly in the centre of the country and spread out through isolated mission stations in the north, especially Kavango. Most Portuguese speakers are Roman Catholic.

LANGUAGE

Akrikaans and English are the two official languages, and are used for all official documents, road signs and publications. Afrikaans is a guttural language with a rolling 'g' sound pronounced like 'hr', which makes it difficult for many people to understand. However, the close relationship to Dutch makes many of the words at least vaguely familiar when written down, although understanding a native speaker may not be quite so easy. Some Afrikaans speakers in rural areas may be reluctant (or unable) to speak any other language, but it is perfectly possible to spend an enjoyable time in the country and be unable to speak a word of anything but English. English, rather than Afrikaans, is the language of Caprivi.

German is very widely spoken; in some areas such as Swakopmund you will hardly hear anything else, although people will understand English. You may also hear Portuguese spoken in the Windhoek area and on the coast. English-speaking Namibians often have strong southern African accents which may be confusing to those accustomed to other forms of spoken English.

The two other main language groups are the Bantu group (including Wambo and Herero) and the Khoisan group (including Nama and the San languages), which are not related. Khoisan dialects include many 'click' elements which make them very difficult to learn, and few members of the White population can speak them. Clicks are made by compressing the tongue against different parts of the mouth to form different sounds. Names which include a symbol (like the !nara fruit) are Khoisan in derivation; in this case the '!' is a sideways click sound, a bit like encouraging a horse. Many native Khoisan speakers also speak at least one Bantu and one White language, usually Afrikaans or German rather than English. Damara people speak a variety of Nama, while most of the so-called Coloureds in Namibia speak Afrikaans.

The Bantu language group is even more complicated and includes eight different dialects of Wambo, of which Kwanyama and Ndonga are Owamboland's official languages. The Kavango group has four separate tribes (Kwangali, Mbunza, Sambiyu and Geiriku) who each use a separate dialect, although Kwangali is the most common. The most common language in Caprivi is Lozi, which originally came from Barotseland in Zambia. Herero people (not surprisingly) speak Herero, which is a rolling melodious language, apparently especially rich in vowel sounds. Many Namibian place names which begin with O (such as Okahandja and Omaruru) come from the Herero. Rehoboth Basters speak mainly Afrikaans, with some English and German.

Facts for the Visitor

VISAS & EMBASSIES

The visa situation in Namibia is rather fluid, not to say in complete chaos. Currently, residents of the Republic of South Africa and EEC countries need a valid passport but are not required to have a visa. There is still some doubt about whether this will be extended to the USA and Commonwealth countries.

The Namibian authorities recommend that, at least 30 days before leaving for Namibia, you check visa requirements with your nearest South African diplomatic or consular representative, or contact the Namibian Department of Civic Affairs (☎ (061) 398111), Private Bag X13200, Windhoek 9000.

You can also get a Namibian visa at the Zambian High Commission in most countries. Visas are generally issued for a period of two or three weeks, but you can get them extended while you are in Windhoek. In order to do so you will need a return air ticket. The process is lengthy and may require several visits to the Civic Affairs offices in Windhoek. It is currently possible to buy a visa at Windhoek International Airport but because of the confusing situation you would be unwise to rely on this in the future.

Upon entering the country you will be required to fill in an arrival form giving basic travel details and anticipated length of stay. A customs declaration form is also obligatory. Your passport is then stamped and part of the form stapled in it until departure, when a departure form and customs form are completed and the process is repeated in reverse. This will happen every time you leave the country, even if it is merely crossing the border into Walvis Bay, which is technically South African territory.

Entry Requirements

If you are a citizen of an EEC country, Canada, or the People's Republic of China, a valid passport will probably be sufficient to gain entry to Namibia from South Africa. During the first nine months after independence the new border regulations caused many problems for South African nationals who were, for the first time, obliged to produce a passport when crossing to and from Namibia. The same was true in reverse for Namibian citizens who had not yet had passports issued and were therefore technically prohibited from leaving their country.

This situation has now been resolved. Citizens of South Africa can in theory also use their passbook, emergency travel certificate or other official travel documentation instead of a passport, but there have been cases where lack of a full passport has resulted in entry to Namibia being refused.

Foreign Embassies in Namibia

Although various embassies and high commissions are in the process of being established in the country, there is as yet no list of addresses; even the Department of Civic Affairs may be unable to tell you which countries currently have diplomatic representation. Asking around suggests that Canada, the UK, France, Germany, South Africa and the People's Republic of China have established missions and that the citizens of these countries are exempt from visa requirements. But check before you leave.

CUSTOMS

Customs regulations are much the same as for other countries, except that you will have to declare firearms at the point of arrival and get a temporary import permit. In the unlikely event that you are bringing a pet with you, health certificates may be required and you will need full veterinary documentation. Pets are not allowed in any of the Nature Conservation game parks or resorts. Both entry and departure customs forms require you to declare the approximate amount that you intend to spend or have spent while in the country.

There are customs posts and entry formalities at Windhoek's J G Strijdom International Airport, 42 km east of the city, and Eros Airport, which serves Namib Air flights from Cape Town and flights to neighbouring countries. If your flight from Cape Town touches down at Keetmanshoop in southern Namibia, as most flights do, you will be required to clear customs there rather than in Windhoek. If you are coming by train from South Africa, there is a customs stop between Upington in South Africa and Ariamsvlei, and another between Walvis Bay and Swakopmund.

MONEY
Currency

The unit of currency is the South African rand, divided into 100 cents. Banknotes in circulation include R50, R20, R10, R5 and R2 but the R2 note is currently being replaced by an R2 coin. Coins include the nickel (R1) and 50, 20, 10 and five cents. Rands issued in South Africa are legal tender in Namibia, and vice versa, but Namibia intends issuing its own currency in 1992-93.

Exchange Rates

At the time of writing, the South African rand had the following values against other currencies:

US$1	=	R2.83
A$1	=	R2.24
UK£1	=	R4.87
¥100	=	R2.17
DM1	=	R1.67
SFr	=	R1.93
FFr1	=	R0.49
NZ$1	=	R1.60
C$1	=	R2.55
BotP1	=	R1.28
Z$1	=	R0.52

There is no limit to the amount of money that you can bring into Namibia in the form of currency or travellers' cheques unless you are travelling via South Africa, in which case you are not allowed to enter or leave the country with more than R200.

Travellers' Cheques & Credit Cards

It is possible to cash travellers' cheques and exchange foreign currency notes at any bank, but only the very largest hotels have

this facility. Some small shops will also change limited amounts of foreign currency and may even give you a better rate than the banks. Many hotels and shops will not accept travellers' cheques in anything except South African rand, so it is usually wise to change small amounts of foreign currency or travellers' cheques into cash as you need it. National Park rest camps will not accept foreign currency or foreign travellers' cheques. Most hotels, shops and restaurants will accept credit cards, but you will find that Visa or MasterCard is much more widely used than American Express.

Costs

Because of the favourable exchange rate (if you come from outside South Africa), Namibia is a very cheap country to visit. A camping site place will cost R5, a good hotel room with full board can be had for R50, and you can buy a two kg steak in Windhoek (should you wish to do so) for less than half that amount.

Tipping

It is usual to tip porters, taxi drivers, waiters and room staff at least 10% of the value of the service bought. Tipping is illegal in any of the resorts and game parks operated by Nature Conservation but this ruling is universally ignored.

Bargaining

The only time when it is accepted as reasonable to bargain comes when buying craftwork directly from the artist concerned, as at roadside stalls. But the prices asked will be so low and the average annual income of the seller so small that you have to ask yourself whether this is morally acceptable. Prices in shops are not usually negotiable; the exceptions are artwork and very expensive curios.

Consumer Taxes

There is a tax called general sales tax (GST) which adds 10% to most things that you buy, including food, accommodation and fuel. The purchase of certain luxury goods such as leather and jewellery by tourists may be exempt from this tax if you can produce a valid passport and tickets.

CLIMATE & WHEN TO GO

Namibia, although predominantly a desert country, has regional climatic variations corresponding to the different geographical subdivisions. By far the most hot and arid climate is to be found in the heart of the dune sea, where it is also quite windy under a clear blue sky. There are cold onshore south-west winds all year round at the coast with an east (berg) wind in the winter. These winds are derived from the South Atlantic anticyclone pressure system which ultimately determines the climate of the country.

The upwelling cold Benguela Current and onshore anticyclonic winds produce a steep climatic gradient in the desert from coast to escarpment. Summer temperatures in the desert can reach over 40°C and fall to below freezing at night. Fogs are common at the coast, generally developing during the night and sometimes lasting well into the morning up to 20 km inland.

The Central Escarpment has a higher rainfall than the coast (200 to 400 mm per year), making it both pleasant for visitors and highly suitable for cattle farming. The air is very clear but humidity is low, and there is generally a light wind. Rainfall steadily increases as you go north, reaching a maximum of more than 600 mm per year on the Okavango. This gives the Okavango a lush, tropical woodland and contributes to the many substantial rivers. Rainfall decreases again to the east of the Central Escarpment, on a gradient diminishing to the fringes of the Kalahari Gemsbok Park in South Africa.

The north and interior of the country has two rainy seasons, one short and one long. The main rainfall period, between January and April, may include some powerful thunderstorms. A shorter rainy season occurs any time between October and December, but for the rest of the year the weather is generally dry and cloudless.

Everywhere in Namibia enjoys a

minimum of 300 days of sunshine a year, but temperatures and rainfall vary considerably both seasonally and geographically. There is no time of year when the country is unpleasant to visit, although many people find it best to avoid the Namib and Etosha national parks in the extreme heat of December to March.

The long, narrow coastal belt of the Namib Desert is hot all year round and air temperatures reach over 40°C in summer. The presence of the cold offshore Benguela Current moderates this heat a bit and produces pleasant onshore winds. It also causes dense fogs, especially during autumn and winter, which roll in before dawn and sometimes last until lunchtime. This does not mean that the sun is less intense: you can still get sunburnt through the fog. For part of the year there is also a nasty east wind in the Namib, generally around June and July, which can bring tremendous three-day sandstorms to the desert and make it effectively impossible to move around. East winds also stir up the dust all over the country, and their unpleasant effects can be felt in Windhoek. The best time to visit the Namib is between May and September, when the sun is less intense, although the nights are still extremely cold.

Some resorts close for part of the year. Halali Rest Camp in Etosha is closed from 1 November until the second Friday in March, as is the Ai-Ais Hot Springs Resort. Others, such as Swakopmund, become extremely busy over Christmas and Easter and during the long school holidays.

The semi-arid mountainous Central Escarpment (including the Windhoek area) has temperatures a bit lower than the rest of the country and considerably lower than the Namib, but it is pleasant to visit all the year round. There are two rainy seasons, a 'short rains' between October and December and a main rainfall period between January and April. During this time you may get the occasional thunderstorm and short, sharp shower, but this is quickly over and merely gives the country a fine clean appearance and lays the dust. The rest of the year you can

rely on relatively cloudless sunshine with the days getting hot – above 40°C in January and sometimes falling below freezing at night. The orange groves around Omaruru will be in production during the winter, and local fruits are at their best between July and September.

The low-lying north-eastern and south-eastern regions, which are effectively extensions of the Kalahari and Karoo of Botswana and South Africa, get much hotter than the Central Escarpment and do not receive so much rain. In the north the bush cover gets much thicker as you move into the high rainfall area of Kavango and Eastern Caprivi. The main rainy season early in the year means that the rivers may be in flood between January and March, so it is wise to get some local information before you start along the Caprivi Strip at that time of year. Some roads in the east of the country may also become unpassable at that time and driving conditions on others, even the road up to the Waterberg Plateau Park, become quite tricky.

TOURIST OFFICES
Local Tourist Offices
The main tourist office for the country is located in the City Hall building in the centre of Windhoek. There are small tourist offices in the municipal buildings of all but the smallest towns in Namibia; and smaller information bureaux in Karibib, Usakos, Omaruru, Okahandja and Gobabis, all of which are open during office hours.

The Visitor Centres at Daan Viljoen Game Reserve, Gross Barmen Hot Springs and the Von Back Dam all have visitor information produced by Nature Conservation. Unfortunately the local information they give out is of variable quality but you'll be able to pick up some brochures and maps. They also carry a 'What's On' listing and information about forthcoming events.

Information centres are also to be found in game parks, and there are tourist offices in resorts. In Windhoek there is a Tourist Information Service stand inside the municipal buildings on Neser Strasse, clearly signposted from Kaiser Strasse. All these offices will have a basic range of information about the country, although in the case of small municipal offices this will have a markedly regional focus.

Information can be obtained in advance from:

SWA Publicity & Tourist Association
   PO Box 1868, Windhoek 9000 (☎ (061) 28160)
Namibia Tourism
   Private Bag 13346, Windhoek 9000, (☎ (061) 220241)

Overseas Reps
Germany
   Namibia Verkehrsburu, Postfach 2041, W-6380 Bad Homburg 3, Im Atzelnest 3 (☎ (06172) 406650)
South Africa
   Namibia Tourism, The Carlton Centre, PO Box 11405, Johannesburg 2000 (☎ (011) 331 7055)
   Namibia Tourism, The Sanso Centre, St George's St, PO Box 739, Cape Town 8000 (☎ (021) 419 3190)
UK
   South Africa Tourism Board, Regency House, 1-4 Warwick St, London W1R 5WB (☎ (071) 439 9661)

USEFUL ORGANISATIONS
The post-independence reorganiastion of Namibia's government has put tourism and wildlife into the same ministry, but the wildlife department, now the Directorate of Nature Conservation, is universally known just as Nature Conservation and has a considerable degree of autonomy. It controls all national parks, game parks and most of the resorts in Namibia and is a mine of information about the country's wildlife. There is an information and booking office in Windhoek on Kaiser Strasse (Independence Ave) next to Verwoerd Park. You can also contact them in advance at: Directorate of Nature Conservation, Director of Tourism (Reservations), Private Bag 13267, Windhoek 9000 (☎ (061) 36975 reservations, (061) 33875 information).

The most useful organisation for information on road conditions is: Automobile Association of Namibia, PO Box 61, Windhoek 9000 (☎ (061) 24201)

BUSINESS HOURS & HOLIDAYS
Business Hours
Normal business hours are Monday to Friday from 8 am to 1 pm and 2.30 to 5 pm. Some organisations may be open on Saturday between 8 am and 1 pm, and some open at 7.30 am and close around 4 pm in winter. Lunch hour closing tends to be quite strictly enforced.

Banks, government departments and information offices all keep to these hours, as do car hire firms and other businesses that you might otherwise reasonably expect to be available in the evenings or weekends. The Namibian phone book will sometimes give a 24-hour number, but the relevant switchboard may not be staffed.

Petrol stations in major towns are often open 24 hours a day, but in outlying areas you may have difficulty getting fuel out of hours or on Sundays, so it is wise to be prepared. In towns, supermarkets are generally open over lunchtime and at the weekends, and small corner shops are often open late into the evening.

Anything run by Nature Conservation will adhere to its published hours almost to the minute.

Public Holidays
Namibia has the following public holidays when banks and most shops will be closed:

1 January
   New Year's Day
March/April
   Good Friday, Easter Sunday, Easter Monday
1 May
   Workers Day
Aporil /May
   Ascension Day
7 October
   Day of Goodwill
10 December
   Human Rights Day
25 & 26 December
   Christmas, Boxing Day

School holidays are when resorts are at their busiest. The main summer holidays run from approximately mid-December to mid-January, and there are three shorter breaks towards the ends of March, June and September.

CULTURAL EVENTS

The Windhoek Carnival in late April, the Windhoek Oktoberfest in late October, and the Windhoek agricultural show in late September are the major social events in Namibia. Another event to watch for is Herero Day, towards the end of August, when Herero people in traditional dress gather at Okahandja for a memorial service to their chiefs who were killed in the Khoi-Khoi and German wars.

POST & TELECOMMUNICATIONS
Post Offices

The post offices in all major towns are open during normal business hours: there are some small offices in resorts which offer a more limited service during the same hours. Namibia's main post office is the Windhoek GPO in Kaiser Strasse, which is open theoretically only during business hours but in practice at lunchtime as well.

All post offices will sell you the current issues of magnificent souvenir stamps for which Namibia is famous. The Windhoek GPO has a special department upstairs for philately enthusiasts.

Sending Mail

Internal post within the country is extremely slow – rumour has it that six weeks is not an unusual delivery time. Overseas airmail, on the other hand, is pretty fast; cards or letters to Europe take around five days if posted in Windhoek, longer if posted elsewhere. Hotels will post mail for you but there are plenty of mailboxes around and the collection times are clearly marked.

Mail is cheap: a postcard to Europe costs only 25 cents. Parcel post is also cheap due to the favourable exchange rate of the rand but there are fussy restrictions on parcel wrapping and customs declarations, so check first before you post. If you plan to buy a lot of heavy souvenirs there are a number of agencies which will ship them for you (check the Windhoek Yellow Pages for a current list).

Receiving Mail

Mail sent to a street address in town will be

slower to arrive than mail sent to a box. If you are staying in an outlying area, remember that your mail will take much longer than mail sent to a major urban centre. The further the distance from Windhoek, the longer your mail will take to arrive. You can arrange for your mail to be send to a hotel or to await your arrival at a post office or any major travel agent, but you will need to warn them in writing well in advance and give your arrival dates. To collect your mail from a post office counter you will probably need to show identification.

Telephone, Fax & Telecommunications

Phones in Namibia are relatively efficient but the lines may not be very clear. Answerphones are uncommon and it is quite difficult to contact a business or organisation outside office hours. You can make local and international calls from post office booths or hotels but there are no phone boxes in the streets.

Fax machines are becoming increasingly popular for businesses and there are bureaux in major towns where you can send and receive faxes. These open and close all the time but they are not difficult to find – ask at the nearest bank or post office and they will direct you. Most of the medium-size and larger hotels will send a fax for you.

Cellular technology has yet to hit Namibia and the mobile phone is unknown, but in very rural areas there are short-wave radios. Some really isolated locations (like the Desert Research Unit at Gobabeb) only have a radiotelephone. Radiotelephone numbers are listed in the phone book, but the procedure (also listed) is a bit more complicated than picking up the phone and dialling, and you may have to book calls with the operator in advance.

There's only one slim telephone directory for the whole of Namibia but it conveniently lists most people's private and work addresses and has a separate section for government departments. It also has a useful Yellow Pages which is effectively a business guide to the whole country.

TIME

Namibia is two hours ahead of Greenwich Mean Time, so when it's noon in London it's 2 pm in Windhoek.

ELECTRICITY

Electrical appliances run on 220/240 V and almost all wall sockets in Namibia take big, round three-pin, 15-amp plugs. If you have a continental or US adaptor you may well find that it can't cope. A cheap solution is to buy a plug for R1.50 and fit it to your appliance while in the country. In addition, if you are using US appliances (which operate on much lower voltage), you will need a voltage adaptor. Some appliances (such as shavers) have a switch so you can readily alter the voltage.

LAUNDRY

Hotels (even the smallest) almost always have a laundry service, generally with a 12-hour or 24-hour turnaround. All small towns have a laundry but self-service launderettes are not common outside Windhoek. However, washing machines are widely available at camping sites and resorts. Dry-cleaners can be found in major towns. It will cost about R5 to dry-clean a skirt or pair of trousers, and about R2.50 to get a shirt laundered.

WEIGHTS & MEASURES

Namibia works on the metric system; distances are measured in km and weights in kg.

BOOKS & MAPS

There are lots of books about the country written in English, German and Afrikaans, and all Namibian bookstores have a 'local' section. You may find it difficult to buy any of these in other countries, even in specialist bookstores. Recommended books include:

Etosha by A Mertens (Nasionale Boekhandel); not available outside Namibia
Namibia by D Cubitt (Don Nelson, Cape Town)
Skeleton Coast by A Schoeman (Macmillan, South Africa); hardback only

The Namib by Mary Seely (Shell Oil, Namibia);
written by the Director of the Desert Research
Unit

If you're interested in desert survival read
The Sheltering Desert by Henno Martin,
written in 1957 and republished in 1983 by
Donker (South Africa). It tells the story of
the two years spent by Martin and his friend
Hermann Korn living like San in the desert
to avoid internment during WW II. Some
parts are not recommended for vegetarians,
but it has possibly the best descriptions of the
ecology of the Namib that I have ever read.

Bookshops
There are a number of good bookshops in
Windhoek, including the two branches of the
South African CNAA chain in Kaiser Strasse
and in the Post Strasse Mall. These sell
everything from newspapers and magazines
to dictionaries and journals. All bookshops
have separate sections for works in
Afrikaans, German and English, books in
English being in the majority. Lüderitz and
Swakopmund have good bookshops and
many small towns will have a book section
in the supermarket or general store.

Maps
Maps are available from bookstores and
Nature Conservation offices, and road maps
are often free at petrol stations. If you want
a really detailed topographic or geological
map, then ask at the Nature Conservation
office on Kaiser Strasse, Windhoek, about
current availability. They are not on open
sale, but can be obtained from the relevant
government department.

MEDIA
Newspapers & Magazines
Namibia has several newspapers, including
the *Namib Times* (Walvis Bay), the *Times of
Namibia*, *Die Suidwester* and the *Windhoek
Observer*, which is probably the best. None
are distinguished by their unbiased coverage
of events or mastery of the rules of journal-
ism but they are a good way of finding out
what's on. The readily available South

African daily papers are better sources of
world news and some European newspapers
can be bought at CNAA branches in
Windhoek. German newspapers are also
available in Windhoek and Swakopmund
together with a full range of magazines and
journals such as *Time* and *Newsweek*. Prices
are quite steep – *Time* may cost you R10 –
and deliveries are a bit erratic.

Radio & TV
Radio Namibia has a service in three
languages on different wavebands. A
Namibian television station operates in the
evenings between 5 and 11 pm, half in
English and half in Afrikaans, but it is
eminently missable due to a lack of pro-
fessionalism and not a lot of local news. Few
places, apart from larger hotels, provide TV
in bedrooms (at some hotels it is an optional
extra) although there is usually one available
somewhere in a bar or lounge. The largest
Windhoek hotels have the American Cable
News Network (CNN) and some have videos
in the rooms. TV reception is not possible
throughout Namibia, anyway, and many
isolated farms do not have a set. Video
rentals are popular and there are lots of video
shops.

FILM & PHOTOGRAPHY
Namibia is a photographer's paradise. The
numerous camera shops in Windhoek and
Swakopmund can process B&W film in just
a few days, arrange for colour processing,
printing and enlargements, and supply pro-
fessional-quality films and all photographic
supplies. Film tends to be expensive in
Namibia and it is wise to arrive with ample
supplies, although you will certainly be able
to buy your favourite variety in Windhoek.
However, unusual varieties of film may be
hard to come by in remote areas, as local
shops will probably only stock basic varieties for colour prints. Most camera shops
offer a repair service and will mount photographs.

Because of the heat and dusty conditions
it is wise to keep your film and camera in a
sealed container when not in use. A cheap

icebox or coolbag serves the purpose admirably.

WOMEN TRAVELLERS

Solo women travellers are an unusual sight in Namibia and hitching alone is not really recommended. It's safe to walk around any of the towns except in unlit areas at night, although during the last year there has been an uncomfortable escalation in the amount of rapes and muggings, especially in Windhoek. Avoid carrying a large amount of money.

Namibia is an exceptionally conservative country when it comes to dress. Shorts are not really acceptable in Windhoek where you will look out of place even in bush clothes, although in rural locations there is no problem. In the evenings shorts and sportswear and even sandals will get you barred from some posher restaurants. Beachwear is fine in Swakopmund but don't wear it elsewhere, and visits to former tribal areas or mission stations in the north of the country always merit a skirt or loose cotton trousers.

DANGERS & ANNOYANCES

With the exception of downtown Windhoek, theft is not a serious problem in Namibia. However, you would be wise to lock your car in urban areas and conceal valuables. Over the last year there have been an increasing number of muggings in Windhoek, so it's sensible to avoid badly lit areas at night and not to carry valuable items.

Directorate of Nature Conservation

In Namibian game parks laws are enforced with extreme strictness by the totalitarian regime of Nature Conservation. You cannot gain access to most parks, including Etosha, without being in a car, closed truck, minibus or tour party. All accommodation must be booked before arrival and you are not allowed in on a bike, motorbike or other irregular form of transport. They sign you in, watch you and sign you out again.

The only alternative if you really can't club together with someone to hire a vehicle or join a tour is to hang about a petrol station near the park entrance and beg a lift. However, this is illegal and if caught you can be deported. Hitching in Namibia is also (technically) illegal.

WORK

There is no chance of foreigners getting any sort of work in Namibia, even casual work. This is because of the high unemployment and low population density.

HIGHLIGHTS

Namibia is a quiet, empty, sparsely populated country. It's clean, well organised and with an efficient infrastructure representing the legacy of colonial occupation. It's easy to get around and full of diverse attractions. The Teutonic legacy adds a level of charm; where else could you eat *sachertorte* (a multilayer German chocolate cake) on the edge of the desert with clouds of flamingos overhead?

Namib Desert Everyone going to Namibia wants to see the Namib Desert, from which the country derives its name. This is arguably the most spectacular arid scenery in the world – miles of mountainous red sand dunes between the cold waters of the Atlantic and the jagged edge of the Central Escarpment. You can drive across the northern part, which is flatter and more stony and has isolated mountain ranges sticking up from the plains, and get access to the great dunefield at Homeb or Sossusvlei.

Lüderitz The southern Namib is different again and much favoured by artists because of the extraordinary pastel colours. The little town of Lüderitz in the south of the country makes a good base to explore it from. The area is attractive because of the isolation and extreme aridity. Lüderitz was once a thriving fishing port but is now virtually a ghost town. Nearby, a real ghost town, Kolmaskop, is steadily being taken over by the dunes. Offshore penguin and seal colonies take advantage of the rich fishing in the cold Benguela Current. Lüderitz is now the home of a thriving crayfish (rock lobster) industry and is on the edge of the great Diamond Area (no entry, alas) stretching south to the border with South Africa.

Swakopmund Swakopmund, another coastal town but this time in the centre of the country, provides quite a different experience as it is effectively a small Bavarian village stuck on the coast of Africa. It's full of early German colonial architecture and little *konditorei* (German-style pastry and cake shops) and beer gardens. It's something of a culture shock, especially if you've come over from Zimbabwe or Botswana.

Windhoek German colonial culture pervades much of Namibia, and every small town has some good specimens of period architecture. Windhoek, the capital, has some splendid buildings dating from around the turn of the century, all jumbled up with post-modernist office blocks in a swirl of ethnic mix. Windhoek itself is a must for the visitor, not just for the buildings but because it is such an attractive capital, clean and green yet set in the middle of arid mountain ranges covered in aloes.

Etosha National Park Another major tourist attraction is Etosha National Park, the third largest in the world and one of the least visited. This makes a visit a memorable experience as the park is unlikely to be crowded and there are always plenty of wild animals around. It is centred around a vast salt pan, shimmering like a lake in the fierce sun, except on the rare occasions when the pan holds water and becomes covered by flocks of flamingos. The country around the pan is quite flat bushveld, but there are lots of unobtrusive waterholes where you can sit and watch the activity. You aren't allowed to walk because of the large lion and black rhino population, but there is an excellent gravel road network. Etosha has three rest camps, maintained by Nature Conservation, of which the most striking is Namutoni, a whitewashed theatrical 'Beau Geste' German colonial fort where a bugle call wakes you at sunrise.

Kavango & Caprivi The north-east of the country is less often visited, since before independence this required special permits. It is quite different in character from the arid south and west as a result of higher rainfall. North of Etosha the bushveld becomes dense woodland, and in Kavango you enter a country where people live by the rivers in small kraals, subsisting by mixed farming and fishing. The lush green of the Okavango River and its tributaries are a shock after the dryness of Etosha, and you can see clouds of magnificent swallowtail butterflies, herds of hippos and a thriving population of crocodiles. The Caprivi Strip, the corridor of land connecting Namibia to Zambia, has some small but extremely remote national parks where you can have a real wilderness experience.

Hot Spring Resorts The extensive parks system actually has something for everyone's taste, from the glories of Etosha to the decadent hot spring resorts of Gross Barmen near Windhoek and Ai-Ais in the extreme south. There you can luxuriate in hot mud springs and thermal baths, get a massage, a beauty treatment or just an unusual stopover. The hot spring resorts, which are popular weekend destinations for Namibians, resemble European spa towns in miniature.

Fish River The Fish River Canyon is the most southerly of Namibia's natural wonders and one of the most spectacular. Frequently compared to the Grand Canyon, it is a gigantic ravine, 161 km long, up to 27 km wide, and nearly 550 metres deep. It was cut by the waters of the great Fish River, which is now a mere trickle at the bottom of the chasm. A road links viewing sites along the eastern edge and there is a 90 km hiking trail ending at the hot spring oasis of Ai-Ais.

ACCOMMODATION

Namibia has an extremely wide range of accommodation with something to suit everybody, and the current exchange rate of the rand makes it a cheap country to visit. Hotels, rest camps, caravan parks, guest farms and even safari companies are all graded using a star system, with regular inspections carried out by the Ministry of Wildlife, Conservation & Tourism. A current accommodation list, upgraded yearly, is available from the tourist office in Windhoek.

Accommodation and food is subject to a standard 10% tax which is generally included in quoted prices. It's always worth trying to bargain over rates as hotels often run special offers out of season. Establishments also receive a T grading (a T means that they provide accommodation mainly to tourists) and a Y grading (YY means a restaurant licence only, YYY means fully licensed). You will not be able to get a drink on Sunday out of licensing hours unless you are having a meal, even in a hotel.

Camping

Most towns have camping sites and caravan

parks, which are graded on the same star and T system as hotels. Many will provide bungalows or rondavels with linen and towels, some with private facilities. Many camps have a pool, restaurant and shop. Bungalows generally cost anything between R25 and R80, depending on size and degree of luxury, but as a rough guide a bungalow for four people can usually be had for under R50.

The most expensive rest camps are found in Caprivi and near Windhoek. Some rest camps also have camping and caravan sites attached; these generally cost less than R15 per site. You have to book rest camp accommodation directly with the site as there is no central reservations system. The sites are seldom full, so you are most unlikely to be turned away.

Bush camping is not permitted anywhere in Namibia on public land without permission. If you wish to camp on private land then you have to ask for permission from the farmer. Camping in national parks is restricted to scheduled sites. Nature Conservation enforce this rule with patrols in all their parks and the conservators have quite wide-ranging powers. They almost constitute a paramilitary organisation and it is wise to keep on the right side of them. Friendly specimens do exist but I sometimes feel that they are kept concealed from the public view.

Hostels

There is very little hostel accommodation in Namibia except in Nature Conservation rest camps inside national parks. Cheaper hotels and guest farms have to be used instead.

Nature Conservation Game Parks & Resorts

The best value in accommodation is undoubtedly provided in the game parks and resorts administered by Nature Conservation, all of which must be booked in advance, generally via their office in Windhoek. Camping sites in the parks can cost up to R25 per night but there is always a pool, shop, restaurant, and good ablutions block. If you are travelling in a large party there are often 10-bed dormitory rooms with shared facilit-

ies for R5 per person, and you can get a two-bed bungalow for less than R50 or a five-bed bungalow for less than R100 at many resorts.

All Nature Conservation accommodation is self-catering, but the resorts have restaurants and shops. The only snag is that, although linen, towels and sometimes soap are provided, nothing in the way of cookware or eating utensils can be found, which may be a problem unless you've got camping equipment with you. But there is a always a reasonably priced restaurant at each site.

Namibian residents are entitled to 20% discount on entrance fees (but not on vehicles or accommodation) at any Nature Conservation site. If you book Nature Conservation accommodation you can't occupy it until after noon and you must leave by 10 am on the day of departure. It's possible to book by post or fax at the Windhoek reservations office; they'll send you a confirmation and an invoice.

Hotels

The hotel sector also includes small establishments which might be called guest houses elsewhere and all are classified under a grading system.

One Star One-star hotels have to conform to 71 minimum requirements, including private bathrooms or showers for 25% of the rooms, at least one communal bathroom or toilet for every eight other beds, and a 16-hour floor service for light refreshments. In practice these tend to be very simple hotels with basic accommodation usually available from about R30 per person, although some are even cheaper. You will pay more in Windhoek and in holiday areas like Swakopmund or Lüderitz. Most are owned and managed by a local couple and will offer inclusive terms (B&B, or B&B and evening meal). They will always have a small dining room and a bar, and some have a garden and public rooms as well. Few will have air-con, but all will provide clean, comfortable accommodation with adequate beds and towels.

Top: Old German fort at Namutoni, Namibia (MS)
Middle: Post Street Mall, Windhoek, Namibia (MS)
Bottom: Baroque railway station, Swakopmund, Namibia (MS)

Top: Kolmanskop Ghost Town, Namibia (DS)
Bottom: Shipwreck near Lüderitz, Namibia (DS)

Two Star Two-star hotels must have private bathrooms or showers for 50% of the rooms, room heating on request, a minimum of one communal bathroom and toilet for every seven rooms, a full-time head chef, 16-hour floor service, and 14-hour reception service. This is the commonest hotel classification in Namibia and the category ranges from quite basic hotels to really luxurious hotels like the Strand in Swakopmund. Prices range widely too, but reckon to pay from R50 (single) and R60 (double), rising to R120 at the top of the range.

Three Star Three-star hotels are in the minority as there are only four in the country. They conform to international standards – mostly private bathrooms, heating, wall-to-wall carpets, a range of public rooms and lounges, and an à la carte menu. They all have restaurants, 24-hour reception, room service, guest transport, and high-quality service. You'll pay around R120/160 for a single/double room.

Four Star Four-star hotels are an even rarer species; in fact this category only includes the Kalahari Sands in Windhoek, which is an air-conditioned palace with a salon, valet service and full range of ancillary services aimed at the business and diplomatic traveller. Rates start at R210/240 for singles/doubles.

Guest Farms

In addition to the hotel sector there is a similar star grading system for guest farms, which are generally more expensive than hotels. They will seldom have more than half a dozen rooms and you need to book well in advance. Guest farms provide a unique insight into how the country actually works, because you are living on a working farm. You receive intensely personal service, often at luxury level, but they're a pricey way to see the country.

It is wise, when booking, to check that your chosen farm is not on the list specially recommended for hunters. Some farms have a 'hunting season' but are open for visitors

interested in game viewing and photography at other times of year. The following farms are currently for hunters only:

Karibib
    Farm Khomas
Okahandja
    Farm Matador
    Farm Okatjuru
    Farm Wilhemstal-Nord
Windhoek
    Farm Bellerode
    Farm Ibenstein
    Farm Mountain View
    Farm Ongoro-Gotjari

FOOD
Snacks

One of the nicest things about eating in Namibia is the numerous German konditorei where you can buy fresh apple strudel and delicious pastries and cakes. Anton's, in Swakopmund, is a national institution, but the products do not travel well, especially out into the desert! Windhoek and Lüderitz also have good cafes, and there are small coffee shops in all towns.

Windhoek and Swakopmund have a number of establishments, including the coffee shops of larger hotels, where you can get an inexpensive snack-type lunch.

Breakfast

With the exception of Windhoek and Swakopmund, eating out in Namibia is not a gourmet delight. All the hotels serve three meals a day, but menus are very meat-oriented. Do not be surprised to find curried kidneys with your breakfast eggs. Breakfast, the cooked sort, always includes bacon and a heavy sausage called *boervors* ('farmer's sausage'). Few can eat more than one. The big hotels in Windhoek and Swakopmund, such as the Safari, sometimes offer a buffet breakfast with the price of your room. All sorts of delights will be on offer, including kippers (smoked kingklip), porridge, the usual English breakfast constituents, and a wide range of German breads, cold meats, cereals and fruit. In fact you hardly need to eat anything else all day. Smaller hotels will almost always give you a cooked breakfast, but cereal and toast may be had for the asking, though there will not be much variety. Namibian toast is terrible – stale white bread left to get cold and rubbery. Lots of people still eat a hearty steak for breakfast. Coffee is barely adequate, except at German-run establishments, and tea is variable.

Main Meals
The components of cooked lunches and dinners tend to be similar if you are staying in hotels. Most people take a packed lunch or (if in a town) patronise the local takeaway, which is inevitably located near the bottle store and makes everything from a sandwich (made in a bread roll called a *brötchen*, which is filled *mit* (with) something, as in brötchen mit ham). Other takeaway favourites including oryx pie and chips. Fish & chips are very popular and readily available in even the smallest towns.

Meals in the evening mainly feature meat (usually beef, rarely lamb or chicken). If you are a carnivore then the meat is delicious; a huge fillet steak will set you back about R20 (more in bigger hotels) but its accompaniments are limited. Fish, inevitably kingklip, is best eaten at the coast when you can be sure it is fresh. Chicken, often in a *peri-peri* (peppery sweet-and-sour) sauce, is sometimes available.

You may also get the opportunity to try some Afrikaner desserts like *koeksisters* (a kind of sweet dumpling), or *melktart* (milk tart). For after dinner it is worth remembering that a factory in Windhoek makes Springer liqueur chocolates – delicious but expensive.

Fruit & Vegetables
Namibia still imports most of its food from South Africa. Potatoes accompanying a main meal will almost always be chips, and vegetables will not be served in profusion and may well be frozen or tinned. The most popular fresh vegetables are the squash family, of which the nicest are gemsquash (a

hard, round, green ball) and butternut squash (which looks like a yellow gourd). Pumpkin is also common.

Fruit is expensive except in winter, but in season the oranges are delicious. Paw-paws (papaya), picked straight from the tree with a six-metre pole and a basket to catch them, take some beating when served with a squeeze of lemon or lime. Travel in Kavango during July to enjoy this treat at its best. The fruit season is roughly from May to September. Outside that period, fruit and salad things can get expensive, as everything will be imported via South Africa and you pay the markup, which makes even apples quite pricey.

If you have transport or are travelling in a party, buy a big five kg or 10 kg box or bag of fruit from a supermarket in Windhoek, the open market in Tal Strasse, or one of the wholesalers in the North Windhoek Industrial Estate. In northern Namibia, fruit can sometimes be bought by the wayside, and even down near Keetmanshoop there is a fruit-growing area whose products are cheaper from roadside stalls than from the supermarket.

Self-Catering
All the big towns feature one or more supermarkets with the basic necessities but sometimes with few frills. Food becomes more expensive as the distance from the capital increases. There are a number of corner shops which are often Portuguese owned and sell everything from animal feed to the occasional spit-roasted chicken. Special treats to watch for are rusks (hard, cake-like biscuits, wonderful for travelling but heavy on the teeth). Ooomas are the best brand – they come in all sorts of varieties, and are apparently indestructible and unaffected by being stuffed in the corner of a rucksack. I recommend the marmalade flavour for breakfast.

Meat and sausage *(wors)* is bought from a corner *slagtery* (butchers) which will have a better selection than the supermarket, and bread from a corner *bakkery* (bread shop).

Biltong (dried meat in strips or shavings) comes in packs of every shape and size, mostly beef biltong but some game (*wildsbiltong*) including gemsbok and ostrich. The latter is considered a delicacy, but I thought it was rather bland. There is also a good variety of German salami and smoked meats together with unique local sausages called *landjager*. These wonders are about 15 cm long, two cm square and completely solid. You end up gnawing them like a bone, but the flavour is good and they are cheap and last forever.

Cheese is expensive, uncommon and generally of the Edam variety. Decent cheese can only be bought in Windhoek and it is very expensive. If you are camping, bear in mind that cheese, like meat, has a limited lifespan, so consider buying tinned feta (goat's milk cheese), which sounds ghastly but is in fact delicious.

DRINKS
Nonalcoholic Drinks

Water in Namibia is safe to drink but may be very salty and unpalatable, especially in the desert areas and up in Etosha. Those in the know take a large water container if travelling by car and fill it up when passing through Windhoek. Some Namibian bottled water is available but only in one-litre quantities and at considerable expense. Fruit juices are plentiful but vary in quality. My favourites are the Liquifruit range, which includes apricot, peach, mango-pineapple and combinations. The peach one mixed with sparkling wine makes a great Bellini cocktail. Liquifruit comes in huge packs as well as one litre sizes and small pocket packs with straws. Cheaper juices are mainly orange or guava.

Tea and coffee can be had from any takeaway (and there is one in every small town) but Windhoek and Swakopmund have several good coffee houses. There is a particularly ghastly herbal tea called *rooibos* (red bush) tea which is reputed to have therapeutic properties if you can cope with it.

Alcohol

All hotels have a bar attached, although with smaller establishments this can be quite rough and unlikely to serve sophisticated cocktails. Many hotels also have a beer garden with waiter service. Windhoek and Swakopmund also have a number of pleasant bars, generally open only in the evenings and often serving food as well as drink, and Windhoek is famous for its sidewalk cafes where you can sit and watch the world go by. Cafes also serve alcohol, by the way, but generally just wines and beer.

Alcohol is not sold in supermarkets. It must be bought from the local *drankwinkel* (bottle store), which also sells ice (from about 50 cents for a small bag) and is usually open all day except lunchtime and Sundays.

Namibia is a real beer-drinker's country. Various beers are brewed locally, of which the best in my view is Windhoek beer, a light lager-type beer that is uniquely refreshing. It comes in standard lager strength, packaged in cans and bottles of varying sizes from a 350 ml *dumpi* (equivalent to the Australian stubby) to a 'large' 500 ml beer. A dumpi will cost anywhere between R1 and R2 in a beer garden, depending on how posh the surroundings are, and a tray of 24 costs R25 from the bottle store. Windhoek beer is also available in a Special (Export Strength) variety and a low-alcohol variety (Windhoek Light) which is surprisingly agreeable and can be bought everywhere. The other major brewery in Namibia is Hansa, in Swakopmund, which also produces standard and export strength. South African beers like Lion and Castle are widely available, together with many German *weissbier* (white beer) varieties which are slightly more expensive.

It's also possible to get really good South African wines in Namibia. Most bottle stores stock a wide range, including large one to five-litre boxes and economy-size one or two-litre jars. Reds definitely have the edge; some varieties to try are made in the Cape wine-growing district near Stellenbosch from cabernet and pinot grapes. Nederbergs are the most widely available in 750 ml and

250 ml (individual two-glass) sizes. Do not rely on being able to get an exotic cocktail (or even a glass of sherry) outside Windhoek.

And what do you do when camping in the desert and dying for a cold beer? Tie the beer (cans are best) in a sock, soak the sock in water (recycle your washing-up water) and attach the sock to a convenient branch or the wing mirror on your vehicle. The beer is cooled by evaporation.

ENTERTAINMENT

There's not a lot of public entertainment outside Windhoek, which proudly boasts two cinemas and two theatres. A couple of nightclubs and several restaurants feature dancing and a cabaret. Football matches, swimming galas, the occasional event at the Academy or a visiting chamber music ensemble complete the potential entertainment. Most hotels have a TV and some have a radio in each room, but in rural areas your nightlife will mostly be confined to a drink in the bar. The exception is Swakopmund (and to a lesser extent Lüderitz) where there might be some local event to attend.

THINGS TO BUY

There's a wide range of souvenirs, from superb basketry (mainly produced by Wambo people) and Kavango woodcarvings through to African curios and dubious items of airport art.

Quality purchases include the products of the thriving karakul sheep industry, such as rugs, wall hangings and textiles, which are often made to order.

Windhoek is the centre of the upmarket leather industry, also based on karakul as well as locally farmed ostrich and crocodile. You can get extremely high-quality products, from belts and handbags to beautiful made-to-measure leather jackets.

The colours of the Namib inspire a number of local artists, and many galleries in Windhoek and Swakopmund specialise in local paintings and sculpture.

Minerals and gemstones are also popular purchases, either in the raw form or cut and polished as jewellery, sculptures or carvings. Malachite, amethyst, chalcedony, aquamarine, tourmaline, jasper and rose quartz are among the most beautiful.Chess sets and other art objects are made from marble quarried near Karibib. Kudu leather shoes ('Swakopmunders') make a good souvenir of the desert.

Getting There & Away

AIR

To/From South Africa

Windhoek's J G Strijdom International Airport is about 42 km east of the city. South African Airways (SAA) operates daily flights from there to Johannesburg and Cape Town with connections to other cities in southern Africa. There are daily flights from Eros Airport, Windhoek, to and from Oranjemund, Johannesburg and Cape Town in South Africa on Namib Air. A single fare to Johannesburg or Cape Town will cost at least R300 on either SAA or Namib Air.

Namib Air is producing a new timetable and price structure in October 1991.

To/From Zambia, Zimbawe & Botswana

Namib Air flies twice a week (Wednesday and Friday) from Harare to J G Strijdom, twice a week (Wednesday and Friday) from Lusaka, and once a week (Saturday) from Gaborone. There is also a small Beechcraft 1900 flight to Windhoek (Eros Airport) from Victoria Falls on Monday, Wednesday and Friday. Namib Air also flies a Beechcraft to Eros Airport from Maun about three times a week. As a rough guide, the price from Maun to Windhoek is currently R331.

LAND

Border Crossings

There are border control posts between Namibia and Botswana at Buitepos, 125 km east of Gobabis (4WD only); Ngoma, 60 km south-east of Katima Mulilo (all vehicles), and Mohembo, 25 km south of Bagani (all vehicles). The only control post between Namibia and Zambia is at Wenela, four km north of Katima Mulilo (all vehicles). Road traffic between Namibia and South Africa is monitored on the road between Upington and Nakop at Ariamsvlei, through Mata Mata on the border of the Kalahari Gemsbok Park, through Rietfontein (Aroab) and Velloorsdrift (gravel roads), and at Noord-oewer on the main tarred road from Cape Town.

To/From South Africa

Bus A luxury Mainliner coach service between Johannesburg, Cape Town and Windhoek runs twice a week from each city. The fare from Cape Town is around R245; the coach stops everywhere you can think of en route and takes about 16 hours. It connects at Windhoek with a service to Walvis Bay, which costs R75 and takes about five hours.

The operating company, F P du Toit Transport, has a Windhoek reservations number (☎ (061) 227847) and has branches in all Namibian towns. You can also book via the American Express offices in Cape Town or Johannesburg and thus via their network worldwide.

Train It's also possible to reach Windhoek by train from South Africa, although this involves quite a tedious rail journey from Upington, where the Namibian railway connects with the South African system since the train originates in Cape Town. Journey time from Upington to Windhoek is around 24 hours and the train from Upington to Windhoek runs on Saturday, Monday and Friday. The train leaves Cape Town at either midnight or 2 am, reaching Upington eight to 10 hours later and Windhoek 24 hours after that (via Karasburg and Keetmanshoop). The one-way, 2nd-class fare to Cape Town is R192. The train changes from South African Railways to TransNamib Ltd at the border.

Car & Motorbike You can drive to Namibia along good tarred roads from South Africa, either from the south (Cape Town direction), crossing the border at Noordoewer, or from the east (Johannesburg and Upington) with a border crossing at Nakop. Alternative routes involve driving on gravel roads into south-eastern Namibia at Rietfontein, near Aroab, or further north at Mata Mata from the Kalahari Gemsbok Park in South Africa.

An international driving licence is a prerequisite for driving into and within Namibia.

Hitching It is possible to hitch across the border from South Africa, especially with trucks. Drivers occasionally want money for lifts; an informal rate of R5 for 100 km is about right, though you should agree on a price before starting.

To/From Zambia, Zimbabwe & Botswana
Bus & Train There are no bus or train links across the border from Namibia to Zambia, Zimbabwe or Botswana, so you'll have to fly or find road transport.

Car & Motorbike A gravel road from Windhoek through Gobabis to Botswana crosses the border at Buitepos, but it's only suitable for 4WD traffic. It's also possible to drive across from Botswana to Namibia at the extreme eastern tip of the Caprivi Strip at Ngoma and Mohembo (both suitable for ordinary cars), though the road along the Caprivi Strip is only marginally passable for vehicles without 4WD.

You can also drive from Zambia via the border crossing at Wenela near the Namibian town of Katima Mulilo in east Caprivi. There is no land access to Angola, but this may change in the near future.

Hitching It is possible to hitch across all the borders but traffic is very sparse and you could wait a long time, perhaps days. The Caprivi Strip is notoriously difficult to hitch along since there is little traffic and most of it is local. However, the situation has improved since independence. Drivers in official cars have strict instructions not to pick up hitchers.

SEA

Cruise liners and other passenger vessels on regular scheduled routes do not call at Walvis Bay, although you can reach Cape Town easily by sea and then continue your journey by car, bus or rail.

RIVER

The border crossing across the Kunene between Namibia and Angola was closed, but at the time of writing there were rumours that it was due to be reopened.

Getting Around

AIR
Local Air Services
Namib Air operates a network of internal flights from Eros Airport in Windhoek. You can fly to Katima Mulilo (Monday, Wednesday and Friday), Keetmanshoop (Tuesday and Thursday), Lüderitz (Tuesday, Thursday and Sunday), Oshakati (Tuesday and Thursday), Rundu (Monday and Wednesday), Swakopmund (Tuesday, Thursday, Friday and Sunday) and Tsumeb (Monday, Tuesday, Wednesday and Thursday) and make connections between any of these places as well. A full timetable and information is available from Namib Air (☎ (061) 38220), which has a new head office in the approach to the mall area in Post Strasse, Windhoek, just off Kaiser Strasse.

All these timings may have changed with the introduction of a new schedule in late 1991. Price rises are likely as well, but here are some single internal airfares from Windhoek (Eros) from the current timetable to give an idea of the scale: Swakopmund R90, Oshakati R317, Tsumeb R231, Rundu R282, Katima Mulilo R455, Keetmanshoop R205, and Lüderitz R364.

BUS
Scheduled bus travel in Namibia is quite limited, but it is possible to see the sights by taking a long-distance coach from Windhoek to any other major town and then joining a tour or exploring your options. The main coach stop in Windhoek is opposite the Kalahari Sands Hotel on Kaiser Strasse, where a current timetable is displayed.

The Mainliner international coach service runs twice a week between Windhoek and Cape Town and will enable you to stop off at Rehoboth, Mariental, Keetmanshoop or Grünau before the border crossing at Noordoewer. If you take the twice-weekly Mainliner service on the Johannesburg route, the first four stops are the same; but you can also reach Karasburg before the border

crossing at Ariamsvlei. The cost from Windhoek to Keetmanshoop is R97 and the buses are air-conditioned, with meals, reclining seats and videos available. Only two items of baggage are allowed, and they must not exceed a total of 30 kg; no excess baggage is carried unless there is space available. Fares include refreshments and meals.

There's also a regular Mainliner coach from Windhoek to Walvis Bay via Swakopmund three times a week which costs R75 and takes five hours. You can reach Tsumeb via Grootfontein on a Mainliner, with three departures per week and a fare of R79.

TRAIN
Like buses, train travel within Namibia is limited, being confined to the main routes from the south to Windhoek and from Windhoek west to the coast and north to the Golden Triangle round Grootfontein, Tsumeb and Otavi. The trains are now operated by TransNamib Ltd (☎ 293-3030), which took over from South African Railways when Namibia became independent. However, services are extremely slow and, with the exception of the main north-south line, they mix passengers and freight and appear to stop at every single tree. Trains run infrequently and schedules are still a bit flexible – check with the station well in advance of travel or call TransNamib. There are three classes of travel and it is necessary to make reservations at the relevant station office when you get there. Trains are never fully booked as they are not a popular mode of transport.

You can get a train on Friday and Sunday from Windhoek to Tsumeb via Otjiwarongo and Otavi and make connections to Okahandja and Grootfontein. Trains from Windhoek to Walvis Bay leave on Tuesday, Friday and Sunday, and from Otavi to Grootfontein on Monday and Saturday. The main line from Upington will drop you at

Keetmanshoop where you can connect with a train to Lüderitz on Friday and Sunday.

You could, if you wanted, even charter your own train through TransNamib: a splendidly Victorian concept.

TAXI

Taxis are available in Windhoek at the stand opposite the Kalahari Sands Hotel (☎ (061) 37070); you can order one by phone or hire it at the stand. All are fitted with meters. It is not easy to get a taxi in the middle of the night and you would be wise to order one beforehand. Hotels will always book a taxi for you, but even in Windhoek it may be difficult to find one yourself at night as they don't cruise the streets.

CAR & MOTORBIKE

By far the easiest way to get around Namibia is by road. There is an excellent system of main tarred roads running north-south the entire length of the country. These are joined by equally good tarred roads reaching the coast at Lüderitz and Swakopmund. Good-quality gravel roads lead to most places of interest. All but the smallest gravel roads are passable for 2WD cars. As a rule of thumb, think twice about travelling along any road whose classification begins with a D unless you have checked its condition in advance.

Motorbikes are not very common in Namibia (probably because of the condition of the roads) and are not permitted in the national parks. If you are bringing a motorbike, spare parts and servicing facilities may be limited, but they do exist in Windhoek because of the popularity of all-terrain cycles as recreational vehicles.

Drivers should be aware that Namibia has recently adopted a new system of road numbering. This book used the new system, but old maps may still have the old numbers listed.

Road Rules

Drive on the left as in the UK. There's a general speed limit of 120 km/h on open roads and 60 km/h in built-up areas. Driving in Namibia theoretically requires an inter-national driving licence, but in practice a valid driving licence from your own country is usually enough.

Gravel Road Driving

Driving on gravel roads is a minor art form. The following points may help if you are a novice:

1. Keep your speed down: 100 km/h at most, but 80 km/h is safer.
2. Stick to the ruts made by previous cars.
3. If the road is corrugated, gradually increase your speed until you find the correct speed (you'll know when you can hardly feel the corrugations) and stick there.
4. Watch the bends; if a curve is signposted, drop your speed by at least half before making the turn.
5. If something is coming in the opposite direction, reduce your speed and keep as far to the left as you can; it's customary to wave if you're on quite a remote road!
6. Check the recommended tyre pressures and keep them slightly softer than you would when driving on tar.
7. Avoid travelling at night if you can.
8. In rainy weather the roads will rapidly get muddy and you may get streams of water in the middle. Great care is needed.
9. Watch out for animals. Kudus are a great problem at night as they don't get out of the way; hitting one will seriously damage your car as well as the animal. Warthogs and baboons also frequent grass verges.
10. Avoid the temptation to make a sharp swerve to avoid chameleons or snakes if the edges of the road are a bit fragile.

After 100 metres on a gravel road you and everyone in the car will be covered with dust, as will the contents of the boot, if you leave the window open. The alternative is to close the hatches and use air-conditioning, but this may be unacceptable or not available.

Remember to wrap your camera and other fragile items in several layers of plastic bin liners or keep them in sealed containers. The dust is quite easy to wipe or wash off and every garage or hotel will have someone who will be prepared to clean your car if you're fussy.

Rental

It's easy to hire a car in Namibia, as there are

branches of all the main multinationals such as Hertz, Avis and Budget at the International Airport, in the city itself, and in other major towns. I have had problems with all of them at one time or another and now double check all reservations. If you have arranged for a car to meet your plane or train make sure they know *which* airport or station, and treble check.

Car rental offices are often only open during office hours, and their 24-hour number is frequently unattended. I've been stranded several times.

Good local alternative to the big companies include:

Kessler Car Hire, PO Box 20274, Windhoek 9000 (☎ 33451); a 4WD vehicle speciality
Imperial Car Hire, PO Box 1387, Windhoek 9000 (☎ 35819); branches at both Windhoek airports

Whichever company you use it's wise to reserve your car well in advance as vehicles are in limited supply. Expect to pay more than you would elsewhere in southern Africa, as an informal surcharge applies because the cars have such a short life (road conditions are hard). If you're going to be doing a lot of driving, avoid the smallest economy car and go for the next size up with air-conditioning. Rental rates start at R40 per day plus 75 cents per km over any free allowance. A Land Rover costs around R105 per day to hire.

If you are planning to drive a rental car across the border into Botswana or Zimbabwe special papers will be required and you must clear this with the hire company before leaving. Kessler Car Hire can hire you a complete camping outfit, including tent, portable fridge, table and chairs, sleeping bag and mattress.

If you're hiring a truck or other unusual vehicle, remember than you won't be admitted to game parks if the back is open or if it is beach-buggy style.

Purchase

It's possible to buy a vehicle in Namibia, although this probably won't be worth your while unless you are staying a long time. If this option appeals to you try the Kessler Garage in Windhoek, which has a good range of 2WD and 4WD vehicles. You will not be able to use a hire-purchase system unless you are a Namibian citizen, and you are unlikely to be able to get credit. Cash purchase is about the only option, and you'll lose out unless you hold the car for a year.

HITCHING

Hitching is technically illegal in Namibia but you will see some visitors doing it, and the authorities turn a blind eye. For many local people it is a way of life, although they face legal penalties if caught. If you are a driver you should exercise your own discretion about whether to pick up the local hitchers who flag you down frequently on main roads and approach you discreetly at petrol stations.

On unfrequented roads you may have to wait a long time (perhaps days) for a lift in extremely hot conditions. Even then, private car owners will not necessarily pick you up. Namibians themselves (the White population, anyway) do not all approve of hitching. Truck drivers are often friendly and give lifts willingly, even across international borders, but they may make a modest charge. Always determine the cost, if any, before you accept a lift.

LOCAL TRANSPORT
To/From the Airport

There is a regular bus service from the International Airport and from Eros Airport to Windhoek, with a bus meeting each flight. The R20 fare gets you to the middle of town at the main bus stop opposite the Kalahari Sands Hotel.

You can also get a taxi at the International Airport, but a ride to town will be at least R50. You'd be better off taking the bus. Taxis are seldom waiting at Eros Airport but can be called from the phone box. It's often difficult to get one at night.

There is a limited taxi service from other local airports and train stations to town centres, but cards are on display at phone boxes so that you can call on arrival.

Bus

There is a network of elderly 'township' buses which were once used to be used to convey people from outlying residential areas into the cities to work, but these are unreliable and no timetable exists. However, if you have some specific destination in mind, start out walking in the right direction and ask someone where a bus stop is and how frequent the buses are. Township buses are notorious for frequent breakdowns, but the company is a lot of fun and it is a good way to meet people. Bear in mind that this is not a mode of transport which is usually taken by members of the White community so you may be the focus of surprised attention.

With the exception of a possible canoe ride on the Okavango and city-centre taxis, this is the sum total of possible local transport. In rural areas the local people commute by donkey cart, and one can see why.

TOURS

The largest local tour operator is Oryx Tours, but there are several other reputable general and specialist operators:

Desert Adventure Safaris
  PO Box 339, Swakopmund 9000 (☎ (064) 15412); local tours of Swakopmund and the surrounding area
Lüderitz Safari & Tours
  PO Box 76, Lüderitz 9000 (☎ (063) 312719); local tours of Lüderitz and the surrounding area
Namib Air (Tours Division)
  PO Box 731, Windhoek 9000, (☎ (061) 38220); works out personal itineraries for anyone wanting to fly to Etosha via its subsidiary, Namib Flying Safaris
Namib Tours
  PO Box 53, Keetmanshoop 9000 (☎ (063) 13361); local tours of Keetmanshoop and the surrounding area
Oryx Tours of Namibia
  38 Bismarck Street, Windhoek 9000 (☎ (061) 224252, fax (061) 35604)
SAR Travel Bureau
  PO Box 415, Windhoek 9000 (☎ (061) 298-2532)
Skeleton Coast Safaris
  PO Box 20373, Windhoek 9000 (☎ (061) 37567); fly-in safaris to the wilderness area of the Skeleton Coast which cannot be reached by any other means
SWA Safaris Pty Ltd
  PO Box 20373, Windhoek 9000 (☎ (061) 37567)
Toko Safaris
  PO Box 5017, Windhoek 9000 (☎ (061) 25539)

Windhoek

Central Namibia is dominated by the capital, Windhoek, a small, rather elegant city with a distinctly German feel about it located in the dry clean air of the country's central highlands. It is almost the geographical centre of Namibia. It has the major road and rail crossroads and the only international airport, and forms the centre of all business and commercial operations.

Windhoek is in a dip in the highlands of the central plateau at an altitude of 1660 metres. Its suburbs spread out over the surrounding hills, making a series of attractive views for the visitor, and it is laid out on a straightforward grid pattern that facilitates navigation. The city is full of trees and gardens and this greenness, combined with exciting postindependence building projects and the German colonial architectural heritage, makes it an exceptionally attractive place to visit.

The Windhoek skyline is dominated by the Old Administration Building, nicknamed the Tintenpalast (Place of Ink), the Alte Feste (Old Fort; once a fort, now a museum) and three castles (now private houses), each on its own hill. There is also a beautiful German Lutheran church which can be seen from a considerable distance away which acts as a focus for the city.

Windhoek is only just over 100 years old but has a history as diverse as its population. The original settlement in what is now Klein Windhoek was called Aigams (Hot Water) by the Nama people, and Otjomuise (Places of Smoke) by the Herero. Both names refer to the hot springs in the area which served as a focus for early tribal settlement. A visit in 1836 by Sir James Alexander, the British prospector and explorer, resulted in another name change to Queen Adelaide's Bath. Jonker Afrikaner, the Khoi-Khoi leader who was famously victorious in wars with the Herero, then called it Winterhoek after the farm in the Cape where he was born.

The modern name, Windhoek, means 'windy corner' and was corrupted from the original Winterhoek during German colonial occupation from the 1890s, under Curt von François. At that time, the town acted as headquarters for the German Schutztruppe (colonial troops) sent there to keep the peace between Herero and Khoi-Khoi. Many buildings from this period can still be seen, including the Alte Feste which was the administrative capital of German Southwest Africa for more than 10 years around the turn of the century.

After a narrow-gauge railway was built to Swakopmund in 1902, Windhoek experienced a significant period of growth, evolving into the business, commercial and administrative centre of Namibia. It was declared a city in 1965 and now houses the head offices of all Namibian organisations (including Nature Conservation) and also has a series of significant historic monuments and things to see.

Windhoek has an extremely diverse population of around 130,000. The ethnic mix of Namibia is reflected on its streets, where you can see the dominant Wambo, Herero and Damara people, together with Namas, the occasional San, 'Coloureds' and Whites all bustling along. Languages are just as varied, although the shops have a markedly German orientation. However, most of the English-speaking population of Namibia live in Windhoek as well.

Orientation

The heart of Windhoek is Kaiser Strasse which bisects the city and contains most of the major shops and administrative offices. It has just been renamed Independence Avenue but in practice the name is never used (except on some tourist literature) and all the original road signs remain. Outlying suburbs like Pioneerspark and Klein Windhoek are primarily residential and all the tourist accommodation and facilities are

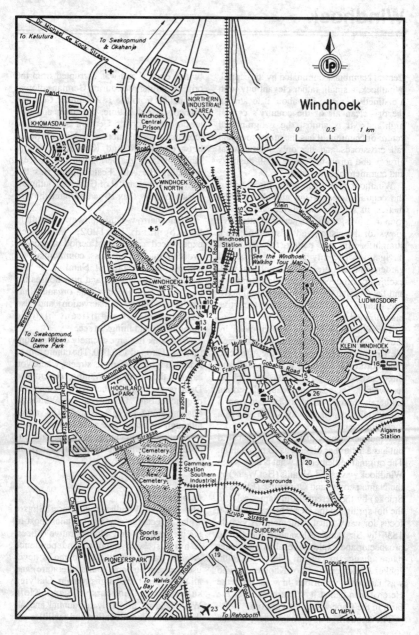

■ PLACES TO STAY	OTHER	14 University of Namibia
		15 Church
3 South West Star Hotel	1 State Hospital	16 Post Office
10 Hotel-Pension Handke	2 Post Office	18 Post Office
11 D'Avignon Hotel	4 Hospital	19 Exhibition Hall
12 Fürsten Hof	5 State Hospital	20 Swimming Pool
17 Hansa Hotel	6 Church	23 Eros Airport
21 Caravan Park	7 Old Locomotive	24 Scherinburg Castle
22 Safari Motel	8 Church	25 Heintzburg Castle
	9 Reservoir	26 Sanderburg Castle
	13 Elizabeth House	

concentrated in the city centre. The tower of the Kalahari Sands hotel and associated Frenchbank Centre is almost in the middle of town and forms a focal point to find your way around. Going north along Kaiser Strasse you get into the industrial areas of north Windhoek on the road to Okahandja, although there is a second commercial area in the south near Eros airport.

If you have transport it's worth driving through the suburbs to get a feel for how Windhoekers live; which is out of doors 300 days a year and quite often in considerable style with lots of ground and a shady verandah.

In the centre of town you'll notice a huge rash of new buildings, some daringly postmodernist in style, around the Park and Tal Strasse areas, including a huge new mall complex along Post Strasse. The city planners have attempted to develop new retail attractions in this area but the level of investment has fallen away since independence and rents are, by Windhoek standards, astronomical. Consequently many units stand empty but are still objects of wonder. Some visitors have been heard to say, though, that the style is more appropriate to a Western capital than an African city.

There are also a number of small alleyways leading west off Kaiser Strasse lined with pavement cafes and small shops which make an agreeable place to watch the action. Verwoerd Park (sometimes called Zoo Park) next to the GPO provides some welcome shade and is a good place to have a picnic before continuing an exploration.

The centre of Windhoek is actually small enough to be explored conveniently on foot.

Information
The local papers, especially the *Windhoek Advertiser*, are a good source of information about current happenings, and the head office of Nature Conservation (☎ (061) 33875), next to the GPO at the junction of Post Strasse and Kaiser Strasse, has information about all their resorts and the national parks.

A publication called *Windhoek Information* with cultural information appears roughly every three months and can be obtained free either from the information centre or most hotels. The Arts Association of South West Africa/Namibia (☎ (061) 31160) has up-to-date information about cultural events and the Automobile Association (☎ (061) 224201) can tell you about the state of the roads.

Tourist Office The main tourist information centre in Windhoek is in the City Hall buildings at the junction of Curt Von François Strasse and Kaiser Strasse, and has information about the whole of Namibia.

Climate The relatively high altitude of Windhoek gives the air a crisp clean feel but also contributes to considerable temperature variations. Windhoek has an average rainfall of 260 to 360 mm a year (mostly in November and January-April) which results in lush gardens and spectacular flowers.

Money Windhoek has branches of all major banks, open during normal business hours. Here again they are almost all concentrated along the short central section of Kaiser Strasse.

Post & Telecommunications The GPO is on Kaiser Strasse right in the centre of town by the side of Zoo Park. It's open during normal business hours. Some of the outlying suburbs such as Klein Windhoek have post offices as well.

Travel Agencies Several Travel agencies have branches in Windhoek, mostly around the Kaiser Strasse area. The largest and most helpful is Trip Travel (☎ (061) 36880) which also has a branch in Swakopmund. Woker Travel (☎ (061) 37946) is also recommended and there is a branch of SAR Travel in the Frenchbank Centre (☎ (061) 298-2532). Any of these agencies can give you up-to-date travel information, as well as booking trips, tours and accommodation.

Bookshops Books, papers, maps and stationery can be bought at the two branches of CNAA Bookshops in the Frenchbank Centre and Post Strasse Mall, or at any of a series of small bookshops on Kaiser Strasse. Some, like Der Bücherkeller round the corner in Peter Müller Strasse, specialise in German-language books.

Things to See & Do

Walking Tour There are more than a dozen buildings reflecting the German colonial legacy in Windhoek, some of which are open to the public and all of which can be reached by walking.

It's nice to start a walking tour in the so-called Zoo Gardens in **Verwoerd Park** on Kaiser Strasse, where you can see the Hottentot memorial and displays of elephant fossils and meteorites found on the site. Look for a glass-topped area near the Kaiser Strasse entrance. It's thought that the elephant bones which it protects were the remains of a prehistoric kill site (possibly dating from the Early Stone Age); you can also see the quartz tools used to cut the carcass up. The **Hottentot Memorial**, an obelisk with a golden imperial eagle on top, was dedicated in 1987 to the memory of Schutztruppe soldiers who died in the wars of 1893-94, fighting Khoi-Khoi led by their renowned chief Hendrik Witbooi.

Walk up Park Strasse to Lüderitz Strasse for a look at the old **Supreme Court**, which was built in 1897-98 as quarters for the state architect, Gottlieb Redecker. He never used the house, which became the magistrates court, complete with a nice shady verandah on the south side for those waiting for their case to be called. The building houses the Namibia Conservatoire.

Just opposite is the **Nursery School** dating from 1896 which does indeed house a nursery school at the moment, but formerly housed the services of the German Lutheran church before the present Christuskirche was built. Looking north down Lüderitz Strasse you can see **Southwest Africa House**, built in 1959 on the site of the former Colonial Governors residence, which is now the official residence of the President. The **Old Garden Wall** once surrounded it but was demolished in 1858 to make way for State House.

Following Lüderitz Strasse south you'll see the **Hauptkasse**, built in 1898-9, which was the financial headquarters of the German colonial administration. It was extended in 1906 and 1909 and later used as a school hostel, and is now part of the Department of Agriculture.

Just opposite, on the corner of Neser Strasse and Peter Müller Strasse, is **Ludwig von Estorff House** which dates from 1891. It was built as a mess for military engineers and named after a former commander of the Schutztruppe who lived there (between campaigns) around 1902-10. The building has taken a turn at being a residence for senior officers, a hostel, a trade school, and finally (today) the Windhoek Reference Library.

One of Windhoek's primary landmarks, the German Lutheran **Christuskirche**,

Windhoek – Walking Tour

0   125   250 m

To Swakopmund
Windhoek Station
Bahnhof Strasse
John Meinert Strasse
Sinclair Strasse
Sinclair Strasse
Anderson Strasse
Holmeyer Walk
Leutwein
Lindequist Strasse
Love Strasse
Leutwein Strasse
TV More Strasse
Tal
Independence Ave
Bülow Strasse
Kaiser Strasse
Lüderitz Strasse
Stübel Strasse
Post Strasse Mall
Park Strasse
Zoo or Vrwoerd Park
Nesei Strasse
Peter Möller Strasse
Car Park
French-bank Centre
Curt Von François Strasse
To Eros Airport
To International Airport & Klein Windhoek
Gobabis Road
Alte Feste

1	Owambo Memorial	15	Library	27	Ludwig Von Esdorff House
2	Police Station	16	St Mary's Cathedral	28	Kaiserliche Realschule
3	Lookout	17	S.W.A. House	29	Kalahari Sands Hotel
4	Thüringer Hof	18	GPO	30	Reiterdenkmal
5	Turnhalle	19	Elephant Remains	31	Officers House
6	Oode Voopost	20	Nature Conservation	32	Historic Train
7	Post Office	21	Old Supreme Court	33	J.G. Van François Stadium
8	Art Gallery	22	Tintenpalast		
9	Kudu Statue	23	Hauptkasse	34	Curt Von François Statue
10	Continental Hotel	24	Christuskirche	35	Tourist Information Centre
11	R.C. Hospital	25	South African Airways Terminal	36	Church
12	Theatre	26	Mainliner Coach & Taxi Stand		
13	State Museum				
14	St George's Cathedral				

stands in an island at the top of Peter Müller Strasse. It's an unusual building made of local sandstone and designed by Gottlieb Redecker in conflicting neo-Gothic and Art Nouveau styles. The corner stone was laid in 1907. If you want to go inside the church the key can be obtained from the church office just down the road in Peter Müller Strasse during business hours.

Walking south from the church along Leutwein Strasse you get a good view of Windhoek to your right, and the road is lined with interesting buildings. The first one on the right is the **Kaiserliche Realschule**, built in 1907-08, which was the first German school in Windhoek. It opened in 1909 with 74 children but was substantially enlarged a few years later. The curious turret with wooden slats to help ventilation was part of the original building. The enlarged building became the first German high school and later an English middle school after WW II.

Just down from the school is the fancy brickwork of the **Officer's House**, built in 1905-06 by the Works section of the German colonial administration, which accommodated the senior officers. You can visit the outbuildings, six-horse stable and saddle room which are used as garages today. The whitewashed ramparts opposite belong to the **Alte Feste** which is the oldest building in Windhoek, dating from 1890-92. It was originally the headquarters of the first Schutztruppe to arrive in 1889 under the command of Curt von François. Although minor changes were made in 1901, the original character was maintained and you can visit the building which today houses the Historical Section of the State Museum. It is open between 8 am and 4 pm on weekdays, and from 10 am to 12.45 pm and 3 to 6 pm at weekends. The train outside with engines and coaches was one of the first narrow-gauge trains to run in the country.

The bronze statue outside the Alte Feste is the **Reiterdenkmal** or Rider's Memorial which was unveiled on 27 January 1912, on Kaiser Wilhelm's birthday. It shows a mounted soldier of the colonial period and commemorates Schutztruppe soldiers killed in Namibia in the Herero-Nama wars of 1904-08.

The road at the side of the Reiterdenkmal leads to the administrative nerve centre of Namibia at the **Legislative Assembly**, a modern building remarkable chiefly for its use of indigenous building materials. It is possible to get a 45 minute tour during weekdays, except when the Assembly is in session, but you should check (☎ (061) 229251) before turning up. Next to the modern building is the **Tintenpalast** (1912-13) which was formerly the headquarters of German South West Africa and subsequently the administrative centre for all governments including the present one. It is set in some lovely gardens laid out in the 1930s and includes an olive grove and bowling green.

Continuing down Love Strasse and Lindequist Strasse to Leutwein Strasse you'll see the **State Museum** on the left which is open Monday to Friday from 9 am to 6 pm, and on Saturday and Sunday from 10 am to 12.30 pm and 3 to 6 pm. Almost next door is the **Windhoek Theatre**, built in 1960 by the Arts Association and still Windhoek's major cultural centre.

The **Anglican Cathedral** of St George is just opposite, located appropriately on Love Strasse. It has the distinction of being the smallest cathedral in southern Africa. The **Diocesan School** is nearby, with a strange construction called the **Mansard Building** in its grounds. This was once a private house but is now part of the school, and remarkable chiefly for its architecture, familiar in Versailles but the only example of a mansard roof in Namibia. The style is totally unsuited to the climate.

There are also a couple of interesting buildings around Werth Strasse, including the **Villa Migliarina** and **Villa Lanvers**, both now private houses and designed in 1907 by Otto Busch. The Lanvers house has a cylindrical tower which gives it a fine castle-like appearance, and both have lovely gardens which (alas) are not open to the public.

Back on Leutwein Strasse you pass the **Turnhalle**, built in 1909 as a practice hall for members of Windhoek Gymnastic Club and also designed by Busch. It was modernised in 1975 and, in its new capacity as a conference hall, housed the political debates of the late 1980s which resulted in Namibian independence. The first sitting of the Constitutional Conference on independence for South West Africa took place there on 1 September 1975 and was known as the Turnhalle Conference.

Round the corner in John Meinert Strasse you pass the **NTN Building** (1905), once six flats for government employees and now the headquarters of the National Theatre of Namibia. Almost next door is the **Oude Voopost**, a simple yet 'classic' colonial building from 1902 which was once the survey offices.

At the corner of Kaiser Strasse and John Meinert Strasse there is a bronze kudu statue, one of a series of battle memorials which include the **Owambo Campaign Memorial** (an obelisk in the garden next to the railway in Bahnhof Strasse near the station) and the **Cross of Sacrifice** in Leutwein Strasse. A statue of Curt von François, the founder of Windhoek, stands proudly outside the municipal buildings in Kaiser Strasse.

Castles Outside the city centre, but just about within walking distance you can see the three Windhoek 'castles' called Schwerinsburg, Heynitzburg and Sanderburg strung out on the Gobabis road. All were built between 1913 and 1918 and are now private homes.

Brewery Tours You can get a tour of the South West Brewery (home of Windhoek Lager and Windhoek Export beers) which used to be located in an old building on Tal Strasse, where it had operated since 1902. The brewing operation recently moved to the Northern Industrial Area out of Windhoek on the Okahanja road. Call (061) 38100 for tour information).

Sports Windhoek has good sporting facilities and there is a fine municipal swimming pool at the south end of town near the corner of Jan Jonker Strasse and Centaurus Strasse.

Walking Trail There is a walking trail called the Hofmeyer Walk through Klein Windhoek valley, which starts at the junction of Orban Strasse and Anderson Strasse. It takes about an hour and gives you a panoramic view of the city and a close-up of the aloes. These cactus-like plants which cover the hillsides near Windhoek are at their best in winter. Look for tiny sunbirds and bulbuls that are attracted by the flowers.

Festivals

As befits a town with such a Germanic flavour, Windhoek has a famous Oktoberfest (generally towards the end of the month). The Windhoek Carnival or 'Wika' is held in late April with a series of events and balls lasting about a week. There is also the Windhoek Agricultural, Commercial & Industrial Show, held in late September/early October on the Show Grounds south of central Windhoek on Jan Jonker Strasse.

Places to Stay – bottom end

Camping Windhoek has no camping sites which are star-graded and officially listed. The best unlisted site in Windhoek is at the *Safari Motel* (☎ (061) 38560) at Eros Airport. You can use the shuttle bus to Windhoek town centre operated by the hotel; it leaves from the main Windhoek bus stop across from the Kalahari Sands around every half-hour.

There is another camping site and caravan park called the *Oasis* behind the Alla Pergola restaurant on Brakwater Rd. Check with the information centre for current status and costs (no telephone number is available).

Hostels There are no student hostels in Windhoek; the closest approximation is the *Windhoek Backpackers Lodge* at 25 Best Strasse (☎ (061) 228355), which costs around R15 per night for self-catering accommodation and comes highly recommended.

Places to Stay – middle

Before independence it used to be quite difficult to get a hotel room in Windhoek. Now, with a reduction in visitors because fewer South Africans are coming in, it's much easier, but some places get booked up in school holidays and with tour groups. In addition, accommodation in Windhoek is more expensive than anywhere else in the country, although it's still cheap compared with Europe or North America because of the exchange rate of the rand.

One-Star Hotels Windhoek has two small one-star hotels. The *Hotel-Pension Handke* (☎ (061) 34904) has 10 rooms with prices starting at R55, but no liquor licence. The *South West Star Hotel* (☎ 061-213205), mainly a bar with rooms out in the suburbs of Khomasdal, is not recommended, though it is cheap: rooms start at R35.

Two-Star Hotels There are several two-star hotels along Kaiser Strasse, including the *Thüringer Hof* (☎ (061) 220631), famous for its beer garden, with rooms from R90. The *Continental* (☎ (061) 37293), just down from the GPO, has recently been remodelled and costs from R80; and the smaller *Hotel-Pension Cela* (☎ (061) 226294) has a very continental atmosphere also for around R80 per night.

The *Hotel Fürstenhof* (☎ (061) 37380) on the other side of the Okahandja road has rooms from R85.

Places to Stay – top end
Three-Star Hotels The *Safari Hotel*, three km out of town near Eros Airport, is probably the best hotel in Windhoek, with pleasant gardens, a shady beer garden and a large pool. The room tariff starts at R100 and includes a huge self-service buffet breakfast. They've recently built a R30 million block of 400 rooms, so you stand a good chance of getting a vacancy. There's a free shuttle service into town and between both airports at half-hourly intervals.

Four-Star Hotels At the top end of the market, Windhoek has the only four-star hotel in the country, the *Kalahari Sands* (tel 36900), right in the middle of town on Kaiser Strasse and priced accordingly. It has recently had a total refit and now has 187 rooms (plus the Presidential Suite) equipped to full international standards with minibar and coffee machines. However, service standards can vary, and with single rooms at around R210 I don't think it offers value for money.

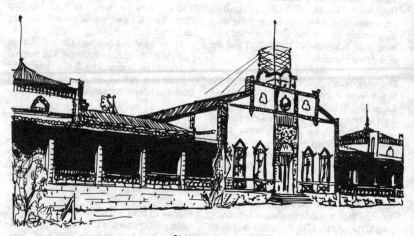

Old post office

Places to Eat

Windhoek has a range of eating places, from elegant and expensive restaurants (generally in hotels) to simple street cafes.

Cafes For a basic cup of coffee try the coffee bar in (strangely) *Wecke & Voights* department store in the Frenchbank Centre, or the *Central Cafe* in the Jack Levinson arcade off Kaiser Strasse, which has pavement tables. They also serve a wide variety of German-style meals (the lentil soup with sausage is recommended) and cakes or pastries for casual meals. There's a takeaway window for filled rolls (*brötchen*) but the place gets really busy at lunchtime.

There's also the *Kaiserkrone Restaurant and Cafe* in Post Strasse, which has good homemade food and is licensed. Expect to pay less than R5 for coffee and a cake and between R5 and R10 for a light meal.

Restaurants My favourite formal restaurant in Windhoek is in the *Hotel Fürstenhof* (☎ (061) 7380), slightly off the beaten track on TV More Strasse. It is a low key but extremely elegant, quiet restaurant serving French-style food with some flair. You'll pay about R25 to R50 for a gourmet meal with wine.

If you are more interested in quantity than finesse, try the evening eat-all-you-like buffet for R25 at the *Safari Hotel* which is very good value. The Italian restaurant *Alla Pergola*, two km along Brakwater Rd, has dinner dances with a cabaret. *La Cave*, in Carl List Haus, round the back of Wecke & Voights in Kaiser Strasse, is a small French-style restaurant popular with local people. *Gathemann's* German restaurant, in one of the old colonial buildings in Kaiser Strasse just opposite the GPO, has a nice terrace and good food with local specialities including kudu steaks. Expect to pay anywhere between R10 and R50 per head in these restaurants, depending on what you eat.

The *Thüringer Hof* hotel has a pleasant German restaurant called the Jagerstübe near its beer garden, but beware of prostitutes who use it to meet clients.

Takeaways & Fast Food There are a number of fast-food outlets in Windhoek, including *Kentucky Fried Chicken*, plus steakhouses of every description and shops selling hot pies and fish & chips. A glance at the *Windhoek Advertiser* will tell you what special offers are around at the moment.

Self-Catering Grocery shopping is best done at either the *OK Supermarket* (Frenchbank Centre on Kaiser Strasse) which is cheap, cheerful and comprehensive, or *Wecke & Voights* almost next door. This is a a small and more expensive department store which specialises in things Germanic and has an excellent food department with a delicatessen in the basement. They make good bread and cakes and will prepare filled sandwiches and rolls for you. They have the best selection of local smoked meats and biltong.

Entertainment

Cinema & Theatre Windhoek has an excellent cinema, Kine 300, on Klein Windhoek Strasse and a drive-in near Eros Airport. There are occasional theatre productions at the Academy and concerts by the Windhoek Conservatoire. The Kalahari Sands hotel has cabaret evenings and there are productions at the National Theatre of Namibia on Leutwein Strasse. The small Warehouse Theatre in the old brewery in Tal Strasse has jazz and light music concerts and visiting serious music as well.

Lectures The State Museum often has special exhibitions and runs a program of evening lectures, films and slide shows. Enquire at the desk. It's well worth a visit anyway for the ethnographic and natural history collections. There's also an occasional lecture programme at the Alte Feste.

Discos The Namib Nite Club, reputedly one of the best discos in southern Africa, has live music at weekends. It's just off Florence Nightingale Strasse in Windhoek North and costs R5 for entry. Ask a taxi driver to take you, as there is no public transport and it seems to be known merely by word of mouth.

Things to Buy

Luxury Clothes Windhoek is the shopping capital of Namibia: you can buy everything from basic camping equipment to expensive fur and leatherwork. Most of the shops selling the latter are around Kaiser Strasse. They look slightly intimidating because of the security precautions but you can buy good-quality small leather goods (belts, purses etc) quite cheaply. Prices vary according to the leather, with ostrich (from local farms) being the most expensive. A buffalo belt (also farmed locally) will set you back around R50 and last forever. Handbags start at around R350 and briefcases at double that. Workmanship is superb and quality is high, for a fraction of European prices. There are also a lot of shops that sell furs and custom-made coats. At the top of the range (and very popular with German tourists) are coats and jackets made from local Swakara (karakul) pelts which start at R1000 for a jacket and can be made to order.

It goes without saying that purchasing souvenirs made from endangered species such as the cheetah or leopard is ethically indefensible, even though they are freely offered for sale. Moreover, you will probably not be allowed to import them into your own country.

Jewellery, Gemstones & Ivory Windhoek has a thriving jewellery industry based round locally mined gemstones and gold. A number of artisans work to order and you'll see a great range of unusual designs in the shops at not-too-outrageous prices. Gemstones and mineral specimens are sold in specialist shops together with a huge range of articles, from animal carvings to clocks. Some of the most spectacular are the green malachite and orange 'tiger's eye' agates.

You'll also see a lot of ivory artefacts and jewellery for sale. Some is imported from manufacturers in Hong Kong and thus of highly dubious origin. It should be avoided at all costs. Some, clearly marked, is locally produced from culled animals from Namibian national parks. If in doubt ask, or (better still) avoid buying ivory altogether in order to stop stimulating the trade. Many countries will not allow you to import items containing ivory.

Curios & Souvenirs There are a number of souvenir shops specialising in inexpensive gifts, including T-shirts (post-independence motifs are popular). Windhoek also has some shops specialising in curios and tribal art, ranging from the mass-produced through to outstanding (and expensive) woodcarvings. Always ask the provenance and check that you don't need an export/import licence. The dealer will have a licence if he or she is authorised to sell antiques and this can be checked with the police. Most of the shops will arrange shipping for you. Less attractive to the tourist for practical reasons is locally made furniture, in simple wood and leather shapes from indigenous artisans, but you can arrange for pieces to be shipped.

Crafts & Markets The Namibia Crafts Centre has been established in the old South West Breweries building on Tal Strasse, intending to open Monday-Friday between 8 am and 5 pm, and on Saturday from 8 am to 1 pm as a permanent showcase and market for handicrafts. At the time of writing work was still in progress.

Every first and third Saturday of the month there is a street market in Kaiser Strasse in front of the GPO which provides an excellent opportunity to meet local people and to buy handicrafts of a higher quality than those found in the souvenir shops. There is a small market at Tal Strasse on weekdays, mainly for vegetables, baskets and woodcarvings.

Handicraft stalls are a common sight on Windhoek's streets, and there are always people selling Herero dolls outside the Kalahari Sands and displays of baskets and woodcarving near Verwoerd Park. However, if you are planning to tour the country you will be able to buy better-quality products direct from the craftspeople more cheaply in the areas where they are produced. Baskets, for example, are much cheaper in Owamboland where they originate.

Getting There & Away

Air Windhoek can be reached on the daily scheduled services of Namib Air from Cape Town and Johannesburg, with flights arriving at the International Airport. There is also a direct service from Frankfurt twice a week and flights from Gaborone, Harare, Lusaka, Maun and Victoria Falls. Internal Namib Air flights to Windhoek (Eros Airport) connect the capital with Katima Mulilo, Keetmanshoop, Lüderitz, Oshakati, Rundu, Swakopmund and Tsumeb.

Bus Windhoek is served by the scheduled Mainliner service from Cape Town and Johannesburg, which also connects the capital with Rehoboth to the south. The northern Mainliner between Windhoek and Tsumeb enables you to reach Okahandja by bus and there is a scheduled bus service to Windhoek from Swakopmund and Walvis Bay.

Train Windhoek is the hub of Namibia's train service and you can reach it on TransNamib Railways from South Africa through Keetmanshoop. Trains leave Johannesburg every Wednesday, Friday and Sunday at 12.30 pm and arrive in Windhoek two days later. Some towns (like Usakos and Okahandja) in the local area can also be reached by train.

Car & Motorbike Unless you approach Windhoek from the north you are must negotiate hilly country, but the roads are excellent and the scenery breathtaking. Windhoek literally forms the hub of the country, with the main crossroads of the B1, which extends the entire length of Namibia, and the B2/B6 stretching from Swakopmund on the coast through almost to the Botswanan border. Roads are clearly signposted and a new Western Bypass enables you to avoid the traffic of the town centre.

Hitching It's easier to hitch to and from Windhoek than anywhere else in the country. There is a lot of traffic on the major roads and you should be able to reach the capital easily from any direction.

Getting Around

To/From the Airport There is an airport coach service from both Windhoek (Eros) and the International Airport which connects with each incoming and outgoing flight. Taking the bus into town from the International Airport costs about R30 but is a lot cheaper than a taxi (R50 and up). The shuttle bus to and from Eros Airport leaves from the main bus stop opposite the Kalahari Sands and also provides a means of getting to the Safari Hotel and all attractions (such as the municipal swimming pool) at that end of town.

Car & Motorbike Local residents think that parking is difficult, but that is because they are accustomed to having no parking restrictions at all. In practice it is easy to find a meter or space in one of the covered or open car parks for a modest 10 cents per hour.

Taxi There is a main taxi stand by the bus stop opposite the Kalahari Sands hotel. Taxis can be called by telephone, but they do not cruise the streets.

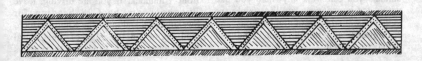

Central Namibia

There are several interesting places to visit in central Namibia, including the Khomas-Hochland highlands with the Daan Viljoen Game Reserve, the hot spring resort of Gross Barmen, minor nature reserves such as the Von Bach Dam, and picturesque towns like Okahandja. All can be reached as day trips from Windhoek or as part of a longer tour. Further away, the road network from Windhoek leads west to the Namib Desert and Swakopmund through the mountain passes, and north to Etosha, Kavango and Owamboland through the farming country around Otjiwarongo and the mining towns of Otavi and Tsumeb. Southwards, the main B1 road from Windhoek to Keetmanshoop forms the artery linking Namibia and South Africa.

The Erongo Mountains north of Usakos, where there are famous prehistoric cave paintings, form the eastern boundary of the Windhoek catchment area, and on the other side of the city the town of Gobabis is the centre of a karakul sheep-breeding area on the road to the Botswanan border crossing.

DAAN VILJOEN GAME PARK

Daan Viljoen is in the hilly Khomas- Hochland uplands about 25 km west of Windhoek. A small game park run by Nature Conservation, it's extremely popular as an excursion by Windhoek residents. For this reason even day visitors need to make prior arrangements (☎ (061) 226806) instead of just turning up at the gate. The park is open between sunrise and sunset throughout the year, and there is a restaurant, kiosk and swimming pool. Admissions costs R5 per adult plus R5 per vehicle. It's one of the nicest of the smaller parks, because since there are no dangerous animals you can walk anywhere you like within the boundaries. You'll certainly see gemsboks, kudus, mountain zebras and springboks, and possibly an eland and hartebeest as well.

Things to See & Do

Walking Trails Ask at the park office for recommended walking trails and information on the best places to see animals. The hills are open thornbush and there is pleasant but not taxing walking across the numerous game trails. Some trails have been laid out including a two day walk, a short three km ramble and the nine km Rooibos Trail which follows a circular route starting near the swimming pool.

Birdwatching Daan Viljoen is also famous for more than 200 species of birds including the rare green-backed heron and pin-tailed whydah. There's a special booklet (available from the office) to help you identify them.

Fishing The dam is stocked with barbel, kurper and black bass but fishing requires a permit (ask at the office).

Places to Stay & Eat

The rest camp is inside the park near the Augeigas Dam and has a nice swimming pool but no petrol station or shop. It includes a caravan and camping site with pitches for up to eight people at a cost of R25 per day. You can also stay in a rondavel-style bungalow with two beds for R40 but these must be booked at the Nature Conservation office in Windhoek. Because of its proximity to Windhoek, Daan Viljoen tends to get quite busy.

The restaurant serves three main meals a day and there is a small kiosk for drinks and refreshments.

Getting There & Away

To reach Daan Viljoen you really need a vehicle, as there is no public transport to or from Windhoek. If you are driving, leave Windhoek on the C28 heading for Swakopmund and cross the Khomas-Hochland region on the edge of the Central Escarpment, which separates the valleys

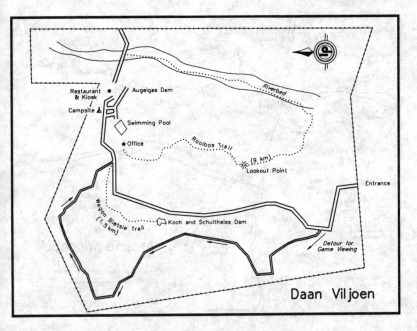

Daan Viljoen

around Windhoek from the desert. Daan Viljoen is clearly signposted about 25 km from the capital.

Getting Around
You can drive within the park on any marked road, or walk wherever you wish. No motorcycles are admitted.

BOSUA PASS
The C28 from Daan Viljoen continues westwards towards Swakopmund over the Central Escarpment at the Bosua Pass, a gravel road with a gradient of 1:5, which is one of the steepest in the country. The road eventually leads to Swakopmund via the central gravel plains of the Namib, but is less picturesque than the more southern route over the Gamsberg.

The road passes a number of places of interest. The area is famous for its prehistoric copper-smelting sites and the rich copper ores were also mined by Europeans in the mid-1800s. You can also see (but not visit) the Liebig House, built in 1912, with its strange double-storey architecture. It's now completely derelict but was once lavishly decorated, with a fountain in the living room. Every year someone has a plan to turn it into a hotel but none of these have come to fruition.

Near the settlement of Karanab are the ruins of Fort François, named after Major Curt von François who established a series of military posts to protect the road between Swakopmund and Windhoek. This one had an ignominious end as a drying-out station for German military alcoholics!

All these minor sites are signposted from the road but have no visitor facilities. There is no public transport to the area and the pass is steep and not for faint-hearted drivers or anyone towing a caravan.

KARIBIB
Karibib is a little town which started life as

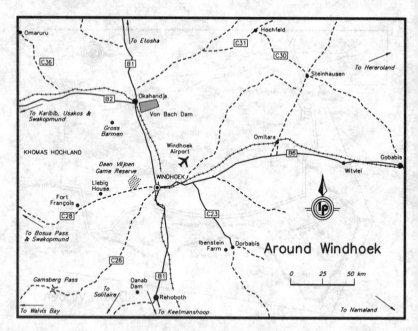

Around Windhoek

| 0 | 25 | 50 km |

a station on the narrow gauge Windhoek-Swakopmund line. It's in the centre of prime ranching country but is principally famous for its high-quality marble (aragonite) quarries, and for gemstones which can be bought at several outlets in the town, including one which specialises in selling local tourmalines.

There are a couple of interesting buildings including the Station (1900) and Christuskirche (1910), reputedly the first church in the country to be partly made of marble. The quarries currently process about 100 tons of marble per year.

Places to Stay & Eat
Camping & Self-Catering There is a one-star rest camp (☎ (062) 252-1314), featuring 10 self-catering bungalows plus camping sites and a pool, at the private Tsaobis Leopard Nature Park south of Karibib on the C32. Day visitors are not accepted. Rates for fully equipped bungalows start at R50, with camping from R20. There's no public transport to or from Karibib.

Hotels The one-star *Hotel Erongoblick* (☎ (062) 25281) in Karibib has no restaurant but offers basic facilities from R30. The *Hotel Stroblhof* (☎ (062) 252) has a small restaurant, swimming pool and rooms at the same price.

Guest Farms *Farm Audawib* (☎ (062) 252-1631) outside Karibib offers full board from R110 per person.

Getting There & Away
Bus & Train You can reach Karibib on the Mainliner coach from Windhoek to Swakopmund, which leaves on Monday, Tuesday and Wednesday at 8 am, arriving in Karibib at 10.25 am. The journey costs R44. On Friday the bus leaves Windhoek at 3 pm, arriving in Karibib at 5.25 pm. Return journeys depart on Tuesday, Wednesday and

Thursday at 10.40 am, arriving in Windhoek at 1 pm; on Sunday, it leaves at 5.37 pm, arriving in Windhoek at 8 pm.

It is also possible to get to Karibib from either Swakopmund or Windhoek by train; ask at the station for a current timetable.

Car & Motorbike At the foot of the Bosua Pass, a small road (C32) runs north via Tsaobis, a former barracks town of the Schutztruppe. This joins the tarred B2 at Karibib. Karibib can also be reached from Windhoek by the B2 in less than three hours.

Getting Around
Karibib is tiny and you can walk round it in minutes.

USAKOS & THE ERONGO MOUNTAINS
Usakos, some 30 km west of Karibib, was originally just a station on the narrow-gauge railway and still has little to recommend it except a few nice buildings. However, it acts as a good base to explore the Erongo Mountains, which contain some of Namibia's finest rock paintings.

Things to See & Do
Locomotive Spotting One of the locomotives responsible for the foundation of the town still stands in front of the present station. Railway enthusiasts might like to know that this is locomotive number 40, one of three Henschel heavy-duty locomotives built in 1912 by the firm of Henschel & Son in Casel, Germany. Its partner, locomotive 41, currently resides in front of the station at Otjiwarongo.

Erongo Mountains The high (2300 metres) volcanic Erongo Mountains are famous, like the Brandberg, for their caves and rock paintings. The best known is Phillip's Cave with the so-called White Elephant paintings about which the prehistorian Abbé Breuil wrote a book.

If you want to visit the cave, stop at Farm Amieb and ask for directions; they'll charge you a day visit fee of R5. The cave can only be reached on foot, and the walk, quite steep

in places, takes about 45 minutes. I wouldn't recommend you to try it around midday. The farm also has a picnic spot near a rock formation called the Bulls Party; they will charge you R3 to use its facilities.

Bushwalking If you continue north past Farm Amieb on the D1935 you skirt the Erongo Mountains (on your right) and have the option of continuing north to Damaraland or east towards Omaruru. This route virtually encircles the Erongo, and there are several minor roads which lead into the heart of the mountains which can be used as a base for some bushwalking.

Places to Stay & Eat
Hotels Usakos has one small, ungraded hotel, the *Usakos Hotel* (☎ (062) 242259) which has no restaurant but offers B&B from R45.

Guest Farms *Farm Amieb* (☎ (062) 242-1111) is a luxurious three-star guest farm which also has (expensive) camping sites with pre-pitched tents. The farm includes all luxuries and costs from R170 for full board. The *Wüstenquell Desert Lodge* (☎ (062) 242-1312) on the Karibib side of Usakos is slightly cheaper at R130 for full board.

Getting There & Away
Bus & Train You reach Usakos in exactly the same way as for Karibib except that the journey is 30 minutes longer (or 30 minutes less if you're coming from Swakopmund).

Car & Motorbike The best way to get to Phillip's Cave is by leaving Usakos on the D1935 (signposted to Okombahe). Farm Amieb is signposted at a turnoff from the D1935.

Getting Around
You can walk round Usakos in minutes but there is no transport available up into the Erongo Mountains unless you have your own car or take a tour.

OMARURU

The name Omaruru means 'bitter thick-milk' in Herero and refers to the milk produced by cattle which have been grazing on bitterbush (*Pechuelloeschae leubnitziae*).

Like so many of these central Namibian towns, Omaruru was once a German police post and was attacked by Herero forces in 1904. The Franke Tower (named after the commanding officer) is a historic monument from this period which contains a small museum, and the municipal offices will give you further information about the area. The tower is kept locked, but you can get a key at the Central Hotel in Main St or at the Hotel Staebe in Monument St.

Each year on 10 October the Herero people come in procession from the Ozonde residential suburb to the graveyard opposite the mission house, where their chief Wilhelm Zeraua was buried after his defeat in the Herero wars.

Places to Stay & Eat

Camping & Self-Catering Omaruru has a municipal camping site (☎ (062) 232) costing R5 per site and R1 per person. The site also has some bungalows but bedding and cutlery are not provided. The two-bed version costs R10 and the three-bed R40.

Hotels The *Hotel Staebe* (☎ (062) 23235) is graded one-star and costs from R50 for B&B. The smaller *Central Hotel* has just 10 rooms from R39. Both have a restaurant and are virtually the only places to eat in Omaruru.

Guest Farms Omaruru is in the heart of guest farm territory and there are more than half a dozen within the immediate area, though some cater especially for hunters. If you plan to stay locally the information office in Windhoek will give you a current list and further information. Prices and standards vary, but most of the local farms are at least two-star. These include *Immenhof* (☎ (065) 321803) from R150 for full board, *Farm Schönfeld* (☎ (065) 321831) from R110 for B&B, and *Farm Otjandaue* (☎

(062) 232-1203) which costs from R150 for full board.

Getting There & Away

Omaruru is off the B2, along the C33 between Swakopmund and Otjiwarongo, about 280 km from Windhoek. There is no public transport.

GROSS BARMEN

Gross Barmen is another playground for the inhabitants of Windhoek. It was once (inevitably) a mission station, established in 1844 to reach the Herero. You can still see the ruins of the mission and associated fort. However, this is not the reason that most people come to the area, as Gross Barmen is now the most popular hot-spring health resort in the country. The spring waters are rich in sulphide and fluoride and are supposed to be good for rheumatism.

The resort is operated by Nature Conservation and has a mineral bath, large indoor hot pool and an outdoor swimming pool with naturally warm water. There's also a shop, restaurant and tennis courts, and the whole place feels a bit like a cross between an oasis and a health farm with lots of elderly Germans wandering around in dressing gowns. Like Daan Viljoen, its immense popularity as a day trip from Windhoek means that you have to book even day visits in advance (☎ (062) 212091).

Gross Barmen costs R5 (adult) and R5 (vehicle) to visit but local people often buy a season ticket (R30 per year). Admission to the mineral bath and covered thermal pool costs R2 per session.

You can stay at Gross Barmen either on the camping site (R25 per pitch) or in one of the bungalows which vary from five-bed (R90) to simple two-bed (R40), which are all fully equipped with the exception of crockery and cutlery.

Gross Barmen makes a nice stopover on the way to Etosha and can also be used as a base to explore the centre of Namibia. There's not a lot to do apart from swim, but you can walk around the dam and surrounding hillsides. A path has been cut through the reedbeds and it is equipped with benches for birdwatchers, but there are no marked trails.

Getting There & Away

If you're not on a tour, you'll have to drive to Gross Barmen or hitch there along the B1 or B2. From Omaruru it's easy to drive back to Karibib via a gravel road, or you have the alternative of taking a minor road which joins the main B2 about halfway between Karibib and Okahandja at a small town called Wilhelmstal. From there it is less than 50 km to the resort of Gross Barmen.

The direct way to get there is via the main B1 straight north from Windhoek, where the road leading to the resort is clearly signposted just south of Okahandja.

OKAHANDJA & HEREROLAND

The nearest town to Gross Barmen is Okahandja, which is about 45 minutes drive from Windhoek and has a number of interesting things to see. This is the administrative centre for the Herero people, formerly nomadic cattle-raisers who moved into the area (previously occupied by Khoi-Khoi) during the 1800s and received their first missionaries less than 30 years later. The mid-19th century saw constant conflict between Herero and Khoi-Khoi, and Okahandja has a number of monuments dating from the period.

Things to See & Do

Maherero Day Each year, on the weekend either before or after 23 August there is a ritual when the Red Flag Herero people come to Okahandja on what is known as Maherero Day to honour their fallen chiefs. It's an extraordinary sight – thousands of traditionally clad Herero women with their men in a variety of military uniforms converge on the mission churchyard in a stately procession. Chiefs including Mahehero (1890) and Tjamuaha (1861) are buried in a graveyard next to what is now the municipal swimming pool, but was once the Herero chiefs' main kraal. The Khoi-Khoi leader Jonker Afrikaner (1861) and other Khoi-

Khoi chiefs are buried near the Friedenskirche church.

Hereroland & Gobabis The minor roads north-east of Okahandja lead deep into Hereroland, but there are few places of interest and no tourist facilities. You can, however, work your way in a semicircle via the small gravel roads C31 and C30 to Gobabis, which is a major cattle and sheep-farming area. The Gobabis region contains more than 800 farms, and there are huge dairy and beef processing plants.

Gobabis is the administrative centre for the Tswana people and is only 120 km from the Botswana border at Buitepos. The countryside around Gobabis can look quite lush in the rainy season (January to April).

If you are returning to Windhoek on the main tarred B6, you'll pass close by Omitara and Dorka, the centre of a karakul area. Ask for directions to the workplace, which is generally open during business hours. The road also passes Windhoek's JG Strydom International Airport. There is a turning south marked C23 (Dorbabis) to a famous karakul weavery on the Ibenstein Farm where you can see the whole manufacturing process.

The logical way to go from there is to head back to the B1 at Rehoboth or meander through the cattle-farming country of east Hereroland between Rehoboth and Aminius, but there are no tourist amenities.

Places to Stay & Eat

Camping The *Welkom* camping site at Gobabis (☎ (068) 812213) has camping sites, a pool and five self-catering bungalows that cost R60 for four beds.

Hotels The one-star *Okahandja Hotel* (☎ (062) 213024) has a restaurant and rooms from R45. Gobabis has two hotels, the *Central Hotel* (☎ (068) 12094) from R37 and the *Gobabis Hotel* (☎ (068) 12568) from R45, both with a bar and restaurants.

Guest Farms There are a number of guest farms around Okahandja including the luxurious *J & C Lievenberg* (☎ (062) 252-3112) with full board from R140 and facilities including a tennis court and golf driving range. *Monte Cristo*, nearer Windhoek, has rooms from R80 (☎ (061) 32680), and *Elsenheim* (☎ (061) 64429), with rooms from R90 is off the B1 Okahandja road.

Gobabis also has a variety of guest farms including *Farm Owingi* (☎ (068) 817330) at R65 for B&B, and *Farm Steinhausen* (☎ (062) 023240) which costs from R130 for full board.

You can eat at any of the small hotels in this area or buy a takeaway in Gobabis or Okahandja.

Getting There & Away

Bus & Train Okahandja is served by the main train service from Windhoek to Tsumeb, and Windhoek to Swakopmund. Check the station for latest schedules.

It is also on the Mainliner bus route from Windhoek to Tsumeb. The bus leaves Windhoek on Thursday at 7 am, arriving in Okahandja at 7.55 am; on Sunday it leaves Windhoek at 2 pm, arriving in Okahandja at 2.55 pm. The fare is R28. There is a return bus to Windhoek leaving on Monday at noon and on Friday at 7 pm. No trains or buses go to Gobabis.

Car & Motorbike Okahandja is only 70 km north of Windhoek on the main B1, which provides easy driving. Gobabis is equally easy to reach via the B6 from Windhoek, with a driving time of around three hours, but the minor roads through Hereroland are in poor condition and not suitable for non-4WD vehicles.

If you are planning to cross the border, follow the gravel extension of the B6 (signposted R55) east from Gobabis. You must allow 12 hours driving between Buitepos and Maun in Botswana, but do not attempt the journey unless you have 4WD. It's safer to travel in a convoy as the road is isolated and in terrible condition.

VON BACH DAM

Just south of Okahandja is the Von Bach Dam & Recreation Resort, operated by Nature Conservation and again requiring clearance for a day visit (☎ (062) 212475). There is limited accommodation – one two-bed hut without bedding or facilities for R30, and a camping site for R25 per night – but the area is used mostly by anglers. If you are planning to fish you need a licence, obtainable at the gate. Day visits cost R5 per person plus R5 per vehicle. There's not a lot to see if you don't fish but you can take bushwalks from the camp. There are no restaurant or shop facilities, though there are some nice picnic places. It's also a favourite spot with birdwatchers.

Getting There & Away

Von Bach Dam is signposted just south of Okahandja on the B1. There is no public transport.

REHOBOTH

Rehoboth is an interesting small town about 85 km south of Windhoek on the B1. It developed around a mission station, but the town and surrounding district (Rehoboth Gebiet) has been set aside for the Rehoboth Basters, an ethnic group of mixed European/Khoisan blood who originated in the Cape and migrated north at the end of the 18th century. The Basters are extremely proud of their heritage and their name (which means half-caste) and, although used as an insult elsewhere, it is here considered to be a matter of pride and signifying their interesting heritage.

Things to See & Do

The Basters heritage is displayed in the Rehoboth Museum (open during business hours), located in the house of the settlement's first colonial postmaster, which dates back to 1903. There are photos from the period 1893-96 covering the early mission station and its rebuilding by the Basters, under their leader Hermanus van Wyk. There is also a display of the prehistory and ecology of the area, and the facilities are shortly to be expanded by an open-air museum on a late Iron Age site near the village. This was due to open in late 1991; the staff at the museum (who are friendly and helpful) can give you further information.

The Reho Spa complex surrounds a thermal spring and a resort complete with a thermal bath (39°C), bungalows and camping site. You can visit the spa on a daily basis (R3 per adult, plus R1.50 for the thermal bath). No advance booking is required unless you plan to stay the night in one of the bungalows or camping sites.

Oanab Dam The new Oanab Dam has just been completed and forms part of efforts to conserve Namibia's water supplies. The way is signposted west from the B1 along 10 km of gravel road. There is a small visitor centre with toilets and a picnic place overlooking the dam. Several short walking trails have been laid out from this lookout point, which makes a pleasant picnic place.

Places to Stay & Eat
Camping You can rent a camp or caravan site at Reho Spa for R10 per day; or a variety of bungalows, from one-room (five beds, R35) to two-bedroom luxury (from R60). The site has a cafeteria, pool and thermal bath. Book at the Reho Spa office (☎ (062) 712774).

Hotels The *Bahnhof Hotel*, just outside Rehoboth near the station, has five rooms and minimal facilities and costs from R12 (☎ (002) 08550). It serves merely as a glorified bar for the area.

Restaurants The cafeteria at the spa provides cheap and adequate food; apart from that, catering in Rehoboth is limited to several fish & chip takeaways on the main road, which service travellers to Windhoek.

Getting There & Away
Bus & Train Rehoboth is a stop on the main Keetmanshoop-Windhoek railway and is on the Mainliner bus route from South Africa. The bus leaves Windhoek on Monday, Tuesday and Thursday at 6 pm, arriving in Rehoboth at 17.10 pm. There is also a Monday and Thursday service leaving Windhoek at 4 pm. You can return on Sunday and Wednesday at 4.45 pm and on Thursday at 10.40 am. The fare is R22.

Car & Motorbike Rehoboth is a mere 90 km south of Windhoek on the B1. You can also get there on minor roads, including the R47 from Solitaire and the R46 leading into Namaland.

Northern Namibia

The geography of northern Namibia is extremely varied. The region is bounded by the Kunene and Okavango rivers, which form the borders with Angola and Zambia, and extends through the long, thin arm of the Caprivi Strip to the Zambezi and Chobe rivers and the border with Botswana.

The strange shape of the Caprivi Strip is the result of an exchange of territory between Germany and Britain in 1890. Britain acquired Zanzibar and Germany got Helgoland together with the strip of land named after the German Chancellor, Count von Caprivi, which became part of the German protectorate in 1890. The original Caprivians were mainly subsistence farmers on the banks of the Zambezi and Kwando rivers. There are still substantial San populations in West Caprivi and Bushmanland, but few lead their original nomadic hunter-gatherer lifestyles.

Owamboland, as its name suggests, is the territory of the eight Wambo tribes who constitute the largest population group in Namibia. They are primarily stock farmers and small business people, in contrast to the closely related Kavango tribes of the northeast of the country, who are fishers and woodcarvers. Owamboland is flat, sandy and monotonous; Kavango is heavily wooded and dominated by its river systems. The Kavango area was settled in colonial days by German Roman Catholic missionaries, and there are a number of missions, hospitals and clinics at Nyangana, Sambiu and Andara still operated by church authorities.

Until Namibian independence in March 1990, going further north than Grootfontein required a special permit obtainable only in Windhoek, and you then had to negotiate various police control posts along the way. Happily, these formalities have now been abandoned and you can drive freely along the B8 north towards Rundu or the B1 to Ondangwa through what are now known as 'common' lands. However, previous diffi-culties in reaching the area do mean that there are few tourist facilities and the roads are of variable quality. There is a marked difference in appearance and prosperity between these common lands and the regimented White-owned ranches of the south.

During 1990-91 there was trouble in Kavango and Caprivi when an outbreak of intestinal disease resulted in the temporary declaration of a state of emergency by the president of Namibia. In addition, the war in Angola made travel in this border region mildly hazardous because bombs occasionally fell on the Namibian side. Now that a ceasefire has been signed in Angola this problem has been removed and it is possible that the border crossings from Angola to Namibia may be reopened. Unfortunately the withdrawal of the army has actually contributed to falling living standards in the north as basic services have become rundown and health problems have been made worse by the lack of transport to clinics, previously available in army vehicles.

It's sometimes said that north of Tsumeb and Grootfontein you cross a border between the First and Third Worlds. For practical purposes you notice a sign reading 'Animal Disease Control Checkpoint' which marks the veterinary boundary fence barring the movement of animals from north to south because of the dangers of rhinderpest and foot-and-mouth disease. Animals bred north of this line can't be sold to the south.

Information

There are two main tourist information centres in the northern region, one at Rundu and the other at Katima Mulilo. Both are theoretically open during business hours, but the range of information carried is extremely limited. It is considerably easier to get information about the area before you go, preferably at the tourist information centres at Grootfontein or Windhoek. They can also advise you about any current travel difficulties in the north.

The main Nature Conservation office in Kaiser Strasse, Windhoek, carries information about the Popa Falls Rest Camp and Mahango and Khaudum game reserves in Kavango and Caprivi. There are also local Nature Conservation offices in Rundu and Katima Mulilo, open during office hours.

Climate
Owamboland has a dry, semidesert climate with hot days and cool nights. It gets very hot indeed during the summer (over 40°C) and is sunny all year round. Kavango and East Caprivi are in a higher rainfall belt. The rainy season occurs there between mid-January and April and causes some communications problems, as rivers may overflow and roads become impassable. This is not the best time to travel in the area.

Dangers & Annoyances
Kavango and Caprivi both have a serious mosquito problem so it is important to take all relevant antimalarial precautions. Bilharzia is present in the Okavango, Chobe and Linyanti river systems and bathing is not recommended. The tsetse fly, present in East Caprivi, is especially active at dusk. All the northern rivers sustain large crocodile populations which pose a danger to swimmers, fishers and canoeists. There are also large numbers of hippos which will attack a boat even if unprovoked. To add a final cheerful note, leprosy is a relatively common disease in the north and Rundu has a large leper hospital, but the disease is not infectious.

Kavango & Caprivi

Like Owamboland, Kavango and Caprivi have severe economic problems, yet they are rather easier to get to because they are on the main through route to the Botswana border. The region is geographically quite distinct from the rest of Namibia. It has the highest rainfall in the country and most people live in small settlements on or near the Okavango River, which flows eastwards to feed the swamps of the Okavango River and forms the northern border of the country.

When travelling north past the bushveld and cattle farming areas of Grootfontein there is a sudden transition within the former tribal areas to dense bush, baobab trees, *mopani* savanna and small kraals of round huts with conical roofs.

Kavango is a green, wooded, rather gentle country which is the centre of the Namibian timber industry, and the Kavango people are famous for their woodcarvings which can be bought freely by the roadside. The area is also home to San communities, many of whom still work as slaves for Mbuskush, Sambiyu and other Caprivi tribal groups and are 'inherited' within the family. Most of the people live directly alongside the Okavango River.

Organised Tours
Some of the main Namibian tour operators feature Caprivi in their tours. Desert Adventure Safaris (☎ (064) 14072) in Swakopmund arranges safaris to its own camp at Lianshulu (near Sangwali in Caprivi) which are especially popular with birdwatchers.

Okavango River
The broad, blue Okavango River itself is something of a shock after the dryness of the rest of the country. Walking along the banks, you can see millions of butterflies, many still unclassified, and (reputedly) one crocodile for every two metres of riverbank. Swimming in the river is not recommended for this reason, and bilharzia is an additional hazard. Dugout canoes called *watu* or *mekoro* (singular *mokoro*) are pulled up along the bank, and woven basket fish traps are visible in midstream. The people also fish from the banks using spears.

The Roman Catholic mission stations and hospitals along the river welcome visitors, and each has something to recommend it, such as the statue of Christ at Andara. Most of the mission staff speak German, and you

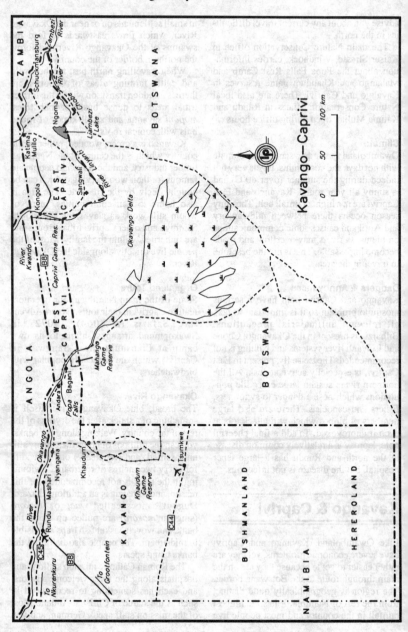

Kavango–Caprivi

Top: Fish River Canyon, Namibia (DS)
Left: Sand dunes, Namib Desert, Namibia (DS)
Right: Sossusvlei, Namibia (DS)

Top: Kuiseb River, Namib Desert, Namibia (MS)
Second: Kuiseb Canyon, Namib Desert, Namibia (MS)
Third: Sossusvlei, Namibia (DS)
Bottom: Fish River Canyon, Namibia (DS)

will often be encouraged to take part in a service. The sisters who operate the clinic and school at Sambiu are pleased to see travellers, especially if you take some gifts (sweets and fruit are best) for the children in their care. One of the sisters, now aged 92, can tell authentic stories (in German) of the early colonial days.

Katima Mulilo

Katima Mulilo is a small town on the Zambezi, near the border between Namibia and Zambia. It's as far away from Windhoek as you can get in Namibia and feels curiously English. The riverine vegetation, with its huge lush trees, tropical birds and monkeys, makes it interesting to walk around; and there are some old buildings from the colonial era, including the house called Schuckmannsburg built in 1912 by a Captain Streiwolf. Ask at the tourist information centre for current opening hours and details as well as directions to the newly opened Caprivi Art Centre. Katima has a thriving open-air market in the town centre which is open every day.

You can also hire a boat to go hippo viewing on the Chobe River and Liambezi Lake.

Linyanti & Liambezi

You can reach the Linyanti area of Caprivi by driving along the D3511 (4WD only) from Katima Mulilo in the east or from the Kongola control post in the west. Tracks will lead you to the Linyanti River channels, which are a network of small reed-lined channels and islands very similar to those of the Okavango region of Botswana. The area is famous for its wildlife, especially birds like the African fish eagle. It is possible to persuade local people to provide a guide and a mokoro to explore Liambezi Lake and marvel at the crocodiles and hippos.

If you have a 4WD vehicle you can reach the lake from Katima by taking the gravel D3511; this road passes through the village of Signu from where you can get close to the lake without going through reedbeds. The D3511 then loops through East Caprivi and

rejoins the B8 at Kongola. However, the lake dried up in 1985 so it might be wise to check first with Nature Conservation in Windhoek or Popa Falls before making the long journey across Caprivi.

Game Reserves

Most people visit this area for the game reserves, permits for which must be obtained at the Nature Conservation office in Rundu.

Caprivi Game Reserve The road from Rundu to Katima Mulilo leads right through the Caprivi Game Reserve but there are control points at Bagani in the west and Kongola in the east. The road is poor quality and you are not allowed to leave it. Popa Falls Rest Camp near Bagani is useful if you are planning to visit the Mahango and Khaudum game reserves. You will certainly see hippos and crocodiles in the river and are advised for this reason to swim only in the bathing places near the rest camp! There are some good waterfalls on the Okavango near Andara which are also likely places to see hippos.

Mahango Game Reserve The Mahango Game Reserve, 12 km south of Popa Falls, will only accept 4WD vehicles, and then just for a day visit. During the dry season you sometimes see huge concentrations of elephants along the Okavango in this area. You can drive through Mahango (4WD only) on the main road between Bagani and Shakawe in Botswana, and within the reserve there are a couple of minor gravel roads for game viewing.

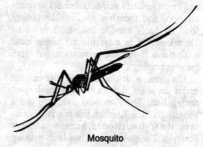

Mosquito

Khaudum Game Reserve Covering 380,000 hectares on the edge of Bushmanland, Khaudum is completely undeveloped; gravel tracks meander through the bush, and you can see roan antelopes, wild dogs, elephants, zebras and many other animals similar to those of Etosha. Khaudum only accepts prebooked reservations, but you can enter Popa Falls Rest Camp between sunrise and sunset as a day visitor. The roads are notorious for their loose sandy tracks which become a sea of mud in the rainy season, and Nature Conservation insists on a minimum of two self-sufficient 4WD vehicles per party, equipped with food and water for three days. You can reach the entrance to the Khaudum Game Reserve from the B8 (also called the D3402 there) at Katere where the turnoff is signposted.

Popa Falls Rest Camp This camp is on the south bank of the Okavango River, about a day's drive east from Rundu. Apart from accommodation and picnic places, there is a walk to Popa Falls, which are really rapids but make an interesting excursion.

Rundu
Rundu is quite an uninteresting town on the Okavango River. About the only things to do there are to eat ripe paw-paw in season (July to September) or to go fishing or birdwatching along the river.

Bushmanland
Bushmanland has just been opened up to visitors, but you will need to be travelling in a large party (two or three 4WD vehicles) and be completely self-sufficient. The roads are poor and there are no facilities (either food or fuel) outside the small town of Tsumkwe. It is possible to camp near settlements if you ask permission, but there are no camping sites.

The area is dry, sandy and barren; the major draw for visitors is the possibility of seeing San. The San who live here are a subgroup of the Khoisan but few still maintain their traditional hunter-gatherer lifestyle. The government has been making some attempts to introduce cattle herding and to anchor the San communities in small settlements.

Places to Stay
There is very little tourist accommodation in Kavango and Caprivi. This shortage of space, combined with the remoteness from Windhoek, tends to make hotel-type accommodation rather expensive.

Camping The caravan and camping site attached to the *Zambezi Lodge* (☎ (067) 352203) in Katima Mulilo has 10 places, an ablutions block and swimming pool, at a cost of R10 per person plus R5 per car. It has not currently received a star grading. The *Suclabo Lodge* (☎ (067) 372-6222) at Popa Falls has self-catering bungalows but also allows camping.

Camping in the Popa Falls and Khaudum reserves is controlled by Nature Conservation; places can be booked in advance at the head office in Windhoek. At both locations a camping site costs R20 per day plus the admission charges to the reserves (R5 per adult and R5 per car). Popa Falls has a kiosk where limited food stocks are available (but you should reckon to be self-sufficient as

San hunter

these are unreliable), barbecues and an ablutions block. There are also four-bed huts for R60 per day, with bedding and towels provided.

Within the Khaudum Game Reserve you can camp at either Khaudum or Sikereti, and there are also four-bed huts available for R25 per day without linen. Food and water are not available, and Nature Conservation insists that you take along all supplies for all passengers for a minimum of three days. No caravans or trailers are allowed in Khaudum and there must be at least two 4WD vehicles in each group.

It is possible to camp anywhere in Kavango and Caprivi outside the game reserves as long as you ask permission from the nearest local settlement, but no formal camping sites are available.

Hotels Rundu used to have adequate hotel accommodation at the *Kaisosi Safari Lodge*, which had a main hotel block and seven self-catering bungalows. This is currently closed but it is worth checking in Windhoek before leaving to see whether it has reopened. The *Zambezi Lodge* (☎ (067) 352203) in Katima Mulilo is a hotel, rest camp and caravan park. It has 25 self-catering bungalows which cost R105/146 for singles/doubles. The hotel, which has a pool, restaurant and floating bar on the Zambezi together with a nine-hole golf course, is expensive by Namibian standards.

Travellers in Caprivi have noted the shortage of accommodation in Katima Mulilo; it is best to reach the town well before sunset in order to find a place to stay.

Places to Eat
Most restaurants in Kavango and Caprivi are attached to the hotels. The *Katima Mulilo Yacht Club* has a licensed restaurant, but it is expensive and upmarket. Petrol stations in Rundu and Katima have limited catering facilities where you can get sandwiches, pies and beverages. The game reserves feature barbecues, and some takeaway food can be bought in shops in the small towns. You would be wise to buy all food supplies in

Rundu or Katima Mulilo and plan to cater for yourself while travelling in the area.

Things to Buy
Kavango people are famous for their woodcarvings, which are also readily available everywhere. Animal figures, masks, wooden mugs for beer, walking sticks and boxes are carved in a local light hardwood called *dolfhout* (wild teak) and make excellent souvenirs. Soapstone carvings of animal and human figures are produced in Caprivi.

You may also meet San in the Rundu area who are offering craftwork for sale, generally sets of bows, arrows and quivers. These are perfectly functional and genuine, though sold minus the traditional poison on the tip! Beads made from ostrich eggshell are combined into attractive necklaces and jewellery and sold in Kavango. There is also a distinctive local palm-leaf hat, like a cross between a coolie hat and a panama, which to my knowledge is found nowhere else in Africa.

Getting There & Away
Air Namib Air flies from Windhoek (Eros Airport) to Rundu or Katima Mulilo two or three times a week. On Friday it flies in either direction between Katima Mulilo and Maun in Botswana.

Call Namib Air's head office in Windhoek (☎ (061) 38220) for current timetables. Scheduled Namib Air services also link Katima Mulilo with Victoria Falls and Maun, but you have to travel via Windhoek.

Bus & Train There are no scheduled bus or train services in the area.

Car & Motorbike It is easy to get from Windhoek north along the B8 to Rundu. Travelling from Rundu into Kavango is less easy west of Mashari on the Okavango River, since the fine tarred road deteriorates into a gravel road which has not been well maintained. This route is only marginally passable for 2WD vehicles right through the Caprivi Strip till it becomes tar again at Kongola; you really need 4WD. The tarred stretch continues until the border with

Zambia. Filling stations are few and far between, especially in Owamboland. The small dirt roads in the area are usually in very poor condition.

You can reach Caprivi from Botswana via the border crossing at Ngoma Bridge which is open every day from 8 am to 4 pm. You will then need to drive around 60 km on a reasonably good road to reach Katima Mulilo. You can also enter the Caprivi Strip from Shakawe in Botswana via Mohembo, in the western part of the strip.

On the Botswana side, fuel is available at Kasane, Ghanzi and Maun, but on the Shakawe route there is no petrol available between Maun and Andara, so a reserve tank is essential. See the Botswana Getting There & Away chapter for more information on the Botswanan side of the border.

There is a branch of Avis Rent-a-Car at Katima Mulilo in Caprivi, but otherwise if you need to hire a vehicle to tour this area it is best to so at Tsumeb or in Windhoek.

Motorcycles are not allowed into game reserves or rest camps run by Nature Conservation.

Hitching You should be able to hitch a lift to or from Botswana via Ngoma Bridge, since the 54 km transit route through the Chobe National Park in Botswana is relatively well travelled. If you avoid the Chobe riverfront tourist drives on the Botswana side you won't have to pay the hefty national park fee. See the Botswana Getting There & Away chapter for more information.

Getting a ride in a truck between Rundu and Katima Mulilo is relatively easy, but hitching off the main roads is extremely difficult as there is very little traffic; you could wait for days.

Getting Around
Air You can fly from Rundu to Katima Mulilo on the scheduled services of Namib Air, but this involves a three-sided journey via Windhoek. In theory you can get flights between Rundu and Katima Mulilo, but in practice you may find that the only way to make a local connection between these towns is to make a triangular flight via Windhoek. All services are on Namib Air.

Bus & Train There are no scheduled bus or train services. Some local buses may be available, especially around Rundu and Katima Mulilo; the tourist information centres will be able to give you further information.

Car & Motorbike Minor roads in this area are in very poor condition and petrol stations are few and far between. There are no facilities at all along the C45, which runs west from Rundu along the Okavango River joining Kavango and Owamboland. Fuel is only available at Rundu, Tsumkwe, Bagani, Mukwe and Katima Mulilo.

You may have access problems when the rivers are in flood any time during the November to March rainy season. Roads frequently become impassable. Ask at the AA office in Windhoek or the tourist information centre in Rundu for a current report.

Motorbikes are not allowed in any of the game reserves.

Hitching It is possible to hitch a lift through Kavango and Caprivi, especially with trucks. Rundu or Katima Mulilo are the best starting points. Local people use donkey carts or hitch.

Boat You may have some success in persuading local people to give you a watu ride across the rivers or between villages. Boats can also be hired at Katima Mulilo; enquire at the Zambezi Lodge.

Owamboland

Owamboland was closed to visitors until recently and still has virtually no tourist facilities. It is in many ways quite dull: flat, sandy plains with occasional savanna and mopani forest belts. The overwhelming impression of Owamboland is of drought and poverty. Unemployment exceeds 60%

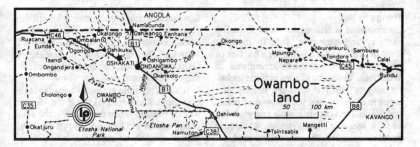

and many people feel that the pre-election promises of SWAPO have not been fulfilled. Little money is being invested in the area at present by the Namibian government and there are worries about the political fate of the area, which was the home base for SWAPO during the independence fighting. Falling living standards have not been helped by the return of 40,000 workless exiles.

Owamboland's problems are compounded by a severe water shortage. The region has a unique network of shallow watercourses called *oshanas* which provide most of the water for the local people and are also a source of fish and a kind of water onion which is cultivated. There are also a few boreholes, but the only piped water supply runs just alongside the main road. Fortunately the oshanas fill up during the rainy season and, because of the underlying rocks, tend to retain water almost permanently. Their water is desperately needed as Owamboland is quite densely populated by Namibian standards. The Wambos, Namibia's largest population group, are mainly stock farmers who raise cattle and goats and grow a millet called *muhango*.

Ondangwa

The largest town in Owamboland, Ondangwa has huge warehouses which provide stock for more than 6000 tiny cuca shops which serve the highly entrepreneurial rural inhabitants of Owamboland. The name 'cuca' comes from an Angolan beer which used to be served there. It is possible to visit the people who make the high-quality basketry and canework by asking directions at the municipal offices.

Ruacana Falls

The spectacular waterfalls or rapids at Ruacana, on the upper reaches of the Kunene, now produce hydroelectric power through a huge power station. Until recently the area was sealed off for military reasons, so there are no tourist facilities. You can only reach the falls by road and you need 4WD. Take the C35 through the Kaokoveld, skirting the western side of Etosha, or the C46 from Oshakati which joins the C35 at Ruacana. Further west than Ruacana the roads fade away into tracks leading into the remote Baynes Mountains and Zebraberge near the Angolan border.

Places to Stay & Eat

There is no accommodation available in Owamboland, although it is rumoured that hotels will shortly open in Ondangwa and Oshakati. However, it is possible to camp informally near any of the villages or small towns after asking permission, although you may find conditions quite rough and there are no facilities available. It would be wise to check with the tourist information centre in Tsumeb, the nearest major town, if you are planning to stay in Owamboland.

There are no restaurants in Owamboland but food and drink can be bought and eaten at any of the small shops. Oshakati, Ondangwa and Opuwo have limited takeaway facilities near petrol stations.

Things to Buy

Owamboland is famous for its high-quality basketry and canework, sold in roadside stalls or at the maker's home for a fraction of the price such work can command in Windhoek. Favourite shapes include globular baskets with lids in every size up to a metre in diameter, and shallow woven plates and bowls. Designs are simple and graceful, usually incorporating a brown geometric pattern woven into the pale yellow reed.

Necklaces and other jewellery made from ostrich eggshell beads are made in Owamboland.

Getting There & Away

Air You can fly to Oshakati, the major commercial centre of Owamboland, from Windhoek on scheduled Namib Air services which leave on Tuesdays and Thursdays. On arrival you will not find a hotel or any tourist facilities. Call Namib Air's head office in Windhoek (☎ (061) 38220) for current timetables.

Bus & Train There are no scheduled bus services as far as Owamboland, so your only option is to travel by rail from Windhoek to Tsumeb or Grootfontein and make your way by road from there.

Car & Motorbike You can drive to Owamboland from Tsumeb along the B1, which skirts the eastern border of Etosha and is signposted to Ruacana. This is still a sensitive military area and no border crossings are currently allowed. The border crossing to Angola at Namacunda is still closed.

The B1 is a dirt road but is in good condition due to recent improvements for military purposes, but many of the other roads in Owamboland are only suitable for 4WD vehicles. Fuel is available at Ondangwa, Oshakati, and probably at Opuwo, but cannot be counted on.

It's also possible to reach Ruacana via the C35 from Kamanjab, skirting the western side of Etosha. When the fourth Etosha rest camp is built at Otjovasondu this road will almost certainly be improved.

Hitching Now that the border has been opened there is nothing to stop you trying to hitch to Owamboland, but very little traffic goes that far north and you may have a long wait.

Getting Around

There is no scheduled transport of any kind in Owamboland. Local people get around using the occasional elderly bus (for which no timetables exist), donkey carts or hitching.

Car & Motorbike The main roads through Owamboland are OK for ordinary sedan cars, but the small dirt roads in the area are usually in very poor condition and you need 4WD. Petrol stations are few and far between.

Motorbikes are not allowed into game reserves or rest camps run by Nature Conservation.

Boat It's possible to get limited local transport by canoe on the Okavango River, but this is more in the nature of sightseeing excursions than a means of getting around.

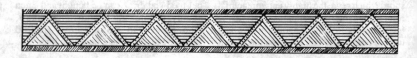

Etosha, Damaraland & the Skeleton Coast

The Etosha National Park, north-east of Damaraland, is Namibia's premier wildlife reserve and home to more than 100 types of mammals, including many endangered species. Now one of the largest national parks in the world, it is superbly managed by Nature Conversation; visitors are at liberty to drive round the park on a network of gravel roads, stopping at waterholes whenever they wish. Part of the charm of Etosha is its huge area (over 20,000 sq km). High game counts and relatively low visitor numbers mean that the needs of the animals have not become subordinated to the needs of visitors in any way. At certain times of the year you can drive for hours among herds of zebras and gemsboks in Etosha without seeing another vehicle.

The park is centred round a vast saltpan which forms one of its many ecosystems, surrounded by woodlands and grasslands which provide a very diverse habitat for the animal and plant communities. Etosha is undoubtedly one of the world's greatest wildlife experiences, not to be missed by any visitor to the country.

The region between the Skeleton Coast and Etosha is technically called Damaraland, and includes Namibia's highest mountain, Königstein (King's Rock), 2580 metres high in the Brandberg range. Crossing inland from the coast, you are aware of a gradual increase in gradient from the flat terraces and dunes of the coast, through the pro-Namib, and into the foothills of the mountains. The rivers which flow through the northern Namib (the Uniab, Huab, Ugab and Omaruru) all have their headwaters in these mountains, which are also home to Namibia's most famous prehistoric rock art sites. The Namib Desert is actually at its widest at the edge of Damaraland, along an imaginary line drawn between Torra Bay and Khorixas.

Spitzkoppe and the Brandberg Mountains in Damaraland are famous for their rock paintings and birdwatching opportunities. There are a number of locations to choose from and it's fun to spend time exploring the area on foot along marked trails. Etosha, of course, provides ample opportunities for watching wildlife by its many waterholes.

The term 'Skeleton Coast' is properly used to refer to that stretch of coastline between the mouth of the Ugab River (120 km north of Swakopmund) and the Kunene River which forms the border with Angola; in this chapter it is considered to include the coastline as far south as Swakopmund. It is often considered to include the whole northern coast and indeed part of the southern coast of the Namib south of Walvis Bay. The name derives from the treacherous nature of the coast and the fact that it has been a graveyard for ships since time immemorial.

The dunes are continually shifting. I once came across the skeleton of a small trawler stuck deep in dune sands more than one km inland, with all its provisions (complete with tinned pilchards) intact. The place has a lunar, mystical quality. Its extreme desolation and frequent fog cover make it eerie, the silence broken only by the cries of seabirds and barks of seals.

Etosha National Park

Etosha National Park is Namibia's premier nature reserve and tourist attraction; it covers more than 20,000 sq km and protects 114 species of mammals, together with 340 bird species, 16 amphibians, one fish species and uncounted insects. Part of its enjoyment is the variety of habitats which, together with unobtrusive tourism management, make the visitor feel a part of the environment and not

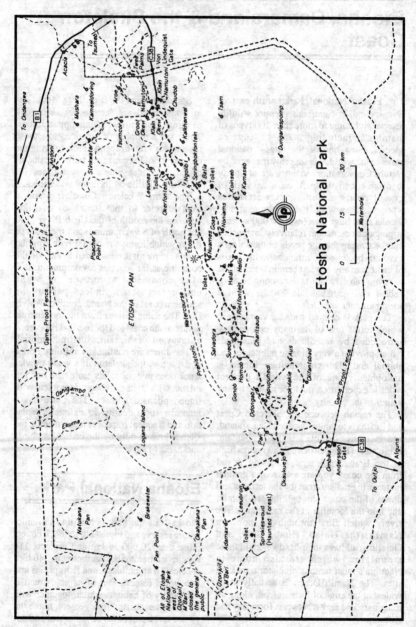

Etosha National Park

an unwelcome intrusion into the lives of the park's inhabitants.

The marvels of Etosha were first revealed to European eyes when the traders and explorers John Andersson and Francis Galton arrived by wagon at what is now Namutoni in 1851. Andersson and Galton were followed a few years later in 1876 by an American trader, G McKeirnan, who later described his first experience of the abundant wildlife thus: 'All the menageries in the world turned loose would not compare to the sight I saw that day'.

The area did not attract the interest of conservationists till after the turn of the century when the then Governor of German South West Africa, Dr F von Lundquist, became concerned over diminishing animal numbers and proclaimed an area of 99,526 sq km as a reserve, including Etosha Pan. This huge region was not bounded by fences, so animals could still wander off along their normal migration routes but were protected within the designated area. Afterwards the boundaries of the park changed several times before the present boundary was established in 1970, giving a smaller size of 23,175 sq km, but the initial intention has remained the same – to conserve, study and display Namibia's fauna and flora.

Nowadays the park is administered by Nature Conservation and includes a full Research Unit, established in 1974. You can visit the park on a daily basis but it also has three excellent rest camps, at Namutoni, Halali and Okaukuejo. It makes more sense to stay at least one or two nights as you can't really see everything in less than three days. The rest camps are all different and each is of some historical significance.

Etosha is an immense, flat, saline desert of more than 5000 sq km which originated 12 million years ago as a shallow lake fed by the waters of the Kunene River. Over the intervening period climatic alterations and volcanic activity changed the Pan from lake to brackish dry desert which only very occasionally holds water. In years of good rain the vast shallow depression (usually just known as 'the Pan') gets fed from the Ekuma

and Oshigambo rivers in the north and the Omuramba Owambo River in the east, and becomes a temporary shallow lagoon full of white pelicans and flamingos. But very few visitors are lucky enough to see this.

The Pan will usually be white, inhospitable and full of mirages shining in the distance, crossed by a million animal tracks.

Orientation & Information

The part of Etosha which is open to tourists is the eastern zone of the park, consisting of the Pan and its surrounds.

You can't drive on the Pan itself, but it is surrounded by savanna grassland and mopani woodland with occasional rocky outcrops (especially around Halali), teeming with animals. You drive yourself around on the network of gravel roads. Because of the huge area the park is never crowded and it is rare to find more than one vehicle watching a waterhole – something of a contrast with East Africa.

Each of the three Nature Conservation rest camps has an information centre that's open during office hours, and the staff at either of the main gates will give you a map and point you in the right direction.

The best time to visit Etosha is in winter (May-September) when wildlife congregates around the waterholes. In summer (December-March) there are occasional isolated rainy episodes on the Pan which the animals follow. Summer temperatures can also get very high, reaching 44°C, which makes it very hard going for a visitor enclosed in a hot car.

Landforms & Vegetation

Some of the roads in the park take you right to the edge of the Pan (though not on it, since this is a protected area) giving a magnificent view of endless, white, flat, saline desert. The mopani woodlands which fringe this pan are the commonest vegetation type in Etosha. They actually constitute 80% of the park's vegetation and are greenest in the rainy season (December-March). This sparse bush country also includes umbrella-thorn trees *(Acacia torilis)* and other trees favoured by browsing animals.

The weird *moringa* trees *(Moringa ovalifolia)*, peculiar to Etosha, occupy a sector of the mopani forest just west of Okaukuejo and are worth a visit. The area has been dubbed the Haunted Forest because of these strange-looking trees. Bushman legend says that God had found a place on earth for all the plants and animals but then realised that he had a bundle of moringa trees still to go. He flung them up in the air, roots pointing skywards, and they landed in Etosha. Or so they say.

Watching Waterholes

The road network in the park lets you visit a number of waterholes. Opinions are divided: some visitors like to stay by one hole all day and watch which animals appear, while others like to take in as many locations as possible. You need to visit the entire width of the park, from Pan to mopani forest, to stand a chance of seeing all its varieties of game.

It's important to remember to drive slowly and quietly, especially when arriving at waterholes, and to make as little noise as possible while you are watching. The best time to visit is in winter (May-September) when wildlife congregates around the waterholes. In summer (December-March) there are occasional isolated rainy episodes on the Pan which the animals follow. Summer temperatures can also reach 44°C, so not only is it too hot for you but any animal worth its salt is hiding in the nearest patch of deep shade. On the other hand this is also the calving season and you can see tiny painted zebra calves and miniature fragile springboks.

It's fun to leave the camp at first light and spend a pre-breakfast hour watching at a waterhole to see what comes to drink. You see the most animals at sunrise and sunset and the least at midday – at least that's the theory. The three rest camps have 'sightings' books of what has been seen recently where. Nature Conservators will also have information about the amount of water in waterholes and recommendations about the best places to go to see particular species.

Identifying Animals

The animals you might encounter in Etosha include some protected species such as the black-faced impala and black rhinoceros. There are also large populations of more common animals such as elephants (1500), giraffes (2000), Burchell's zebras (6000), Hartmann's (mountain) zebras (600), red hartebeests (600), blue wildebeests (2600), gemsboks (4000), elands (250), kudus (1000), roan antelopes (70), ostriches (1500), lions (300), more than 20,000 springboks and a few cheetahs and leopards. You are almost certain to see the majority of these during any one visit, but lions are the most difficult to spot.

The animal communities vary, of course, with the local ecology. Oliphantsbad (near Okaukuejo) is, as its name suggests, a good place for elephants; the further east you go in the park the more wildebeests, kudus and impalas join the springboks and gemsboks. The area around Namutoni gets the most rain (443 mm per year, compared with 412 mm at Okaukuejo) so there is a different fauna. That is where you'll have your best chance to see the Damara dik-dik, Africa's smallest antelope.

In addition to its large mammals, Etosha has some interesting small fry, including two species of mongoose (yellow and slender) and a large lizard, the leguaan.

Etosha is also famous for its birdlife. Yellow-billed hornbills are very common, and there is a wide variety of birds of prey. On the ground you're likely to see the huge kori bustard, which weighs 15 kg and seldom flies, marabou storks, white-backed vultures and many other species.

Organised Tours

Etosha features in virtually every tour of Namibia and you can organise a trip from Windhoek or Swakopmund using any of the local operators such as Oryx Tours (☎ (061) 224252) or SWA Safaris (☎ (061) 37567).

Places to Stay

Camping & Self-Catering All the accommodation within the park is either camping or self-catering and it is operated by Nature Conservation. If you plan to stay at any of the three Etosha rest camps (a fourth is planned for Otjovasondu) then you need to reserve accommodation well in advance at the Nature Conservation office in Windhoek. Okaukuejo and Namutoni rest camps are open all year round but Halali is shut between 1 November and 15 March. The camps are located approximately 70 km apart, and each has a shop, restaurant, petrol station, swimming pool, mail facilities and firewood. A camping site costs R25 at any of the rest camps in Etosha.

It's worth noting that none of the accommodation in Etosha provides crockery, cutlery or any cooking equipment, though everything is equipped with linen, towels and soap. Rest camps must be reached before sunset and not left till after sunrise. The times are posted clearly on the gates; if you're late they will lock you out. Should this happen, drive right up to the gate and hit the horn. You will have a long wait but eventually the gate will open and a Nature Conservator will emerge. He will take you to the camp commander who will give you a lecture and make a note on your permit so that the next tourist office knows what a criminal you are. This all sounds terribly petty and militaristic but it does serve to get everyone firmly within walls (or fences) at night.

Okaukuejo This is the major camp and employs 92 people. It is also the location of the Etosha Research Station and has easily the nicest pool and restaurant. An unusual feature is the waterhole just over the fence from the camp which is floodlit at night and clearly visible. You can see the animals but they can't see you. There are viewing benches inside the camp boundary and I've never yet been there at night without seeing some marvel – last time it was a young black rhinoceros having a quiet drink.

Okaukuejo has three different sizes of bungalow/rondavel, sleeping either two, six or eight people. There are also 'bus' quarters consisting of a double room and the use of shared facilities, and four-bed tents that are erected for you. At Okaukuejo, bus quarters cost R108, a four-bed tent costs R25, a two-bed bungalow R50, a three-bed R70 and a four-bed R90. All the bungalows have a kitchen, bathroom and barbecue. There are also camping sites if you're bringing your own tent or caravan.

Okaukuejo has a visitor centre with interesting information about the research being carried out in the park. The most unusual display deals with what is politely called dung and helps you to identify the different species from their trademarks! There's also a lookout tower, now restored, which gives a fine panorama of the camp and park. The restaurant and pool areas (three small pools and a nice bar) have just been refitted and you can get drinks and three meals a day. There's also a shop, a kiosk for cool drinks, and picnic sites for day visitors.

Halali Halali, in the centre of the park, has marginally less character than the other rest camps. It gets its name from a German term meaning the blowing of a horn at the end of a hunt; the horn is a motif for the camp. It has much the same facilities as Okaukuejo, but there is a 10-bed dormitory with shared facilities for an amazing R50 per night for the lot. Accommodation at Halali is slightly cheaper, with a two-bed bungalow for R40 and basic two-room cabins next to the dormitory also for R40. Camping costs are the usual R25 per site.

Namutoni This is by far the nicest of the camps – a romantic, whitewashed, Beau Geste-style fort stuck in the middle of the bush. It was also an outpost for German troops, and in 1899 the German cavalry built a fort on the spot to help in controlling the local Wambos. It was defended by a force of seven German soldiers against more than 500 Wambos at a famous battle on 28 January 1904, but was later destroyed. The present shape of the fort is attributable to a refit in 1905-06 when it served as a police

Fort Namutoni

station, but it was restored for tourist accommodation in 1956.

You can walk all round the old fort; there is a great view from the tower and ramparts. Some accommodation is actually in the fort: the rooms are in the walls, but they often have only shared facilities and cost R30 to R108. The rest, ranging from bungalows to caravans, is just outside together with the restaurant and pool. Namutoni also has bus quarters and a camping site like Halali and Okaukuejo, but its two-bed bungalows start at R30 with four-bed models from R65. Huge mobile homes with four bedrooms and accommodation for eight people can be rented for R60.

There is a little sunset ceremony when the flag on the fort is furled, accompanied by a bugle call, and another ceremony at sunrise to wake you up.

Hotels There are no hotels in the park, but it is possible to make a day visit using hotel accommodation in Tsumeb or Outjo. The hyperluxurious three-star *Mokuti Lodge* (☎ (067) 13084) is the nearest hotel to Etosha, a mere 11 km from Namutoni. It generally serves as a base for upmarket tour operations and has nearly 100 rooms plus pool and private game reserve – but it will set you back between R100 and R200 per night.

Places to Eat

Restaurants Each rest camp has a restaurant open for all main meals, plus a bar and a kiosk for cool drinks and snacks. There is no other catering in the park.

Getting There & Away

Air The nearest public airport to Etosha is at Tsumeb. If you happen to be flying your own private plane you can land in the park and hire a guide. Contact Trip Travel in Windhoek (☎ (061) 36880) for details.

Bus & Train It is possible to take a bus or train to Tsumeb, but thereafter you need to join a tour or hire a car as there is no scheduled public transport to Etosha.

Car & Motorbike By far the easiest way to reach Etosha is to drive the 500 km from Windhoek along the B1 via Okahandja and Otjiwarongo and then take either the C38 to Outjo (for Okaukuejo) or B1 to Tsumeb (for Namutoni). Anyone coming from Swakopmund or Damaraland joins this road at Outjo, and travellers from Caprivi on the B8 meet it at Tsumeb.

Avis Rent-a-Car has a branch in both Tsumeb and in Okaukuejo but you need to book well ahead.

Hitching You might be able to hitch to Etosha; try petrol stations at any of the surrounding towns, especially Outjo or Tsumeb. Remember that, once inside the park, Nature Conservation requires you to stay in a vehicle and you can't hitch back from inside the park.

Getting Around

A car or truck is the only permitted method of getting around Etosha; pedestrians and motorbikes are forbidden. If you're driving an open bakkie (pick-up truck) you won't be allowed in unless you screen off the back. Nor can you take in any pets or firearms, or leave your vehicle at any time (unless inside a rest camp), or do a whole list of other things which Nature Conservation warns you about.

In order to get in to Etosha you must fill in a form at one of the main gates. You are then issued with a permit for which you pay R8 per adult and R10 per car per day. After getting your permit you must then check in at the nearest rest camp.

All the roads inside the park are moderately easily traversed with a 2WD car, but the higher your wheelbase (as in a Land Rover, bakkie or minibus) the more you'll see.

There is a strictly enforced 60 km/h speed limit to protect animals and plants from the dust. Since you inevitably have all your car windows open to get a better view, both you and all your possessions will get covered in dust. If you have anything which will not survive this treatment, seal it in several layers of plastic bags. You can get your car cleaned at any of the rest camps for a small fee, or simply leave it till you return to civilisation.

If you break down inside the park, stay in your car until help arrives. Nature Conservators make regular patrols. Toilets are marked clearly on the map – don't be tempted to leave the car to answer nature's calls anywhere else.

Damaraland

Damaraland forms a hilly transitional zone between the extreme aridity of the Skeleton Coast in the west and the flat saltpan of Etosha. The Damara people, whose traditional homeland this is, were miners, smelters, copper traders and seminomadic stock farmers until the arrival of Europeans, when they settled and became mixed-economy farmers. The area is also home to the enigmatic Nama people, descendants of the

original Khoisan in Namibia, who speak a click language and are traditionally stock farmers.

Damaraland does not have any of the fenced, organised ranches of central and southern Namibia, and much of the soil is poor. The country consists almost entirely of common land and the farms lack capital investment. Damaraland is full of strange and unique features. There is, for example, a particular species of harvester ant which lives here and collects large quantities of grass seed. These stores are then utilised by the Damara as a major food source.

Orientation & Information

To the north of Damaraland is the southern edge of the remote Kaokoland, barred to visitors until recently and still little known. To the south the mountains of Damaraland abruptly terminate at the line of the main B2 road linking Swakopmund with Karibib, Omaruru and Otjiwarongo and the beginnings of the rich cattle and fruit-growing area of central Namibia.

Damaraland includes some high mountain areas and extremes of climate, from high aridity on the coastal plains that slope towards the Skeleton Coast to higher rainfall in the Brandberg and Erongo mountains. Dust storms may be encountered in the winter and showers any time during the summer.

There is a tourist information centre at the municipal office in Khorixas, the centre of Damaraland, which is open during office hours. You can also get some information at the tourist information centre in Swakopmund, or at the municipal offices in Omaruru and Otjiwarongo on the borders. The manager of the Shell service station at Usakos is a mine of information about walking routes through the Spitzkoppe.

KHORIXAS

Khorixas is the administrative capital of Damaraland and the best centre for exploring either the Brandberg or Spitzkoppe. There is absolutely nothing to see or do in the town itself.

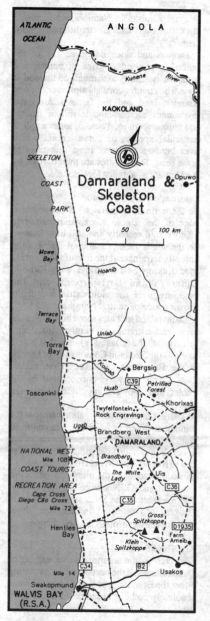

Places to Stay & Eat

Khorixas has an excellent camping site (☎ (0908) 3512) with sites from R15 plus R4 per person and 40 self-catering bungalows from two-bed to luxury, ranging from R77 to R154. Reservations are not necessary for the camping site. There is a swimming pool and restaurant plus a shop stocking basic foodstuffs. The site is about three km west of the town on the continuation of the R76 and is clearly signposted.

The camping site's restaurant is virtually the only place to eat in the town, unless you count a snack bar at one of the garages. Food can be bought at local supermarkets.

No camping is permitted at the Brandberg or Twyfelfontein. The northern part of Damaraland approaching the Hoanib River and Kaokoland boundary has no accommodation, with the exception of a two-star rest camp, *Palmwag Lodge*, off the D2620 about 150 km north-west of Khorixas (☎ (064) 14459). It has seven bungalows plus camping sites and offers meals, but provides no towels. Charges range from R85 to R110, including full board, with camping sites from R25.

Getting There & Away

Car & Motorbike Khorixas can be reached from the coast along the C35 through Uis, and from Outjo via the C39 skirting the Fransfontein Mountains. The C35 virtually bisects Damaraland and leads south to Swakopmund via Henties Bay. You can also reach Khorixas from central Namibia along the B2 to Omaruru, where you turn off onto the C36 to Uis and pick up the C35.

Getting Around

Khorixas itself is tiny, so you can walk round it in a few minutes. There is no scheduled public transport in the area.

PETRIFIED FOREST

The Petrified Forest is an assemblage of huge fossil tree trunks of which the largest is 30 metres long and six metres in diameter. These are now scattered on top of the ground but were originally part of a forest which either grew here some 200 million years ago or was brought down from higher ground by an intense flood.

You'll also see welwitschias growing among the tree trunks which are seen to best advantage just as the sun is setting. There are about 50 trees visible, and it is quite difficult to realise that they are fossilised since the bark and tree rings are so perfectly preserved. Most belong to an ancient group of plants called gymnosperms, which include many present day plants such as pines and welwitschias.

The Petrified Forest was declared a National Monument in 1950 after having had a bad time from vandals. There are no tourist facilities at the site, but a picnic area is planned.

Getting There & Away

You'll need your own transport to visit the forest. There is a sign labelled 'Versteende Woud' (Petrified Forest) about 40 km west of Khorixas on the C39 gravel road linking Khorixas with Torra Bay. This road is not recommended for 2WD. A gate leads to a footpath with two branches; take the lefthand path, which leads you directly to the site.

SPITZKOPPE

The Klein (Small) and Gross (Large) Spitzkoppe Mountains, arguably the best known landmarks in the country, loom over this part of the pro-Namib, and there are some nice walking trails. Tourist information centres will give you a detailed map of Spitzkoppe. It is worth trying to reach the place called Bushmans Paradise at the very eastern edge of the Pontok Mountains in the Spitzkoppe range. At the parking place is a wire cable to help you climb over a smooth granite slope to a point where you can see the Bushman paintings. Astronomers say that the clear air at night is especially good for stargazing in these mountains. It's also a good place for birdwatching.

Getting There & Away

You can turn off the B2 west of Usakos onto the minor road towards Henties Bay (D1918), then turn north off this road onto D1930 which takes you to Uis. This route takes you directly past Spitzkoppe.

BRANDBERG MOUNTAINS

The magnificent Brandberg Mountains, north of Uis and near the upper course of the Ugab, are visible on good days from 70 km away. The Brandberg gets its name because of its supposed resemblance to a huge slag heap glowing red in the sunshine. Its steep slopes are seemingly without vegetation, although actually it has an unusual flora of euphorbias and quivertrees.

The Tsisab ravine area of the Brandberg is famous for its collection of rock paintings which were found by a German surveyor (Dr Reinhard Maack) in 1918. On his way down the mountain after climbing the Königstein he took shelter in one of the many cave overhangs and saw the painting which has become known as the White Lady. But Maack's Shelter which contains the painting is only one of many magnificent rock art sites in the area. You'll see lots of stone tools and pottery fragments on the ground but it is illegal (and destructive) to collect any, or to spray the pictures with water or any other liquid to make them clearer.

Allow about an hour and a half to walk up the ravine to Maack's Shelter and about four hours for the round trip. The shelter is quite easy to find and the famous painting shows a white figure (possibly a young man) about 40 cm high, with what looks like a bow and arrow in one hand. It has never been satisfactorily dated but is part of a frieze which might be as much as 16,000 years old. It gets its name from an article written in 1948 by the Abbé Breuil who speculated that the exotic-looking figure could even be Egyptian or Cretan. This is not a theory which meets with much favour today, as we now know much more about the very early occupation of the area.

There are numerous other shelters and overhangs with rock paintings, and you may also see baboons, klipspringers and possibly mountain zebras. The Brandberg is very hot all the year round, so avoid doing this walk at noon, and take water with you. It's not really a good idea to go further up the ravine than Maack's Shelter without a guide: ask in Swakopmund or Usakos if you want to arrange a tour of the paintings.

Getting There & Away

Access to the centre of the Brandberg is clearly signposted off the D2359, about 15 km north of Uis. The road takes you 30 km to the headwaters on the Tsisab Ravine in the heart of the Brandberg, where you can park and walk to Maack's Shelter.

TWYFELFONTEIN

Twyfelfontein is another spectacular mountain massif which is reputed to contain the largest gallery of rock art in Africa, mostly painted by Khoisan people and their descendants over the course of the last millenium. The name actually means Doubtful Fountain, as a former inhabitant doubted that the water supply was sufficient to support life in this very harsh area.

The Twyfelfontein paintings have been declared a National Monument; in addition to the paintings there are engravings made by using a stone 'chisel' to remove the hard outer skin of the sandstone. Many of the original chisels are still around and there is a huge gallery of art to explore which can easily occupy you for a full day. You have to search for the paintings in nooks and crannies within the jumble of rock and you can walk anywhere you like within the area. Like Brandberg, its gets very hot. And as at all such significant sites, leave it as you found it.

Getting There & Away

The paintings are about 30 km north of the Brandberg. A signpost on the C35 points the way down a branch road (the D2612) to Twyfelfontein.

KAOKOLAND

Kaokoland is a vast mountainous area west of Etosha which until recently was off-limits to visitors. It is crossed by a few unsignposted, poor-quality tracks and has no visitor facilites except at the administrative capital, Opuwo. Fuel and supplies are not available between Opuwo and Palmwag, and there are no hotels. Parts of Kaokoland are extremely rugged and hard going for even the toughest 4WD; don't attempt the roads without a good vehicle travelling in a convoy of at least two, preferably with a guide. There is no public transport and there are few people about, with the exception of the nomadic Himba people who move across the area in search of grazing. There is a rumour that part of Kaokoland is to be scheduled as a new national park within the next few years, to protect the large elephant herds and other animals in the area.

Getting There & Away

There is no public transport of any kind into the interior of Damaraland. The only possibility is to take the bus or train to Karibib, Omaruru, Otjiwarongo, Outjo or Tsumeb and arrange road transport from there.

Car & Motorbike The car remains virtually the only method of exploring this area. Many of the minor roads are difficult for 2WD, although there is access to the area from the tarred B2 from Swakopmund and the B1 to Otjiwarongo and C38 through Outjo.

One of the nicest ways to explore Damaraland is to drive across from the coast via the C35 from Swakopmund and Henties Bay, which enables you to appreciate the gradual change in gradient, climate and flora. The road is gravel but easily passable with 2WD, though there is no fuel (or shade) between Henties Bay and Uis.

There is a branch of Avis Rent-a-Car in Okaukuejo and another in Tsumeb. Fuel is available only at Uis, Khorixas and Kamanjab; no tourist facilities are found outside these towns.

Hitching Hitching across this area is extremely difficult. The main B1/B2 system offers your best chance of a lift, but it is unlikely that you will find getting into the Erongo or Brandberg mountains very easy if you're hitching.

Getting Around

There is no scheduled public transport in this area. Few alternatives exist to renting a car or taking an organised tour.

Skeleton Coast

Orientation & Information

The Skeleton Coast is reputed to cover nearly two million hectares of sand dunes and to form one of the most inhospitable and waterless areas of the world. For the convenience of visitors the coast has been broken up into several administrative sections, more or less zoned by ease of access and their distance from Swakopmund.

National West Coast Tourist Recreation Area

The southern stretch of Skeleton Coast extends through the National West Coast Tourist Recreation Area, a 200-km-long and 25-km-wide strip from Swakopmund to the Ugab River. Visiting this area does not require a permit and the road may be driven easily in 2WD cars, although shifting sand sometimes makes driving hazardous. The morning fog, caused by onshore winds blowing over the cold Benguela Current, is deceptive. You may require a waistcoat or jacket but can still get deeply sunburnt when it is foggy. There are no formal visitor attractions, just the space and clean air, but the coast is very popular for angling.

At the resort village of Henties Bay, 80 km north of Swakopmund, a good road leaves the coast and branches inland through Damaraland towards Uis and Khorixas, but the coastal salt road continues to the Cape Cross Seal Reserve. The Omaruru River joins the Atlantic at Henties Bay and, since it rises in an area of high rainfall, the river quite often actually flows (unlike the Swakop and Kuiseb).

If you notice any familiar-looking plants by the roadside around here they are probably wild tobacco, native to the Americas. How did they get there? No one knows, but one explanation is that they arrived along with hay for horses during the German-Khoi-Khoi war. Botanists are trying some experiments to see what happens to the natural vegetation when the wild tobacco is removed. Saltpans are another feature of the local scenery, with some being commercially exploited. The road northwards crosses numerous dry watercourses where animal tracks are often visible in the sand; you can try your hand at species identification.

Cape Cross Seal Colony

Cape Cross marks the site where the first European to arrive here, the Portuguese navigator Diego Cão, planted a cross. You can visit a replica which is accompanied by a short inscription.

The main interest of Cape Cross today is that it is a breeding reserve for Cape fur seals (*Arctocephalus pusillus pusillus*) which live there in tens of thousands. Current population estimates vary between 80,000 and 100,000. The water and rocks are thickly covered with seals profiting from the rich fish concentrations in the cold Benguela Current. Fur seals have a thick layer of short fur beneath the coarser guard hairs which remain dry and trap air for insulation, so that the animals can maintain an internal body temperature of 37°C and spend long periods in the cold (10°C to 15°C) waters off the Namibian coast.

Seals eat about 8% of their body weight of fish each day; this causes some conflict of interest with anglers and has lead to a management programme at Cape Cross designed to keep the size of the colony more or less at its present level. Cape fur seals are quite big. Males reach 187 kg in weight on average but this can increase to more than 360 kg during the breeding season due to the accumulation of large food reserves in the form of blubber. Females are smaller (75 kg on average) and they give birth to a single, blue-eyed pup in late November or early December. About 90% of pups are born within that 34-day period, which is the best time to visit the colony.

Pups begin to suckle within an hour of

their birth but are soon left in communal 'nurseries' by their mothers, who take trips to forage for food. The pup will often stay with its mother for nearly a year, moulting after the first few months from dark grey to olive brown. Mortality rates in the colony are high: up to 27% of pups fail to survive, especially during the first week of birth. You will generally see a few black-backed jackals around and sometimes a brown hyaena near the colony, which together account for nearly a quarter of pup deaths.

You can visit the reserve daily (except Friday) from mid-December until the end of February, and also during the Easter holidays and weekends until the end of June. From 1 July to 15 December the reserve is only open on Wednesday afternoons from noon to 4 pm. It costs R5 per adult to visit and there is no accommodation, though drinking water and toilets are available.

No advance booking is required. The reserve can also be visited on day trips or tours from Swakopmund, but there is no public transport.

Skeleton Coast Park

Following the coast road through the tourist recreation area 110 km (70 miles) north of Cape Cross, you come to the Ugab River which forms the boundary between the tourist recreation area and the Skeleton Coast Park proper. The park is divided into north and south zones; only the southern zone (Ugab River to Hoanib River) is accessible, and you need a permit. This costs R8 from the Nature Conservation office in Windhoek or the information centres at Swakopmund and Okaukuejo, but it does not entitle you to visit the camps at Torra Bay or Terrace Bay. You are also obliged to reach the gates of the park by 3 pm.

There is a fine field of barchans (crescent-shaped dunes) at Torra Bay, similar to the one just outside Lüderitz, which marks the start of the northern dunefield stretching from Torra Bay to the Curoca River in Angola.

The Ugab and the Huab (the next river north) are the southernmost parts of the Namib where big game is to be found today.

Anywhere north of here you have a chance of seeing the Namib elephants, rhinoceroses, lions and giraffes. Biologists are currently investigating the special adaptations that these animals (particularly elephants) have made to living in such dry conditions.

Skeleton Coast Hiking Trail

There is a 50-km hiking trail along the Ugab River which is walked the second and fourth Tuesdays of each month. The hike starts at 9 am from the Ugab River crossing, 200 km north of Swakopmund, and takes groups of six to eight people. It costs R75 per person and you must book at the Nature Conservation reservations office in Windhoek well in advance. A medical certificate of fitness (issued less than 40 days before the hike) is required and must be handed to the trails officer. You provide your own food and equipment. It's a good idea to spend the Monday night at the Mile 108 camp, 40 km south of the Ugab, which gets you to the start on time. The trip ends on the Thursday and is accompanied throughout by a member of Nature Conservation staff who is a mine of information on the local ecology. Lions, hyaenas, gemsboks and other antelopes may be seen along the Ugab, and have even been known to appear on the beaches.

Welwitschias

Just before Torra Bay a small gravel road (D2620) branches off between the Koigab and Uniab rivers, leading to a junction. If you turn south at the junction you reach Damaraland and Khorixas; north takes you to Kamanjab. More welwitschias grow in this area, and as you go inland the scenery changes from grassland to acacia thorn trees.

Northern Skeleton Coast

The Skeleton Coast's most northerly area, north of the Hoanib to the Kunene, is not accessible by car; you can get there only on a fly-in safari operated on a concession basis by Skeleton Coast Safaris (☎ (061) 37567), PO Box 20373, Windhoek 9000. The trip lasts five days and costs R3450 per person all inclusive, starting from Windhoek via

Swakopmund and flying to a tent camp at Sarusas about 600 km north of Swakopmund in the Khumib River valley. You stay in an igloo-style tent (complete with chemical toilet) and take daily guided 4WD tours to the dunes, Cape Fria seal colony and the Hoarusib Canyon. Dolphins are often seen offshore and your beach walks are accompanied by the constant cries of kelp gulls and gannets.

Places to Stay & Eat
Camping There are camping sites along the coast road (with showers and basic amenities) at Mile 14, Jakkalsputz, Henties Bay, Mile 72 and Mile 108. You need to take all equipment with you, but it is possible to buy water at the camping sites for 10 cents per litre. Most of the camps are set up to cater for sea anglers.

Camping at Torra Bay is very basic and costs R10 per day. The camping site is open only from 1 December to the end of January and you have to book in advance at Nature Conservation in Windhoek. It is also possible to stay even further north at Terrace Bay but it costs R120 per day for one person, though this includes accommodation and three meals. Like all the Skeleton Coast sites

it is mainly set up to cater to the needs of surf anglers. You need to have a reserved place (booked at Windhoek) and you can't cross the Ugab River after 3 pm. There is no accommodation further north than Terrace Bay unless you are on a fly-in safari.

Hotels There are no hotels on the Skeleton Coast north of Swakopmund.

Getting There & Away
The Skeleton Coast is lined by a salt road running north from Swakopmund; distances are measured in miles from Swakopmund. The road terminates 70 km north of the Terrace Bay fishing camp, but not all areas are equally accessible. There is no public transport so a car is essential. The road is good but the bleak, sun-scarred landscape is not suitable for hitching. Access to the extreme northern part is denied unless you are on a fly-in safari.

The C39 gravel road links Khorixas with Torra Bay, but it's not recommended for 2WD.

Getting Around
Unless you're on an organised tour, the only way around the Skeleton Coast is by vehicle.

North Central Namibia

The northern central area of Namibia, east of Damaraland, south of Etosha and north of Windhoek, is often ignored by visitors to the country, yet it has much going for it and many things to see which make it worth a stopover or two. It is easily reached by road, either north from Windhoek via Okahandja, or south down from Kavango-Caprivi and Owamboland. This central area includes some of the richest agricultural land in the country together with the major mining district and a number of significant historical sites.

Before colonial days the region was inhabited by the nomadic cattle-raising Herero people together with lesser numbers of Damara and San. The first German missionaries arrived in the late 1800s, followed by more settlers near the turn of the century. The German Schutztruppe established a base at Otavi and some architectural relics of this period can still be seen today. The region was also the scene of many confrontations between Germans and Herero in the early colonial period, resulting in a final battle at Waterberg in 1904.

The Grootfontein area has an especially interesting history. In 1855 about 40 families of trekkers arrived from Angola to settle there on land which their leader Will Jordan had bought from the Wambo chief Kambonde. They proclaimed the area as the 'Republic of Upingtonia' but the regime only lasted a couple of years.

Central northern Namibia includes the important nature reserve of Waterberg Plateau Park, renowned for the preservation of rare species, where there is a hiking trail and tours organised by Nature Conservation. Other interesting places to visit include the Hoba meteorite and the deep Otjikoto Lake near Tsumeb.

Orientation

The central northern area is interesting, yet many of the small towns cater almost exclusively for transient visitors on their way north to Etosha. There is a corresponding lack of public transport and it can be quite difficult to reach places such as Waterberg or Hoba without a car. The towns are small with a limited range of facilities but the surrounding countryside is pleasant, including quite hilly country near Otavi and rolling farmland in the south near Otjiwarongo.

Information

There are municipal information centres at Outjo, Otavi, Grootfontein, Otjiwarongo and Tsumeb as well as an information centre in the rest camp at the Waterberg Plateau Park. All are open during standard business hours and are clearly signposted. In the smaller towns some historic buildings are kept locked, but you can get the key from the local tourist information centre. They will also be able to tell you about the availability of local transport, which is quite limited and generally unscheduled, and they can book you a camping site place.

Climate

Expect clear sunny days with cooler nights, especially during May-September. Daytime temperatures will get into the top 30s during January and February in the north of the region. This is not a high rainfall area but you may get showers any time between November and April.

Things to Buy

There are no local specialities peculiar to this region, although skin and hide products (bags, rugs etc) are quite common. Otjiwarongo is on the edge of Hereroland and many roadside stalls sell the costumed Herero dolls. Outjo has a famous bakery with some of the best bread in Namibia, and since the south of the region is a major fruit-growing area, citrus fruits can be bought cheaply by the roadside during July to September.

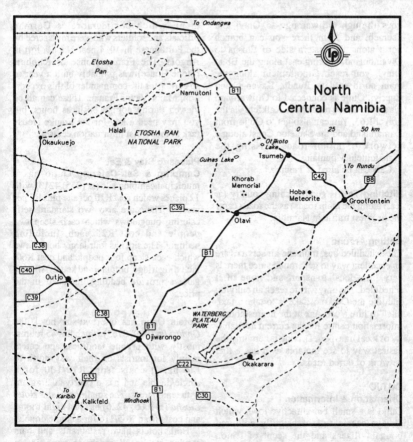

North Central Namibia

To Ondangwa

Etosha Pan

Namutoni

Halali · ETOSHA PAN NATIONAL PARK

Okaukuejo

Otjikoto Lake
Guinas Lake
Tsumeb

To Rundu

Khorab Memorial

Hoba Meteorite

Grootfontein

C39

Otavi

C38

C40

Outjo

C39

C38

B1

WATERBERG PLATEAU PARK

B1

Otjiwarongo

C22

Okakarara

C33

To Karibib

Kalkfeld

To Windhoek

C30

0   25   50 km

Getting There & Away

Air The major airport, at Tsumeb, has scheduled Namib Air services from Windhoek. Minor airports at Outjo and Otjiwarongo mainly cater for charter air freight traffic.

Bus The Mainliner coach service from Windhoek to Tsumeb takes six hours and connects Otjiwarongo, Otavi, Kombat and Grootfontein. Buses leave Windhoek at 7 am on Thursday and 2 pm on Sunday, returning at 7 pm on Monday and 2 pm on Friday from Tsumeb. The whole journey costs R79 one-way, and segments of any length can be booked at the Mainliner office in Windhoek (☎ (061) 227847).

Train You can get a train on Friday and Sunday from Windhoek to Tsumeb via Otjiwarongo and Otavi. Grootfontein can be reached by train from Otavi on Monday and Saturday. There is a local rail service between Otjiwarongo and Outjo both ways every Monday, Wednesday and Friday.

Car & Motorbike This region includes excellent tarred roads and the main through-routes in the country. The B1 from Windhoek goes through Otjiwarongo to Otavi and Tsumeb, and from there you can branch north along the eastern side of Etosha to Owamboland. Forking east along the B8 at Otavi, you reach Grootfontein along the main north road to Rundu, Kavango and Caprivi. Outjo is connected to Otjiwarongo via a good tarred road and to Kalkfeld via the gravel R63. You can also get to Outjo from Damaraland and the Skeleton Coast along a network of minor roads crossing the Fransfontein Mountains.

Cars can be hired at Tsumeb.

Hitching This is good hitching country (at least along the main roads) as the roads carry the heaviest traffic in Namibia.

Getting Around

The scheduled bus, train and air services are an excellent way to get around since there is very little local transport and none of it scheduled. The only way to reach an outlying site like the Otjikoto Lake is to take a taxi, hitch or hire a car. Ask at the nearest tourist information centre for the current availability of local transport. Driving is certainly the easiest way to see the area as it has a fine network of tarred roads.

OUTJO
Orientation & Information

Outjo is a small but attractive town which always seems full of brightly coloured bougainvillaeas and the scent of lemon blossom. The area grows citrus fruit and is quite rich farming country as well, mainly cattle ranching. There are lots of architectural remnants of the colonial period worth a visit: the tourist information centre in the municipal offices is open during office hours for current information.

Things to See & Do

It's pleasant to walk round Outjo and look at some of the architectural remnants of the colonial past. These include an old windmill tower dating from the end of 1900 which supplied water to the German barracks and soldiers. There is also the Naulila Monu-

ment, which commemorates German officials and soldiers who were massacred by the Portuguese in 1914 near Naulila fort in Angola. The Franke House or Kliphuis (Stone House) was probably built a year or so earlier for the commander of this expedition, Major Victor Franke. These can all be viewed during normal business hours, but you may need a key for the Franke House (ask at the tourist information centre).

Places to Stay & Eat

Camping & Self-Catering Outjo has a municipal camping site (☎ (065) 4213) with 12 places which cost R10 per site plus R1 per person. There are also two standard self-catering bungalows which each sleep two people and cost R25 each, including bedding. The site has four larger bungalows which each sleep four people and cost R60, including fridge, hotplate and kettle. All bungalows provide bedding, included in the price.

Hotels Outjo has one two-star hotel, the *Onduri* (☎ (090) 8763) which has 45 rooms, mostly with private facilities, and caters mainly for tourists on their way north to Etosha. It costs from R70/100 for a single/double and has a courtyard fragrant with lemon trees. The smaller one-star *Hotel Etosha* (☎ (065) 4226) has just eight rooms and costs from R65/116 for a single/double.

Both hotels have restaurants and bars serving meals and snacks to nonresidents and there are a couple of small takeaway places in the town as well.

Guest Farms Outjo is in the heart of a major tourist area and thus well supplied with guest farms. These include the three-star *Bambatsi Holiday Ranch* (☎ (065) 421104) with nine rooms and a pool, where full board starts at R115 per person per day (single or double). *Otjitambi* guest farm (☎ (065) 424602) is graded two-star and has eight rooms with full board starting at R145 per day, but it also provides facilities for hunters. There is also the *Toshari Inn* guest farm (☎ (065) 423602) with 17 rooms but no pool, with prices starting from R115 per day for full board.

Getting There & Away
Air Although Outjo has an airport, Namib Air does not currently operate a scheduled service. However, it is worth checking with their head office in Windhoek (% (061) 38220).

Bus & Train There are no scheduled bus or train services to Outjo with the exception of the local Otjiwarongo-Outjo railway line which provides a thrice-weekly service (Monday, Wednesday and Friday) leaving Otjiwarongo at 8.20 am and arriving in Outjo at 10.27 am. The train makes a return journey the same day, leaving Outjo at 11.20 am and arriving in Otjiwarongo at 1.30 pm.

Car & Motorbike Outjo can be reached from Otjiwarongo in the south via the main B1 road. North of the town this road becomes gravel as it continues on north to the Ombikahek gate of Etosha. Outjo can also be reached via a minor road, the R63, from Kalkfeld and from Damaraland via the poor-quality gravel C39 over the Fransfontein Mountains from Khorixas.

Getting Around
Outjo is tiny; you can walk round all the major sites in less than an hour as it has really only one main street.

OTJIWARONGO
Orientation & Information
Otjiwarongo (Pleasant Place or Place Where Fat Cattle Graze, depending on who you listen to) is a mainly agricultural and ranching centre. A Rhenish mission station was started here in 1891 after a treaty was signed between the missionaries and the Herero chief Kambazembi, followed by the establishment of a military post a few years later. The town became prosperous when the narrow-gauge railway from Swakopmund to the Otavi copper mine was built in 1906 and it functions as a halfway house between Windhoek and Etosha. It also boasts an air-field and a population of 8500. The surrounding area is one of the richest farming regions in the country.

If you approach Otjiwarongo from the south, look for the twin peaks of the Omatako (Buttocks in Herero) Mountains to the left of the road near the junction with the D2404. Since Otjiwarongo is on the fringe of Hereroland you'll see many of the statuesque crinoline-clad Herero ladies.

There is a tourist information centre in the municipal offices, signposted from the main road.

Things to See & Do
There's not a lot to do in Otjiwarongo, which is more a place people pass through on the way to somewhere else: generally Etosha or the Waterberg Plateau Park. One unusual attraction is Namibia's first crocodile ranch, open daily between 9 am and 6 pm. There is a signpost off the main road and it is only a short walk.

Places to Stay
Camping The municipal camping site at Otjiwarongo (☎ (065) 12231) is in a rather sinister fashion next to the crocodile park, which is actually quite convenient since campers can use the farm's refreshment facilities. The site is small (six places) and costs R9 per site plus R1.60 per person.

Hotels Otjiwarongo has two hotels, largely used by travellers to Etosha, of which the nicer is the two-star *Hamburger Hof* (☎ (090) 83841), part of the Namib Sun chain. This costs from R80/136 for a single/double with B&B. The smaller *Hotel Brumme* has 12 rooms and costs from R60/94 for a single/double.

Guest Farms The two-star *Okonjima* guest farm (☎ (065) 818212) near Otjiwarongo has five rooms and costs from R110 per person for full board, including use of the pool. Alas, it also has facilities for hunters, as does the larger *Wabi Hunting Lodge* (☎ (065) 815313) which advertises 'splendour and luxury facilities' from R115 (full board).

The *Mount Etjo Safari Lodge* (☎ (065) 32), on the C33 68 km south of Otjiwarongo heading for Kalkfed, is in a private nature reserve. You can go on walking or vehicle safaris and watch lions feeding. The accommodation is hotel-type rooms but purists can also sleep in tree-top hides. Costs start at R165/286 for singles/doubles for full board.

Places to Eat

Restaurants Both hotels have a bar and restaurant serving meals and snacks. The cafeteria at the crocodile farm next to the main camping site provides a good range of light meals, and Otjiwarongo also has the usual range of takeaway facilities near petrol stations.

Getting There & Away

Air Namib Air flies to Otjiwarongo but flight schedules are not currently available. Check their head office in Windhoek (☎ (061) 38220).

Bus The Mainliner bus from Windhoek to Otjiwarongo leaves Windhoek at 7 am on Thursday and 2 pm on Sunday; the journey takes three hours and costs R54 (single). The bus continues on to Otavi, Kombat, Grootfontein and Tsumeb and you can return to Windhoek from Otjiwarongo on Monday (departs 10 am) or Friday (departs 5.05 pm).

Train The train to Tsumeb via Otjiwarongo from Windhoek runs on Friday and Sunday. Ask at Windhoek station for current schedules. You can also reach Otjiwarongo from Outjo by the local train service, which leaves Outjo on Monday, Wednesday and Friday at 11.20 am, arriving in Otjiwarongo two hours later.

Car & Motorbike Otjiwarongo is at a major road junction. From the south you can reach it either from Windhoek via the B1 or from Swakopmund via Karibib, Omaruru and Kalkfeld along the B2 and the C33. From the north the B1 leads to Otjiwarongo from Otavi or you can reach it from Outjo and the B5.

Getting Around

Otjiwarongo is quite a small place and you can easily walk round.

WATERBERG PLATEAU PARK
Information & Orientation

The Waterberg Plateau Park is, in my view, one of the nicest and most interesting of all Namibian nature reserves. The area also has considerable historical interest, as Waterberg was the site of the decisive battle between Germans and Herero in 1904 which resulted in a victory for the colonial side but with much loss of life.

You can see the plateau clearly on the horizon from 50 km away, looming 150 metres over the plain with sheer sides and a flat top like a kind of Lost World. The plateau itself is nearly 50 km long and up to 16 km wide and, as you might expect from the name, there is a lot of water. This produces quite lush vegetation with a mosaic of trees and scrub savanna, and is responsible for the large amounts of game.

Admission to the park costs R5 per person plus R5 for a vehicle, and is paid at the Nature Conservation office near the main (and only) gate. The office is open from 8 am to 1 pm and from 2 pm to sunset, all through the year.

Gamewatching

Waterberg is famous for the rare and threatened species which breed there, including the sable and roan antelopes, tsessebe, buffalo and white rhino. You may also see wild dogs, leopards, cheetahs and lesser bushbabies. Nature Conservation plans to add more species over the next few years, probably the reedbuck, waterbuck and black rhino.

Birdwatching

The Okarukuwisa Mountains on the western edge of the plateau are the only place in Namibia where the Cape vulture breeds and you can see the birds soaring overhead. Nature Conservation is making great efforts to increase their numbers after a crash in the 1950s when the species was nearly

Rhinos

exterminated by the poisons used in farming. A 'vulture restaurant' where kudu and gemsbok appear regularly on the menu is part of this programme though it's relatively unattractive to human visitors.

Waterberg has more than 115 bird species including the rare Ruppell's parrot, the rockrunner and two species of hornbill (Bradfield's and Monteiro's).

Dinosaur Footprints

Waterberg also contains dinosaur footprints and a series of archaeological sites. Ask for details at the Nature Conservation office.

Waterberg Wilderness Trail

The Waterberg Wilderness Trail can be followed every second, third and fourth weekend between April and November. The walk begins on Thursday afternoon at 4 pm from the Onjoka gate of the park and ends early Sunday afternoon. The trail is accompanied by armed Nature Conservators, and they only take one group of six to eight people at a time. Walking the trail costs R75 per person and you have to provide your own food and sleeping bags. It's necessary to reserve a place well in advance at the

main Nature Conservation office in Windhoek. You also need to be reasonably fit and able to cover 15 km of rough walking per day. Nature Conservation provides simple rest huts and all other requirements.

Battle of Waterberg Commemoration

The Herero people and various German organisations also commemorate the battle of Waterberg around 11 August at the memorial in the graveyard near the resort office. This is a simple ceremony which is worth attending if you happen to be in the area, but not worth a detour. Sober dress is appropriate.

Organised Tours

Waterberg features on the itineraries of many Namibian tour operators. Check in Windhoek with companies such as Oryx Tours (☎ (061) 224252) for their current schedule of trips.

Places to Stay & Eat

There is a Nature Conservation rest camp (named after Bernabé de la Bat) in the Waterberg Park with bungalows and a camping site. It's essential to reserve places well in advance at Windhoek. A tent or caravan site costs R25 per day for a maximum of eight persons, one caravan or tent and two vehicles.

The camp also has self-catering accommodation but it is a bit more expensive than the other parks and game reserves. You can book a one-bedroom bungalow (sleeping three) for R70 per day, a two-bedroom version (sleeping five) for R120, and a room with shower but no cooking facilities for R108 (sleeping two). All prices (except camping) include bedding. There is a bar and restaurant, kiosk for essential supplies, barbecues and a swimming pool, but no petrol station. It's wise to take all food and supplies with you.

Getting There & Away

Air, Bus & Train There is no scheduled public transport to Waterberg. The only alternative is to take a Mainliner coach or train to

Otjiwarongo and take a taxi from there, but it may cost you R50 and availability is limited.

Car & Motorbike You reach Waterberg by turning east along the C22 just south of Otjiwarongo. The road leads east into Hereroland and is signposted to the Waterberg Plateau Park. A small gravel access road leads from the C22 and is in very bad condition. It could be impassable in a bad rainy season. If you do not have 4WD it's wise to check in Windhoek for a road report before you go.

Motorcycles are not allowed in the Waterberg Plateau Park.

Getting Around

Nature Conservation arranges tours using their open 4WD vehicles around the park and to the top of the plateau. Ask at the office or in Windhoek for the latest timings. Unlike at Etosha, you are not allowed to drive round the park in your own car, primarily because Waterberg is geared to the management of endangered species and visitor numbers are restricted. There are hides from which you can watch animals, and the Nature Conservation staff provide lots of background information. Because there are dangerous animals here (including a large white rhino population) you aren't allowed to walk on your own.

OTAVI

Orientation & Information

Between Otjiwarongo and Tsumeb the B1 goes through Otavi, near the mountains of the same name. Otavi was originally a German garrison town whose natural springs were used to irrigate the surrounding land to provide bread for the new settlers. The town grew after the railway was established in 1906 and became a major copper mining centre linked to Swakopmund via a narrow-gauge railway.

Things to See & Do

Two km north of Otavi there's a signpost to the Khorab Memorial where German troops surrendered to the South African Army under General Louis Botha on 9 July 1915. You follow the road past the hotel, cross the railway line and turn right along the marked track to find the memorial which was put up in 1920.

Places to Stay & Eat

Camping & Self-Catering There is a small one-star municipal camping site at Otavi (☎ (067) 4222) with 10 sites each with a power point for caravans. These cost R11 per site plus R1.10 per person. The site also has six self-catering bungalows each with four beds, shower/toilet, fridge, hotplate and kettle. These cost R27.50 per bungalow plus R1.10 per person, including bedding.

Hotels Otavi has a lone one-star hotel, the *Otavi Hotel*, with 11 rooms. It costs R35 (single) and R30 (double) including breakfast. They also have a bar and restaurant which serves all meals and snacks to nonresidents.

Apart from the hotel there is virtually nowhere to eat in Otavi unless you count garage takeaways.

Getting There & Away

Air Otavi has no airport but you can fly to Tsumeb from Windhoek four times a week on Namib Air and travel the last 65 km overland.

Bus The Mainliner coach service goes through Otavi, leaving Windhoek on Thursdays at 7 am and Sundays at 2 pm. The trip takes about 4½ hours and costs R66 one way. You can also reach Otavi by Mainliner from Tsumeb, leaving Monday at 7 am and Friday at 2 pm. The journey takes around two hours, since you travel via Grootfontein and Kombat, and costs R35 for a single.

Getting Around

Otavi is a tiny town where everything, such as it is, can easily be reached on foot. Taxi services are extremely limited but the municipal office can advise you on local transport availability.

HOBA METEORITE
Orientation & Information
At Othihaenena, about 25 km north-east of Otavi, you can see the world's largest meteorite at a farm called Hoba. The Hoba meteorite was discovered in the 1920s and is thought to weigh about 54,000 kg (50 tonnes). It consists of 82% iron and 16% nickel with traces of other metals. No one knows when it fell to earth. The meteorite, which is cubic (apparently rare for meteorites), was declared a National Monument in 1955 since it had been badly hacked about by souvenir hunters. A conservation project was launched with funds from the Rössing Foundation. There is a display wall giving information about the meteorite and a small nature trail through the bush nearby. You can also take advantage of some shade and a picnic place with toilet facilities.

While in the area it is also worth visiting the Ghaub mines nearby. These are worked-out copper mines and some interesting caves full of stalagmites and stalactites. You need to get permission and precise directions from the municipal offices in Otavi.

Getting There & Away
Bus The Mainliner coach service runs from Tsumeb to the Kombat copper mines twice a week (leaving Tsumeb at 7 am Monday and 2 pm Friday). The trip costs R23. Unfortunately you cannot catch a return bus the same day and there is no accommodation in Kombat. You can also stop off there using the Mainliner travelling north from Windhoek. That leaves Windhoek at 7 am Thursday and 2 pm Sunday, reaching Kombat just under four hours later.

Car & Motorbike You reach the meteorite by taking the B8 or B1 from Otavi to Grootfontein. About 25 km from Otavi you pass the Kombat copper mines on your left and a sign to Farm Hoba. Ask at the farmhouse for directions to the meteorite which is very easy to find. No public transport goes to Hoba but you may be able to hitch a lift from Otavi or Grootfontein, or take a local taxi – but that is expensive (R20 to R30).

The Ghaub mines can be reached from a small road (D3022) off the B2 signposted 'Ghaub', but exploring the caves needs a guide, who can be arranged at the municipal offices in Otavi.

GROOTFONTEIN
Orientation & Information
Grootfontein, a town with a very German colonial feel, has many buildings made of local limestone and the town feels upright and respectable, with avenues of jacaranda trees which bloom in September. There's a nice museum located in the old German fort, a famous Tree Park planted by the South West Africa Company many years ago with species from all over the world, and a cemetery which contains the graves of early settlers and Schutztruppe. Grootfontein housed the original head office of the South West Africa Company in 1893 and later became a Schutztruppe base.

Today Grootfontein is the centre of Namibia's major cattle farming area and is a pleasant, rather Teutonic market centre with good supermarkets.

Fort
You can still visit the fort which was restored in 1974 as a result of a public appeal. It is between Upingtonia and Eriksson Sts and includes an exhibition of the early history of the area. There are no official opening times and you need to call Mr Menge (☎ (067) 312061) to borrow the key.

Cemetery
The town cemetery contains several Schutztruppe graves and can be found just off the main Rundu road.

Places to Stay
Camping & Self-Catering The small municipal camping site with a swimming pool at Grootfontein (☎ (067) 313100) has a camping site and caravan park costing R2.50 per person and R11 per vehicle. There are also four self-catering chalets which each sleep four people and cost R60 per chalet with an extra charge for bedding.

Hotels Grootfontein has two small one-star hotels. The *Meteor Hotel* (☎ (067) 312078) has 24 rooms and costs about R60/100 for a single/double. The smaller *Nord Hotel* (☎ (067) 312049) has 11 rooms and costs about R40 per person.

Places to Eat

There is a restaurant at the *Meteor* and both hotels have a bar. There is a small restaurant next to the camping site, and Grootfontein also has a couple of licensed cafes for light meals. Takeaway food is available from petrol stations and the supermarket.

Getting There & Away

Air Grootfontein does not have an airport; the nearest is at Tsumeb less than 50 km away.

Bus Grootfontein is the last stop on the Mainliner Windhoek-Tsumeb coach service, leaving Windhoek Thursday and Sunday and returning Monday and Friday. The journey takes about five hours and costs R70. Book at the Mainliner office in Windhoek (☎ (061) 227847).

Train The twice-weekly train service (Friday and Sunday) from Windhoek to Tsumeb enables you to stop at Otavi and make a connection to Grootfontein. Check at Windhoek station for timings and cost.

Car & Motorbike From the south you can reach Grootfontein along the main B1 from Otjiwarongo, turning off onto the B8 (signposted to Grootfontein and Rundu) at Otavi. From Owamboland take the B1 south to Tsumeb and continue along the C42 to Grootfontein. From the north-east you come into Grootfontein down the B8 from Rundu, which is joined about 60 km north of the town by the gravel C44 which meets the Botswana border east of Tsumkwe in Bushmanland.

Getting Around

Grootfontein is a very small place and you can easily walk around. There is a limited local taxi and bus service (ask at the municipal offices for details). The nearest car hire locations are in Tsumeb.

TSUMEB
Orientation & Information

Tsumeb is at the apex of the 'Golden Triangle' of roads linking the town with Otavi and Grootfontein. It is a mining town whose prosperity is based on the presence of copper ore and associated minerals (lead, silver, germanium and cadmium) around a volcanic pipe.

The mining history of Tsumeb goes back to the Iron Age and many prehistoric smelting sites have been found. Inevitably ownership of the rich area was much disputed by the different tribal groups and it became a prime target for European interest during the 1800s. Colonial mining activities seem to have started in the 1890s and the copper vein was so rich that it justified the construction of a railway line all the way to Swakopmund.

Tsumeb is also famous for having more than 200 varieties of minerals found locally. These have found their way into museum collections all over the world. There's a fine collection in the Smithsonian (Washington, USA) and lots in the small town museum as well. Tsumeb also has many shops which specialise in selling minerals and ores like azurite to collectors, together with carvings, curios and jewellery made from them.

Information about Tsumeb can be obtained at the museum or at the municipal offices on Main St where there is a small information centre.

Museum

The history of the town is told in the museum which is well worth a visit. Apart from the outstanding geological specimens it also has a lot of militaria, including weapons recovered from Otjikoto Lake. This was part of a dump of military materials, including cannons and vehicles, which was abandoned by German troops prior to their surrender to the South Africans in 1915. The museum is in the former Old German Private School in

Main St and is open from 9 am to noon and 3 to 6 pm Monday to Friday, and from 3 to 6 pm on Saturday. The building itself dates from 1915 and had two short periods as a school around an interval as a hospital for German troops.

St Barbara's Church

The Roman Catholic church in Tsumeb was built in 1914 and dedicated to St Barbara, the patron saint of mineworkers. You can find it at the junction of Main and Third Sts. There are some interesting colonial murals and an odd tower.

Lakes Guinas & Otjikoto

These lakes are about 25 km north-west of Tsumeb. If driving, you take the B1 towards Namutoni, and there is a sign to the two lakes. Lake Otjikoto is reputedly 120 metres deep and contains unusual mouth-breeding cichlid fish species. These come in a variety of cheerful colours; biologists think this has something to do with the absence of predators, which made it unnecessary for the fish to develop camouflage.

The explorers Charles Andersson and Francis Galton 'discovered' Otjikoto in 1851. The lake had formerly been an underground cavern in limestone country which had collapsed, leaving a huge steep-sided hole. All sorts of local legends surround these 'bottomless' lakes, which are striking to visit because of the steep sides and dense woodland. Lake Guinas is much the smaller of the two.

Lake Otjikoto was the place where the retreating Germans dumped weaponry and ammunition in 1915 to prevent it falling into South African hands. Rumour has it that this included 300 to 400 wagon loads of ammunition and 24 cannons. Some of this was later recovered by a joint effort from the South African Army, the Tsumeb Corporation and Windhoek State Museum. Artefacts included an intact Krupp ammunition wagon, presently displayed in the Alte Feste Museum, Windhoek.

Places to Stay & Eat

Camping Tsumeb has a municipal camping site (not star graded) which costs R10 per site per day plus R2 per adult. Day visitors are allowed to picnic there for R5. Sites can be reserved by phone (☎ (067) 13056).

Hotels Tsumeb has two small two-star hotels. The *Hotel Eckleben* (☎ (090) 83842) has 16 rooms and costs R80/120 for a single/double. It has a restaurant but no pool. The larger *Minen Hotel* has 38 rooms and costs about R40/80 for a single/double. There is also the super-luxurious three-star *Mokuti Lodge* (☎ (090) 8749) near the boundary of the Etosha National Park. Rooms here will set you back R150/220 for a single/double, since the hotel is designed to cater for wealthy visitors to Etosha who wish to stay outside the park boundary rather than in Nature Conservation rest camps.

Getting There & Away

Air There are four flights per week to Tsumeb on Namib Air from Eros Airport, Windhoek.

Bus Mainliner coach services between Windhoek and Tsumeb leave Windhoek on Thursday and Sunday. The journey takes about six hours and costs R79 one way: reserve seats at the main office (☎ (061) 227847). Return services leave Tsumeb on Monday and Friday and you can stop at Grootfontein, Kombat, Otavi, Otjiwarongo and Okahandja on the way.

Train There is a twice-weekly train service on Friday and Sunday from Windhoek to Tsumeb which costs about the same as the bus. Check the station for the current timetable.

Car & Motorbike Tsumeb can be reached from the south by the main B2 from Otjiwarongo; the drive takes about three hours. There is access from Owamboland via the B1, which passes the Namutoni Gate. If coming from the north-east of Namibia down the Caprivi Strip you'll have to follow the B8 south from Rundu to Grootfontein and branch off to Tsumeb along the C42, which is clearly marked.

Getting Around

Tsumeb is a very small town and everything is within walking distance. It may be possible to get a taxi to take you out to Lake Otjikoto, or to get a local bus. Enquire at the tourist information centre. An alternative would be to hire a car from the branch of Avis in Tsumeb (☎ (067) 12520) or hitch.

Southern Coast

The southern coast includes the Namib-Naukluft National Park and the two major coastal towns of Swakopmund in the central Namib and Lüderitz in the south.

If you've come up from the south of Namibia via the Kalahari Gemsbok Park you'll notice a great difference in flora and fauna. Unlike the Kalahari, which is quite heavily vegetated and well explored (by desert standards), the Namib gives the impression of being totally sterile, although it actually supports a great deal of wildlife. The Namib Desert itself is long and thin, mostly less than 200 km wide, sandwiched along the coast between the cold waters of the South Atlantic and the Central Escarpment. It stretches more than 2000 km from Oliphants River across the border in South Africa to San Nicolau in southern Angola. There's a gradual slope from coast to escarpment, with the eastern boundary of the desert lying more than 1000 metres above sea level. There's also a rainfall gradient in the same direction, with maximum rain (100 mm per year) on high ground in the east.

Part of the attraction of the Namib is its great variety. The largest area is occupied by an immense linear dunefield of huge red dunes piling up on the horizon as far as the eye can see. The dunes seem lifeless but actually support a complex food chain that is able to exist because of the moisture obtained from frequent fogs caused by the condensation of onshore winds over the cold Benguela Current. The dunes stop quite abruptly in the north at the Kuiseb River, and between the Kuiseb and Swakop rivers they are replaced by flat, arid gravel plains with isolated hills and mountain ranges rising from them.

Looking at a map you'll see that a number of rivers, which are really best thought of as linear oases, apparently cross the desert. They range from those where water flows quite regularly to those where water only appears every few years in the upper reaches (like the Kuiseb). However, there is suffi-cient subsurface water to support a rich tree growth which follows the watercourses meandering through desert and dune.

The dune area of the Namib has a unique fauna. Walking across the dunes at Homeb or Sossusvlei you will certainly see traces of it – the trails of the sidewinder adder, dune lizards and plenty of the Namib black beetles (toktokkies) that are specially adapted to the desert environment. The dunes are also host to the blind golden mole, a large white dancing spider called 'white lady' (fortunately nocturnal) and a host of birds and other small creatures. First thing in the morning it's fun to look at the tracks and see what has been happening during the night – you get quite expert at distinguishing the trails of the sidewinder adder from those of geckos and other lizards, and you might be lucky and catch a glimpse of the rare golden mole. The millions of black beetles scuttling all over the dunes are quite harmless. They make a living in the plant detritus at the foot of the slipface and get their moisture by condensing fog water on their bodies. On a foggy morning at the top of a dune you can see a line of shiny beetles with tails in the air and water slipping down the body towards the mouth!

On the gravel plains, jackals, bat-eared foxes and sometimes caracals and aardwolves can be seen, while ground

Bat-eared fox

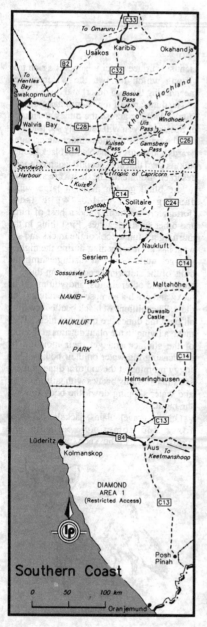

Southern Coast

| 0 | 50 | 100 km |

squirrels, mongooses, ostriches, gemsboks, springboks and zebras are always around. After a good rain (10 to 20 mm) seeds begin to germinate and the plains become a meadow of waist-length grass heaving with wildlife. However, this is only a fraction of the huge herds that lived here before the park was fenced off. Many people argue that the fencing of the park boundary is the reason why so little game is likely to be seen, as the fences cross natural migration routes. Unfortunately there haven't been many good rains recently but you will certainly encounter small herds of plains zebras, ostriches and the occasional magnificent gemsbok.

The whole Namib area is covered with archaeological material representing the remains of prehistoric hunter-gatherers who have tracked game in the area for the last 750,000 years. Along the shore you can see the middens of shells and fishbones belonging to the *strandlopers* ('beach people') who lived near the coast, and inland you should watch for stone circles and rock paintings of Khoisan people. Nowadays the Namib region is uninhabited, except for Topnaar Hottentots in the Kuiseb and Walvis Bay area and people employed on farms at the edge of the park.

Travelling in the Namib outside Swakopmund or Lüderitz really requires you to be self-sufficient. You need to take all your supplies with you, consider your route carefully, and realise that petrol stations are infrequent. It is necessary to follow the basic survival rules for travelling in a desert area. The sophisticated coastal ambience of Swakopmund can lull you into a false sense of security but any traveller in the Namib should realise that this is one of the world's harshest areas.

As you would expect, this is a hot, dry area where only the gravel plains at the extreme eastern edge get more than 100 mm of rain a year. You can reckon on clear, bright, sunny days all year round and the chances of rain are extremely small. In Swakopmund it has not rained in living memory. The daytime temperatures reach 45°C in the summer and fall below freezing at night. In fact as soon as the sun has set, the temperature drops quite sharply.

The mildest temperatures are found at the coast because of the effect of the cold offshore current, but this can also cause heavy fogs. The Namib area experiences an east wind in the winter which can bring sandstorms, and rainfall in the highlands of the Naukluft between December and April can cause the rivers to flood. The coast, especially around Lüderitz, can be extremely windy all year round; the interior of the desert can also get windy, especially in the winter.

The frequent light breeze tempts you to carelessness, but a powerful sunscreen and a hat are essential. So are shoes or sandals: step barefoot on the sand at noon and you will get a nasty burn.

Information
There is no shortage of environmental data about the desert. Because the Namib is relatively small (only one-thirtieth the size of the Sahara) and contains such varied and clearly defined subenvironments, it is a Mecca for academics. More than 600 scientific papers on it have been produced to date. Nature Conservation has offices in Swakopmund, Lüderitz and Windhoek where you can get information about the whole Namib area. The Nature Conservation offices at Naukluft and Sesriem also have maps, leaflets and information. Specific scientific information about the Desert Research Station at Gobabeb can be obtained from: The Director, Desert Ecological Research Unit, PO Box 1592, Swakopmund; and The Friends of Gobabeb Society, The Desert Research Foundation of Namibia, PO Box 37, Windhoek 9000.

There are helpful tourist information centres in Swakopmund and Lüderitz (open office hours) and the staff in municipal buildings at small towns like Maltahöhe on the desert fringes will also be happy to advise you.

Getting There & Around
The southern coast is very accessible by virtue of a good east-west road system linking the coastal towns to the inland cities. This makes it easy, for example, to reach Swakopmund and Walvis Bay from Windhoek, or to reach Lüderitz from Keetmanshoop. The towns are also linked by air and rail in the same east-west pattern. The problem comes when you want to move north to south (or vice versa): there are few alternatives to hiring a vehicle or joining a tour if you really want to explore the region. It is really far too hot to hitch in a desert area, and lifts may be few and far between.

Swakopmund & Walvis Bay

SWAKOPMUND
Swakopmund is the most popular holiday destination in Namibia – a German colonial town dropped down in the middle of the desert where it is possible to make the transition from blistering heat and dusty gemsbok to elegant harbourfront konditorei in a matter of minutes. Because of its equitable climate and wonderful beaches it is popular both as a family destination and for surfing, angling and watersports. Everything feels German; you will hardly hear any English spoken and little Afrikaans. It is really the only resort town in Namibia. Palm trees line the streets and seaside promenades, and there are excellent hotels and a general air of well-being (one might almost say complacency).

Many German-speaking Namibians have holiday homes or beachfront cottages here and it is a popular destination for overseas German-speaking tourists, who feel very much at home. This contributes to the almost overpowering *Gemütlichkeit* (distinctively German domestic good fellowship). Swakopmund can get very busy in the high seasons (Christmas and Easter) and be almost deserted in August.

Part of the popularity of Swakopmund is due to its temperate climate, averaging 15°C

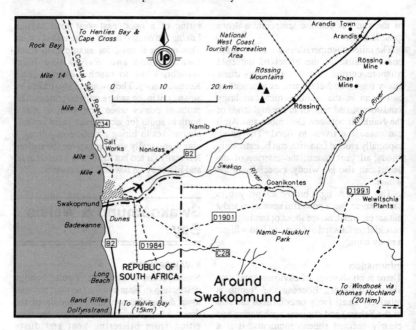

in summer to 25°C in winter, and the virtual absence of rain. You may notice that few houses have gutters or drainpipes. But there is often a sea fog which stretches as far as 30 km inland and provides moisture for the desert food chains, starting with 80 species of lichen.

Another part of the appeal lies in the German colonial architecture and part in the sheer contrast between the little whitewashed elegant town and the vast inhospitable desert that you have to cross to get to it.

History

Swakopmund began life in the 1890s in the early days of the German colonial expansion and was prominent during the German colonial period, as it was the country's only harbour. Walvis Bay, just 30 km down the road, had been annexed to the British-controlled Cape Colony, so Swakopmund

became more important than its limited harbour facilities warranted. This was unfortunate, since it was by no means as good a harbour as Walvis Bay, and passengers could at first only be landed by small surf boats. Later on a pier was constructed (which can be still seen today). The museum has one of the original basketwork cages used to swing passengers over from the ships by winch and pulley. The town was the main import/export centre for the whole territory, and many government agencies and transport houses had buildings here, some of which survive today. During WW I, when South West Africa was taken over by South Africa, Swakopmund became more of a holiday resort than a harbour as that function reverted to Walvis Bay. Nowadays Namibia is still forced to use Walvis Bay (once more part of South Africa) because the old harbour at Swakopmund has silted up and become a bathing beach. The discovery of uranium and establishment of the nearby Rössing mine, the world's largest opencast uranium mine, underpins the economy and infrastructure of the town.

Information

The Namib Information Centre is located in the Woermann Haus just off Kaiser Wilhelm Strasse. They will give you a free Swakopmund guide book and unlimited advice. Woermann Haus is open Monday to Thursday from 9 am to noon and 3 to 7 pm, and on Friday and Saturday between 9 am and noon. There is also a branch of Nature Conservation at the bottom end of Brücken Strasse, open during normal office hours.

Money Swakopmund has branches of all major banks, including Standard, First National, Trust and Swabank, most of which are in Garnison Strasse.

Post & Telecommunications The GPO, in Garnison Strasse, has a booth for making international telephone calls, and you can arrange for mail to be kept for you.

Dangers & Annoyances A minor problem with Swakopmund is the unit of the Presidential Guard which camps out on the pavement near the president's summer palace when he is in residence. There have been a couple of incidents suggesting that the guards are trigger-happy, so it is wise to avoid them if possible.

Beaches

There's lots to see in Swakopmund, though the superb beaches do tend to focus one's attention. The main beach with facilities is just near the lighthouse, but there are kms of deserted sandy beaches further away. There are formal promenades, a pier, tropical gardens to stroll through, and all the seaside resort amenities that you would expect including minigolf and a big, enclosed, heated swimming pool (open 8 to 10 am and 2.30 to 7 pm). Even in January, the height of summer, air temperatures don't rise much above 22°C and there is a light sea breeze and clear sunshine – ideal sunbathing weather.

But be warned: the sun is VERY hot. Parasols can be hired from a kiosk near the pool.

Colonial Architecture

If you can tear yourself away from the beach, Swakopmund has lots of interesting buildings that are relics of the German occupation. The ornate railway station or Bahnhof was built in 1901 and declared a National Monument in 1972. You can reach it by walking up Bahnhof Strasse from the beach. The Lutheran Church on Otavi Strasse was built in 1911 in the New Baroque style. There is also the castle-like barracks which once housed German troops and the old Bezirkgericht (District Court), modified after WW I to become the offical holiday home of the territory's administrator (and now of the president).

The amazing Woermann Haus, completed in 1905, forms a focal point for the town. This splendid building was once crew accommodation for shipping lines, and its tower (the Damara Tower) was a lookout for controlling shipping movements. It has now been restored, declared a National Monument (one of 11 in Swakopmund) and converted into a library. You get a splendid panorama of the town from the top of the tower. The Namib Information Centre is in part of this building. Woermann Haus is open Monday to Thursday from 9 am to noon and 3 to 7 pm, and on Friday and Saturday between 9 am and noon.

Swakopmund Museum

Swakopmund has a nice museum at the foot of the lighthouse, on the site of the old harbour warehouse which was destroyed in 1914 by a lucky shot from a British naval vessel. The museum is open from 10 am to 12.30 pm and 3 to 5.30 pm (admission R3 per adult). It specialises in exhibits relating to the ethnology and history of Namibia and local flora and fauna: there's a good display on the !nama melon. There's an exceptionally good reconstruction of some house interiors, including the shop of the apothecary Emil Kiewittand and an interesting display related to the Rössing mine.

Central Swakopmund

For those interested in militaria, the place is a mine of information. I especially like the stifling-looking uniforms of the Camel Corps and the room of Shell furniture, so called because it was homemade from petrol and paraffin cans during the depression of the 1930s.

Rössing Mine

Organised tours in Swakopmund include a bus trip to the Rössing mine, the world's largest opencast uranium mine, which leaves on Fridays at 8 am from outside Cafe Anton, returning for a late lunch. You can book at the museum; the tour costs R5 per adult and all proceeds go to the museum. The scale of the mine is unbelievable: a 100-truck train leaves it fully loaded every 20 minutes, 24 hours a day, 365 days a year. Rössing is the major local employer, with a staff of 2500, and is committed, via the Rössing Foundation, to education and training. Many of the facilities in Swakopmund, such as hospitals and workers' housing are the result of Rössing money.

Camel Farm

If all else fails you could always go for a

■ **PLACES TO STAY**

21	Strand Hotel
24	Pension Schweizerhaus & Cafe Anton
25	Hotel Pension Rapmund
33	Hansa Hotel
34	Atlanta Hotel
43	Hotel Zum Grüner Kranz
44	Hotel Schutze
53	Dig By See
57	Hotel Europa Hof
65	Holiday Bungalows

OTHER

1	Rheinische Missions Station
2	Hospital
3	Gefangnis
4	Kabelmesse
5	Bahnhof Der Alten Staatsbahn
6	Villa Wiese
7	Deutsche Regierungsschule
8	Dr Schwietering Haus
9	Altes Deutsches Wohnhaus
10	Altes Postgebäude
11	Municipal Main Office
12	GPO
13	Police Station
14	Altes Amtsgericht
15	Magistrate
16	Marine Denkmal
17	Kaiserliche Bezirkgericht
18	Leuchtturm
19	Swimming Pool
20	Museum
22	Mole

23	War Memorial
26	Ritterburg
27	Nature Conservation
28	Fürst Bismarck
29	Alder Apotheke
30	Trendhaus
31	Haus Altona
32	Ludwig Schröder Haus
35	Altes Deutsches Wohnhaus
36	Litfass Säule
37	Lutheran Church
38	Pfarrhaus Der D.E.L.K.
39	Haus Wille Ehemalige Deutsche Schule
40	Otavi-Bahnhof
41	O.M.E.G. Haus
42	Tannery
45	Haus Germania
46	Barclays Bank
47	Kaiserhof
48	Altes Deutsches Wohnhaus
49	Woermann Haus
50	Namib Information Centre
51	Library & Art Gallery
52	Jay Jay's
54	Alte Landingsbrücke
55	Schwester Frieda Heim
56	Altes Deutsches Wohnhaus
58	M C Human Flats
59	Altes Deutsches Wohnhaus
60	Haus Hohenzollern
61	Scultetus Haus
62	Alte Kaserne
63	Prinzessin Rupprecht Heim
64	Maternity Home
66	Fundamente Des Altes Funkturmes

camel ride at the camel farm, 12 km out of town on the Rössing road (the B2). You need to ring Elke (☎ Swakopmund 363) to book, and they may be able to arrange transport. It's only open in the afternoon.

Martin Luther Tractor

A few km along the main B2 Swakopmund-Windhoek road (the B2) a steam tractor stands looking rather lonely in the middle of the desert. It was imported in 1896 to carry freight across the Namib and only survived a couple of trips before grinding to a halt within sight of Swakopmund, where it was abandoned. It has now been restored and named Martin Luther, whose words 'Here I stand; God help me, I cannot do otherwise' are engraved on its pedestal.

Goanikontes

A little further east along B2 is a signpost pointing southwards to Goanikontes, a little farm and oasis in the bed of the Swakop River which makes a nice destination for some desert walking. You can combine the visit with seeing some welwitschias nearby. It's just too far to walk from Swakopmund, but you can get a taxi.

Welwitschias

Welwitschia mirabilis, an extraordinary giant plant found nowhere else in the world, can be seen at several places on the gravel Namib, but it is protected and some of the locations are secret. You are allowed to photograph some superb specimens on Welwitschia Plain near Swakopmund, but you need a permit and map from the Nature Conservation office at Swakopmund which gives detailed information on access.

The plant was discovered in 1959 and is something of a botanical curiosity related, strangely, to pine trees but having features in common with club mosses. Male and female plants are entirely separate. Welwitschias look like giant leathery aspidistras and are adapted to survival in the toughest of environments. It was once believed that the plant had a tap root long enough to reach the watertable 100 metres or more below, but researchers have found that the plant gets its water supply from condensed fog. The stem can be up to three metres long and the whole plant is two metres across. Scientists at Gobabeb are measuring growth rates and studying the fauna which uses the shade provided by the plant. Another belief is that the plants can live for more than 1000 years, but this has never been proved. Welwitschias are marvellously adapted to their desert environment and also apparently contain some compounds which make them unpleasant for grazing animals.

Festivals & Events

Swakopmund in the high season is essentially a German family seaside resort, attracting people who want to escape the heat inland. Many have holiday homes or beach huts here and you sometimes feel that everyone knows everyone else except you. There are a number of local events including a *Reitturnier* (gymkhana) in January and the Carnival in August: get details from the Namib Information Centre.

Organised Tours

The town features on virtually every organised tour of Namibia, and many safari operators offer sightseeing tours and day trips; Charly's Desert Tours (☎ (064) 14341) on Kaiser Wilhelm Strasse and Desert Adventure Safaris (☎ (064) 14459) both have a good programme of day, overnight and sightseeing tours.

Places to Stay

Camping & Self-Catering The *Mile 4 Caravan Park*, on the Henties Bay road, has 400 caravan places and camping sites are available from R7.50 per night (off season). The park has two kitchens, a full laundry and a shop. Book by phoning the caretaker (☎ (064) 161781) or write to Mile 4 Caravan Park, PO Box 3452, Vineta, Swakopmund 9000.

Swakopmund also has a *Nature Conservation Rest Camp* where you can rent everything from a VIP flat (six beds, R110) to a Fisherman's Cabin (two beds, R22) with all amenities except towels. There are also luxury flats (six beds, R77), chalets (six beds, R55) and a four-bed version of the Fisherman's Cabin for around R25. All accommodation has a fridge, use of freezer facilities, double hotplate, bedding, shower and toilet, but the luxury flats have full cutlery and glassware as well, and a TV. No towels are provided, but they can be hired from the adjacent laundry. You can reserve accommodation by writing to the Head of Tourism (☎ (064) 12807, fax (064) 12249), Municipality of Swakopmund, Private Bag 5017, Swakopmund 9000, or call at the booking office at the camp between 8 am and 1 pm or 2 and 4 pm. The camp is located on the Walvis Bay side of Swakopmund, near Swakop and Moltke Sts.

It is also possible to rent holiday flats for a week or more (ask at the Namib Information Office).

Hotels There are more than a dozen hotels and pensions in Swakopmund, but during school holidays and the winter season (October-March, especially December and January) they can get booked up well in advance. It is more difficult to get a room in Swakopmund than anywhere else in Namibia, though that isn't really saying much.

One-star hotels like the *Hotel Schutze* (☎

(064) 12718) start at R30 per person, including breakfast. At the two-star *Strand Hotel* (☎ (090) 83557), right down on the beach, you can ask for a room with a balcony or sea view – or both! A buffet breakfast, which can also be served in your room, is included; costs start at R126 for a single. The two-star *Hotel Europa Hof* (☎ (064) 15898), a Bavarian fantasy on Bismarck Strasse, has a nice restaurant; rooms start from R53 per person. The *Hotel-Pension Schweizerhaus* (☎ (064) 12419) just opposite the president's summer residence is something of a local landmark, and offers very good accommodation from R70 single.

Places to Eat

Restaurants Swakopmund has a whole range of restaurants from fine dining (still at modest prices) through to a *Kentucky Fried Chicken* outlet. Some restaurants are really elegant; the candle-lit restaurant at the *Strand Hotel* (evenings only) serves food in a formal setting, as does the restaurant at the *Hansa Hotel* on Roon Strasse.

There are some nice smaller restaurants specialising in fish and seafood. Try *Erichs* on Post Strasse (open for lunch and dinner) or the *Bayern Stubchen* on Garnison Strasse. *Jay Jay's* restaurant in Brücken Strasse serves traditional *boerekos* (South African food).

Cafes Swakopmund also has an amazing range of cafes and konditorei where elegant German ladies eat sachertorte in the morning. Easily the best is the *Cafe Anton*, famous throughout Africa, attached to the Pension Schweitzerhaus and open from 7 am to 2 pm and 3 to 6 pm, and for dinner from 6.30 to 8 pm. Superb coffee and an *apfelstrudel* (apple pastry) will set you back less than R5, and the view is good too. Other konditorei of note are the *Seebad Cafe* on Kaiser Wilhelm Strasse, which has a good takeaway bakery and confectioners, and the *Cafe Treffpunkt* further down the same road.

There are lots of small cafes and takeaways near the beach, and barrows sell ice cream and light refreshments during the season.

Pubs & Bars Swakopmund also has a lot of pubs which generally serve food as well and tend to be informal, including the *Western Saloon* ('last pub for 145 km') famous for its oysters, and *Kücki's Pub* which serves pizza. All the hotels have at least one decent bar. Stick to the cocktail bar, as the alternatives can be a bit rough; this may also be called the 'ladies' or 'private' bar, and you have to wear something respectable in the evening.

Entertainment

Evening entertainment tends to focus round eating and drinking but there are occasionally films or events at the museum and there is one cinema, the Atlanta on Roon Strasse.

Things to Buy

Swakopmund is famous for its hard-wearing kudu leather shoes ('Swakopmunders') which may be bought at the tannery in Otavi Strasse. They also sell handbags, sandals, belts and all manner of leather goods at rock-bottom prices. There is a craft centre called ENOK (First National Development) Centre which includes a shop called Karakulia, Swakopmund's famous carpet weavery, and a tourmaline shop. The information centre will give you a detailed map and directions.

There are a number of shops and small art galleries which specialise in prints and paintings of the area, from classic watercolours to modern surrealistic African art. A small gallery called Reflections near Cafe Anton often has exhibitions of the work of local artists. There are a number of African souvenir and curio shops and many quite expensive jewellers, who often use local gems and semiprecious stones. Pieces may be commissioned and it is often possible to watch the goldsmith at work. The T-shirt factory shop in Woermann Strasse print their own garments and have a good variety.

Getting There & Away

Air Swakopmund may be reached by air four times a week on Namib Air flights from

Windhoek (Eros), where you can link up with the international network. Namib Air also flies between Swakopmund and Cape Town via Lüderitz three times a week. Check the main office in Windhoek for current schedules.

Bus There is a Mainliner coach route from Windhoek to Swakopmund via Okahandja, Karibib and Usakos. The journey takes 4½ hours and costs R68. It leaves Windhoek at 8 am on Monday, Tuesday and Wednesday, and 3 pm on Friday, returning from Swakopmund on Tuesday, Wednesday and Thursday at 8.28 am and on Sunday at 3.38 pm.

Train Swakopmund is easily accessible by train from Windhoek on Tuesday, Friday and Sunday, though it is an overnight journey, leaving Windhoek at 7.10 pm and arriving in Swakopmund at 5.25 am. This train comes from South Africa via De Aar and continues on to Walvis Bay. You can also reach Swakopmund by train from Otjiwarongo, Tsumeb and Grootfontein on Friday and Sunday.

Car & Motorbike The many visitors who choose to drive from Windhoek have a choice of either the Gamsberg Pass, Bosua Pass or a third route via Okahandja and Karibib. Although the last route is the longest it has the dual advantages of being on tarred roads all the way and passing through a number of places of interest. Driving time from Windhoek to Swakopmund using this route is around four or five hours. The Gamsberg Pass route is not for the fainthearted – see details in the next section under Naukluft Park.

You can rent a car in Swakopmund from Avis (☎ (064) 12527), Budget (☎ (064) 12080) or Imperial (☎ (064) 161587).

Hitching Hitching is possible between the interior and Swakopmund along the major routes, but don't try to hitch, walk or cycle in the interior or within the Namib Desert

Park: it's far too hot and you could wait days for someone to come along.

Getting Around
Taxis are available from the airport but otherwise are not easy to find. There is no other public transport but it is a very small town and everything in the town centre is within walking distance.

WALVIS BAY
Although technically not in Namibia, Walvis Bay forms a possible excursion for anyone visiting the Namib area. It is an architecturally uninspiring town with none of the colonial charm of Swakopmund. Indeed, until recently its principal claim to fame was the existence of major fish canning factories and its function as Namibia's only port. Today life is complicated by the fact that Walvis Bay is part of South Africa. There is high unemployment because of factory closures and the town centre is quietly depressing. Moreover, the necessity to cross a formal frontier between Swakopmund and Walvis Bay is irritating both for visitors and local people, but there is some suggestion that the current border formalities will be either toned down or abandoned in the near future.

The first European to land at Walvis Bay was Bartholomew Diaz in 1486, but nothing much happened there for another 300 years until American whaling ships began to congregate in the area, giving the port its name. It was officially annexed to Britain as part of the Cape Colony in 1884. It is the centre of very rich fishing grounds and is a major deepwater port, though its fishing fleet, once one of the largest in southern Africa, has now greatly declined and many of the pilchard and white fish factories and canneries stand empty.

Bird Island
If you are travelling from Swakopmund look out for Bird Island off the coast, one of a series of huge wooden platforms built to provide a home for seabirds. The guano they produce is regularly collected – about 1000

tonnes per year. If the wind is in the wrong direction you can smell it halfway to Swakopmund.

Bird Lagoon & Saltpans

Just south of the town there is a lagoon justifiably famous for its birdlife. You can sometimes see upwards of 20,000 flamingos at a time. The signpost near 13th Rd (easy to find) points to both the bird sanctuary and the saltworks, which lie to the south-west of the lagoon. These use evaporating pans to obtain high-purity salt, most of which is exported to South Africa for the chemical industry. It's possible to get a formal tour of the saltworks by making an advance appointment (☎ (064) 22376).

These Walvis Bay wetlands are the single most important coastal wetland in southern Africa for migratory birds: in the course of a year 150,000 migrants may make a brief stop here.

Places to Stay

Camping There are two camping sites at Walvis Bay, one private and one public. The private *Langstrand* (☎ (064) 25981) site is the larger with 100 places, and it costs R11.30 per site and an additional fee for a power supply if you have a caravan. It is about 16 km north of the town and is thus not a lot of use if you do not have your own vehicle. The municipal site in town, near the Esplanade, is smaller but has a two-star grading, with 26 places costing exactly the same (☎ (064) 25981).

Hotels The cheapest hotel accommodation in Walvis Bay can be found at the *Golden Fish Guest House* (☎ (064) 22775) which is not luxurious but has B&B from R17 per person if you're sharing a double room. There is also the *Mermaid Hotel* (☎ (064) 26211) which is not graded and has rooms from R37.

Walvis Bay has three star-graded hotels, but they aren't nearly so much fun as the Teutonic extravaganzas of Swakopmund. The one-star *Flamingo Hotel* (☎ (064) 23011) has 29 rooms starting at R65 per person and the two-star *Casa Mia* (☎ (064) 26596) has 22 rooms from R57. Both have TV in all rooms. The *Hotel Atlantic* (☎ (064) 22811) has just 12 rooms from R48.

Places to Eat

Restaurants & Cafes The four hotels in Walvis Bay all have restaurants, where you can get lunch and dinner, together with a bar. The best meals can be found at the *Probst Cafe* on Ninth St, but this is not open during the evening. The *Harbour Cafe* off 13th Rd also provides a decent meal, and there are several small eating places in the town centre.

Getting There & Away

Air Walvis Bay is served by Swakopmund airport with scheduled flights on Namib Air from Windhoek (Eros). You will need to take an airport taxi into Walvis Bay.

Bus There is a Mainliner coach service to Walvis Bay via Swakopmund, Usakos, Karibib and Okahandja which leaves Windhoek each Monday, Wednesday and Friday at 8 am, arriving in Walvis Bay at 1 pm. The Friday service leaves Windhoek at 3 pm, arriving at 7.37 pm. Return journeys leave Walvis Bay on Tuesday, Wednesday and Thursday at 8 am, arriving in Windhoek at 1 pm. There is also a Sunday service leaving Walvis Bay at 3 pm and arriving in Windhoek at 7.04 pm. The fare is R68 one way.

Train Trains from Windhoek to Walvis Bay leave Tuesday, Friday and Sunday and go via Swakopmund. They leave Swakopmund at 5.30 am and arrive in Walvis Bay at 6.55 am. Ask at the station for current fares and schedules. During the winter the rail service between Swakopmund and Walvis Bay is often disturbed by the weather, as high winds blow sand on the track and undermine its foundations. If this seems a possibility, call the station for details. This is not a new problem for Walvis Bay and you can see the remains of an old train, the *Hope*, which tried to run on the original narrow-gauge railway and was abandoned because the line kept getting buried under drifts 25 metres high. The old train (now a National Monument) stands in front of Walvis Bay station on Sixth St.

Car & Motorbike Renting a car in Windhoek and driving across the Namib Desert Park to Walvis Bay gives you the best cross-section of landscapes but involves negotiating the Gamsberg Pass. The alternatives via the Uis Pass or through the Khomas Hochland mountains are lengthier and not so spectacular. You can also reach Walvis Bay by turning south from Swakopmund on the B2 and driving the connecting 32 km down a pleasant coast road. Remember that, if you are planning to leave the main road when crossing the Namib Park on the way to Walvis Bay, you need a permit from Nature Conservation.

You may have a considerable wait at the frontier as there are full immigration procedures to be negotiated in both directions.

Getting Around
Walvis Bay is small enough to walk around, but there's not a lot to see anyway. The camping site and hotels are within easy walking distance of the bus terminal on 13th Rd, and you can wander round the lagoon. If you want to visit the fishing harbour you need to get a permit from the Harbour Police office off 13th Rd. They'll probably ask to see your passport.

Namib-Naukluft Park

The Namib-Naukluft Park is the country's largest wildlife conservation area and now one of the biggest national parks in the world. It is composed of more than 23,000 sq km of desert and semidesert which includes the diverse habitats of the Namib Desert Park between the Kuiseb and Swakop rivers, the Naukluft (formerly the Naukluft Mountain Zebra Park), the high dunefield at

Sossusvlei and the bird sanctuary at Sandwich Harbour.

The present boundaries of the park were determined in 1978 by merging the Namib Desert Park and the Naukluft Mountain Zebra Park with parts of Diamond Area 1 and a lot of the state land bordering the actual desert. The whole area is often referred to simply as 'the Namib' and it's convenient to describe it as a unit.

Getting There & Away
Car & Motorbike It's quite easy to get to the northern Namib, and you can travel through it freely on main roads linking Windhoek and the central area with the coast. Minor roads skirt the eastern edge and surrounding farmlands, but leaving the major roads within the Namib Desert Park boundaries requires a permit. This costs R5 per vehicle and the same per adult, and can be obtained from the Nature Conservation offices in either Windhoek or Swakopmund. At the weekend, when these offices are closed, you can get a permit from the Kreiss service station on Kaiser Wilhelm Strasse in Swakopmund or the office of Charly's Desert Tours just down the road. In Walvis Bay, permits can be obtained from the Troost Transport, Namib Ford and CWB service stations.

The main roads throughout the Namib area are quite accessible for 2WD, but the minor roads are often in poor condition and only marginally passable. Outside the main towns there are no services of any kind, so it is essential to take water, food, spare fuel, two spare tyres and spare clothing if you are venturing off the main roads. If camping you must take wood, water and all your food. If you break down on a minor road, stay with your car – eventually someone will come along.

Hitching Hitching is possible between the interior and the coast along the major routes, but don't try to hitch, walk or cycle in the interior or within the Namib Desert Park: it's far too hot and you could wait days for someone to come along.

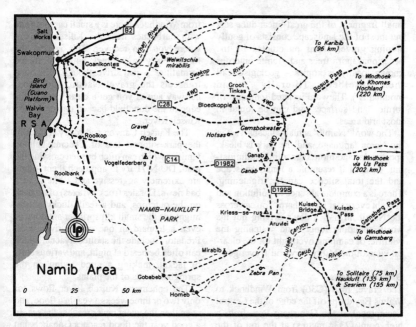

Namib Area

0   25   50 km

Getting Around

There's no public transport in this area, so a vehicle is the only viable option for getting around.

SANDWICH HARBOUR

This partly landlocked reed-lined lagoon is located at the mouth of the Kuiseb River, south of Walvis Bay. The extraordinary proliferation of bird life is due to the unique water conditions. The lagoon is filled by water percolating from the Kuiseb River through the dunefield which greatly reduces its salinity. Sandwich Harbour is a refuge for great flocks of coastal and freshwater birds and a breeding place for many fish species including sharks.

Local legend says that over 200 years ago a ship carrying a cargo of gold, precious stones and ivory intended as a gift for the Moghul emperor from Lord Clive was stranded here en route to India from England. The cargo (valued at £6 million sterling) is believed to lie somewhere under the shifting dunes, but despite many attempts no one has found it (yet).

Getting There & Away

Sandwich Harbour, 42 km south of Walvis Bay, is accessible only by 4WD vehicles. A road leads to the isolated reed-encrusted lagoon. You need a permit to visit Sandwich, which can be obtained in Swakopmund either from the information centre or the Kreiss service station on Kaiser Wilhelm Strasse. No camping is permitted and the road may be closed at certain times because of high winds. No access is allowed on Sundays. There are no visitor facilities at the lagoon.

NAMIB DESERT PARK

The most accessible area of the Namib, the Namib Desert Park, lies between the canyons of the Kuiseb River in the south and the Swakop River in the north. It includes a small fragment of the great linear dune sea, but most of the landscape consists of gently sloping gravel plains punctuated by the occasional thorn trees and granite outcrops known locally as kopjes – geologists call them inselbergs (literally 'island mountains'). They are isolated remnants of former land surfaces and can be found in most arid areas.

The word 'Namib' actually means Vast in the Nama language, and the park is bleak, spectacular and more than a little intimidating. Parts of it resemble a lunar landscape and the total silence can be frightening. There is a complete absence of pollution and at night every star is pin sharp. You can cross the Namib in half a day's driving but it's worth spending longer and watching the wildlife, or camping overnight for the clearest view of the Milky Way you'll ever get.

Gamsberg Pass

The gravel road (C36) from Windhoek to Walvis Bay drops off the edge of the Central Escarpment at the Gamsberg Pass from a high point (2334 metres) at the top of the Gamsberg range. You are suddenly suspended in space with a spectacular view out across the gravel plains and the dune sea almost as far as the coast. To the south you can see the outliers of the Naukluft Park. It has to be the best view in Africa – literally breathtaking.

The bad news is that the gravel road then descends the Gamsberg pass down a series of hair-raising loops until it reaches the upper part of the Kuiseb Canyon. Going east to west you are on the outside of the badly cambered curve with a sheer drop on your left and a cliff on the right. Beware of local farmers in battered bakkies accelerating up the pass on the wrong side of the road. If you don't like heights do the route in reverse and keep well in to the side. If you dare raise your eyes from the road, watch for the tracks which mark the old wagon route and count your blessings.

Kuiseb Canyon

If you are driving across the Gamsberg Pass from Windhoek there is a small camping site with barbecues near the Kuiseb Canyon where you can recover. This is near the formal entry to the park but there are no formalities – just drive though. The road transects the gravel Namib, and about halfway across you get a clear view of the edge of the dunefield backed up against the Kuiseb River.

The Kuiseb Canyon and rocky fringes of the park support lots of Chacma baboon families which can often be seen crossing the road. DO NOT try to approach them – they are extremely aggressive and a bite is very bad news. Dassies (rock hyraxes) often bask on the outcrops, and a really lucky person might see the small klipspringer antelope or even a leopard in one of the river beds. Predators include the spotted hyaena, which can often be heard at night, and various sorts of jackal, making a good living on the springbok herds of the plains.

The ephemeral Kuiseb River flows for only two or three weeks a year in a flood, and even then the water never reaches the sea. In a good year the flood reaches Gobabeb, but it generally seeps into the sand further upstream and is pumped out at Rooibank for unpleasant-tasting drinking water.

The spectacular rocky Kuiseb Canyon is accessible at its eastern end near the foot of the Gamsberg Pass and there is a camping site at Homeb. Look for the cave where the geologist Henno Martin and a companion went into hiding for three years during WW II, living entirely off the land. His book *The Sheltering Desert* (republished in 1983 by Donker, South Africa) is well worth reading. The upper reaches of the canyon are uninhabited, but further down, where the valley broadens out, Topnaar Hottentot villages are scattered along the north bank. The Kuiseb itself is just a broad sandy riverbed for much of the year – the steep rocky outcrops on the southern bank hold back the great dunes which tower 150 metres and can be clearly seen from the road.

Homeb

The nearest place to enter the dunes in the

central Namib section of the park is at the camping site at Homeb. This is actually on the Kuiseb and is clearly signposted off the main park road. It is quite near a Topnaar Hottentot village whose people use the subsurface water from wells dug in the riverbed as the Kuiseb floods seldom reach this point. The water also supports a lot of trees, including a couple of species of fig, and you are likely to see steenboks, gemsboks and baboons in the river bed. It's a good place to take a walk down the sandy river bed and across it into the edge of the dunes.

!Nama Melons

In the lower reaches of the Kuiseb you may see one of the Namib's most famous plants, the !nama *(Acanthosicyos horrida)*, a member of the cucumber family whose spiny bushes grow in places where it can tap subsurface water. The !nama (the exclamation mark is pronounced as a glottal click, if you can manage it) was important in the culture of the Topnaar Hottentots and each year during the harvesting season you can see donkey carts full of the spiky fruit being transported by Topnaars back to camp to be dried and prepared for consumption. The seeds are then removed from the rind and dried for eating and the pulp is spread on the sand to make a kind of chewy cake which preserves well. The !nama seems to have been utilised in this way for tens of thousands of years. The museum at Swakopmund has a good display about the plant.

Gobabeb

Near Homeb you'll see a turning marked 'Gobabeb', but you require a special permit to take this road. Gobabeb means Place of the Fig Tree but there aren't many trees around nowadays. It houses the Namib Desert Ecological Research Unit, which is a complex of laboratories, weather station and research facilities. The location is spectacular, just at the junction of the dunefield and the gravel plains, but you need a permit from Nature Conservation in Windhoek to visit it and you must have a scientific reason as the station is not generally open to visitors.

Scientists come here from all over the world to study the Namib and there is a small on-site museum. Intending visitors should write for information to the Director, giving at least three months notice. Open days are sometimes scheduled and there are self-guided nature trails, lectures and field demonstrations.

With the advent of independence, Gobabeb is expanding its research and educational programmes for Namibians, and a new lecture hall and laboratories are being built.

Places to Stay & Eat

In the central Namib park there are basic camping sites with minimal amenities at Kuiseb Bridge, Mirabib, Kriess-se-Rus, Swartbank, Vogelfederberg, Bloedkoppie, Groot Tinkas and Ganap. All these sites also function as picnic areas, but remember you need a day-visit permit to visit them. You can book and pay the overnight camping fees (R10 per night per site, for up to eight people) at the information centre in Swakopmund during the week or at the Nature Conservation offices in Windhoek, Swakopmund, Sesriem or Hardap. Each site has tables, toilets and barbecues but no washing facilities. Drinking water is available at camping sites but it can be extremely salty; take bottled supplies with you.

No camping is permitted in the Namib outside these localities; there is no other accommodation and no shops or petrol stations within the park boundaries. It is essential to carry all supplies with you.

Getting There & Away

There is no public transport to or from the park. The Mainliner coach service from Windhoek to Swakopmund crosses its extreme northern tip but does not stop.

The best way to see the park is to drive across it. You can reach it from Windhoek via the Gamsberg Pass (but see the description of this road earlier in this chapter), Bosua Pass or a third route via Okahandja and Karibib. There is no north to south route but you can fork south at Kuiseb Bridge along the road to Maltahöhe, Solitaire and the southern Namib.

Getting Around

There is no public transport within the park, so travellers have the option of taking a tour (based at Windhoek or Swakopmund) or hiring a vehicle. If you are driving off the main roads be warned that some of the smaller roads are in poor condition – only marginally passable for 2WD. You need a permit to drive on them which can be obtained at a cost of R5 from the Nature Conservation offices in Windhoek or Swakopmund.

Do not attempt to hitch in the desert.

NAUKLUFT PARK

The Naukluft Park (formerly the Naukluft Mountain Zebra Park) is part of the main Namib-Naukluft Park run by Nature Conservation. In contrast to the Namib Desert area it is mountainous, with quite a different fauna and flora. The Naukluft only accepts visitors who are camping overnight in groups of three to 20 people. The area was a battlefield during colonial times between German Schutztruppe and local Khoi-Khoi people under their famous leader Hendrik Witbooi, who used the Naukluft caves as a base from which to wage guerilla warfare. Inevitably, they lost in the end (1894); you will see a number of graves around the Naukluft which relate to this conflict.

Wildlife

The mountains of the Naukluft are among the most attractive areas of Namibia – a complex of gorges and streams (Naukluft means Narrow Gorge) famous for its wildlife. The Tsondab, Tssams RiverTssams and Tsauchab rivers all rise here, and because of the ample water is there plentiful supply of wildlife. The Naukluft is famous for its Hartmann's (mountain) zebras, kudus, cheetahs, leopards and springboks; you can often see tiny yellow klipspringers perched on the rocky crests with black eagles soaring overhead.

Hiking Trails

Part of the charm of the Naukluft are the marked hiking trails, including the standard model of about 17 km which takes seven to eight hours to complete. This trail takes you out of the camping site and past the old German cannon road, along river beds, past caves and waterfalls and gets you back again in a circle.

There is also a guided round trip of 120 km run by Nature Conservation that takes eight days to complete (but you can drop out after the first four days). It is open between 1 March and 31 October on the first and third Sundays and Wednesdays of the month. You can book at the Nature Conservation office in Windhoek. The price of R25 includes accommodation at an old farmhouse in Naukluft the day before the hike begins and on the last day. You can only go in a group of three to 12 people.

Places to Stay & Eat

The Naukluft has a more formal camping site than those in the Namib, with water, firewood and a washing block. The site is not open to day visitors. The charge is R25 per night for eight people but the camping site has an overall maximum of 32 and therefore gets booked up well in advance. You are not allowed to stay for more than three nights.

Getting There & Away

Car & Motorbike The Naukluft section of the park can be reached from the C14 Maltahöhe-Solitaire road if you've come from the south. If you're in Windhoek you can come south on the B1 and then branch off on the C24 at Rehoboth. There is a magnificent drive along the eastern edge of the park from the Kuiseb Bridge along the C14 to Solitaire. Notice the colour of the dunes deepening the further you get south: by Sossusvlei they are a dark reddish-orange.

SOSSUSVLEI

Sossusvlei is a huge dried-up pan (vlei), which sporadically holds water, at the base of some of the most spectacular dunes in the Namib. It has the highest dunes in the Namib,

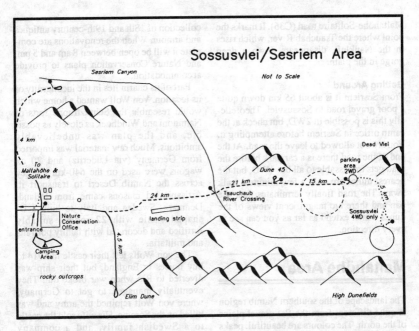

Sossusvlei/Sesriem Area

Not to Scale

Sesriem Canyon

4 km

To Maltahöhe & Solitaire

Nature Conservation Office

entrance

Camping Area

rocky outcrops

Elim Dune

24 km

Tsauchaub River Crossing

21 km

landing strip

4.5 km

Dune 45

15 km

Dead Vlei

parking area 2WD

Sossusvlei 4WD only

High Dunefields

up to 300 metres high, which can be explored on foot. Here the sand is at its reddest. The dunes seem gradually to change colour from deep red through to pale orange as the day advances, and sunset here is an amazing experience. It's a nice place to walk as the shade and water are good places for wildlife spotting.

Things to See

The purpose of visiting Sossusvlei is just to see the dunes and their associated wildlife. To do this you need to pass through the Nature Conservation camping site at Sesriem and travel along a poor road to the vlei itself.

The name Sesriem means Six Thongs, which was the number of leather ox-wagon thongs which had to be joined together so that a bucket could reach from the rim of the gorge to the water below.

Allow plenty of time (preferably a full day) for this trip unless you are camping

overnight in Sesriem, as there is no accommodation between Maltahöhe and Swakopmund and it is a long hot drive. If there is water in the pan you will be able to see a large variety of birdlife, including flamingos, but even in the dry season it's possible to see unbelievably photogenic gemsboks and ostriches wandering across the foot of the dunes.

Places to Stay & Eat

There is a good but small camping site at Sesriem with 10 sites plus water and a shower block, but no bungalows or preset tents. Like Naukluft, this site gets booked up well in advance and costs R25 per night for a maximum of eight people. Wood is available. Book at the Nature Conservation office in Windhoek or Swakopmund.

Getting There & Away

You reach Sossusvlei via a clearly marked turnoff signposted 'Sesriem' from the

Maltahöhe-Solitaire road (C36). It marks the point where the Tsauchab River, which rises in the Naukluft, disappears down a deep gorge in the plain.

Getting Around

From Sesriem it is about 65 km down quite a poor gravel road to Sossusvlei. Theoretically this is possible in 2WD, but check at the camp office in Sesriem before attempting it. You are not allowed to leave the road. At the end of the road there is a car park before the road gets impassable to all but 4WD, but the nearest dunes are only a few minutes' walk away. The road finally terminates near the pan and there are magnificent views of the dunes which extend as far as you can see in every direction.

Maltahöhe Area

The landscape of the southern Namib region is quite different from the flat gravel plains of the north. The colours are beautiful: peaks of pinkish-grey mountains (the Awasib and Uri-Hauchab ranges) rising from a greenish-grey flat plain like ships out of the sea. The extreme clarity of the air makes it possible to see for immense distances and in the rainy season there is a lot of wildlife about, sometimes quite big herds of gemsboks and springboks. This is also a major karakul farming area. Maltahöhe itself is a very small town with one hotel and virtually nothing else to recommend it, but the area is worth visiting just for the landscapes.

Duwasib Castle

It's worth checking with the municipal office in Maltahöhe or with Nature Conservation in Lüderitz to see if Duwasib Castle is open. This *Schloss* (castle) is being renovated by Nature Conservation and it should be open by the time you read this.

Duwasib, about 70 km south of Maltahöhe on the C14, is a curious baroque castle dating from 1909, built by Baron Captain Hans-Heinrich von Wolf. It houses an important collection of 18th and 19th-century antiques and armour. When the renovations are complete it will be open between 8 am and 5 pm, and Nature Conservation plans to provide accommodation.

Part of its charm lies in the incongruity of its location. Von Wolf wanted a home which would resemble the Schutztruppe forts of Namutoni and Windhoek as closely as possible, and the plan was unbelievably ambitious. Much raw material was imported from Germany (via Lüderitz) and 20 ox wagons were used on the 640-km journey across the Namib Desert to transport it. Artisans and masons came from Ireland, Denmark, Sweden and Italy to built a U-shaped castle with 22 rooms, suitably fortified and decorated with family portraits and militaria.

The von Wolfs left their castle in 1914 to buy horses in England, but their ship was diverted to Rio when war broke out. They eventually managed to get to Germany, where von Wolf rejoined the army and was killed on the Somme. His wife sold the castle to a Swedish family, and a company (Duwasib Pty Ltd) bought it in 1937.

Wild Horses

The area south of Maltahöhe and west of Aus, in Diamond Area 1, has herds of wild horses which may be descended from von Wolf's stud. There are thought to be around 200 of them and they seem thin and scruffy, although actually they have become adapted to desert living and drink only once every five days in arid conditions. A borehole at Garub pumps water for their exclusive use. Their exact origin is unknown; an alternative theory sees them as descendants of former Schutztruppe mounts. In years of good rain the horses get fat and happy and the herds are steadily increasing, protected by their privileged location in Diamond Area 1. Nature Conservation is reputed to be thinking about taming some for use on patrols in Etosha.

Places to Stay & Eat

Camping & Self-Catering The *Namib Rest Camp* (☎ (066) 323211) at Maltahöhe allows camping and also has six self-catering bungalows, two for two people costing R50 and three for four people costing R72, all including linen.

Hotels The one-star *Hotel Maltahöhe* (☎ (066) 3213) offers simple accommodation from R34 and has a restaurant and bar. The *Helmeringhausen Hotel* (☎ (063) 627) is even smaller and has rooms from R44, including breakfast.

Guest Farms There are also some guest farms on the fringes of the park of which the best known is probably the two-star *Farm Sinclair* (☎ (06362) 6503) near Helmeringhausen just off the C14 from the south. They have five rooms and charge R100 for accommodation including full board. The *Burgsdorf* guest farm near Maltahöhe also has five rooms and charges from R66 (B&B) and R99 (full board).

Getting There & Away
You can reach the southern Namib area by driving south from Sesriem along the C36 to Maltahöhe, and then taking the C14 to Helmeringhausen. The roads are gravel but adequate for 2WD.

There is no public transport into this area and hitching is inadvisable.

Lüderitz

Once a busy port, situated on one of the best natural harbours along the Namibian coast, today Lüderitz is a ghost town with only the nearby Consolidated Diamond Mines (CDM) workings and the remnants of the former fishing fleets keeping it going at all. It has immense appeal – a faded Teutonic ghost town at the very edge of the desert where the dunes encroach onto the houses and there is a biting onshore wind from the cold Atlantic. The first European to visit the site was the Portuguese navigator Bartholomew Diaz, who sailed down the coast which he called the 'Sands of Hell' in

1486 and named the landlocked harbour Angra Pequena (Little Bay).

The little town gained importance as the first German settlement in South West Africa. It was founded by a Bremen merchant named Adolf Lüderitz as a trading post, and it was Lüderitz who later persuaded Bismarck to extend German protection to the territory in 1884. Serious development of the town began with the first finds of diamonds in 1908 when a 'Wild West' town grew up, with claims being pegged and fortunes won and lost. Today the diamond mines are operated by CDM, derived from the original Deutsche Diamant Gesallschaft founded by Ernst Oppenheimer.

Although much smaller than Swakopmund, Lüderitz is also a holiday town, with constant sunshine all the year and a temperature of 19°C to 26°C relieved by a light south-west wind. It has a picturesque port where the fleet of crayfish (rock lobster) boats are based. Crayfish are in season from November to April and the industry is a major local employer. New industries include seaweed and seagrass harvesting (the products mainly exported to Japan) and some experiments with farming oysters, mussels and prawns.

The sea off the Lüderitz coast is among the cleanest in the world (a function of the cold Benguela Current) and wonderful for nature lovers as it shelters seals, penguins and other marine life.

Orientation & Information
Warning In and around Lüderitz, make sure you stay well clear of the prohibited Diamond Area. Patrols tend to shoot first and not bother about asking questions. The prohibited area begins south of the main A4 Lüderitz-Keetmanshoop road. There are signs along the road and along other tracks. The border continues to just west of Aus and runs north-south from there. Keep out!

Tourist Office Lüderitz has an excellent information centre at the top of Bismarck Strasse, open between 9 am and noon on weekdays. There is also a branch office of

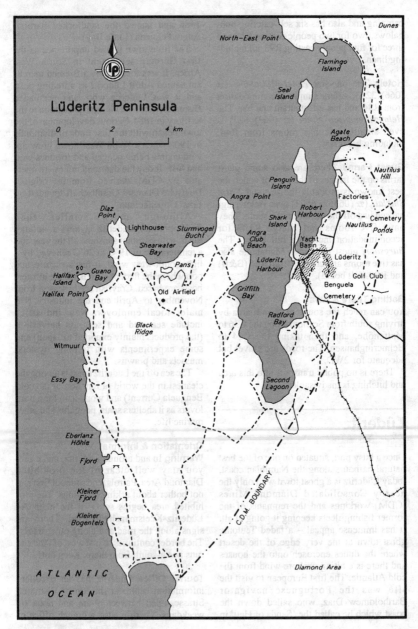

Lüderitz Peninsula

0   2   4 km

Dunes

North-East Point

Flamingo Island

Seal Island

Agate Beach

Nautilus Hill

Penguin Island

Angra Point

Factories

Diaz Point

Lighthouse

Sturmvogel Bucht

Robert Harbour

Shark Island

Cemetery

Nautilus Ponds

Shearwater Bay

Angra Club Beach

Yacht Basin

Lüderitz

Pans

Lüderitz Harbour

Golf Club

Halifax Island

Guano Bay

Old Airfield

Griffith Bay

Benguela Cemetery

Halifax Point

Black Ridge

Radford Bay

Witmuur

Essy Bay

Second Lagoon

Eberlanz Höhle

Fjord

Kleiner Fjord

Kleiner Bogentels

C.D.M. BOUNDARY

ATLANTIC OCEAN

Diamond Area

Nature Conservation at Schinz Strasse, open Monday to Friday from 8 am to 1.30 pm and 2 to 4.20 pm.

Money Lüderitz has branches of all the main banks, mostly in Bismarck Strasse, open during business hours.

Post & Telecommunications The post office is in Schinz Strasse and has facilities for making international calls and receiving mail.

Colonial Architecture

Within Lüderitz itself there is a fascinating sample of German colonial architecture, including the Magistrate's House, Railway Station, Old Post Office and Concert & Ball Hall. Goerke Castle, now a private house, can be visited daily between 2 and 3 pm, and the museum on Diaz St is open on Tuesday, Thursday and Saturday from 4 to 6 pm.

Boat Trips

Boats leave the harbour jetty for two or three-hour trips daily to see the nearby seal colony; tickets are obtainable at the bookstore.

Kolmanskop

The greatest attraction near Lüderitz is Kolmanskop, the remains of a substantial small mining town a few km outside Lüderitz which is gradually returning itself to the desert. It was once a thriving mining town complete with casino, skittle alley and theatre with renowned acoustics, but the slump in diamond sales after WW I and the discovery of the richer diamond deposits at the mouth of the Orange River sounded the death knell for the town. By 1956 it had been deserted and the dunes had begun to move in. A few buildings have been restored but the ghost town atmosphere remains.

Permits (day visit only) can be obtained from the CDM office (between the power station and the museum) and cost R3 for an adult. Only guided tours are accepted at the moment: reservations can be made in advance (☎ (063) 312331). Guided tours take place Monday to Saturday at 9.30 am

with a tour guide, Siggi Manns, who was born in Kolmanskop and tells a fine tale.

Diaz Point

To the south of Lüderitz, gravel roads take you 22 km out to Diaz Point, where a cross commemorates the European discovery of the area. Be warned – even in midsummer this area is extremely windy and the offshore cold Benguela Current, though great for wildlife, is not such fun for humans. Take a warm waistcoat or jacket and think twice before swimming. Standing on Diaz Point you have a great view of the nearby seal colony and there are usually jackass penguins surfing off the rocks. Cormorants, flamingos and a wide range of wading birds, together with schools of dolphins offshore, complete the wildlife. A complex of gravel roads leads you through a bleak lunar landscape to a series of fjords and coves popular with anglers.

North of Lüderitz a similar road leads to Agate Bay where there's a spectacular beach made of ground agates and the remains of diamond diggings. Worth trying your luck!

Places to Stay

Camping & Self-Catering There is an oceanfront holiday complex (☎ (063) 312398) with bungalows and rondavels which start at R25 per night (two beds), and a small restaurant. Camping is also permitted.

Hotels The *Pension Zum Sperrgebiet* (☎ (063) 312856) in Bahnhof Strasse has 10 rooms with prices from R38. Not surprisingly, it is especially popular with German visitors. Two hotels in Lüderitz are still owned by descendants of the original Lüderitz family. The two-star *Bay View* (☎ (063) 312288) has recently been refitted and consists of an enclosed complex of 30 rooms opening from shady courtyards; there's also a pool. Rooms (from R60) are cool, airy and comfortable and there is a good restaurant specialising in crayfish. Just up the road the Bay View's one-star partner, the *Hotel Kapps*

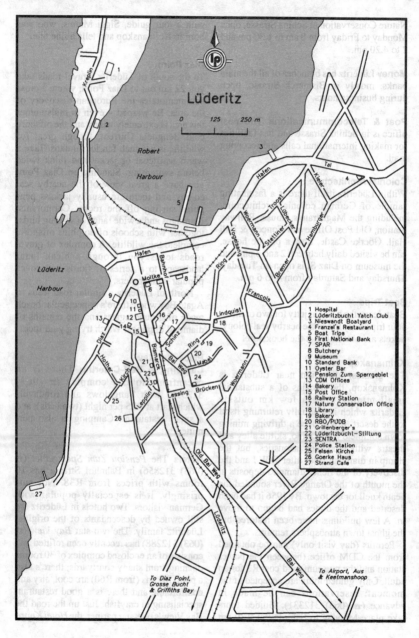

Lüderitz

0   125   250 m

Robert Harbour

Lüderitz Harbour

1 Hospital
2 Lüderitzbucht Yatch Club
3 Nieswandt Boatyard
4 Franzel's Restaurant
5 Boat Trips
6 First National Bank
7 SPAR
8 Butchery
9 Museum
10 Standard Bank
11 Oyster Bar
12 Pension Zum Sperrgebiet
13 CDM Offices
14 Bakery
15 Post Office
16 Railway Station
17 Nature Conservation Office
18 Library
19 Bakery
20 RBO/PUDB
21 Grillenberger's
22 Lüderitzbucht–Stiftung
23 SENTRA
24 Police Station
25 Felsen Kirche
26 Goerke Haus
27 Strand Cafe

To Diaz Point,
Grosse Bucht
& Griffiths Bay

To Airport, Aus
& Keetmanshoop

(☎ (063) 12701), is smaller and cheaper but lacks the same charm. Rooms start at R46.

Places to Eat

Restaurants The *Bay View* has a pleasant restaurant at the top of a converted colonial building with a small bar complete with panoramic views. Dinner is served from 7.15 to 9 pm, and service is pleasant but on the slow side. Specialities include crayfish, local oysters and kingklip.

Cafes The *Oyster Bar*, in Bismarck Strasse near the post office, serves a wide range of light meals and snacks and there is a pleasant coffee shop attached to Diaz Souvenirs just opposite. Lüderitz also has the usual range of takeaways for brötchen, and there are a couple of small seafront cafes which open sporadically.

Entertainment

Pubs & Bars The Crayfish Bar in Bismarck Strasse is the most popular in town. A skittle alley at the Kapps Hotel is open every Monday night (women) and Tuesday and Thursday (men).

Things to Buy

Lüderitz produces high-quality rugs, which in many ways are among the best buys. They are woven in desert colours with local fauna and fauna as favoured designs. A karakul weavery, Lüderitz Carpets, that employs local craftswomen, is at the top of Bismarck Strasse; it will make special orders, deliver worldwide and is famous for the density of its weave. The works can be visited Monday to Friday from 8 am to 1 pm and 2 to 7 pm, and on Saturday between 8 am and noon. The Lüderitz Boekwinkel bookstore has a wide range of jewellery, newspapers and books and will also arrange boat tours. Diaz Souvenirs has the usual range of souvenirs as well as good-quality bush clothing (shorts from R50), T-shirts and magazines.

Getting There & Away

Air Lüderitz may be reached by plane on scheduled Namib Air services from Windhoek three times a week via Swakopmund. Windhoek to Keetmanshoop costs around R350. You can also get there directly from Cape Town on Namib Air on Monday, Wednesday and Friday; the plane continues to Swakopmund. These flights travel via the South African diamond-mining town of Oranjemund, near the border.

Bus & Train There is no scheduled bus service to Lüderitz, but you can get there by overnight train from Keetmanshoop on Friday and Sunday. Ask at the Windhoek or Keetmanshoop stations for current timetables. The train leaves Keetmanshoop at 6.30 pm and arrives in Lüderitz at 6.05 in the

Ostrich

morning. Return trains leave Lüderitz at 6 pm Friday and Sunday, arriving in Keetmanshoop at 5.54 am. The trip costs around R80 one way (2nd class). This link enables you to connect with the main rail services from South Africa to Windhoek.

Car & Motorbike It's definitely worth making the 300 km drive from Keetmanshoop, which is mostly on a good tarred road with the exception of the 100-km stretch from Goageb to Aus. At Aus the road is joined by the dirt road leading through the Namib to Helmeringhausen and Maltahöhe. Between Aus and Lüderitz the road passes through beautiful scenery in the southern Namib – rows of misty mountains erupting from flat sandy plains as far as the eye can see, with the forbidden territory of Diamond Area 1 to the south. Do not stray off the road! If a wind is blowing, the barchan dunefield in the last 10 km before Lüderitz may be moving steadily across the road. Take care when driving over this blowing sand: the baby dunes are harder than you think and do not do the transmission any good.

Cars can be hired from Avis (☎ (063) 312054), but book well in advance.

Getting Around
Everything in the town centre of Lüderitz is within walking distance and there is a limited taxi service to and from the airport and hotels. Apart from that you will need a car to reach outlying beaches or Diaz Point, as there is no public transport. Lüderitz Safaris & Tours (☎ (063) 312719) has a programme of local tours and excursions.

Southern Namibia & the Central Escarpment

This region includes all the country south of Rehoboth and east of the Namib boundary. Geographically this encompasses tremendous variations, from the rich cattle country of Namaland to the semidesert of the Kalahari border, the fringes of the southern Namib, and the spectacular Fish River Canyon near the South African border.

The region is bisected by the north-south B1 and has several major towns, including Keetmanshoop, Karasburg and Mariental. Most overseas visitors tend to spend little time in the Central Escarpment area, and if time is short they head north for Etosha or east for the desert. Yet there is much to see there and it is possible to produce interesting itineraries just off the beaten track, even if your primary destination is Ai-Ais or Lüderitz.

Orientation

One of the good things about this area is that it is relatively accessible. Most of the major towns on the B1 are connected by train, bus and road links and it is easy to get around. Unfortunately a number of the places to see are not so easy to reach by public transport. A visit to Fish River Canyon, for example, really requires you to have your own vehicle or to make use of an organised tour. There are many good tour companies operating in the region (some based at Keetmanshoop) that will arrange everything from a short sightseeing excursion to a major expedition.

The towns of the central and southern area are quite uninspiring and lack the colonial charms of Swakopmund or Lüderitz. They function mainly as commercial and market centres and, with the exception of Keetmanshoop, don't have a lot in the way of interesting colonial architecture. The Central Escarpment is Namibia's richest farming area and much of the region is cattle and karakul country, though some citrus fruit is grown as well.

The south of Namibia includes some of the country's most spectacular scenery at the Fish River Canyon, which is worth a couple of days of anyone's time. There you can camp, walk, hike or luxuriate at the hot spring resort of Ai-Ais and enjoy the wonderful views. There is also the Hardap Dam Resort (run by Nature Conservation) which makes a nice central place to stay with an excellent game reserve where you are allowed to go off and walk on your own.

In the south-east it is possible to cut off a triangle of the journey between Windhoek and Johannesburg by travelling through the Kalahari Gemsbok Park, technically a part of South Africa but included here as it is such a popular diversion. There you can see a range of habitats and animals quite different from those in Namibian game parks like Etosha.

Information

Information about this area can be found at the municipal offices of any of the small towns (like Karasburg) during business hours, together with the Nature Conservation offices at Hardap Dam and Ai-Ais and the museum at Keetmanshoop. There is an information centre in Mariental just off Michael van Niekerk St.

In Keetmanshoop, which effectively functions as the capital of southern Namibia, the information centre is open Monday to Friday from 7.45 am to 12.30 pm and from 2 to 4 pm. On Saturdays opening hours are 9 to 11 am. Outside these hours tourist information is available at either the Canyon or Hansa hotels.

Information about the Kalahari Gemsbok Park can be obtained in South Africa from the National Parks Board (☎ (012) 441191), PO Box 787, Pretoria 0001, South Africa.

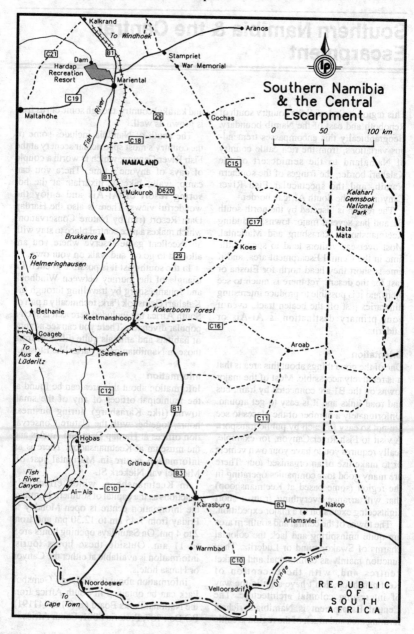

Climate

The uplands of the Central Escarpment avoid the climatic extremes of the lowlands on either side and you can expect clear sunny days, often with a light breeze, but showers of rain any time between November and March. The nights are not so cold as in the Namib area and you do not get the morning fogs. On the eastern side of the escarpment it gets a bit hotter and considerably drier as the plains slope southwards towards the Kalahari. The same is true on the west as you get towards the fringes of the Namib. In the south the rivers can flood if the rains are heavier; the resort of Ai-Ais is closed from the end of October until the beginning of March for this reason.

The dry Mariental area is famous for its dust storms which can occur in summer.

Getting There & Away

Air Keetmanshoop is a scheduled stop on Namib Air services between Cape Town and Windhoek (Eros Airport).

Bus Mariental, Keetmanshoop and Grünau are all connected by the Mainliner luxury coach service which runs between Johannesburg, Cape Town and Windhoek.

Train Mariental, Keetmanshoop and Grünau are all stops on the main train service between Upington in South Africa and Windhoek. You can also connect with overnight trains to Lüderitz at Keetmanshoop on Friday and Sunday. Ask at the station for a current timetable.

Car & Motorbike There is good access from South Africa via the main tarred roads from Upington and Cape Town which join the B1. The B4 from Lüderitz joins the B1 at Keetmanshoop and is tarred along all its length, except around 100 km in the middle. Outlying roads, especially those leading to the Namib and the Kalahari Gemsbok Park, are gravel and of variable quality.

Hitching Hitching is good along the main B1 but less so between Keetmanshoop and

Lüderitz. It is extremely difficult to hitch out to places of interest like the Fish River Canyon.

Getting Around

Bus & Train You can get between Mariental, Keetmanshoop, Rehoboth and Windhoek using train and Mainliner services which run two or three times a week.

Car & Motorbike The B1, which runs along the spine of the Central Escarpment, is an excellent tarred road but the quality of some of the gravel roads leading off it could definitely be improved. As a rule of thumb, the further a minor road is from a main highway or a town the worse it is going to be, and some roads in the extreme east of the region are not recommended for 2WD vehicles at all. Because of the good quality of the B1 it is tempting to drive straight from Windhoek to Keetmanshoop (which takes around five hours) and not linger upon the way.

Organised Tours

Many of the Namibian tour operators based in Windhoek do tours of this area, especially featuring Fish River. The Canyon Hotel (☎ (063) 13361) in Keetmanshoop also carries information about local tour operators and sightseeing trips.

MARIENTAL DISTRICT

Orientation & Information

Mariental is a small administrative centre in the heart of the karakul district. Various new agricultural projects are in progress, including community ostrich farming. The name means Mary's Dale and was given to the settlement by its first White farmer, Hermann Brandt, who bought some land from the Nama chief Hendrik Witbooi in 1890 and named it after his wife. There's not really a lot to see in the town itself, but many places of interest are strung out along the way.

After leaving Rehoboth, if you are travelling south, you cross the Tropic of Capricorn, marked on the road by a large sign. South of Mariental is Namaland, stretching nearly to

Keetmanshoop. The simplest way to see it if you have your own transport is to drive down the B1, but there is an attractive detour down the D620 reached by turning east at Asab across the heart of Namaland.

Mariental

Mariental is a small agricultural one-horse town which dates from the 1920s. There's not a lot to see as it functions mainly as an administrative and commercial centre.

Stampriet & Gochas

Before coming into Mariental from the north you will see a turning (C20) leading east off the B1 signposted to Stampriet, now a fruit and vegetable-growing area but once the scene of much conflict between the Nama and Germans. There are number of monuments commemorating these struggles. If you turn south at Stampriet along the C15 to Gochas you'll come to a small monument on the eastern side of the road near the Farm Gross Nabas which commemorates a battle fought here between 2 and 4 January 1905. German troops were defeated by Witbooi Nama with heavy losses.

Places to Stay & Eat

There's no camping site at Mariental; the nearest is the Nature Conservation resort at Hardap Dam.

Mariental has one small one-star hotel, the *Sandberg Hotel* (☎ (066) 12291), with 18 rooms costing from R38. The hotel has a restaurant, but apart from that the only catering outlets are takeaways near petrol stations in Mariental.

Getting There & Away

Bus & Train Mariental can be reached on the Mainliner coach which leaves Windhoek on Monday, Tuesday and Thursday at 6 pm. The journey takes three hours and costs R56 for a single. You can also get there from South Africa using the same service. The main Upington-Windhoek train service stops at Mariental.

Car & Motorbike Mariental is on the B1. Just

north of the town you can turn west along the C19 to Maltahöhe and east along the B5 which wanders through Namaland before joining the B6 near Windhoek International Airport.

HARDAP DAM
Orientation & Information

Hardap Dam & Recreation Resort is under the control of Nature Conservation. An adult day-visit permit costs R5, plus R5 for a car, and entitles you to unlimited use of the splendid swimming pool and picnic places. The resort office also has a small information centre and an aquarium showing fish found in the lake, but when I went there this was fairly useless as there were no labels identifying the species.

Hardap Dam Lake

The main attraction at Hardap is the huge (25 sq km) artificial lake, anomalously located in the middle of the arid countryside, which dams part of the upper reaches of the Fish River and is famous for birdlife (flamingos, fish eagles, pelicans, spoonbills and Goliath herons). There is also a research establishment where fish production, breeding and commercial exploitation are being studied by Nature Conservation. You are allowed to fish in the lake yourself but need a licence from the resort office; the main stocks are carp, barbels, mudfish and blue kurpers.

The possibility of siting a dam here was discussed as far back as 1897 by a German professor, but his idea was not implemented for nearly another 100 years until construction finally started in 1960. The dam wall is 39 metres high and holds back a sheet of water stretching almost as far as the eye can see into a particularly bleak semidesert landscape.

The resort has a spectacular visitor centre poised like an eagle's nest on a crag over the dam; it sounds attractive but somehow isn't. The colours of the rock are sombre, there is little vegetation and the water level in the dam is often very low. The whole place has a lonely, empty feel about it. The restaurant, built on a terrace overlooking the lake, certainly has a wonderful view, as does the swimming pool on the top of the cliff, and the accommodation is of a very high standard.

Hardap Game Reserve
In my view by far the most attractive part of Hardap is the attached game reserve, reached by a turning crossing the wall of the dam. You can drive through the reserve along 80 km of roads or walk anywhere you like (the walking is safe, easy and convenient). There are a couple of marked circular trails, nine km and 15 km long, and you can get a free map at the resort office.

The reserve is a medley of flat shrub savanna plains with stands of thorn trees (camelthorn, wild green-hair tree, buffalo thorn) plus rocky kopjes where you are likely to see dassies and perhaps a klipspringer. There are no 'dangerous' animals but you are bound to see kudus, gemsboks, springboks, ostriches and mountain zebras and might catch sight of an eland or red hartebeest.

Hardap Game Reserve was so ideal for cheetahs that the population increased to such an extent that it was affecting the abundance of the other animals, so the cheetahs were relocated elsewhere.

Because of the presence of the lake and such a variety of different habitats, there are more than 260 bird species around. But don't bother to follow a sign marked 'Voelparadys' (Bird Paradise) which is merely a stand of dead camelthorns where a large quantity of white-breasted cormorants took up residence many years ago when the water levels in the dam were higher.

Places to Stay & Eat
Tents and caravan sites are available at Hardap (R25 for up to eight persons plus two vehicles and tent). You can rent a neat bungalow with all amenities at a cost of R45 for two beds or R90 for five beds, or dormitory-type two-bed rooms for R30. No crockery and cutlery is provided.

Hardap has a shop, restaurant and petrol station; it also used to be popular with watersports enthusiasts, but this seems to have died away. Unless you have booked accommodation you must leave the resort by sunset and must arrive before sunset to claim reserved places.

Getting There & Away
The Hardap turnoff from the B1 is signposted 15 km north of Mariental. A minor road leads six km to the entrance gate but you must go and check in at the resort office (open from sunrise to 1 pm and from 2 pm to sunset) where you'll be issued with a permit.

Getting Around
You can drive or walk anywhere in the Hardap resort, including the game reserve. Hitching and motorbikes are not permitted.

KALAHARI GEMSBOK PARK
Orientation & Information
It's easy to reach the Kalahari Gemsbok Park in South Africa via any of the minor roads leading east from Mariental. The park terrain is semidesert, dunes, the dry beds of the Auob and Nossob rivers, and grassland with camelthorn vegetation. The entry point to and from Namibia is at Mata Mata, where there is a Rest Camp & Information Centre.

If you are planning to use the park as a route into South Africa (an alternative to the tarred road via Keetmanshoop) you should note that the last time I was there visitors were compelled to spend at least one night at Mata Mata. No day-visiting was allowed. In addition to Mata Mata there are two other rest camps at Nossob and Twee Rivieren; Nossob has the main park information centre and all three have shops (though with a very limited range of fresh food) and fuel.

Things to See & Do
Most of the animals live in the river valleys or around the pans (as in Etosha), and because the park border is open to the Gemsbok National Park in Botswana (for animals but not for humans!) you never really know what and how much wildlife you are going to see. Springboks and gemsboks are the most common, with the occasional

herd of blue wildebeests. Elands live in the sandy dune areas and you might see red hartebeests around the northern end of the Nossob River. The park also has a full range of predators (lions, cheetahs, leopards, wild dogs, jackals, brown and spotted hyaenas) and 238 bird species, including 44 types of birds of prey which apparently flourish under the protection of Nature Conservation and because there is so much food around.

Places to Stay & Eat

All accommodation within the Kalahari Gemsbok Park is controlled by the South African National Parks Board; you need to reserve accommodation with the Reservations Office (☎ (021) 419-5365), National Parks Board, PO Box 7400, Roggebaai 8012, South Africa.

There is a range of camping sites and self-catering bungalows similar to those in Etosha, but there are no restaurants and you are well advised to take all your own food as park supplies are limited.

Getting There & Away

The park can be most easily reached by road along the C15 from near Mariental to the South African border post at Mata Mata.

Getting Around

The park itself covers nearly 10,000 sq km with 400 km of roads which are just about passable (but check) for 2WD vehicles. Using motorbikes or hitching is not permitted.

KEETMANSHOOP

Orientation & Information

Keetmanshoop itself is a not an unattractive town but it seems curiously transient. It forms the main southern crossroads of the country and is a stopping point and junction for visitors and freight coming from Cape Town in the south, Upington and the high veld of South Africa in the east, Lüderitz on the coast and Windhoek in the north. It is actually one of the largest towns in the country (15,000 people) and forms the centre of the thriving karakul district.

Keetmanshoop was founded in 1860 by the Rhenish Mission Society, and the original church, dating from 1895, can still be seen together with other contemporary buildings. The town does not lack character but it has developed few sights of great interest to visitors, possibly because nobody ever stays there for very long.

Colonial Architecture

There are a couple of nice examples of colonial architecture, including the Kaiserliches Postampt which houses the information centre, on the corner of 5th Laan and Fenchelstrasse. This is actually a National Monument, and was built in 1910 to house the newly formed post and telegraph services. The middle section of the building formed the base of the telegraph mast and the rest housed postal officials who still, at that period, made some of their deliveries by camel. Part of the museum store in Windhoek is housed in a converted camel stables of the same period.

Just opposite the building is a pleasant grassy park complete with pond and waterlilies, ideal for picnicking.

Kokerboom Forest

The strange tree-like plants called *kokerbooms* (quivertrees), which look prehistoric and can reach eight metres high, are in fact aloes *(Aloe dichotoma)*; there is a dense stand around 14 km north-east of Keetmanshoop. The best collection is on the Farm Gariganus and can be visited (there is a R5 fee) by calling at the farmhouse, signposted off the main roads as 'Kokerboomwoud', but there are many splendid specimens just by the road which can be seen for free. The trees are at their best in June and July when they are covered in little yellow flowers; this isn't the only location in Namibia where they are found, but it's the place with the greatest numbers. The name 'quivertree' derives from the San practice of hollowing out the branches and using the tough bark to hold arrows. Quivertrees are protected plants in Namibia and the area has been proclaimed a National Monument.

Quivertree

Karakul Sheep

When travelling anywhere in the south or semidesert of Namibia you will notice scraggy, uninspiring, goat-like creatures which actually constitute the country's so-called 'black gold': the karakul sheep. The first karakul arrived in the 1900s and a breeding and experimental station was started after WW I. Today the industry is centered in Keetmanshoop and Maltahöhe and the quality of the pelts is reckoned to be the best in the world, although the Soviet Union and Afghanistan produce greater quantities.

The karakul sheep is hardy, able to survive in very arid conditions and bred chiefly for its pelts, although some are used for mutton, and the wool is the basis for Namibia's thriving textile industry. Karakul pelts are marketed under the name 'Swakara' and are one of the country's major exports for the luxury leather-goods market. Most karakuls are black, but you'll also see grey, white, brown and spotted varieties. Anyone who has eaten goat will know what roast karakul tastes like.

Brukkaros

The extinct volcano of Brukkaros is a geological curiosity which apparently derives from the interaction of magma and underground water 80 million years ago. Sediments clogged the crater lake that formed in the centre of the volcano and eventually the surrounding lavas weathered away; only the sediments that solidified in the volcanic 'plug' were left.

If you are travelling south of Mariental you can see the extinct volcano of Brukkaros looming 650 metres above the plains in the west about 80 km north of Keetmanshoop. It's reached via the C98 and D3904 along signposted backroads leading you about 50 km west of the B1, but you can't quite get to the foot of the mountain in 2WD. There's a parking place about two km short; you then follow the road which leads to a clearly marked path. This path was actually laid out in the 1930s by staff from the Smithsonian Institute who developed a research station on the western rim of the crater from which they could observe the surface of the sun. It takes about half an hour to walk up to the crater and another hour to reach the observation centre, from which there is a fabulous view across the plains of Namaland.

Do not attempt to walk this trail in the middle of the day or without water as there is no shade and you are completely exposed to the sun.

Mukurob & East Namaland

The D620 turning off the B1 leads you to Mukurob, once a dramatic 34-metre-high stone tower perched on a pinnacle of rock which formed a landmark like a finger pointing to the sky. Its Nama name means Finger of God. There's a fine legend about the name which derives from the time when the Nama and Herero people were perpetually squabbling about pasture in the area. The Nama challenged the Herero to pull the rock over, and 10 oxen were slaughtered to provide the ropes, with gangs of Herero tugging away. Of course they failed and the Nama laughed, saying 'mu-kuro' ('now you see').

The road is still signposted but all that is

now visible is a pile of rubble – God's finger collapsed on 8 December 1988, an event which was seen by many as an ill omen for independence. The location is still dramatic and a good picnic spot, though without any shade.

If you have decided to visit Mukurob then it's worth continuing to follow the small D620 as the landscape suddenly changes from ultra-arid bushveld around Mariental to lush thornscrub with fat goats and cattle the deeper you move into Namaland. The sheep and cattle get steadily fatter and the grass greener the further you go east. It's an attractive area to drive through but there are no tourist facilities and no fuel, though you can get water from any of the small farms. The D620 eventually reaches a minor road (Rd 29) forming the back way from Mariental to Keetmanshoop which will take you into Keets, becoming steadily more arid and hilly country until it comes out at a junction surrounded by kokerbooms.

Places to Stay

Camping There is a large two-star municipal camp/caravan site (☎ (063) 13316) at Keetmanshoop with a laundry and shower block, priced at R7 per site for each vehicle and R2 per person.

Hotels Keetmanshoop boasts two hotels of which the three-star *Canyon* (☎ (063) 13361) is the best, just off the main road and with a pool and restaurant with a distinctly German feel. The hotel will arrange to collect visitors from the airport and also fixes day visits and other tours. It's a popular stopover for tour buses but it's expensive, with rooms starting at R87. The two-star *Hansa Hotel* (☎ (063) 13344) is more centrally located, smaller and comfortable with rooms from R49.

Places to Eat

Both hotels have restaurants which serve all meals and a range of snacks to nonresidents, and Keetmanshoop has several 24-hour petrol stations with small shops and takeaways attached.

Getting There & Away

Air The Namib Air service leaves Windhoek on Tuesday and Thursday at 5 pm and arrives at Keetmanshoop at 6.40 pm, continuing on to Cape Town. Return flights leave Cape Town on Tuesday and Thursday at 5 pm, also arriving at 6.40 pm.

Bus & Train The bus leaves Windhoek at 6 pm on Monday, Tuesday and Thursday, arriving in Keetmanshoop at 11.45 pm; the single fare costs R97. It then continues to Cape Town, arriving at 11.10 am the following day. The fare from Keetmanshoop to Cape Town is R177 (one way) and from Keetmanshoop to Johannesburg R188, with approximately the same timings. Buses from Cape Town to Keetmanshoop leave at 6 pm on Thursday and noon on Sunday and Wednesday, and from Johannesburg at 10 am Sunday, Monday and Wednesday.

Keetmanshoop is also a stop on the main Upington-Windhoek railway. Ask at any station for a current timetable.

Car & Motorbike Keetmanshoop is located on the B1, which connects Windhoek with South Africa. You can reach Keetmanshoop from Lüderitz along the B4, which has a fine tarred stretch through Seeheim to Goageb, though the road deteriorates into gravel soon after. East of Keetmanshoop the C16 will again take you to the South African border at Rietfontein or, travelling via Karasburg along the tarred B3, you cross the border at Nakop en route to Upington in the Republic.

There is a branch of Avis Rent-a-Car (☎ (063) 12337) in Keetmanshoop.

Getting Around

Public transport in Keetmanshoop is limited, but the Canyon hotel will arrange taxis and local tours and everywhere within the town can be easily reached on foot.

FARM ROOIPUNT

If you can find the railway station at Goageb and head south for 50 km on a complex of gravel roads you come to one of Namibia's strangest National Monuments on Farm

Rooipunt. This is quite difficult to find and it's a good idea to call the farmer (Mr de Vries) in advance (☎ (063) 6381). He makes a small charge for showing you the places of interest at Rooipunt, but it's worth it not only because he was the first White farmer in the area (and is thus a fund of stories) but because the road is terrible and you'll probably never find the place anyway without him.

The main attraction is the Singing Rock, which is thought to be a musical instrument. It looks like a large flat black rock with white holes but the holes are not natural and if you tap it sharply with a pebble you get different notes like the tones of a xylophone. Nobody knows who made it. The farm also has some magnificent rock paintings and engravings.

AUS & BETHANIE

Aus

The B4 continues west to Aus where you can see the ruins of an internment camp where German military personnel and policemen were kept during WWI. As you go into Aus turn left at the junction and follow a road signposted 'Rosh Pinah'. Follow the road straight ahead until you see the National Monument sign. Aus was set up for 1500 prisoners and 600 guards all living in tents in poor conditions. The inmates turned to brickmaking and constructed their own houses, selling the bricks to the guards for 10 shillings per 1000! The camp was dismantled in 1919 and virtually nothing remains today, although some attempt has been made to reconstruct one of the houses. There is one published book, *Aus 1915-1919*, with a map and guide to the camp but it is only available in Afrikaans. Copies can be bought in Keetmanshoop or Lüderitz.

Bethanie

Turning north from Goageb you reach the town of Bethanie which is one of the oldest settlements in Namibia. It was founded in 1815 by the London Missionary Society to convert the Khoi-Khoi, but the first missionary was a German, the Reverend Heinrich Schmelen. Apparently London had experienced a staffing crisis at this time and recruited missionaries trained in Berlin. His mission station, the Schmelenhaus, is a one-storey cottage which is open during office hours. You can also see the house of Captain Joseph Fredericks, the 19th century Khoi-Khoi chief who signed a treaty with the representatives of Adolf Lüderitz on 1 May 1883 for the sale of what was then Angra Pequena and is now Lüderitz. Both the Fredericks house and the church (Evangelical Lutheran) are National Monuments.

The C14 road from Bethanie continues to Helmeringhausen and crosses the southern Namib.

Places to Stay & Eat

Aus has a small one-star 10-room hotel, the *Bahnhof Hotel* (☎ (063) 33244), where you can get a comfortable room for as little as R20. The hotel also has a bar and restaurant serving meals and snacks. The one-star *Bethanie Hotel*, with just six rooms, costs from R55, but there is no restaurant.

Apart from that there are no catering facilities in this area, nor any camping sites or petrol stations.

Getting There & Away

Aus can only be reached by road, namely the B4 from Keetmanshoop in the direction of Lüderitz. The turn to Bethanie is clearly signposted along the R31, about 140 km from Keetmanshoop.

Getting Around

There is no public transport in this area.

FISH RIVER CANYON & AI-AIS

Orientation & Information

Fish River Canyon is often described as Africa's answer to the Grand Canyon, and indeed it has some spectacular scenery. The gorge, which cuts through the flat ultra-arid plateau, is 161 km long and up to 27 km wide in places, almost 500 metres deep at some points, and with the gleam of water in its depths. The visitor crossing the desert experiences something of a shock walking over the apparently flat desert, as the canyon

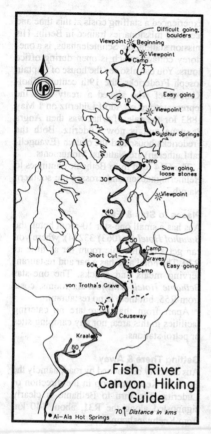

Fish River Canyon Hiking Guide

70 Distance in kms

Hobas

The Nature Conservation checkpoint at Hobas to the north of the canyon has a small information centre and sells cool drinks. Beyond the checkpoint you can follow a winding, poor-quality gravel road which leads 10 km to the main viewing point over the gorge where there is a picnic area with shade, toilets and barbecues. This is the best lookout over the canyon and the starting point for a hiking trail of 90 km to Ai-Ais which is open from early May to the end of August.

Fish River Hiking Trail

This trail takes four days to complete and can only be walked by parties of three to 40 people. A medical certificate of fitness issued within 40 days of the hike is required and you need to reserve a place well in advance. By this they mean 12 to 18 months ahead; contact the Nature Conservation office in Windhoek by phone or letter. The hike costs R25 per person but you have to arrange your own accommodation and transport and sign an indemnity form at Hobas.

Ai-Ais Hot Spring Resort

The hiking trail ends at the resort of Ai-Ais in the southern end of the canyon, famous for its hot springs and forming an oasis in this extremely arid area. The springs originate deep under the riverbed and are rich in chloride, fluoride and sulphate, with water temperatures averaging 60°C. The water is piped to a series of pools and jacuzzis and is reputed to be especially good for anyone with rheumatism or nervous disorders. Apart from its therapeutic properties the resort waters are also home to a number of species of fish, including yellowfish and barbel. Flights can be arranged from Ai-Ais to view the canyon (ask at the main office) and there is an information centre as well, open during office hours.

Ai-Ais is closed between 31 October and 1 March.

Places to Stay & Eat

Camping & Self-Catering There is a fairly

is a sheer drop, like looking out over the edge of the world. The colours are magnificent: layers of pastel pinks, mauves and greys.

The canyon itself contains only a modest remnant of the great Fish River, the longest river in Namibia, in the form of a few pools. Nowadays the river flows very intermittently, coming down in flood only in the late summer (March to April) and leaving a few pools behind it to provide water for animals. The road has a series of viewing sites.

There are information centres run by Nature Conservation at Hobas and Ai-Ais, open during office hours.

basic camping site at Hobas with 10 places and water and firewood available. You need to make reservations in Windhoek and the site costs R25 per day. Limited food supplies are available.

Camping at Ai-Ais costs R25 per day for up to eight people, with an ablution block and barbecues. There is a shop, restaurant, petrol station, swimming pool and mineral bath. Self-catering accommodation at Ai-Ais varies from luxury flats (R100 per day, sleeping four) to basic four-bed huts for R55. Crockery and cutlery are provided only in the luxury flats, but all flats and huts have bedding and towels. It costs R5 per day just to visit the resort, plus R5 for a vehicle and R2 to use the spa and mineral baths. During the season you can book accommodation (at Windhoek) or turn up as a day visitor before sunset.

Hotels The nearest hotel accommodation to Ai-Ais and Fish River is at Karasburg. The *Kalkfontein Hotel* (☎ (063) 42172) is tiny, with room rates starting at R40, and the *Van Riebeeck Hotel* (☎ (063) 4223) is even smaller though the same price. There is also the *Suidwes Motel* at Noordoewer which has rooms from R32 (☎ (002) 013).

Getting There & Away
Car If you are going to visit the Fish River Canyon from Keetmanshoop then the easiest method of access is to take the B1 south from Keetmanshoop through Grünau to where a minor tarred road (C10) branches west, signposted to Ai-Ais. The scenery is barren

and dramatic. About 50 km on you are faced with a choice. C10 continues to the rest camp at Ai-Ais but a minor road (D324) branches north, skirting the eastern border of the canyon and leading to the main viewpoint at Hobas.

All the gravel roads in this area are passable for 2WD, but care is recommended. Lots of animals cross the road and there are occasionally drifting sand and steeply cambered bends.

After leaving Hobas the D601 connects at Holoog with the slightly better quality C12, passing the small Augrabies Steenbok nature park and joining the tarred Keetmanshoop-Lüderitz highway at Seeheim. Alternatively, rejoin the B1 and turn south and you will reach the South African border post at Noordoewer on the Orange River in under an hour.

Getting Around
You can walk around the Fish River Canyon or drive along the gravel roads, but there is no public transport.

Things to Buy
This isn't an area with any renowned souvenirs, but you can get wonderful fruit from roadside stalls, especially around Mariental. The karakul farms of Keetmanshoop have also resulted in the development of a couple of weaveries and rug-making outlets; in the south, paintings and photographs of the Fish River landscape make pleasant mementos.

Index

Safari Guide

ANTELOPES

Although the small bushbuck antelope exists in fairly large numbers in wooded areas of many southern African game parks, it is a shy solitary animal and is rarely sighted.

Standing about 80 cm at the shoulder, the bushbuck is chestnut to dark brown in colour. It has a variable number of white vertical stripes on the body between the neck and rump, usually two horizontal white stripes lower down which give the animal a harnessed appearance, a number of white spots on the upper thigh and a white splash on the neck. Horns usually are grown only by males, but females have been known to grow them on rare occasions. The horns are straight with gentle spirals and average about 30 cm long.

Bushbucks are rarely found in groups of more than two, and prefer to stick to areas with heavy brush cover. When startled they take off and crash loudly through the undergrowth. They are nocturnal browsing animals, yet rarely move far from their chosen spot. Though shy and elusive they can be aggressive and dangerous when cornered. Their main predators are leopards and pythons.

Bushbuck
Scientific name: *Tragelaphus scriptus*

There are seven subspecies of Kirk's dik-dik, but only one is found in south-western Africa, the Damara dik-dik. It is a tiny antelope, standing only around 35 cm at the shoulder. It is reddish-brown on most of its body, with a white belly. Size is the best way to identify a dik-dik, but other telltale marks are the almost total lack of a tail and the tuft of dark hair on the forehead. Horns (found on the male only) are so short (around six cm) that they are often lost in the hair tuft. The males weigh no more than 6 kg, the females being slightly larger.

Dik-diks are usually seen singly or in pairs and are sometimes found in exceedingly dry places – it seems they get most of their necessary moisture from the food they eat. They are territorial, each occupying an area of around five hectares. They are mainly nocturnal but can be seen grazing in the early morning and late afternoon; they rest in the heat of the day. In Namibia, they generally prefer to stay in dense woodland which has a thicket understorey.

The females bear a single offspring twice a year. After six months the young dik-dik reaches sexual maturity and then is driven out of the home territory.

Dik-Dik
Scientific Name: *Madoqua(Rhyn chotragus) kirki ssp. damarensis*

1

Common or Grey Duiker
Scientific name: *Silvicapra grimmia*

The common duiker is the most common of the 10 species in Africa. Even so, it is not sighted often as it is largely nocturnal, usually only lives in pairs, and prefers areas with good scrub cover. Duikers are found in thick scrub throughout Zimbabwe and much of Botswana. The rare blue duiker is found only in the forests of Zimbabwe's eastern highlands.

The common duiker, only 60 cm at the shoulder, is greyish light-brown with a white belly and a dark brown vertical stripe on the face. The horns, on males only, are very short (around 20 cm), pointed, and grow straight.

Duikers are widely distributed and can be found in a variety of habitats ranging from open bush to semidesert, but they prefer low open scrub and are even found in cultivated areas where other herbivores have been exterminated.

They are almost exclusively browsers and only rarely eat grasses, though they appear to supplement their diet with insects and guinea fowl chicks. They are capable of doing without water for long periods but will drink it when it's available.

Eland
Scientific name: *Taurotragus oryx*

The eland looks similar to some varieties of cattle seen on the Indian subcontinent, and is found in all the Zimbabwean parks as well as in Moremi and Chobe in Botswana. It is not common in the south of Namibia, but there is a large population in Etosha, best seen to the east of the game park around Namutoni.

It is the biggest of the antelopes, standing about 170 cm at the shoulder. A mature bull can weigh up to 1000 kg. Elands are light greyish-brown and bear as many as 15 vertical white stripes on the body, although these are often almost indistinguishable on some animals. Both sexes have horns, which are spiralled at the base, swept straight back and grow to about 65 cm long. Males have a much hairier head than the females, and their horns are stouter and slightly shorter.

Elands prefer savanna scrub to open spaces, but avoid thick forest. They graze on grass and tree foliage in the early morning and late afternoon, and are also active on moonlit nights. They need to drink once a day, but can go for a month or more without water if their diet includes fodder with a high water content.

Elands are usually found in groups of around six to 12, but there may be as many as 50 in a herd. A small herd normally consists of several females and one male, but in larger herds there may be several males, and there is a strict hierarchy. Females reach sexual maturity at around two years and can bear up to 12 calves in a lifetime. The young are born in October or November.

The gemsbok (or oryx) is a large grey antelope which is commonly seen in all the Botswanan game reserves. It is also a very common sight in Namibia and is seen everywhere from the fringes of the great dune fields to the Etosha Pan, where large herds of animals may be seen. There are also a few in the southernmost areas of Hwange National Park in Zimbabwe.

The gemsbok, of which there are two types, stands around 120 cm at the shoulder. For the type found in Namibia, the upper body is pale grey with black and white markings on the face and a band of black on each flank, and the abdomen is white. Both sexes have long, rapier-like horns, used to defend themselves from predators. Elsewhere, its coat is a sandy fawn with a black stripe along the spine down to the tip of the tail. The underparts are white and separated from the lower flanks by another black stripe. There are also two black rings just above the knee of each foreleg.

Both types of gemsbok have ovate pointed ears, the main distinguishing feature being, as the name suggests, a tuft of black hairs on the ears of the fringe-eared gemsbok. Gemsboks are easy to distinguish from other antelopes by their straight, very long and heavily ridged horns which are carried almost parallel. Both males and females have horns, which come into their own when the animal is forced to defend itself. Held down between the forelegs, they are formidable weapons used to impale an enemy.

Gemsboks are principally grazers but will also browse on thorny shrubs. They are capable of doing without water for long periods of time but will drink daily if it is available.

Herds vary from five to 40 individuals and some-times more, though the bulls are usually solitary.

Gemsbok (South African Oryx)
Scientific name: *Oryx gazella*

This small and stocky antelope is reddish-brown and has a pale red underside. The back and sides are speckled with individual white hairs from the nape of the neck to the rump, hence the name grysbok, which means 'grey buck' in Afrikaans. They stand only about 46 cm in height and nor-mally weigh no more than nine kg. Only the males have horns, which are small, sharp and straight.

The grysbok inhabits both bushy and wood-land savanna country and rocky kopjes, feeding primarily on shoots and leaves. They also like to munch the reeds which grow in wetlands.

Grysboks are solitary animals; more than two together are rarely observed. They're most active from morning to late afternoon, spending the nights resting in bushy thickets and stony out-crops. They're found throughout Zimbabwe and northern Botswana.

Grysbok
Scientific name: *Raphiceros melanotis*

Hartebeest
Scientific name: *Alcelaphus buselaphus*

The hartebeest is a medium-size antelope found in small numbers in the game reserves of Zimbabwe and Botswana. It's easy to recognise as it has a long, narrow face and distinctively angular short horns (on both sexes) which are heavily ridged. Colouring is generally light brown on the back, becoming paler towards the rear and under the belly. The back slopes away from the humped shoulders. There are two types of hartebeest in Zimbabwe and Botswana: Lichtenstein's hartebeest and the red hartebeest. In Namibia, the latter variety is common in the north of the country, especially in Etosha. Red hartebeests are among the fastest of all antelopes.

They feed exclusively on grass and usually drink twice daily, although they can go for months without water if necessary.

They are social beasts and often mingle with animals such as zebras and wildebeests. Their behaviour is not unlike the wildebeest's, particularly the head tossing and shaking.

Sexual maturity is reached at around two years; calving goes on throughout the year, although there are peak periods in February and August. Predators are mainly the large cats, hyaenas and hunting dogs.

Impala
Scientific name: *Aepyceros melampus*

The graceful impala is one of the most common antelopes and is found in large numbers in all the national parks and reserves.

A medium-size antelope, it stands about 80 cm at the shoulder. The coat is a glossy rufous colour, though paler on the flanks, and the underparts, rump, throat and chin are white. A narrow black line runs along the middle of the rump to about halfway down the tail and there's also a vertical black stripe on the back of the thighs. The males have long, lyre-shaped horns (averaging 75 cm) that curve upwards as they spread.

There is a special Etosha subspecies of impala, called the black-faced impala, with a darker coat than its relative and a pronounced purple-black blaze on the forehead.

Impalas are gregarious animals, each male having a harem of up to 100 females, but more usually around 15 to 20. Males without such a harem form bachelor groups. There is fierce fighting between males during the rutting season, but otherwise they are fairly placid animals. The normal gestation period is six to seven months, but it is prolonged if rainfall has been low and there is insufficient grass to nourish the young.

Impalas are known for their speed and amazing ability to jump, being capable of clearing 10 metres in a single jump lengthways or three metres in height – and this they frequently do, even when there's nothing to jump over!

The distinctive klipspringer inhabits rocky outcrops in Hwange and Matobo national parks in Zimbabwe, and are seen most often in Namibia on the slopes bordering the escarpment, around the upper reaches of the Kuiseb Canyon, Brandberg, and other mountainous areas. These delicate little antelopes, which have a significant role in San mythology, are shy and easily disturbed.

Standing about 50 cm at the shoulder, they are easily recognised by their curious tip-toe stance (the hooves are adapted for balance and grip on rocky surfaces) and the greenish tinge of their speckled, coarse hair. Horns, found on the male only, are short (about 10 cm) and widely spaced.

When alarmed they retreat into the rocks for safety. They are amazingly agile and sure-footed creatures and can often be observed bounding up impossibly rough rock faces. These antelope can also go entirely without water if there is none around, getting all they need from the greenery they eat. They are most active just before and after midday. Klipspringers are usually found in pairs, or a male with two females, and they inhabit a clearly defined territory.

Klipspringers reach sexual maturity at around one year, and females bear one calf twice a year. Calves may stay with the adult couple for up to a year, although young males usually seek their own territory earlier than that.

Predators are mainly the leopard and the crowned eagle, but also include jackals and baboons.

Klipspringer
Scientific name: *Oreotragus oreotragus*

The beautiful greater kudu, one of the largest of the antelopes, is found all over Zimbabwe, Namibia and northern Botswana, but prefers hilly country with fairly dense bush cover.

Greater kudus stand around 1.5 metres at the shoulder and weigh up to 250 kg, yet they're very elegant creatures, light grey in colour with broad ears and a long neck. The sides of the body are marked by six to 10 vertical white stripes and there is a white chevron between the eyes. Horns are carried only by the males and are both divergent and spiralling.

Kudus live in small herds of up to five females and their young, but the herds often split up during the rainy season. The males are usually solitary, though occasionally they band together into small herds.

They are mainly browsers and only seldom eat grasses, but are capable of eating many types of leaves which would be poisonous to other animals.

Although somewhat clumsy animals when on the move, they are capable of clearing well over two metres when jumping.

Greater Kudu
Scientific name: *Tragelaphus strepsiceros*

Lechwe

Scientific name: *Kobus (Hydrotragus) leche*

Found mainly along the Chobe riverfront, the Okavango Delta, and Namibia's Caprivi Strip, the red (or Zambezi) lechwe is a mid-size antelope with a yellowish-brown body. Males have lyre-like horns with an average of about 200 rings.

The red lechwe is most easily observed along the Botswanan banks of the Chobe River. It inhabits marshes, rivers, swamps and lakes, where it feeds on riverine grasses and also feeds in waters about 50 cm deep. They normally live in large herds of sometimes hundreds of males, females and young. Females reach sexual maturity at about 1 1/2 years, and mating and birthing occur at any time of year.

Hunted by lions, cheetahs, leopards, hunting dogs, hyaenas, pythons, and even humans and crocodiles, the apparently tasty lechwes have good reason to be paranoid. They're primarily active in game reserves at dawn and dusk, but where they're hunted by humans, the few surviving lechwes are only out and about at night.

Nyala

Scientific names: *Tragelaphus angas* (common nyala), *Tragelaphus buxtoni* (mountain nyala)

The medium-size nyala is one of Africa's rarest and most beautiful antelopes. Males are grey with vertical strips down the back, long hair under the throat and hind legs, and a mane. The males have long, lyre-shaped horns with white tips. Females are a ruddy colour with vertical white stripes, but lack horns.

Although nyalas are found in small numbers throughout south-eastern Africa, their only Zimbabwean population is in Gonarezhou National Park. Their main foods are shoots, buds, bark, fruit and leaves of trees and bushes. During the dry season they're active mainly in the morning and evening, while in the rains they more often feed at night.

Female nyalas and their young live in small groups, with one older dominant male to guard and defend them from young males, which live in their own social groups. The nyala will defend itself bravely against humans and enemies – mainly leopards and, to a lesser degree, lions. The young may even be taken by baboons and birds of prey.

Similar to the duiker in appearance, the small oribi is relatively uncommon; your best chance of spotting one is in the lowveld of south-eastern Zimbabwe, in Kazuma Pan National Park, and around the Nogatsaa area of Botswana's Chobe National Park.

The oribi's most distinguishing mark, although you'll need binoculars to spot it, is a circular patch of naked black skin below the ear – it's actually a scent gland. Another identifying characteristic is the tuft of black hair on the tip of the short tail. Otherwise the oribi is a uniform golden brown with white on the belly and the insides of the legs. Males have horns which are short, straight and about 10 cm long.

Oribis usually graze on grassy plains that have good shelter. If water is available they will drink willingly, but can also go without water entirely. When alarmed they bolt and then make bouncing jumps with a curious action – all four legs are kept completely stiff. It is thought this helps them to orient themselves in places with poor visibility. After 100 metres or so they stop and assess the danger.

The territorial oribi is usually found in pairs. Sexual maturity is reached at around one year, and the females bear one calf twice a year.

Being quite small, the oribi has many predators, including the larger cats.

Oribi
Scientific name: *Ourebia ourebi*

Also known as the kob, the extremely rare and endangered puku is limited to about 100 individuals along the Chobe River in Botswana, never straying far from that permanent water source. Although similar to the lechwe in shape and colour, the puku is a bit larger and has thicker horns (males only) and different markings.

There's no particular mating season; females will bear two single offspring in a year. Young males, mature males and females with young keep generally separate herds. They rarely range more than one km from home base, visiting a designated rutting ground within that area only for mating.

Pukus are normally active at dawn and from late afternoon to dusk, with occasional activity during the day. They eat mainly foliage and riverine grasses. They're hunted by lions, leopards, hyaenas and hunting dogs.

Puku
Scientific name: *Kobus kob vardoni*

Reedbuck

Scientific names: *Redunca arundineum (common reedbuck), Redunca fulvorufula (mountain reedbuck)*

The dusky brown reedbucks are found throughout southern Africa, near wetlands or riverine areas; they never stray more than a few km from a permanent water source.

They are medium-size antelopes, standing around 80 cm high at the shoulder. The most distinctive features are the forward-curving horns (males only) and the bushy tail. The underbelly, inside of the thighs, throat and underside of the tail are white.

Reedbucks are very territorial and are found in small groups of up to 10 animals. The groups usually consist of an older male and accompanying females and young. Their diet consists almost exclusively of grass, but does include some foliage.

They are active early in the morning and late in the afternoon and evening. They need to stay close to water.

At mating time, males fight spiritedly. After reaching sexual maturity at around 1½ years, females bear one calf at a time.

The reedbuck's main predators include the big cats, hyaenas and hunting dogs.

Roan Antelope

Scientific name: *Hippotragus equinus*

The roan antelope is one of southern Africa's rarest species, but it still exists in some numbers in Hwange, Kazuma Pan and Chobe national parks. Roan antelopes are also found on the western edge of Etosha where they were introduced in an effort to increase numbers. You can also see them in the Waterberg Plateau Park.

The roan antelope reaches up to 150 cm at the shoulder and bears a striking resemblance to a horse, hence the name. The bulls can reach 270 kg in weight and carry heavier horns than the females. Roan antelope are grazers but prefer tall rather than short grass, especially where there is ample shade and good fresh water. The coat varies from reddish fawn to dark rufous, and the underparts are white. Roans have a conspicuous mane of stiff, black-tipped hairs which stretches from the nape to the shoulders. Under the neck there's another mane consisting of long dark hairs. The ears are long, narrow and pointed, with a brown tassel at the tip. The face has a very distinctive black and white pattern. Both sexes have curving, backswept horns up to 70 cm long.

Roans are aggressive and fight from a very early age, a characteristic which frequently deters predators. For most of the year they live in small herds (usually of less than 20 but sometimes more) led by a master bull, but in the mating season the bulls become solitary and take a female out of the herd. The pair stay together until the calf is born, after which the females form a herd by themselves. They later return to their former herd. Herds gather during the dry season.

The sable antelope is found in Zimbabwe, in Matobo, Hwange and particularly Zambezi national parks. It is rare in Namibia but can be seen in the Waterberg Plateau Park. It is slightly smaller than its cousin the roan, but is more solidly built. The colouring is dark brown to black, with white face markings and belly. Both sexes carry long, back-swept horns which average around 80 cm, those of the male being longer and more curved.

The sable is active mainly in the early morning and late afternoon, and is found in herds of up to 25 – sometimes more in the dry season. Sables are territorial, each group occupying a large area, although within this area individual males have demarcated territories of up to 30 hectares. Sables feed mainly on grass, but foliage accounts for around 10% of their diet.

Females start bearing calves at around three years of age; the main calving times are January and September.

Like the roan, the sable is a fierce fighter and has been known to kill lions when attacked. Other predators include the leopard, hyaena and hunting dog.

Sable Antelope
Scientific name: *Hippotragus niger*

The sitatunga is a swamp antelope with unusual elongated hooves which give it the ability to walk on marshy ground without sinking. It is restricted primarily to the Okavango Delta in Botswana.

Very similar to the bushbuck in appearance, except that the coat of the male is much darker and the hair of both sexes much longer and shaggier, the sitatunga stands a little over one metre at the shoulder. The males have twisted horns up to 90 cm long. It is a fairly shy antelope, so sightings are not all that common. A good swimmer, the sitatunga will often submerge itself almost completely when alarmed, leaving only its nostrils exposed.

It feeds largely on papyrus and other reeds and is usually nocturnal though in places where it remains undisturbed it can be diurnal. Animals normally live singly or in pairs, but sometimes come together in small herds numbering up to 15.

Sitatunga
Scientific name: *Tragelaphus spekei*

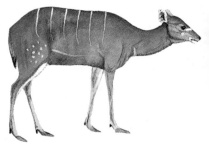

Springbok
Scientific Name: *Antidorcas marsupialis*

The springbok is a medium-sized gazelle, growing to about 80 cm at the shoulder. The horns of the female are lyre-shaped and about 25 cm long, while the male's horns are longer at about 35 to 40 cm. It's face is generally either all white, or has a dark brown patch on the forehead, along with a brown stripe passing from the base of the horn, around the eye and to the edge of the mouth. The springbok's body is brown, with white on the underside and on the insides of its legs. It also has a strip of long, white hairs in the middle of its back.

It is active early in the morning and from late afternoon to dusk. It also often comes out on nights with strong moonlight. It eats grass and the leaves of bushes, and occasionally digs out roots and tubers. It drinks water often, but can apparently survive for long periods without. Springboks often *pronk* (leap vertically in the air) when alarmed. It calves from December to January.

Springboks are social animals and generally move in herds of 20 to 100 animals; sometimes herds of several hundred can be seen. Under conditions of severe drought, huge herds have migrated in search of water; in 1896, the area covered by millions of migrating springboks measured 220 km by 25 km. In Namibia, great herds, driven mad by thirst, have flocked to the coast, drunk seawater and died, leaving the shoreline covered in tens of thousands of carcasses.

Nowadays, springboks have been pushed out of much of their former range by hunting or agricultural expansion. Many still congregate in the Kalahari, however, and they are by far the most common antelope seen in Namibia, being found almost everywhere from the desert fringes right up to the banks of the Okavango.

Steenbok
Scientific name: *Raphicerus campestris*

Sometimes spelt steinbock, the steenbok resembles both the duiker and the grysbok. The males have small, widely separated, straight horns. The legs are long and slender and the tail is quite short. The back colour ranges from light reddish brown to dark brown, and on the upper edge of the nose is a black, wedge-shaped spot.

Steenboks are found primarily on open plains but are also common in the Kalahari area of western Botswana and eastern Namibia, although not in rocky or sloping areas. They're solitary animals, individuals only having contact with others during the mating season.

Normally, steenboks are active in the morning and evening, but may continue into the night when there's bright moonlight. The rest of the time they seek out high grass or ant bear holes which offer some protection from their main enemies, which include leopards, eagles, pythons, jackals and hyaenas. The young are even preyed upon by monitor lizards.

The tsessebe is not unlike the hartebeest in appearance but is a darker, almost purple colour and has black patches on the rear thighs, front legs and face. It's horns, carried by both sexes, are also different, curving gently up, out and back. The tsessebe is found in all of Zimbabwe's game parks, Namibia's Caprivi and the parks of northern Botswana.

A highly gregarious antelope, it lives in herds of at least 15 and frequently mingles with wildebeests, hartebeests and zebras.

During the mating season the bulls select a well-defined patch of ground and defend it against rivals. At this time, females are free to wander from one patch to another. After mating, the herds divide into male and female groupings.

Tsessebes are exclusively grazers. Although they can live on dry grasses which other antelope won't eat, they prefer flood plains and moister areas which support lush pasture. When water is available they drink frequently, but they are also capable of surviving long periods without water as long as sufficient grass is available. Lions are their main predators.

Tsessebe (Topi)
Scientific name: *Damaliscus lunatus*

The ringed waterbuck, so called because of the white ring around its rump, has white markings on the face and throat. It is a fairly solid animal and is easily recognisable by its thick, shaggy, dark brown coat and white inner thighs. A rather common animal, it is easily seen in all the Zimbabwean parks, Chobe in Botswana, and the northern Namibian parks.

Only the males have horns, which curve gradually outwards then grow straight up to a length of about 75 cm. As you might expect from the name, waterbucks are good swimmers and readily enter the water to escape from predators. Their habitat is always close to water, and males have marked territories by the water's edge. Females and younger males tend to wander at random through male territories. Herds are small and usually consist of cows, calves and one mature bull – the other bulls live in small groups apart from the herd.

The bulk of the waterbuck's diet is grass, but it does eat some foliage.

Sexual maturity is reached at just over one year, although a male will not become the dominant bull in the herd until around five years of age.

Predators such as lions, leopards and hunting dogs go for the young calves and females, but mature waterbucks are not a favoured prey species because of their tough flesh and the distinct odour of the meat.

Ringed (Common) Waterbuck
Scientific name: *Kobus ellipsiprymnus*

Wildebeest

Scientific names: *Connochaetes taurinus (blue or bridled wildebeest), Connochaetes gnou (black or white-tailed wildebeest)*

The wildebeest, also called the gnu, is to the African savanna what the bison once was to the American prairies. Numbering in their thousands in certain areas, particularly in central Botswana and in Hwange, Chobe and Etosha national parks, wildebeests are unmistakable because of their clumsy and rather unappealing appearance. They are well known for their eccentric behaviour, which includes loud snorting, tossing and shaking of the head, bucking, running around in circles and rolling in the dust (thought to be a reaction to the activity of the botfly larva which manages to find its way right up the nostrils and into the brain). Wildebeests are heavily built, with a massive head and wild mane; they've been described as having the forequarters of an ox, the hind parts of an antelope and the tail of a horse.

Their sheer numbers, nevertheless, are testimony to their superb adaptation to the environment. Almost entirely grazers, they are constantly on the move in search of good pasture and water, and their annual migration between Makgadikgadi Pans and Nxai Pan (and vice versa) is an amazing sight. Thousands lose their lives while migrating, particularly to the Kuke buffalo fence which extends from east to west across western Botswana, where they succumb to thirst or mere exhaustion while trying to get around the fence.

They're very gregarious animals, usually seen in large herds, sometimes numbering tens of thousands, in association with zebras and other herbivores.

During the mating season, groups of up to 150 females and their young are gathered together by up to three bulls, which defend a defined territory against rivals even when on the move. There's apparently no hierarchy amongst the bulls and, at the end of the mating season, the breeding herds are absorbed back into the main herds.

Although they graze in a scattered fashion without any apparent social organisation during the rainy season, they coalesce around waterholes and any remaining pasture in the dry season. Wildebeests prefer to drink daily and will walk up to 50 km to secure water, but they are capable of surviving for up to five days without it. They're also noisy when grazing, constantly producing a series of snorts and low grunts.

Their main predators are lions, cheetahs and wild dogs, though hyaenas are also very partial to young calves.

The Cape buffalo occurs in great numbers in all the major parks; in Namibia, your best chance off seeing them is in the Waterberg Plateau Park.

This massive animal can be extremely dangerous to humans and should be treated with caution, although for the most part it is docile and will stay out of your way. Solitary rogue bulls and females protecting young calves are the most aggressive; 800 kg of angry buffalo thundering towards you is not to be taken lightly.

Both sexes have the distinctive curving horns which broaden and almost meet over the forehead, although those of the female are usually smaller. The buffalo's colour varies from dark reddish brown to black.

Buffaloes are often found in herds of 100 or more and never stray too far from water, especially in the dry season. When food and water are plentiful the herds often disperse. Cape buffaloes are relatively territorial and never stray more than about 50 km from their home base.

CAPE BUFFALO
Scientific name: *Syncerus caffer*

CARNIVORES

The carnivores are the animals most seriously affected by tourists in East Africa, having to trail dozens of white minibuses while trying to hunt. Fortunately, the game parks of southern Africa remain largely wild and see few tourists, so natural patterns are altered little by human visitors. Still, it's best not to interfere; although the temptation and excitement may be great, keep your distance if animals are obviously hunting.

One glance indicates how this animal was named. The bat-eared fox is basically a long-legged fox with enormous ears. Naturally, its sense of hearing is exceptionally good and it can hear faint sounds below ground while foraging for subterranean insects. By lowering its head towards the soil, ears parallel, the fox can thus get an exact fix on the location of potential food. This performance is followed by a burst of frantic digging to capture the prey. It mainly eats insects, small animals, fruits and berries.

Its tail is very bushy and its body is brown, with some white markings, and a black edge on the tips of its ears. The bat-eared fox either digs or takes over a burrow, which usually has several entrances and rooms. The fox is active at night, especially just after sunset. Large birds of prey and hyaenas are its only enemies.

It is found in Zimbabwe only in Hwange National Park, but is much easier to see in Botswana and Namibia. Indeed, it is quite common in Etosha and around the Namib Desert area.

Bat-Eared Fox
Scientific Name: *Otocyon magalotis*

Civet (African Civet)
Scientific name: *Civettictis (Viverra) civetta*

The civet is a medium-size omnivore around 40 cm high at the shoulder and 90 cm long (excluding the tail). Its coat of long, coarse hair is basically grey but has a definite and variable pattern of black spots and bands. The tail is bushy at the base and is held out straight when the animal is on the move. The head is mostly greyish white and the ears are quite small, rounded and tipped with white hairs.

Civets are solitary, nocturnal animals, hiding in thickets, tall grass or abandoned burrows during the day, and so are rarely sighted. The most likely places to spot them are in Hwange and other western Zimbabwe parks. The rarer tree civet is found only in Zimbabwe's eastern highlands.

Civets have a very varied diet consisting of rodents, birds and their eggs, reptiles, amphibians, snails, insects (especially ants and termites), berries, young shoots of bushes, and fruits.

The other conspicuous feature of the civet is the presence of musk glands in the anal region which produce a foul-smelling oily substance used to mark territory. This musk is used in manufacturing perfumes, though in Western countries it is collected from animals held in captivity.

Cheetah
Scientific name: *Acinonyx jubatus*

The cheetah is one of the most impressive animals you can hope to come across – sleek, streamlined and graceful. It is found in small numbers in all the major game reserves – Hwange, Zambezi, Kazuma Pan, Mana Pools, Chobe, Moremi, Etosha and so on. Cheetahs are protected in Namibia and may still occasionally be seen on farmland, especially in the north of the country.

Similar in appearance to the leopard, the cheetah is longer and lighter in the body and has a slightly bowed back and a much smaller and rounder face. It stands around 80 cm at the shoulder, measures around 210 cm in length (including the tail) and weighs from 40 to 60 kg.

Normally the cheetah hunts in early morning or late evening, relying on bursts of tremendous speed – up to 110 km/h – for catching its prey, but this speed is only sustainable for a very short time. During a hunt the cheetah stalks its prey as close as possible and then sprints for 100 metres or so; if by that time it hasn't caught its victim, it will give up and try elsewhere. Often the prey (usually a small antelope) is brought to the ground with a flick of the paw that trips it up. Other prey includes hares, jackals and young warthogs.

Cubs are usually born in litters numbering from two to four, and the main breeding period is from March to December. They reach maturity at around one year but stay with the mother much longer than that, as they have to learn to hunt.

Cheetahs rarely fight, but predators (mainly of cubs) include lions, leopards and hyaenas.

Unlike the civet, the genet distinctly resembles the domestic cat, though the body is considerably longer and the tail is longer and bushier. The long, coarse coat has a prominent crest along the spine. The basic colour varies from grey to fawn, patterned from the neck to the tail with roundish dark brown to black spots. The tail is banded with nine or 10 similarly coloured rings, and has a whitish tip.

The genet lives singly or in pairs in riverine forests and dry scrub savanna and open country. It is a very agile tree climber, but is seldom sighted since it is entirely nocturnal. During the day it sleeps in abandoned burrows, rock crevices or hollow trees, or up on high branches, apparently returning to the same spot each day.

Its prey is generally hunted on the ground, though it will climb trees to seek out nesting birds and their eggs. Like the domestic cat, it stalks prey by crouching flat on the ground. Its diet consists of a variety of small animals (mostly rodents), birds, reptiles (including snakes), insects and fruits. It is well known for being a wasteful killer, often eating only a small part of the animals it catches.

Like the domestic cat, the genet spits and growls when angered or in danger.

Litters typically consist of two or three kittens.

Genet
Scientific name: *Genetta genetta (European Genet), Genetta tigrina (Large-spotted Genet)*

The hunting dog is the size of a large domestic dog and is of a medium build. It is found mainly in Zimbabwe and Botswana – anywhere where there is a high concentration of game animals – and so is seen in all the reserves. Hunting dogs are rare in Namibia, however; your best chance of seeing one is in West Caprivi.

The dog's unusual coloration makes it quite a beautiful creature; the black and yellowish splotches are different in each animal, ranging from almost all black to almost all yellow. The only constant is the white tail tip. The large rounded ears are prominent physical features.

Hunting dogs tend to move in packs ranging from four or five dogs up to as many as 40. They are efficient hunters and work well together. Once the prey has been singled out and the chase is on, a couple of dogs will chase hard while the rest pace themselves; once the first two tire another two step in, and so on until the quarry is exhausted. Favoured animals for lunch include gazelles, impalas and other antelopes. They rarely scavenge, preferring to kill their own.

Hunting dog pups are usually born in grass-lined burrows in litters averaging seven, although litters of 15 are not unheard of. By six months they are competent hunters and have abandoned the burrow.

The hunting dog has no common predators, although unguarded pups sometimes fall prey to hyaenas and eagles.

Hunting Dog
Scientific name: *Lycaon pictus*

Hyaena

Scientific names: *Crocuta crocuta*
(spotted hyaena), *Hyaena brunnea*
(brown hyaena)

The spotted hyaena is a fairly common animal throughout most of Zimbabwe, Botswana and Namibia, especially where game is plentiful. The rare brown hyaena is also found in limited areas and was the focus of the study recounted in Mark & Delia Owens' book *Cry of the Kalahari*. Shy and secretive, it is thought to be confined to an area around the Uniab delta.

Bearing a distinct resemblance to dogs, the hyaena is a large, powerfully built animal with a sloping back, broad head and large eyes, but with rather weak hindquarters. The sloping back gives the animal its characteristic loping gait when running. Its short coat is dull grey to buff, entirely patterned with rounded blackish spots except on the throat. Its powerful jaws and teeth enable it to crush and swallow the bones of most animals, but not the elephant.

Hyaenas are mainly nocturnal animals but are frequently seen during the day, especially in the vicinity of lion or cheetah kills impatiently waiting for their turn at the carcass along with vultures. Otherwise, the days are spent in long grass, abandoned aardvark holes or in large burrows which they dig out up to a metre below the surface of the soil. It's a very noisy animal; when camping out in the bush at night you'll frequently hear its characteristic, spine-chilling howl which rises quickly to a high-pitched scream. This is only one of the sounds which the spotted hyaena emits. Another is the well-known 'laugh', though this is generally only produced when the animal finds food or is mating.

The hyaena has highly developed senses of smell, sight and sound, all important in locating food (carrion or prey) and for mutual recognition among pack members and mating pairs.

Hyaenas are well known as scavengers and can often be seen following hunting lions and wild dogs, usually at a respectable distance, though they will occasionally force these animals to abandon their kill. Although carrion does form an important part of their diet, hyaenas are also true predators and are more than capable of bringing down many of the larger herbivores. They often form packs to run down their prey, sometimes reaching speeds up to 60 km/h.

In the mating season, hyaenas assemble in large numbers, especially on moonlit nights. All hell breaks loose on these occasions and the noise is incredible. The young are born in the mother's burrow. The pups are weaned at around six weeks old and become independent shortly afterwards.

The hyaena's main enemy is man, though lions and wild dogs will occasionally kill or mutilate a hyaena that gets too close to a kill. Although hyaenas are reputed to be cowardly, you're advised to keep your distance as they do occasionally attack humans sleeping in the open.

The black-backed jackal is a common sight in the parks and reserves. The black back which gives it its name is usually more silvery than black and is wide at the neck, tapering to the tail. Although the jackal is in fact a dog, the appearance is more that of a fox because of its very bushy tail and long ears.

The jackal is for the most part a scavenger, and so is commonly seen in the vicinity of a kill. If food is not forthcoming from that direction, jackals will hunt insects, small mammals and birds, even the occasional small antelope. They are also found on the outskirts of human settlements and will attack sheep, poultry and young calves or foals.

Jackals are territorial, a pair guarding an area of around 250 hectares. Cubs are born in litters of five, six or seven. Although they don't reach maturity until almost a year old, they usually leave the parents when just two months old.

Enemies of the black-backed jackal include leopards, cheetahs and eagles.

The leopard is one of the most widespread but least observed of the big cats. A powerfully built animal which uses cunning to catch its prey, it is present in all the major game reserves in Zimbabwe and Botswana but is rare in Namibia. There, they are confined to the Central Escarpment and associated areas; you might see one in the Kuiseb or Fish River canyons or in the rocky areas to the east of Etosha.

It is difficult to find as it is nocturnal and spends the day resting on branches of trees, often up to five metres above the ground. It is as agile as a domestic cat in climbing such trees, where it also carries its prey so that it's out of the way of other scavengers which might contest the kill.

The leopard's coat is usually short and dense with numerous black spots on a yellowish background, though some are black all over. The underparts are white and less densely spotted. In addition, the coats of leopards found in open country are generally lighter than those in wooded country.

Leopards are solitary animals, except during the mating season when the male and female live together. The gestation period is three months and a litter usually consists of up to three cubs.

They prey on a variety of birds, reptiles and mammals including large rodents, rock hyraxes, warthogs, smaller antelopes and monkeys (especially baboons), though they occasionally take domestic animals such as goats, sheep, poultry and dogs. This wide range of prey explains why they are still able to survive even in areas of dense human settlement long after other large predators have disappeared. But their presence is generally unwelcome since they do occasionally eat humans.

Black-backed Jackal
Scientific name: *Canis mesomelas*

Leopard
Scientific name: *Panthera pardus*

Lion
Scientific name: *Panthera leo*

Lions are big attractions in the national parks and game reserves and are found in most of the main ones. Lions are extremely common in Etosha, but they are most easily seen in the dry season (May to September) when they congregate near waterholes. They spend much of the day lying under bushes or in other attractive places; when you see a pride stretched out in the sun like this, they seem incredibly docile.

But unlike Kenyan lions, which are quite docile and allow vehicles to approach to close range, lions in southern Africa are less accustomed to people and will avoid them when possible. Never be tempted to get out of a vehicle at any time in the vicinity of a lion. Loud noises and sudden movement also disturb them. They're at their most active for around four hours in the late afternoon, but spend the rest of the time lazing.

Lions generally hunt in groups, with the males driving the prey toward the concealed females who do the actual killing. Although they cooperate well together, lions are not the most efficient hunters – as many as four out of five attacks will be unsuccessful. Their reputation as human-eaters is largely undeserved as in most circumstances they will flee on seeing a human. However, once they have the taste for human flesh and realise how easy it is to make a meal of one, lions can become habitual killers of people, but most dangerous lions are the older ones who can no longer bring down more fleet-footed animals.

Lions are territorial beasts. A pride of up to three males and 15 accompanying females and young will defend an area of anything from 20 to 400 sq km, depending on the type of country and the amount of game food available.

Lion cubs are born in litters averaging two or three. They become sexually mature by 1½ years and males are driven from the family group shortly after. Lions reach full maturity at around six years of age. Unguarded cubs are preyed on by hyaenas, leopards, pythons and hunting dogs.

There are at least eight species of mongoose present in southern Africa, but the most common is the banded mongoose, which may be seen in all the game parks. It is brown or grey and is easily identifiable by the dark bands across the back which stretch from the shoulder to the tail. The animal is about 40 cm in length and weighs between 1.3 and 2.3 kg.

In Etosha you can find the yellow mongoose (*Cynictis penicillata*), which has a distinctive white tip to its tail. Yellow mongooses are active all day and apparently like the company of ground squirrels with whom they are frequently to be seen. The less common slender mongoose (*Galerella sanguinea*), a solitary animal, has a black-tipped tail.

The mongoose is a very sociable animal, living in packs of between 30 and 50 individuals which stay close to one another when foraging for prey. They are often very noisy, having a wide variety of sounds which they use to communicate with each other. When threatened they growl and spit in much the same manner as a domestic cat.

Being diurnal animals, they prefer sunny spots during the day but retire to warrens – rock crevices, hollow trees and abandoned anthills – at night. A pack frequently has several warrens within its territory.

The mongoose's most important foods are insects, grubs and larvae, but it also eats small amphibians, reptiles, birds and their eggs, fruits and berries. Its main predators are birds of prey, though they are also taken by lions, leopards and wild dogs. Snakes rarely pose a danger since these would-be predators are attacked by the entire pack and the snake is frequently killed.

The mongoose is one of the creatures which have become very habituated to humans in some places, and comes right up to the game lodges scavenging for scraps.

The serval is a wild cat, about the size of a domestic cat but with much longer legs. It is found in thick bush and tall grass near streams in central and eastern Zimbabwe. It stands about 50 cm high and measures 130 cm long, including the tail.

The serval's colouring is a dirty yellow with large black spots which follow lines along the length of the body. Other prominent features are the large upright ears, long neck and relatively short tail. Being a largely nocturnal animal, the serval is usually only seen in the early morning or late evening. It lives on birds, hares and rodents and is an adept hunter – it catches birds in mid flight by leaping into the air.

Servals are born in litters of up to four. Although independent at one year, they don't reach sexual maturity until two years of age.

Mongoose
Scientific names: *Mungos mungo (Zebra or banded mongoose, Hebogale parvula (dwarf meerkat), Cynictis penicillata (red meerkat), Paracynictis selousi (Selous' mongoose), Suricata suricata (slender-tailed mongoose), Atilax paludinosus (marsh mongoose), Ichneumia albi (White-tailed mongoose), Herpestes ichneumon (Ichneumon), Herpestes sargaineus (slender mongoose)*

Serval
Scientific name: *Lepitailurus serval*

ELEPHANT
Scientific name: *Loxodonta africana*

Everyone knows what an elephant looks like so a description is unnecessary, except perhaps to mention that African elephants are much larger than their Asian counterparts and that their ears are wider and flatter. A fully grown bull can weigh more than 6½ tonnes. Elephants are found in all the major game parks with the exception of Matobo, where they'd be too destructive to the environment, and the parks of central and southern Botswana, where there is insufficient water to support elephant populations. The greatest concentrations of elephants are in Hwange, Chobe, Moremi and Etosha parks. Etosha in particular has a huge population of elephants, boosted by herds that move in from the adjoining Kaokoveld and Owambo regions. Your best chance of seeing them comes in the dry season (May to September) as they disperse across the pan towards rainwater pools during the rainy season.

The tusks on an old bull can weigh as much as 50 kg each, although 15 to 25 kg is more usual. The tusks of one elephant shot in Zimbabwe's Gonarezhou National Park weighed 110 kg! Both the males and females grow tusks, although the female's are usually smaller. An elephant's sense of sight is only poorly developed, but its smelling and hearing are excellent.

Elephants are gregarious animals, usually found in herds of between 10 and 20 consisting of one mature bull, a couple of younger bulls, cows and calves, though herds of up to 50 individuals are sometimes encountered. Old bulls appear to lose the herding instinct and often lead a solitary existence, only rejoining the herd for mating. Herds are often very noisy since elephants communicate with each other by a variety of sounds, the most usual ones being various rumbles produced through the trunk or mouth. The best known elephant sound, however, is the high-pitched trumpeting which they produce when frightened or in despair and when charging.

Herds are on the move night and day in order to secure sufficient water and fodder, both of which they consume in vast quantities – the average daily food intake of an adult is in the region of 250 kg. They are both grazers and browsers and feed on a wide variety of vegetable matter, including grasses, leaves, twigs, bark, roots and fruits, and they frequently break quite large trees in order to get at the leaves. Because of this destructive capacity they can be a serious threat to a fragile environment, especially in drought years, and are quite capable of turning dense woodland into open grassland in a relatively short time. Because of Africa's rapidly increasing human population and the expansion of cultivated land, they also come into conflict with farmers when they destroy crops such as bananas, maize and sugar cane.

Mineral salts obtained from 'salt licks' are another essential part of an elephant's diet. They are dug out of the earth with the aid of their tusks and devoured in considerable quantities.

Elephants breed all year and have a gestation period of 22 to 24 months. Expectant mothers leave the herd along with one or two other females and select a secluded spot where birth occurs. They rejoin the herd a few days later. Calves weigh around 130 kg at birth and stand just under a metre high. They're very playful and are guarded carefully and fondly by their mothers until weaned at two years old. They continue to grow for a further 23 years or so, reaching puberty at around 10 to 12 years. An elephant's life span is normally 60 to 70 years, though some individuals reach the ripe old age of 100 or more.

Giraffes are found in all the game parks of Zimbabwe, Botswana and Namibia. The two most common species are the Masai giraffe and the reticulated giraffe.

The name giraffe is derived from the Arabic *xirapha* ('the one who walks quickly'). Giraffes are protected in Namibia, and they are common in Etosha. You may be surprised to see them chewing bones, a practice known as *pica*, which indicates of a shortage of minerals in their diet.

The main distinguishing feature of the Masai giraffe is its irregular, often star-shaped spots, compared with the more regular pattern of the reticulated giraffe. The reticulated giraffe is a deeper brown and its body has a more intricate tortoise-shell pattern.

The average male stands around 5½ metres; females are mere midgets at 4½ metres. Females are normally lighter in colour and have less well-defined markings than do males. Horns are found in both sexes although these are merely short projections of bone which are covered by skin and hair – all that's left of what might once have been antlers. Despite the fact that the giraffe has such a huge neck, it still has only seven cervical vertebrae – the same number as humans.

Giraffes graze mainly on acacia tree foliage in the early morning and afternoon; the rest of the time they rest in the shade. At night they also rest for a couple of hours, either standing or lying down.

GIRAFFE
Scientific names: *Giraffa camelopardalis (Masai Giraffe), Giraffa reticulata (Reticulated Giraffe)*

HIPPOPOTAMUS
Scientific name: *Hippopotamus amphibus*

In southern Africa the hippo is found in greatest numbers in the Okavango Delta, the Zambezi and Chobe rivers, waterholes in all the parks, and some popular recreational dams in Zimbabwe. In Namibia, the falls at Andara are a good place to see them.

Hippos are too well known to need description except to note that these huge, fat animals with enormous heads and short legs vary between 1350 and 2600 kg when fully grown. Their ears, eyes and nostrils are so placed that they remain above water when the animal is submerged.

Hippos generally spend most of the day submerged, feeding on bottom vegetation and surfacing only occasionally to grab a breath of air before plunging again. They come out of the water to graze only at night. Entirely herbivorous, they feed on a variety of grasses in pastures up to several km away from their aquatic haunts. They are voracious feeders and can consume up to 60 kg of vegetable matter each night. They urinate and defecate in well-defined areas – often in the water, in which case they disperse the excreta with their tails.

Hippos are very gregarious animals and live in schools of 15 to 30 individuals, though in certain places the schools can be much larger. Each school consists about equally of bulls and cows (with their calves) and, like other herd animals, there's an established hierarchy. Hippos may appear to be placid, but they fight frequently among themselves for dominance, especially the males. The wounds inflicted in such fights can be quite horrific; virtually every hippo you see will bear the scars of such conflicts.

To humans, hippos are statistically Africa's most dangerous animal, with most accidents occurring when hippos surface beneath boats and canoes or when someone sets up camp in a riverside hippo run. It's similarly not a good idea to come between a hippo and its retreat to the water. They may look sluggish but they are capable of running at considerable speed and don't much care what stands in their way.

Hippos breed all year; the period of gestation is around 230 days. The cows give birth to a single calf either in the water or on land and suckle it for four to six months, after which it begins to graze regularly. Sexual maturity is reached at about four years old and the life span is about 30 years (longer in captivity).

The only natural predators of hippos are lions and crocodiles, which prey on the young. Though hippos occasionally foul fishing nets, they're considered beneficial because their wallowing stirs up the bottom mud and their excreta is a valuable fertiliser which encourages the growth of aquatic organisms.

PRIMATES

The yellow baboon, just one of at least five species of baboon, is the one most commonly sighted in southern Africa. Chacma baboons are also common in Namibia in rocky outcrops or river canyons, and can frequently be seen in large groups just near the edge of the road.

The baboons' dog-like snouts give them a more aggressive appearance than most other primates, which generally have much more human-like facial features. They are usually found in large troops of up to 150 animals, with a dominant male; the troop has a territory ranging from two to 30 sq km. Baboons spend most of their time on the ground searching for insects, spiders and birds' eggs. They have also found that the lodges, camping sites and picnic areas in the game parks are easy pickings, especially when idiotic tourists throw food to them so they can get a good snap for the holiday album.

Baboons are fierce fighters; their only real natural enemy is the leopard, although young cubs are also taken by lions and hunting dogs.

Resembling an Australian possum, the greater bushbaby is in fact a small monkey about the size of a rabbit. It is found in dense, moist forest habitats all over southern Africa, but since it's a nocturnal creature it is rarely seen by day. The head is small with large rounded ears and, as might be expected on a nocturnal animal, relatively large eyes. The thick fur is dark brown and the tail is thick and bushy. An average adult measures around 80 cm in length, 45 cm of which is tail, and weighs less than two kg.

The lesser bushbaby is about half the size of the greater bushbaby. It is a very light grey and has yellowish colouring on the legs.

Baboon
Scientific name: *Papio eynocephalus (Yellow Baboon)*

Bushbaby
Scientific names: *Galago crassicaudatus (greater or giant bushbaby)*, *Galago senegalensis (lesser or Senegal bushbaby)*

Samango Monkey (White-throated Guenon)
Scientific name: *Cercopithecus sp.*

Also known as the white-throated guenon, the Samango monkey inhabits much of eastern Africa, from Kenya south to Natal in South Africa. In Zimbabwe it occurs only in the eastern highlands, concentrated on the Chirinda Forest Reserve and the densely forested regions along the Mozambique border.

The face is grey to black, but most of the back and the flanks and upper limbs have a greenish cast. The rump is yellow and the lower limbs are black. Mature males make coughing sounds; females and young of both sexes make chirping and chattering sounds.

The Samango monkey feeds in the early morning and late afternoon in the higher treetops, descending into shady areas during the day. They normally live in social groups of four to 12.

The monkeys eat mainly shoots, leaves, young birds, insects, moss, fungi, fruit, berries and eggs, and occasionally even raid plantations, taking chickens. They are hunted by leopards, pythons and eagles.

Vervet Monkey
Scientific name: *Cercopithecus aethiops*

The playful vervet monkey is the most common monkey in southern Africa, and is seen in parks and reserves (and camping sites and picnic areas!) in all three countries. It is easily recognisable because of its black face fringed by white hair and its yellowish-grey hair elsewhere, except for the underparts which are whitish. The male has an extraordinary bright blue scrotum.

Vervet monkeys are usually found in groups of up to 30 and are extremely cheeky and inquisitive, as you may well find when camping in the game reserves; they are often very habituated to humans and will come right inside tents or minibuses in search of a handout. Normally they live in woodland and savanna but never in rainforests or semidesert.

Africa's most sought-after commodity, rhino horn, has caused rhino numbers to decline dramatically throughout the continent, and in most countries they have been exterminated. Determined conservation efforts in Zimbabwe, Botswana and Namibia, however, are allowing them to make somewhat of a comeback.

Rhinos are one of the more difficult animals to sight, simply because of their lack of numbers. The best place to see them in Zimbabwe is Matobo National Park, where good numbers of both black and white rhinos are present. There are also quite a few in Hwange and Chobe national parks. The black rhino population is particularly healthy in Zimbabwe's Chizarira National Park and there are a few white rhinos in Kazuma Pan National Park. Namibia currently has a dehorning program in progress in the hope of preventing the extinction of rhinos in that country. You have a very good chance of seeing black rhinos in Etosha Park, where there is one of the largest (and most stable) populations in Africa – more than 300. White rhinos are found in the Waterberg Plateau Park near Otjiwarongo, where they have been introduced to form a breeding population.

Rhinos usually feed in the very early morning or late afternoon; at other times they tend to keep out of sight. Their eyesight is extremely poor and they rely more on keen senses of smell and hearing. When alarmed, they will normally flee from perceived danger. If they decide to charge, however, they must be given a wide berth, although with their poor eyesight chances are they'll miss their target anyway. They have been known to charge trains and even the carcasses of dead elephants!

A rhino's territory depends on the type of country and the availability of food, and so can be as little as a couple of hectares or as much as 50 sq km. The diet consists mainly of leaves, shoots and buds of a large variety of bushes and trees.

Rhinos reach sexual maturity by five years but females do not usually become pregnant for the first time until around seven years of age. Calves weigh around 40 kg at birth and by three months of age weigh around 140 kg. Adult animals weigh in at anything from 1000 kg to 1600 kg! They are solitary animals, only coming together for some days during mating. Calves stay with the mother for anything up to three years, although suckling generally stops after the first year.

RHINOCEROS
Scientific name: *Diceros bicornis*

SMALLER ANIMALS

Aardvark
Scientific name: *Orycteropus capensis*

Also known as the ant bear, the porcine-looking aardvark has thick and wrinkled pink-grey skin with very sparse and stiff greyish hair. It has an elongated tubular snout and a round, sticky, pink tongue which it uses to lap up ants and termites dug from nests and rotting wood with the long claws of its front feet.

Aardvarks dig metre-long holes which are used as shelter by numerous other animals – hares, hyaenas, jackals, warthogs, owls, and rodents. They normally emerge only at night, but in the morning after a cold night they may bask in the sun awhile before retiring underground. When the holes are occupied, the entrances are sealed except for a small ventilation hole. When confronted by an enemy, an aardvark somersaults and bleats loudly or quickly excavates a refuge. When cornered, it resists attack with the foreclaws, shoulders and tail.

Aardvarks are normally solitary animals and only mother and offspring live together.

Cape Clawless Otter
Scientific name: *Aonyx capensis*

The Cape clawless otter, a river otter, is common in the Chobe and Okavango rivers of northern Botswana as well as near the Namibian coast. Its back is light greyish brown and the snout, face and throat are white or cream. The white cheeks each have a large rectangular spot. Unlike most otters, Cape clawless otters don't have webbed feet, and although some are truly clawless, others have only short pointed claws on the third and fourth toes.

The otters are normally active during the day, and with a bit of luck may be seen playing, swimming and diving throughout the afternoon. In areas where they're hunted by humans, the otters have become nocturnal.

Their main foods include fish, crabs, frogs, and bird and crocodile eggs. Their only known enemy is the crocodile.

Also known as the ratel, the honey badger is of a similar size and shape to the European badger and is every bit as ferocious. African honey badgers have been known to remorselessly attack creatures as large as the Cape buffalo! They're present throughout Zimbabwe, northern Botswana and Namibia, but they're normally only active between dusk and dawn so are rarely observed. They're almost regarded as pets at Sinamatella Camp in Zimbabwe's Hwange National Park, however, and anyone camping there will almost certainly have the opportunity to see them.

Honey badgers subsist on fish, frogs, scorpions, spiders, and reptiles, including poisonous snakes; at times they'll even take young antelopes. They also eat a variety of roots, honey, berries and eggs, and they're adept at raiding rubbish bins.

Honey Badger (Ratel)
Scientific name: *Mellivora ratel*

The species of hyrax you're most likely to encounter is the rock hyrax *(Procavia capensis)*. It's a small but robust animal about the size of a large rabbit, with a short and pointed snout, large ears and thick fur. The tail is either absent or reduced to a stump.

The hyrax is an extremely sociable animal and lives in colonies of up to 60 individuals, usually in rocky, scrub-covered locations. A diurnal animal, it feeds mostly in the morning and evening on grass, bulbs and roots, and on such insects as grasshoppers and locusts. During the rest of the day hyraxes can frequently be seen sunning themselves on rocks and chasing each other in play. Where they are habituated to humans they are often quite tame, but when alarmed in other places they dash into rock crevices uttering shrill screams. Their senses of hearing and sight are excellent.

The hyrax breeds all year, the period of gestation being about seven months – a remarkably long period for an animal of this size. Up to six young are born at a time, and they are cared for by the whole colony. Predators include leopards, wild dogs, eagles, mongooses and pythons.

Despite being such a small creature, the hyrax is believed to be more closely related to the elephant than any other living creature, but the relationship is uncertain. It's most often observed in Matobo, Hwange and Chizarira national parks and in other parks wherever one finds the low rocky kopjes that it loves. Hyraxes are very widespread in Namibia; you could encounter one on almost any rocky outcrop.

Rock Hyrax (Dassie)
Scientific name: *Procavia capensis*

Pangolin
Scientific name: *Manis sp.*

The Cape pangolin, one of several species of African pangolins sometimes known as scaly ant-eaters, is covered with large rounded scales over the back and tail with hair only around the eyes, ears, cheeks and underside.

Pangolins are present all over Zimbabwe, Botswana and northern Namibia, normally keeping to dry scrubby country, especially areas with light sandy soil such as the Kalahari. They are primarily nocturnal animals, active between midnight and dawn. They walk on the outside edges of their hands, with claws pointed inward. Their primary foods include ants and termites dug from termite mounds, rotting wood and dung heaps. They rarely excavate their own holes, however, and prefer to live in abandoned ant bear holes.

WARTHOG
Scientific name: *Phacochoerus aethiopicus*

Warthogs are found in all the major parks in Zimbabwe, Botswana and Namibia but are most profuse in Zimbabwe's Hwange National Park. Warthogs are also common in Namibia and are very frequently seen along roadside verges. The family groups are called 'sounders'.

The warthog takes its name from the somewhat grotesque wart-like growths which grow on its face. Warthogs usually live in family groups which include a boar, a sow and three or four young. Their most (or perhaps only) endearing habit is the way they turn tail and trot away with their thin tufted tails stuck straight up in the air like antennae.

The males are usually bigger than the females, measuring up to one metre long and weighing as much as 100 kg. They grow upper and lower tusks; the upper ones curve outwards and upwards and grow as long as 60 cm; the lower ones are usually less than 15 cm.

Warthogs feed mainly on grass, but also eat fruit and bark; in hard times they will burrow with the snout for roots and bulbs. They rest and give birth in abandoned burrows, or sometimes excavate a cavity in abandoned termite mounds. The piglets are born in litters of up to eight, although two to four is far more usual.

Zebras are among the most common animals in the parks and are widely distributed. You'll find them in great numbers in Hwange, Chobe, Etosha, Mana Pools, Zambezi and Moremi and to some degree in all the minor game parks as well. Zebras often mingle with other animals, most commonly wildebeests but also with elephants and impalas.

There are two species found in southern Africa, the most common being Burchell's zebra which is found in all the parks. Some taxonomists classify Burchell's zebra into various 'races' or subspecies, but this is a contentious issue since it is impossible to find two zebras exactly alike even in the same herd. What is more certain is that, although Burchell's and Grevy's zebra often form mixed herds over much of their range, they do not interbreed in the wild. The other variety is the beautiful mountain zebra, found primarily in the Erongo, Khomas Hochland and Naukluft areas of western Namibia.

Burchell's zebra is common in Namibia, particularly in the pro-Namib plains and Etosha, but the country also has a substantial population of Hartmann's (mountain) zebra. At first sight it may be difficult to tell the difference, but Hartmann's zebra doesn't have the shadow lines between the black strips. Hartmann's zebra also has a gridiron pattern of black stripes on the lower back just above the tail and a loose fold of skin (dewlap) hanging below the chin. Hartmann's zebra is limited to the west of Etosha and the Naukluft Mountain Zebra Park. The two species do not, apparently, interbreed.

Zebras are grazers but will occasionally browse on leaves and scrub. They need water daily and rarely wander far from a waterhole, though they appear to have considerably more resistance to drought than do antelopes.

Reproductive rituals take the form of fierce fights between rival stallions for control of a group of mares. The gestation period is about 12 months and one foal is born at a time.

The most usual predator is the lion, though hyaenas and wild dogs occasionally take them too.

ZEBRA

Scientific names: *Equus burchelli* (Burchell's zebra), *Equus grevyi* (Grevy's zebra), *Equus zebra hartmannae* (Hartmann's (mountain) zebra)

BIRDS

Flamingo
Scientific names: *Phoeniconaias minor*
(lesser flamingo), *Phoenicopterus ruber*
(greater flamingo)

Flamingos are found in large numbers in the salt pans of Botswana and Namibia and in pools along the Namibian coast. Flamingos are found in Namibia in profusion around Walvis Bay and Sandwich Harbour, as well as on stretches of water further south such as Hardap Dam. On the rare occasions when Etosha Pan has water it can be completely covered in greater and lesser flamingos. They are especially attracted by the proliferation of algae and crustaceans which thrive in the intermittent lakes of Makgadikgadi's Nata Delta and the vast Etosha Pan.

Flamingos have a complicated and sophisticated system for filtering the foodstuffs out of the water. This is because the highly alkaline water would be toxic if consumed in large quantities. The deep pink lesser flamingo filters algae and diatoms out of the water by vigorous suction and expulsion of the water in and out of its beak several times per second. The minute particles are caught on fine hair-like protrusions which line the inside of the mandibles. This is all done with the bill upside down in the water. The suction is created by the movement of the thick and fleshy tongue which lies in a groove in the lower mandible and works to and fro like a piston. It has been estimated that one million lesser flamingos consume over 180 tonnes of algae and diatoms daily!

While the lesser flamingo obtains its food largely by sweeping its head to and fro and filtering the water, the greater flamingo is more a bottom feeder and supplements its algae diet with small molluscs, crustaceans and other organic particles from the mud.

Jackass Penguin
Scientific name: *Spheniscus demersus*

Common along the cold southern Namibian coast, the jackass or Cape penguin lives in colonies on the rocky islets. Its endearing short and stocky appearance belies its graceful manoeuvring through the water. Penguins' wings have evolved into flippers which are used for rapid underwater locomotion. The skin is insulated against the chill water by a layer of air trapped beneath the feathers. Penguins also have supraorbital glands which excrete salts, allowing them to take their liquids from salt water.

Like Australia's fairy penguins, jackass penguins breed twice a year, producing an average of three eggs each time, but egg mortality is fairly high.

The penguins' primary enemies are the Cape fur seals which inhabit the same coastline.

The very distinct and instantly identifiable ostrich is the largest living bird. It is widely distributed throughout the savanna plains of Zimbabwe, Botswana and Namibia, and so is most widely seen in both the inside and outside of parks and game reserves, particularly in central Botswana and on the desert plains of western Namibia. Ostriches are widespread on the pro-Namib gravel plains and in bushveld. Namibia has started its first commercial ostrich farms.

The adult ostrich stands around two metres high and weighs as much as 150 kg. The neck and the legs are bare, and all these areas of bare skin turn bright red in breeding males. The bushy plumage on the males is dark black, with white feathers in the redundant wings and the tail. The females are a uniform greyish brown and are slightly smaller and lighter than the males. The ostrich's long and strong legs can push it along at up to 50 km/h.

Ostriches tend to be territorial and are rarely seen in groups of more than six individuals. They feed on leaves, flowers and seeds of a variety of plants. When feeding, the food is gradually accumulated in the top of the neck and then passes down to the stomach in small boluses, and it's possible to see these masses of food actually moving down the neck.

The ostrich breeds in the dry season, and the males put on quite an impressive courtship display. Having driven off any possible rival males, the male trots up to the female with tail erect, then squats down and rocks from side to side, simultaneously waving each wing in the air alternately. Just for good measure the neck also waves from side to side. The males may couple with more than one female, in which case the eggs of all the females (up to five) are laid on the same nest, and so it may contain as many as 30 eggs. The eggs are incubated by the major female (the one first mated with) by day, and by the male at night. The other female birds have nothing further to do with the eggs or offspring.

Ostrich
Scientific name: *Struthio camelus*

Vulture

Scientific names: *Neophron per-cnopterus, (Egyptian vulture), Neophron monarchus (hooded vulture), Trigonoceps occipitalis (white-headed vulture), Pseudogyps africanus (white-backed vulture)*

Vultures are large birds belonging to the Accipitridae family, of which hawks and eagles are also members. There are a whole range of different species, the most common ones in southern Africa being the Egyptian, hooded, white-backed and white-headed vultures. They all prefer savanna country with high concentrations of game and are found in large numbers in Hwange, Chobe, Moremi, Mana Pools, Chizarira and Etosha, but are present in all the smaller parks, as well. Etosha is home to a number of species of vultures. The white-backed vulture is the most common, although the lap-faced vulture can sometimes be seen.

These large birds, with a wing span of up to three metres and weighing up to five kg, feed almost exclusively by scavenging. They are fairly inefficient fliers and so rely to a large degree on finding rising hot-air thermals on which to glide and ascend. For this reason you won't see them in the air until well into the morning when the updraughts have started.

Vultures have no sense of smell and so depend totally on their excellent eyesight, and that of their cohorts, for locating food. Once a kill or a fallen animal has been sighted, a vulture will descend rapidly and await its turn at the carcass. Of course, other vultures will follow the first downwards, and in this chain reaction they may come from as far afield as 50 km. They are very efficient feeders and can rapidly strip flesh from bone, although they are not good at getting a start on a completely intact carcass. A large group of vultures (they often congregate in groups of up to 100) can strip an antelope to the bone in half an hour. Because they are poor fliers, however, vultures often cannot fly with a belly full of food, so after gorging themselves they retreat a short distance and digest their meal.